T0373137

MHAIMBHAT

GOD AT PLAY

VOLUME 1

MCLI 36

MHAIMBHAT

म्हाइंभट

GOD AT PLAY

VOLUME 1

Edited and translated by
ANNE FELDHAUS

MURTY CLASSICAL LIBRARY OF INDIA
HARVARD UNIVERSITY PRESS
Cambridge, Massachusetts
London, England
2024

SERIES DESIGN BY M9DESIGN

Library of Congress Cataloging-in-Publication Data

Names: Mhāimbhaṭa, active 13th century, author. |
Feldhaus, Anne, translator, editor. |
Mhāimbhaṭa, active 13th century. Līḷācaritra.|
Mhāimbhaṭa, active 13th century. Līḷācaritra. English.
Title: God at play / Mhaimbhat ; edited and translated by Anne Feldhaus.
Other titles: Murty classical library of India ; 36.
Description: Cambridge, Massachusetts ; London, England :
Harvard University Press, 2024- |
Series: Murty Classical Library of India ; 36|
Translation of: Līḷācaritra. |
Includes bibliographical references and index. |
Marathi (Devanagari script) with English translation.
Identifiers: LCCN 2023004959 |
ISBN 978-0-674-29241-3 (v. 1; cloth)
Subjects: LCSH: Cakradhara, active 13th century. |
Mahānubhāva--Biography.
Classification: LCC BL1277.892.C35 M4613 2024 |
DDC 294.5092 [B]--dc23/eng/20230510
LC record available at https://lccn.loc.gov/2023004959

CONTENTS

INTRODUCTION

God at Play is a highly unusual religious text. It is an account of the life on earth in the thirteenth century of a person whose followers understood him to be the supreme God. Created by his early devotees and piously preserved through many generations, this religious biography is nevertheless remarkably down-to-earth. It is full of lively details about the places its subject went, the people he met, and his everyday routines. The language of the text is Marathi, the principal spoken language of the large region of India that was already then called Maharashtra. As the oldest extant literary text in Marathi, composed in or around 1278, *God at Play* holds an important position in the history of Indic literature.

The subject of the text is a wandering holy man named Chakradhar. For his followers, who call themselves Mahanubhavs ("those who have a great [*mahā*] experience [*anubhāv*]"), Chakradhar was the last of a series of five incarnations of the supreme God in human form.[1] According to Mahanubhav religious ideas, to achieve liberation from rebirth and suffering, a key requirement is to spend time in the presence (the *sannidhān*) of one of these incarnations. In the absence of any of the incarnations—a condition that Mahanubhavs understand to have prevailed since the disappearance of Chakradhar and, more than a decade later, the death of his guru, Shriprabhu—Mahanubhavs are to practice recollection of the divine incarnations:

vii

their names, their appearance, and their actions.[2] The purpose of *God at Play* is to aid this recollection.

The term *caritra* in *Līḷācaritra*, the Marathi title of the work, means "biography," or, more precisely, "deeds," and *līḷā* refers to the playful, sometimes whimsical actions of a divine being. In at least some Mahanubhav usage, stress is placed on the intentionality with which the divine being acts.[3] Hence the title *Līḷācaritra* refers to Chakradhar's deeds, understood to be the intentional, playful acts of a divine incarnation; each chapter of the text is called, appropriately, a *līḷā*.

Mahanubhavs revere *God at Play* as a record of God's life on earth. For them, every single thing Chakradhar did is important, not just the miracles he performed or the theological and ethical teachings he articulated and exemplified. Chakradhar's followers do treasure the memories of his teachings and his displays of power, but they also care intensely about what he ate and how it was prepared, what kinds of people he interacted with and what they were doing, in which corner of what temple courtyard in what village he spoke his precious words, where exactly he slept and sat, and even where he urinated and defecated. These details make the biography particularly lively and engaging, unlike what some readers might expect in a religious text motivated by pious recollection. The prose of *God at Play* is concrete and matter-of-fact in an almost poetic way, even for those readers who are not Mahanubhavs.

As an unintended consequence of its religious purpose, *God at Play* provides a great deal of information about life in medieval India. The text creates a rich portrait of the lives and interests of people in thirteenth-century Maharashtra. We learn about material culture, law and civic arrangements, social hierarchies and economic conditions, other religious groups and practices, and political history. Because Chakradhar practiced, through most of his life, the constant wandering that he enjoined on his disciples, and because the text narrates his travels in lively detail, it can also serve as an extremely rich resource for historical geography and religious archaeology.

The simple, direct style of the text appeals to modern tastes in a way that the flowery poetry and multiple similes of many other Old Marathi texts, both Mahanubhav and non-Mahanubhav, do not. Refreshingly, for a religious biography, *God at Play* manages to treat its subject reverently without engaging in heavy piety or defensive apologetics. There are even some touches of humor. For example, although many religious biographies, including this one, identify their subject as omniscient, few would allow "the omniscient one" to ask, almost petulantly, *"Must* I know *everything?"* (SP19).

Composition and Authorship

The principal author of *God at Play* was Mhaimbhat. A Brahman who was a learned Sanskrit pandit and a goldsmith by profession, he became one of Chakradhar's most important followers. Mhaimbhat narrates his first meeting with Chakradhar early in the final section, called "The Second Half," of *God at Play:* the two engaged in a philosophical dispute in Sanskrit, with Chakradhar emerging the victor.[4]

After meeting Chakradhar several more times, Mhaimbhat made the difficult decision to renounce the comforts of the householder's life and become a full-fledged disciple.

For his most committed followers, Chakradhar taught a life of strict asceticism: renouncing sex and family life; wandering constantly, with no fixed dwelling; eating only food obtained by begging. Mhaimbhat tells the story of his own renunciation later in "The Second Half."⁵ After eating a festival meal, Mhaimbhat says, he went out to defecate. He picked up a handful of mud and set out toward the river to cleanse himself. At that point, he remembered that Chakradhar had invited him to renounce his home and work and become a disciple. "When am I going to do that?" Mhaimbhat asked himself. At first he thought of taking a year to make the necessary arrangements for his family, and after that leaving to follow Chakradhar. Then Mhaimbhat thought, "What if I die by then?" and he reduced the amount of time to six months. Worried that even then he could die before he left, he decided to leave in three months, then one month, then two weeks, then one week, and finally one day. Even then he asked himself, "Who knows what will happen tomorrow?" He resolved to go home, make the arrangements, and leave that very day. But again he worried, "What if I change my mind?" Still with the mud in his hand, he decided to go to the river, cleanse himself, and depart immediately. At that, a final worry arose: "What if a snake bites me on the way to the river?" So he dropped the mud and left. "I must go to the Gosavi," he said to himself. "Let my father-in-law take care of everything!"

Mhaimbhat joined the company of Chakradhar's disciples later than many of the other prominent members of the group. Whereas most of those followers are introduced in "The First Half," the initial 329 chapters of which are included in this volume, Mhaimbhat first appears as a character in "The Second Half," in several *līlās* besides the ones I have just summarized. After Chakradhar's departure, in 1274–75 (Mahanubhavs believe he did not die), his disciples, led by Nagdev, migrated to Riddhipur, the large village that was home to Shriprabhu, Chakradhar's guru. They stayed there in Shriprabhu's presence until he died, in 1286–87. The composition of *God at Play* was most likely finalized around 1278.[6]

An undated Mahanubhav text entitled *Itihās* (History) tells of a conversation between Nagdev and Mhaimbhat in which Nagdev recruited Mhaimbhat to compile *God at Play*. Along with other disciples of Chakradhar, these two men were living in Riddhipur, spending part of each day "serving" Shriprabhu, after Chakradhar was no longer with them. Mhaimbhat said to Nagdev, "You tell me the *līlās* of the omniscient one, and I will write them down." Nagdev agreed, and so for six months the two men retired to the Vajeshvari temple on the outskirts of Riddhipur for a few hours each day. There Nagdev narrated to Mhaimbhat the *līlās* that he himself remembered. Subsequently he urged Mhaimbhat to interview other disciples to learn about *līlās* that they remembered, and finally Nagdev edited the results of Mhaimbhat's research.[7]

Smr̥tisthal̤ (In the Absence of God), a prose account of the Mahanubhavs' early years under Nagdev's leadership, gives a similar account of Mhaimbhat's composition of *God at Play* and Nagdev's editorial role. It also includes a series of lively chapters chronicling Mhaimbhat's research. In one of those chapters (140), Mhaimbhat follows the busy farmer Kheibhat around as he works in his fields, asking him about the *līḷās* that he experienced.[8] (Kheibhat appears under his nickname, Dakhale, in several chapters in this volume.) In another chapter of *Smṛtisthaḷ* (142), Mhaimbhat refuses to eat a meal at Sarangpandit's home until Sarangpandit tells him the *līḷās* that he experienced.[9] (Sarangpandit, too, appears frequently in this volume.) Conversely, in chapter 139 of *Smṛtisthaḷ*, Mhaimbhat castigates himself for having failed to recognize Gadonayak, the Yadava kings' treasurer who had interacted with Chakradhar, when Gadonayak passed Mhaimbhat on the road and stopped to greet him.[10] Gadonayak appears relatively infrequently in *God at Play*, perhaps as a result of Mhaimbhat's failure to take this chance to interview him.

Besides *God at Play*, Mhaimbhat also composed the biography of Chakradhar's guru, Shriprabhu. That text, entitled *Ṛddhipurcaritra* (The Deeds of God in Ṛddhipur), includes a chapter (252) that provides an even more vivid example of the thoroughness of Mhaimbhat's research.[11] The chapter tells that Shriprabhu went to a place named Mahandule, where a grain cart had broken down. When the people asked him what to do about the cart, he told them, "Put on a new axle." After narrating this story, the text adds the following information:

According to some, he did this at Mahandule in the Godavari valley. Mhaimbhat wrote down the date and

the day of the week. Then he searched in the Godavari
valley. There was a village there named Mahandule.
So he asked the people there, "On such-and-such
a date, on such-and-such a day of the week, was
someone's cart broken down here?"

The people said, "Yes, there was one broken down."
And he was amazed.

These descriptions of Mhaimbhat's research process
demonstrate clearly that the composition of *God at Play*
was a collaborative effort. Mhaimbhat could write his own
account of the things that he himself had heard Chakradhar
say and do. Nagdev, who had spent more time in Chakradhar's presence, could recount many additional *līḷās*, as
could other disciples who had been with Chakradhar even
longer than Nagdev. Baïse, the "old woman" ascetic who had
constantly been in Chakradhar's presence, taking care of him
from the end of his solitary period—the beginning of "The
First Half" (*Pūrvārdha*) in this volume—onward, had killed
herself from grief, so she was not available for Mhaimbhat to
interview.[12] Many other disciples were still alive, however,
and Mhaimbhat went around asking them and other people
who had met Chakradhar about the things that Chakradhar had said and done in their presence. In a sense, all these
people collaborated with Mhaimbhat in formulating the text
of *God at Play;* he was thus, strictly speaking, the compiler
of the text rather than its author.

Besides being one of Mhaimbhat's collaborators, Nagdev
played an additional role as editor. One chapter of *Smṛtisthaḷ*
describes in some detail the editorial role performed by

Nagdev (more often called Bhatobas or Bhat) and his instructions to Mhaimbhat:[13]

141 Bhat hears the *līḷās* from Mhaimbhat and tells him to verify them.

Then Mhaimbhat told Bhatobas everything that had happened. They discussed the *līḷās* of the Gosavi that Mhaimbhat had collected. Bhatobas approved the ones that were correct; of those that were wrong, he said, "These are not the words of his holy mouth. These others are."

Then he said to Mhaimbhat, "Ask Upadhye about the ones that Upadhye experienced; ask Natho[ba] about the ones that Natho experienced; ask Sadhe about the ones that Sadhe experienced." In this way, Bhatobas commanded Mhaimbhat to ask only the person who had experienced each *līḷā* about it.

So Mhaimbhatbas did this, and then he discussed the *līḷās* with Bhatobas in the same way as before. Then he divided them into two parts, "The First Half" and "The Second Half."

Loss and Reconstruction of the Original Text

The textual history of *God at Play* does not end here. As Nagdev was dying (in or around 1302), *Itihās* tells us, he appointed Baïdevbas his successor, handing over to him the manuscript of *God at Play* along with other important Mahanubhav texts.[14] Baïdevbas and two other major leaders died in rapid succession soon after Nagdev, and the manuscript of *God at Play* was entrusted to Kavishvar. "Then all the disciples would ask Kavishvar about the *līḷās* as they memorized them."[15]

During the upheaval that ensued after an "assault by the Sultan of Delhi"—presumably the incursion by ʿAla al-Din Khalaji in 1307—Chakradhar's disciples scattered.[16] As one group, led by Kavishvar, was fleeing to the coastal area of Maharashtra, highway robbers attacked them in a mountain pass. Parasharambas, the disciple who was carrying the bundle of manuscripts, managed to save some of the texts, but the manuscripts of *God at Play* and several other important texts were lost. When peace and prosperity were restored, Kavishvar and the other disciples returned to the Godavari valley and began reconstructing and compiling Chakradhar's *līḷās.* Eventually, states *Itihās,* "everyone" started compiling collections of *līḷās,* so that there came to be thirteen versions of *God at Play.*[17]

These were passed on orally at first, it seems, and then eventually written down. *Itihās* goes on to give the lines of transmission of the various written versions.[18] Two of these are named for Parasharambas and Rameshvarbas, two disciples of Kavishvar, and another—the one considered to be the earliest—is named for Kamalaïse's disciple Hiraïsa, a woman famed for her quickness at memorizing.[19] Besides the disciples who contributed to these thirteen written, more or less official versions, *Itihās* names another fifteen disciples who created versions of their own, as well as another dozen or more disciples, some unnamed, whose memorized versions of particular passages are noted with phrases like "one version" (*ekī vāsanā*) in Mahanubhav manuscripts.

Whereas some disciples had memorized *līlās* word for word, *Itihās* points out, others remembered the plot of the story or its general point (the *bhāv*), and some disciples were more free than others in making up their own wording.[20]

It is not clear when or by whom *Itihās* was written.[21] At the very least it records a tradition passed down orally through generations of Mahanubhavs. The account in *Itihās* demonstrates that a great number of people cared very much about *God at Play* and were eager to get the text exactly right. The story also explains why manuscripts and published editions sometimes repeat the same line, or the same small part of an episode, one or more times in only slightly different words: the scribes who included various versions of a passage in their manuscripts were being extremely conscientious. In the Note on the Text and Translation, I discuss how I have handled the complications this conscientiousness entails for a contemporary editor and translator.

The Revelation of the Text to the Outside World

From the time of its reconstruction until about one hundred years ago, *God at Play* was known almost exclusively to Mahanubhavs. Relatively soon after the death of Nagdev, early in the fourteenth century, the Mahanubhavs began to close in on themselves and become isolated from the surrounding world. The most dramatic indication of this is the fact that Mahanubhavs began copying their manuscripts, including those of *God at Play,* in secret coded scripts in which one letter of the Devanagari alphabet is substituted for another.[22] It was only in the early twentieth century, after some false and insulting statements in the *Imperial Gazetteer of India* were used by a defendant in a libel suit, that some Mahanubhav leaders and scholars began to teach the scripts to outsiders. The rich trove of Mahanubhav literature, including H. N. Nene's edition of *God at Play*, burst onto the scene as a sensation in Maharashtra.[23] As a result of the publication of that edition and other Old Marathi Mahanubhav texts, twentieth-century scholars began to rewrite the early history of the Marathi language and its literature; at the same time, "modernist" Marathi poets began citing Chakradhar among the most important influences on their writing.[24] Passages from *God at Play* came to be included in syllabi for college and university courses, and S. G. Tulpule published an accessible, readily available edition of Nene's text (Mhaimbhat 1964–1967). V. B. Kolte's thoroughly researched edition (Mhaimbhat 1978; second edition, 1982) is a work of meticulous scholarship, but its inclusion of a few episodes that some Mahanubhavs saw as offensive led eventually to the withdrawal of the book from circulation.[25]

Attention to *God at Play* in English and other European languages has lagged behind the production of Marathi editions. After N. G. Kalelkar's 1950 doctoral dissertation, which was written in French, I. M. P. Raeside pioneered the study of the Mahanubhavs in English-language scholarship. His "Bibliographical Index of Mahānubhāva Works in Marathi" is a painstaking work that is extremely helpful in sorting out the morass of premodern Mahanubhav literature.[26] More recently, *God at Play* was one of two texts on which Christian Novetzke based his probing social history of thirteenth-century Maharashtra.[27] My hope is that the inclusion of *God at Play* in the Murty Classical Library of India will help to bring further attention to this extraordinary work of religious literature.

Structure and Themes

The titles "First Half" (*Pūrvārdha*) and "Second Half" (*Uttarārdha*) are commonly used to label the parts of Indic texts, including the two major parts of *God at Play*. In the case of *God at Play,* some manuscripts and editions of the text also separate out the first several dozen chapters of *Pūrvārdha* and give them a different name, "The Solitary Period" (*Ekāṅka*).[28] These are the chapters that tell of Chakradhar's early life and his time as a lone wandering ascetic, before there were disciples constantly in his company.

Neither Mhaimbhat nor his informants had any direct experience of the "solitary period" of Chakradhar's life. The chapters of this part of the text are based on what Chakradhar later told his disciples about that time, and in several cases a chapter of "The Solitary Period" is framed by a brief indication as to where and to whom Chakradhar narrated it. "The Solitary Period" begins with a brief account of the three incarnations of the supreme God that immediately preceded Chakradhar (Dattatreya Prabhu, Cangdev Raül, and Shriprabhu) and then tells the miraculous story of how Chakradhar became a divine incarnation: Cangdev Raül was an ascetic who lived in Dvaravati (Dvarka), in Gujarat. Harassed by a lascivious female ascetic, he abandoned his body and entered the body of Haripal, a young man who had just died in another place in Gujarat and was now reborn as Chakradhar. When the corpse came back to life, Chakradhar resumed Haripal's privileged life as the son of a high government official, a husband, and a compulsive gambler. When his wife refused to give him her jewelry to settle a gambling debt, he became disillusioned. He extracted his father's permission to travel to Ramtek, a pilgrimage place dedicated to the god Ram in what is now Nagpur District, Maharashtra. On the way there, the young man escaped from his retinue and came instead, alone, to Riddhipur. There he met Shriprabhu, who bestowed "power" (*śakti*) on him.

After this decisive meeting with Shriprabhu, Chakradhar—whom the text calls "Gosavi," "our Gosavi," or "the omniscient one"—becomes a wandering ascetic. Aside from a twelve-year stay at a kind of ascetics' colony at a place the text calls simply "the Mountain," the Gosavi spends the next period of his life moving from place to place and interacting with many different kinds of people. Toward the end of "The Solitary Period," he and a female ascetic helper named Bonebaï make a pilgrimage to Lonar and then set out with a group of pilgrims who are traveling to Tryambakeshvar (Tryambak) for the Simhastha pilgrimage. When the group reaches Pratishthan (present-day Paithan), in the final chapter of "The Solitary Period," the Gosavi meets Nagubaï, a senior female ascetic who comes to be called Baïse. In the first chapter of "The First Half," when the Gosavi decides not to continue on the pilgrimage to Tryambakeshvar, Baïse offers to provide him his meals in her hermit's cell in Pratishthan and suggests that he sleep in the Bhognarayan temple there.

Thus begins the next phase of Chakradhar's life, the period during which a group of disciples gathers around him, with at least one or two at a time accompanying him on his travels and the others coming to and going from wherever he is staying. During the part of "The First Half" in this volume, the Gosavi has major stays (each called an *avasthān*) in a number of places, interspersed with a series of overnight stays (called *vastis*) in many more.[29] There are also many episodes in which the location is identified simply as "on the road" or "along the way" (*mārgī*). To a great extent, especially in "The First Half" and "The Second Half," the overall structure of *God at Play* is geographical.[30] It is the *sequence of places* that determines the order of the *līḷās* in the text.

Within the rough order determined by the routes and stopping places of Chakradhar's travels, *God at Play* recounts episodes, *līḷās,* that sometimes cluster around Chakradhar's interactions with a particular disciple or his contests with other religious teachers (what Novetzke calls "spiritual entrepreneurs").[31] There are some miracle stories, including episodes in which Chakradhar cures people (SP33, SP34, SP42, FH9, FH160, FH258, FH299, FH300, FH321, and FH323), exorcises ghosts (FH6), brings a dead woman to life (SP43), or violates the laws of physics (SP36). Other chapters demonstrate his expertise in a variety of fields: he knows about horses (SP16), masonry work (SP54), plowing (FH185), horticulture (jujubes, FH226; betel nuts, FH71; mangos, FH294; ritupe fruits, FH96), drawing (FH304), martial arts and gymnastics (FH166, FH184), and debate (SP49, SP50), not to mention yoga (FH73) and mantras (FH12, FH63). He can discern things his disciples or others say and do in his absence (e.g., FH71, FH215, FH329), and he can predict such events as the arrival of visitors (FH168–169, FH243). Not least, he is especially skilled at pacifying dangerous animals: a wild buffalo (SP40), fighting bulls (SP68), tigers (SP17, SP41, FH279), a wild boar (FH75), and snakes that fall down on him at night (SP57). In the case of one of the tigers (FH279), Chakradhar remarks presciently that the humans are more of a danger to the tiger than the tiger is to them.

Several chapters are constructed so as to frame one of Chakradhar's aphorisms found in the *Sūtrapāṭh* (The Book of Sutras) or to describe the context in which he narrated one of the moral stories found in the *Dṛṣṭāntapāṭh* (The Book of Parables).[32] A number of more literally theological chapters explore, from different angles, just who or what Chakradhar is.[33] These include several that demonstrate or imply his identity with Krishna, who is for Mahanubhavs the first of the major incarnations of the supreme God (SP38, FH8, FH12, FH63, FH71, FH244, FH263). For the most part, though, *God at Play* focuses on the details of Chakradhar's everyday life, the people he met and interacted with, the things he did and said, and the foods that he and his companions ate.

The people who appear in the text represent an astonishing array of social categories.[34] Although most of his closest disciples were Brahmans—several of them related to one another—they included women as well as men. From the beginning of "The First Half" until nearly the end of the book, his one constant companion is the old woman, Baïse, who takes care of him, performs puja (ritual worship) to him three times a day, and is in charge of cooking for him and the other disciples.[35] Another close female disciple who appears frequently in the text is Mahadaïse, the first known female poet in Marathi. In addition, in the course of his wanderings Chakradhar interacts in various ways with members of a wide variety of castes and occupational groups. These include Leatherworkers[36] and members of other communities today known as Dalit (previously, "Untouchable"), as well as Oil Pressers, wrestlers, horse traders, masons, thieves, highway robbers, dancers, agricultural laborers, musicians, poets, prostitutes, and a Blacksmith. Some competing holy men are portrayed as avoiding him (SP19, SP44, FH164), and one pair attempts to assassinate him (FH80–FH81). The only person the Gosavi himself tries to avoid is the Yadava king Mahadev (r. 1260–1270; FH104–FH106, FH114). By attracting and then avoiding the king, the Gosavi prefigures the complicated relationships between Sufi *shaikhs* and sultans in nearly contemporary Delhi and beyond.[37]

Similar and Related Texts

Despite its distinctiveness in many respects, *God at Play* is the biography of a religious teacher and thus hardly unique in Indic literature. Starting with biographies of Gautama Buddha and the Jina Mahavira, including *jātaka* stories about the previous lives of the Buddha and biographies of Jain savior figures, *tīrthāṅkaras,* who preceded Mahavira, such texts extend to Sikh *janamsākhīs* and biographies of modern holy men like Ramakrishna, as well as "conversations" between Sufi *shaikhs* and their disciples, several only slightly later in date than the *Līḷācaritra.*[38] *God at Play* shares some motifs (hieratic language, a certain number of miraculous occurrences) with some of these types of texts. It would be difficult, however, to trace any direct connections or influences between *God at Play* and these other biographical traditions. The text is not modeled on any of them, nor are there any non-Mahanubhav religious biographies modeled on *God at Play.*

While the Mahanubhavs' isolation and secrecy long prevented *God at Play* from having the influence or connections it might have had in the outside world, it does form a tightly woven intertextual web with several other Mahanubhav works. Within the vast corpus of Mahanubhav Old Marathi literature, there are several texts that are similar to *God at Play* in being written in prose and consisting of short chapters narrating remembered episodes in the lives of their principal subjects. First of all, there is a collection of approximately 150 additional episodes about Chakradhar entitled *Ajñāt Līḷā* (Unknown Deeds), which is included in a separate section at the end of several editions of *God at Play.*[39] In addition, there are brief biographies of the other four principal incarnations of the supreme God. The most important of these is *Ṛddhipurcaritra* (The Deeds of God in Ṛddhipur), a biography of Shriprabhu, Chakradhar's guru and immediate predecessor as a divine incarnation.[40] Composed more than a decade after *God at Play,* this text was also compiled by Mhaimbhat. *Smṛtisthaḷ,* a prose text written in a similar style, gives an account of the early Mahanubhavs in the years after Chakradhar's departure, when Nagdev had become the leader of the group.[41]

Besides these works, which are similar to *God at Play* and were perhaps even modeled on it, a number of other texts are nested within the biography of Chakradhar. These include several poetical works whose composition or first performance is narrated in *God at Play*, sometimes with some verses included in the relevant *līḷā*. Passages from the *Sūtrapāṭh*, the collection of Chakradhar's aphorisms, and the *Dṛṣṭāntapāṭh*, the collection of his parables, are also frequently quoted or referred to in *God at Play*.[42] Because an exegetical principal requires Mahanubhavs to understand Chakradhar's aphorisms in terms of the biographical context (*prakaraṇ*) in which he spoke them, there are commentaries on the *Sūtrapāṭh* that draw on *God at Play* to provide that context.[43] Other, more conventional commentaries on the *Sūtrapāṭh* also sometimes refer to the biographical context of the aphorisms.[44]

Other types of ancillary texts related to *God at Play* include *Ratnamālāstotra* (A Paean Consisting of a Garland of Jewels), an earlier version of the biography written in Sanskrit verse by Kesobas, the man who later compiled the *Sūtrapāṭh*.[45] Much briefer than *God at Play*, *Ratnamālāstotra* refers cryptically to episodes found in more detail in the Marathi text. *Mūrtiprakāś* (Light of the Holy Form), another work by Kesobas, includes references in Marathi verse to some *līḷās*.[46] There are also a number of texts entitled *Pūjāvasar* (Worship Service) that describe Chakradhar's daily routine, and a type of text called *abāb* or *ābāb* that provides a kind of index to *God at Play*.[47]

Most striking are distinctive texts dedicated to naming and describing the *places* where Chakradhar lived or visited.

The principal text of this type is *Sthānpothī* (The Book of Places).[48] This text catalogues the places where Chakradhar went, discussing them in the order in which they are found in *God at Play*. Along with noting the directional orientation of temples and other buildings where Chakradhar stayed, describing their location in relation to one another and to the village or town where they are found, and identifying the exact spots where Chakradhar sat, slept, and so on, *Sthānpothī* also sometimes refers succinctly to the *līḷās* that took place there. Besides *Sthānpothī*, which is written in prose, there is a verse text focused on the Mahanubhav holy places. This text, called *Tīrthamālikā* (Garland of Holy Places), is a type of litany, meant to be chanted.[49] It lists the names of the places in roughly the order in which they appear in *God at Play* and *Sthānpothī*, with occasionally a very brief reference to a *līḷā* that occurred at one of the places. These texts reflect the intense interest in geographical location that is one of the most striking characteristics of *God at Play*.

Acknowledgments

Over the past five decades, many teachers, friends, students, and passing acquaintances in India, Australia, Austria, Canada, Germany, Japan, Russia, Slovakia, the UK, and the United States have helped me, directly or indirectly, with this project. I am extremely grateful to all of them. I thank the Max-Weber-Kolleg of the University of Erfurt, Germany, and the Khyentse Foundation–India (through the Department of Pali at Savitribai Phule Pune University) for fellowships that allowed me to work on my translation, and

Heather Hughes, Samantha Mateo, and Julie Hagen for their meticulous efforts in preparing this volume for the Murty Classical Library of India series. I am grateful to Sheldon Pollock for including *God at Play* in the series to begin with; discussing this extraordinary text with him has been a pleasure and a privilege. My husband, Stephen MacKinnon, has listened tirelessly to many episodes from the text; his interest in the project has kept me going.

NOTES

1   The previous four incarnations are Krishna, Dattatreya (in his one-headed, not three-headed, form), Cangdev Raül (also called Chakrapani), and Shriprabhu (also called Gundam Raül or Govindaprabhu).

2   *Sūtrapāṭh* (Kesobas 1983), "Ācār" 28: *nām* (name), *līlā* (deeds), *murti* (form), *ceṣṭā* (actions).

3   In discussing the sutra cited in the previous note, the *Acārband* commentary edited by Kolte (Bidkar 1982: 102–103) distinguishes between *līlā* and *ceṣṭā* by stating that *līlā* refers to an action that a divine incarnation performs intentionally and in interaction with a living being, whereas *ceṣṭā* is used for a divine incarnation's interactions with material objects, without any particular intentionality.

4   SH115 of this MCLI edition (forthcoming).

5   SH476 of this MCLI edition (forthcoming).

6   Chakradhar's departure is narrated at the end of *God at Play*. For the date of his departure, see Kolte 1982: (58). For the date of Shriprabhu's death, see Mhaimbhat 1972: 13–14. For the date of completion of *God at Play*, see Kolte 1982: (64)–(66).

7   Y. K. Deshpande 1932: 46–49.

8   *Smṛtisthaḷ* 1960: 48; 1992: 115–116.

9   *Smṛtisthaḷ* 1960: 48–49; 1992: 116. 142. This passage portrays Mhaimbhat as single-minded to the point of rudeness in carrying out his research and in practicing devotion and asceticism. He does not, in the end, eat the meal.

10 *Smṛtishtaḷ* 1960: 47–48; 1992: 115.

11 The title is *Śrīgovindaprabhu-caritra* in Kolte's edition (Mhaimbhat 1972) and *The Deeds of God in Ṛddhipur* in the translation by Feldhaus (Mhaimbhat 1984).

12 Her death is narrated at the end of "The Second Half" (*Uttarārdha*, in a forthcoming volume of this edition).

13 *Smṛtisthaḷ* 1960: 48; 1992: 116.

14 According to *Smṛtisthaḷ* 260 (*Smṛtisthaḷ* 1960: 78; 1992: 148–149), Nagdev died sixteen years after the death of Shriprabhu (1286–87; see note 6). By another method of calculating, the year of Nagdev's death was 1312.

15 Y. K. Deshpande 1932: 51.

16 Eaton 2019: 64. The phrase "assault by the Sultan of Delhi" translates the wording in *Itihās* (Y. K. Deshpande 1932: 51).

17 Y. K. Deshpande 1932: 51–52.

18 Y. K. Deshpande 1932: 52–54. This passage names fifteen versions, two of which are apparently considered subsidiary versions (*upapāṭhs*) of others.

19 For more on the Hiraïsa version, see Nagpure 2004: 82–83; for a thorough discussion, see Thakare n.d. (2002): 51–68. The Hiraïsa version is mentioned in verses 140–143 of Krishnamuni's "Anvayasthaḷ" as well (Nene 1939: 66): "Mhaimbhat compiled the *līlās*. Hiraïsa listened to all of them.... Hiramba [Hiraïsa] researched the three types of *līlās* ["The Solitary Period," "The First Half," and "The Second Half"?] and wrote a book compiling them. The brilliant Parashuram made the titles of the three types, based on the *līlās*."

20 Y. K. Deshpande 1932: 55.

21 Priyolkar 1965: 20. Some modern Mahanubhav scholars (for example, Nagpure 2004: [82] and Thakare n.d. [2002]: 60; cf. Y. K. Deshpande 1932: 46) attribute it to "Bhishmacharya," presumably the Bhishmacharya whom Raeside (1960: 506) dates to the late fourteenth century.

22 For a brief discussion of the most widely used of these scripts, see the Note on the Text and Translation. Pathan 1977 argues against the view that the Mahanubhavs encrypted their manuscripts to hide the contents from Muslim rulers. Novetzke 2016: 301 refers to an early twentieth-century view that "opposition from Brahminic authorities" led to the use of the secret scripts.

23 For the five volumes edited by Nene, see Mhaimbhat 1936–1937, 1950.

24 For the modernist poets, see Shahane 2017: 135.

25 See Acharya Mahant Salkar Baba Others v. Dattatraya Others; Novetzke 2016: 303–304. More recently, some good scholarly editions of the complete text (for example, Mhaimbhat 2004 and Mhaimbhat n.d.) have emerged from within the sect. Solapure's edition of "The Solitary Period" (Mhaimbhat 2007) is also a work of careful scholarship.

26 Raeside 1960. Raeside also translated an important early Mahanubhav verse text about Krishna (Raeside 1989). Previous English translations of all or part of *God at Play* include Mhaimbhat 2009 and Mhaimbhat 1977, both published under Mahanubhav auspices. Sontheimer and Tulpule had spent several years working on an English translation when Sontheimer suddenly died in 1992; only a few passages from the translation were published (Sontheimer 1982). Scholarly work on *God at Play* undoubtedly includes numerous books and articles in Hindi or Panjabi that unfortunately I cannot read.

27 Novetzke 2016.

28 Or, as Tulpule 1973 argues, "Ekāka."

29 I am working with a geographer, an archaeologist, and other colleagues to create a map of these places and Chakradhar's routes between them.

30 I discuss the geographical structure of *God at Play* in detail in Feldhaus 2019.

31 Novetzke 2016: 4.

32 See the discussion in the next section, "Similar and Related Texts."

33 See Feldhaus, forthcoming.

34 For an exploration of the insights *God at Play* gives us into social arrangements in Chakradhar's time and his ways of handling them, see Belvalkar 2009.

35 The one period of separation in this volume occurs when Chakradhar sends Baïse on ahead to Riddhipur in FH37 and later meets her there, in FH46.

36 As explained in the Note on the Text and Translation, I capitalize the names of professions that are also caste names.

37 Digby 1986: 68–69; Digby 1990.

38 For examples see Ashvaghosha 2008, *Jātaka* 1895–1913, Collins

2016, Yativrishabha 2012, Bhavadevasuri 1919, McLeod 1980, Gupta 1942, Nizamuddin Auliya 1992, and Digby 1994; see also Jain and Upadhye 1974: 9.

39 Mhaimbhat 1982 (Kolte): 735–796; Mhaimbhat 2004 (Nagpure): 744–797; see also Panjabi n.d.(b): 34–109. These episodes were "unknown" in the sense that no one remembered where they had taken place (Panjabi n.d.[b]: 6).

40 Mhaimbhat 1972, 1984. For the other biographies, see Raeside 1960: 500, nos. 298–299 and 301, and Panjabi n.d.(b).

41 *Smṛtisthaḷ* 1960, 1992.

42 See Kesobas 1983 (*Sūtrapāṭh*) and 1937 (*Dṛṣṭāntapāṭh*). V. B. Kolte made the editorial decision to include the whole text of each sutra and each parable somewhere in his edition of the *Līḷācaritra* (Kolte 1982: [83], [86]–[87]). The endnotes to the translation identify by chapter and/or number the sutras and parables referred to or cited verbatim in the text.

43 For example, *Prakaraṇvaś* n.d. [1968] and Bhishmacharya 1961.

44 These commentaries are numerous, and some are extensive. Published examples include Bidkar 1982, Marathe 1985, Nene 1937, and Vaïndeshkar 1989.

45 Kesobas 1968.

46 Kesobas 1962. See, for example, vv. 397–435 (pp. 45–49).

47 For the texts called *Pūjāvasar,* see Raeside 1960: 492–493. See Pathan 1982 for an excellent example of an *abāb* text.

48 *Sthānpothī* 1976. For a more detailed discussion of this text, see Feldhaus 2003: 196–206.

49 *Tīrthamālikā* 1981.

NOTE ON THE TEXT
AND TRANSLATION

This edition is based on that of Hari Narayan Nene (1936–1950).[1] Besides being the *editio princeps* of the *Līḷācaritra,* Nene's edition has the advantage of being relatively clear and straightforward. Its disadvantage is that it is out of print and extremely rare. In addition to Nene's edition, I have consulted five other printed editions, which sometimes offer readings I find preferable: Tulpule (1964–1967), Kolte (1982), Nagpure (2004), Panjabi (n.d.), and Solapure (2007; for "The Solitary Period" only).[2] Many of the manuscripts used by these editors are undated; the earliest dated one is from *Śaka* 1463 (1541 C.E.).[3]

The manuscripts Nene used—as well as, presumably, those used for the other editions—are written in the Mahanubhav cipher script called *sakaḷ lipī.* Like the other Mahanubhav scripts, this one is based on the normal Devanagari used for Marathi but substitutes one Devanagari letter for another and employs abbreviations for some commonly occurring words.[4] I have accepted most of Nene's transcriptions and have retained his punctuation to a great extent.[5] In particular, I have followed Nene, as well as most Mahanubhav manuscripts, in using two dots, vertically arranged, instead of a *danda* (a vertical line), as the principal form of punctuation. Besides silently correcting obvious typographical errors, I have departed from Nene's edition by numbering the chapters consecutively within each of the two parts of the text included in this volume. (The Concordance compares the numbering of the chapters in this edition with that in Nene's and the other editions.)

Old Marathi manuscripts exhibit wide, sometimes wild, variations in orthography, including with respect to the presence or absence of the dot (*anusvār*) indicating nasalization. In most cases where I have noted a variant reading, the version whose abbreviation appears first after the variant is the one whose exact spelling I have used in the variant (see the Abbreviations list preceding the Notes). Beyond orthographic differences, there is an extraordinary amount of variation in content and wording among manuscripts of the *Līḷācaritra,* and hence among the editions as well. Some editions, such as Nene's, include numerous passages that note alternative wordings or even slightly different versions of the events or conversations in a given chapter. Such alternatives are preceded by names, such as Hiraïsa, Parasharambas, or Rameshvarbas, or by terms such as "research" (*sodh,* Sanskrit *śodha*), "one version" (*ekī vāsanā*), "[another] version" (*vāsanā*), "some say" (*ek mhaṇati*), "in the view of some" (*ekāceni matē*), or simply "or" (*tathā*).[6] Alternative readings of this kind occur *within* a manuscript, not just *between* manuscripts, and so I call them "internal variants." The story of the loss and reconstruction of the original manuscript, as recounted in the Introduction, explains the inclusion of these internal variants in manuscripts of the text.

In preparing the Marathi text, I have reproduced Nene's text in its entirety and have striven at the same time to make it as readable and coherent as possible. This has in some cases meant choosing readings from editions other than Nene's;

in such cases I have included Nene's reading in the endnotes
to the Marathi text. As for the internal variants, I have
included in the body of the Marathi text those that I consider
most significant to the narrative, as well as a few brief ones
that are synonymous with what precedes them. The
other internal variants are to be found in endnotes to the
text, introduced by the abbreviated notation "Ne adds"; in
notes of this kind I give only Nene's readings and not those
of the other editions I have consulted. The significant internal variants that are included in the body of the Marathi
text are translated in the body of the English version, and
some internal variants in the endnotes to the Marathi text
are translated in the endnotes to the English version. Such
endnotes begin with the term that introduces the variant in
the text: "according to Parasharambas," "Hiraïsa version,"
"some say," "or," and so on.

Other kinds of endnotes to the translation provide (1)
necessary identifications and clarifications, (2) the chapter
name and sutra number of aphorisms from the *Sūtrapāṭh*
that that occur verbatim in *God at Play,* or are echoed in it,
and (3) the chapter number and full text of parables from the
Dṛṣṭāntapāṭh referred to in the text. Places mentioned in the
text are identified in an endnote at their first occurrence. To
identify these places, I have relied on the place indexes in the
other *Līḷācaritra* editions and in Kolte's edition of *Sthānpothī*
(1976), as well as the village lists in the online version of the
2011 Census of India.

The information in the Glossary draws in part on Kolte
(1977), Enthoven (1920–1922), and the indexes of personal
names in other *Līḷācaritra* editions. Gods whose names

occur frequently are identified in the Glossary; other gods are identified in either a footnote or an endnote at the first occurrence of their name. Several of the many people who appear in the text are addressed and referred to by multiple names; the Glossary has only one entry for each person, and alternative names are identified in a footnote at their first occurrence. Marathi terms for which I have not found reasonably close, simple English equivalents are also defined in the Glossary.

In the Glossary, as well as in the translation itself, I have standardized the spelling of proper names and religious terms that manuscripts of the *Līḷācaritra* spell in a variety of ways. With the exception of the term *līḷā,* for which I have retained the Marathi retroflex "ḷ" (ळ), I have spelled the terms in their Sanskrit form. I have also used Sanskrit forms of the names of most gods and many people mentioned in the text, but have generally omitted a final or medial "a" that is not pronounced in Marathi. In some cases, modern Marathi speakers would pronounce the Devanagari letter च, often written "ch" in English, as "ts" rather than "ch"; in such cases I have transliterated the letter as "c." (For example, I have written "Cangdev" for चांगदेव, but "Chakradhar" for चक्रधर). In the case of caste names that indicate a profession (Blacksmith, for example), I have translated the caste name and capitalized it in English.

In general, my aim has been to narrate the various episodes in a style as lively and natural as the original Marathi. While I have tried to remain faithful to the wording of the original, I have also attempted to make the translation read smoothly in English. Thus, besides leaving out many

internal variants that could interrupt the flow of the narrative, I have combined some of the very short, staccato
sentences, or "telegraphic jottings," that give *God at Play*
its distinctive paratactic style.[7]

Embedded in the language of *God at Play* is the theological assumption that its subject was a divine incarnation. That subject is seldom referred to by the name (or
title, "emperor") Chakradhar, but rather by another title,
or occasionally—in the voice of another character in
a story—by a nickname. (The text never calls him "Chakradhar" in its own voice.) The titles the text uses most frequently
for him are Gosavi ("master," "lord") and "the omniscient
one" (*sarvajña*). People in the text generally address
Chakradhar as "Gosavi," often preceding or following
words spoken to him with the polite particles *jī* or *jī jī*.
I have attempted to capture the deference these particles
express by translating them as "Lord," "Lord Gosavi,"
or (when spoken by certain strangers) "Sir," but often
I have simply dropped one or more *jī* from the translation.
The text reserves the title "omniscient one" for passages
in which Chakradhar teaches someone something,
renders a judgment, or even makes a simple statement;
it hardly ever refers to him as "omniscient" when he asks
a question. In the translation, I have tried to preserve
this distinction as far as possible, but I have not always
succeeded. People in the text address the Gosavi in
the third person, and he refers to himself with third-
person pronouns or with adverbs of place (for example,
eth, "here"). Judging that this third-person usage sounds
too stilted in English, I have generally resorted to second-

person pronouns for statements and questions addressed to the Gosavi and first-person pronouns for his references to himself.

Another way *God at Play* pays respect to Chakradhar's divinity is in its use of special hieratic terms to refer to his hands, feet, face, head, neck, and body as a whole. As far as possible I have translated these terms as "holy hand," "holy foot," and so on. Special terms are used as well to refer to the Gosavi's sleep (*pahuḍ*), waking up (*upahuḍ*), meals (*ārogaṇā*), and so on. In these cases, I have been able to echo the special language only for *ārogaṇā,* which I have generally translated "*his* meal" rather than simply "*a* meal." A particularly clear example of the use of these hieratic terms is found in chapter SP36, when the Gosavi insists that his hosts treat his companion, a thief, as well as they treat the Gosavi himself. The hosts comply, but the text uses different terms for what happens to the Gosavi and what happens to the thief: "The Gosavi had a massage and a bath [*mardanā mādanem*]. His companion was anointed and bathed [*uṭīlā nhāṇilā*]. The Gosavi had his meal [*ārogaṇā*]; the companion ate a meal [*jevaṇ*]. The Gosavi went to bed [*pahuḍ*]; the companion lay down [*nījailā*]."[8]

Besides using special words this way, the text goes to great pains never to ascribe spontaneous emotions, desires, sensations, or weaknesses of the human body directly to the Gosavi. Instead it says that he "accepted" anger or fatigue or a fever, or that he was "inclined" to do—or not do— something. I have tried in the English translation to mirror these usages in the Marathi text. Thus, I have usually avoided saying that the Gosavi "wanted" or "desired" anything: as an incarnation of the supreme God, he was self-sufficient and free, not constrained by normal human needs or feelings.[9]

NOTES

1   Mhaïmbhat 1936–1937, 1950.

2   Tulpule's edition is the closest to Nene's. It basically takes over Nene's text, making some small corrections. Tulpule leaves out some internal variants and relegates others to footnotes. Panjabi's edition was probably published in the early 1980s: he indicates that it is intended as a corrective to Kolte's 1978 version (Panjabi n.d.[a]: 12; see the Introduction to this volume for the view on the part of some Mahanubhavs that Kolte's edition needed correction). Although the Panjabi edition is undated and was printed with relatively few *anusvāra*s (nasalization marks), I found its readings extremely helpful in preparing this edition; Panjabi's versions of the chapters covered in this volume generally adhere more closely to those in Nene's edition (and Tulpule's) than to Kolte's or Nagpure's versions.

3   Kolte 1982: 76.

4   For further description of the scripts, and keys to decoding them, see Bhave 1924: 78–81, Bhave 1928: 334–336 and photo following 336, Raeside 1970, and Ravalobas 1964: 9–26.

5   There is one exception: I have changed most of the conjunct consonants that Nene interprets as *hma* (ह्म) in Devanagari to *mha* (म्ह). However, in words where the conjunct is normally spelled *hma*—as in the word *brāhmaṇ,* for example—I have retained that form.

6   Hiraïsa, Parasharambas, and Rameshvarbas are identified in the Introduction. Other names attached to internal variants in this volume are Ekoba (in FH266), Gopalba (FH278), Kanadi Lukhaïse (FH130), Miyamba (FH314), and Ramdevmuni (FH47).

7   "Telegraphic jottings" comes from Raeside 1976: 597.

8   See also SP46, where differential language is used for the similar treatment accorded to the Gosavi and the other guests at a wedding.

9   I offer a fuller discussion of these verbal phenomena in "The Divine Self in the *Līḷācaritra*"; see Feldhaus forthcoming.

The Solitary Period

१ सैह्याद्री व्याघ्रवेषें भेटि :॥:

श्रीपरेशाय नमः ॥0॥ फलेठाणी कन्हाडेय ब्राह्मणाचां घरीं अवताऊ स्वीकरीला : मग केतुले एक दीस राज्य केलें : एकदिनीं श्राध जालें : तै गोसावियां भार्या रतीचीया चाडा विनविलें : आणि : गोसावीयासि तेव्हळिं ब्रह्मचर्याची प्रवृत्ति : मग तें निमीत्य करूनि : मातापुरा बीजें केलें : तेथ देवगीरीवरि बीजें करितां : श्रीदत्तात्रयएप्रभु व्याघ्राचा वेखु धरूनि जाळि तळुनि बीजें केलें : हाक दीधली : श्रीमुगुटीं चवडा ठेविला : लोकू भीयाला : तो पर्ता केला : तेथ शक्ति स्वीकारिली : अवताऊ स्वीकरीला : ऐसी एकि वासना : जवं लोकू द्वारावतीए जाए तवं गोसावी तेथ होते : मग बीजें केलें द्वारावतीए :॥:

२ द्वारावतीए अवस्थान :॥:

गोसावी द्वारावतिएसि खराटेवरि बीदी झाडीति : मग सूपीं पूंजे भरिति : श्रीमूगुटावरि ठेविति : गोमतीए मध्यें घालीति : सूपें मार्गु प्रगटे : खराटेनि विद्या :॥:

1 HE MEETS SHRI DATTATREYA PRABHU IN THE FORM OF A TIGER AT THE SAHYADRI MOUNTAIN.

Homage to the supreme God.

He* took on an incarnation in the home of a Karhade Brahman in Phalethan.[1] Then he lived happily for some time. One day when there was an ancestor rite, the Gosavi's wife asked him to make love to her. But he was inclined to celibacy then. So, on that pretext, he went to Matapur.[2]

As he was going up Devgiri there, Shri Dattatreya Prabhu emerged from the foot of a thicket in the form of a tiger.[3] He roared, and he placed his paw on the holy head.[4] The people got frightened, and then he took it back. The Gosavi took on divine power there. (According to one version, he took on an incarnation.)

The Gosavi stayed there until some people were going to Dvaravati.[5] Then he went to Dvaravati.

2 HE STAYS IN DVARAVATI.

In Dvaravati, the Gosavi would sweep the streets with a broom. Then he would put the piles of dirt into a winnowing fan and place it on his holy head. He would toss the dirt into the Gomati River. He showed the way with a winnowing fan and knowledge with a broom.[6]

---

* The supreme God; here, Cangdev Raül.

३ सूपमार्जनी क्रीडा :॥ः

श्रीप्रभु द्वारावतीए बीजें केलें : संन्यासू स्वीकरीला : मग
रीधपुरा बीजें केलें : तेथौनि मागौतें द्वारावतीये बीजें केलें :
गोमतीएचां तीरीं जपत होते : पुढां दंडु रोवीला असे :
तेथ गोसावी बीजें करीता वरि सूप ठेविलें : वरि खराटेनि
हाणितलें : दंडु मोडुनि गोमतीए मध्यें घातला : तेथ श्रीप्रभु
शक्ति स्वीकरीलि : दुसरी वासना : अवताऱु स्वीकरीला :
मग रीधपुरा बीजें केलें :॥ः

४ श्रीप्रभुभेटि : कामारव्यागमन :॥ः

हीवरळियें महदाईसीं पुसीलें : जी : जी : द्वारावतीये गुंफेसि
गेलियें : तवं तेथें एकु महात्मे होते जी : तयांचीये तोंडौनि
रूपेचीया सरीया ऐसीया निगति : तरि ते काइ जी :
तवं सर्वज्ञें म्हणीतलें : ते तयांची लाळ जी : मीयां त्यातें
पूसीलें : आपणयांसि नांव काइ : माहादेओ मूनि : आपण
कवणाचेयां आनोग्रहीत : अनंत मूनीचेया : ते कवणाचे :
ते श्रीचांगदेओ राउळाचें :॥ः श्रीचांगदेओ राउळीं बीजें
कैसेयां परी केलें : तें आम्हीं नेणों : तरि : तुमचे अनंतमूनि
काइ म्हणति : वीद्या आणि पुरुषू महाराष्ट्री असे : तुम्ही
काइ म्हणा : आम्हिं अनंतु अनंतु म्हणों : बाइ : तें ते

3 HE PLAYS WITH A WINNOWING FAN AND A BROOM.

Shriprabhu* went to Dvaravati and became a renouncer. Then he went to Riddhipur, and from there he returned to Dvaravati.[7] He was reciting mantras on the bank of the Gomati, with a stake planted in the ground in front of him.

The Gosavi came there, placed a winnowing fan on Shriprabhu's head, and struck it from above with a broom. He broke the stake and tossed it into the Gomati. Shriprabhu took on divine power there. (Another version: He took on an incarnation.) Then he went to Riddhipur.

4 HE MEETS SHRIPRABHU; KAMAKHYA APPROACHES HIM.

In Hivarali, Mahadaïse asked, "Lord, when I went to a hermit's cell in Dvaravati, there was a Mahatma there who had silver threads coming out of his mouth.[8] What was that, Lord?" The omniscient one† replied, "That was his saliva."

"'What is your name?' I asked him. 'Mahadev Muni.' 'Whose disciple are you?' 'Ananta Muni's.' 'Whose is he?' 'He is Shri Cangdev Raül's.' 'How did Shri Cangdev Raül leave the world?' 'I don't know.' 'Then what does your Ananta Muni say?' '"The holy man and his knowledge are in Maharashtra."' 'What do you say?' 'I say, "Ananta, Ananta."'"

"How could he know that, my woman? Nobody knows it.

* Chakradhar's guru, another divine incarnation.
† Chakradhar.

केवि जाणति : तें कव्हणिचि नेणें : तें एथौनि तुम्हासि
सांघिजैल ॥: काउरळिची कामाख्या : प्रसिधि आइकौनि :
रतीचिया चाडा तेथें आली : देवतेची आज्ञा लंघौनि साउमेया
न वचवे : तेथ ब्रह्मचर्याची प्रवृति : म्हणौनि बाहेरीं बीजें न
करीति : ऐसी सात अहोरात्रें उभी होती : तिएचा आग्रहो
देखौनि तें पुर त्यजीलें : तिए समइं गुजरातेचेया प्रधानाचेया
कूमराचें देह गेलें : तें समसाना आणिलें होतें : तेव्हळिं तें
स्वीकरीलें ॥ आणि महदाईसीं गोसावियातें पुसीलें : हां जि :
आमचे गोसावी काइ हें गुजराथेचेया प्रधानाचे कुमरू :
हां जि : मग निगों कैसें दीधलें : या उपरि रामयात्रेची गोष्ट
सांघीतली ॥: महदाईसीं बीढारीं म्हणीतलें : आबै आबै :
द्वारावतीचे चांगदेओ राउळ तेचि आमुचे गोसावी : होए वो
रूपै : ऐरी दीसीं आली तेव्हळि सर्वज्ञें म्हणीतलें : बाइ तैसां
स्थानीं तैसिया तैसिया गोष्टी तिया न कीजत कीं : जि जि:
गोसावी कैसेनि जाणितलें : सर्वज्ञें म्हणीतलें : बाइ जाणिजे
ऐसें हेतु धातु तवं : हेतु धातु तवं कैसें जाणिजे : पां :
जाणिजे ऐसें तुम्हा उठितां बैसतां ॥:

५ पुरस्वीकार ॥:

पुर स्वीकारीलें : वास पाहों लागलें : आवघेयांही हरिखु
जाला : कूमरू जीयाला : कूमरू जीयाला : मग गोसावी
नगरामध्यें बीजें केले : कमळा आइसासीं सेस भरिली :

I will tell you what happened: Kamakhya of Kaürali heard of Cangdev Raül's reputation and came there out of sexual desire.[9] But she could not transgress the god's command and approach him. He was inclined to celibacy, and so he did not come out. She stood there for seven days and seven nights. Finally, seeing her determination, he gave up his body.

"At that moment, the son of a minister in Gujarat died. When his body had been brought to the cremation ground, I took it on."

And Mahadaïse asked the Gosavi,* "So, Lord Gosavi, are you this minister's son from Gujarat?" "Yes." "How did they let you leave?" Thereupon he told her the story of the Ram pilgrimage.[10]

At their lodgings, Mahadaïse said, "Abai! Abai! Our Gosavi is really Cangdev Raül of Dvaravati." "Is that so, Rupai?"

When Mahadaïse returned the next day, the omniscient one said, "My woman, don't talk about such things in a place like that."[11] "All right, Lord. How did you know, Gosavi?" The omniscient one said, "I can tell from your intentions and actions, my woman." "How can you tell from my intentions and actions?" "I can tell from the way you stand up and sit down."

5 HE TAKES ON A BODY.

He took on the body and began to look around. Everyone was delighted. "The minister's son is alive! The minister's son is alive!" they said. Then the Gosavi entered the town.

---

* Chakradhar.

7

गोसावी तयाचे गुणधर्म स्वीकारिलें : गोपाळमंत्री दीक्षा :
गोपाळळ्णही आण : जोआंचें व्यसन : राणियेचा पढीयावो :
हरिपाळ नावं : प्रधान कुशळु : तेणें दरे दरकुटे : सोधविलें :
पुरुषें उठविलें असैल : म्हणौनि : आपूलीये राणिए करवि
पूसविलें : कमळाइसातें विहरणीचीया खूणां : तीहीं
आधिलीचि सांचीतलीया : अनारीसीया नाहीं :॥:

६ द्यूतक्रीडा :॥:

गोसावी केतुले एक दीस राज्य केलें : पूत जाला : गोसावी
सारिचें जुं प्रत्येहीं खेळति : जींकति : म्हणौनि हारि
स्वीकरिली : बहुत द्रव्य हारविलें : जुआरीं म्हणीतलें : जि
जि : हारविलें असे तें वेचिजो : दीजो : मग खेळिजो : मग
गोसावी तेथौनि बीजें केलें : दारवठा जुआरीं म्हणीतलें :
जि जि : गोसावी आमुचें आधीं देयावें : मग भीतरीं बीजें
करावें : सर्वज्ञें म्हणीतलें : तुमचे दीधलेयाविण : हे आरोगण
करी : तरी गोपाळळ्णही आन : गोसावी भीतरीं बीजें केलें :
कमळाइसातें म्हणीतलें : आपूला अळंकारू आणा : तेहीं
म्हणीतलें : कां : एथौनि जूं हारविलें : तयातें म्हणीतलें :
तुमचें दीधलेयावीण हें आरोगण करी : तरी गोपाळळ्णही
आन : कमळाइसी म्हणीतलें : आम्ही देओं तरि आम्हांई

They put an auspicious red mark on Kamalaïse's* forehead.

The Gosavi took on all of the man's characteristic traits: his initiation into the Gopal mantra, his Gopal oath, his addiction to gambling, his love for his wife, and his name, Haripal.[12]

The minister was clever. Suspecting that some holy man must have brought his son back to life, he had his people search in ravines and caves. He had his wife ask Kamalaïse about the way her husband made love. It was like before, she said. No different.

6 HE GAMBLES.

The Gosavi lived happily for some time. A son was born to him. Every day the Gosavi would gamble on parcheesi. Usually he would win, but once he accepted losing.[13] He lost a great deal of money. The gamblers said, "Sir, you must pay what you have lost. Give us the money, and then you may play some more." So the Gosavi left.

At the door of his house the gamblers said, "Lord Gosavi, first you should give us what you owe us; then you may go inside." The omniscient one said, "I swear by Gopal that I will not eat a meal until I have given you what I owe you."

The Gosavi went inside. He said to Kamalaïse, "Bring me your jewelry." "Why?" "I lost at gambling. I told them, 'I swear by Gopal that I will not eat a meal until I have given you what I owe you.'" Kamalaïse said, "I swear the same oath that I will not give it to you."

* The revived man's wife.

तेचि आन : मग गोसावी उपरीयेवरि पहुडु स्वीकरीला :
माता मर्दनीया पाठविला : सर्वज्ञें म्हणीतलें : क्षुधा नाहीं :
माता उठवावया आली : गोसावी नुठति : मग माता
कमळासाइतें पुसों लागली : तेहीं मागील वृत्तांतु सांघीतलें :
प्रधान राउळौनि आला : आणि पुसीलें : गोसावियां
आरोगणा : राणियां म्हणीतलें : नाहीं : आजि आझूइं कां
नाही : मग तेहीं मागील वृत्तांतु सांघीतलें : मग प्रधान
गोसावीयापासि आला : गोसावी पहुडले असति :
उपंगळिए घेउनि उठविलें : मग पुसीलें : आजि आझूइं
आरोगण कां नाहीं : सर्वज्ञें म्हणीतलें : एथौनि जुं हारविलें :
तयातें म्हणीतलें : तुमचें दीधलेयावीण हें आरोगण करी
तरि गोपाळण्ही आन : प्रधानें म्हणीतलें : जोडीलें असे तें
तुझें नव्हे : प्रधानें वाखारी आणवीलि : जुआरीयांचें द्रव्य
पाठवीलें : मग गोसावीया आरोगणा जाली :॥:

७ श्रीप्रभुदर्शनागमन :॥:

एक वेळू सर्वज्ञें म्हणीतलें : रामयात्रे जावें : प्रधानें
म्हणीतलें : तो देसू पारका : तेथ जाओं नै ए : ऐसें मोडीलें :
गोसावी व्रत घेतलें : रामू देखिजैल तै : मर्दना : मादनें :
व्याळी : गोसावी ताक भातु आरोगण करीति : मूर्ति कृश
जाली : गोसावीयांचीया माता म्हणीतलें : प्रधानातें : सोंदर

The Gosavi went upstairs and fell asleep. His mother sent a masseur to him. "I'm not hungry," said the omniscient one. His mother came to awaken him, but the Gosavi would not get up. Then his mother asked Kamalaïse what had happened, and Kamalaïse told her.

The minister came home from the palace and asked if the Gosavi had had his meal. "No," said the minister's wife. "Why hasn't he eaten yet today?" asked the minister. Then she told him what had happened.

The minister came to the Gosavi. He was asleep. The minister put his arms around him and lifted him up, then asked him, "Why haven't you had your meal yet today?" The omniscient one said, "I lost at gambling. I said to them, 'I swear by Gopal that I will not eat a meal until I have given you what I owe you.'" The minister said, "Doesn't everything I've earned belong to you?" He had his money bag brought to him, and he sent the gamblers their money.

Then the Gosavi ate his meal.

7 HE COMES FOR *DARŚAN* OF SHRIPRABHU.

Once the omniscient one said, "I want to go on the Ram pilgrimage." The minister forbade him, saying, "That is enemy territory.[14] You can't go there." The Gosavi made a vow: "I will not bathe or have a massage or eat an evening meal until I see Ram."

The Gosavi was eating only buttermilk and rice. He grew thin. The Gosavi's mother said to the minister, "His beauti-

मूर्ति कृश जाली : दुवाही राउत पाइक जाति तैसा
पाठवावा : केतुलेनि एके परिवारेंसीं दांडिएवरि आरुहण
करूनि बीजें केलें : सरिसा उगाणा : कोठी : चाटे : बडुवू :
तैसे निगाले : पेणें प्रति एकूएकें नीरोंपेंसी एकूएकातें
पाठवीति : मग : दोघेजण सरीसे होते : तयातें चुकौनि
गोसावी परमेश्वरपुरा बीजें केलें : श्रीप्रभु रांधवण हाटीं क्रिडा
करीत असति : स्याम मूर्ति : नाभि चुंबित खाड : उतरिए
वस्त्र : गगनाची वास पाति : आपणेया आपण बोलत
रांधवणाचां घरीं तिहीं पदार्थांसीं खेळ करीत असति : ते
क्रीडा आमचे गोसावी पांत असति : श्रीप्रभु रांघवणीं सेंगुळें
बुडडें वोळगविलें : तें श्रीप्रभु प्रसाद करूनि : आरे : घे घे :
घेना म्हणे : ऐसें भणौनि : गोसावीयाकडे टाकीलें : गोसावी
वरिचेयावरि झेलिलें असता वरि धरिलें : मग आरोगिलें :
तेथ गोसावी ज्ञानशक्ति स्वीकरीलि :॥:

८ अवस्था स्वीकारु :॥:

गोसावी अवस्था स्विकरिलि : मार्गीं चालावेयाची प्रवृत्ति
नाहीं : कांटेयां केसकळाप गुंपति : ते वारेनि उगवति : कां :

ful body has become emaciated. Send him with an escort of cavalry and foot soldiers."

The Gosavi got into a palanquin and set out with a sizable retinue. He took with him his baggage, a supply of grain, some servants, and a priest. Each time they halted for the night, he sent one of them off on an errand. Eventually only two men were left with him. The Gosavi escaped those two and went to Parameshvarpur.[*]

Shriprabhu was playing in the prepared-food market. His body was dark, his beard reached down to his navel, and a cloth was draped over his shoulders. He was looking up at the sky, talking to himself, and playing with the food in the cook's house. Our Gosavi[†] watched him play.

The cook offered Shriprabhu sweetened bits of fried wheat dough and a vegetable fritter. Making them into *prasād*, Shriprabhu said, "Hey! Take them! Take them! Come on, take them, I tell you," and he tossed them toward the Gosavi. The Gosavi caught them high in the air and held them up; then he ate them. The Gosavi took on knowledge-power there.

8 HE ACCEPTS A STATE OF EXTREME DETACHMENT.

The Gosavi accepted a state of extreme detachment. He was not inclined to walk along the road. His matted hair would get caught in thorns. The wind would loosen it, or someone

* Riddhipur.
† Chakradhar.

13

कव्हणिं मनुष्य उगवी : तेव्हळि गोसावी बिजें करिती१ : मूर्ति
वोरखडे : कांटे रूपति : असूधाचे बींदु नीगति : ते साहाज
पन्हरेयावरि मानुकूली तैसीं मीरवति :॥ः

९ मुक्ताबाई भेटि :॥ः

पर्वतीं बारा वरिषें क्रीडा केली : एकुदिनीं मुक्ताबाईसीं
दर्सन जालें : आपुलेया आश्रमा घेउनि आली : वनपुष्पाची
पूजा केली : कंदमूळफळाची आरोगणा दीधली : तयासि
म्हणीतलें : इतुकें दी तप केलें : तयाचें फळ आजि जालें :
पाहाळीं गेलीं लोंवं : चुंभळी वळीलीं नखें : भुइं काढती
जटै : मूक्ताबाई ऐसें नांव :॥ः

१० कांतीए श्रीचांगदेव राउळ शिष्या भेटि :॥ः

गोसावीं दादोसांतें म्हणीतलें२ : महात्मेहो तुम्ही श्रीप्रभुचेया
दर्शना कां जा : जि : आमचे परमगुरु म्हणौनि : तुमचे परम
गुरु ते कांतीए असति : मग कांतिएची लिळा सांघीतली :
कांतिएची लिळा : कांतिएसि पाणिपात्र करावेया नगरामध्यें
बीजें केलें : तेथ द्वारावतीकाराचे अनुग्रहीत राजगुरू होउनि

would unravel it, and then the Gosavi would move on.

His body got scratched. Thorns would pierce it and drops of blood would appear. They looked naturally beautiful, like rubies on pure gold.

9 HE MEETS MUKTABAÏ.

For twelve years he carried out his divine play on the Mountain.[15] One day Muktabaï* had his *darśan*. She took him to her ashram and worshiped him with wildflowers. She gave him a meal of roots and fruit. She said to him, "Today I have gotten the reward for the asceticism I have practiced for such a long time."

Her body hair was profuse. Her nails curled into coils, and her matted locks reached to the ground. Her name was Muktabaï.

10 HE MEETS A DISCIPLE OF CANGDEV RAÜL AT KANTI.

The Gosavi asked Dados, "Mahatma, why do you go for *darśan* of Shriprabhu?"[16] "Because he is my guru's guru, Lord." "Your guru's guru is at Kanti." Then he told the *līlā* about Kanti.

The *līlā* about Kanti: At Kanti the Gosavi went into the town to beg for food with his bare hands. A disciple of the one from Dvaravati* had become the king's guru there. He

---

* A female ascetic.

15

वर्तत असति : तेहीं उपरिए वरूनि देखवीलें : आपूलेया
सीष्याकरवि बोलाविलें : तेथ गोसावीं बीजें केलें : तीहीं
म्हणीतलें : ऐसा पींडु : मा : ऐसा कां उपेक्षीला : गोसावी
उगेचि होते : मग तीहीं विद्या संक्रमू आदिरिली : गोसावी न
स्वीकरीति : तिहीं म्हणीतलें : पुरुषु हटिया असे : मग तिहीं
म्हणीतलें : जी जी : आमतें वयस्तबनि विद्या असे : तिया
पींडु धरे : ते स्विकरावी जी : मग स्विकरीली : महदाइसीं
पुसीलें : जी जी : गोसावी विद्या स्विकरीली : तरि : तयांसि
काइ जालें : तयांची वीद्या अपूर्ण होत तें संपूर्ण केली :
जाली :॥:

११ आंध्रदेशीं तैल्यकारा भेटि :॥:

पंचालेश्वरीं पींपळा तळिं गोसावी³ उभे असति : आणि
आपेगांवीचा अनंत देवो ब्राह्मणु तयासि अभियोगु जाला :
तयातें मारावेया पाठीं लागले : अनंतदेवो पुरांतु चालुनि
गोसाविया पासिं आलें : इतुलेनि तयांची रोषबूधी गेली :
गोसावियासि गुंफा करावेयाची प्रवृतिं : तयातें पुसीलें :
तुमचेनि कुदळी पाउडें जोडे : जी जी : परि : मज
अव्हिलाओ आला असे : जी : ते मातें मारावेया पाठीं
लागले : मीं गोसावीयाकडे आलां : मग ते राहिले : जा तुमचे

saw the Gosavi from an upper story and had his own disciples invite him over. The Gosavi went there. The man said to him, "You have such a good body! Why have you ignored it so?"

The Gosavi kept silent. Then the man attempted to transmit yogic knowledge to him. The Gosavi would not accept it. The man said, "This holy man is stubborn." Then he said, "Lord, I have a type of knowledge that stops the aging process. It keeps your body in good shape. Please accept it, Lord." The Gosavi accepted it.

Mahadaïse asked, "Lord, after the Gosavi accepted the knowledge, what happened to that man?" "His knowledge was incomplete. I made it complete."

11 HE MEETS AN OIL PRESSER IN THE ANDHRA LAND.

The Gosavi was standing at the foot of a pipal tree at Panchaleshvar.[17] An accusation was made against Anantadev, a Brahman from Apegav.[18] People ran after him, intending to kill him. Anantadev jumped into the flooded river and came to the Gosavi. With that, the people's anger went away.

The Gosavi was inclined to build a hermit's cell. He asked Anantadev, "Can you get us a pick and a hoe?" "Yes, Lord. But an accusation has been made against me, Lord. People were running after me to kill me. When I came to you, Gosavi, they stopped." "Go ahead. No one will do anything to you."

* Cangdev Raül.

17

कव्हणीं कांहीं न करी हो : मग : ते मागुतें गावां गेले :
तवं एरांची वोखटी बूधि निवर्तली : तयातें क्षेमावीलें : मग
तीहीं घरूनि कुदळी पाउडें गोसावीयापासि घेऊनी आलें ॥
रामेश्वरबास ॥ गोसावीयाची पूरता उपहारू आणिला : मग
गुंफा करितां : बाइसीं म्हणितलें : बाबा : बटिकूरें काईसेया
सीनवीजतें असीजति : बाबासि काइ एथ ठाकलें असे :
यावरि तैल्यकाराची गोष्टि सांगितली :॥: अंध्रदेशीं एकाकी
असतां एकी गावीं तेलीया एकाचेया घरा : पाहानपटीं बीजें
केलें : उदेयासिचि : तवं तो तेली नदी हात पाए धों गेला
होता : तयाची तेलिणि आंगणीं बाजसूपवतीए वरि नीजैली
होती : तिएसवें गोसावी पहुड स्वीकरीला : तयाची पासवडी
पांगुरौनि : तवं ते गजबजौनि उठीली : मेलिये वो : मेलिये
वो : मज सरीसा कोणुनेणो एकू निजैला : ऐसी बोबाति
बाहीरि नीगाली : तेथ मांदी मीनली : एक तेयां पुढां सांघों
गेलें : आगा : तुझीए स्त्रीए सरीसा कोन नेणों एकू निजैला :
तेणें आपुला नीएमु सारीला : मग आला : खांडें घेउनि :
गोसावी श्रीमुख पांगुरौनि पहुडले होते : तेणें पासवडी
आसूडिली : आणि श्रीमुख देखीलें : आणि रोखबुधी
नीवर्तली : हातीचें खर्ग गळौनि गेलें : एया लींगा : माझेया
घरा सोमनाथु आला : मलीनाथु आला : अवघे जा जा
तुम्ही : ए ए : गोसावीयाचेयां श्रीचरणा लाग : आजि तुं
जेतुलेंही जाणसि : तेतुलेंही रांधि : आपण हाटां गेला :
पूजासाधन : तांबूळ : सरें घेउनि आला : सरें वोळगविलीं :

When he returned to his village, the people's enmity had dissipated. They embraced him. Then he brought the Gosavi a pick and a hoe from home. (According to Rameshvarbas, he brought a meal just for the Gosavi.[19]) Then, as they were building the cell, Baïse said, "Baba,* why are you wearing out your poor disciples? Is this the point you've reached, Baba?"

In reply he told the story of the Oil Presser: In the Andhra land, when he was alone, he went early one morning, right at dawn, to an Oil Presser's house in a certain village. The Oil Presser had gone to the river to wash his hands and feet. His wife was asleep on a bed in the courtyard. The Gosavi accepted sleep with her, covering himself with the man's thick shawl.

She jumped up, startled. Shouting, "Oh, no! Oh, no! Some stranger is sleeping with me!" she went outside. A crowd gathered. Some people went to tell her husband, "A stranger is sleeping with your wife!" He finished his morning routine and then came back, bringing a sword.

The Gosavi had fallen asleep, his holy face covered by the shawl. The man snatched it away. When he saw the holy face, his anger disappeared. The sword fell from his hand. "Oh, Linga![20] Somnath has come to my house. Malinath has come. Go away, all of you! Go away!" To his wife he said, "Come here! Come here! Touch the Gosavi's holy feet. Today you must cook all the dishes you know how to make."

The man went to the market. He brought back materials for puja, some pan, and Java plums. He offered him the fruit. ("My woman, Java plums were in season then. The plums

---

* "Father," an affectionate form of address.

बाइ : तै सराचें दी : मूठी एसणीं सरें : मग : सरें आरोगण
केली : मग मर्दना दीधली : मादनें जाली : सलदिचा धुवटु
वोलि साउला वोळगविला : पूजा केली : सर्वज्ञें म्हणितलें :
बाइ : तो सांप्रदाएकु : पूजा करूं जाणे : मग आरोगणा
जाली : गुळळा जाला : फोडी वोळगवीलीया : विडीया
करूनि दीधलीया : बाज सूपवती झाडीली : गोसावी
पहुड स्वीकरीला : तेचि थाळा ताटीं आपण दोघें बैसली :
दैवभाग्य आमुचें : ऐसें सूख अनुमोदितें जेविलीं : मग एकू
श्रीचरण एकें चेतला : तथा दुसरा श्रीचरण एकें चेतला :
चरण संवाहन केलें : मग गोसावी पहुडले : पाठीं सागळ
भरूनि ठेविली : तियेंही नीजैली : रात्रि तृषेची प्रवृत्ति जाली :
तिए गांवीं तुंगभद्रा नावें नदी : तयांची वस्तें परित्यजुनि
आपलीं घेउनि तेथ बीजें केलें : उदक प्राशन करितां थोंब
खचलें : मूर्ति झळंबिली : तैसेंचि पूरामध्यें बीजें केलें :
मग उद्यांचि गोवळरुवें म्हणों लागलीं : आरे : माणूस एक
पूरें एताए रे : मूर्ति जेथ थडीए लागली : तेथ बीजें केलें :
ऐसी लीळा सांघीतली : मग सर्वज्ञें म्हणीतलें : बाइ : तै
तैसी प्रवृत्ति : जें : तान्हैलेयां पाणी पेओं न मगीजे⁴ : आतां
एथें ऐसी प्रवृत्ति : घेया घेया बापेया : वेगु करा : मग गुंफा
करविली :॥:

were as big as a fist!") He ate the plums, and then they gave him a massage and he had a bath. They offered him a fine, clean dhoti from a chest. They did puja to him. (The omniscient one said, "My woman, the man was a member of a sect. He knew how to do puja.")

Then the Gosavi ate his meal and rinsed his mouth. They offered him pieces of betel nut, and they made rolls of pan and gave them to him. They brushed off the bed, and the Gosavi lay down on it. The two of them sat down to eat from the plate the Gosavi had used. "We have great good fortune," they said, applauding their happiness as they ate their meal.

Then one of them took hold of one of his holy feet, and the other took hold of the other holy foot. They massaged his feet, and the Gosavi went to sleep. Later they filled a cloth water bag and put it there, and they too went to sleep.

During the night the Gosavi got thirsty.[21] There was a river named Tungabhadra at that village. He took off the clothes they had given him, put on his own, and went to the river. As he drank water, the clump of earth and grass he was standing on collapsed, and his body splashed into the water. He fell straight into the flooded river.

Early the next morning cowherd boys began to say, "Hey! There's a man floating along with the floodwater." He went wherever his body touched the riverbank.[22]

After telling this *līlā*, the omniscient one added, "My woman, at that time that was my inclination: I would not ask for water to drink when I was thirsty. Now my inclination is to say, 'Get me some! Get it, my fellow! Hurry up!'"

Then he had his disciples build the hermit's cell.

१२ चर्मकारा भेटि :॥:

गावां एका बीजें करितां मार्गा पव्हे : पव्हेसि गोसावियांसि
आसन जालें५ : तवं चाम्हारू आणि चाम्हारी हाटां गेलीं
होतीं : तीये आलीं : चाम्हारें दंडवतें घातलीं : श्रीचरणा
लागला : गौसावि सौंदर्य देखौनि पाहों लागला : पुडवाटवा
सोडीला६ : फोडी बोळगवीलीया : विडीया करूनि
दीधलिया : तवं मागिली कडौनि : चाम्हारि आली :
उठीसिना गा : गावां जाओं : पारूख : पारूख : पुडतीं तिया
म्हणीतलें : त्रिसूधी तेणें तैसेंचि उत्तर दीधलें : हां गा : तु
न एसि : न यें तरि माझिए माथाचां हातु फेडी : फेडिला
जाए : कोण साक्षी : गोसावीयां कडे दाखवीलें : हां देव
हो : गोसावी ते मानिलें : मग ते निगाली : गोसावीं तांबूळ
प्रतेजीता तेणे हात ओडविला : तो प्रसादु घेतला७ : मग
तयासि गोसावीया पासौनि स्थिती : तयातवं देहभाव : मी
कवण काइं : ऐसें वीसरलें : ते लोकीं गोसावी होऊनि
वर्तति : ते विचरत विचरत खोलनाएकाचेया आंबेया
आले : तेथ ईश्वरपुरुषु म्हणौनि घरोघरीं जेवावेया नेति :
एक आपुलेया घरीं घेउनि गेले : पूजा केली : जेऊं सूदलें :
तया पुरुषाचीए गाविचे चाम्हार तेथ हाटासि आले : तेहीं
म्हणीतलें : हारे : हा आमचिए गावीचा चाम्हारू नव्हे : एथ

12 HE MEETS A LEATHERWORKER.

As he was going to a certain village, there was a drinking-water stand along the road. The Gosavi was sitting at the water stand when a Leatherworker who had gone to the market with his wife came there. The Leatherworker prostrated himself and touched the holy feet. Seeing the Gosavi's beauty, he began to stare at him. He opened his partitioned pouch and offered him pieces of betel nut. He made rolls of pan and gave them to him.

At that point, the Leatherworker woman caught up with her husband. "Come on, get up! Let's go home to our village." "Wait a minute. Wait a minute." She said the same thing again, and he gave the same answer. This happened three times.

"All right. You are not coming. If you aren't coming, then give up your rights over me." "I give them up." "Who is the witness?" He gestured toward the Gosavi. "This god." The Gosavi agreed. Then she left.

As the Gosavi was spitting out the pan, the man stretched out his hand for it. He took it as *prasād,* then went into a trance caused by the Gosavi. It made him lose all consciousness of his body, all sense of who and what he was. He became a Gosavi and moved about in the world as one.

In the course of his wanderings, he came to Kholnayak's Ambe.[23] There, considering him a god man, people took him from house to house for his meals. One man took him home with him, did puja to him, and served him a meal.

Another Leatherworker from the holy man's village came there to the market. "Hey! Isn't he a Leatherworker from our

देओ जाला : एणें गावों विटाळिलां : ऐसें एरू पुसे एरू पुसे :
आवघांइं आइकीलें : तै जगळदेवो वींझदेओ अधिकार्ये :
तेहीं स्मार्त बोलाविलें : नीबंध काढविलें : तिहीं म्हणीतलें :
चुनेयाचेयां खडेया मध्ये बैसवावे : मग पाखाला सोडाविया :
तिहीं तयां पुरुषां तैसेंचि केलें : तवं मांदी देखौनि पैली
कडौनि एकीं एकातें पुसीलें : तीहीं म्हणीतलें : तया पुरुषां
तैसेनि तैसें केले : मग : एरीं म्हणीतलें : तुम्ही तयासि काइ
कराल : ते पैऱ्हां हाटां आंतु : गळा माळ : तोंडी तांबूल :
ऐसे खेळत असति : तयांचिए गळांचीं माळ सूकेचिना :
मग : महदाईसीं पुसीलें : हांजि : तयांसि काइ जालें : सर्वज्ञें
म्हणीतलें : तया तवं तयाचा नीर्वंसू जाला :॥:

१३ द्यूतक्रीडा :॥:

हीवरळीए आपलो उपरि हे लीळा सांघीतली : बाइ : हे जुं
खेळे : हें जीके : परि हारवीना : गावीं एकीं जूआठेयासि
बीजें केलें : जूआरियांतें म्हणीतलें : धुरे एकी पवाडु आति :
एइजो जी : म्हणौनि : ते परते सरले : पवाडु केला : मग
गोसावी खेळों लागले : बहुत कवडे जींकीले : लाहान कुरंगे
कवडे वेंचिले : पवींत दीधले : वेगळे कवडे केले ते श्रीकरीं

24

village?" he said. "Here he has become a god. He has polluted the village." The man asked one person after another. Everyone heard about it.

The officials, Jagaldev and Vinjhdev, summoned Brahmans knowledgeable in traditional law. They had them take out their law books. The Brahmans said, "Seat him in a bed of quicklime, then pour on water from leather water bags." That is what they did to the holy man.

Seeing the crowd from a distance, one man asked another what was going on. The second man replied, "We have taken care of that holy man." The first man said, "What can you do to him? He is playing over there in the market, with a garland around his neck and pan in his mouth. The garland around his neck is not at all wilted."

Later, Mahadaïse asked, "What happened to them, Lord?"[24] The omniscient one said, "Their lineage was cut off because of what they did."

13 HE GAMBLES.

He told this *līḷā* in Hivarali in connection with Aplo: "My woman, I used to play dice. I would win, but I would never lose."[25]

In a certain village, he went to a gambling den. He said to the gamblers, "Is there room for a winner?" "Come on in, Sir," they said, and they moved aside and made room for him. Then the Gosavi began to play. He won lots of cowrie shells. He got rid of the small, brown cowries, giving them

घेऊनि दोंदेंसीं धरिले : रांधवण हाटां बीजें केलें :
तेथ म्हणीतलें : कवडा जेवन अंन जोडे वो : एइजो जी :
म्हणौनि : एकीं बोलाविलें : कवडे तयांसि दीधले : तिहीं
मर्दना दीधली : मादनें दीधलीं : तिहीं आपुलीं वस्त्रें
वोळगवीलीं : महीमेसारखी आरोगणा दीधली : मग
गोसावीयांसि आरोगण करीतां तया अंनासि रूप करीति :
तेणें तयासि सूख होए : मग : तेहीं बाज सूपवती घातली :
मग पहुड स्वीकरीला : उद्यां सीं फीटे तवं तेथें असति : मग
तयाचीं वस्त्रें ठेउनि जुआठेया बीजें करीति : हाटवटीएचीं
मानुसें आपुलाला व्यापारू सांडुनि गोसावीयातें अवलो-
कीति : जवं देखति तवं : भाट : विदावंतें : वाट पाहाति :
कालीचा जगदानि तो आझुइं न ए : तवं बीजें केलें : तिएहीं
दीसीं जींकति : आरोगणे पुरते ठेवीति : एर वेचीति : तिए
दिसीं आणिका घरां बीजें करीति : आधली दीसीचिया
रांधवणी दुना लाभ होए : तियें गोसावीयांची वाट पाहातें
असति : यापरि तेथ केतुले एक दीसु होते : मग बीजें केलें :॥:

१४   भक्ता भेटि :॥:

वोरंगळ प्रदेशीं गावीं एकी पाणिपात्रासि बीजें केलें :
सेवटिली एकी घरीं ब्राह्मणें एकें म्हणीतलें : जी जी :
गोसावी ए नगरीं जवं असति : तवं माझीए घरीं उपरी असे :

away. He took the others in his holy hand and held them against his stomach.

He went to the prepared-food market and said, "Can I get a meal for cowrie shells?" "Come on in, Sir," said one man, inviting him in. He gave the man the cowrie shells. The man gave him a massage and a bath. He offered him his own clothes and gave him a meal that was fitting for his high rank. As the Gosavi ate the meal, he praised the food. That made the man happy. Then the man arranged a bed for him, and the Gosavi accepted sleep.

The next day, he stayed there until the morning chill wore off. Then he left the man's clothes behind and went to the gambling den. The people in the market dropped what they were doing and looked at the Gosavi for as long as they could see him. The bards and singers were waiting for him, saying. "Yesterday's generous patron hasn't come back yet." Then he arrived.

That day too he won. He kept enough for his meal and got rid of the rest. Each day he would go to a different house. The cook from the previous day would get twice as much money as usual, so the cooks would be waiting for the Gosavi.

He stayed there for several days this way, then he left.

14 HE MEETS A DEVOTEE.

He went to beg in a village near Orangal.[26] At a house at the edge of the village a certain Brahman said, "Lord Gosavi, my house has an upper story. Please stay there whenever you are

तेथ बीढार करावें : माझी बहीणि सेवादास्य करील :
गोसावी विनंती स्वीकरिलि : तेथ बीजें केलें : उपरिए वरि
बाज सुपवती घातली : केतुले एक दीस तेथ होते : ऐसां
लोकु भकों लागला : कोण्हीं कांहीं बोले : कोण्हीं कांहीं
बोले : तेहीं म्हणीतलें : मी आपुलां डोळां देखैन : मग जें
करावें तें करीन : मग ते पाहों ठाकलें : तवं गोसावी पहुडले
असति : ते बाई : पोटकुळिया देति होतीꝰ : तयासि तैसाची
डोळां लागला : आणि : तिची डोइ मूर्ति लागलीꝰ : ऐसें
देखोनि तिहीं म्हणीतलें : हे नव्हे : हे प्रवर्तवीति असे : मग ते
क्षोभले : खांडे काढुनि : खर्ग घेउनि : ओखटीया बुधी
आले : तवं गोसावी श्रीमुख उघडुनि : कृपादृष्टी अवलोकुनि
प्रेम उत्तमसाधन संचरिलें : तैसेंचि बीजें केलें : ते भक्तही
सरिसें नीगालें : मास दोनीं संनिधानीं : ऐसा केतुलेयां एकां
काळां : सर्वज्ञें म्हणीतलें : भटो तुम्हीं ए गावीं असा : हे
पैलि गावीं असैल : मासा पाखा : मग : ते भक्त गावींची
सींववेन्हीं एति : तवं गोसावीचिए गांवीहुनि ब्राम्हणु एकू
कनवृतिसि ए : तयातें ते नीच पूसति : हां भटो : तुमचां
गावीं : पुरुष एक असति कीं : गौर श्रीमुर्ति : लांब कान :
विसाळ नेत्र ऐसिया खुणा सांघति : ते नीकेनि असति : तो
म्हणे : नीकेनि असति : सींवेसि एउनि ऐसें प्रत्येंही पुसति :
एकुदीनीं तेणें ब्राह्मणें म्हणीतलें : स्त्रियां पुरुषाचा ऐसा वेधु
नाहीं : पुरुषां पुरुषाचा काइसा वेधु : पां : ऐसें म्हणौनि

in this town. My sister will serve you." The Gosavi accepted the invitation and went there. They arranged a bed upstairs.

After he had stayed there for several days, people started to gossip. Some would say one thing, others would say something else. The Brahman said, "I will see for myself, and then I will do what needs to be done." So he kept watch on them. The Gosavi was lying down, and the woman was stroking him on the stomach. Just then her eyes closed, and her head touched his body.[27] When the man saw this, he said, "He's seducing her, isn't he?" He got angry and drew his sword. He came toward them holding the sword, intending to attack.

At that point, the Gosavi uncovered his holy face. He looked at the man with his merciful glance, and the man was overcome with love. The Gosavi left immediately. The devotee set out too, along with him. He stayed in his presence for two months.

After some time, the omniscient one said, "Bhat, you stay in this village. I will be in that village over there for a couple of weeks."

After the Gosavi left, the devotee would come to the boundary between the villages. Every time a certain Brahman came from the Gosavi's village to beg for grain, the devotee would describe the Gosavi, saying, "Bhat, there is a holy man in your village with a fair complexion, long ears, and large eyes." He would ask the man, "Is he all right?" "He is all right," the man would answer.

The devotee came to the village boundary and asked him that every day. One time the Brahman said to himself, "No woman feels this much attraction to a man. How can a man be so attracted to a man?" So he gave a different answer:

29

म्हणीतलें : आन सांघीतलें : तें तुम्हीं नेणां : तें तैसेनि तैसें
वर्तलें : सर्प नीमीत्यें : हां भटो सत्य : ना : सत्य : ऐसें
त्रीसूधि पुसीलें : तिहीं सत्यचि म्हणीतलें : तैसेचि ते भक्त
उभेचि पडले : देहत्यागु केला : देह विसर्जिले : मग : तो
ब्राह्मणु भीयाला : गोसावीयांपासि आला : अवघें वृत्तांत
सांघीतलें : सर्वज्ञें म्हणीतलें : हां भटो ऐसा सत्यही अर्थु
न संगिजे : न बोलिजे : मा एसणें असत्य कैसेनि तुम्हां
बोलविलें : मग : कुदळी पाटी घेववीली : त्यासी निक्षेपू
करवीला : बाई : यासि तेथ मग राहावेंचि ना : हें तेथौनी
नीगालें :॥ः

१५ वोरंगळीं मल्लपूजास्वीकारु :॥ः

गोसावी वोरंगळासि बीजें केलें : तिये गावींचा सदर्थु मालु :
तयासि भैरवनाथाची भक्ति : तो तेथ एतु होता : मार्गीं
तयासि दर्सन जालें : दांडिए खालौति उडी घातली :
गोसावीयातें दांडी वाउनि आवारा घेउनि आला : मग :
मर्दना दीधली : पुजा केली : आरोगणा करवीली : मग :
तीहीं विनविलें : जी जी : गोसावी ए नगरीं असति तवं
एथें बीढार करावें : गोसावी मानिलें : मग केतुलेया एकां
दीसां मालें नवसीलें : जी जी : मज पुत होइल तरि मीं
पाचां सहस्रांची पूजा गोसावीयासि करीन : ऐसा तयाचीए
स्त्रिएसि गर्भसंभुति जाली : त्या दोघांइं गोसावीयाची

"Don't you know? He has died, from snakebite." "Oh, no, Bhat! Is that true?" "Yes, it's true."

He asked the man three times, and each time the man said that it was true. With that, the devotee immediately collapsed and died. He gave up his body. Frightened, the Brahman came to the Gosavi and told him everything that had happened. The omniscient one said, "Oh, no, Bhat! Even if such a thing is true, you should not say it to anyone, you should not talk about it. What made you say that when it was not true?"[28] He had the man fetch a hoe and a broad basket, and he had him bury him.

"My woman, after that I couldn't stand to stay there. I left that place."[29]

15 HE ACCEPTS WORSHIP FROM A WRESTLER IN ORANGAL.

The Gosavi went to Orangal. There was a rich wrestler from that town who was devoted to Bhairavnath. As he was coming there, he had *darśan* of the Gosavi along the road. The wrestler jumped out of his palanquin, offered it to the Gosavi, and brought him to his compound. He gave him a massage, did puja to him, and had a meal prepared for him. Then he invited him: "Lord Gosavi, please make your lodgings here while you are in this town." The Gosavi agreed.

Then, after several days, the wrestler made a vow: "Lord Gosavi, if I get a son, I will do a puja to you that costs 5,000 coins."

When the man's wife became pregnant, the couple's faith

अधिक श्रधा जाली : आरोगण जालेयां विण तयाची स्त्री
जेविना : मग : गोसावी वीहरणी उसीरू न लविति : मग :
केतुलेयां एकां दीसां : बिजें करूं आदरिलें : तवं तेणें
म्हणितलें : जी जी : मज पूत होए तवं राहावें जी : मग पूत
जालेयां नंतरें बीजें करूं आदरिलें : पुडतीं म्हणीतलें : जी
जी : बारसें होए तवं राहावें जी : बारसें जालें : अनदान
केलें : यानंतरें बीजें करूं आदरीलें : पुडतीं तेणें म्हणीतलें :
जी जी : उष्टवनवरि राहावें : जी : उष्टवन जालेयां नंतरें पाट
सूताचा जोगवटा केला : तेथ पांचां सहस्त्रांची रत्लें
खेवणिलीं : मग मर्दना दीधली : पुजा केली : मग जोगवटा
वोलगवीला : मग तेथौनि बीजें केलें : आउसें जोगवटा
घालुनि बैसली होती तया उपरि म्हणीतलें : नाएका : यातेंही
एकु जोगवटा होता : परि : तो पाटसुताचा : पांचा
सहस्त्रांचा : हें काइ जी : पांचां सहस्त्रांचां कैसा जोगवटा
जी : मग हे लीळा सांचीतली : तो काइ केला जी : तो एका
ब्राम्हणासि दीधला : हें काइ जी : ऐसा जोगवटा कैसेनि
देवों सकीनलें : जी : नाएका तुम्ही असतीति तरि तुम्हां
दीजता :॥:

in the Gosavi grew stronger. The wife would not eat her meal unless the Gosavi had had his, and so he would not delay in coming back from wandering.

After some time the Gosavi attempted to leave. The man said, "Please stay until my son is born, Lord." After the son was born, the Gosavi again attempted to leave. The man said, "Please stay until his naming ceremony has taken place, Lord, on the twelfth day." The naming ceremony took place, and they gave away food. After that the Gosavi attempted once again to leave. This time the man said, "Please stay until his first-solid-food ceremony, Lord." After the solid-food ceremony, the man had a silk yogi's scarf made, with jewels worth 5,000 coins set into it. Then he gave the Gosavi a massage, did puja to him, and offered him the yogi's scarf. Then the Gosavi left.

One time, when Aüse was sitting wearing a yogi's scarf, the Gosavi said, "Nayaka, I used to have a yogi's scarf, but it was made of silk and worth 5,000 coins."[30] "What do you mean, Lord?" she asked. "How can a yogi's scarf be worth 5,000 coins?" Then he told her this *līlā*.

"What did you do with it, Lord?" "I gave it to a Brahman." "What do you mean, Lord? How could you give away such a scarf, Lord?" "If you had been there, Nayaka, I would have given it to you."

१६ विवाहो स्विकारू :॥ः

गावीं एकी वृक्षा खालिं आसन : तवं हेडाउ उतरले होते :
ते गोसावियांपासि आले : तेहीं गोसावियातें राजकुमरां ऐसें
देखीलें : मग तेहीं घोडेयाचीया जाति पुसीलिया : गोसावी
घोडे जाती निरूपीती : जातिशुद्ध तो बहुतांमध्यें एकु खडेन
हाणें : तो घोडा तयाची वास रोखें पहातुचि असे१० : मग
हेडाउइं गोसावीयांते११ वीनवीलें : आपुलेया दुसा घेउनि
आले : मग मर्दना जाली : मादनें केली : गोसावीयासि वस्त्रें
वोळगवीलीं : घोडा दीधला : गोसावी मुख्य नाएकु : एर
आवघे सेवक : ऐसें वर्तों लागले : मग : वोरंगळा बीजें केलें :
हेडाउ आले आइकौनि लोकु साउमा आला : घोडे वीकीता :
गोसावी घोडेयाची जाति जीवन बोलेति१२ : हा घोडा
अमुकीये जातीचा : अमूका गुण : अमुकें लक्षण : हा घोडा
अमूकेंचि लाहे : हेडाउ म्हणति : हा घोडा गोसावीयाचेनि
बहुत मोल पावला : लोकु म्हणे : हा घोडा गोसावीयाचेनि
सवंग आला : तेथ एकू वेव्हारा आला : तेणें देखीलें : मग
म्हणीतलें : जी जी : मातें कन्यारत्न एक असे : तीचेया रूपा
अनुरूप वरु कव्हणें ठाईं नाहीं : तर तीतें गोसावी आपुली
दासी करि तरि तेणें मी कृत्याकृत्यू होए : माझेया केलेया
फळ होए : सर्वज्ञें म्हणीतलें : एथ जाति कुळ नाहीं : खुंट
दावें नाहीं : तेणें म्हणीतलें : जी जी : गोसावीचि जाति

16 HE ACCEPTS MARRIAGE.

He was sitting under a tree in a certain village where horse traders had stopped. The horse traders approached the Gosavi. They saw him as a prince, and so they asked him about the breeds of horses. The Gosavi explained the breeds of horses. "A purebred horse," he said, "is one that, when one man in a large group hits him with a pebble, keeps staring angrily at that man."

Then the horse traders invited the Gosavi to their tent and brought him there. He had a massage and a bath. They offered the Gosavi clothes, and they gave him a horse. They began to act as if the Gosavi was the leader and all the others were his servants.

Then he went with them to Orangal. Hearing that the horse traders had come, people approached them. As they sold horses, the Gosavi talked about the horses' breeds and features: "This horse is of such-and-such a breed. It has such-and-such good qualities, such-and-such characteristic marks. This horse will fetch such-and-such a price."

The horse traders said, "Because of the Gosavi, this horse fetched a high price." The people who bought the horses said, "Because of the Gosavi, we got this horse for cheap."

A merchant came there, saw what was going on, and said, "Sir, I have a jewel of a daughter. Nowhere is there a husband worthy of her beauty. If you make her your maidservant, Gosavi, I will be gratified. My good deeds will have been rewarded." The omniscient one said, "I have no caste or lineage, no wife or family to tie me down." The man said, "Lord Gosavi, you yourself are caste and lineage. You

35

कूळ : गोसावीचि खुंट दावें : सर्वेंझें म्हणीतलें : यातें
करावेया नाही : तेणें म्हणीतलें : जी जी : मातें अवघीचि
आइत असे : तव हेडाउवीं म्हणीतलें : हें अवघें
गोसावीयाचेचि नव्हे : मग : तो वेव्हारा गोसावीयांतें
गोत्रांकुटुंबातें दाखवावेया घेउनि गेला : गोधोळीचें लग्न
जालें : च्यान्ही दीस वन्हाडीकेचें जालें : मग हेडाउइं
पाठवणीं मागीतली : हेडाउ नीगाले : मग केतुले एक
दीस तेथ राज्य केलें : एकदिनी : उपरीएवरि सारी खेळत
असति१३ : तवं अवधूत एकू नगरामध्यें भिक्षेसि रीगाला :
संसारेसी पाठिमोरा जाला : ऐसा देखीला : तो देखौनि ऐसें
म्हणीतलें : आतां एथौनि ऐसीयां होइजैल : तवं तीयें आउसें
मूच्छर्पपरिपूर्ण होउनि पडीली : गोसावी उपंगळीए घेउनि
उठविली : श्रीकरें डोळें पूसीलें : नेत्र प्रमार्जिले : सावधें
केली : मग म्हणीतलें : एथौनी तुमतें झांकवीजत होतें
हांसीजत होतें : तेथ महदाइसीं पूसिलें : हांजी : गोसावी
बीजें केलें : तरि तीयें काइ जी : तीयें यातें देखतें असति :
स्तीति संचरली : आनंद जाला : मग बीजें केलें :॥:

१७ डाकरामीं व्याघ्रविद्रावण :॥:

डांकरामीं पाणीपात्र करूनि पहुडावेया भिवेश्वराचेया देउळा
बीजें करीत होते : तवं लोकें वारिलें : देव व्हो : एथं न वचा :

yourself are wife and family." "I don't have the means," said the omniscient one. "Lord, I have everything that is required," replied the man. The horse traders said, "Isn't all of this really the Gosavi's?"

Then the merchant took the Gosavi to show him to his clansmen and his family. The wedding took place, with a Gondhal.[31] The celebration went on for four days. Afterward the horse traders asked leave to go.

After the horse traders had left, the Gosavi lived there happily for some time. One day when he and his wife were playing parcheesi upstairs,[32] a wandering ascetic entered the town to beg for food. The Gosavi saw that the man had turned his back on worldly life. Seeing him, the Gosavi said, "I'll become like that now."

With that, his wife fell down in a dead faint. The Gosavi put his arms around her and lifted her up. He wiped her eyes with his holy hand, put water on her eyes, and revived her. Then he said, "I was fooling. I was kidding you."

Later, Mahadaïse asked a question about it: "Lord Gosavi, when you left, what happened to her?"[33] "She was looking at me. She went into a trance and felt blissful. Then I left."

17 HE CHASES AWAY A TIGER AT DAKARAM.

In Dakaram, he had begged for food with his bare hands and was going to the temple of Bhiveshvar to sleep.[34] The people there warned him off, saying, "Don't go there, God.

न वचा : एथ वाघु असे : गोसावी आइकौनि बीजें केलें :
तवं तेथ वाघु आला होता : तेणें हाक दीधली : गोसावी
सींहनादु केला : मग तो वाघु पळाला : वाघु तेथौनि गेला :
गोसावी तेथ पहुडले : उदेयाचि लोकु तेथ आला : तुरें
वाजवीत : काहाळा : सींहनादु देति : परि वाघु निगेना :
प्रत्येहीं ते ऐसेंचि करीति : मग वाघु जाए : ते देवासि पूजा
करिती : तै न निगेचि : तीहीं म्हणीतलें : आजि वाघु आझूइं
कां निगेना : तवं एकी म्हणीतलें : कालि वारीत वारीतां
माणुस एक एथ आलें होतें : मग तेहीं दुरौनि पाहिलें : तवं
चौकीं गोसावीयातें देखीलें : जी : जी : एथ वाघु आला होता
कीं : सर्वज्ञें म्हणीतलें : आला होता : तेणें हांक दीधली :
एथौनि सींहनादु केला : तो गेला : आद्यप्रभृतीं तो एथ न ये
हो : मग : सर्वज्ञें म्हणीतलें : बाइ : तीये दीउनि स्थान वसतें
जालें :॥:

१८ तैल्यकारयुग्मा स्थिती :॥:

गावीं एकी हाटामध्यें बीजें केलें : तिळ तेलीण तिळ
पाखडीत होती[१४] : तीया देखीलें : मग तिया म्हणीतलें :
आगा ए बरवीया जोगीया येईजो वो माझेया घरा : ऐसें
म्हणौनि श्रीकरी धरूनि घरा घेउनि गेली[१५] : मग तेथ दोन्ही
दारसंका धरूनि : सर्वज्ञें म्हणीतलें : आगा ए मेहरा : तुझीया

38

Don't go. There's a tiger there." The Gosavi heard them, but he kept going.

The tiger had come there; it growled. The Gosavi roared like a lion, and the tiger ran away. It left.

The Gosavi slept there. Early the next morning, the people came there, playing horns and beating kettledrums. They roared like lions, but the tiger did not appear. Every other day when they did this, the tiger would go away and they would do puja to the god. But that day the tiger was not to be seen. "Why hasn't the tiger shown up yet today?" they asked. Someone said, "There was a man who came here yesterday, even though we tried to warn him off."

They looked from a safe distance then, and they saw the Gosavi in the central hall of the temple. "Lord," they asked, "did the tiger come here?" The omniscient one replied, "He did come here. He growled, I roared like a lion, and he went away. He won't be coming here anymore."

Later the omniscient one said, "My woman, from that day on, the place became inhabited."

18 AN OIL PRESSER COUPLE GOES INTO A TRANCE.

When he went into the market in a certain village, a Sesame-seed Oil Presser woman was winnowing sesame seeds there.[35] She saw him and said, "Come along, handsome yogi. Please come to my house." And she took him by his holy hand and brought him to her house.

There, holding on to both sides of the doorframe, the

मेहरी यातें काईसेया आणिलें : तो घाणा खेटीत होता : तेणें
म्हणितलें : जी जी : मी तीळमारा तेली : जी जी : माझेया
पापा क्षेवो करावेया आणिलें जी : ऐसें म्हणौनि घाणीया
खालुती उडी घातली : बाजेवरि पासवडी आंथुरिली : तेथ
आसन : तो पासीं बैसला : तें उपहाराची आइत करीतें
होती : मग तीयां दोघां विद्यास्तीति जाली : गोसावी बीजें
केलें : सर्वज्ञे म्हणीतले१६ : तीयें अद्यापि देवोदेवी होउनि
वर्ततें असति : हें तिया वाटा तेणें ठायें आलें : परि तीयें यातें
ओळखीतिचि ना :॥:

१९ पंचकौळाचार्यग्रहो निवृत्ति :॥:

बीडीं दक्षिणेश्वराकडे बीजें केलें : पासी पद्मनाभीदेव
असति : तीया वाटां सारस्वतभट आडपालौ वोडौनि गेले :
तवं बाईसीं म्हणीतलें : बाबा : पैल सारस्वत भट नव्हति :
सर्वज्ञें म्हणीतलें : होति : हे बाबातें देखौनि आडवे आडवे
का जात असति : सर्वज्ञें म्हणीतलें : पद्मनाभि तें हा एथु
असे : म्हणौनी : तव बाईसीं म्हणीतलें : हा बाबा हा
एथ असे : तरि यासि आडवेया जावेया कारण काइ : या
उपरि सर्वज्ञें म्हणीतलें : शिष्या अभिमानू : म्हैळीचेयापसि
अधीकू१७ : गोसावी पंचकोळाचार्याची गोष्टि सांघीतली :
गावीं एकी व्यवहारेया एकाचेया घरा पाणीपात्रा बीजें केलें :

omniscient one said, "Hey, Oil Presser! Why has your wife brought me here?"

He was running the oil mill. "Lord," he said, "I am an Oil Presser who presses sesame seeds. She has brought you to do away with my sins, Lord." Saying this, he jumped down from the oil mill. He spread a thick shawl over a mattress. The Gosavi sat down on it, and the man sat near him while the woman prepared some food. Then both of them went into a knowledge-trance. The Gosavi left.

The omniscient one said, "Still today they are living as a god and goddess. I came through that place when I was on that road, but they didn't recognize me at all."

19 HE EXORCISES PANCHAKAULACHARYA'S GHOST.

When he went to the Dakshineshvar temple in Bid, Padmanabhidev was with him.[36] Sarasvatbhat passed by on that road, holding the end of his garment in front of his face. Baïse asked, "Baba, wasn't that Sarasvatbhat over there?" "It was," said the omniscient one. "Why is he avoiding looking at you, Baba?" The omniscient one said, "Because Padmanabhi is here." Baïse said, "Yes, he is here, Baba. But why should Sarasvatbhat avoid him?" Thereupon the omniscient one said, "Pride in one's disciples is greater than that of a woman in her man."[37]

The Gosavi told the story of Panchakaulacharya: In a certain village, the Gosavi went to the home of a merchant to beg for food with his bare hands. The man's son was

तवं तेया पुत्रासि ग्रहो लागला असे : अति सौंदरू :
तो साखळीं खांबी आळिला असे : तेल वोतीलें असें :
तयातें धाडावेया गुणिये एति : तो ग्रहो म्हणे : एणें मंत्रें मातें
धाडीसी : ऐसें : म्हणौनी : मंत्र उच्चारी : एणें वोखदें मातें
धाडीसी ऐसें म्हणौनी वोखदाचें नांव घे : तो काइसेनही न
वचे : मग : तो ग्रहो कवणेंसी बोलेना : ऐसां तेथ गोसावी
पाणीपात्रा बीजें केलें : पुढां पन्हीवा होता : म्हणौनी :
मागौतें बीजें केलें : तेथ न वचतिचि : तेणें ग्रहें गोसावियां
देखीलें आणि म्हणों लागला : हां गा : मातें सोडा कां गा :
एया गोसावीयां पासीं जावों देया कां गा : मीं तुमचेया पुत्रातें
सोडीन : आणि मी या ग्रहत्वापासौनि मुंचैन : तेहीं
म्हणीतलें : हा इतुले दीसू बोलेना : आतां बोलिला तरि
सोडा : आम्हां इतुकेयां असतां के जाईल : मग सोडीला :
तवं गोसावी नदीसी बीजें केलें : श्रीचरणें सीळातळावरि
उदक घातलें : तीये सीळेवरि अन्न घातलें : आरोगण करीत
असति : तवं ग्रहो आला : मागीलीकडे बैसला : मग :
म्हणीतलें : जी जी : मज प्रसादु दीयावा जी : उचिष्ठ गोसावी
प्रसादु देती तरि माझेया पापासि निकृति होइल : सर्वज्ञें
म्हणीतलें : तूं कवणू : जी जी तें गोसावी जाणत असति
कीं : सर्वज्ञें म्हणीतलें : एहीं अवघां जाणावें कीं : मग : तेणें
सांगितलें : मी ग्रहो जी : जी जी : मी पूर्वी पंचकौळाचार्या :
माझा शिष्य आणिका एका अवधुता पासि गेला : तेणें
अभिमानें मिया तेयासिं विषप्रळयो केला : तया पापातवं
मीं ग्रहो जाला : सर्वज्ञें म्हणीतलें : एथीचिये दृष्टीसमोर

extremely handsome, but he was possessed by a ghost. They had chained him to a post and poured oil on him. Exorcists were coming to drive out the ghost. "You think you can exorcise me with this mantra," the ghost would say, and then he would recite a mantra. "You think you can exorcise me with this medicine," he would say, and then he would name a medicine. Nothing could make the ghost leave. Afterward the ghost would not speak with anyone.

It was while this was going on that the Gosavi went there to beg for food with his bare hands. There was a drain in front of the house, so he went around the back. He did not go anywhere near the boy. The ghost saw the Gosavi and began to say, "Hey! Will you set me free? Will you let me get close to this Gosavi? I will leave your son, and I will be saved from being a ghost."

"He has not spoken for a long time," they said. "Since he has spoken now, set him free. With so many of us here, where can he go?" So they let him go.

Meanwhile the Gosavi went to the river. With his holy foot he splashed water onto a flat rock. He put his food down on the rock. As he was eating his meal, the ghost arrived, sat down behind him, and said, "Lord Gosavi, please give me *prasād*. If you give me your leftovers as *prasād*, my sin will be done away with." "Who are you?" asked the omniscient one. "You know, Lord Gosavi." The omniscient one asked, "Must I know everything?"

Then the ghost said, "I am a ghost, Lord. I used to be Panchakaulacharya. My disciple left me for another ascetic. Out of injured pride, I poisoned him to death. I have become a ghost because of that sin." The omniscient one said, "No

ग्रहो उभा न न्हाये कीं : तवं तेणें म्हणितलें : जी जी : मीं
अवचेयामध्ये ग्रहोसी मुख्य नायकू : तो मी : मग गोसावी
तेयासि प्रसादु आरोगणस्थानीं सांडीला : गोसावी परतें बीजें
केलें : तेणें अवचे सीतेंसीतें वेचुनि खादलें : सर्वज्ञें
म्हणितलें : यातें धरा : एन्हवीं पडैल : मग तो ग्रहो तेयाचिए
देहींहुनि गेला ॥छ॥: रामे : तेहीं गोसावीयातें आवारासी
नेलें : मर्दना मादनें पुजा केली : आरोगणा जाली : मग
तेथौनि बीजें केलें : मग बाईसीं^{१८} म्हणितलें : बटीका तरि तुं
न एसि एथें :॥:

२० घोडाचुडी शिष्या सांघात् :॥:

गोसावीयासि घोडाचुडीचे सिष्य भेटले : तेहीं म्हणितलें : देव
हो : चाला जावों खीखवींद पर्वतासि : तेथ घोडाचुडी असति :
गोसावी मानिलें : गोसावी आधीं पाणीपात्र करीति :
पाठीं ते चाटणीं करीति : सांघातें असति : एकु दीं^{१९} ते
चाटणीं करित होते : एकी बाइया कढती कढती आंबील
हातीं घातली : तेहीं आंबील चाटीली : हातु वळनीयें पूसिलें :
आणि आगी लागली : गावों जळों लागला : तें पुरुषु :
मागील वास पाहाति : हांसति : ऐसे गोसावियांपासि आलें :

ghost can remain standing before my gaze." He replied, "I am the seniormost leader of all the ghosts, Lord."

Then the Gosavi dropped some *prasād* for the ghost at the place where he had eaten his meal. The Gosavi stepped away, and the ghost picked up every grain of food and ate it. The omniscient one said to the others, "Hold him up or he will fall down." Then the ghost left the young man's body.

(According to Rameshvarbas, the merchant took the Gosavi home. He gave him a massage and a bath and did puja to him. The Gosavi ate a meal there, and then he left.)

After hearing this story, Baïse said to Padmanabhidev, "So you should not come here, Batika."

20 HE ACCOMPANIES A DISCIPLE OF GHODACHUDI.

A disciple of Ghodachudi who met the Gosavi said to him, "Come on, God. Let's go to the Kishkindha mountain.[38] That's where Ghodachudi stays." The Gosavi agreed.

The two of them traveled together. First the Gosavi would beg for food with his bare hands, and afterward the disciple would beg, licking the food off his own hands. One day, when the disciple was begging that way, a woman put boiling hot gruel in his hand. He licked up the gruel and wiped his hand on the lower edge of a thatched roof. That started a fire, and it began to burn up the whole village.

Looking back and laughing, the man came to the Gosavi. When the Gosavi asked him what had happened, he told

गोसावी पूसीलें : तेहीं अवघें व्रूतांत सांघीतलें : मग : सर्वज्ञें
म्हणीतलें : माहात्मे हो वोखटें केलें : ऐसेनी भूत हिंसा
जाली२० : परि कैसीहीं कांहीं घृणा नुपजैचि होए : आता हे
तुम्हा सांघातें नये : मग गोसावी तीं अहोरात्रें परमेश्वरपुरा
आले : बीजें केलें :॥:

२१ श्रीप्रभु दर्शना गमन : दाभविहीरी अवस्थान :॥:

दोहीं पीवळ तळौलियां मध्यें श्रीप्रभुभेटी होए : पाहारू दोनि
कांटीये एकि तळि बैसले असति : मग : श्रीप्रभु रीधपुरा
बीजें करीति : मार्गीं मातांगु एकू : हुरडा सोले : उंसाचीया
कांडीया : दोने भरूनि ठेवी : वरि पातळी झांकी : श्रीप्रभु
बीजें करीति : तेथ अडुखळति : इ काइ रे : मेला जाए :
म्हणौनि : तेथचि बैसति : कणु कणु आरोगीलें : मग : बीजें
केलें : तो प्रसादु आमुचे गोसावी चेति : मातांगु दुरौनि दोही
गोसावीयांसि दंडवत घाली : मग श्रीप्रभुची श्रीमूर्ति दीसे तवं
आमुचे गोसावी अवलोकीत उभे असति : मग : दाभविहीरी
बीजें करीति : तेथ पाणिपात्र करीति : आरोगण होए :
भैरवी पहुड : प्रतिदीनी श्रीप्रभुचेया दर्शना जाति : दीसवीस

him everything. Then the omniscient one said, "Mahatma, you have done something evil that has caused harm to living beings, but you don't feel any pity at all. I am not going to travel with you anymore."

Then the Gosavi went to Parameshvarpur. He reached there in three days and three nights.

21 HE GOES FOR *DARŚAN* OF SHRIPRABHU. HE STAYS IN DABHVIHIR.

He would meet Shriprabhu between the two salt ponds, where they would sit for six hours at the foot of a thorn tree.[39] Then, as Shriprabhu went toward Riddhipur, a Matanga* would be husking ears of grain along the road. He would put the husked grain and pieces of sugar cane in leaf-cups and place them there. He would cover them with a leaf-plate.

As Shriprabhu came along, his steps would falter at that place. "Hey!" he would say, "What is this? Drop dead!"[40] And he would sit down right there, eat it grain by grain, and then move on. Our Gosavi would eat what was left as *prasād*. The Matanga would prostrate himself from afar to both Gosavis. Our Gosavi would stand there watching for as long as he could see Shriprabhu's holy form.

Then our Gosavi would go to Dabhvihir. There he would beg for food with his bare hands and eat his meal, then sleep in the Bhairav temple. Every day he would go for *darśan* of Shriprabhu. He stayed there about twenty days.

---

* A member of an extremely low caste.

अनुमान अवस्थान : एकदिनी रूपनाएका दर्शन जालें :
आपुलीया गावां घोडेया वाउनि घेउनि गेला : मर्दना जाली :
मादनें जाली : पुजा केली : सर्वज्ञें भणीतलें : तो आगमीक
पुजा करू निका जाणे : तेथ वसति जाली : आरोगणा
जाली : मग तेथौनि बीजें केलें :॥ः

२२ विझीं गोंडवाडा अवस्थान :॥ः

माहादाइसे²⁹ भिक्षे गेली होती : भुतानंदाचीए लेकीचीया
घरा : तेथें भूतानंदाचीया नाती : चींचुकरटां तांदुळ रांधीलें :
तें गोसावीया पुढां सांघीतलें : जी जीः तांदुळ सीजलें : जी :
सर्वज्ञें म्हणीतलें : आति : बाइ : हे वीझींमध्यें गोंडआंतु
होते : तया गोसावीयांची प्रीति संचरीली : गोसावीयांतें न
देखति : आणि देवणे करीतें आळविति : कीलु कीलु करीतें
नाचति : श्रीचरणीं तळवा : तळहातीं : उदरीं : मोमे देति :
मग वेळुवाचें कांडोरें कोरीति : तेथ तांदुळ घालीति : डांबीर
घालीति³² : सेणें मातीया बोबुनि आगींमध्यें घालीति : तें
होतें पदन तीयेंचि जाणति : मग : पायाळें चिरीति : मग :

48

One day Rupanayak* had *darśan* of the Gosavi. He brought him to his village on a horse. The Gosavi had a massage and a bath, and Rupanayak did puja to him. (The omniscient one said, "He knew how to do a proper puja, according to the scriptures."[41])

The Gosavi stayed overnight there. After eating his meal, he left.

22 HE STAYS IN A GOND SETTLEMENT IN THE VINDHYA MOUNTAINS.

Mahadaïse had gone to Bhutanande's daughter's house to beg for food. Bhutanande's granddaughter had cooked rice in a pot made from tamarind pulp. Mahadaïse told the Gosavi about it. "The rice was fully cooked, Lord!" she said.

The omniscient one replied, "That's right, my woman. I was in the Vindhyas among the Gonds. They were filled with love for me. When they did not see me, they would wail, 'Oh God!' They would chirp like birds and dance. They would kiss me on the soles of my holy feet, on the palms of my hands, on my stomach.

"They would scoop out sections of bamboo and put uncooked rice inside. They would cover them, seal them shut with cow dung and mud, and put them in a fire. Only they could tell when they were ready. Then they would cut them open with a small sickle. They would put the rice to

---

* Maternal uncle of Sadhe.

तो भातु पातळीये नीवतु घालीति : पातळी पोमिनिचीया
पानाची : एकी दोणां आधाचा मधु घालति : एकू दोना
पानीयाचा ठेवीति : पाणीयाची सीर तीयेंचि जाणति : ऐसें
उकरीति : आणि पानी लागे : ऐसी आरोगण देति : मग :
केतुलेया एका काळा बीजें केलें :॥ः

२३ ससीक रक्षण :॥ः

गावीं एकी व्रक्षाखाली आसन : तव पारधी वाटे ससा
सोडीला : तया पाठीं सुणी सोडीली : काकूळती येउनि ससा
जानूतळि रीगाला : सूणी उभी राहीली : मागील कडौनी
पारधी आले : तेहीं वीनवीलें : ससा सोडीजो जी : सर्वज्ञें
म्हणीतलें : हा एथ सरण आला : पुडती तीहीं म्हणीतलें : जी
जी : हा होडेचा ससा जी : या कारण सूरीया काढणीया
होती : जी जी : हा सोडावा जी²³ : सर्वज्ञें म्हणीतलें : हां गा :
एथ सरण आलेया काइ मरण असे : जी जी : तरि हा :
गोसावी राखबीला ॥ रामेश्वरबास ॥ निरूपण केलें : हां गा :
ए रानीं असति : पाणी पीति : यातें तुम्ही कां मारा : तीहीं
म्हणीतलें : जी जी : आजि लागौनि न मारूं : मग : तें
निघाले : मग : सर्वज्ञें म्हणीतलें : माहात्मे हो : आतां जाए :
ऐसें : भणौनि : जानु उचलिली : मग ससा निगाळा :॥ः

cool on a dish made of the broad leaves of a *pominī* tree. They would pour honey from a dried gourd into a leaf-cup, and they would set down another leaf-cup for water. Only they knew where the underground watercourses were. They would dig there and strike water. This is the kind of meal they would give me.

"Then, after some time, I left."

23 HE PROTECTS A RABBIT.

He was sitting under a tree in a certain village when hunters let loose a rabbit on the road and unleashed a female dog to run after it. Whining pitifully, the rabbit came and hid under his thigh. The dog stood there.

The hunters came up from behind. "Please let the rabbit go, Lord," they entreated him. The omniscient one said, "It has taken refuge with me." Again they said, "Lord, we have made a bet about this rabbit. Swords will be drawn because of it. Please let it go, Lord." The omniscient one said, "Can someone who has taken refuge with me be allowed to die?"[42] "All right, Lord. Then the Gosavi has saved it."

(According to Rameshvarbas, "Hey!" he explained. "They live in the wilderness. They drink water. Why do you kill them?" "All right, Lord," they replied. "From this day on we will not kill them.")

After they left, the omniscient one said, "Go now, Mahatma," and he raised his thigh. Then the rabbit left.

२४ सेंदुरजनीं मासोपवासिनी तांबोळ प्रदानीं स्थीति :॥ः

सेंदुर्जणी नारायणाचां देउळी मासोपवासीनी असति : तेथ
बीजें केलें : दोन्ही दारसंका धरूनि भीतरि अवलोकीलें :
मग : साजां आसन : एकी मासोपवासीनी श्रीमूखीचें तांबोळ
मागितलें : गोसावी श्रीकरें लोकांकडे दाखवीलें :
त्या म्हणीतलें द्यावें जी : लोकांचे काइ : मग दीधलें : तीएसि
स्तीति जाली : तिसि बारा वरीखें आनोदकें नाहीति :
आपणपें कांहीं जाणे ना : तीचे बाप भाऊ : वायू : तथा
वारा : म्हणौनि वोखदें करीति : बारा वरीखां : त्या :
म्हणीतलें : पुरुष होतिल : तरि देह वाचैल : तेहीं पुसीलें :
कैसें पुरुष असति : तया पुढां सांघीतलीया खुणा : ते
आतांचि नीगाले : मग : ते पाहों लागले : गोसावी तींएचि
प्रदेशीं भेटले : तीहीं म्हणीतलें : गोसावीयासि आवारासि
घेउनि गेले : तेथ बीजें केलें : तीया गोसावीया देखीलें :
श्रीचरणा लागली : आणि : स्तीति सूभर जाली : मागुतीं
गोसावी तेथौनी बीजें केलें :॥ः

24 IN SENDURJAN A WOMAN WHO IS FASTING FOR A MONTH GOES INTO A TRANCE WHEN HE GIVES HER PAN.

Women who were fasting for a month were staying in the Narayan temple at Sendurjan.[43] He went there, held onto both sides of the doorframe, and looked inside. Then he sat down at a small shrine.

One of the women fasting for a month asked for the pan from his holy mouth. With his holy hand, the Gosavi gestured toward the other people. "Please give it to me, Lord," she said. "Who cares about those people?"

Then he gave it to her, and she went into a trance. For twelve years she did not eat food or drink water, and she was not aware of herself. Her father and brother got medicine for her, thinking she was possessed by a spirit. After twelve years, she said, "If that holy man were here, I would be saved." "What is the holy man like?" they asked. She told them his distinctive features and said, "He just left."[44]

So they began to search for the Gosavi, and they found him in that same region. They told him about her and brought him home with them. When the Gosavi reached there, she saw him and touched his holy feet. And her trance deepened.

Once again the Gosavi left there.

२५ भोगारामीं अवस्थान :॥:

लखुदेवोबा गोदानां कटका गेले : ते करजाळेया आले : तेहीं
सामकोसांतें पुसीलें : नागदेवो के गेला वो : तेहीं म्हणीतलें :
गोसावीयांपासीं असे : गोसावी कोण : सामकोसीं
म्हणीतलें : श्रीचांगदेओ राउळ गोसावीं : हींवरळीये असति :
आणि अंतःकरण वेधलें : तैसेंचि निगालें : अहोरात्रें आले :
श्रीमूर्तिचे सारिखें पुढां देखति : मढाचां दारवठां पातले :
तवं भट बाहीरि निगतां भेटले : भटीं म्हणीतलें : आलासि
तें निकें केलें हो : मग भटीं दर्शनें आणुं पाठवीलीं : दर्शन
घेउनि आले : दंडवतें घातलीं : आणि : स्थीति भंगली : दर्सन
आणिलें तें आवघें वीखूरलें : तें भटीं आसनापासि ठेविलें :
मग गोसावी पुसीलें : तुम्हांसि एथचें दर्शन आति :
तेही म्हणीतलें : नाहीं जी : तरि श्रवण आति : जी : जी :
मग तीहीं मागील पूर्वी सांघीतली२४ : मग सर्वज्ञें म्हणीतलें :
ऐसी एकें सुक्षेत्रें असति : भुमीं बीयां मेळापकू कीजे : आणि
भारू आथौनी पीकति : एकी वासना : चुमरींसीं उठीति :
एकें नांगरवेन्हीं उलखीजति : घाटे वापे पेरीजति : परि तेथें
बींहीं न निगे :॥: मागां हे रामी होतें : हें जया वोटेया वरि
होतें तया वोटेयासी बडुवा धुपार्ति करी : तया वोटेया वरि

25 HE STAYS IN THE BHOGARAM TEMPLE.

Lakhudevoba went to the capital to receive a cow as a dona-tion.[45] He came to Karanjale and asked Samakose, "Where has Nagdev gone?"[46] "He's with the Gosavi," she replied. "Who is the Gosavi?" "Shri Cangdev Raül Gosavi,"[*] said Samakose. "He is at Hivarali."

And Lakhudevoba's heart was pierced. He set out imme-diately. He got there in one day and one night, the Gosavi's holy form constantly before his eyes. When he reached the doorway of the hermitage, he met Bhat, who was coming out. "It's good you've come here," said Bhat.

Then Bhat sent him to get offerings. He went and got offer-ings and prostrated himself to the Gosavi, and his trance broke. All the offerings he had brought got scattered. Bhat placed them next to the Gosavi's seat.

The Gosavi asked, "Have you had my *darśan* before?" "No, Lord," he replied. "Have you at least heard of me?" "Yes, Lord," he said, and he told the Gosavi what had happened in the past.

Then the omniscient one said, "Some people are good fields like this. Just put the seeds in the ground and they blossom and ripen abundantly. Other fields get plowed, seedlings get planted in them, but not a single grain grows.

"Once, after I had been at Ram,[†] a temple priest would perform *āratī* with incense to the pedestal that I had stayed

---

* Chakradhar, Cangdev Raül's reincarnation.
† Ramtek.

ब्राम्हणू येकू बैसला ː तेयासि स्तीति जाली ː तेणें वोटेयासि
धुपार्ति करितां देखीलें ː मग बडुवातें पुसीलें ː तुम्ही धुपार्ति
कवणासि करीत असा ː तेणें म्हणीतलें ː एथ एकु पुरुष
होते ː तेयासि करूं ː मग ː भोगरामांसि करूं ː ते पुरुषू
निगाले ː मग तेयाचीया वोटेयासि करूं ː ते केउते गेले ː तेणें
म्हणीतलें ː मनसीळेसि गेले ː मग तो ब्राह्मण मनसीळेसि
आला ː दर्शन जालें ː मग ː त्या स्थीती सूभर जाली ː सर्वझ्नें
म्हणीतलें ː ऐसें हें एथचेया नामातवं होए ː कां स्थानातवं
होए ː॥ː

२६   भांडारेकारा भेटि ː॥ː

भांडारां भांडारेकराचेया घरां पाणीपात्रां बीजें केलें ː तवं ते
उतरा संग वस्त्र धोत्र घालुनि पोथी वाचीत होते ː तयासि
स्नानां लागौनि ː पाणी सारिलें होतें ː पाणिपात्र जालें ː परि
गोसावीयांचि वास न पाहाति ː मग ː सर्वझ्नें भांडारेकारा
म्हणीतलें ː भटो ː मागिल फांकि म्हणा ː मग गोसावी बीजें
केलें ː पाठीं तेही नीगाले ː तवं घरीचां म्हणीतलें ː तुम्ही
के निगालेति ː तुम्हां पाणीं सारिलें असे ː मग भांडारेकारीं
म्हणीतलें ː हें इतले दीस तुम्हापासीं होतें ː आतां जेयाचें
तेयापासि जात असे ː तुम्ही राहा ː सर्वझ्नें म्हणीतलें ː
अज्ञाधरें ː मग तियें राहीलीं ː गोसावी तळां श्रीचरणें
शिळातळावरि उदक घातलें ː श्रीकरिचें अन्न तेथ ठेविलें ː

on. A certain Brahman sat on the pedestal and went into a trance. He saw that the temple priest was performing *āratī* to the pedestal, and so he asked the priest, 'To whom are you doing *āratī?*'

"'There was a holy man here,' the priest replied. 'I used to do *āratī* to him, and then I would do it to Bhogaram. Since the holy man left, I do it to his pedestal.' 'Where did he go?' 'He went to Mansil,' said the priest.[47] So the Brahman came to Mansil. He had my *darśan,* and then his trance deepened."

The omniscient one said, "This can happen from my name or from a place."[48]

26 HE MEETS BHANDAREKAR.

In Bhandara he went to beg with his bare hands at Bhandarekar's house.[49] Bhandarekar had draped the end of his dhoti over his shoulders and was reading a religious text. Water had been drawn for his bath. He put food into the Gosavi's hands but did not look at him. Then the omniscient one said to Bhandarekar, "Recite the previous section, Bhat." And the Gosavi left.

Bhandarekar set out after him. "Where are you going?" asked his wife. "The water for your bath is ready." Bhandarekar replied, "I've been with you for a long time, but now I'm going to be with the one I belong to. You stay here." (The omniscient one remarked, "She was obedient, so she stayed there.")

At a pond, the Gosavi splashed water with his holy foot onto a flat rock. He placed the food from his holy hands on

मग : आरोगणीं भांडारेकारा प्रसादु जाला : मग परतें ऐसें
वृक्षातळीं बीजें केलें : भांडारेकारी अरुतें धोत्र फाळुनि
आसन केलें : गोसावी नावेक आसनीं बैसलें : मग तेथौनि
बीजें केलें :॥:

२७ तथा स्तुति करणें :॥:

एक वेळ भांडारेकार वीगुळी चावीले : असाह्य पीडा होों
लागली : मग म्हणीतलें : जी जी : मी स्तुति करूं : सर्वज्ञें
म्हणीतलें : करा : मग स्तुति करूं लागले : जवं जवं स्तुति
करीति तवं तवं व्यथा काढली : ऐसी स्तुति करीतां अवघी
व्यथा काढली :॥:

२८ अळजपुरीं भैरवी अवस्थान :
भांडारेकाराची पूजा स्वीकार :॥:

बेलोपुरीं भटोबासातें म्हणीतलें : वानरेया : तुम्हांसि करणीये
एकूं असे गा : भटीं म्हणीतलें : जी जी : सर्वज्ञें म्हणीतलें :
परी ते द्रव्यसाध्य : तव भटीं म्हणीतलें : जी जी : गोसावी
जाणत असति कीं : मातें द्रव्य नाहीं : सर्वज्ञें म्हणीतलें :
तूं उभा ठाकलाचि पुरे : सीधीतें ऐथौनिचि नेइजैल कीं :
पुरुषु आपुलें करणीयें म्हणौनि प्रवर्तें : तयासि द्रव्याचीं

it. As the Gosavi ate his meal, Bhandarekar had his *prasād*. Then the Gosavi went over to the foot of a tree, and Bhandarekar tore his dhoti and made it into a seat for him there. The Gosavi sat on it for a little while, and then he left.

27 AND BHANDAREKAR PRAISES HIM.

Once a scorpion bit Bhandarekar. He began to feel intolerable pain, and so he said, "May I praise you, Lord?" "Do that," said the omniscient one.

Then he began to praise the Gosavi. The longer he praised him, the more the pain subsided. Finally, as he kept praising him, all the pain went away.

28 HE STAYS IN THE BHAIRAV TEMPLE AT ALAJPUR. HE ACCEPTS BHANDAREKAR'S PUJA.

In Belopur he said to Bhatobas,* "Monkey, there is a task for you."[50] "Yes, Lord," said Bhat. "But," said the omniscient one, "you'll need money to do it." Bhat replied, "Lord Gosavi, you know that I have no money." The omniscient one said, "All you have to do is to stand up. I will lead you to success. A man who sets out to do his duty gets plenty of money."[51]

---

* Nagdev, also nicknamed Monkey.

सतें मीळति : मग भांडारेकाराची गोष्ट सांघीतली ॥ एथ
भांडारेकार होते : तयासि करणीयें वीहीलें : तें एथौनिचि
सीधी नेलें : अळजपुरी भैरवी अवस्थान : ॥ भांडारेकारा
निर्वाणेचेया देउळा पाठवीलें : कव्हणी कांही म्हणैल : तेथ
जाइजे हो : मग : भांडारेकार निर्वाणेचेया देउळा मागें
बैसले : पंचोळीची स्त्री धानाबाई : तीसि निर्वाणेची भक्ति :
ते प्रदक्षणे आली : तवं भांडारेकारातें देखीलें : तेयांसि
नमस्कारू केला : आवारा चेऊनि गेली : पुजा करूं
आदरीली : तवं तेहीं म्हणीतलें : हे काई कराल : तीयां
म्हणीतलें : पुजा करुनि : मग तेहीं म्हणीतलें : पुजा तरि
आमुचेया गोसावीयासि करा : तीया म्हणीतलें : तुम्हांइं
आणि गोसावी असति : तयातें बोलाऊं पाठवीन : दांडी
डोळेकार पाठवीन : तेही म्हणीतलें : ना : आम्हीचि
बोलाउनि : मग : भांडारेकारीं आवघें व्रूतांत सांघीतलें :
जी जी : तरि तेथ बीजें करावें : गोसावी तेथ बीजें केलें :
त्या गोसावीयासि देखीलें : आणि : भांडारेकाराचेया पासि
उचें बरवीं पुजाद्रव्यें आणौनि पुजा करूं आदरीली : तवं
सर्वज्ञें भणीतलें : तुम्ही यांचा हातीं वोपा : हे एथ पुजा
करीति : हें याचें कीं : मग तीयें : भांडारेकाराचीए हातीं
देति : ते गोसावीयासि पुजा करीति : मग : भांडारेकाराचीं
पुजाद्रव्यें तीहीं आणिलीं : पूजा केली : तें तेयाची तयासि
देवों आदरीली : तीहीं म्हणीतलें : जी जी : ईश्वरीं अर्पीलें तें
माघौतें कैसे घेयावें : सर्वज्ञें म्हणीतलें : एथौनी तुम्हा देइजत

Then he told the story of Bhandarekar: "When Bhandarekar was with me, I told him to do things, and I myself brought him success at them."

The Gosavi was staying in the Bhairav temple in Alajpur. He sent Bhandarekar to the Nirvan temple. "Someone will say something. Go there." So Bhandarekar sat behind the Nirvan temple.

Pancholi's wife, Dhanabaï, was devoted to Nirvan. When she came to circumambulate the temple, she saw Bhandarekar. She bowed to him and took him home with her. When she started to perform puja to him, he asked, "What are you going to do?" "I'm going to do puja," she said. Then he said, "If you're going to do puja, do it to our Gosavi." "*You* have a Gosavi?" she asked. "I will send for him. I will send a palanquin and palanquin bearers to get him." "No," he replied. "I will invite him myself."

Bhandarekar told the Gosavi everything that had happened. "So please go there, Lord," he said.

The Gosavi went there. When she saw him, she brought more elaborate, finer puja items than those she had been going to use for Bhandarekar. As she started to perform puja, the omniscient one said, "Hand them to him. He does my puja. He is mine!" So she handed each item to Bhandarekar, and he performed the Gosavi's puja. Then she brought the items intended for Bhandarekar's puja, and she performed his puja with them.

The Gosavi started giving her back the items she had offered him. "Lord," she said, "how can I take back what I have offered to God?" "Because I am giving it to you," said the omniscient one. She agreed.

61

असीजे : तेहीं मानीलें : मग त्यें परित्यजुनि बीजें केलें : मग :
सर्वज्ञें म्हणीतलें : भटो : तुमचें करणीयें चरितार्थ हो : तेथ
म्हाइंभटीं म्हणीतलें : जी जी : मज वीहीजो : मातें द्रव्य
असे : तुम्हांसि आणिक करणीयें : यांसि आणिक करणीयें :
हा संनिधान पातला असे : तुम्हां संनिधान करावें असे :॥:

२९ नांदियेडीं भावतीर्थीं अवस्थान : पटीसाळपतन :॥:

नांदेडीं भावतीर्थीं नरसींहीं अवस्थान :॥: भांडारेकार भिक्षेसि
गेले : तवं पडिसाळे लेकरुवें पढतें होतीं : भांडारेकारीं
म्हणीतलें : आरे : परते परते सरा : पडीसाळ पडली :
पडली : तीयें आवघीं बाहीरि नीगाली : आणि : पडीसाळ
रिचवली : तें आश्चर्यें लोकासि जालें : सोपस्कार भीक्षा देति :
भीक्षा घेउनि आलें : मग गोसावीया पुढा : तेहीं मागील
वृत्तांत सांघीतलें : मग सर्वज्ञें म्हणीतलें : हां गा : ऐसेसीं
करींता लोकु न भजो : ऐसें न कीजे कीं : तेहीं म्हणींतलें :
जी जी : मज ऐसें न व्हावें : सर्वज्ञें म्हणीतले : ऐसें न करा
तर नव्हे :॥:

Then the Gosavi left, abandoning the offerings. The omniscient one said to Bhandarekar, "Bhat, your duty has been fulfilled."

After hearing this story, Mhaimbhat* said, "Tell me to do that, Lord. I have money." "You have one task, and he has another. He has reached my presence.[52] You have yet to achieve my presence."

29 HE STAYS AT BHAVATIRTHA IN NANDED; A VERANDA FALLS DOWN.

In Nanded he stayed in the Narasimha temple at Bhavatirtha.[53] When Bhandarekar went out to beg for alms, some children were studying on a veranda. Bhandarekar said, "Hey, you! Get out! Out! The veranda is falling down! It's falling down!" They all got out, and then the veranda collapsed.

That amazed people. They gave him delicacies as alms. He brought the food back, and then he told the Gosavi what had happened. The omniscient one said, "When you do something like that, why wouldn't people worship you? Don't do things like that!"[54] "May that never happen to me, Lord," he said. The omniscient one replied, "If you don't do things like that, it won't happen."

---

* The compiler of this text.

३० भांडारेकारा देहावसान :॥ः

नृसींही भांडारेकारासि असक्ति उपनली ः तें भोगस्थान
म्हणौनि पैलाडी नंदेश्वरा बीजें केलें ः मांडी उसीसेसा
दीधली ः एकी वासना ः सर्वज्ञें म्हणीतलें ः भटो काळवंचना
करूं ः तीहीं म्हणीतलें ः ना ः जी ः मग मांडी उसीसें करूनि ः
श्रीमुख अवलोकीत देह त्येजीलें ः मग गोसावी तेयांसि
जळनिक्षेपु करवीला ः सर्वज्ञें म्हणीतलें ः बाइ ः मग यासि
तेथ राहावेंचि ना ः मग हें तेथौनी निगालें ः॥ः

३१ गोपाळांतु खेलु :॥ः

गोसावी गावां एका बीजें करीत असति ः तवं ः राणीं गोपाळ
खेळत असति ः सर्वज्ञें म्हणीतलें ः गोपाळ व्हो ः हें तुम्हांतु
खेळों येईल ः तिहीं म्हणीतलें ः व्हो कां जी ः रानेभेरियाचा
खेळु ः गोसावीयां खेळतां ः जीयावरि दाही ये तेयाचिए
पाठीवरि अरुहण करीति ः ते सीमां पुरे ः परि तो पाठी वरूनि
उतरवीना ः एर म्हणिएति ः कारे उतरिसि ना ः तो म्हणे ः

30 BHANDAREKAR DIES.

While they were staying in the Narasimha temple, Bhan-
darekar became weak. Because it was a busy temple, the
Gosavi went across the river to the Nandeshvar* temple.
He let Bhandarekar put his head on his lap. (One version:
The omniscient one said, "Bhat,† shall I trick death?" "No,
Lord," he replied.) Then, resting his head on the Gosavi's lap,
looking at his holy face, Bhandarekar gave up his body. The
Gosavi had them dispose of his body in the water.[55]

The omniscient one said, "My woman, after that I simply
could not stay there, so I left."

31 HE PLAYS WITH COWHERD BOYS.

As the Gosavi was going to a certain village, cowherd boys
were playing in a pasture along the way. The omniscient one
said, "Hey, cowherd boys! I want to come and play with you."
"All right, Sir," they said.

They were playing a piggyback game. In the game, the
Gosavi would climb up on the back of whoever's turn it was.
That boy's turn would come to an end, but he would not let
the Gosavi down from his back.

The other boys would say, "Hey, why aren't you letting him
down?" and the boy would say, "Hey, I'm feeling blissful."

---

* Shiva.
† Bhandarekar.

सूख होत असे रे ः तवं एरू म्हणे ः पा पां ः जी ः माझीये
पाठिवरि बैसा ः तवं तेयांहीं तैसेंचि सूख होए ः तवं तो म्हणे ः
आरे ः तुज काइसें सूख ः सूख तें मज होत असें ः तवं
आणिक म्हणे ः पा पां ः जी ः माझीये पाठिवरि बैसा ः यापरि
आवघीयाचीए पाठीवरि अरुहण केलें ः जेयाचीए पाठिवरि
अरुहण करीति ः तयासि सूख होए ः मग खेळु पारूखला ः
मग मोटा सोडीलीया ः काला केला ः गोसावीयासि
आरोगणा ः मग उसीरू जाला ः जेया गावां बीजें करीत
होते ः तेया न वचतीचि ः आणिकू आडवा गांवो होता ः तेथ
बीजें केलें ः मागीली कडौनि एकू संन्यासी आला ः तेहीं
गोपाळातें सूख अनुमोदीतां आइकीलें ः कैसा गा देओ ः कैसें
आम्हांसि सूख दीधलें ः संन्यासी म्हणीतलें ः गोपाळ हें सूख
काइ जाणती ः पूसीलें ः हारे गोपाळ व्हो ः तुम्ही काइ बोलत
असा ः तेहीं म्हणीतलें ः देवो एकू आम्हांतु खेळो आला ः तो
जेयाचिए पाठिवरि बैसे तेयासि सूख होए ः ऐसें अवघेयासि
सूख दीधलें ः तेहीं म्हणीतलें ः हारे ते पुरुषु केउतें गेलें ः ते
पैलगावां नीगाले ः मग ते संन्यासी गोसावीयापासि आले ः
तयासि स्थिति जाली ः ते अद्यापि द्रावडदेसीं आचार्ये होउनि
वर्तत असति ः॥ः

At that, another boy would say, "Come on, Sir! Sit on my back." He too would feel the same kind of bliss. "Why should bliss be just for you?" he would say. "*I'm* feeling blissful."

At that, yet another boy would say, "Come on, Sir! Sit on my back."

In this way, he climbed up onto each one's back. Whoever's back he climbed up on would feel blissful. Then, after the game was over, they opened their lunch packs and mixed their food together. The Gosavi ate his meal with them.

It got to be late, and the Gosavi did not reach the village he had been going to. He went to another village, in between.

A sannyasi who came up from behind heard the cowherd boys extolling the bliss that they had experienced. "What a god he was! What bliss he gave us!"

The sannyasi said to himself, "Can cowherd boys know this kind of bliss?"

"Hey, cowherd boys!" he asked. "What are you talking about?" "A god came to play with us," they said. "Whoever's back he sat on felt blissful. He gave all of us that bliss." The sannyasi asked, "Hey, where did the holy man go?" "He set out toward that village over there."

Then the sannyasi approached the Gosavi and went into a trance. To this day, he is a religious teacher in the Dravidian land.*

* South India.

३२ तथा गोपाळ चोंढीए लपवणें :॥:

गावीं एकी वीहीरीसि आसन : तेथ गोपाळ आले : एरू ए :
आपूलीया वाहाणा फेडि : पांगुरण ठेवी : उदकामध्यें रिगे :
तो अदृश्य होए : आणिकू ए : तोही अदृश्य होए : ऐसे
आवचे अदृश्य जाले : गोरूवें आपणालेया गेली : गावींची
माणुसें आलीं : तवं तेहीं गोपाळाचेया पांगुरणाचे पुंजे
देखीले : मग तेहीं पुसीलें : हा जी एथ गोपाळ होते कीं :
सर्वज्ञें भणीतलें : एथ असति : आपुलालेयाचीं नांवें घेउनि
बोलावा : मग ते नांवें घेवोंघेंवों बोलावीति : सांगेया
म्हणति : आणि तो उदकांतुनि निगे : आपलें पांगुरण घे :
वाहाणा ले : मग जाय : आणिकातें बोलावीति : तेही तैसेंचि
नीगति : लपवीले होते ते आवघेही निगाले : तेथ महदाइसीं
पूसीलें : हा जी : तें कें होतें : सर्वज्ञें म्हणीतलें : अवगळा
एकी धरिले होते :॥:

३३ गोवारी-ज्वर-निवृत्ति :॥:

एकी गावीं म्हातारी एकीचा पुत गोरूवे राखे : तेनेंसी
गोसावीयासि पाडु प्रज्ञान आति : तीए गावीं गोसावीयासि
वृक्षा खालि आसन : ऐसां तेयासि जरू आला : तयाचीया
माता म्हणीतलें : जी जी : तेयासि जरू आला : आतां गोरूवें
आणिकासि नीरोवीति : आम्ही मेलों : गोसावी तेयाचीया

32 AND HE HIDES COWHERD
BOYS IN A WELL.

When he was sitting at a well in a certain village, cowherd boys came there. One boy would come, take off his sandals, put down his blanket, and disappear into the water. Another one would come, and he too would disappear. Eventually they all disappeared. The cattle went back to their homes.

When the people of the village came there, they saw the pile of the cowherd boys' blankets. "Sir," they asked, "were the cowherd boys here?" "They are still here," answered the omniscient one. "Call out to each of them by name."

So they called out to each of them by name. "Sanga!" they said, and Sanga came out of the water. He took his blanket, put on his sandals, and left. They called out to the others too, and they emerged the same way. All the boys who had been hidden came out.

Later, Mahadaïse asked, "Where were they, Lord?" The omniscient one said, "A cosmic power had seized them."[56]

33 HE STOPS A COWHERD'S FEVER.

An old woman's son used to herd the cattle in a certain village. He got to know the Gosavi well, as the Gosavi used to sit under a tree in the village.

One day the boy got a fever. His mother said, "He has a fever, Lord. Now they will give the cattle to someone else to herd. We are finished."

घरा बीजें केलें : तेयाचें पांगरूनि तेया सरिसा पहुड : तेयासि
समाधान जालें : तो गोरूवासरिसा पाठविला : तेयाची माए
गोसावीयासि पथ्य करी : केतुलेया एका दीसा : गोसावी
समाधान स्वीकरीलें : मग : त्यें : गोसावीया नीगों नेदीति :
सर्वज्ञें म्हणीतलें : हें तयासि भांडौनि निगालें : हे गोष्टी
भुतानंदाप्रति सांघितली :॥:

३४ क्षीरारीया नेत्रपतन :॥:

दोही गावामध्ये वृक्षातळि आसन : खीरारी एकु दाटुनि
सीवारू चारी : तयासि गांवीचे लांचु देति : मग : तो गोरूवें
परतीं : तैसेंचि तीए गावी सीवारू चारूं लागला : बोंब
जाली : धावणें निगालें : गोसावीहीं बीजें केलें : गोसावी
तळुसुति केली : सर्वज्ञें म्हणीतलें : हें जैसे तेयाचें आठावेठीचें
पाइक : ऐसें हें पुढां पुढां वाढीनलें२५ : खीरारीया भांडण
जालें : वारितां खीरारी धरेना : आणि गोसावी चडकणा
हानौनि तेयाचा डोळा खालि पाडीला : आणि : कळि
समली : मग श्रीकरीं डोळा घेउनि लावीला : श्रीमुखीचेया
तांबूळाची पींड बांधली : डोळा निका जाला : मग तेथौनी
बीजें केलें :॥:

70

The Gosavi went to his house and lay down with him under his blanket. The boy recovered, and he was sent out with the cattle. His mother prepared special dietary foods for the Gosavi. After several days, the Gosavi accepted recovery.

Afterward they would not allow the Gosavi to leave. The omniscient one said, "I had to fight with them to leave."

He told this story to Bhutanande.

34 A COWHERD'S EYE FALLS OUT.

He was sitting at the foot of a tree between two villages.

A certain cowherd used to graze his herd very close to the edge of villages. When the people of a village paid him off, he would move the cattle back. He began to graze his herd that way at the edge of a village the Gosavi was sitting near. A call went out, and people came running. The Gosavi went there too, girding his loins. (The omniscient one remarked, "I kept running ahead, as if I were their conscripted soldier.")

One cowherd fought without restraint, even though people were warning him to stop. The Gosavi struck him sharply, and his eye fell to the ground. And the skirmish came to an end.

The Gosavi picked up the eye with his holy hand and put it into its socket. He tied a lump of pan from his holy mouth to it. The eye healed, and then the Gosavi left.

३५ कळावी बीरवणी विकारज्ञान :॥:

नाथोबा घोगरगावा भिक्षे जाति तो उसीरू लागला : मग
गोसावी पुसीलें : मंडळीका उसीरू का लावीला : तेहीं
म्हणीतलें : जी जी : एकी पुसे : देव व्हो तुम्हांसि देवी कां
न करा : देवीवीण गमे कैसें : सर्वज्ञें म्हणीतलें : पोरा :
तयाचा घरा कां जासि : जी जी : पाठीं इतुला ऐसा भातु
घाली : सर्वज्ञें म्हणीतलें : तेया गांवा न वचावें : मग :
कळावीबीरवणेयाची गोष्टि सांघीतली :॥छ॥: गांवीं एके
पाणीपात्रासि बीजें केलें : एंकि बाइ : गोसावीयातें देखौनि
म्हणे बटकीतें : पुस गे : देवासि काइ देवी असे : तेवींचि
कळावी बीरवी : पुडती पुडती म्हणे : पुस गे : देवासि काइ
देवी असे : सर्वज्ञें म्हणीतलें : प्राणियांसि यातेंहीं देखौनि
विकारूं भोगूं आवडे :॥:

३६ चोर-सांघाती सोडवणें :॥:

सांघातधर्मा उपरि गोष्टि सांघीतली : गांवी एकी पहुडावेया
बीजें केलें : चिपडी ऐसी पडली असे : तीये गावींचिया
अधीकाऱ्याची घोडी चोरीं काढीली : एकू चोरू खोडां
घातला असे : तराळु आपुलें पुरावें सोधीत असति : तीहीं
गोसावीयातें देखीलें : पैलु कोणु कोणु : म्हणौनी : साउमे

35 HE TELLS ABOUT THE PASSION OF THE WOMAN WHO SHOOK HER BANGLES.

Nathoba would go to Ghogargav to beg.[57] Once, when he was delayed getting back, the Gosavi asked, "Mandalik, why did you come back late?"[58] "Lord," he replied, "there is a woman who asks me, 'Oh god, why don't you get yourself a goddess? How can you get along without a goddess?'" The omniscient one said, "My child, why do you go to her house?" "Afterward she gives me a lot of rice, Lord." The omniscient one said, "Do not go to that village."

Then he told the story of the woman who shook her bangles: The Gosavi had gone to beg with his bare hands in a certain village. Seeing him, a woman there would say to her maidservant, "Ask him, 'Does the god have a goddess?'" As she said this, she would shake her bangles. Again and again she said, "Ask him, 'Does the god have a goddess?'"

The omniscient one said, "Women like to enjoy passion by looking at *me* as well."

36 HE FREES HIS THIEF COMPANION.

The Gosavi told this story about the duty of companions: He went at twilight to a certain village to sleep. A mare that belonged to an official of that village had been stolen. One thief had been put in the stocks, and the night watchmen were searching for evidence.

They saw the Gosavi. Asking, "Who is that over there?" they approached him. The Gosavi did not say a word, and so

आले : गोसावी उगेचि : मग ते गोसावीयातें धरूनि घेउनि
गेले : अधीकाऱ्या पुढे सांघीतलें : चोरू एकू धरिला असे :
तेनें म्हणीतलें : जतन करा : तेहीं चोरू खोडां घातला होता :
तेथ आणिलें : खोडां श्रीचरणु चालवीला : खीलि आदळितां
हातु वरताचि ठाके : एरू म्हणे : कां खीलि आदळीसिना :
तो म्हणे : हातु खालुता नैए : मा मा : म्हणौनि : येरू घे :
त्याही तैसेंचि होए : ऐसें अवघेयाचें हात वरतेचि ठाकति :
खालुते न येति : मग तेहीं अधीकाऱ्यापुढें सांघीतलें :
मागाचा चोरू खोडां चालीत होतों : तवं खीलि आदळितां
मोगरिचा हातु खालुता नए : वरिचा वरि हातु असे :
मग : तो अधीकाऱ्या कळदीवी लाउनि तेथ आला : तेणें
म्हणीतलें : गोसावीयातें एर्थें कोणें आणिलें रे : फेडीजो जी
श्रीचरणु : गोसावी उगेचि : पुढती तेणें म्हणीतलें : गोसावी
उगेचि : पुढती तेणें म्हणीतलें : श्रीचरणु फेडीजो जी :
सर्वज्ञें म्हणीतलें : आधीं सांगाती : तेणें म्हणीतलें : फेडागा
सांगातीयाची खीलि : मग गोसावीयासि आवारासि बीजें
करावया म्हणीतलें : आधीं सांगाती : मग गोसावीयासि
मर्दना मादनें : सांगाती उटीला न्हाणिला : गोसावीयासि
आरोगणा : सांगातीया जेवण जालें : गोसावी पहुड :
सांगाती नीजैला : मग सांगातीयें म्हणीतलें : जी जी मीया
अन्यावो केला असे थोरू : हे मातें न रखती तरि मी जावों :
गोसावी आनोज्ञा दीधली : तो निगाला : उदियाचि

they arrested him and carried him off. They told the official, "We have captured a thief." "Keep him in custody," he said.

They brought him to where they had put the thief in the stocks. They put his holy foot in the stocks. As one of the watchmen went to pound in the bolt, his hand stayed raised in the air. Another watchman said, "Why aren't you pounding in the bolt?" "Because my hand won't come down!" he replied.

So another man took over. The same thing happened to him as well. Everyone's hand got stuck in the air that way and would not come down. So they told the official, "As we were putting that thief in the stocks, when we tried to pound in the bolt we could not bring down the hand that was holding the mallet. The hand would stay up in the air."

The official lit a lantern and came there. "Hey!" he said. "Who has brought the Gosavi here? Please remove your holy foot, Lord." The Gosavi did not say a word. The official repeated what he had said. The Gosavi did not say a word. Once again the official said, "Please remove your holy foot, Lord." The omniscient one said, "First my companion."

The official said, "Release his companion's bolt." Then he told the Gosavi to come to his house. "First my companion," said the omniscient one.

The Gosavi had a massage and a bath. His companion was anointed and bathed. The Gosavi had his meal; the companion ate a meal. The Gosavi went to bed; the companion lay down. Then the companion said, "I have committed a major crime, Lord. If they are not going to keep me under guard, may I leave?" The Gosavi gave him permission, and the man set out.

गोसावीयापासि तो अधीकाऱ्या आला : तेणें म्हणीतलें :
सांगाती काइ गोसावी पळवीला :॥ः

३७ वेठी जाणें :॥ः

वेठी गमन : गोसावी गावीं एकी पडवीए : पहुड : काबाडीया
मध्यें : उदीयांचि मोलकैयें तीयें वेठी धरूनि नेली : तेया
सरिसें : गोसावीयांतेंही नेलें : अवघेयांहीं सेती पांठा
चिरीलिया : एकी पांठ गोसावीयाहीं चिरीली : अवघेयांचीया
पांठा चालति : गोसावीयांची पांठ चालेना : गोसावी श्रीकरीं
गहुवाचिया काडीया दोणि घेउनि निश्चळ बैसले असति :
पैल पांठ चालेना तें काइ : एरीं म्हणीतलें : नेणों : हा मागां
लागौनि निवांतु बैसला असे : कांही पांठ चालवीना : मग
तो अधीष्ठाता साउमा आला : तेणें म्हणीतलें : गोसावीयासि
कोणें रे आणिलें : मग तेणें वीनवीलें : तेतुलेया सेतासि अन्न
आलें : मग गोसावीयासि आरोगण दीधली : मग तेथौनी
बीजें केलें :॥ः

76

Early the next morning the official came to the Gosavi and said, "Did you let your companion run away, Gosavi?"

37 HE WORKS AS A FORCED LABORER.

In a certain village, the Gosavi was sleeping on a veranda along with some laborers. Early in the morning, some paid workers seized them and carried them off as forced labor. They carried off the Gosavi too, along with the others.

All of them were reaping rows of crops in a field. The Gosavi was reaping a row as well. All the others were making progress in harvesting their rows, but the Gosavi was not making any progress. He was sitting motionless, holding two stalks of wheat in his holy hand.

"Why isn't that row over there getting harvested?" asked the supervisor. The others said, "We don't know. That fellow has fallen behind and is just sitting there. He's making no progress on his row." Then the supervisor came up to him. "Hey! Who brought the Gosavi here?" he asked.

Later, that field produced however much food the man asked for.

He gave the Gosavi a meal, and then the Gosavi left.

३८ द्विजगोरक्षण :॥ः

गांवीं एकी पाणिपात्रासि बीजें केलें ः ब्राह्मणा एकाचेया
घरासि ः तेणें म्हणीतलें ः कोण्हाचीं गोरूवें राखा कां ः सर्वज्ञें
म्हणीतलें ः यासी कव्हणी राखों नेदी ः तेणें म्हणीतलें ः
आम्हीं देउनि ः आमची राखा ः सर्वज्ञें म्हणीतलें ः हें राखैल
परि दोहे ना ः सोडील परि बांधेना ः तेणें म्हणीतलें ः आम्हीं
बांधौनी ः आम्हीं दोहौनि ः गोसावी मानीलें ः उदीयांचि तिये
गोसावीयासि मोट घालीति ः गोसावी गाइ सोडीति ः राना
चारावेया नेतिः गोसावी मोटेचें अन्न आरोगण करिति ः सुडा
धुति ः श्रीमुकुटावरि घालीति ः सीळातळावरि बैसति ः गाइ
श्रीमूर्ति अवलोकीत बैसलिया असति आनंदु रोवतीति ः
वीळीचां गोसावीया गाई घेउनि बीजें करिति ः तीया गाइसि
बहुत दुध होए ः मग तेणें ब्राम्हणें म्हणीतलें ः आपुलियें
ब्राम्हणीतें ः पै ः आजि दुध बहुत जालें ः गाइ निकेया
चारीलिया ः यासि न्हावेया लोणीं घालावें ः याचीये मोटें दहीं
घालावें ः यापरि निचाचेयापसि निच अधीक गाइसि दुध
होए ः मग तो ब्राम्हणु राखों गेला ः गाइ कव्हणा राना नेतु
असे पा ः तवं गोसावीयांसि एका सीळातळासि आसन ः
गाइ श्रीमूर्ति अवलोकित²⁶ आनंदु रोंवतीति देखीलिया ः
वीळवेन्ही चारूं नाहीं ः पाणीं नाहीं ः ऐसें देखौनि थोर

38 HE HERDS A BRAHMAN'S COWS.

He went to beg at a Brahman's house in a certain village. The man said, "Why don't you herd someone's cattle?"[59] The omniscient one replied, "No one will give me any to herd." The man said, "I'll give you mine. Herd mine." The omniscient one said, "I will herd them, but I won't milk them. I will let them loose to graze, but I won't tie them up." "I will tie them up," said the man. "I will milk them." The Gosavi agreed.

Early in the morning the man's wife would pack a lunch for the Gosavi in a cloth. The Gosavi would untie the cows and lead them to the pasture to graze. He would eat the food she had packed for him, then wash the cloth and put it on top of his holy head. He would sit on a flat rock, and the cows would sit there looking at his holy form, chewing the cud of happiness.

In the evening the Gosavi would come back with the cows. The cows would give a great deal of milk, and the Brahman would say to his wife, "There's plenty of milk today! The cows have grazed well. Give him butter for his bath, and put yogurt in his lunch pack." Every day the cows gave extra milk this way.

Then one day, wondering, "Which pasture is he taking the cows to?" the Brahman went to keep watch on him. He saw the Gosavi sitting on a flat rock while the cows looked at his holy form and chewed the cud of happiness. Seeing that they had nothing to graze on and no water to drink all day long,

वीस्मयो जाला : मग घरीं ब्राम्हणीपुढां सांघों लागला : पै :
आमचेया गाइ राखते तो साक्षात श्रीकृष्णू : मग तेथींचें
वृतांतु सांघीतलें : तीये दीसी गाइ गावामध्यें घातलीया : मग
बीजें केलें :॥:

३९ कुंडी राजेया दरिसन :॥:

भैरवी अवस्थान : दीस वीस : लोणारी तारातीर्थीं आसन :
तेथ कान्हरदेवो आला होता : तेथ गुरूवें सांघीतलें : पुरुषु
एकु भैरवी असति : तया उपरि त्यासि तारातीर्थीं दर्सन
जालें : हडुपातें वाखारी मागीतली : तीया आसूचें पुजा
दर्सन केलें : कान्हरदया जवळीलीं म्हणीतलें : देवव्हो : घेया
घेया : सींगुणाचा कान्हु प्रसन जाला : तवं तेणें म्हणीतलें :
सरा रे : ऐसे काइ म्हणत असा रे : कान्हु तो तुम्हासी कीं :
यासि काइ कान्हु : शोधु :॥: मग रावो नीगाला : गोसावी ते
परित्यजुनि बीजें केले२७ :॥: मग तेणें दीठीचें राखण घातलें :
मग तेथौनि गोसावी बीजें केलें : तेणें द्रव्यें कूमारेस्वराची
पाळी केली :॥:

the man was astounded. When he got back home, he said to his wife, "The man who is grazing our cows is Shri Krishna himself!" And he told her what had happened there.

That day, after bringing the cows back to the village, the Gosavi left.

39 A KING HAS *DARŚAN* AT A POOL.

He stayed in the Bhairav temple at Lonar for twenty days.[60] He would sit at Taratirtha.*

When Kanhardev[†] came to Lonar, the priest told him, "There is a holy man staying at the Bhairav temple." Afterward, Kanhardev had *darśan* of the Gosavi at Taratirtha. He asked his servant for his money bag and did puja to the Gosavi with gold coins.

Kanhardev's attendant said, "Take this, God. Take it. Singhan's[‡] Kanhu is pleased with you." Kanhardev said to the attendant, "Hey! Back off! What are you saying? Kanhu is important to you, but what is Kanhu to him?" (Research: Then the king left.[61]

The Gosavi abandoned the money and left.) People there kept watch on the money. After the Gosavi had left, they used it to build a compound wall for the Kumareshvar temple.

---

* A pool with a waterfall at Lonar.
† Krishnadev Yadava (r. 1246–1260), Kanhu for short.
‡ Singhandev Yadava (r. 1210–1246), Kanhardev's grandfather.

४० अरण्य महीष रोष हरण :॥:

गोसावी गावां एका बीजें करीत असति : तेथीचेनि लोकें
वारिलें : देव व्हो : या वाटा न वचा : न वचा : एथें अरण
म्हैसा असे : तो माणुसें मारी : आइकौनि बिजें केलें : ते
मार्गीं चालतां वाणी पडली आणि म्हैसा आला : गोसावी
अवलोकीला : आणि : तेयाचा रोखु निर्वर्तला : मग
गोसावी२८ बीजें केलें : तीयें दीउनि तो मार्ग वसता जाला :॥:

४१ व्याघ्रपीलीं खेळवणें :॥:

एकू वेळ रानीं जाळीं एकी बीजें केलें होतें : तेथें लाहासिचीं
पीलीं होतीं : ते पारधी गेली होती : तीयें पीलीं गोसावी
खेळवीलीं : तवं ते आली : गोसावी अवलोकीली : रोखू
नीवर्तला : मग : ते मोळी टेकौनि बैसली : सूनेयाचिया परी :
मग नावेक गोसावी पीलीं खेळविलीं : वडुवें धरूनि
एरीकडीचा ऐरीकडी घातली : मग तीएचीं तीएकडे घालुनि
मग गोसावी बीजें केलें :॥:

४२ ठाकुरभार्या पुत्रदान :॥:

ठाकूर एकू : तयासि पुत्र नाहीं : तेणें गोसावीयातें देखीलें :
मग आपुलीया आवारासि घेऊनि गेला : गोसावियासि मर्दना
दीधली : मादनें जाली : पुजा केली : आरोगणा जाली :

82

40 HE PACIFIES A WILD BUFFALO.

As the Gosavi was going toward a certain village, the people there warned him off: "Don't go by this road, God. Don't go that way. There's a wild buffalo here that kills people."

He heard them, but he kept going. As he walked along the road, he heard a sound, and the buffalo arrived. The Gosavi looked at it, and its anger disappeared. Then the Gosavi proceeded on his way.

From that day on, that road became safe to use.

41 HE PLAYS WITH TIGER CUBS.

Once he went into a thicket in the wilderness. A tigress had left her cubs there and gone off to hunt. When she returned, the Gosavi was playing with the cubs. The Gosavi looked at her, and her anger disappeared. She curled up on the ground like a dog.

The Gosavi played with her cubs a little longer. He picked them up by the scruff of their necks and moved them from one side to the other. Then he put the cubs down next to her and left.

42 HE GIVES A THAKUR'S WIFE A SON.

There was a certain Thakur who had no son. He saw the Gosavi, brought him home with him, and gave him a massage. The Gosavi had a bath, puja was done to him, and he ate his

दंडवतें घातलीं : मग तेणें ठाकुरें म्हणीतलें : पुरुषाचें
वीर्यें अमोघ : पुत्राचेया चाडा आपुली वडील स्त्री सेवा
करावेया पाठविली : नावेक ते सेवा करीत होती : मग
सर्वज्ञें म्हणीतलें : बाई निद्रा करा जा : मग ते गेली : तिया
म्हणीतलें : गोसावीयासि प्रवृत्ति नाहीं : तेणें म्हणीतलें : ते
वडील म्हणौनि नाहीं : मग धाकुटी भार्या पाठवीली : तियेसि
गोसावी आंतु रिगों नेदीतिची : तेथौनिची पाठवीली :
तीयाहीं सांचीतलें : गोसावीयासि प्रवृति नाहीं : मग तेणें
वीनवीलें : जी जी : मज पुत्र नाही : सर्वज्ञें म्हणीतलें : वडिले
भार्येसीं वीहरण करा : मग होईल : मग बीजें केलें :॥:

४३ राएरी पाणिपात्र :॥:

रायेरीं अवस्थान असे : तीये गावीं वामनपेंढी ब्राह्मणु :
तयाची भार्या निवर्तली : ते समसानां आणिली होती :
तीये प्रदेसीं गोसावीयातें वामनपेंढीं देखीलें : श्रीचरणा
लागला : मग गोसावीयातें वामनपेंढीं म्हणीतलें : जी जी :
गोसावीयाची दासी नीमाली जी : गोसावीयासी पाणिपात्र
दे जी : ऐसा शाब्दीं म्हणीतलें : वीनवणी स्वीकरीलीं : मग
गोसावी तीये जवळि बीजें केलें : तीयेतें म्हणीतलें : बाइ एथ
पाणीपात्र दीया : मग ते बाइ जीयाली : मग गोसावी तेथौनी

meal. They prostrated themselves to him. Then the Thakur said, "A holy man's semen is unfailingly potent." In the hope of getting a son, he sent his senior wife to serve the Gosavi.

After she served him a little while, the omniscient one said, "My woman, go away and get some sleep." So she left. She said to her husband, "The Gosavi is not interested."

The husband said, "She is the older one; that's why he is not interested." So he sent his younger wife. The Gosavi did not even let her enter the room: he sent her away immediately. She too said, "The Gosavi is not interested."

Then the Thakur appealed to him: "Lord, I have no son." The omniscient one said, "Have sex with your senior wife, and you will get one." Then he left.

43 AT RAYER, HE BEGS FOR FOOD WITH HIS BARE HANDS.

When he was staying at Rayer, the wife of Vamanpendi, a Brahman in that village, died.[62] She had been taken to the cremation ground. Vamanpendi saw the Gosavi nearby. He touched the Gosavi's holy feet, then said to him, "Your maidservant has died, Lord Gosavi. She used to give you food when you were begging with your bare hands, Lord." He appealed to the Gosavi in these words.

The Gosavi responded to his plea. He went up close to her and said, "Put food into my bare hands, my woman." And she came back to life. Then the Gosavi left the cremation ground.

बीजें केलें : घरा तयाचीया तया बाइया पाणीपात्र आणिलें :
सर्वज्ञें म्हणीतलें : बाइ पाणीपात्र दीयाल तरि तें असे : मग ते
उगीचि राहीली : वामनपेंद्यीं पाणीपात्र दिधलें : मग तेथौनी
बीजें केलें :॥:

४४ गोविंदस्वामी स्थिति :॥:

गोसावीया राएरीं कीं नादीयेडीं अवस्थान असे : वृक्षा एका
तळि आसन होए : गोवींद स्वामिसि गोसावीयांची श्रधा
नाहीं : गोसावीयाचें दर्सन होइल म्हणौनि ते वाट सांडीली :
आणिकी वाटा जाति : एकुदीनीं वृक्षा आड आसन :
गोसावी तेथ नसति : म्हणौनी तया वृक्षावरौनि गोविंदस्वामी
आले : दिठि दीठि मीनली : आणि स्थीति जाली : मग
गोसावीयांसि आड पडीले : जी जी : मिं पापीया जी :
गोसावीयांसि भके : ऐसां ऐसां शब्दीं तेहीं अनुताप केला :
मग सर्वज्ञें म्हणीतलें : विष्णूस्वामी तुमतें पूसीती : हें तुम्हासि
कवणा पासौनि : एथौनि सांचाल : तरि : हे तुम्हां दर्सन
नेदी : गोवींद स्वामीं म्हणीतलें : हो कां जी : मग ते निश्वला

At their house, she brought food to put into his bare hands. The omniscient one said, "My woman, if you put food into my hands, the same thing will happen to you again." That silenced her.

Vamanpendi put the food into the Gosavi's hands. Then the Gosavi left.

44 GOVINDASVAMI GOES INTO A TRANCE.

When the Gosavi was staying in either Rayer or Nanded, he would sit under a tree. To avoid having his *darśan,* Govindasvami, who did not believe in the Gosavi, would leave the road and take some other route.

One day the Gosavi sat behind the tree. Thinking the Gosavi was not there, Govindasvami came past the tree. Their eyes met, and he went into a trance. He prostrated himself to the Gosavi and expressed his remorse to him, saying things like, "Oh Lord! I am a sinner, Lord. I have criticized you, Gosavi."

Then the omniscient one said, "Vishnusvami* will ask you, 'Who put you into this trance?' If you say it came from me, I will not give you *darśan.*" "All right, Lord," said Govindasvami.

---

* Govindasvami's guru.

बैसले असति : स्नान न करीति : देवपुजा न करीति :
विष्णुस्वामिसि नमस्कारू न करीति : ऐसें कर्म कांहींचि न
करीति : मग वीष्णुस्वामी म्हणितलें : सापें हा गोवींदु नष्टु
जाला : स्नान न करी : आम्हांसि नमस्कारू न करी : देवपूजा
न करी : मग वीष्णुस्वामी स्वप्नू देखीला : नरसींहु दंडवतें
घालुं लागला : तेहीं गजबझौनि म्हणितलें : हें काइ : हें
काइ : तुम्हीं मज दंडवतें कैसी घालीतें असा : तवं नरसींहें
म्हणीतलें : तुम्हीं आमचीं दंडवतें आपेक्षीत असा : म्हणौनि :
घालीत असों : तीहीं म्हणितलें : तुमचीं दंडवतें मीं कैसी
आपेक्षीत असें : तवं नरसींहें म्हणीतलें : गोवींदाचीं दंडवतें
आपेक्षीलीं असति : तरि गोवींद तो मीं : ऐसें स्वप्न देखीलें :
मग चेवो आलेया उपरि उदेयांसिचि गोवींदस्वामीसीं दंडवतें
घालूं लागले : तवं गोवींदस्वामीं म्हणीतलें : हें काइ : हें
काइ : तुम्ही मज दंडवतें कैसी घालीतें असा : तवं तेहीं
म्हणीतलें : हें तुम्हां कोणापासौनि हें सांघावें : तवं गोवींद
स्वामीं म्हणीतलें : हें तुम्हाचि पासौनि : तवं तेहीं म्हणीतलें :
हें आम्हांसिचि नाहीं : मग तुम्हांसि कैचें : विष्णुस्वामीं
म्हणीतलें : आम्हां पुढां सांघा कां : तुमचेनि आम्हाहीं गोमटें
होइल : मग तेहीं सांघीतलें : हें मज गोसावीया पासौनि
जाले : मग : एर एर : गोसावीयांचेया दर्सना आले : गोसावी
तेयांसि दर्शना नेदीतिचि :॥ः

After that Govindasvami simply sat still. He did not do any of his ritual duties: he didn't bathe, he didn't do puja to the gods, and he didn't pay homage to Vishnusvami. Vishnusvami said, "These days this Govindu is a wreck. He doesn't bathe. He doesn't bow to me. He doesn't do puja to the gods."

Then Vishnusvami had a dream. Narasimha started prostrating himself to him. He got frightened and said, "What is going on? What is going on? How can you be prostrating yourself to me?" Narasimha replied, "You expect me to prostrate myself to you; that's why I am doing it." Vishnusvami said, "What do you mean, I expect you to prostrate yourself?" Narasiṃha replied, "You expect Govinda to prostrate himself. Well, I am Govinda."

Early the next morning, when he woke up after having that dream, Vishnusvami began to prostrate himself to Govindasvami. Govindasvami said, "What is going on? What is going on? How can you be prostrating yourself to me?" "Tell me," he replied, "who put you into this trance?" Govindasvami answered, "You yourself caused it." "I don't have that power," said Vishnusvami. "So where did you get it from? Will you tell me? I too will be blessed, through you." So Govindasvami told him, "This happened to me because of the Gosavi."

Then they both came for *darśan* of the Gosavi. But the Gosavi refused to give them *darśan*.

४५ विष्णुस्वामी घुटीकासिद्धिकथन :॥:

भक्तीजनीं पूसीलें : हां जी : विष्णूस्वामिसी येसणीं उपाधि
काइसी : सर्वज्ञें म्हणीतलें : तेयातें घुटिका सीधी होति :
घुटिका तोंडी घालीति : आणि उत्पवन करीति : आपुलियां
सीक्षाचिया ठाया जाति : कडवंसां राहाति : तयाचें एकांतींचें
बोलणें आइकति : एरी दीसीं तेयापुढे सांघति : तुं ब्राह्मणींसीं
ऐसा बोलीलासि : तुझी ब्राह्मणी तुसीं ऐसीं बोलीली : ऐसी
खूण सांघति : एतुलेनि तयासि आश्र्चर्यें होए : हे सामान्य
नव्हति : एणें तयांची श्रधा वाढीनली : मग पर्वणी एकी
आली : लोकांसी आश्र्चर्यें दाखवावें म्हणौनि घुटिका तोंडी
घालुनि उत्पवन केलें : तवं सींक आली : तवं घुटिका
तोंडीचीं पडीली : पोरू पाणीयांतु पडिला : म्हणौनि पावो
मोडला : सोधु : यऱ्हवीं थडीए पडतां : तरि हाडगुड नुरतें :
मरता :॥:

४६ उभए वऱ्हाडीक करणें :॥:

गावीं एकी सेवंतिये वऱ्हाड राहीलें असे : तयांतु : गोसावी
बीजें केलें : बैसले : गांवींचे वऱ्हाडी तेया साउमे आलें :
वाजत गाजत घेउनि गेले : मांडवीं वरिलाकडे बौसों घातलें :

45 HE TELLS ABOUT THE SUPERNATURAL POWER THAT VISHNUSVAMI GOT FROM A PILL.

The devotees asked, "Lord, how did Vishnusvami get such great powers?" The omniscient one replied, "He had a power that came from a pill. He would put a pill in his mouth and fly up in the air. He would go to his disciples' place, stay off to the side, and listen to what they said in private. The next day he would tell them things like, 'You said such-and-such to your wife. Your wife said so-and-so to you.' When he said things like that, they would be amazed. His extraordinary powers strengthened their faith in him.

"Then a festival day came. In order to amaze people, he put a pill in his mouth and flew up in the air. But then he had to sneeze, and the pill fell out of his mouth. Poor child, he fell into the water, and so his foot got broken." (Research: "Otherwise, if he had fallen on the riverbank, he would have broken all his bones. He would have died.")

46 HE JOINS BOTH SIDES OF A WEDDING PARTY.

A bridegroom's party had stopped at the edge of a certain village. The Gosavi went and sat down among them. The bride's party came out from the village to meet them, and

खालिलीकडे येर वऱ्हाडी बैसले : आधीं गोसावीयांसि
चरणक्षाळण केलें : पाठी येरांचें पाय धूतले : आधी
गोसावीयांसि विडा ओळगविला²⁹ : पाठी येरा वऱ्हाडीयांसि
तांबुलें दिधली : गोसावीया मर्दना दिधली : एरांचीं आंगे
उटीलीं : वरिलीकडे ताट गोसावीयासि केलें : खालिलीकडे
ठाए एरांसी केले : गोसावीयासि आरोगण जाली : वीडा
वोळगवीला : एरां तांबुलें दीधलीं : मग : वऱ्हाड जानवसेया
निगालें : गोसावी अनुवर्जनाचेनि मीसें नावेक बीजें
केलें : मग तेथौनी पहुडतें स्थाना बीजें केलें : ऐरी दिसीं
तेतुलेया वेळा : जानवसेया बीजें केलें : वरिलीकडे बैसले :
वऱ्हाडा मुळ आलें : तेयासवें गोसावी बीजें केलें : आधीलें
दीसीचियापरी अवघी क्रिया : परियंत स्वीकरिली : यापरि
चाऱ्ही दीस वऱ्हाडीक जाली : चौथां दीसीं : एर म्हणति :
एराचें मान्य : एर म्हणति : एराचें मान्ये : ऐसेनि संभ्रमें
एरयेन्हीं वस्तें वाइलीं : मग तेथौनि बीजें केलें ॥ एकी
वासना : एर एराते म्हणीतलें : हे तुमचे मान्य : यासी ऐसीं
वस्तें वावों येति: तव येरीं म्हणीतलें : हे तुमचे मान्य कीं: तव
येरयेन्हीं म्हणीतलें : आमचे नव्हति : आम्हीं म्हणों तुमचे
मान्य : तैसेंचि येरीं म्हणीतलें : तव सर्वझें म्हणीतलें : हे

then took them into the village to the accompaniment of a band. They spread out a seat for the Gosavi on the western side, under the wedding canopy. The rest of the wedding party sat on the eastern side.

First the hosts washed the Gosavi's feet, and then they washed the others' feet. First they gave a pan roll to the Gosavi, and then they gave pan to the other members of the wedding party. They gave the Gosavi a massage, and they anointed the others' bodies. On the western side, they served food on a plate for the Gosavi; on the eastern side, they put food on leaf-plates for the others. After the Gosavi ate his meal, they offered him a pan roll. They gave pan to the others.

When the wedding party set off for their lodgings, the Gosavi went along with them for a while, as if to see them off. Then he went from there to the place where he was sleeping.

At the same time the next day, the Gosavi went to their lodgings and sat on the western side. When the invitation to the wedding came, the Gosavi went along with them. As on the previous day, he accepted all the rites of hospitality.

The wedding went on like this for four days. On the fourth day, one group said that he was an honored guest from the other side. The other group said that he was an honored guest from the first group's side. Confused this way, both sides gave him clothes. Then he left.

(One version: One party said to the other, "He is your honored guest, so we can give him clothes." At that, the others said, "He is *your* honored guest." The first party said to the other, "He is not ours. We say he is *your* honored guest." The others said the same thing. Then, saying, "I am

तुमचे नव्हे : यांचें नव्हें : हें कव्हणाचेंही नव्हे : ऐसें म्हणौनि
बीजें केलें : तवं तेहीं म्हणीतलें : एइजो जी : एइजो जी :
आम्ही आवघी गोसावीयांचीं : मग उभें वर्गीं गोसावीयासि
वस्तें वाइलीं : मग गोसावी बीजें केलें :॥:

४७ सिद्धु रे सिद्धु म्हणणें :॥:

गांवी एकी घरीं वऱ्हाड : तेथ बीजें केलें : मांडवीं उभे
राहीले : सीधु रे सीधु : परि : सीधातें कोण्ही देखे ना : तवं
मांडवीं होते : तेही म्हणीतलें : हें नव्हे : आम्ही देखत असों :
देखत असा : तरि : कां बैसा न म्हणां³⁰ : पुडतीं सर्वज्ञें
म्हणीतलें : सीधु रे सीधु : परि : सीधातें कव्हणी देखेना :
तथा : वोळखेना : तवं घरींचां अधीष्ठाता बाहीरि निघाला :
तेणें म्हणीतलें : एइजो जी : एइजो जी : म्हणौनि : बैसों
घातलें : मर्दना मादनें जालें : आरोगणा केली : मग बीजें
केलें :॥:

४८ उकरडां पहुड :॥:

गांवीं एकी : गोसावी : उकरडीं पहुड : उदीयांसीचि बाइला
राख घातली : ये जवं जवं राख सोहोमी लागे : तवं तवं हें
घरघरा घोरे : राखेपाठीं चीपाडें सेण घालितां समइं : आंग

not yours. I am not theirs. I belong to no one at all," the omniscient one left.

"Please come back, Lord," they said. "Please come back, Lord. All of us belong to you, Gosavi." Both sides gave clothes to the Gosavi, and then he left.)

47 HE SAYS, "HEY, A SIDDHA! A SIDDHA!"

He went to a house in a certain village where there was a wedding. He stood under the wedding canopy and said, "Hey, a Siddha! A Siddha! But no one looks at the Siddha." The people under the canopy said, "Aren't we looking at you?" "If you are looking, why don't you say, 'Take a seat'?" Again the omniscient one said, "Hey, a Siddha! A Siddha! But no one looks at (or, recognizes) the Siddha."

At that point, the head of the household came outside. Saying, "Please come in, Lord. Please come in," he put down something for him to sit on.

The Gosavi had a massage and a bath, and he ate his meal. Then he left.

48 HE SLEEPS IN A HEAP OF GARBAGE.

In a certain village, the Gosavi went to sleep in a heap of garbage. Early in the morning a woman tossed some ashes onto it. Every time the warm ashes hit him, he snored loudly. When she tossed some husks and cow dung on top of the

झाडौनि बीजें केलें : तें माणुसीं देखीलें : मग लोकें
म्हणीतलें : आरे : उकरडा व्याला : माणूस जालें : हें गांवा
अरिष्ट जालें : आता शांति करा : खीच पुरीया रंधन केलें :
उकरडां जोगीया देसांतरीयां वाढीलें : जोगी पात्रें भरूनि
जातां गोसावीया भेटले : जोगी म्हणीतलें : देवव्हो : जा :
उकरडा व्याला : गावीं अरिष्ट जालें : तें गावींचा शांतिक
केलें : तेथ तुम्हां जेवण होईल : गोसावी तेथ पातळि घालुनि
आरोगण केली : मग बीजें केलें :॥:

४९ भगवोद्द्रहणी उभया जयो :॥ः

गावीं एकी संन्यासी दोघीं उघाणी करूं आदरीली :
गोसावीयांतें सभा केलें : जेयाचें स्थळ निरधार होए : तेयातें
गोसावी अवलोकीति : तवं एराचें स्थळ निरधार होए :
तेयाकडे अवलोकीति : आणि : तेया अपुर्व अपूर्व स्फुरे :
यापरी दोघाइं जैत दीधले :॥ः

ashes, he emerged, brushing off his body. Some people saw that happen.

Then people in the village said, "Hey! The garbage heap has given birth! A human being has been born from it! This is a disaster for the village. Do a pacification ceremony now."

They cooked *khīcaḍī** and puris and served them at the garbage heap to yogis from other places. As the yogis were leaving with their full bowls, they met the Gosavi. The yogis said, "Go there, God. The garbage heap has given birth. It is a disaster for the village, so the people of the village have performed a pacification ceremony. You will get a meal there."

The Gosavi set down a leaf plate there and ate his meal. Then he left.

49 IN A DEBATE BETWEEN TWO ASCETICS, HE MAKES BOTH OF THEM VICTORIOUS.

In a certain village, two sannyasis began to debate each other. They made the Gosavi the judge. When the Gosavi looked at the one whose argument was weaker, the other one's argument would falter. Then, when the Gosavi looked at that one, he would think of one new point after another.

In this way, the Gosavi gave victory to both of them.

---

* A mixture of grains cooked together.

५० पराजित-मठ-प्रतिष्ठा :॥:

गावीं एकी संन्यासी दीग्वीजयों करीतु आला : गावींचेया
संन्यासीयासीं उघाणी केली : गावींचेनि संन्यासीयें
हारवीलें : तेयाचें मठापत्यें : पूस्तक भांडार : तेयासि जालें :
मळा : वाडु वृत्ति : हे अवघे तेयासि जालें : मग : गावींचेनि
संन्यासीयें गोसावीयांतें वीनवीलें : जी जी : मठापत्यें गेलें :
पुस्तक भांडार गेलें : ऐसें दुख करीत सांघीतलें : गोसावी
देघांइ उघाणी लावीली : पुडती गावींचेया संन्यासीयातें एरें
नीरोत्तर केलें : सर्वज्ञें म्हणीतलें : ऐसें हें म्हणत असति कीं :
इतुलेनि तेयांसि अपुर्व स्फुरे : पुडतीं तीहीं निरोत्तर केलें : तवं
सर्वज्ञें म्हणीतलें : ऐसें हें म्हणत असति कीं : इतुलेनि तेयांसि
अपुर्व स्फुरे : ऐसेनि गांवींचा संन्यासी एरू जींतला :
मग तेयाचें मठापत्य पुस्तक भांडार : तेयाचें तेयासि जालें :
मग तेहीं संन्यासी गोसावीयासि आपुला वोटा संपादीला :
गोसावीयासि आरोगण देति : गोसावीया बीजें करू नेदीति :
मग गोसावी तेयासीं भांडौनि बीजें केलें : तथा रूसौनि :॥:

50 HE RESTORES A MONASTERY THAT HAS BEEN SEIZED.

A sannyasi who had gone around defeating everyone in debate came to a certain village. He held a debate with the sannyasi from that village. He defeated the village's sannyasi and won the monastery headship and the library from him. He also won the orchard and the large land grants. Then the village's sannyasi appealed to the Gosavi. "Lord, I have lost the headship of the monastery," he lamented. "I have lost the library."

The Gosavi arranged a debate between the two men. Once again the other sannyasi silenced the one from the village. The omniscient one said, "This is what he is saying," and with that the village's sannyasi thought of a new point. Again the other one silenced him, and the omniscient one said, "This is what he is saying." With that, the village's sannyasi thought of another new point.

In this way, the sannyasi from the village defeated the other one and got back the headship of the monastery, the library, and everything that had been his. Then he gave the Gosavi his pedestal to sit on. He gave the Gosavi meals. He would not let the Gosavi leave.

Finally the Gosavi quarreled (or, got angry) with him and left.

५१ मार्गीं अधीकार्या भेटी :॥ः

गावीं एकी पाणीपात्र करूनि बीजें करित असति : तवं
मागीली कडौनि अधीकार्या एक मार्गीं जातु असे : तेयाचेनि
राउत पाइकें : सबळाचेया बुढीया गोसावीयातें परतें
सारिलें : आणि श्रीकरीचें अन्न सांडीलें : मग : गोसावी
तेथचि बैसले : उरेंसीं एकू श्रीकरू धरिला : एरें श्रीकरें भुइचें
अनु वेचुंवेचुं तेथ चालीति : ऐसें अधीकार्ये देखीलें : ऐसें
कोणें रे केलें : मग तेणें दांडीए खालुनि उडी घातली : वीणउं
लागला : हें असों दीजो जी : गोसावी नीवांत वेचीतचि
असति : सीतें : मग तोहीं वेंचू लागला :॥ः

५२ झाडी रामदरणा भेटी :॥ः

सवे उपरि गोष्टि सांघीतली : तरि याही एका वृक्षाची सवे
आति : झाडीसि वृक्षाखाली अवस्थान असे : गोसावी
पाणीपात्र करूनि पहुडावेया वृक्षाजवळि येत असति :
तवं तेथ रामदरणा उतरला : कटकैये जात असे : गोसावी
दुसाचेया तनेयावरि श्रीचरण देत बीजें केलें : वृक्षातळि

51 HE MEETS AN OFFICIAL
ALONG THE ROAD.

He was leaving a certain village after begging for food with his bare hands. An official was coming along the road from behind. With the handles of their spears, his horsemen and foot soldiers pushed the Gosavi aside, and the food fell out of his holy hands.

The Gosavi sat down right there, holding one holy hand against his chest. With his other holy hand he was picking up the food from the ground and putting it into the hand at his chest. The official saw this. "Who did this?" he shouted, jumping down from his palanquin. He began pleading, "Please let it be, Lord."

The Gosavi quietly kept on picking up the grains of food. Then the official began picking them up too.

52 HE MEETS RAMDARANA
IN THE FOREST REGION.

He told a story about habits: "Even I got used to one particular tree."[63]

The Gosavi was staying under a tree in the Forest Region.[64] He had begged for food with his bare hands and was coming to the tree to sleep. Ramdarana, who was on a military campaign, had made a halt there. The Gosavi came there, stepping on the tent ropes with his holy feet, then sat down under the tree.

आसन : तवं येरीं म्हणीतलें : हें कोण कोण : म्हणौनि :
धावत गोसावीयापासि आलें : एक रामदरणेया सांघो
गेले : एकु दुसाचिया तणेयावरि पाये देत आला : निवांतु
वृक्षाखालि बैसला असे : मग रामदरणा कळदीवा लाउनि
तेथ आला : गोसावीयातें देखीलें : श्रीचरणा लागला :
मग वीनउनि दुसासि घेउनि गेला : मर्दना दीधली : आणि :
रामदरणेनि मनोर्थु केला : जे : एवेळेची कटकै परते कां :
तरि मी गोसावीयातें गावां घेउनि जाइन : तवं कटकै
परतावी ऐसीया जाळीया आलीया : गोसावीयासि
आरोगण : मग लिखीतें वाचिलीं : मग म्हणीतलें : जी जी :
अळजपुर निकें नगर असे जी : गोसावी तेथ बीजें करावें :
सर्वज्ञें म्हणीतलें : एथ पुर्व दृष्ट असे : जी जी : तेथ बीजें
करावें जी : गोसावी विनवणी स्वीकरीली : मग तेणें वस्त्रें
वोळगवीलीं : गरूड घोडा आसना लागि दीधला : सेवक
दीधले : गोसावीयाचा परिवारू गोसावीयां सरसा वेगळा
चाले : रामदरणेनि अळजपुर श्रृंघारवीलें : गावींचा लोकू
साउमा आला : रामदरणेनि नगरदर्शन गोसावीया देववीलें :
रामदरणेयाचिये देव्हारचौके अवस्थान :॥:

Asking, "Who is this? Who is this?" Ramdarana's men came running to where the Gosavi was. Some of them went to tell Ramdarana: "A man has come here and stepped on the tent ropes. He is sitting quietly under a tree." So Ramdarana lit a lantern and came there. He saw the Gosavi and touched his holy feet. Then he invited him to his tent and took him there. He gave him a massage. And Ramdarana decided, "If this campaign gets turned back, I will take the Gosavi home to my village."

With that, word came to turn back the military campaign. Ramdarana read the message after the Gosavi had eaten his meal. He said to the Gosavi, "Alajpur is a good town, Lord. Please come there, Gosavi." "I have seen it already," said the omniscient one.[65] "Yes, Lord, but please come there."

The Gosavi accepted the invitation. Then Ramdarana offered him clothes and gave him a horse to ride that was as fast as an eagle. He gave him attendants. The Gosavi's retinue traveled separately, along with the Gosavi.

Ramdarana had Alajpur decorated, and the townspeople came out to greet the Gosavi. Ramdarana had him given a tour of the town. He stayed in Ramdarana's domestic shrine.

५३ अळजपुरी आवारीं अवस्थान : प्रतिदिनीं अंबीनाथा दर्शनागमन : विडा वाणें :॥ः

गोसावीयासि उदीयांचि मर्दना मादनें होए : मग : गोसावी
प्रतदिनीं अंबीनाथाचेया दारवठां गरूडावरूनि उतरति :
चामाठी गरुडाचीए कानि घालीति : वीहीरिसी गुळळा
करीति : श्रीकरें श्रीचरणासि उदकस्पर्शन करीति : मग
अंबिनाथासि वीडा वाति : कदाचीत चौकीं आसन होए :
पुराण आइकति : कदाचित बाळाणा टेकौनि आसन होए :
पेखणें अवलोकीति : प्रदक्षेणा करूनि आवारासि बीजें
करीति : गरूडासि स्तीति होए : स्तीति चाले : त्या तवं
मार्गा चालतां गरूडाची गति क्षाळे : तवं गोसावी पासिला
मनुक्षासीं गोष्टी लावीति : मग गोसावी श्रीकरें खांदु
थापटीति : मग आवारा भीतरि बीजें करीति : गावींचा
लोकू गोसावीयातें देखौनि म्हणे : रामदरणेयातें लेकी
वाढत असे : हे जावाइ करावेया आणिले असति :
रामदरणेयाची माता प्रतेहीं श्रीचरणा तुळसी वाए :
मग गोसावीया आरोगण होए :॥ः

53 HE STAYS IN THE COMPOUND AT ALAJPUR. HE GOES TO THE AMBINATH TEMPLE FOR *DARŚAN* EVERY DAY. HE OFFERS PAN.

Early each morning the Gosavi would have a massage and a bath. Then every day he would ride his eagle horse to the Ambinath* temple. He would dismount at the temple gate and put the reins over the horse's ears. At the well, he would rinse his mouth and put water on his holy feet with his holy hand. Then he would offer pan to Ambinath. Sometimes he would sit in the temple hall and listen to Purana recitations. Sometimes he would sit on the balcony, leaning on the railing and watching the dancing. He would circumambulate the temple and return to Ramdarana's compound.

On the way, the eagle horse would go into a trance. As it walked along the road in the trance, the horse would slow down to a halt. The Gosavi would converse with the nearby people. Then he would pat the horse on the shoulder with his holy hand, and they would proceed into the compound.

Seeing the Gosavi, the townspeople would say, "Ramdarana's daughter is growing up. He has brought this man to be his son-in-law." Every day Ramdarana's mother would offer sprigs of tulsi to the Gosavi's holy feet. Then he would eat his meal.

—

* Shiva.

५४ चुर्णजाति निरुपण³¹ :॥:

मग अंबीनाथा प्रदक्षणा करीतां सूताऱु चुना उखरडीत
असति : गोसावी तेयातें पुसीलें : हांगा : चुना कां उखरडीत
असा : तेहीं म्हणीतलें : जी जी : नवा चुना केला : सर्वज्ञें
म्हणीतलें : तो चुना जाला असे : येऱ्हवी हाचि निका असे :
मग तेहीं चुना जैसा केला तैसा सांघीतला : सर्वज्ञें म्हणीतलें :
मर्दनीं उणा : मग चुनें जाति निरूपीली : चुना तो ऐसा :
खडे ऐसे भाजावे : ऐसीं ऐसीं द्रव्यें होआवीं : ऐसी मर्दना
होआवी : इतुके दीस कुहीजो दीयावा : मग ऐसा वाटावा :
मग तो चुना सुनेयां पुढां चालिजे : दहींभाताचा उंडा
म्हणौनि घे : आणिकांची वास पाहे : तो चुना जाला ऐसें
जाणीजे : ऐसा होय तरि करावा : ना तरी फेडावा ना :
तीहीं म्हणीतलें : जी जी : हें आम्हीं परीसों नेणों : मग
जाणौनि काइ : हें गोसावींचि निरूपावें : आणि :
गोसावींचि परीसावें :॥:

54 HE DESCRIBES THE TYPES
OF SLAKED LIME.

Once when he was circumambulating the Ambinath temple, masons were scraping the slaked lime off the walls. The Gosavi asked them, "Hey, why are you scraping off the lime?" "We've made new lime, Lord," they replied. The omniscient one said, "You've already made the lime. If you hadn't, what is already here is just fine."

Then they told him how they had made the slaked lime. The omniscient one said, "It hasn't been crushed enough." Then he described the types of slaked lime. "Slaked lime is like this. This is how you should heat the lumps of lime. This is how you should liquify it. This is how you should crush it. You should allow it to slake for so many days, and then this is how you should grind it. After that, toss the lime to a dog. If it eats it as if it is a morsel of yogurt and rice, then waits expectantly for more, you can tell that the lime is ready. If that happens, use it. If not, get rid of it."

"Lord Gosavi," they said, "we don't know how to listen to this, so how could we possibly understand it? You yourself should tell about it, and you yourself should listen."

५५ औदास्यस्वीकार : आरवीं सोमनाथीं अवस्थान : वस्त्रपूजास्वीकार :॥:

मास दाहा अवस्थान होतें : मग उदास्य स्विकरीलें : अवघें
परित्येजुनि पासोडेयाचें वस्त्र पांगरौनि : आरवी वृक्षातळि
आसन : एरीकडे गोसावीयांचे सेवक पाहों लागले : तवं
गोसावीयांतें न देखति : मग तेहीं रामदरणेया पुढें सांघीतलें :
तेणें भवतें पाहों धाडीलें : तीए दीसीं गोसावी न दीसतीचि ॥
एरी दीसीं एका सांघीतलें : गोसावी आरवी वृक्षातळि
असति : रामदरणां धांवत तेथें आला : तवं गोसावी वीळीचां
वेळीं सोमनाथीं होते : दर्सन जालें : ऐसें कां अव्हेरिलें जी :
ऐसें वीनउं लागला : गोसावी वीनति न स्वीकरितिचि :
मग तेणें दोघदोघे राखणें दृष्टीचीए आळीवे घातले : वाट
वाटे : सर्वज्ञें म्हणीतलें : जैसें हें तेयाचें काहीं लागे तैसें : मग
सोमनाथीं तिन दी अवस्थान : मग एरी दीसीं रामदरणेनि
वीनवीलें : जी जी : आवारा बीजें करावें जी : माझी माता
श्रीचरणां तुळसी वाइल : तीएसीं पारणें होइल :
मग गोसावीयाचेया प्रत्या ये : तैसे गोसावी करितु :

55 HE TAKES ON INDIFFERENCE.
HE STAYS IN A SOMNATH TEMPLE IN A
GROVE. HE ACCEPTS PUJA OF CLOTHES.

He stayed there for ten months. Then he took on indifference. He abandoned everything, put a thick, rough garment over his shoulders, and was sitting at the foot of a tree in a grove.

Meanwhile the Gosavi's attendants began looking for him. They could not find him, so they told Ramdarana about it. He sent them to search in the surrounding area. That day they could not find the Gosavi.

The next day someone said, "The Gosavi is at the foot of a tree in the grove." Ramdarana came running there. It was evening then, and the Gosavi was at the Somnath temple. Ramdarana had *darśan* of the Gosavi and began to plead with him, "Lord, why have you rejected me this way?" The Gosavi made no response at all to his plea. So Ramdarana placed two guards within sight of him on each of the roads to the place. (The omniscient one remarked, "It was as if I owed him something."[66])

After the Gosavi had stayed in the Somnath temple for three days, the next day Ramdarana pleaded with him: "Please come to the compound, Lord. My mother will offer sprigs of tulsi to your holy feet. After she completes her vow and breaks her fast, you may do whatever you want."

मग आवारासि बीजें केलें : मर्दना दीधली : मादनें दीधली :
पाटाउं त्रीवडि : दुटि : बोळगवीली : माता तुळसी वाइली :
मग गोसावीयासि आरोगण जाली : माता पारणें केलें : मग
येरी दीसीं गोसावी बीजें केलें :॥ः

५६ वटनेर मार्गीं काटीवनीं पोतकीं
खेलु : काटीया सोकरणें :॥ः

बडनेरा काटी वनीं दुटी फाडुनि पोतुकें केली : तेथें गोपाळ
होते : तेयातें म्हणीतलें : गोपाळ हो : हें दुसी होइल : तुम्ही
ग्राहीक होआ : तीहीं म्हणीतलें : जी जी : काइसेनि घेओं :
सर्वज्ञें म्हणीतलें : चींचोरीचीया आसू करा : दामनियांचे
दाम कराः तेहीं म्हणीतलें : हो कांः जी : मग गोसावी
दुसीयाचीया परी दांडी घातली : गोसावी हातासन
दाखवीति : गोसावी बहुत सांघति : गोपाळ तोकडेया
मागति : यापरि तेयांसि पोतुकें दीधलीं : तेहीं आसू
दीधलेया : सर्वज्ञें म्हणीतलें : निवडक : फुटकया : वाटावों
लाभे : उरलीं वस्तें तेहीं कांटीया सोकरीलिया : फु भोरडीए
म्हणौनि : दोनि हातसुडा श्रीमुगुटीं राखीला : दोनि हात

So he came to the compound. He was given a massage and a bath, and Ramdarana offered him a three-piece silk shawl. Ramdarana's mother offered sprigs of tulsi to him. Then the Gosavi ate his meal, and Ramdarana's mother broke her fast.

The next day the Gosavi left.

56 HE PLAYS WITH SCRAPS OF CLOTH IN A GROVE OF THORN BUSHES ON THE VADNER ROAD. BIRDS GET SCARED AWAY FROM THE THORN BUSHES.

In the thorn-bush grove at Vadner, he tore the shawl into scraps of cloth.[67] Some cowherd boys were there. He said to them, "Hey, cowherd boys! I'll be the shopkeeper. You be the customers." "What should we use for money, Lord?" they asked. The omniscient one replied, "Use tamarind seeds as gold coins and babul seeds as copper coins." "All right, Lord," they said.

The Gosavi put down a measuring rod like a wandering cloth merchant's. He signaled the prices with his hands. The Gosavi would name a high price, and the cowherds would ask for a low price. He would give them the scraps of cloth and they would give him the gold coins. "This one is bent," said the omniscient one. "This one is broken. This one can be spent."

Saying, "Shoo! Go away!" they hung the rest of the cloths on the thorn bushes to scare away birds. He kept two lengths of cloth on his holy head and two lengths of cloth around his waist.

सूडा : कटीं प्रदेसीं राखीला : मग गोपाळीं मोटा सोडीलिया :
आरोगणा दीधली : मग बीजें केले :॥:

५७ वटेश्वरीं सर्पद्वयपतन :॥:

गोसावी वडनेरेया बीजें केलें^{३२} : वटेश्वरीं आसन : मग गुरुवें
म्हणीतलें : देव हो : एथ देवाची उपकरणें असति : तुम्हीं
पैलीए देउळीए निद्रा करा : गोसावी पौळी बाहीरि देउळी
तेथ पहुडले : रात्रीं दोनि सर्प वक्षेस्थळावरि जूझौनि उरावरि
पडीले : तवं गुरुवें म्हणीतलें : मग काइ केले देव व्हो :
सर्वज्ञें म्हणीतलें : उरावरि पडिलेया काइ कीजे तें केलें : एणें
हातें हा फेडीला : एणें हातें हा फेडीला : इतुलेनि गुरुवासि
विस्मयो जाला :॥:

५८ रामदेवा भेटी : स्थिति :॥:

मग आंबजयेसि बीजें केलें : वडाचिए खांदिए वरि आसन :
लोंबता श्रीचरणीं : एकीकडे दादोस वटेश्वरासि आले :
गुरुवा आणि दादोसां मैत्र : गुरुवें दादोसातें म्हणीतलें :

112

Afterward the cowherd boys opened their lunch packs and gave him a meal. Then he left.

57 TWO SNAKES FALL DOWN NEAR THE VATESHVAR TEMPLE.

When the Gosavi had reached Vadner and was sitting in the Vateshvar* temple, the priest said, "Oh God, services for the god take place here. You go and sleep in that shrine over there." The Gosavi went and slept in the shrine, which was outside the compound wall.

At night, two snakes that were fighting up above him fell down onto his chest.

The temple priest asked him about it: "What did you do then, God?" The omniscient one said, "I did what people should do when something falls on their chest. I removed one with this hand, and I removed the other one with my other hand."

The temple priest was amazed.

58 HE MEETS RAMDEV, WHO GOES INTO A TRANCE.

Then he went to the Ambajai† temple and sat on the branch of a banyan tree with his holy feet hanging down.

Meanwhile, Dados came to the Vateshvar temple. The temple priest and Dados were friends. The priest said to

---

* Shiva, "Lord of the banyan tree."
† A goddess.

रामा जैसीया पुरूषाचीया गोष्टि कीजति : तैसें पुरुष एथ
आले असति : मग : रात्रीची वेवस्था सांघीतली : दादोसीं
म्हणीतलें : ते पुरुखू केउते गेले : तेणें म्हणीतलें : आंबजैए
गेले : मग दादोस तेथ आले : श्रीचरणा लागले : मग
गोसावीयासि खालि आसन : दादोसां स्तीति : मग दादोसीं
आरोगणे लागौनि वीनवीलें : तेथ घेउनि आले : आरोगणा
जाली : मग : वटेश्वरीं पहुड : त्रीरात्र एक : अवस्थान :
अनुमान :॥ः

५९ वासनीए वसति : गोपाळीं आरोगण :॥ः

मग वासनीए बीजें केलें : तेथ वसति जाली : मागौते
वडनेरेया³³ बीजें केलें : वटेश्वरीं दक्षीणे वटु : तेथ आसन :
तवं गुरुवें देखीलें : मग तेणें म्हणीतलें : गोसावी कें बीजें
केलें होतें जी : रामू भवतें पाहात होता : तेणें दादोसा पुढें
सांघीतलें : मग दादोस आले : दंडवतें घातलीं : श्रीचरणा
लागले : दादोसीं क्षेउर केलें होतें : तें गोसावी पूसीलें : तीहीं
म्हणीतलें : जी जी : आमचे पीते वाटे चोरी उपद्रवीलें :
दादोसीं म्हणीतलें : जी जी : आमतें दैवीक पडलें : तरि :
गोसावीया आरोगणे लागौनि अन्न आणुं येइल : सर्वज्ञें
म्हणीतलें : येईल : तैसें एथ कांही नाही : मग दहींभातु वाटा

114

Dados, "Ram, a holy man like the ones we talk about has come here." Then he told him what had happened the night before. "Where did that holy man go?" asked Dados. "He went to the Ambajai temple," replied the priest.

Dados came there. He touched the holy feet, and then the Gosavi sat down lower. Dados went into a trance.

Afterward he invited the Gosavi for a meal and took him to eat it. The Gosavi ate the meal, and then he slept in the Vateshvar temple.

He stayed there for about three nights.

59 HE STAYS OVERNIGHT IN VASANI. HE EATS A MEAL IN THE GOPAL TEMPLE.

Then he went to Vasani.[68] He stayed there overnight, then returned to Vadner. He was sitting at the banyan tree to the south of Vateshvar when the temple priest saw him and said, "Where did you go, Lord Gosavi? Ram* was looking all over for you."

After he told Dados that the Gosavi had returned, Dados came there. He prostrated himself and touched the holy feet.

Dados had had his head shaved. The Gosavi asked him about it. "Lord," he replied, "my father was killed by highway robbers. But still, Lord Gosavi, even though I have death pollution, may I bring food for your meal?" "You may," replied the omniscient one. "I don't observe anything like that."[69] So Dados brought him a bowl of yogurt and rice.

* Dados.

घेउनि आले : गोसावीया आरोगणा जाली : मग दादोसीं
म्हणितलें : जी जी : गावांमध्ये गोपाळाचें देउळ असे : तेथ
बीजें करावें जी : मज गोसावीयाचेया दर्शनांसि येयावीया
सोहपें होईल : रात्रीं गोपाळीं आरोगण : तेथ पहुड होय :
उदया गोसावीया बीजें करितां म्हणितलें : जी जी : दीस
च्यारि राहावें जी : सूतक सरैल मग मीं गोसावीया सरिसा
एवों एइल : सर्वज्ञें म्हणितलें : हें आतां न ऱ्हाये : मग तुम्ही
मागीला कडौनि या : तवं तेहीं म्हणितलें : जी जी : दर्शन
कव्हणें ठाई देईजैल : सर्वज्ञें म्हणितलें : हें मेहकर प्रांताकडे
होइल :॥:

६० पातुरडीं स्मशानवस्त्रस्वीकार : वाळुकेश्वरी वसति : आलेगांवीं लिंगाचां देउळीं वसति :॥:

पातुरडी समसानवस्त्र होतें तें श्रीचरणें स्वीकारिलें : तेथें
माहारू राहातु होता : तेणें म्हणितलें : सांडि : सांडि :
गोसावी दोही श्रीकरीं धरूनि वस्त्र वीसीर्ण दाखवीलें : मग
तो माहारू वीनऊं लागला : स्वीकरिजो जी : निडळ भुइसीं
लावी : पुडतीं पुडतीं म्हणितलें : परि न स्विकरितिचि : मग
वाळुकेश्वरीं वसति जाली :॥:

116

After the Gosavi ate the meal, Dados said, "Lord, there is a temple of Gopal in the village. Please come there, Lord. It will be easier for me to come for your *darśan* there."

That night the Gosavi ate his meal in the Gopal temple, and he slept there. The next morning, as the Gosavi was leaving, Dados said to him, "Please stay four more days, Lord Gosavi. My death pollution will be over, and then I can come with you." The omniscient one said, "I won't stay here now. You follow me later." "Where will you give me *darśan* next, Lord?" asked Dados, and the omniscient one replied, "I will be in the region of Mehkar."[70]

60 IN PATURADI HE ACCEPTS A GARMENT FROM THE CREMATION GROUND. HE STAYS OVERNIGHT IN THE VALUKESHVAR TEMPLE. HE STAYS OVERNIGHT IN A LINGA TEMPLE AT ALEGAV.[71]

In Paturadi he accepted a garment from the cremation ground, picking it up with his holy foot. A Mahar who was living there said, "Drop it! Drop it!"[72]

Holding the cloth in his holy hands, the Gosavi unfolded it and showed it to him. Then the Mahar began to plead, "Please accept it, Lord." He said that again and again, touching his forehead to the ground. But the Gosavi refused to take it.

Afterward he spent the night in the Valukeshvar temple.

६१ पव्हे देवा भेटी : वसति : ब्राह्मणाचें
अन्न आरोगण : आंजनीए वसति :॥:

पव्हे आसन : तेथें देवां दर्सन जालें : वीसये जवळि
पोखरणीचिए पसीमीली पाळीं : तेथ बीजें केलें :
गोसावीयापासि दादोस बैसले असति : परि गोसावीयाचिए
आरोगणेची चींता नाहीं : ना : आपुलेया जेवणाची चींता
नाहीं : कांहीं स्फुरेना : तवं एकू ब्राह्मणु तेथ आला : गोसावी
तेयातें म्हणीतलें : भटो यातें जेवावेया नेया : तो देवातें
घरां घेउनि गेला : तांबीया पाय धुवावेया दीधला : त्यासि
वाढीलें : तवं देवी म्हणीतलें : आमचिए पालवीं घाला :
आम्ही आपुलेया गोसावीयासि आरोगण देउनि : मग आम्ही
जेउनि : मग दादोस वरणभात घेउनि आले : गोसावियासि
आरोगण दीधली : तेयांसि प्रसादु जाला : मग तेथ वसति
जाली : एरी दिसीं देवां पाठवणी जाली : मग देवीं
म्हणीतलें : जी जी : दर्सन कवण ठाइं दीजैल : सर्वज्ञें
म्हणीतलें : प्रतेस्थान प्रांताकडे :॥:

61 HE MEETS DEV AT A WATER STAND. HE STAYS OVERNIGHT. HE EATS A BRAHMAN'S FOOD. HE STAYS OVERNIGHT AT ANJANI.[73]

Dev* had *darśan* of him when he was sitting at a water stand.

Later the Gosavi went to the western embankment of a reservoir near Vishaye.[74] Dados was sitting with the Gosavi, but he was not worrying about the Gosavi's meal, or about his own meal either. He was not thinking about anything. The Gosavi said to a Brahman who came there, "Bhat, take him to eat a meal." The man took Dev to his house and gave him a copper water pot to wash his feet.

When they served the food to Dev, he said, "Put it into the end of my garment. I'll give my Gosavi his meal, and then I will eat mine." Dados came back with dal and rice. He gave the meal to the Gosavi and ate the *prasād* himself. Afterward the Gosavi stayed there overnight.

The next day he gave Dev leave to go. Dev asked, "Where will you give me *darśan* next, Lord?" "In the region of Pratishthan," replied the omniscient one.[75]

---

* Dados.

६२ मेघंकरी वोणेबाइया भेटी :॥:

मेहकरी बाणेश्वराचीए सोंडीएवरि आसन : तवं बोणेबाइया
भीक्षे निगालिया : तेहीं गोसावीयातें देखीलें : मग तेही
म्हणीतलें : बाबा : कवणीचि कुसी उसासुनि निगालासि बा :
ऐसी कवणि पापीण वीसंवली : गोसावी उगेचि :
कोणिकडौनि एइजताए : गोसावी खुणांचि श्रीमुगुटें
दाखवीलें : मग तेहीं म्हणीतलें : हा बा : तरि आपण
मौनिदेयां होइजैल : गोसावी मानीलें : मग एकु लाडु पाणीं
आणिला तो गोसावीयासि वोळगवीला : गोसावी च्याऱ्हीं
एकें सेवखंडे आरोगीलीं : मग तेहीं म्हणीतलें : बा मुनिदेया
आम्हीं भीक्षा मागौनि घेउनि येउनि : तवं एथचि असा : मग
तुम्हां आरोगण देउनि : गोसावी मानिलें : मग तेहीं लवलव
करूनि भीक्षा घेउनि आली : गुंफे आरोगणा दीधली :
भैरवाचें देउळ पहुडावेया दाखवीलें : बा मूनिदेया :
ए नगरीं जवं असाल तवं उदेयां एथ पाणीभातु घेयावा :
वीळिचा भिक्षा मागौनि एउनि : ते जेवावी : ऐसें म्हणीतलें :
स्वीकरीलें :॥:

62 HE MEETS BONEBAÏ AT MEHKAR.

He was sitting on the elephant-trunk-shaped parapet next to the steps of the Baneshvar temple at Mehkar when Bonebaï set out to beg for food.[76] She saw the Gosavi and said, "Baba! Whose womb did you come bursting out of, Ba?*
What kind of sinful woman gave birth to you?" The Gosavi kept silent. "Where are you coming from?" she asked. The Gosavi answered with just a movement of his holy head. Then she said, "All right, Ba. So you will be Munidev."† The Gosavi agreed.

Then she brought a sweet ball and water and offered them to the Gosavi. The Gosavi ate a few morsels of the sweet ball. "Ba Munidev," she said, "I'll go and beg for some food. Stay right here until I bring it back. Then I will give you your meal." The Gosavi agreed.

Then she quickly went begging and brought back food. She gave him his meal in her hermit's cell and showed him the Bhairav temple to sleep in. "Ba Munidev," she said, "as long as you are in this town, eat water-and-rice gruel here in the mornings.[77] In the evenings, eat whatever food I bring back as alms."

He accepted her offer.

---

* A short form of Baba, "Father."
† "The silent god."

६३ भैरवी निद्रा : जुआरीयांचा उपद्रव :॥ः

एकु दीनी रात्रीं भैरवी पहुडले असति : तवं तेथ जुवारी
आले : तेहीं श्रीकंठीं नखें रोवीली : एरी दीसीं उदीयां
आरोगण करीतां : बोणेबाइं देखीलें : तेहीं म्हणीतलें :
मुनिदेया : बा : हें कंठीं काये जालें : सर्वज्ञें म्हणीतलें :
बाइ रात्रीं जुवारी आले : तेहीं एथ उपद्रव केला : मग तेहीं
बडुवातें म्हणीतलें : आमचेया मूनिदेयासि बाणेश्वरीं नीद्रा
करूं द्या : मग तेथ पहुड करीति :॥ः

६४ रात्रीं चोरु विद्रावन[३४] :॥ः

मग बोणेबाइचीए गुंफेसि चोरु रीगाला[३५] : तो अवघे पदार्थ
बाहीरि आंगणा घेउनि आला : तेथ आपुलिये जाडीं : मोट
बांधत असे : तवं तीहीं कवाड दाटुनि घातलें : मग बोबाति :
धांव बा मूनिदेया : चोरें नागवीलें : बा मुनिदेया : ऐसीया
बोबात असति : तवं : गोसावी बीजें केलें : सांचलु पडीला :
आणि चोरें वास पाहीली : तवं गोसावीयाची श्रीमूर्ति
वाढीनली देखीली : एसनी एकि : चोरु पळाला : मोट
जाडीची सांडौनि पळाला : मग सर्वज्ञें म्हणीतलें : बाइ :
काइ म्हणत असा : बाइ : कां बोबाता : चोरें नागवीलों

63 HE SLEEPS IN THE BHAIRAV TEMPLE. GAMBLERS ATTACK HIM.

One night when he was sleeping in the Bhairav temple, gamblers came there and dug their fingernails into his holy neck. As he was eating his meal the next morning, Bonebaï saw the marks. "Ba Munidev," she said, "what has happened to your neck?" The omniscient one replied, "My woman, gamblers came and attacked me during the night."

Then she said to the temple priest, "Let our Munidev sleep in the Baneshvar temple." After that he slept there.

64 HE DRIVES AWAY A THIEF AT NIGHT.

Later, a thief got into Bonebaï's cell. He had brought all her belongings out to the courtyard and was bundling them up in his blanket. She shut the door tight, then started shouting, "Come running, Ba Munidev! A thief has robbed me, Ba Munidev."

As she was shouting this way, the Gosavi arrived. Sensing his approach, the thief looked at him. And he saw the Gosavi's holy form in its full splendor. Immediately the thief ran away. He dropped the blanket bundle and fled.

Then the omniscient one said, "What are you saying, my woman? Why are you shouting, my woman?" "A thief has robbed me, Ba Munidev." "Open the door, my woman."

बा मूनिदेया : उघडा बाइ कवाड : कवाड उघडुनि बाहीरि
आली : मग मोट सोडवीली : पा पा : बाइ : तुमचें काइ
गेलें : अमूकें असे : अमूकें असे : ऐसे अवघेही पदार्थ होते :
सर्वज्ञें म्हणीतलें : बाइ : जाडी कोणाची : तेंही म्हणीतलें :
जाडि चोराची : सर्वज्ञें म्हणीतलें : बाइ : तरि उपराठा
चोरुचि नागवीला मा³⁶ : तवं तेहीं म्हणीतलें : आतां तो
जाडिकारणें मागुता येइल : सर्वज्ञें म्हणीतलें : बाइ : हें एवढें
एयातें एसणें एक वाढीनलें देखीलें : तो भीयाला : तो
गेला :॥:

६५ गोकुळाष्टमीं पूजा :॥:

गोकूळ अष्टमीचां दीसीं उदेयाचीए आरोगणे गुंफे बीजें
केलें : तवं मातीएचें गोकुळ करीतां देखीलें : मग पुसीलें :
बाइ : हें पैल काइ : तवं तेहीं म्हणीतलें : मूनिदेया : तुम्हीं
हें नेणा : आज जन्माष्टमी : तवं सर्वज्ञें म्हणीतलें : बाइ :
श्रीकृष्ण काइ मातीएचा : देवकी देवी काइ मातीएची : हें
असों देया : तरि काइ करूं बा मूनिदेया : सर्वज्ञें म्हणीतलें : हें
श्रीकृष्ण होइल : तुम्ही देवकी देवी होआ : हो कां बाबा :
मग जें करीतें होती तें सोडीलें : खाजि तळिलीं : वीळीचां
वेळीं गोसावी वीहरणीहुनि बीजें केलें : फुलोरा बांघों
लागले : मग व्रतस्ती बाइया गोसावीयासि पूजा केली :
गोसावी देवकीएचां उसंगीं रिगाले : मग श्रीकरीं वाण

124

She opened the door and came outside. Then the Gosavi had her open the bundle. "Take a look, my woman. Take a look. What things of yours are missing?" "This is here. That is here." All her things were there.

"Whose blanket is this?" asked the omniscient one. "The blanket belongs to the thief," she replied. The omniscient one said, "So, my woman, in fact it's the thief who's been robbed!"[78]

"Now he will come back for the blanket," she replied. The omniscient one said, "My woman, he saw me in my full splendor. He got frightened. He is gone."

65 PUJA ON GOKUL ASHTAMI.

When he went to Bonebaï's cell for his meal on the morning of Gokul Ashtami, he saw her making a Gokul out of clay.[79] "My woman," he asked her, "what is that over there?" "Don't you know, Munidev?" she asked. "Today is Janma Ashtami."* The omniscient one replied, "My woman, is Shri Krishna made out of clay? Is Devaki Devi† made out of clay? Stop doing this." "What should I do then, Ba Munidev?" The omniscient one said, "I'll be Shri Krishna. You be Devaki Devi." "All right, Baba."

Then she stopped what she had been doing. She made some fried snacks. In the evening, when the Gosavi came back from wandering, she began constructing an archway of fruits and flowers. Women who were fulfilling vows did puja

---

* Gokul Ashtami. *Janma* means "birth."
† Krishna's mother.

समर्पिलें : गोसावीया आरोगण जाली : देवकी देवी जाली :
तीयें उपवासू करितें होतीं : तवं सर्वज्ञें म्हणीतलें : बाइ :
श्रीकृष्ण उपजलें : तें देवकीया देवीं काइ उपवासू केला :
मग ते बाइ जेवीली : व्रतस्ता बाईया उपवासू केला : एरी
दीसीं उपहारू नीफजवीला : गोसावीयासि मर्दना मादनें :
पुजा केली : आरोगण जाली : मग तयांसि पारणें झालें :॥:

६६ सप्तवार घटा श्रीकर लावणें :॥:

मार्कंडेवीहीरिसि आसन : तेथ बाइ एकी पाणियां आली :
त्या म्हणीतलें : हा बाबा : भरि घागरिसि हातु लावा कां :
गोसावी श्रीकरू लावीला : यापरी सातां हेळां श्रीकरू
लाववीला : वीळींचां वेळीं तीयेचा भातारू तेथ संध्या करू
आला : तेणें गोसावीयातें देखीलें : श्रीचरणा लागला : मग
तो घरासि घेउनि आला : गोसावीयासि आसन केलें :
मग ब्राम्हणीतें म्हणीतलें : ए : गोसावीयांचेया श्रीचरणा
लाग : ते श्रीचरणा लागली : मग तीयां म्हणीतलें : एयां
गोसावीयां करवीं मियां सातां हेळां श्रीकरू कैसा लावीला :

to the Gosavi. The Gosavi sat on Devaki's lap, and they put their offerings into his holy hands. The Gosavi ate his meal.

The woman who had become Devaki Devi was fasting. But the omniscient one said, "My woman, did Devaki Devi fast when Shri Krishna was born?" So that woman ate a meal, but the other women who were fulfilling vows fasted.

The next day they prepared a meal. The Gosavi had a massage and a bath, and they did puja to him. After he ate his meal, they broke their fast.

66 HE LIFTS A POT WITH HIS HOLY HAND SEVEN TIMES.

When he was sitting at the Markanda well, a woman came there to fetch water. "Hey, Baba," she said, "will you give me a hand with this full water pot?" The Gosavi lifted it up with his holy hand. She came seven times and had him lift it up with his holy hand.

In the evening, her husband came there to perform *sandhyā*. He saw the Gosavi and touched his holy feet. He brought the Gosavi home and prepared a seat for him. Then he said to his wife, "Come here and touch the Gosavi's holy feet."

She touched the holy feet. Then she said, "How could I have made this Gosavi lift my pot with his holy hand seven times?"

तेणें म्हणीतलें : चांडाळी : पापीणी : गोसावीया करवि करूं
कैसा लावीला : गोसावीयांचेया श्रीचरणा लाग : मग : तेणें
चरणक्षाळण केलें : वीनवीलें : मग गोसावी तेथौनि बीजें
केलें :॥:

६७ सामान्यस्त्रियां भेटी :॥:

मग गोसावी सामान्यस्त्रिहाटें बीजें करीत असति : तवं
सामान्यस्त्रिया दोघी एकी घरीचिया : एकि साउमि आली :
ते वीनवुनि पालवीं धरूनि घरा घेउनि गेली : बाजसूपवतीए
वरि आसन : वीडीया करूनि दीधलीया : मग त्या म्हणीतलें :
जी जी : मातें द्रव्य अपार असे : पर ते वायां जात असे जी :
तवं एरीं म्हणीतलें : सर ऐसें काइ म्हणतासि : गोसावी
माएबापु : पुडती तीयां तैसेंचि म्हणीतलें : एरीं तैसेंचि
नीराकरीलें³⁷ : गोसावी तीएचा शब्द आइकौनि एरीची वास
पाहाति ॥ मग सर्वज्ञें म्हणीतलें³⁸ : बाइ तुम्ही म्हणत असा
तें नव्हें : ए म्हणतें असति तें होए : मग तेथौनि बीजें केलें :॥:

Her husband said, "You Outcaste woman! You sinner! How could you have made the Gosavi lift your pot? Touch his holy feet." He washed the Gosavi's feet and invited him for a meal.

Then the Gosavi left.

67 HE MEETS PROSTITUTES.

Later, the Gosavi was going through the prostitutes' quarter. One of two prostitutes who belonged to the same house approached him. She invited him, grabbed him by the end of his garment, and brought him to the house. He sat on a bed while she made rolls of pan and gave them to him. Then she said, "Lord, I have unlimited amounts of money, but it is going to waste."

At that, the other one said, "Back off! What are you saying? The Gosavi is our mother and father." Again the first one said the same thing, and the other one objected the same way.

The Gosavi listened to the second one's words and looked at the first one. Then the omniscient one said to the first one, "My woman, what you are saying is wrong. What she is saying is right." Then he left.

६८ महीषयुद्ध निवारण :॥:

एकू वेळ एरीं हाटवटीया बीजें करीत असति : तवं म्हैसे
दोनि जूंझत असति : तडुवीया तडवी पडली असे : माणुसें
माळवधा वरूनि पाहातें असति : गोसावीया बीजें करीतां
लोकें वारीलें : देव हो : न वचा : न वचा : पुढीं म्हैसे जूंझत
असति : गोसावी बीजें केलें : दोहीचि थडक मीळौनि
वोसरले होते : गोसावी दोहींतें अवलोकौनि दोहीमध्यें बीजें
केलें : मग दोहींचा रोखु नीवर्तला : एकू ऐसा नीगाला : एकू
ऐसा नीगाला : मग लोकासि वीस्मयो जाला :॥:

६९ लोणारमार्गीं चोरकुमति हरण :॥:

सोमवारी आली : मग : बोणेबाइ म्हणीतलें : बा मूनिदेया
लोणारासि जावों : गोसावी मानिलें : मग बीजें केलें : मग
कूमारेश्वरीं आसन : मात्रा गोसावीया पासि ठेउनि बाइया
अष्टतीर्थें करूनि आलिया : मग धारेसीं आसन : मग बाइ
बीढारीं उपहारू निफजवीला : गोसावीया आरोगण :
दैत्यसूदना मागां मढू : तेथ वसति : एरी दीसीं दैत्यसूदना
वीहरणा बीजें केलें : बाइया अष्टतीर्थीया करूनि उपहारू

68 HE STOPS A FIGHT BETWEEN
WATER BUFFALO BULLS.

Once when he was going to another market, two water
buffalo bulls were fighting. People watched from the roof-
tops as the bulls butted heads with each other. As the Gosavi
went along, people warned him off: "Don't go there, God.
Don't go there. Buffalo bulls are fighting up ahead."

The Gosavi kept going. The two bulls had slammed into
each other and then pulled apart. The Gosavi looked at the
two of them and then stepped in between them. Their anger
subsided. One of them set off in one direction and the other
in another direction.

The people were amazed.

69 ON THE ROAD TO LONAR, HE DOES
AWAY WITH ROBBERS' EVIL INTENTIONS.

When a no-moon Monday was coming, Bonebaï said, "Let's
go to Lonar, Ba Munidev."[80] The Gosavi agreed, and they
went there.

The Gosavi was sitting at the Kumareshvar temple. The
women left their belongings with him and went to the Eight
Tirthas.[81] Later he sat at the waterfall, and then Bonebaï
cooked food at their lodgings.[82] The Gosavi ate his meal.
He spent the night in a hermitage behind the Daityasudan
temple.[83]

The next day he went wandering to the Daityasudan
temple, and Bonebaï went to the Eight Tirthas. Then she

131

निफजविला : गोसावीया आरोगण : मग पहूडानंतरें
म्हणीतलें : बा मूनिदेया लोकु निगाला : आतां गावां
जावोंना : गोसावी बीजें केलें : मार्गीं वृक्षाखालि आसन :
जूझमालीं आसन : गोसावीया तेथौनि बीजें केलें : यानंतरें
चोरू बाइया देखीलें : मग तीहीं बाइ म्हणीतलें : बा मूनिदेया
चोर चोर बाबा : सर्वज्ञें म्हणीतलें : बाइ : भीया ना : पुढां
चाला : तवं आले : उभे राहीले : सर्वज्ञें म्हणीतलें : कांगा
माहात्मे हो जेहुनि तुम्ही आलेति ते कां वर्तना कीजेना : तवं
तेहीं म्हणीतलें : जी जी : गोसावीयाचां ठाइं काइ : गोसावी
अवलोकीलें : आणि तेहीं म्हणीतलें : गोसावी अवळा वेळीं
कैसें बीजें केलें³⁹ : गोसावीया सरीसें कोण्ही माणुस नाहीं :
गोसावीया म्हणीतलें : महात्मे हो : तुम्हीं असा नव्हे :
काइसी अवेळ : मग गोसावी तयासि पुडवाटवा झाडौनि
तांबुळ दीधले : पाठवणी दीधली : तवं तेहीं म्हणीतलें : जी
जी : आमचे पुढां आणिक असति : तें गोसावीयाचां ठाइं
उपद्रो करीति : सर्वज्ञें म्हणीतलें : तैसें एथ कव्हणी काइ न
करी : ऐसांहीं ते सरीस आले : सोंदरासंगमीं आणिक चोर
भेटले : एरएन्ही गोसावीयातें गावांमध्यें गांववेन्ही बोळवीत
आले : मग तेयासि पाठवणी जाली : ते गेले :॥:

cooked some food and the Gosavi ate his meal. After he had slept for a while, she said, "Ba Munidev, people are leaving now. Let's go home."

The Gosavi left. Along the road, he sat under a tree, he sat at Junjhmal.* After the Gosavi left there, Bonebaï saw some robbers. "Ba Munidev!" she said. "Robbers! Robbers, Baba!" The omniscient one said, "Don't be afraid, my woman. Keep on walking."

The robbers arrived. They stood there, and the omniscient one said, "Why don't you do what you came to do, Mahatmas?" "How could we do that to you, Lord Gosavi?" they replied. The Gosavi looked at them, and they said, "Why have you come at such a wrong time, Gosavi? There are no men with you, Gosavi." The Gosavi said, "You are not like that, Mahatmas. How is this a wrong time?" Then the Gosavi shook out his partitioned pouch and gave them some pan. He gave them leave to go.

"Lord," they said, "there are more of our people up ahead. They will attack you, Gosavi." The omniscient one said, "No one does anything like that to me."

Even so, they came along. They met more robbers at the Sondara confluence.[84] One band after another of robbers accompanied the Gosavi through one village and up to the next. Then he gave them leave to go, and they left.

––––

* "Fighting Pasture."

७० सिंहस्थयात्रे गमन :॥:

सीहस्तु आला : मग बोणेंबाइ म्हणीतलें : बा मूनिदेया
त्रीयंबका जावों : गोसावीं मानिलें : गोसावीयासि दुणिची
आंगी टोपरें सीवीलें : उपाहानउ बांधलिया : सर्वज्ञें
म्हणीतलें : बाइ : ओझें काहीं घवों नोको : वाटें मिळेल⁴⁰ :
तेहीं म्हणीतलें : मूनिदेया : बाबा : साना गावीं वीसजू न
जोडे : ऐसांही आइती : तरि थोडी बहुत तऱ्ही घेओं : सर्वज्ञें
म्हणीतलें : बाइ : हें पुढां जोडैल : मग बीजें केलें :॥:

७१ नदी उपानहौ त्याग :॥:

मार्गीं नदी उतरतां उपाहानौ फेडीलीया : तीया तेथचि
टाकौनि बीजें केलें : बाइया पुढें चालती होतीया : तेहीं
मागील वास पाहीली : तवं श्रीचरणीं उपानहौ नाहीं⁴¹ : मग
तेहीं म्हणीतलें : बा मूनिदेया उपानहौ काइ केलीया : सर्वज्ञें
म्हणीतलें : बाइ : जाः तीया तेथचि असति : कटकट : बा
मूनिदेया : आम्हांपुढें सांघतेति कां तरि आम्हीं घेतों कीं :
मग आणिकी उपाहानउ बांधलीया⁴² : तीए दीउनि नदी

134

70 HE SETS OFF ON
THE SIMHASTHA PILGRIMAGE.

When the Simhastha came, Bonebaï said, "Let's go to Tryambak, Ba Munidev."[85] The Gosavi agreed. She sewed a double-thick cloak and a cap for the Gosavi, and she strapped sandals on his feet.

The omniscient one said, "Don't bring anything heavy, my woman. We'll get what we need along the way." "Munidev Baba," she said, "in small villages we can't get provisions, and we can't get prepared food either. So let's take at least a little something along." "We will get it up ahead, my woman," said the omniscient one.

Then he set out.

71 HE DISCARDS HIS SANDALS
AT A RIVER.

As they crossed a river along the way, he took off his sandals. He simply left them there and kept going. Bonebaï was walking on ahead. When she looked back, she did not see the sandals on his holy feet. So she said, "Ba Munidev, what did you do with your sandals?" The omniscient one said, "Go back, my woman. They are right there." "Oh, no, Ba Munidev! If you had told me, I would have gotten them." Then she strapped another pair of sandals on his feet.[86]

देखति आणि मागें राहाति : उपाहानउ हातीं घेति : मग नदी
उतरलेयां मेळवीति :॥:

७२ मार्गीं प्रतिदिनीं बोणें :॥:

पेणें पावलेयां एकाधा देउळी कां पडवीये^{४३} आसन होए :
गावींचा लोकु गोसावीयांतें देखौनि कणिक : तांदुल : तुप :
ऐसें आवघें घेउनि येति : मग ते आवघे बाइया बीढारा
घेउनि जाति : गोसावी म्हणति : आवघें वेचा : ठेवाना :
मग बाइं म्हणीतलें : बा मूनिदेया : एथ तुम्ही चुकाल : तरि
बीढारां जावों या कां^{४४} : मग मागुते यां : सर्वज्ञें म्हणीतलें :
बाइ : ऐसें एईल चोजवीत : चोजवीत : गोसावी देउळीं
असति कां नदी असति^{४५} : बाइयांसि रधन करूं सरे : मग
वाट पाहाति : आणि : गोसावी बीजें करिति : गोसावीयासि
आरोगण होए : मग पहुड आणिके स्थानीं होए गावां :
उदेयांचि मार्गीं गोसावी बाइयांसि पारूखति : जरि बाइया
पुढां एति : तरि तीया पारूखति : मग तेथ भेटी होए : मग
साउमे चालति :॥:

From that day on, whenever she saw a river, she would hang back. She would take his sandals in her hands. Then, after he had crossed the river, she would put them down in front of him.

72 ALONG THE ROAD, HE GETS FOOD OFFERINGS EVERY DAY.

When they reached their halting place for the night, he would sit in a temple or on a veranda. Seeing the Gosavi, the people of the village would bring wheat flour, rice, and ghee. Then Bonebaï would take it to the lodgings. The Gosavi would say, "Use it all up. Don't save any."

Later she said, "Ba Munidev, if you get lost here, will you be able to get to the lodgings? Will you come back?" "My woman," replied the omniscient one, "I will ask directions and find my way back."

The Gosavi would be at a temple or at the river. Bonebaï would finish cooking, and then she would wait for him. The Gosavi would come there, eat his meal, and then sleep somewhere else in the village.

Early the next morning, the Gosavi would be waiting for Bonebaï on the road. If she arrived first, she would wait for him. They would meet there and walk on.

७३ रावसगावीं माहादेव पाणीभात बाबुळशेंगा आरोगण

एयापरी क्रमें क्रमें रावसगावां बीजें केलें : तो गांवो तीर्थाचा
म्हणौनि सिदोरि न ठेवीतिचि : मग सीधनाथीं माहादेवो
पाठकांचीए गुंफेसि बीजें केलें : तेहीं पाणीभातु बाबूळसेंगा
ऐसी आरोगण दीधली : सीळें आरोगण : मग रंधन जालेया
तेथ बीजें केलें : बाइं म्हणीतलें : बा मूनिदेया आजि
भूकैलेति : मग गोसावीया आरोगण : तेथ अवस्थान :
कवणीं ठाइं ते नेणीजे :॥:

७४ प्रतिष्ठानीं बाइसां भेटी :॥:

मग क्रमें क्रमें प्रतिस्थानासि बीजें केलें : भोगवतिएसि
राहिले : तेथ बाइ म्हणीतलें : बा मूनिदेया हें थोर नगर :
एथ तुम्ही चुकाल : बिढारासि जावों या : सर्वज्ञें म्हणीतलें :
बाइ : एइल ऐसें चोजवीत चोजवीत : बाइया बाईंसाचीए
गुंफे गेलीया : पै : वो : नागुबाई आम्हांसरिसे एक मूनिदेव
असति : काइ सांगों तेयाचें सौंदर्ये : मग आश्र्वय अनुभवीची
सांघौनि मग बीढारा नीगालिया : मग बाइसासि ते
पुरूखु देखीजति एसी चाड उपनली : तवं पाहारा अढैचां
भोगावतीचिया खांडि नगरामध्यें बीजें केलें : बाइसें
वामदेवाचीए गुंफे जात असति : पार्वतीसोमनाथापासि

73 AT RAVASGAV HE HAS A MEAL OF MAHADEV'S WATER-AND-RICE GRUEL AND BABUL PODS.

Traveling stage by stage this way, the Gosavi reached Ravasgav.[87] That village was a holy place, so they did not pack any food at all. He went to Mahadev Pathak's hermit's cell at the Siddhanath temple. Mahadev gave him a meal of leftovers: water-and-rice gruel and babul pods.

Then, after Bonebaï finished cooking, he went to the lodgings. "You are hungry today, Ba Munidev," she said. Then the Gosavi ate his meal.

He stayed there several days, it is not known where.

74 HE MEETS BAÏSE IN PRATISHTHAN.

Then, traveling stage by stage, he reached Pratishthan. He stopped at Bhogavati.[88] There Bonebaï said, "Ba Munidev, this is a large town. You will get lost here. Will you be able to get to the lodgings?" The omniscient one said, "My woman, I will ask directions and find my way there."

Bonebaï went to Baïse's hermit's cell. "Nagubaï!" she said. "There is a certain Munidev traveling with me. How can I express his beauty?" Then, after telling her about the marvels she had experienced, she set off for their lodgings. Baïse conceived a desire to see that holy man.

That afternoon, the Gosavi entered the town through the Bhogavati gate. Baïse was on her way to Vamdev's hermit's

भेटी जाली : बाईसीं मनीं म्हणीतलें : ऐसें पुरुष ए नगरीं तवं
नसति : हे तेचि होती : मग बाइसीं गोसावीयातें पूसीलें :
आपण कवणीं कडौनि येइजत असे : गोसावी श्रीमुगुटें
खूणां दीशा सांघीतली : तवं बाईसीं म्हणीतलें : लोणारा
मेहकरा कडौनि : गोसावी मानिलें : मग बाईसीं म्हणीतलें :
आमचिए मढीएसि चाला : गोसावीयासि पाएपुसणें
बैसावेया घातलें : मग बाइसीं म्हणीतलें : हांसूबाई :
महात्मेयांसि पाणीभातु दीया : गोसावीयासि दूधी करटा
आरोगण : मग भोगनारायणीं पहुड केला : बोणेबाइ पाहारू
एकू वाट पाहीली : मग म्हणों लागली : आजि मुनिदेव
आझुइं न एतिचि : तरि काइ चुकलें : हें थोर नगर : परि :
चुकती कीरू ना : ना तरि कव्हणी जेवावेया नेले असति :
ऐसें वेवस्तुनि : मग तीयें जेवीली :॥ः

एकांक समाप्त

cell. She met the Gosavi near the Parvati-Somnath* temple. Baïse said to herself, "There are no other holy men like this one in this town. This must be the one." So Baïse asked the Gosavi, "Where are you coming from?" The Gosavi moved his holy head to indicate the direction. "From Lonar and Mehkar?" asked Baïse. The Gosavi agreed.

Then Baïse said, "Come along to my hermitage." She put down a doormat for him to sit on. Then Baïse said, "Hamsubaï, give the Mahatma some water-and-rice gruel." The Gosavi had his meal in a dried gourd. Then he went to sleep in the Bhognarayan temple.[89]

Bonebaï waited for three hours. Then she began to say, "Munidev hasn't come here yet today. So did he get lost? This is a big town, but surely he wouldn't get lost. Maybe someone has taken him for a meal."

Deciding that this was what had happened, she went ahead and ate her meal.

End of "The Solitary Period."

---

* Shiva and his wife, Parvati.

The First Half

१ त्रींएंबका न वचणें^१ :॥:

एरी दीसीं उदीयांचि गोसावीयांसि बाइसाचिए गुंफे
अग्निकोनीं आसन : पश्चीमा मुख : बोणेबाइं म्हणीतलें :
नागुबाइचिए गुंफेहुनि : मुनिदेव न एति कीं : ऐसें भणौनि :
तेथ आलिया : पै वो नागुबाई : आमचें मुनिदेव नैएतीचि^२ :
निच रंधन होए : आणि : येति : कालि न येति चि : तरि :
काइ थोर नगर भणौनि चुकले : परि चुकति किरू ऐसे
नव्हति : तरि : काइ कोण्ही जेवावेया नेले : ऐसें बोलिली :
तवं उपाहानौ देखीलिया : पुढारीं आलीं : ऐसी वास
पाहाति : तवं : गोसावीयातें देखीलें : मग : म्हणीतलें : हें
काइ बा मुनिदेया : कालि बीढारा न याचि : आम्हीं वाट
पाहात होतों : सर्वज्ञें म्हणीतलें : बाइ : हे ऐसेची आले^३ : मग
बोणेबाइं म्हणीतलें : चाला चाला बा : मनिदेया : सांगातु
निगाला : तवं बाइसीं म्हणीतलें : हें काइ वो : माहात्मेयासि
काइसा त्रीयंबकु : हें जेथ असती तेथचि तिर्थ : तवं : तेंहीं
म्हणीतलें : हे काइ वो : तरि : आम्हीं : आपूलिया मूनिदेयातें
नेवों ना : ऐसी बाइसांवरि घुचाइली : मग : म्हणीतलें : चाला
बा मूनिदेया : म्हणौनि : उपाहानौ मेळवीलिया : मग गोसावी
लोणार वरि बीजें केलें : तेथ उपाहानहो फेडीलीया : तीये
पुढें उपाहानहौ घेउनि गंगा उतरली : उपानहो मेळवावीया
मागील वास पाहीली : तवं : गोसावी तेथचि उभे असति :

1 HE DOES NOT GO TO TRYAMBAK.

Early the next morning the Gosavi was sitting in the southeast corner of Baïse's hermitage, facing westward. Bonebaï thought to herself, "Munidev has not returned from Nagubaï's hermitage." So she went there and said, "Nagubaï! Our Munidev hasn't come back. Every day I cook food for him, and he comes to eat. But yesterday he didn't come at all. So I thought, it's a big town, so maybe he has gotten lost. But surely he wouldn't have gotten lost. So I thought, maybe someone has taken him for a meal."

As soon as she said this, she saw his sandals. She stepped forward, looked around, and saw the Gosavi. "What is going on, Munidev?" she asked. "You didn't come back to the lodgings yesterday. I was waiting for you." The omniscient one replied, "I came here instead, my woman." Then Bonebaï said, "Come on, Ba Munidev. Come on! Our group is setting off."

At that, Baïse said, "What do you mean? What use is Tryambak for a Mahatma? Wherever he is, *that* is a holy place." Bonebaï replied angrily to Baïse, "What do you mean? Can't we take our Munidev away, then?" Then, saying, "Come on, Ba Munidev," she put his sandals down in front of him.

The Gosavi went as far as Lonar *tīrtha*.[1] He took off his sandals there, and she picked them up and crossed the river ahead of him. When she looked back to put the sandals down in front of him, the Gosavi was still standing in the same place.

145

मग बाइं म्हणीतलें : चाला बा मुनिदेया : सर्वज्ञें म्हणीतलें :
बाइ : आतां हें न ए : यालागि इतुका ऐसा त्रियंबकु घेउनि
या : तवं तेहीं म्हणीतलें : कटकट : बा मूनिदेया : चाला कां :
तवं आणिकी एकीं म्हणीतलें : हें काइ : हे माहात्मे४ : हें
काइसेया येति : हे जेथें असती तेथचि तीर्थ : मग : माघौतीं
उपाहानहौ घेउनि आलिया : मग तेहीं म्हणीतलें : बा
मूनिदेया : आम्ही एवों तवं एथचि असा : मग गावांसि
जावों : मग तीया निगालीया : गोसावी देउळें मढ
अवलोकीत पाहारा दीढा नागुबाईचीए गुंफेसि बीजें केलें :
नागुबाई म्हणीतलें : बा मुनिदेया : राहीलेति : तें चांग केलें
हो : आपण जेथ असीजे तेथेंचि तीर्थ : नागुबाई पायेपुसणें
बैसों घातलें : हांसूबाई माहात्मेयांसि पाणीभातु दीया : तेंहीं
दुधी करटां वाढीलें : गोसावीयासि आरोगणा जाली :
नागुबाई म्हणीतलें : बा मूनिदेया : आपण ये नगरीं जवं
असिजैल : तवं एथ पाणीभातु चीयावा : विळीचां भिक्षा
मागौनि तैसी जेवावी : भोगनाराएणि निद्रा करावी : हें
आपुलें ऐसें म्हणावें : गोसावी स्वीकरीलें :॥:

२   बाइसां स्तीति५ :॥:

मग गोसावी भोगनारायणीं पहुडु केला : वीळिचां आरोगण
करूनि उदेयां विहीरणा बीजें केलें : पाहारा दीढा गुंफेसि
बीजें करीति : नागुबाइए पायेपुसणें बैसों घालीति :

146

Then Bonebaï said, "Come on, Ba Munidev." The omniscient one said, "My woman, I'm not coming with you now. Bring back a bit of Tryambak for me." "Oh, no, Ba Munidev!" she replied. "Come on."

Some of the others said, "What do you mean? He is a Mahatma. Why would he come? Wherever he is, *that* is a holy place." So she brought back his sandals and said, "Ba Munidev, stay right here until we get back. Then let's go home." Then they set off.

Looking at temples and hermitages as he went along, by late morning the Gosavi made his way to Nagubaï's cell. Nagubaï said, "It's good that you have stayed, Ba Munidev. Wherever you are is a holy place." Nagubaï put down a doormat for him to sit on. "Hamsubaï, give the Mahatma some water-and-rice gruel," she said.

Hamsubaï served him the food in a dried gourd. The Gosavi ate his meal. Nagubaï said, "Ba Munidev, as long as you are in this town, eat your water-and-rice gruel here. In the evening, beg for food and have that as your meal. Sleep in the Bhognarayan temple. Consider this place your own."

The Gosavi accepted her offer.

2   BAÏSE GOES INTO A TRANCE.

After that, the Gosavi would sleep in the Bhognarayan temple. He would eat his meal in the evening and go out early in the morning to wander. Later in the morning he would go to Nagubaï's cell. She would put down a doormat for him to sit on. "Hamsubaï," she would say, "give the Mahatma some

हासूबाइ : माहात्मेया पाणीभातु दीया : दुधी करंटां
पाणीभातु आरोगणा होए : हंसराजु नागुबाईचिए ठाइं
अवसरू करिति : या परी तीसरां दीसीं उदेयांचि आरोगणा
जालेयां नंतरें आसनीं उपवीष्ट असति : नागुबाईसें
गोसावीयाची वास पाहातें असति : गोसावी नागुबाईसातें
अवलोकीति : दीठीं दीठि मीळे : आणि : नागुबाईसें खालुती
वास पाहाति : गोसावीयाची दीठी चेंपेणा : नागुबाईसा
स्तीति जाली : मग नागुबाई आपणेयातें वोटेया खालुतें
घातलें : बाबा : म्हणौनि : बाबा : पापीण : बाबा : एथ मीं
सूळीं सूदलीयें असें : बाबा खाली : मग गोसावी वोटेयावरि
आसन केलें : मग सेवादास्य करूं लागली : चरणक्षाळण
करीति : आपण चरण उदक घेति : अवसरू करीति :
गोसावीयासि बरवी तात्परियें आरोगणा देति : प्रसादु घेति :
भोगनाराएणीं जाडि आथुरीति : वरि पासोडी : पासवडा
घालीति : तेथ पहुडु होए : ऐसीं वर्तों लागलीं : सर्वज्ञें
म्हणीतलें : म्हातारियेचा ठाइं त्रिदोषू होता : तो सन्निधान
देउनि फेडीला : मग तीसरां दीसीं कळिका एकि
संचरीली :॥:

water-and-rice gruel." He would eat his water-and-rice in a dried gourd. Hamsaraj would perform Nagubaï's worship.

On the third morning, he was seated in his place after finishing his meal. Nagubaïse was looking at the Gosavi, and the Gosavi was looking at Nagubaïse. When their eyes met, Nagubaïse looked down. She could not meet the Gosavi's gaze. Nagubaïse went into a trance.

Then Nagubaï threw herself down from her pedestal. "Baba!" she said. "Baba! I am a sinner, Baba. I have put myself up here in the high seat, Baba, with you down below." Then she prepared a seat for the Gosavi on the pedestal.

After that she began to serve the Gosavi. She would wash his feet and drink the foot water. She would perform his worship. She would attentively give the Gosavi fine meals, and then she would eat the *prasād*. She would spread out a blanket in the Bhognarayan temple and cover it with thick shawls. He would sleep on that. This became their routine.

Later, the omniscient one remarked, "The old woman had three faults. I removed them by giving her my presence. Then, on the third day, one part of love entered her."[2]

३ हंसराजा स्थिति :॥:

हंसराजु आणि पांडे भकति : हें काइ जालें या नागुबाइसि :
चळली काइ : एसणा आमचा पयोवर्तियांचा मार्गु सांडूनी :
नेणोकोण आणिला असे : तेयाचें उसीटें खाति असे :
पायवणी पीति असे : ऐसें दोघें भकति : मग : नागुबाई
म्हणीतले : बाबा : हे हांसूबाई भकति असे : इएसि काइ
करूं बाबा : गोसावी उगेचि होते : एकुदिनी वोटेया वरि
आसन : तवं हंसुबाइसें आलीं : सर्वज्ञें म्हणीतलें : हंसुराजा :
या : या शब्दासरीसीं स्तीति जाली : श्रीचरणापासीं गडबडा
लोळति : जी जी : मी पापीण जी : गोसावीयासि भकें जी :
गोसावीयाची नींदा करीं जी : मग : तेंहीं सेवा करूं
लागली :॥छ॥: हंसराजा स्तीति जालेया नंतरें दुपाहारचा
पहुड वोटेया वरि होए :॥:

४ पांडेया स्वप्रीं नामस्वीकारू :॥:

मग पांडे भकति :॥: एतुके दीस एकीचि भुलली होती :
आतां दोघी भुललिया : या काइ जालें दोघीसि : चळलियां
काइ : एसणा आमुचा पयोवर्तियाचा मार्गु : सांडौनि
नेणोकोण आणिला असे : तेयाचें उसीटें खाति असति :

3   HAMSARAJ GOES INTO A TRANCE.

Hamsaraj and Pande were complaining, "What has happened to Nagubaï? Has she gone crazy? She has left our great milk-drinkers' way and brought in some unknown man.[3] She is eating his leavings and drinking the water from washing his feet."

After the two of them started complaining this way, Nagubaï said, "Baba, Hamsubaï is complaining. What should I do with her?" The Gosavi kept silent.

One day when he was sitting on the pedestal, Hamsubaïse came along. The omniscient one said, "Hamsaraj, come here." As soon as he spoke these words, she went into a trance. She wallowed on the ground at his holy feet, crying, "Oh Lord! I am a sinner, Lord. I was complaining about you, Lord Gosavi. I was criticizing you, Lord Gosavi." From then on she began to serve him.

After Hamsaraj went into the trance, the Gosavi would have his afternoon nap on the pedestal.

4   PANDE LEARNS THE GOSAVI'S
NAME IN A DREAM.

Then Pande would complain.[4] "For such a long time," he said, "only one woman was obsessed with him, but now both of them are obsessed. What has happened to them? Have they gone crazy? They have left our great milk-drinkers' way and brought in some unknown man. They are eating his leavings and drinking the water from washing his feet." He would

पायवणी पीति असति : ऐसे निच भकति : मग : नागुबाई
म्हणीतलें : बाबा पांडा भकतु असे : काइ करूं : गोसावी
उगेचि होते : एकू दी पांडे रात्रीं निजैले असति : ते रात्रीं स्वप्र
जाला : गुंजावर्ण डोळे : बाबर झांटि : हातीं मूदलगु : ऐसे
जमजुत आले : पांडेयातें मूदगलवेन्हीं घेति : तेवीचि
म्हणति : आरे हे कवण पुरूखु : ऐसें नेणसि : हे द्रारावतीकार
श्रीचांगदेवो राउळ : निच गोसावीयासि तुं भकसि : यांची
तुं नींदा करीसि : ऐसे म्हणोनि मुदगलें तोंडावरि हाणति :
गोसावी आड श्रीकर वोडवीति : नको नको : बापूडा मारूं :
नेणचि : पांडे काकुलति एति : मग चेवो आला : उठिले :
मग : नागुबाइ नागुबाइ : म्हणोनि बोबावों लागलें : नागुबाई
म्हणीतलें : हांसूबाई : पाहा पा : पांडा कां बोबातु असे :
हंसराजु गेली : आवो : तुं कां आलिसि : ते नागुबाइ
बोलावी : नागुबाइसें गेलीं : रात्रीचें व्रतांत सांघीतिलें : तरि
गोसावीयातें विनवी कां : एथ बीजें करावें : नागुबाइसा सूख
जालें : नागुबाइ बोलाउं गेलीं : परशरामबास :॥: गोसावी
भोगनाराएणीं होतें :॥छ॥: रामेश्वरबास :॥: गोसावी ब्रह्मचारी
देवाचीए गुंफेसि होते :॥छ॥: नागुबाइ वीनवीलें : बाबा :
पांडा बोलावीत असे : तेथ बीजें कीजो जि : सर्वज्ञें
म्हणीतलें : बाइ : हे काइ तेयाचिय नाथेचा बैलु : ऐसें

complain this way constantly. Nagubaï said, "Baba, Pande is complaining. What should I do?" The Gosavi kept silent.

One night when Pande was sleeping, he had a dream. Messengers of Yama* came to him, their eyes bright red, their hair thick and disheveled, holding maces in their hands. They struck Pande with the maces and said, "Hey! You don't know who this holy man is. He is Shri Cangdev Raül of Dvaravati. You are constantly complaining about the Gosavi, and you criticize him." As they said that, they beat Pande on the face with their maces.

The Gosavi put out his holy hand to block them. "No! Don't beat the poor fellow! He doesn't know any better."

Pande woke up whimpering. He stood up and began to shout, "Nagubaï! Nagubaï!" "Hamsubaï," said Nagubaï, "go and take a look! Why is Pande shouting?" When Hamsaraj went there, Pande said, "Oh! Why have *you* come? Call Nagubaï."

Nagubaïse went there, and he told her what had happened that night. "So will you invite the Gosavi to come here?" he asked. That pleased Nagubaïse.

Nagubaï went to invite the Gosavi. (According to Parasharambas, the Gosavi was in the Bhognarayan temple. According to Rameshvarbas, he was in Brahmacharidev's† hermit's cell.) Nagubaï conveyed the invitation: "Pande is inviting you, Baba. Please go there, Lord." The omniscient one replied, "My woman, am I an ox that he leads around by the

* The god of death.
† Another ascetic in Pratishthan.

153

तेयाचिया बोलावीलेया येइल : ना : बाबायें बीजें करावें :
मग गोसावी बीजें केलें : दारेसीं उभे ठेलें : आणि : पांडा
श्रीचरणावरि दंडवतें घातलीं : श्रीचरणापासि लोळों लागले :
जी जी : मी गोसावीयावरि नीच भकें : मग रात्रींचें वृतांत
सांघीतलें : आजी : गोसावी राखीला जी : आओ नागुबाइ⁶ :
हे कवण गोसावी ऐसें तुम्हीं नेणा वो : हे द्वारावतीकार
चांगदेवो राउळ : नागुबाई गोसावीया पुसीलें : बाबा :
आपणेयां नांव काइ : पांडा म्हणतु असे : तेंचि : सर्वज्ञें
म्हणीतलें : त्रीदोखू होता : तो दर्सन देउनि फेडिला : मग प्रेम
कळीका संचरीली : मग पांडेही गोसावीयाचे जाले :॥:

५ भोगनारायणीं मायधुवां भेटी :॥:

गदोनायेकाचिए ब्रह्मपुरीये मायेधवांचा आवारू : कहीं
प्रागीं स्नान करीति : तोचि देओ पाहाति : कहीं लोणारीं
स्नान करीति : तोचि देवो पाहाति : कहीं पींपळेश्वरीं स्नान
करीति : तोचि देओ पाहाति : आदीत्यवारीं भोगावतिएसि
महीमा : तीए दीसीं अवघा लोकू भोगावतिए स्नान करीति :
ऐसा एकू दीस आदित्यवारू आला : त्या भोगनाराएणीहुनि

nose, that will simply come when he calls?" "No, but please go there, Baba."

The Gosavi went there. He stood in the doorway, and Pande prostrated himself at his holy feet. He began wallowing on the ground at the holy feet. "I was constantly complaining about you, Lord Gosavi." Then he told him what had happened that night. "You protected me today, Lord Gosavi. Oh, Nagubaï, you don't know who this Gosavi is. He is Cangdev Raül of Dvaravati."

Nagubaï asked the Gosavi, "Baba, what is your name?" "It's what Pande is saying."

(Later the omniscient one remarked, "He had three faults. I removed them by giving him my *darśan*. Then a part of love entered him."[5])

After that Pande too came to belong to the Gosavi.

5 HE MEETS A MOTHER AND DAUGHTER IN THE BHOGNARAYAN TEMPLE.

A certain mother and daughter had their home in Gadonayak's Brahmapuri.* Sometimes they would bathe at Prayag *tīrtha* and look at the god there.[6] Sometimes they would bathe at Lonar *tīrtha* and look at the god at that place. Sometimes they would bathe at the Pimpaleshvar temple and look at the god there.[7]

Bhogavati was important on Sundays. Everyone would bathe there that day. One Sunday the mother and daughter were going by way of the Bhognarayan temple to bathe at

* A neighborhood in Pratishthan.

भोगावतिएसि स्नानासि जाती होतीया : गोसावियासि
उदयाचा पूजावस्वर : गोसावी भोगनाराएणाचां आंगणीं उभे
असति⁹ : तिएं आलीं : तेंहीं गोसावीयातें देखीलें : जातांचि
भोगावतिए स्नानै केलीं : तियाचि वाटा मागुतीया आलिया :
तव लेकी म्हणीतले¹⁰ : बाइ : या : देवाये गे जावों :
गोसावीयासि पटिसाळेवरि आसन : माता देउळांतु गेली :
ते गोसावीयातें पाहाते तेथेंचि राहीली : मातां म्हणीतलें : हा
देवो पाहावेया आलिसि तरि देवो पाहासि ना : ते उगीचि
होती : मग घरासि आली : तवं लेकीसि देह जाए ऐसा
ज्वरु आला : थोरि पीडा हों लागली : माए काकूलति करूं
लागली : हागे आइ : हा ज्वरू तुझा काइसेनि जाइल : तीया
म्हणीतलें : मीं म्हणैन ते करीसी तेणें जाइल : तरि : हां गे
आइ : सांग का : ना : भोगनाराएणीं जे गोसावी असति
तेयांचें मज दर्सन होइल तरि माझें देह वांचैल : हो कां : गे :
आइ : म्हणौनि गेली : गोसावीया दंडवतें घातलीं :
श्रीचरणा लागली : मागील आवघें वृतांत सांघीतलें : तर
गोसावी येथ बीजें करावें जी : गोसावी तेथ बीजें केलें :
तिये उठिली : दंडवतें घातलीं : श्रीचरणा लागलीं : आसन
केलें : मातां पुजा द्रव्यें आणिलीं : पाणी ठेविलें : उपहारू
निफजवीला : मग : दोघीं मर्दना दीधली : मार्जने जाले :
पुजा केली¹¹ : आरोगणा जाली : गुळळा जाला : वीडा

Bhogavati. It was time for the Gosavi's morning worship service. He was standing in the courtyard of the Bhognarayan temple, so they saw him as they passed by.[8]

As soon as they reached Bhogavati, they took their baths, then returned by the same route. The daughter said, "Come on, Mother. Let's go to this god."

The Gosavi was sitting on the veranda. The mother went into the temple. The daughter stayed right there, looking at the Gosavi. Her mother said, "You have come to look at this god, but you are not looking at the god." The girl kept silent.

Later, after they reached home, the daughter came down with a deadly fever. She was in agony. The mother began crying pitifully, "What will make your fever go away, my dear?" The daughter replied, "If you do what I say, that will make it go away." "All right then, dear," said her mother. "Tell me!" "If I have *darśan* of the Gosavi who is at the Bhognarayan temple, my life will be saved."

Saying "All right, dear," the mother went there. She prostrated herself to the Gosavi and touched his holy feet. She told him everything that had happened, then said, "Please come there, Lord Gosavi."

When the Gosavi arrived there, the girl stood up. She prostrated herself and touched his holy feet. She prepared a seat for him. Her mother brought the materials for doing puja, put on water to heat, and prepared some food. Then the two of them gave him a massage. He had a bath, and they did puja to him. He ate his meal and rinsed his mouth, and they offered him pan.

Her fever went away.

वोळगवीला : तीएचा ज्वरू गेला : गोसावीयासि पहुड
जाला : मग तीएचि ताटीं दोघीं जेऊं बैसलिया : मग चरण
क्षाळण : चरणसव्हान केलें : चरणोदक घेतलें : मग गोसावी
बीजें केलें :॥:

६ ग्रहे सारंगपाणी भेटी :॥:

ग्रहेसारंगपाणिभट ते बव्हेग्रामिचे¹² : तेयांसि ग्रहो लागला
होता : ते देवांचे सोइरे : तयाचीया मातां दादोसातें म्हणी-
तलें : रामा : तुं कांहीं जाणसी : तरि : या सारंगपाणीचा
आंगीं ग्रहो असे : तो फेडी कां : तेंहीं म्हणीतलें : आवो
माझेनि जाए ऐसेंहीं आति : न वचे ऐसेंही आति : आमचेया
गोसावीयाचेनि जाएचि : ते गोसावी कवण ठाइं असति :
ना : भोगनाराएणीं असति : मग सारंगपाणी : तेयाची माता :
चांगदेवो भट : बल्हेग्रामूनि ऐसी गोसावीयांचिया दरिसनांसि
आलीं : भोगनाराएणीं वीळचिया वेळीं घडीया दो आसन :
तीयें आलीं : दंडवतें घातलीं : श्रीचरणा लागलीं :
आसु दरिसनां केली : गोसावी अवसरू दीधला : जी जी :
रामु आमुचा सोएरा : मागील व्रूतांत सांघीतलें : जी जी :
तरि : याचा आंगीं ग्रहो असे : तो याचिए आंगीचा फेडावा
जी : सर्वज्ञें म्हणीतलें : बाइ तुमतें पाणीभातु असे :
नागुबाई म्हणीतलें : हो बाबा : असे : तिन मुदा करूनि
यातें वोवाळुनि सांडा : नागुबाइ म्हणीतलें : बाबा : हा

The Gosavi went to sleep, and the two of them ate their meal off the same plate that he had used. Then they washed his feet, massaged them, and drank the foot water. Then the Gosavi left.

6 HE MEETS GRAHE SARANGPANI.

Grahe Sarangpanibhat was from Balhegram.[9] He was possessed by a ghost. He was a relative of Dev's.* Sarangpanibhat's mother said to Dados, "Ram, you have some knowledge. Can you exorcise the ghost from Sarangpani?" "There are some that I can exorcise, but there are also some I cannot. Our Gosavi can exorcise all of them." "Where is that Gosavi?" "He is at the Bhognarayan temple."

Then Sarangpani, his mother, and Cangdevbhat came from Balhegram for *darsan* of the Gosavi. He was sitting in the Bhognarayan temple for an hour or so in the evening. They arrived, prostrated themselves, and touched his holy feet. They gave him a gold coin as an offering. The Gosavi gave them an audience.

"Lord," they said, "Ram is our relative." They told the Gosavi what had happened, then requested, "So, Lord, please exorcise the ghost that is possessing Sarangpani." The omniscient one asked Nagubaï, "My woman, do you have some water-and-rice gruel?" "Yes, Baba, I do," she said. "Make three lumps of it, wave them in a circle in front of

* Dados's, Ram's.

सावदु ऐसा दीसतु असे : यांचा आंगीं कें असे ग्रहो :
सर्वझें म्हणीतलें : बाइ : तिन असति :॥: हीराइसा पाठ :॥:
आंगुळीका तीन दाखविलें :॥: एयींचेया दरीसना एतां :
येवों नये : माहारवडा कांटी असे : तेथ राहीले असति : मग
नागुबाई तीन मुदा केलीया : तेयातें वोवाळुनि सांडीलिया :
मग तेंहीं उपाहारू केला : निगतां सर्वझें म्हणीतलें : ते वाट
पाहाताति : परशरामबास : तेयासी आतां याचें कांहीं करूं न
ये : पर : तरि तेया वाटां न वचिजे : तेंहीं म्हणीतलें : हा जी :
द्रुष्टवैर चुकवीजे : आणिकीं वाटां जा : हो कां जी : मग ते
पैलाडीलेया वाटा गेली :॥:

७ देइभटां भेटी : अस्तित जाली :॥:

एकुदीनी भोगनाराएणीं देइभटां भेटि जाली : दंडवतें
घातलीं : श्रीचरणा लागलें : गोसावीयां पासि बैसले : आणि
स्तीति जाली : भोगिली : भंगीली : मग बीढारा गेले :॥:

him, and toss them away." Nagubaï said, "Baba, he seems to be fully awake. Is there really a ghost possessing him?" The omniscient one said, "There are three of them, my woman." (Hiraïsa version: He raised three fingers.)[10] "As he came for my *darśan,* they could not come along. They have stayed on a thorn bush in the Maharvada."[11]

So Nagubaï made three lumps of water-and-rice gruel. She waved them in a circle in front of Sarangpani and tossed them away. Then she prepared some food.

As the group was setting out to leave, the omniscient one said, "They are waiting for you." (According to Parasharambas: "They can't do anything to him now, but still, don't go past them.") "Yes, Lord," they said. "Avoid a known enemy," said the omniscient one. "Go by a different route." "All right, Lord," they said, and they took a detour as they left.

7 HE MEETS DEÏBHAT, WHO GOES INTO A TRANCE.

One day Deïbhat* met him at the Bhognarayan temple. Deïbhat prostrated himself and touched the holy feet. He sat down near the Gosavi and went into a trance. He experienced the trance, and then it broke. Then he went to his lodgings.

---

* A Brahman resident of Pratishthan.

८ सारंगपंडीतां भेटि :॥ः

सारंगपंडीतां देइभटीं गोसावीयांचें बरवेंपण : चातुर्य :
सौंदर्यें : सारंगपंडीतां पुढें सांघीतलें : तेंहीं पूसीलें : ते कवणे
ठाइं असति : ना : भोगनाराएणीं असति : गोसावीयासि
दुपाहाराचा पुजावसर : श्रीकंठीं गळदंडा : आंगिएचे मोकळे
केस : भोगनाराएणाचिये आग्रये कोनी वोतपली घेत उभे
असति : सारंगपंडीत गदोभांडारीयाचिया घरा पुराण सांघों
जात होते : तेथ भेटि जाली : मग म्हणीतलें : जी जी : मज
दरिसन कवणें ठाइं होइल : तथा देइजैल :॥ः सर्वज्ञें
म्हणीतलें : चासाकडे : सारंगपंडीत गदोनाएकाचेया घरा
गेले : दाहा एक श्लोक म्हणीतलें : आणि पोथी बांधली :
तेंहीं म्हणितलें : हे काइ : आजी लवकरी पोथी बांधली :
ना : काहीं कार्ये असे : काखे पोथी : चासाकडे आले : तवं
चासीं गोसवीयांसि आसन^{१३} : पुढां बैसले : मग प्रश्न केला :
जी जी : मागा श्रीकृष्ण चक्रवर्ति पासौनि आकृत्रीम्य आनंदु
आति : तैसा अन्येत्र आति : सर्वज्ञें म्हणींतलें : पाहीजे :
पुसीजे : चर्चिजे : मा जेथ आति : तेथ आति : आणि

8 HE MEETS SARANGPANDIT.

Deïbhat told Sarangpandit about the Gosavi's goodness, cleverness, and beauty. Sarangpandit asked, "Where is he?" "He is at the Bhognarayan temple."

The Gosavi's afternoon worship service had taken place. There was a garland of flowers around his holy neck, and his hair was hanging loose on his body. He was standing at the southeast corner of the Bhognarayan temple, taking in the mild sunshine.

Sarangpandit was going to Gado the Treasurer's* house to expound on Puranic stories. On his way there, he met the Gosavi at the temple. Sarangpandit asked, "Where will I get your *darśan,* Lord?" "On the high riverbank," replied the omniscient one.

Sarangpandit went to Gadonayak's house. He read out ten verses or so, then tied the manuscript closed. "What is going on?" asked Gadonayak. "You have closed the manuscript early today." "There's something I have to do," he replied. With the manuscript under his arm, he came to the high riverbank.

The Gosavi was sitting on the high riverbank.[12] Sarangpandit sat down in front of him, then asked him a question: "Lord, people in the past used to get a natural kind of joy from Shri Krishna Chakravarti. Can that be found anywhere else?" The omniscient one said, "Look at it, ask about it, discuss it. Then it is where it is."

* Gadonayak's.

स्तीति जाली१४ : भोगीली : भंगली : केतुलें एक काळु : मग
वीनवीलें : जी जी : माझेया घरां गोसावी बीजें करावें :
मग तेथ बीजें केलें१५ : उतरीले पटीसाळेवरि आसन :
चरणक्षाळण केलें : चरणोदक घेतलें : वोळणीं : तेल :
चिकसा : आणिला : सर्वज्ञें म्हणितलें : कपीला स्नान कां
वर्तेना : हो कां जी : मग उपरीएएवरि : बीजें केलें : चौरंगावरि
आसन : दोनि गंगाळें उदकां भरिलीं : एके गंगाळीं आंगवसा
तीमीती : श्रीमूर्ति प्रमार्जीति : दुसरीये गंगाळीं आंगवसा
धुति : ऐसें मार्जनें जालें : मग : तीयेचि पटिसाळे चौरंगावरि
आसन : सर्वांगी चंदन वोळगवीलें : पुजा केली : धुपार्ति
मंगळार्ति केली : मग उमाइसा करवीं ताट करवीलें :
मोकानंदें देव्हार चौकीये घेउनि आले : आरोगणा जाली :
सारंगपंडीतीं प्रसादु घेतला : उरला तो मोकानंदें घेतला :
उमाइसीं म्हणितलें : हे काइ मोकानंदा : तुवां प्रसादु घेतला :
पंडीतीं घेतला : मजलागि न ठेवीसीचि : ऐसा अपरीतोखु
केला : मग गोसावी भोगनाराएणां बीजें केलें :॥:

With that, Sarangpandit went into a trance. He experienced the trance, and then, after some time, it broke. Then he invited the Gosavi home: "Please come to my house, Lord."

The Gosavi went there.[13] He was given a seat on the northern veranda. Sarangpandit washed his feet and drank the foot water. He brought body oil, fragrant ointment, and a cloth to wear while bathing. The omniscient one said, "Why not do a sponge bath?" "All right, Lord."

The Gosavi went upstairs and sat down on a low, square stool. Two large vessels were filled with bath water. Sarangpandit bathed him by wetting a cloth in one of the vessels, washing the holy body with the cloth, and then rinsing it in the other vessel.

After his bath, the Gosavi sat on a low, square stool on the same veranda as before. Sarangpandit anointed his whole body with sandalwood paste. He did puja to him and performed *āratī* with incense and with lighted lamps. Then he had Umaïse prepare a plate of food, and Mokananda brought it to the household shrine.[14] The Gosavi ate his meal. Sarangpandit ate the *prasād,* and Mokananda took what was left.

Umaïse complained, "What is this, Mokananda? You have taken *prasād,* and Pandit has taken it, but you haven't left a bite for me."

Then the Gosavi went to the Bhognarayan temple.

९ तथा ज्वर निवृत्ति :॥:

वैजाए राणीयां वैजनाथाचें देउळ करविलें : ब्राह्मणा वृत्ती
दीधलीया : सारंग पंडीतातें बोलाऊं धाडीलें : सारंग पंडीत
कटका गेलें : वृत्ति जाली : काळाक्षेरीं नांव घातलें : शासनीं
नांव घालावें तंव ज्वरू आला : तेहीं म्हणीतलें : देह जाइल
तरि गोसावीयापासि जावो ना : ज्वरू येईल तरि तेथचि
जावो : दांडी केली : बाहीरि बाहीरि गोसावीयापासि आले :
सोधु : हे काइ : पांडेया : ज्वरेसींचि आलेति : मा : ॥
गोसावीयासि दंडवतें घातलीं : श्रीचरणीं लागले : जरू आला
तें सांघीतलें१६ : सर्वज्ञें म्हणीतलें : पांडेया : ज्वरू पूसत असे
गा : केव्हळा केव्हळा भोगीन : जी जी : तो गेलाचि : सर्वज्ञें
म्हणीतलें : तो भोगीलेयावीण न वचे : तरि येवों दीजो जी :
पैन्हा तऱ्ही भोगावाचि कीं : तरि सन्नेधानीं भोगुं : बाइसें
उपाहारू करीति : गोसावीयांसि पुजा होए : आरोगणा होए :
चरणोदक तें उदक : प्रसादु तें पथ्य : अठरा दीस ज्वरू
आला१७ : मग जरू गेला : सर्वज्ञें म्हणीतलें : पांडेया : ज्वरू

9 AND HE STOPS HIS FEVER.

When Queen Vaijaï had a temple of Vaijanath built, she gave land grants to Brahmans.[15] Sarangpandit was summoned to the capital. He went there, and his name was written down as receiving a land grant. As his name was about to be written on the grant deed, he came down with a fever. He said, "If I am dying, I must go to the Gosavi. If I get a fever, that is where I should go." He hired a palanquin and came straight to the Gosavi.

(Research: The Gosavi asked, "What is going on, Pande?* Did it take a fever to get you to come here?") Sarangpandit prostrated himself to the Gosavi and touched his holy feet. He told the Gosavi that he had come down with a fever.[16] The omniscient one said, "Pande, the fever is asking, 'When, oh when, will I get to enjoy him?'" "It has gone away completely, Lord." "It will not go away unless you suffer through it," said the omniscient one. "Then shall I let it come, Lord? If I must suffer through it somewhere else anyway, let me experience it in your presence."

Every day, Baïse prepared food, the Gosavi's puja was performed, and he ate his meal. Sarangpandit drank only the water from washing the Gosavi's feet, and all he ate was the Gosavi's *prasād*. The fever lasted for eighteen days, and then it went away.

---

* Sarangpandit.

काइ करीत असे गा ः तथा सोधु ः आतां कैसें असे गा ः जी
ज्वरू गेला ः न्हा ः जेवा जा ः सुखें असा ः मग गोसावीयातें
उपाहारा लागि वीनवीलें ः वीळीचा घडीयां चौ ः आपणचि
बोलवावेया आले ः बीजें केलें ः मर्दना दीधली ः माजणें
जालें ः पुजा जाली ः आरोगणा जाली^{१८} ः गुळळा जाला ः
वीडा वोळगवीला ः मग बीढारा बीजें केलें ः॥ः

१० उपाध्यां भेटि ः॥ः

चांगदेवो भटीं ः उपाध्यातें म्हणीतलें ः जानो ः जानो ः आम्ही
तुम्ही जैसीया जैसीया पुरुखाचीया गोष्टी करूं का ः तैसे
पूरुखु प्रतेष्ठानीं भोगनाराएणीं असति ः तरि तेयाचें मज
दरिसन करी कां ः हो कां ः तरि ः तु ः कै जासी ः ना पाहे ः ना
पाहेचा दीसू राहे ः माझी पासोडी धुतली येइल ः मग परवां
जाउनि ः तें नागदेवोभटीं^{१९} आइकिलें ः पासोडी धुतली
आली ः रात्रीं दोरा घालिताति ः तवं लाहामाइसीं म्हणीतलें ः
हारे ः बा ः एवढ्या वेळा ः दोरा घालितासि ः तो उदियां चाली
कां ः तवं नागदेवोभटीं^{२०} म्हणीतलें ः हां वो ः हा गेला कीं ः
जोगीया भवंतियापाठीं ः मग उदीयांचि उठीले ः वोहणी
सीदोरी सुवा ः मी गावां जाइन ः तव लाहामाइसें दुःख
करूं लागलीं ः आणि सीदोरी नेघतां निगों आदिरीलें ः मग

"How is the fever doing, Pande?" asked the omniscient one. (Or, research: "How are you now?" "The fever has gone away, Lord." "Take a bath. Go and eat a meal. Live happily."

That evening Sarangpandit invited the Gosavi for a meal. He himself came to extend the invitation. The Gosavi went there. They gave him a massage, he had a bath, and they did puja to him. He ate his meal and rinsed his mouth, and they offered him pan. Then he went to his lodgings.

10   HE MEETS UPADHYE.

Cangdevbhat said to Upadhye, "Jano! Jano! You know the kind of holy men we tell each other about? There's a holy man like that at the Bhognarayan temple in Pratishthan." "Will you take me for his *darśan,* then?" "All right." "When are you going there?" "Tomorrow." "I have to stay here tomorrow. My thick shawl will come back washed. Let's go the day after tomorrow." Nagdevbhat heard what they said.

The thick shawl came back washed. As Upadhye was sewing on it that night, Lahamaïse* said, "Hey there, my child! Why are you sewing at such an hour? Do the sewing tomorrow." "Yes," said Nagdevbhat, "after he has gone chasing after yogis."

Early the next morning, Upadhye got up and said to his sister-in-law, "Pack me a lunch. I'm going on a trip."

When Lahamaïse heard that, she began to cry. And so he started to leave without waiting for the lunch. "When

* Upadhye's mother.

169

लाहामाइसीं म्हणीतलें : हारे बा : कै एसी : चांगदेवोभटातें
म्हणीतलें : ऐसे म्हणां : हा दीसां दो एइल : हां रे : बा :
दीसां दो आणिसी : मानिलें : मग : प्रतेष्ठानासि आले :
गोसावीयास उपहुड जाला²¹ : गुंफेसि आसनीं बैसले
असति : चांगदेवोभट : उपाध्ये आले : दंडवतें घातलीं :
श्रीचरणां लागले : सर्वज्ञें म्हणीतलें बटिका : हा कोणु : जी :
जी : हा आमुचा मैत्रु : सोधु : हाही एथीचाचि : हो जी :॥:
दुपाहाराचा पुजावसर बाईसीं केला : उपाध्यीं बाइसातें फुल
मागीतलें : अक्षेता मागितलीया : मग : अपसव्यें करूनि :
तीथी श्रवण²² केले : मंत्रु म्हणौनि पुजा केली : सहस्त्र-
शीर्षा : मग हातीं अक्षेता घेउनि पूढें उभे ठेले : मंत्रु
म्हणीतला : पुजा : दंडवतें घातलीं : श्रीचरणा लागलें :
सर्वज्ञें म्हणीतलें : बाइ : जीव जीवा आर्चन घडे : बाइसीं
म्हणीतलें : बाबा घडवीति तेयासि घडे :॥:

११ तथा तांबूळग्रहण :॥:

एकुदिनीं भोगनाराएणीं आसन : श्रीमुखीं तांबोल होते :
तेंहीं गांवां जावेयाचें पूसीलें : बाईसें राहावीतें होतीं : सर्वज्ञें
म्हणीतलें : बटीका : बाइसें म्हणतें असति : तें कां कीजे ना :

will you come back, my child?" asked Lahamaïse. Upadhye said to Cangdevbhat, "Tell her, 'He will come back in two days.'" "Will you bring him back in two days, my child?" Cangdevbhat agreed.

When they reached Pratishthan, the Gosavi had waked up and was sitting in his place in the cell. Cangdevbhat and Upadhye arrived there. They prostrated themselves and touched his holy feet. The omniscient one said, "Who is this, Batika?"* "This is my friend." (Research: "He too belongs to me." "Yes, Lord.")

Baïse performed the afternoon puja. Upadhye asked Baïse for a flower and some unbroken rice grains. Then he circumambulated the Gosavi and announced the date. He recited the mantra "Thousand-headed..." and performed puja.[17] Then he stood before the Gosavi, holding the unbroken rice in his hand. He recited a mantra, did puja, prostrated himself, and touched the holy feet.

The omniscient one said, "My woman, the *jīva* worships *jīvas*..."[18] Baïse said, "If you cause someone to, Baba, they do it."

11   AND UPADHYE TAKES HIS PAN.

One day the Gosavi was sitting in the Bhognarayan temple. There was pan in his holy mouth. Upadhye and Cangdevbhat asked about going back to their village, but Baïse was urging them to stay.

* Here, Cangdevbhat.

ना जी : गांवीं अवसरी करीति : वीळचा एकलेयां जावों
जाणाल : जी : आम्हीं एथ अखंड यवों जावों : तरि तुम्ही
धीरवीर म्हणा२३ : गोसावी तांबूळ परित्येजीतां : उपाधीं
आंजूळी वोडवीली : सर्वज्ञें म्हणीतलें : बटिका : एथीचेया
उसिटेंया तांबूळा हात वोडवीत असा : हें काइ२४ : तेहीं
म्हणीतलें : जी : कांहीं जाणिजेना : ऐसें तुम्ही कांहीं जाणिजे
नां : तरि कां घेत असा : जी : आपुलेया भलेया :॥: गांवीं
जाल तरि घरिचीं रिगों नेंदीती : जी जी : नेंदीती तरि नेंदीती :
आणि काइ : तीवए पाटीं जेऊं सुती : जी जी सुती तरि सूती :
आणि काइ : नष्टभ्रष्ट म्हणती : जी जी : म्हणती तरि
म्हणती : आणि काइ : वेगळेयां चालीति : जी जी : चालीति
तरि चालीति : आणि काइ : ऐसांहीं एथीचें तांबूळ कां
घेयावें : जी जी : आपुलेया भलेया : मग गोसावी तांबुळ
दीधले२५ : माळ दीधली : सर्वज्ञें म्हणीतलें : बटीका : तुम्हतें
कव्हणीं कांहीं न म्हणे हो२६ : मग राहिले :॥ः

The omniscient one said, "Batika, why not do what Baïse is saying?" "They are expecting us back home, Lord." "Will you know how to get there on your own in the evening?" "Yes, Lord. We will keep coming here continually." "So I say you are resolute heroes."

As the Gosavi was about to spit out his pan, Upadhye cupped his hands and held them out for it. The omniscient one said, "Batika, why are you stretching out your hands for the pan I'm spitting out?" "I don't know, Lord," he said. "If you don't know, why are you taking it?" "For my own good, Lord." "If you go back to your village, your family will not let you in." "If they don't let me in, Lord, then they don't let me in. What of it?" "They will serve you your meals on a three-legged stand."[19] "If that's how they serve them, Lord, then that's how they serve them. What of it?" "They will say you are lost and ruined." "If that's what they say, Lord, then that's what they say. What of it?" "They will throw you out." "If they throw me out, Lord, then they throw me out. What of it?" "Even so, why should you take my pan?" "For my own good, Lord."

Then the Gosavi gave him the pan and a garland. The omniscient one said to him, "No one will say anything to you, Batika."

They stayed there.

१२ कास्तां हरिदेओ पंडीतां
गोपाळमंत्रभेद नीरोपण२७:॥ः

चांगदेवीं कास्त हरिदेवो पंडित पुराण गीता आइकति :
मग तेथीचे संदेह पडति : ते येउनि : गोसावीया पुसति :॥ः
उदयाचा पुजावसर : गोसावीयांसि भोगनाराएणीं चौकीं
आसन : पासि उपाध्ये असति : तवं हरिदेवो पंडित आले :
म्हणौनि : गोसावी बाहीरि बीजें केलें : पडीसाळे : उपाधी
पासोडी बैसों घातली : सर्वज्ञें म्हणीतले : बटिका पासोडी
मैळेना : ना जी : गोसावी पासोडीएवरि चरणचारीं उभे ठेले :
तवं बाइसीं जाडी आणिली : आसन केलें : गोसावी आसनीं
बैसलें : हरिदेवो पंडितीं दंडवतें घातलीं : श्रीचरणां लागले :
पुढां बैसले : हरिदेवो पंडितीं गीतांचा संदेहो पूसीला : पाठीं
गोसावीयांचि प्रश्न केला : हीराइसा :।ः सर्वज्ञें म्हणीतलें :
तुम्हां परिचयो कव्हणीये ठाइं : तेंहीं म्हणीतलें :
गोपाळमंत्रीं परिचयो : सर्वज्ञें म्हणीतलें : गोपाळमंत्रीं भेद
कितीएक असति : जी जी : दाहावीस असति : दोनी च्यारि
आम्ही जाणों : हीराइसा :॥ः शतएक बोलीजति : दाहा वीस
एक येती : सर्वज्ञें म्हणीतलें : बोला पां : बोलीजो : सर्वज्ञें
म्हणीतलें : गोपाळ मंत्रीं सतसहस्र संख्या भेद : ते भेद के

12 HE TELLS KASTA HARIDEV PANDIT
ABOUT THE TYPES OF GOPAL MANTRA.

Kasta Haridev Pandit used to listen to Puranas and the Gita*
in the Cangdev temple. Then he would come and ask the
Gosavi the questions that had occurred to him there.

Once when he came, the Gosavi was sitting in the central
hall of the Bhognarayan temple for his morning worship
service. Upadhye was with him. Then, because Haridev
Pandit had come, the Gosavi moved outside onto the
veranda. Upadhye put down a thick shawl for him to sit on.
"Won't the shawl get dirty, Batika?" asked the omniscient
one. "No, Lord."

The Gosavi stood on the shawl. Then Baïse brought a blanket and made a seat of it. The Gosavi sat on the seat. Haridev
Pandit prostrated himself, touched the Gosavi's holy feet,
and sat down in front of him.

Haridev Pandit asked a question about the Gita, and afterward the Gosavi asked a question of his own. (According to
Hiraïsa, the omniscient one asked, "What subject do you
know about?" "I know about Gopal mantras," he answered.)
The omniscient one asked, "How many types of Gopal
mantra are there?" "There are ten or twenty, Lord. I know a
few of them." (According to Hiraïsa, he said: "They say there
are a hundred or so. I know ten or twenty.") The omniscient
one said, "Recite them!" "Should I recite them?"

The omniscient one said, "There are a hundred thousand
types of Gopal mantra. What are they? There's one type

* The *Bhagavadgītā*.

175

आति : एकू भेद तो कव्हणीचि नेणे : रुक्मिणि देवीप्रति
श्रीकृष्णचक्रवर्ती नीरूपिला : म्हणौनि रूक्मीणि देवी जाणे :
कां श्रीकृष्णचक्रवर्ति जाणति : आणिक कव्हणिचि नेणति :
हरिदेवो पंडितीं म्हणीतलें : जी जी : हें गोसावीचि जाणावें :
गोसावींचि निरूपावें : आम्हीं परिसों नेणों : मा : नीरूपूनि
तें काइ : मग उपाधीयासि प्रतीति बैसली : द्वापारीचे ते हे
गोसावी :॥:

१३ रवळेया अध्यात्म :॥:

एकुदीसी महदाइसीं रवळेयाचा अध्यात्मीचा गीतु
आइकिला : मग गोसावीयांसि पुढां सांघीतला : यावरि
गोसावी गोष्टि सांघीतली : रवळा कुंभारू : तेणें अध्यात्मु
गीतु केला : द्वारावती चांगदेवो राउळापुढें म्हणितलें : मा
पुसीले : गीतु कैसा जाला : श्रीचांगदेवो राउळीं म्हणीतलें :
तुझा निर्वंशू होए ऐसा जाला : रामेश्वरबास : हे लीळा
गणपति मढीं :॥:

176

that no one knows. Shri Krishna Chakravarti told it to the goddess Rukmini,* and so the goddess Rukmini knows it and Shri Krishna Chakravarti knows it. No one else at all knows it."

Haridev Pandit said, "Lord Gosavi, only you could know this, and only you could tell about it. I don't know how to listen to this, so how could I possibly tell about it?"

Then Upadhye realized that this Gosavi is the one from the Dvapara yuga.†

13   RAVALE'S SONG ABOUT THE SOUL.

One day Mahadaïse heard Ravale's song about the soul, and she told the Gosavi about it. Then the Gosavi told this story: "Ravale was a Potter. He composed a song about the soul, and he sang it in Dvaravati to Cangdev Raül. Then he asked, 'How was the song?' Shri Cangdev Raül said, 'It was so bad that your lineage will be cut off.'"

(According to Rameshvarbas, this *līḷā* took place at the Ganapati Madh.)[20]

---

* Krishna's wife.
† Shri Krishna Chakravarti.

१४ कवडींबा भेटि अवसरू :॥ः

गोसावीयांसि उदयांचा पुजावसर जालेया नंतरे²⁸ : गोसावी
चांगदेवा बीजें केलें : चौकीं आसन : कवडींबासि भेटि
जाली : एकें म्हणती : दक्षिणिले दारवठा : मग : चौकीं
आसन : दंडवतें केलीं : श्रीचरणां लागले : बैसलें : मग :
सीकारीं गावों आदिरिलें : एक म्हणति : बाळानेयावरूनि
आइकिलें :

तुं गोसावी : मी पाइक तुझा :
हरि हरि वाचा उचारण :
नयनु निरखुन ध्यान :
तुं एकु हरी : इतुलें देइं :
आन न मागे :

ऐसीं पांचपदें गाइली : बाइसीं म्हणीतलें : बाबा : भगतु काइ
मागत असे : सर्वज्ञें म्हणीतलें : भगतु आणि मागे :॥ः

१५ तथा गाएन श्रवण :॥ः

गोसावीयांसि उदयाचा पुजावसर जालेया नंतरे²⁹ : गोसावी
चांगदेवा बीजें केलें : बाळाणेयावरि आसन : कवडींबाचे
सीकार : भित्तिरि गात होते : त्वमेव माता पिता त्वमेव :

14 HE MEETS KAVADIMBA
AND GIVES HIM AN AUDIENCE.

One day, after his morning worship service, the Gosavi went to the Cangdev temple. As he sat in the central hall there, Kavadimba met him.[21] (Some say they met at the southern doorway, and then the Gosavi sat in the central hall after that.) Kavadimba prostrated himself, touched the Gosavi's holy feet, and sat down.

Then he began to sing, to the accompaniment of a drone. (Some say the Gosavi listened from the balcony.) Kavadimba sang these five lines:

You are the Gosavi; I am your servant.
May my voice say, "Hari!* Hari!"
May my eyes look closely at your image.
Yourself alone, Hari: give me just that much.
I ask for nothing more.

Baïse inquired, "What is the devotee asking for, Baba?" The omniscient one replied, "Would a devotee ask for anything?"[22]

15 AND HE LISTENS TO SINGING.

After his morning worship service, the Gosavi went to the Cangdev temple and sat on the balcony. Kavadimba's accompanist was singing inside. He sang lines based on the Sanskrit verse, "You alone are my mother; you alone are my father."

***

* Krishna.

या श्लोकावरि हें पदें गाइलीं : बाइसीं म्हणीतलें : बाबा :
भगतु काइ म्हणतु असे : सर्वज्ञें म्हणीतलें : बाइ : हा हें शाब्दें
म्हणतु असे³⁰ :॥:

१६ धानाइसांसीं कवडा खेळु :॥:

एकुदिनीं गोसावी सारंगपंडीताचेया घरासि बीजें केलें :
आसनीं उपविष्ट जालें : धानाइसीं काइसेयाची नेणो आळि
घेतली : सर्वज्ञें म्हणीतलें : बाइ : या : हें तुमसीं कवडां
खेळेल : कवडे घेउनि आली : कवडे मांडिले : गोसावींहीं
आपुले मांडीले : गोसावीयाचे कवडे चालति : तेयाचे न
चलति : आणि म्हणति : आपण चालते घेतले : मज न
चलते दीधले : पालटिति : मागुते मांडिति : गोसावीयांचे
चालों लागति : तेयाचे न चलति : मग म्हणति : मातें हें
जिंकताती : म्हणौनि पुरें केलें :॥:

180

"What is the devotee saying, Baba?" asked Baïse. The omniscient one replied, "He is just saying these words, my woman."[23]

16   HE PLAYS COWRIES WITH DHANAÏSE.

One day the Gosavi went to Sarangpandit's house and sat down. Dhanaïse* was being stubborn about something or other. The omniscient one said, "Come here, my woman. I'll play cowries with you."

She brought the cowrie shells. She arranged her cowries, and the Gosavi arranged his. The Gosavi's cowries were moving ahead, but hers were not moving. "You took the ones that move ahead," she said. "You gave me the ones that don't move."

They traded cowries and arranged them again. The Gosavi's began to move ahead, but hers did not move. Then she said, "He is beating me." So they stopped playing.

---

* Sarangpandit's young daughter.

१७ देवो साकरभातु :॥ः

एकुदीनी गोसावी सारंग पंडीताचेया आवारासि बीजें केलें :
मर्दना माजणें जालें : पुजा केली : उमाइसीं ताट वाढीलें :
सारंग पंडीतासि ठावों केला : मोकानंदु ताट देव्हारचौकीये
घेउनि आले : सारंगपंडीता ठावो मांडीला : उमाइसें पहीत
मोकानंद हातीं नेदीतिचि : गोसावी भातावरि साकर घालुनि
आरोगीत असति : तवं उमाइसें पहीत घेउनि आली : सर्वज्ञें
म्हणीतलें : बाइ : देवो साकरभातु आरोगीतु असे : उमाइसीं
म्हणीतलें : जी जी : मी पहित वाढुं वीसरलियें : पहीत
वाढिली : श्रीचरणा लागली : मग गेली :॥ः

१८ लखुबाइसां भेटि :॥ः

एकुदीनी गोसावीयांसी उदयाचा पुजावसर जालेयानंतरें[३१] :
भोगनाराएणीं आसन : लखुबाइसें दरिसना आली : दंडवतें
घातलीं : श्रीचरणा लागली : पासि बैसली : नावेक होती :
मग गेली :॥ः

१९ देमाइसां भेटि :॥ः

देमाइसें पुराणा जाति : एकुदी पुराणीं ऐसें नीगालें : जें
गुरूवीण मुचिजेना : तरि कवण गुरु करूं पां : हे वामदेव
प्रसीध : आइकीजति : हे गुरु करूं आणि काइ : म्हणौनि :

17 SUGAR AND RICE FOR GOD.

One day the Gosavi went to Sarangpandit's compound. He had a massage and a bath, and they did puja to him. Umaïse served food for him on a plate, and she put food on a leaf plate for Sarangpandit. Mokananda brought the Gosavi's plate to the household shrine and set down Sarangpandit's leaf plate in front of him.

Umaïse had not given Mokananda any dal for them. By the time Umaïse brought the dal, the Gosavi had poured sugar on his rice and was eating the meal. The omniscient one said, "My woman, God is eating sugar and rice."

Umaïse said, "Lord, I forgot to serve the dal." She served the dal and touched his holy feet. Then she left.

18 HE MEETS LAKHUBAÏSE.

After his morning worship service one day, the Gosavi was sitting in the Bhognarayan temple. Lakhubaïse came for *darśan*. She prostrated herself, touched his holy feet, and sat down near him. She stayed there for a little while, and then she left.

19 HE MEETS DEMAÏSE.

Demaïse used to go to Purana recitals. One day she heard in a Purana recital that without a guru one does not get liberation from rebirth. "So whom should I take as my guru?" she asked. "Vamdev is famous. I've heard of him. Why not make

केलें नारीएलें : पाने पोफळें : घेउनि तेयाचिए गुंफेसि गेली :
तवं ते नागीवे : काळे : ढेप एसें बैसले असति : ऐसें देखौनि
आपुला ठाइं विचारिलें : यांजवळि उठों बैसों नये : बोलों
चालों नये : दाउ मिरउं नये : नागीवे केसैन गुरू करूं गे
आइ : म्हणौनि मांगुति निगाली : तव मार्गीं लखुबाइसें
भेटली : तेहीं पुसीलें : देमाइसें : कें गेलीं होतींति : ना :
वामदेवांचीए गुंफेसि : काइ करूं : मग देमाइसीं मागील
आवघें सांघीतलें : मग लखुबाइसीं म्हणीतलें : गुरु कराल
तरि मीं तुम्हासि दाखवीन : जयाजवळि बैसों उठों ये : दाउं
मीरउं ए : ऐसें गुरु मी दाखवीन : म्हणौनि भोगनाराएणा
घेउनि आली : गोसावीयांसि चौकी आसन : सोधु :
भोगनाराएणाचां आंगणीं भेटि जाली : देमाइसीं पानें पोफळें
केलें नारीएलें दर्शन केलीं : एकें म्हणति : नारीएळ पुढां
ठेवीलें : दंडवतें घातलीं : श्रीचरणा लागलीं : लखूबाइसें पूढां
बैसली : देमाइसें आडवांगीं बैसली : सर्वज्ञें म्हणीतलें : बाइ :
गुरूदेवासि पाठी दाखउ नये : ऐसी पासि बैसा³² : मग
देमाइसें समूख बैसली : पुढां गोसावी अवलोकीली : आणि
स्तीति जाली : निगतां सर्वज्ञें म्हणीतलां : बाइ : एथ येवों
आवडे : तेधवां येइजे :।: तथा तेव्हळि येइजे :॥:

him my guru?" So she got bananas, coconuts, betel leaves, and betel nuts and went to his cell.

He was naked, dark, sitting there like a lump. Seeing him like this, she thought to herself, "I couldn't stand up or sit down near him, I couldn't talk or walk. I couldn't show him off to anyone. How can I take a naked man as my guru?" So she set off to return home.

On her way back, she met Lakhubaïse. "Demaïse," she asked, "where have you been?" "To Vamdev's cell." "What did you go there to do?"

So Demaïse told her everything that had happened. Then Lakhubaïse said, "If you want to take a guru, I will show you one. I'll show you a guru you can sit down and stand up near, one you can show off to people." And she took her to the Bhognarayan temple.

The Gosavi was sitting in the central hall of the temple. (Research: They met in the courtyard of the Bhognarayan temple.) Demaïse gave him the betel leaves, the betel nuts, the bananas, and the coconuts as an offering. (Some say she placed a coconut before him.) She prostrated herself and touched his holy feet.

Lakhubaïse sat down in front of him; Demaïse sat with her back to him. The omniscient one said, "My woman, you should not turn your back to your guru. Sit nearby, like this."[24] Then Demaïse sat facing him. The Gosavi looked straight at her, and she went into a trance.

As she was leaving, the omniscient one said, "My woman, come here whenever you like."

२० अवधुता तांबुल :॥:

एकुदीनी उदयाचा पुजावसर जालेयानंतरें[३३] : गोसावी
चांगदेवा बीजें केलें : माडी पूर्वीलें बाळणां : पसीमा
अभीमूखु : अवधूत एकू बैसला होता : गोसावीयांसि
उजवेयाकडे आसन : मग सर्वज्ञें म्हणीतलें : बापेया[३४] :
ऐसें जन्म कोणां दादुलेया कारणें क्षेपीजत असीजे[३५] :
बोलेचिना : ना : पाहेचिना : डावेनि श्रीकरें हनुवटी धरीली :
उजवेन श्रीकरें मुखीं फोडी घातलीया : वीडीया करूनि तोंडीं
सूदलीया : तांबूळ घेतलें : मग गोसावी बीजें केलें :॥:

२१ पेखणिकां अवलोकणें :॥:

एकुदीनी उदयाचा पुजावसर जालेया नंतरे[३६] : गोसावी
चांगदेवा बीजें केलें : उतरिलें बाळणां : दखीणाभिमुख
आसन : तवं चांगदेवा पेखणाइतें पेखणें करावीया आली :
नाचणी तेथ कास घालावेया आली : तवं गोसावीयांतें
देखीलें[३७] : ते गोसावीयांतें पाहातचि राहीली : मग : येरू
ये : येरू ये : ऐसीं अवघींचि आलीं : सर्वज्ञें म्हणीतलें : हें
तेथचि येइल[३८] : देउळां गेली : मग गोसावी तेथचि बीजें
केलें : चौकीं आसन : तेंहीं पेखणें मांडीलें : पेखणें आइकों
आदिरिलें : मादळीत : काहाळिया : वसकरू : चाकीकरू :
आळतीकरू : जें जेयाचें अंग ये : तें तो दाखवी : तेया अंगा

20 HE GIVES PAN TO AN ASCETIC.

After his morning worship service one day, the Gosavi went to the Cangdev temple. An ascetic was sitting upstairs on the eastern balcony, facing west. The Gosavi sat down to his right.

Then the omniscient one said, "You poor fellow! For what great man are you throwing away your life this way?" The man did not say a word; he did not even look at the Gosavi.

With his left holy hand, the Gosavi told hold of the man's jaw. With his right holy hand, he put pieces of betel nut into the man's mouth. He made rolls of pan and put them into his mouth. The man chewed the pan.

Then the Gosavi left.

21 HE WATCHES DANCERS.

After his morning worship service one day, the Gosavi went to the Cangdev temple. He was sitting on the northern balcony, facing south, when women dancers came to the temple to dance. When a dancer came to where the Gosavi was sitting to tuck in her sari, she saw him.[25] She kept looking at the Gosavi. Then another one came there, and yet another one. Finally all of them came to where he was. The omniscient one said, "I will come over there."

They went to the temple, and the Gosavi went there too. He sat in the central hall of the temple. They performed a dance. He began listening to the dance music. Each musician—the barrel drummer, the kettledrum player, the flutist, the tambourine player, the vocalist—would play his part

187

गोसावी तोखति : तेणें तेया सूख होए : पेखणें करूं सरलें :
मग गोसावी तेयांसि तांबुळ दीधलें : पुड वाटुवा रिचवीला :
मग तें निगालीं : पैल ठावों वेन्हीं गेलीं : आणि मागुतीं
आलीं : मग तोखलीं : जी जी : इतुलें दीस कळा पोरटीया
जालिया होतिया : आजी सकळाचे माहेर भेटले : मग :
निगाली : गोसावी बीजें केलें : दखीणिलेया दारवंठेया
पासि : तेया : गोसावीयांतें : पालवीं धरीलें : जी जी :
माझेया बीढारासि बीजें करावें जी : सर्वज्ञें म्हणीतलें :
बाइ : हें एकीं आवंतिलें असे³⁹ : मग ते उगीचि राहीली :
मग बीजें केलें :॥:

२२   धानाइ सलदी लपवणें :॥:

एकुदीनीं गोसावी सारंगपंडीताचेया आवारासि बीजें केलें :
उमाइसें लेकरूं घेउनि बैसली असति : गोसावीयांतें देखीलें
आणि लाजीली : पुढां सलदु होता तेथ धानाइसें घातली :
वरि लुगडें घातलें : गोसावी लुगडें हालत देखीलें : मग
पुसिलें : बाइ : हें काइ हालत असें : जी जी : हें लेंकरूं
कडीये घिया : याचिया अमृतकळा सोकति : मग :
काढीलें :॥:

when it came, and the Gosavi would express appreciation for it. That would make them happy.

When they had finished dancing, the Gosavi gave them pan. He gave away all the pan in his partitioned pouch. Then they left. After going some distance away, they came back. They expressed their pleasure, saying, "Our arts have been orphaned for a long time, Lord. Today we have met the maternal home of them all." Then they left.

As the Gosavi was leaving, near the southern doorway one of the dancers took hold of the end of his garment. "Lord, please come to my home," she said. The omniscient one replied, "My woman, someone has invited me." That silenced her.

Then he left.

22 DHANAÏ GETS HIDDEN IN A CHEST.

One day when the Gosavi went to Sarangpandit's compound, Umaïse was sitting there holding her baby. She saw the Gosavi and got embarrassed. She placed Dhanaïse in a chest that was in front of her, and she put a sari on top.

The Gosavi saw the sari moving, so he asked, "What's this that's moving, my woman?" "It's the baby, Lord." "Take her on your hip. Her cheeks will dry up."

Then she took her out.

२३ तथा शृंघारू पुसणें :॥:

धानाइसें वडिलें जालीं : मग : उटिति : न्हाणिति : लेव-
वीति : नेसवीति : मग : पुसति : धाइ : हा शृंघार
कव्ळणालागौनि : ना : हा श्री चांगदेवोराउळा
गोसावीयांलागौनि : गोसावी आसनीं बैसौनि पाहातें
असति :॥:

२४ तथा आख्याइका श्रवण :॥:

गोसावी एकुदी सारंगपंडीताचेया आवारा बीजें केलें :
सारंगपंडीत मर्दना देत असति : तवं धानाइ : गोसावीयाची
श्रीमूर्ति गौरवर्ण देखीली : मग म्हणति : गोसावीयाची
श्रीमूर्ति हळदी उटीली म्हणौनि गौर जाली : तर ते हळदी
माझां आंगीं लावी कीं : म्हणौनि आळि घेतली : कांहीं
केलियां सवरति ना : मग : सर्वज्ञें म्हणीतलें : बाइ : तथा
धाइया : हें तुम्हां काहाणी सांघैल : आलीं : पासि बैसली :
साळैचें घर मेणाचें : काउळेयाचें घर सेणाचें : पाउसाळां
काउळयाचें घर पुरें जाए : साळैचें वाचे : मग उगीचि
राहीली :॥:

23 AND THEY ASK HER WHY SHE IS DRESSED UP.

When Dhanaïse grew up, they would rub oil on her. They would bathe her, put jewelry on her, and dress her in a sari. Then they would ask her, "Dhaï, who is it you are all dressed up for?" "It's for Shri Cangdev Raül Gosavi."

The Gosavi would be sitting there watching.

24 AND SHE LISTENS TO A STORY.

One day the Gosavi went to Sarangpandit's compound. While Sarangpandit was giving him a massage, Dhanaï saw the light color of the Gosavi's holy body. So she was saying, "The Gosavi's holy body has turned fair because turmeric paste was rubbed on it. So rub that turmeric paste on my body!"[26]

She was so insistent that nothing they tried would appease her. Then the omniscient one said, "My woman (or, Dhaï), I will tell you a story." She came over and sat down near him. "A sparrow's house is made of wax, and a crow's house is made of dung. In the monsoon, the crow's house gets washed away, but the sparrow's survives."

That silenced her.

२५ चांगदेवोभटाची वीनती स्वीकारू :॥:

एकुदिनी सर्वज्ञें म्हणीतलें : बाइ : हें परमेश्वरपुरासि जाइल :
आइत करा : तेथ चांगदेवो भट आले : मग बाईसातें
म्हणीतलें : बाइ : गोसावी परमेश्वरपुरा बीजें करित असति :
तरि मज आपुलेया सांगातें येवों देति : ऐसें पुसा कां : बाइसीं
वीनवीलें : बाबा : चांगो म्हणत असे : गोसावी परमेश्वरपुरा
बीजें करित असति : तरि : आपणेयां सांघातें मज येवों
देति :॥:सर्वज्ञें म्हणीतलें : ऐसें हा बटिका : जी : सर्वज्ञें
म्हणीतलें : तुम्हां गावां जावें असें : गावां जा : सण सारूनि
या : मग गावां जावों⁴⁰ : ऐसेचि उपाधी चांगदेवोभटाकरविं
पुसवीलें : सर्वज्ञें म्हणीतलें : यासि आळेंनिवणें असे : हा
ना⁴¹ ॥छ॥: मग चांगदेवोभट गावां गेले : सणु सारूनि
आलें : बाइसीं आइत केली : मग बाइसें हंसराजू
चांगदेवोभट सरिसे निगाले : मग गोसावी परमेश्वरपुरा बीजें
केलें :॥:

२६ राहाटगावीं वसति :॥:

२७ कडेठाणी माहालक्ष्मीये वसति :॥:ः

25 HE ACCEPTS
CANGDEVBHAT'S REQUEST.

One day the omniscient one said to Baïse, "My woman, I am going to Parameshvarpur. Make the preparations."

Cangdevbhat came there and said to her, "My woman, if the Gosavi is going to Parameshvarpur, would you ask him if he will let me come along with him?"

Baïse made the request: "Baba, Cango is asking, 'If the Gosavi is going to Parameshvarpur, will he let me come along with him?'" "Is that so, Batika?" asked the omniscient one. "Yes, Lord." The omniscient one said, "You need to go to your village. Go to your village, celebrate the festival, and come back. Then we will go."[27]

Upadhye had Cangdevbhat ask the same thing on his behalf. The omniscient one said, "That man has family responsibilities. This one doesn't."[28]

Then Cangdevbhat went to his village. He celebrated the festival and came back. Baïse made the preparations. Then the Gosavi left for Parameshvarpur, and Baïse, Hamsaraj, and Cangdevbhat set out with him.

26 HE STAYS OVERNIGHT
IN RAHATGAV.[29]

27 HE STAYS OVERNIGHT IN
THE MAHALAKSHMI TEMPLE
AT KADETHAN.[30]

२८ भीवांडांउवाचां राजौरा वसति :॥:

२९ सेंदुर्जनीं ब्राह्मणां स्तीति⁴² :॥:

सेंदुर्जनीं गावां इशान्ये पींपळातळिं गोसावीया आसन :॥:
नागझरीए ब्राह्मणु येकू संध्यावंदना गेला होता : तेणें येतां
गोसावीयांतें देखीलें : दंडवतें घातलीं : श्रीचरणां लागले :
मग पुढां बैसला : आणि स्तीति जाली⁴³ : स्तीति भोगु
सरली⁴⁴ : मग आरोगणे गोसावीयांतें वीनवीलें : मग
गोसावी तेयाचेया घरा बीजें केलें : मर्दनामादणें जालें⁴⁵:
भक्तजनें पुजा केली : भक्तजनासहित आरोगणा : पहुड :
उपहुड : विळीचां पुजावसरू जाला : मग : उदीयांचि
मेघंकरा बीजें केलें :॥:

३० मेघंकरीं बाइसें हाटा गमन⁴⁶ :॥:

बाणेश्वरा बीजें केलें : गोसावीयासि आसन : बाईसीं
चरणक्षाळण केलें : पहुड : उपहुड : आरोगण : गुळळा :
वीडा : मागौता पहुड जाला : पुढील गांव धाकुटें म्हणौनि
बाइसें वेसजू वेसरू घेयाविया गेलीं : बाइसातें देखौनि
वाणियें म्हणीतलें : आइ : या : उठौनि बैसों घातलें : बाइसें

28   HE STAYS OVERNIGHT
IN BHIVANDAÜVA'S RAJAUR.[31]

29   AT SENDURJAN, A BRAHMAN
GOES INTO A TRANCE.

At Sendurjan, the Gosavi was sitting at the foot of a pipal tree northeast of the village. A certain Brahman had gone to perform *sandhyā* at a winding stream. As he was returning home, he saw the Gosavi. He prostrated himself to the Gosavi, touched his holy feet, and sat down in front of him. And the Brahman went into a trance.

After the trance came to an end, he invited the Gosavi for a meal, and the Gosavi went to his house.[32] The Gosavi had a massage and a bath. The devotees did puja to him, and he ate his meal along with them. He went to sleep and woke up, and then his evening worship service took place. Early the next morning he left for Meghankar.[33]

30   IN MEGHANKAR,
BAÏSE GOES TO THE MARKET.

The Gosavi went to the Baneshvar temple and sat down there. Baïse washed his feet. He went to sleep and woke up. He ate his meal, rinsed his mouth, and chewed pan. Again he went to sleep.

Because the next village they were going to was small, Baïse went to get provisions. When the Grocer saw Baïse, he said, "Come in, Mother." He stood up and put down some-

बैसली : मग म्हणीतलें : कांहीं वेचु दीया : तेणें म्हणीतलें :
आइ नावेक राहा :॥ः या ग्राहीकातें पाठवीन : मग तुम्ही
मागाल तें देइन : तेया थोर वीकरा जाला : तवं बाइसें
बैसलींचि होतीं : तेणें ग्राहीकातें पाठवीलें : मग पुसीलें :
काइ काइ देवों : बाइसीं म्हणीतलें : कणिक : तांदुल : तुप :
हींगु : मीरियें : जीरें : साकर : ऐसा : सोधु : आठा दामाचां
वेचु होए ॥ हीराइसा पाठ ॥ सोळा :॥छ॥ः देवों बैसलीं :
तवं तेणें म्हणीतलें : आइ इतुकें माझें आपुलिया तुम्ही
उपयोगा नयावें : एकें म्हणति : आणिकु सोळा दाम दीधलें :
मग बीढार पावति : तंव बोलवीत आला : हीराइसा पाठ :
गोसावी पूसिलें : बाइ : उसिरू कां लावीला : बाइसीं मागील
वृतांतु सांघीतलें :॥छ॥ः बाइसीं तेयाचा आदरू सांघीतला :
सर्वज्ञें म्हणीतलें : बाइ : तुम्हां इतुकेंचि बहुत : तुम्हीं
गेलीयां : तुमचां ठाइं : तेयाचें इतुकेंचि काइ बहुत ॥ मग
वसति जाली :॥ः

३१ वीषये वसति : देवीं कमळीं पुजा :॥ः

वीषयेसि देउळां गोसावी बीजें केलें : देउळ पाहीलें :
बाइसें तेथ उपहारू करावेया राहिली : गोसावी वीहरणा
बीजें केलें : मार्गीं दुसरें तळें : तेयाचिए पाळीं चिंचे खालीं

thing for her to sit on. Baïse sat down. Then she said, "Give me some provisions." "Wait a minute, Mother," he replied. "I'll send this customer on his way, and then I'll give you whatever you ask for."

Baïse sat there a long time, while the Grocer filled a large order for the man. After sending that customer on his way, the Grocer asked, "What can I give you?"

Baïse said, "Flour, rice, ghee, asafetida, peppercorns, cumin, sugar." (Research: That was eight copper coins' worth of goods. Hiraïsa version: sixteen.)

When she was about to pay him, he said, "Mother, please take this small offering from me for your use." (Some say he also gave her sixteen copper coins). Then he accompanied her until she reached their lodgings.

(Hiraïsa version: The Gosavi asked, "My woman, what took you so long?" Baïse told him what had happened.) She told him how respectful the man had been. "My woman," said the omniscient one, "such a small thing is big for you. Is it too much for him to do such a small thing for you when you've gone there?"

Then the Gosavi stayed there overnight.

31 HE STAYS OVERNIGHT IN VISHAYE. DEV DOES PUJA WITH LOTUSES.

The Gosavi went to a temple in Vishaye. He looked at the temple, then Baïse stayed there to prepare some food while the Gosavi went out to wander. Along the way, he sat on the embankment of another reservoir, under a tamarind tree.[34]

आसन : हीराइसा पाठ : पींपळ :॥छ॥: गोसावी परमेश्वरपुरा
बीजें करीत असति : ऐसें दादोसीं आइकीलें : गोसावीया
लागौनि कांहीं वाटेचें संबळ मेळउनि टाकूनि घेउनि आलें :
तळियाचिए पाळीं देवा भेटी जाली : देवीं दंडवतें घातलीं :
श्रीचरणां लागलें : वेचु आणिला : तो पुढां ठेवीला : तळांचीं
कमळें काढीलीं : गोसावीयांसि लोहींवां कमळीं पुजा केली :
देवी कमळाची पाकोळी तोडीली : गोसावीयाचां श्रीकरीं
दीधली : जी जी : कोळ पुरूषु उद्धारुनि दाखवावा : सर्वज्ञें
म्हणीतलें : ऐथौनि देवताचक्र निरूपितां : सर्वज्ञें म्हणीतलें :
देसकाळीचे आचार्ये इतुलेया ऐसेया माझारि सारिति४७ :॥:

३२ आलेगावीं गोपाळीं वसति :॥:

३३ पातौरी वसति :॥:

३४ टाकळीए वसति :॥:

३५ लाखेपुरीए लक्षणेश्वरी वसति :॥:

Dados had heard that the Gosavi was going to Parameshvarpur. He got the Gosavi some provisions for the journey and brought them along. Dev met the Gosavi on the embankment of the reservoir. He prostrated himself, touched the holy feet, and put the provisions he had brought in front of the Gosavi.

He picked some lotuses from the reservoir and did puja to the Gosavi with red ones. Dev plucked a lotus petal and handed it to the Gosavi, saying, "Lord, please make a diagram of my family deity."

The omniscient one said, "When I am explaining the *devatācakra...*"[35] The omniscient one said, "Teachers these days stop at just this much."

32   HE STAYS OVERNIGHT IN THE GOPAL TEMPLE AT ALEGAV.

33   HE STAYS OVERNIGHT IN PATAURI.[36]

34   HE STAYS OVERNIGHT IN TAKLI.[37]

35   HE STAYS OVERNIGHT IN THE LAKSHANESHVAR TEMPLE AT LAKHEPURI.[38]

३६ कोडेश्वरीं घाटेया हरीभटा भेटी⁴⁸ :॥ः

कोडेश्वरीं गोसावीयांसि चौकी आसन : घाटे हरीभट
देउळाचेया गाभारेया आंतु जपत होते : एकें म्हणति : गंगे
कडौनि आले : हातीं तांबवटी : तांबुवटीये उदक : तुळसी :
गोसावीयांतें देखीलें : श्रीचरणावरि उदक घातलें : तुळसी
वाइलिया : दंडवतें घातलीं : श्रीचरणा लागले : पासि बैसले :
आणि स्तीति जाली : भोगीली : भंगीली : मग गोसावीयांसि
घरा जेवावेया वीनवीलें : सर्वज्ञें म्हणीतलें : पैले देउळीए
बटिकू असे : तो बोलावा : गेले तवं तेयाचें आसन अंतरक्ष
उपवत असे : वरि कळसी लागत असे : आले : जी : ते
देउळाचेनि कळसें कळसें जात असति : मागौतें धाडिले :
जा : एथौनि बोलावीला अससि ऐसें म्हणां : गेले :
म्हणीतलें : तुमतें गोसावी बोलावीत असति : आणि स्तीति
भंगली : आले : मग गोसावी तेयाचेया घरां बीजें केलें : पुजा
केली : आरोगणा जाली : विळचा मागुती तया स्तीति⁴⁹
जाली : भोगीली : भंगीली⁵⁰ :॥ः

36   HE MEETS GHATE HARIBHAT
IN THE KODESHVAR TEMPLE.

The Gosavi was sitting in the central hall in the Kodeshvar temple.[39] Ghate Haribhat was reciting mantras inside the temple sanctuary. (Some say he came from the river.) He was holding a copper pot. There was water in the pot, and he was carrying sprigs of tulsi.

He saw the Gosavi. He poured the water over his holy feet and offered him the sprigs of tulsi. He prostrated himself and touched the holy feet. He sat down near the Gosavi and went into a trance. He experienced the trance for a while, and then it broke. Then he invited the Gosavi to his home for a meal.

The omniscient one said, "Batika* is in that temple there. Ask him to come here." When Haribhat went there, Batika's seat was floating high up in the air, touching the pinnacle of the temple.

Haribhat came back and said, "Lord, he is going up high, to the pinnacle." The Gosavi sent him back again. "Go and tell him that I have summoned him."

He went there. "The Gosavi is summoning you," he said. And Batika's trance broke. He came there.

Then the Gosavi went to Haribhat's house. He did puja to the Gosavi, and the Gosavi ate a meal. That evening Haribhat went into a trance again. He experienced it for a while, and then it broke.[40]

---

* Here, Cangdevbhat.

३७ बाइसें रीधपुरा पाठवणें :॥:

पद्मेश्वरीं अवस्थान : दीस सात : च्यारि जाले : यरी दीसीं
गोसावी बाइसातें म्हणीतलें : तुम्ही पुढां जा : श्रीप्रभुचिया
दरिसना : वाकिये वस्त्रें घेया : हें मागिला कडौनि येइल५९ :
बाइसें हंसराजु पुढां निगाली : वांकीये वस्त्र घेतलें : मग
रिधपुरा गेली :॥:

३८ खडखांबुली खेळु :॥:

निच चांगदेवो भट भिक्षा करूनि येति : झोळि दृष्टपूत
करीति : मग जेवीति : ते दीसीं चांगदेवो भट भिक्षा करूनि
आले : झोळी काठीए घालीति : काठी टेकौनि ठेवीली :
आणि स्तीति जाली :॥: च्यारी पाहार चौ खांबा भंवंते
भवत होते : पडिसाळेचिया : ऐसी अस्तीति भोगित होते :
उदीयाचि गोसावी परिश्रया बीजें केलें : गोसावी खडखांबुलां
खेळों आदरीलें५२ : गोसावीयांतें देखीलें : आणि स्तीति
भंगली : आले : दंडवतें घातलीं : श्रीचरणा लागले : आसन
केलें : गोसावी आसनावरि बैसले : मग पुसिलें : बटिका :
जेवीलेति : ना जी : गोसावीयांसि झोळी दृष्टपुत करावी
होती : हीराइसा पाठ : आणा पा आरुती : गोसावी झोळी
आणविली : अवलोकीली : हीराइसा पाठ : बटिका रुक्ष
असे :॥छ॥: तवं साधन कांहीं नाहीं : सर्वज्ञें म्हणीतलें :
बटिका : हे काइ : साधन कांहीं नाहीं : तरि एथ सांघाचि

37   HE SENDS BAÏSE TO RIDDHIPUR.

He stayed in the Padmeshvar temple for seven days.[41] After
four of the days had passed, the next day the Gosavi said to
Baïse, "You go on ahead. Get clothes in Vanki to give Shriprabhu as an offering.[42] I will follow behind."[43]

Baïse and Hamsaraj set out ahead of him. They got a
garment in Vanki and then went on to Riddhipur.

38   HE PLAYS THE PILLAR GAME.

Every day when Cangdevbhat came back from begging, he
would have the Gosavi look at his begging bag to purify it
before he would eat his meal. One day Cangdevbhat came
back from begging, hung his begging bag on his stick, leaned
the stick against the wall, and went into a trance. All night
long he circled around and around the four pillars of the
veranda, experiencing the trance.

Early the next morning, the Gosavi went out to urinate.
The Gosavi started playing the pillar game.[44] When Cangdevbhat saw the Gosavi, his trance broke. He came over
to him, prostrated himself, and touched the holy feet.
He prepared a seat. The Gosavi sat down on it and asked,
"Batika, have you had your meal?" "No, Lord Gosavi. You
haven't yet looked at my begging bag to purify it."

The Gosavi had him bring the begging bag. (Hiraïsa
version: "Bring it here.") The Gosavi looked inside. (Hiraïsa
version: "It is dry and tasteless, Batika," he said.) There was
nothing to give the food flavor.

ना : एथ म्हणीतलें : हो बटिका : साधन कांहीं आपजविजे :
भिक्षा करीतां५३ : हो बटिका : जेवा जा : पाणि नाहीं जी :
सर्वज्ञें म्हणीतलें : बटिका : तुम्ही महात्मे किं गा : एके
गांवीं जेवीजे : एके गांवीं आचवीजे : एकें म्हणति : ए
थडीए जेवीजे : पैले थडीए आचवीजे :॥छ॥: मग प्रतदीनीं
हरिभटाचां घरीं पुजा आरोगण होए : सोधु : एकि वासना :
वीळिचा चांगदेवो भट : तेयाचां घरींहुनि दुधभातु आणिति :
मग गोसावीयांसि व्याळी होए : एकी वासना :॥: वीळींचां
चांगदेवो भट भिक्षा करिति : मग गोसावीयांसि व्याळी
होए५४ :॥:

३९ चांगदेवो भटां जाडी :॥:

गोसावी तेथौनि बीजें केलें : मार्गीं गोसावीयांसि वसति
होए : आपणेयां सवें चांगदेवोभटातें निजवीति : रात्रीं
गोसावीयांसि पावो लागैल : म्हणौनि : परते सरति : गोसावी
म्हणति : बटिका : आरुतें ठाका५५ : मग जाडीचा पलौ
पांगुरवीति : रामेश्वरबास : हे लीळा टाकळीएचां मार्गीं :॥:

The omniscient one said, "What is this, Batika? If there is nothing to give the food flavor, you must tell me. I said to you, 'Batika, when you are begging for food, you should get something to give it flavor.'[45] Go ahead and eat, Batika." "But, Lord, there is no water." The omniscient one said, "Batika, you are a Mahatma! You should eat in one village and sip water in another." (Some say, "You should eat on the near bank of the river and sip water on the far bank.")

After that, the Gosavi had his puja and afternoon meal at Haribhat's house every day. (Research: according to one version, in the evening Cangdevbhat would bring milk and rice from Haribhat's house, and then the Gosavi would have his evening meal. According to another version, Cangdevbhat would go begging for food in the evening, and then the Gosavi would have his evening meal.)

39   A BLANKET FOR CANGDEVBHAT.

The Gosavi left that place.

When he spent the night somewhere along the road, he would have Cangdevbhat sleep with him. For fear that his foot would touch the Gosavi during the night, Cangdevbhat would slide away from him. The Gosavi would say, "Come over here, Batika," and he would cover him with the end of his blanket.

(According to Rameshvarbas, this *līlā* took place on the road to Takli.)[46]

४० तथा जाडि परित्यजणें :॥:

स्याळीयां दीसां : उदीयांचि गोसावी बीजें करीति : मग
जाडीचें कोंगटें घालीति : सीं फीटे : आणि श्रीमुगुटेंचि
जाडी उभेया राहुनि खाली घालिति : चांगदेवोभट जाडी
घेति : हीराइसा पाठ : गोसावी म्हणति बटिका जाडि घेया :
मग : चेति :॥:

४१ चांगदेवोभटां खेळो पाठविणें⁵⁶ :॥:

गोसावी उदेयाचां पाहारू एकु चालती : मग : वस्तीचां गांवीं
राहाति : गोसावी⁵⁷ वीहरणा बीजें करिति : आसन होए⁵⁸ :
चांगदेवो भटातें म्हणति : बटिका : खेळों जा :॥:

४२ वांकीये पांडेश्वरीं वसति :॥:

४३ तुगावीं उर्वेश्वरीं वसति :॥:

40   AND HE DISCARDS A BLANKET.

It was the cold season. As the Gosavi set out early in the morning, he would wear a blanket over his head as a cloak. When the air got warmer, he would stop and drop the blanket from his holy head to the ground. Cangdevbhat would take the blanket. (Hiraïsa version: The Gosavi would say, "Batika, take the blanket," and then he would take it.)

41   HE SENDS CANGDEVBHAT
OFF TO PLAY.

The Gosavi would walk for three hours each morning, and then he would stop in the village where he was going to spend the night.

The Gosavi would go out to wander. He would sit down and say to Cangdevbhat, "Batika, go and play."

42   HE STAYS OVERNIGHT IN THE
PANDESHVAR* TEMPLE AT VANKI.

43   HE STAYS OVERNIGHT IN THE
URVESHVAR TEMPLE AT THUGAV.[47]

* A name of the god Shiva.

४४ तळवेलीं लींगाचां देउळीं वसति :॥:

४५ खैराळां उपान्हौत्यागु[५९] :॥:

खैराळा उपानहौ फेडीलीया : सर्वज्ञें म्हणीतलें : बटीका : हें
घेया : परमेश्वरपूर : करा नमस्कारू : आपण दोन्ही श्रीकर
जोडूनि जय केलें[६०] : आणि : चांगदेवो भटीं जय केलें :
सर्वज्ञें म्हणीतलें : बटीका : एथौनि जैसें कीजैल : तैसें तुम्ही
कराल : हें परमेश्वरपूर : केसणें : एथ श्रीप्रभू राज्य करीत
असति : घाला घाला दंडवतें : मग तेहीं दंडवतें घातलीं :॥:
मग श्रीप्रभू महीमा नीरूपीत नीरूपीत बीजें केलें[६१] : मग
माल्हणदेवी पासी उभें राहीले : तवं तेथ श्रीप्रभु बीजें करीत
होते : सर्वज्ञें म्हणीतलें : बटिका आतांचि श्रीप्रभु आले होते :
आतांचि नीगाले : यें नव्हति पाउलें : मार्गरूढी : आसन :
गुळळा : वीडा :॥:

44 HE STAYS OVERNIGHT IN
A LINGA TEMPLE AT TALVEL.[48]

45 HE DISCARDS HIS SANDALS
AT KHAIRALA.[49]

At Khairala the omniscient one took off his sandals and said, "Take these, Batika. This is Parameshvarpur. Do reverence to it." He himself put his holy hands together and gave a cry of victory. And Cangdevbhat gave a cry of victory.

The omniscient one said, "Batika, are you going to do everything exactly like me? How great is this Parameshvarpur! Shriprabhu lives here! Prostrate yourself! Prostrate yourself to it!"

Cangdevbhat prostrated himself. Then the Gosavi went along telling him more and more about the glory of Shriprabhu.[50] They stopped at the Malhandevi* temple just after Shriprabhu left it. The omniscient one said, "Batika, Shriprabhu was here just now. He left only a moment ago. Don't you see his footprints?"

(According to tradition, the Gosavi sat there.[51] He rinsed his mouth and chewed pan.)

---

* A goddess.

४६ श्रीप्रभु भेटि :॥ः

श्रीप्रभु आळंदीया माजि खेळ करिताति : बाइसें साउमी
येउनि वाट पाहातें होतीं : बाइसीं देखीलें : आणि साउमीं
येतें होतीं : तवं बाइसातें श्रीकरें वारीलें : हीराइसा : सर्वज्ञें
म्हणीतलें : बाइ : श्रीप्रभु कव्हणीकडे खेळु करित असति :
बाबा : हे नव्हति : बाबा : आळंदीयापासि खेळ करित
असति : दोही देवां दर्सन जालें : गोसावी पुष्टीचेयाकडे खेंव
दीधलें : श्रीप्रभुसि न मनेचि : सोधु : इ काइ रे : गोसावी
सोडीलें : मग श्रीचरणीचे रज : श्रीमुकुटावरि घातलें :
हीराइसा : मेला जाए : आरे सोडि सोडि : म्हणौनि : कोप
नटलें : मग सोडीलें : श्रीचरणीचें रज :॥ः मग भुइचें इटाळ
घेउनि कोपें भूमीसी आफळिलें :॥छ॥ः मग नगरामध्यें बीजें
केलें :॥छ॥ः

४७ मठीं रोटी आरोगण :॥ः

पुढां श्रीप्रभु : मागां आमुचे गोसावी : तेया मागें बाइसें :
हंसराजु : गोसावी श्रीमूर्ति आछादुनि मठां उतरिले गोदरीया
बीजें केलें : श्रीप्रभु दारवटां बाहिरिल विनायेकेंसीं नावेक
खेळु केला : मग भीतरि बीजें केलें : गोसावीहीं भीतरि बीजें
केलें : खोलंबुथि घालुनि : रामेश्वरबास : दखीणिला कवाडा

46   HE MEETS SHRIPRABHU.

Shriprabhu was playing at the water-storage jars.[52] Baïse had come out and was waiting to greet the Gosavi. She saw him, but as she came toward him he signaled with his holy hand to warn her off. (According to Hiraïsa, the omniscient one said, "My woman, where is Shriprabhu playing?" "Don't you see him, Baba? He is playing at the water-storage jars.")

The two gods had *darśan* of each other. The Gosavi hugged Shriprabhu from behind. Shriprabhu did not like that. (Research: "Hey, what is this?" he said.) The Gosavi let him go. Then the Gosavi took dust from the prints of Shriprabhu's holy feet and put it on his own holy head. (According to Hiraïsa, Shriprabhu pretended to be angry, saying, "Drop dead! Hey, drop it! Drop it!" So the Gosavi dropped the dust from the holy feet.) Then Shriprabhu picked up a piece of brick that was lying there and angrily beat it on the ground.

Afterward they went into the town.

47   HE EATS A MEAL OF ROTIS
IN THE HERMITAGE.

Shriprabhu went ahead, with our Gosavi behind him. After them came Baïse and Hamsaraj. The Gosavi covered his holy form and went to the open space north of the hermitage.[53] Shriprabhu played for a little while with the Vinayak* outside the doorway, then went inside. The Gosavi too went inside, wearing a hooded cloak. (According to Rameshvarbas, he

---

* An image of the god Ganesh.

आड : उभे राहीले : परशरामबास : गरूडाळेयेचया :
खातेनसीं उभें राहीले : उचमढीं चाटे होते : तेहीं श्रीप्रभुतें
पुसिलें : राउळो जेवाल : मेला जाए : जेवावें म्हणे : नेजवावें
म्हणे : मेला जाए : जेवील म्हणें६२ : मग तेल रोटी आणिली :
त्रीपुरुखाचेया मढां उत्तरे : उच मढां पूर्वें : निंब पसिमे
उखळी होती : तेथ तेहीं तेल घातलें : रोटी घातली : श्रीप्रभु
चावीतुचि करिति : ऐसें आरोगिताति : ते लिळा आमचे
गोसावी अवलोकिताति : मग : चावितुचि करूनि : श्रीप्रभु
उचमढू सव्यें घालुनि : बीजें केलें : मग आमचे गोसावी तेथ
आले : उकड आसन असे : श्रीप्रभुचां प्रसाद घेत असति :
तवं चाटां गोसावीयांतें देखीलें : मग वाटी तुपाचा नळा
आणिला : वाटिये तुप घातलें : रोटीचा मो ऐसें घेउनि आले :
मग म्हणीतलें : स्वीकरीजो जी : गोसावी म्हणीतलें : यासि
श्रीप्रभु अयोग्य : मग : हें योग्य६३ : तवं श्रीप्रभु बीजें केलें :
इश्वरीये प्रकाशीलें : म्हणौनि : चाटेयाची मोगरी सुतबडवीती
होती ते श्रीकरी घेउनि गोसावीयाचीया पुष्टिवीभागावरि :
बूदबुद करीति : तिन घाये दीधले : आणि : बाइसें
बोबाइली : वडिलें बाबेनि धाकुटा बाबा मारिला६४ :
सर्वज्ञें म्हणीतलें : श्रीकरू दुखविती जी : पुरों दीजो जी :

stood behind the southern door; according to Parasharam-bas, he stood next to the Garuda* shrine.)

The students were in the Tall Hermitage.[54] They asked Shriprabhu, "Raül, will you eat a meal?" "Drop dead! I should eat, I say. I shouldn't eat, I say. Drop dead! I will eat, I tell you."

They brought oil and rotis. North of the Tripurush Hermit-age, east of the Tall Hermitage, and west of the neem tree, there was a large mortar.[55] They poured the oil into it and put in the rotis.

Shriprabhu was eating his meal by taking a bite and spit-ting it out. Our Gosavi watched the divine play. Shriprabhu finished taking bites and spitting them out, then circumam-bulated the tall hermitage and left.

Then our Gosavi came there. The students saw him as he squatted and ate Shriprabhu's *prasād,* so they brought a small bowl and a tube of ghee. They poured the ghee into the bowl and brought the soft inner part of the rotis. "Please accept this, Lord," they said. The Gosavi said, "Shriprabhu is not worthy of this, and I am?"[56]

At that point, Shriprabhu came along. Because the Gosa-vi's divinity shone forth, Shriprabhu took in his holy hand the stick the students used to beat cotton, and he beat the Gosavi on the back with it. He struck him three times. And Baïse shouted, "The senior Baba has hit the junior Baba!"[57]

The omniscient one said, "You are hurting your holy hand, Lord. Please stop, Lord." (Hiraïsa version: And Shriprabhu

---

* Vishnu's eagle mount.

तथा पुरविजो जी : हीराइसा पाठ : आणि : श्रीप्रभु मोगरी
सांडीली : मेला जाए म्हणे : म्हणौनि हास्य केलें६५ : मग
भैरवा बीजें केलें : श्रीप्रभुते तिकोपाध्याचिए नृत्यकोन वेन्हीं
बोळवीलें : श्रीप्रभु : आवारां बीजें केलें : गोसावी भैरवी
बीजे केलें : अवस्थान दीस वीस :॥:

४८ श्रीप्रभुपूजा :॥:

एरीकडे आवारी६६ बाइसीं श्रीप्रभुसि आसन केलें : पुजा
केली : धुपार्ति मंगळार्ति जाली : आरोगण : गुळळा : वीडा
जाला : मग पहुड : मग गोसावीयांसी जवं तेथ अवस्थान
होतें तवं श्रीप्रभुचांचि ठाइं पुजा करिति : गोसावीयासि
नाहीं : गोसावीया उदयाची पुजा६७ अवलोकावया बीजें
करिति:॥:

४९ श्रीप्रभुवस्त्रपूजा :॥:

गोसावी श्रीप्रभुपुजा दोनी केलिया : बाइसातें म्हणीतलें :
बाइ : वस्त्र आणा आरूते : निरीया केलिया : दर्शन केलें :
स्वीकरीजो जी : श्रीप्रभु नीराकरीलें : हीराईसापाठ : आरे
नको नको : म्हणौनि थोरें श्रांतें निराकरिलें : सर्वज्ञें
म्हणीतलें : बाइ : ठेवा :॥: दिस दोनी तिन वोळगवीलें :
तेंहीं निराकरीलें : आणिक एकू दीसी : श्रीप्रभु मादनें जालें :

dropped the stick. "Drop dead, I tell you," he said, and laughed.)[58]

After that, the Gosavi went to the Bhairav temple. He accompanied Shriprabhu as far as the southwest corner of Tikopadhye's compound. Shriprabhu went into the compound, and the Gosavi went on to the Bhairav temple.

He stayed there for twenty days.

48 PUJA OF SHRIPRABHU.

Meanwhile, in Tikopadhye's compound, Baïse prepared a seat for Shriprabhu. She did puja to him and performed *āratī* with incense and with lighted lamps. He ate his meal, rinsed his mouth, and chewed pan. Then he went to sleep.

For as long as the Gosavi was there, she did puja only to Shriprabhu, not to the Gosavi. The Gosavi would come to watch the morning puja.

49 HE DOES PUJA TO SHRIPRABHU WITH CLOTHES.

The Gosavi did puja to Shriprabhu twice. He said to Baïse, "Bring the garment here, my woman."[59] He made folds in it so it could be put on. He offered it, saying, "Please accept it, Lord." Shriprabhu refused it. (Hiraïsa version: He refused it vociferously, saying "Hey! No! No!") "Put it away, my woman," said the omniscient one.

He offered it to him for two or three days, but Shriprabhu refused it. Then one day Shriprabhu had a bath facing east in

पूर्वामुख चौकी : दखिणीलीये पटिसाळेवरि : बाइसीं
आसन रचीलें : पुजा केली : तवं आमचे गोसावी उतरिलें
पटिसाळेचेनि सेहाडेनसीं उभें : मग पटिसाळे आड :
दखिणीली पटिसाळेसी दखिणामुख उभें : मग वस्त्रें
वोळगवितां : दखिणीले पटिसाळेवरि गुडगे मोडुनि :
पसीमामुख आसन : अंगिकारूं आदरिलें : श्रीप्रभु :
हीराईपाठ : आरे नको नको : म्हणौनि : सामान्य
निराकरीलें : सर्वज्ञें म्हणीतलें : स्वीकरीजो जी :
अंगिकरिलें ॥छ॥: गोसावी नीरीया करूनि श्रीप्रभुसि प्रदान
केलें : नेसले होते तें घेउनि बाइसा हातीं दीधलें : बाइसीं
झाडिलें : सर्वज्ञें म्हणीतलें : हें काइ बाइ : श्रीप्रभुचें वस्त्र
कैसें झाडितें असा : बाबा : रजें भरलें असे : बाइ : श्रीप्रभुचें
वस्त्र : आणिक : रज : ऐसें म्हणत असा : हें रज कैसें : हें
ब्रह्मादीकां दुर्लभ कीं :॥:

५० तथा उपहार करवणे^{६८} :॥:

सर्वज्ञें म्हणीतलें : बाइ : श्रीप्रभुचां ठाइं आन आन आन्न^{६९}
करा : श्रीप्रभु माखान्नप्रीये : मग बाइसें प्रतदीनीं वडे
करीति : श्रीप्रभु आरोगणे देति : तेंचि ताटीं गोसावीयांसि
आणिति : मग गोंसावीया आरोगण होए^{७०} :॥:

the central courtyard, and Baïse prepared a seat for him on the southern veranda and did puja to him there. Our Gosavi was standing next to the lion-faced railing on the northern veranda. Later he stood near the southern veranda, in front of it, facing south. To offer the garment, he sat on the southern veranda, his knees bent, facing west.

Shriprabhu was ready to take it. (Hiraï version: He refused it gently, saying, "Hey! No! No!" The omniscient one said, "Please accept it, Lord," and then he took it.) The Gosavi made folds in the garment and presented it to Shriprabhu. He took the garment that Shriprabhu had been wearing and handed it to Baïse.

Baïse shook it out. "What is this, my woman?" asked the omniscient one. "How can you be shaking out Shriprabhu's garment?" "It is full of dust, Baba." "My woman, are you saying that Shriprabhu's garment has dust on it? How can this be dust? This is precious even to Brahma and the other gods."[60]

50 AND HE HAS FOOD PREPARED FOR SHRIPRABHU.

The omniscient one said, "My woman, make different kinds of food for Shriprabhu. Shriprabhu likes dishes made with lentils."

So Baïse would make fried lentil cakes every day and give them to Shriprabhu for his meal. She would bring the Gosavi some on the same plate, and then he would eat his meal.

५१ भैरवी श्रीप्रभुक्रीडा :॥:

एकु दीस श्रीप्रभु खेळत खेळत : बारवेहुनि बहिरवासि बीजें
केलें : केशवीचेया प्रतीमासिं खेळखेळत तेयाचेया नाकावरि
आंगुळी टेविति : कानावरि ठेविति : डोळेयावरि ठेविति :
नीडळावरि ठेविति^{७१} : तेवींचि म्हणति : हा कानु : हा नाकु :
हा डोळा : हा निडळ : आणि म्हणति : तुं देओ : मेला जाए :
नव्हेसि : हा नव्हे देओ : ऐसें करीत करीत भैरवांसि बीजें
केलें : मागीलाकडे बहिरवो : सर्वज्ञें म्हणीतलें : बाइ : नावेक
परती जा : श्रीप्रभु येत असती : बाइसें बाहीरि निगाली : नेत्र
झाकौनि उगांचि होती : खेळु न भंगावा :॥: श्रीप्रभु भीतरि
आले : तेयांचि प्रयोक्ति भैरवेसीं खेळु केला : मग गोसावीया
पासी आले : गोसावी निश्चळ बैसले असति : हा कानु : हा
नाकु : हा डोळा : हा निडळ : म्हणौनि : भाळ स्थळावरि
बोट ठेवीलें : हा वो : देवो तुं : हीराईसा पाठ : आवो : तुं
देवो म्हणे : नव्हे म्हणे : हा देवो होय म्हणे : ऐसा देवें देवो
प्रकाशिला :॥:

51 SHRIPRABHU PLAYS
IN THE BHAIRAV TEMPLE.

One day Shriprabhu came playing from the stepwell to the Bhairav temple. As he played with the image of Keshav, he would place his finger on the nose, he would place it on an ear, he would place it on an eye, he would place it on the forehead.[61] As he did that, he would say, "This is an ear. This is the nose. This is an eye. This is the forehead." And then he would ask, "Are you God? Drop dead! You aren't. This is not God." He went along doing this all the way to the Bhairav temple.

The image of Bhairav was toward the back of the temple. The omniscient one said to Baïse, "Move out of the way for a little while, my woman. Shriprabhu is coming." She went outside. She covered her eyes and kept silent, so as not to interrupt his play.

Shriprabhu came into the temple. He played with Bhairav that same way and then approached the Gosavi. The Gosavi was sitting still. "This is an ear. This is the nose. This is an eye. This is the forehead." As he said that, he put his finger on the Gosavi's forehead. "Yes! You are God," he said. (Hiraïsa version: "Oh, you are God, I say. You aren't, I say. This is God, I tell you.")

In this way, God revealed God.

५२ हंसराज श्रीप्रभू सेवे राहावणे॰२ :॥:

मग हंसाराजु श्रीप्रभुचीए सेवे राहावीली : वेचावेया दामु
सोळा दीधले : सोधु : बाइ : श्रीप्रभुचां ठाइं आन आन अन्न
करा : श्रीप्रभु माखान्नप्रीये : मग बीजें केलें :॥:

५३ बेलोरा संकनाथी संगमेश्वरीं वसति :॥:

हे परशरामबास : भिवेश्वरीं हें रामेश्वरबास :॥:

५४ सीराळां नागनाथीं वसति :॥:

५५ आसटीये माहालक्षमीये वसति :॥:

आसुटीये बीजें केलें : माहालक्षमीचां देउळीं राहिले : बाइसा
जवळि तिन रुवे उरले होते : ते मागांचि सरले : बाइसीं
म्हणीतलें : बाबा वेचावेया कांहीं नाहीं : सर्वज्ञें म्हणीतलें :
पोफळफोडना गाहाण ठेवा : बाइसीं म्हणीतलें : बाबा :
पोफळफोडना गाहाण ठेवीजैल : मां : बाबासि : काइ

220

52   HE HAS HAMSARAJ
STAY TO SERVE SHRIPRABHU.

Afterward he told Hamsaraj to stay to serve Shriprabhu. He gave her sixteen copper coins for expenses. (Research: "My woman," he said, "make different kinds of food for Shriprabhu. Shriprabhu likes dishes made with lentils.") Then he left.

53   HE STAYS OVERNIGHT IN THE
SHANKANATH TEMPLE AND THE
SANGAMESHVAR TEMPLE AT BELOR.

(This is according to Parasharambas. According to Rameshvarbas, he stayed in the Bhiveshvar temple.)[62]

54   HE STAYS OVERNIGHT IN THE
NAGNATH TEMPLE AT SHIRALA.[63]

55   HE STAYS OVERNIGHT IN THE
MAHALAKSHMI TEMPLE AT ASUTI.

He went to Asuti, where he stayed in the temple of Mahalakshmi.[64]

Baïse's last three pennies had already been spent. "There is no money for provisions, Baba," she said. "Pawn the betel-nut cutter," replied the omniscient one.[65] "Baba," said Baïse, "if we pawn the betel-nut cutter, will you be able to

मागुतें एक एणें असे ः बाइ ः एथ प्रवृत्ती असे ः तरि ः हे देवतें
देखिलीं ः इये खालि एके दाडेनि सात लोही ः द्रव्या भरलीया
असति ः हीराइसा पाठ ः आलुमाळ माती परती कीजैल ः
आणि दीसती ः एथ प्रवृत्ती नाहीं ः॥ः मग चांगदेवो भट गेले ः
सोळे दामीं^{७३} पोफळफोडना वाणीयांपासि^{७४} गाहाणु
ठेविला ः आठा दामाचा वेचु आणिला ः आठ दाम रोकडे
आणिला^{७५} ः गोसावीयांसि पूजावस्वर ः आरोगण ः गुळळा ः
वीडा ः पहुड ः उपहुड ः जाला ः गोसावी आसनीं बैसले
असति ः तवं तो वाणिया आला ः गोसावीयांतें देखीलें ः मग
चांगदेवो भटातें पुसिलें ः पोफळफोडना गाहाण ठेविला ः तो
या गोसावीयाचा ना हो ः पीसवीचे सोळा दाम काढिले ः
गोसावीयां पूढें ठेवीलें ः श्रीचरणा लागला ः मग चांगदेवो
भटातें म्हणींतलें ः भटो या ः आपुला पोफळफोडना घेउनि
या ः गेलें ः घेउनि आले ः मग ः गोसावी तेथौनि बीजें केलें^{७६} ः॥ः

५६ वाठवडा वसति ः॥ः

वासना ः॥ः

get one again?" "My woman, do you see this deity? Beneath it is a stack of seven iron pots filled with money. If I were so inclined..." (Hiraïsa version: "If you moved a little bit of earth aside, you would see it.") "But I am not so inclined."

Then Cangdevbhat went and pawned the betel-nut cutter at a Grocer's for sixteen copper coins. He brought back eight copper coins' worth of provisions and eight copper coins in cash. The Gosavi's worship service took place. He ate his meal, rinsed his mouth, chewed pan, went to sleep, and woke up.

While the Gosavi was sitting in his place, the Grocer arrived. The Grocer saw the Gosavi and asked Cangdevbhat, "The betel-nut cutter that you pawned belongs to this Gosavi, doesn't it?" He took sixteen copper coins from his money bag and placed them before the Gosavi. He touched the Gosavi's holy feet, then said to Cangdevbhat, "Come with me, Bhat. Come and get your betel-nut cutter."

Cangdevbhat went and brought it back. Then the Gosavi left that place.[66]

56 HE STAYS OVERNIGHT IN VATHAVADA.

(One version).[67]

५७ मांगळौरीं वऱ्हारदेवीं वस्ति :
चांगदेवोभटां खेळा अनुमोदन^{७७} :॥:

मांगरूळीं वऱ्हाडदेवी आसन : बाइसीं चरणक्षाळण केलें :
गोसावी चांगदेवो भटातें म्हणीतलें : बटिका : खेळों जा :
बाइसीं म्हणीतलें : बटिका : तेवींचि बाबाचीं वस्त्रें ने :
सोध : चेउनि गेले : एक म्हणति : बाहिरवास तेहींचीं नेला :
नदी धुतला : वाळों घातला : मग पायावरि वोलसरें वाळुवेचें
देउळ करिति : तेवींचि दोही देवाचें नाम लवलवां आठ-
वीति : म्हणति : हे गुंफा श्रीगुंडम राउळा गोसावीयांची : हे
गुंफा चांगदेवो राउळा गोसावीयाची : तेवींचि दोही देवाचें
नाम वेगळाले उचारीति : मग वाहें वाहें म्हणति : म्हणति :
एन्हीं एन्हीं : गोसावीयांचे चरण शरण : ऐसा खेळु खेळत
असति : तवं बाईसीं उपाहारू नीफजवीला : गोसावीयांसि
उदयाचां पूजावस्वर : आरोगण : गुळळा : वीडा : मागुता
पहुड : उपहुड : मग तेथ बीजें केलें : तवं ते खेळत असति :
गोसावी जाउनि मागें उभें ठेले : आणि तेयावरि साइली
पडली : मागुतें पाहीलें : तवं गोसावीयातें देखीले : सर्वज्ञें
म्हणीतलें : बटिका : खेळतु असा : आणि : श्रीप्रभुचें स्मरण
करित असा : ऐसें होए : ऐसें म्हणिजे हो :॥: हीराइसा पाठ :

57 HE STAYS OVERNIGHT IN THE VARHADDEV TEMPLE AT MANGRUL. HE PRAISES CANGDEVBHAT'S WAY OF PLAYING.

The Gosavi was sitting in the Varhaddev temple in Mangrul.[68] Baïse washed his feet, and then he said to Cangdevbhat, "Go and play, Batika."

"Batika," said Baïse, "take along Baba's laundry." (Research: He took it and left. Some say, he took his dhoti.) He washed it at the river and laid it out to dry.

Then he made a temple out of wet sand over his feet, rapidly reciting the names of the two gods as he worked. "This cell is Shri Gundam Raül Gosavi's,"* he would say. "This cell is Cangdev Raül Gosavi's." He would say the two gods' names separately, and then he would say them one right after the other. He would say, "I take refuge at the feet of the one and the other Gosavi."

While he was playing this way, Baïse prepared some food. The Gosavi's morning worship service took place. He ate his meal, rinsed his mouth, and chewed pan. He went back to sleep, then woke up and went to the place where Cangdevbhat was playing.

The Gosavi went and stood behind him, and his shadow fell on him. Cangdevbhat looked back and saw the Gosavi. "Batika," said the omniscient one, "are you practicing recollection of Shriprabhu as you play? That is right. That is what you should say."[69] (Hiraïsa version: "What game are you

———

* Shriprabhu's.

बटिका : काइ खेळत असा : श्रीप्रभुतें आठवीत असा :
तेवींचि याते आठवीत असा : ऐसे होए :॥:

५८ सेंदुर्जनीं ब्राह्मणा आभासु[॰] कथन :॥:

गोसावी सेंदुर्जनासि बीजें केलें : गावां उत्तरे वावरा मध्यें
वडाखालि गोसावीयासि आसन : ब्राह्मणु पींपळाखाली :
स्तिति भोगीत बैसला असे : बाइसीं म्हणीतलें : बाबा : हा
तो ब्राह्मणु नव्हे : सर्वज्ञें म्हणीतलें : होए : बाबा या काइ
जालें : बाबातें देखे परि जवळा नये : सर्वज्ञें म्हणीतलें :
बाइ : यातें हा तेथचि देखत असे : बाबा बोलाउं : बोलावा :
बाइसें गेलीं : भटो तुमतें बाबा बोलावीत असति : तेही
म्हणीतलें : बाइ हे नव्हति : गोसावी एथचि असति : बाइसें
मागुती आलीं : बाबा ब्राह्मणु नये : सर्वज्ञें म्हणीतलें : बाइ :
खांद चुरा : गेलीं : खांद चुरिले : आणि स्तिति भंगली :
हीराइसा पाठ : बाइसीं हनुवटीये धरूनि ऐसें गोसावीयाकडे
तोंड करूनि दाखविलें : भटो हे नव्हति बाबा : पैन्हां
असति : आणि : स्तिति भंगली :॥छ॥: गोसावीयांतें देखीलें :
उठीले : आले : दंडवतें घातलीं : श्रीचरणा लागले : मग

playing, Batika? Are you thinking of Shriprabhu, and at the same time thinking of me? That is right.")

58 HE TELLS ABOUT APPEARING TO A BRAHMAN IN SENDURJAN.

The Gosavi went to Sendurjan. As he sat beneath a banyan tree in a field to the north of the village, there was a Brahman sitting under a pipal tree, experiencing a trance. "Baba," said Baïse, "isn't this that same Brahman?"[70] "It is," said the omniscient one. "What has happened to him, Baba? He sees you, Baba, but he isn't coming over here." "My woman, he sees me there," said the omniscient one.[71] "Should I invite him over, Baba?" "Invite him."

Baïse went there. "Bhat, Baba is inviting you." "My woman," he said, "isn't this the Gosavi right here?"

Baïse returned. "Baba," she said, "the Brahman won't come here." "Squeeze his shoulder, my woman," said the omniscient one.

She went back there and squeezed his shoulder. And his trance broke. (Hiraïsa version: Baïse took hold of his chin, turned his head toward the Gosavi, and showed him to him. "Bhat, that's Baba over there, isn't it?" And his trance broke.) He saw the Gosavi. He stood up, came over, and prostrated himself. He touched the Gosavi's holy feet, then invited him for a meal.

गोसावीयांतें वीनवीलें : गोसावीं तेयाचेया घरा बीजें केलें :
मर्दना जाली : भक्तजनीं पूजा : आरोगण : गुळळा : वीडा :
पहुड : उपहुड : वसति जाली : मग उदायांचि गोसावी बीजें
केले :॥:

५९ डोडवीहीरा राघवदेवां भेटी :॥:

गोसावी डोडवीहिरियासी बीजे करीत असति : ऐसे
राघवदेवीं आईकीलें : मग : सडे संमार्जन : गुढीया
उभिलीया : मखर मांडळि करूनि भागवत मेळविले :
गात : वात : नाचत : मोहो उच्छायासीं साउमे आले : पूर्वीं
भोगनारायणी राघवदेवां भेटि जाली होती : गोसावीयांसि
भेटले : दंडवतें घातलीं : श्रीचरणा लागले : मग म्हणितलें :
हें काइ जी : अपत्यातें कहीं सांभाळिजे ना : पडिताळिजे
ना : सर्वज्ञें म्हणीतलें : हें नव्हे आलें७९ : निकें केलें :
गोमटदेव हो : बरवें केलें : गोमट देव हो : अपूलिया
अपत्यातें पडीताळिलें : म्हणौनि : गात नाचति : हरिखैजति :
खेदखीन्न होत : श्रीचरणा मोमे देति : ऐसेंचि गात वात

The Gosavi went to his house. The Gosavi was given a massage, and the devotees did puja to him. He ate his meal, rinsed his mouth, and chewed pan. He went to sleep and then woke up.

The Gosavi stayed there overnight. Then, early the next morning, he left.

59 HE MEETS RAGHAVDEV
IN DODVIHIR.

Raghavdev heard that the Gosavi was coming to Dodvihir.[72] He had the ground smeared with cow-dung wash, he had decorated poles erected, and he set up an arrangement of archways. Then he gathered the Bhagavats together. Singing, playing music, and dancing, they came out to greet the Gosavi enthusiastically.

Raghavdev had met the Gosavi previously in the Bhognarayan temple.[73] Now he greeted the Gosavi, prostrated himself, and touched the holy feet. Then he said, "What is going on, Lord? Why don't you ever take care of your child? Why don't you ever check up on me?" The omniscient one replied, "Haven't I come here now?"

Raghavdev sang and danced, saying, "You've done well, Gomatdev.* You've done nicely, Gomatdev. You've checked up on your child." He rejoiced. He became sad and kissed the Gosavi's holy feet. In this way, singing, playing music, and

---

* "Kind god," Raghavdev's name for Chakradhar.

नाचत आपुलिया घरा घेउनि आले : लोकु पुसे : राघवदेव
हो : हे कवण : ते गात वात नाचत चालतचि असति :
तेंवींचि म्हणति : हे गोमट देव : बाबा : गोमट देवा : ऐसेया
परीं : गोसावी तेयाचेया घरासि बीजें केलें : आसन : पूजा :
आरोगणा : भक्तजनासहित पहुड : तेथचि वसति जाली :
दुसरीये दीसी गोसावींयातें राहावीत होते : न न्हातीचि :
हीराइसा पाठ : बाइसीं पुसीलें : हें कवण : बाइ : हे दुंडी
राउळाचे अनुग्रहीत :॥:

६० फुलंबरीये मढीं वसति :॥:

६१ गवाणा वनदेवीं वसति :॥:

६२   यळापुरीं राजवीहारीं अवस्थान :॥:

गोसावी यळापुरा बीजें केलें : राजवीहारीं दीस तिन
अवस्थान : माचेयावरि आसन : चरणक्षाळण : पहुड होय :
पुजा : आरोगणा : मागुता पहुड : ऐसे तिन्हीं अवसर
माचेयावरि होति : एके म्हणति : तियची वोवरा आरोगण

dancing, he brought the Gosavi to his home. When people asked, "Who is this, Raghavdev?" he would reply, "This is Gomatdev Baba. Gomatdev." And he would continue to sing, play music, and dance.

The Gosavi proceeded this way to Raghavdev's house. He was given a seat, his puja was performed, he ate his meal, and he went to sleep together with the devotees. He spent the night right there.

The next day Raghavdev tried to get the Gosavi to stay, but he would not.

(Hiraïsa version: Baïse asked, "Who was he?" "My woman, he was a disciple of Dundi Raül.")[74]

60 HE STAYS OVERNIGHT IN A HERMITAGE IN PHULAMBARI.[75]

61 HE STAYS IN THE VANDEV TEMPLE IN GAVAN.[76]

62 HE STAYS IN THE RAJVIHAR CAVE IN YELAPUR.

The Gosavi went to Yelapur.[77] He stayed three days in the Rajvihar cave.[78] He would sit on a high bed. His feet would be washed, and he would go to sleep. Three times a day his puja would be done on the bed, and he would eat his meal and go back to sleep there. (Some say he ate his meals on the

होए : चांगदेवो भट हाटवेचुं आणुं जाति : रात्रीं बाइसें
भीति : वसो डरे : ऐसे शब्द आइकति : मग बाइसीं
म्हणितलें : बाबा : घोर शब्द आइकीजत असीजेति : वसो
डरेताति : भालुवा भुक्तांति : बाइला लेकुरूवांसि परियें
देताति : एका एका गोष्टी सांघतें असति : ऐसे नाना शब्दीं
मज नीद्रा नये : भिति असे : बाबा : चांगदेवो भटीं म्हणी-
तलें : हो बाइ : भीति असीजे॰॰ : मग गोसावी बीजें केलें :
अवघी देउळें पाहीलीं : मग वीळिचां चतुर्विधाचेया मढा
बीजें केलें : बाइ : हे बीढार होए :॥:

६३ चतुर्विधांचां मढीं अवस्थान : उपाध्यां भेटी :॥:

एकु दीस गोसावीयांसि उदयाचा पूजावस्वर जाला :
आरोगण : पहुड : उपहुड : परि गोसावी शयनासनींचि
असति : दादोस मूर्ख्य करूनि बल्हेग्रामीचे माहाजन
देवगिरीसि आले : कांहीं राज्यव्यापारें : तवं गोसावीयांतें
यळापुरीं राज्य करितां आइकीलें : मग दरिसना एळापुरि
आले : माहाकाळीचा देउळीं बिढार केले : मग देवीं
म्हणितलें : जानो : जाए पां : गोसावीयांसि कैसा अवसरू
असे : पाहुनि या : म्हणौनि : उपाधीये धाडीले : आले : तवं
मढाचीं कवाडें लावीलीं असति : मग : उपाधीं शब्द केला :
बाइसीं म्हणितलें : बाबा : कवाड कवण उघडवीत असे :

porch of that cave.) Cangdevbhat would go to the market to get provisions.

At night Baïse would get frightened. She would hear sounds like the roaring of a bull. "Baba," said Baïse, "I keep hearing many kinds of terrible sounds: bulls roaring, female jackals howling, women rocking their babies, people having conversations with one another. The sounds keep me awake. I'm frightened, Baba." Cangdevbhat said, "Yes, my woman. It is scary."

Then the Gosavi went and looked at all the temples. In the evening he came to the Chaturvidh hermitage.[79] "My woman," he said, "here is where we will stay."

63 HE STAYS IN THE HERMITAGE OF CHATURVIDYA. HE MEETS UPADHYE.

After the Gosavi's morning worship service one day, he ate his meal, went to sleep, and woke up, but he stayed in bed.

When Dados and some other leading citizens of Balhegram came to Devgiri for some government business, they heard that the Gosavi was staying in Yelapur.[80] So they came to Yelapur for *darśan*. They made their lodgings in the temple of Mahakali.

Then Dev* sent Upadhye there. "Go there, Jano," he said. "Go and see what the Gosavi is doing."

When Upadhye arrived at the hermitage, the doors were closed. So he knocked. Baïse said, "Baba, someone is knock-

* Dados.

तथा : टीबकारीत असे : सर्वज्ञें म्हणीतलें : बाइ : चांगो
सरिसा बटिकु आला होता : हा नव्हे कीं^{८१} : बाइसें आलीं :
कवाडें उघडीलीं : उपाधीं बाइसा नमस्कारू केला : बाइसें
आलीं : सर्वज्ञें म्हणीतलें : बाइ : कोणु : बाइसीं म्हणीतलें :
आपण म्हणीतला : तोचि : बाबा^{८२} : उपाध्यें भीतरि आले :
तवं आंधारू पडिला असे : उपाधीं मनीं म्हणीतलें : बाइसें
वाति लाविती कां तरि मीं गोसावीयांतें देखतां : तवं भगकरि
श्रीमूर्तिवरि प्रकाशू पडीला : मग दंडवतें घातलीं : श्रीचरणा
लागले : सर्वज्ञें म्हणीतलें : बटिका : हें काइ दीवेन देखीजे :
हें आपणेयांतें दाखवी : तेव्हळिसिचि देखीजे कीं^{८३} :॥: मग
गोसावी पुसिलें : कोण कोण बटिका आले असेति^{८४} :
दादोस : पदकर नागदेवोभट : रांके लक्ष्मींद्रभट : जापीये
वीष्णुभट : आपदेवोभट : बागडे विष्णुभट : नरसिंहभट :
उपाध्याचें भाउ नागदेवोउपाध्ये : गातीय कमळनाइक :
आनो : रवळो : गोंदो : तेरावे उपाध्ये : इतुके आले असति :
सर्वज्ञें म्हणीतलें : बटिका : एथौनि जालें : तें तुमचा ठाइ
वर्तें : हो जी : कैसें वर्तें : ना जी : एकलेया पाहारू खांड बैसों
आवडे : गोसावीयांतें आठउं आवडे : एकलेया बैसलेया
सुखंचि होय जी : तुम्ही यांतें काइ म्हणां : जी जी : श्रीकृष्ण
म्हणों : हीराईपाठ : जेचि श्रीकृष्णचक्रवर्ति तेचि आमचे
गोसावी : सर्वज्ञें म्हणीतलें : तेंचि काइसेया तवं : ना जी :
गोसावी : कास्तां हरिदेवो पंडिता प्रति : गोपाळमंत्राचे भेद
निरूपीले : एकू भेद तो श्रीकृष्ण चक्रवर्ति जाणति : कां

234

ing at the door." The omniscient one said, "My woman, isn't it the Batika who came with Cango?"

Baïse came and opened the door. Upadhye greeted her reverently. When Baïse returned, the omniscient one asked, "Who is it, my woman?" "It's the person you said it was, Baba," replied Baïse.

Upadhye entered the hermitage. It had gotten dark inside, and he said to himself, "If Baïse would light a lamp, I could see the Gosavi." Suddenly light fell on the holy form. Upadhye prostrated himself to the Gosavi and touched his holy feet. The omniscient one said, "Batika, can I be seen with a lamp? I can only be seen when I manifest myself!"[81]

Then the Gosavi asked, "Who else has come, Batika?" "Dados, Nagdevbhat the Reciter, Rake Lakshmindrabhat, Japiye Vishnubhat, Apdevbhat, Bagade Vishnubhat, Narasimhabhat, Upadhye's brother Nagdev Upadhye, Gatiya Kamalnayak, Ano, Ravalo, Gondo. Upadhye is the thirteenth. That's how many have come."

The omniscient one said, "Batika, does what happened to you because of me still affect you?"[82] "Yes, Lord." "How does it affect you?" "I like to sit alone for some time, Lord Gosavi. I like to think about you. It makes me very happy to sit alone, Lord."

"Who do you say I am?" "I call you Shri Krishna, Lord." (Hiraïsa version: "Our Gosavi is Shri Krishna Chakravarti himself.") "Why do you say that?" asked the omniscient one. "Lord Gosavi, when you told Kasta Haridev Pandit about the types of Gopal mantra, you said that there is one type that Shri Krishna Chakravarti and the goddess Rukmini know that no one else at all knows.[83] That is why, Lord."

रुक्मीणदेवी जाणे : आणिक कव्हणीचि नेणे : ऐसें :
सर्वज्ञें म्हणीतलें : या तवं जी : सर्वज्ञें म्हणीतलें : हें जें होये ते
होये ॥ः तुमची बूधि तव निकी : ऐसी बूधि जावों नेदीजे⁶⁵ :
बाइ : बटिकु काइ म्हणतु असे : बाबा : दैवाचा :
भाग्याचा : सर्वज्ञें म्हणीतलें : तुमचां गांवीं माहात्मा असे :
जी जी : सीक्षासुत्र⁶⁶ वर्तें : जी जी : तेथ⁶⁷ तुम्ही जा : हो
जी : महात्मेया वरि आणि येथ कैसी बुधि आति : जी जी :
सरिसीचि : सर्वज्ञें म्हणीतलें : हुं बाइ : बटिकु काइ म्हणतु
असे : बाइसें दुचितीं होतीं : दैवाचा भाग्याचा : बाबा : बाइ
आतां आन एक म्हणतु असे : काइ म्हणत असे बाबा :
पुसा पां : यांतें : बाइसीं म्हणीतलें : काइ म्हणतु अससि :
बटिका उगेंचि : सर्वज्ञें म्हणीतलें : महात्मेया वरि आणि
एथ सरिसीचि बूधि : म्हणत असे : बाइसीं म्हणीतलें : मर
मर पोरा : तुझीये कीडडीये बांधे घागरा : ये जाइल मसण
वेऱ्हीं : टुं टुं करीत : महात्मा काइसा पाखांडाचा : काइसें
तेयाचें आचारित्व : मसणाचें⁶⁸ : बाबातें रडौनि आचारित्व
मागितलें : तथा विद्या : बाबासि आणि रामासि सरी करितु
असे : हीराइपाठ : सर्वज्ञें म्हणीतलें : बाइ : उगी असा :
सतेव जीवासि : काइ जाणणें असे : एथौनि : जाणवीजे :
तैंचि जाणति : बटिका महात्मा तो एकु जीवु : ऐसें
जाणिजे : माहात्मा तो एथिंचा हो : हां गा : देव काइ अनेग
असति : देवो तो एकूचि कीं⁶⁹ : सर्वज्ञें म्हणीतलें : तुमचिया

The omniscient one said, "I am what I am. You have the right idea. Do not let go of that idea.[84] My woman, what is Batika saying?" "That he has good luck, Baba. That he is fortunate."

The omniscient one asked Upadhye, "Is the Mahatma in your village?" "Yes, Lord." "Does he have a tuft of hair and a shoulder thread?"[85] "Yes, Lord." "Do you go to him?" "Yes, Lord. I do." "What do you think about the Mahatma and about me?" "You're exactly the same, Lord."

"Hunh!" said the omniscient one. "My woman, what is Batika saying?" Baïse was not paying attention. "That he has good luck, good fortune, Baba." "He is saying something else now, my woman." "What is he saying, Baba?" "Ask him!"

Baïse asked Upadhye, "What are you saying?" Batika kept silent. The omniscient one said, "He says that he sees the Mahatma and me as exactly the same."

Baïse said, "Die! Die, you ignorant child. They'll tie bells to your bier that will jingle as you go to the cremation ground. How can that heretic be a Mahatma? How can he be a teacher? He belongs at the cremation ground! He came crying to ask Baba to make him a teacher (or, for esoteric knowledge).[86] Batika is equating Baba with Ram."*

(Hiraï version: The omniscient one said, "Be quiet, my woman. Can *jīvas* know anything on their own? Only when I give them knowledge do they know anything. Batika, know that the Mahatma is a *jīva*.[87] The Mahatma belongs to me." "All right." "There are not many gods. There is just one God.")[88]

―――

* With Dados, also called Ramdev.

गांवापासि आत्मतिर्थ असे कीं : हो जी : तुम्ही तेथ जा : हो
जी : तेथ जाइजे हो : तें आणिका स्थावरा सारिखें नव्हे :
तें श्री दत्तात्रयप्रभूची प्रीतष्ठा हो^{९०} : मग श्रीमुखीचें तांबूल
दीधलें : गळाची माळ दीधली : हीराई : तेथ प्रतिदिनीं जाइजे
हो : बटिका ॥छ॥ : बटिका जाते वाट पाहात असति : ते
निगाले ॥ः

६४ देवा सीष्या भेटी ॥ः

देव म्हणो लागले : जानोयें उसीरू कां लाविला : म्हणैनि :
पुसों लागले : उपाध्यासि कोपों लागले : येरी अवघां
म्हणीतलें : दादो : गोसावीयाचेया दरिसना जात असीजे : मां
गोसावीयां पासौनि काइ निगों आवडत असे : देव आले :
गोसावी बाहीरि पटिसाळेवरि बीजें केलें^{९१} : पडिसाळे
दादोसा भेटि जाली : क्षेमालिंगन दीधलें : आसनीं बैसले :
मग आवचेयांतें पृथकाकारें पूसिलें : तथा संभाखीलें : सर्वज्ञें
म्हणीतलें : बाइ : तुमतें पाणिभातु असे : असे बाबा : रवळो
घागरि घेउनि पाणिया धाडीलें^{९२} : सोंडी धुववीली : मग
गोसावी पुसीलें : माहात्मेया काइ पृथकपात्र : जी जी : सर्वज्ञें
म्हणीतलें : आतांचा तवं वेळ ऐसें जालें : मग तुमचें काइ
केहीं गेलें असे : मग सोंडीवरी अन्न घातलें : मग गोसावी
आपणेयां पुढें जेववीलें : आंचवलें : तांबूल देववीलें ॥ः

The omniscient one asked, "Is Atmatirtha near your village?"[89] "Yes, Lord." "Do you go there?" "Yes, Lord." "You should go there. It is unlike any other place. It was established by Shri Dattatreya Prabhu."[90]

Then the Gosavi gave him the pan from his holy mouth and the garland from around his neck. (Hiraï: "You should go there every day, Batika.") Batika was ready and waiting to go. He left.

64 HE MEETS DEV'S DISCIPLES.

Dev started getting angry with Upadhye. "Why is Jano taking so long?" he began to ask. All the others said, "Dado, does someone who has gone for *darśan* of the Gosavi feel like leaving his presence?"

Dev came there. The Gosavi went out onto the veranda and met him there.[91] He hugged Dados, and then sat down. Then he asked about (or spoke with) each of the disciples separately.

The omniscient one asked Baïse, "My woman, do you have any water-and-rice gruel?" "I do, Baba." She sent Ravalo with a pitcher to get water, and she had him wash the elephant-trunk-shaped parapet at the side of the temple steps.[92]

Then the Gosavi asked, "Do Mahatmas need separate plates?" "Yes, Lord." The omniscient one said, "This time do it this way. What do you have to lose?"

So she put the food on the elephant-trunk-shaped parapet, and the Gosavi had them eat in front of him. They rinsed their mouths, and he had them given pan.

६५ दीढपुरुखु नामकरण :॥:

देवीं उतरिला मढासि बीढार आणिलें[९३] : मग वीळचां देवीं
कणिक घेतली : रोटीया केलीया : दोहीं मढामाजि उपाध्यें
भाजीत असति : तवं गोसावी वीहरणौनि बीजें केलें :
गोसावी दोहीं मढामाजि उभे ठेले : मग म्हणीतले : एसनी
अर्ध रोटी टाके : ना जी: अर्धा काइ होइल : तरि काइ पाउण :
ना जी : पाउणा काय होइल : तरि काइ समग्र एकि : ना जी :
समग्र काइ होइल : तरि काइ सवाये : ना जी : सवाया : कां :
दीढ : शोधु : हें काइ गा ऐसेनि दीढ : एसनी दीढ रोटी टाके :
हो जी[९४] : एसणीयां रोटीया केलीया : सर्वज्ञें म्हणीतलें : ऐसें
तऱ्ही तुम्हां दीढ पुरुखु म्हणा : मग जेवीले : निजों गेले :
उपाध्ये राहीले : बाइसीं म्हणीतलें : बटीका : तुं कां राहि-
लासि : तुं जाय : तुझे सांघाति वाट पाहात असति : सर्वज्ञें
म्हणीतलें : बाइ : असों दीया : चांगो सरिसा नीद्रा करील :
तथा सेजा :॥:

65 HE GIVES UPADHYE THE NAME "ONE-AND-A-HALF MAN."

Dev moved his lodgings to the northern hermitage.[93] That evening Dev got some wheat flour, and they made rotis. Upadhye was roasting them in the space between the two hermitages when the Gosavi came back from wandering.

The Gosavi stood between the two hermitages and said, "Will half of one of these rotis be enough?" "No, Lord. What use would half a roti be?" "Then what about three quarters?" "No, Lord. What use would three quarters be?" "Then what about a whole one?" "No, Lord. What use would a whole one be?" "Then what about one and a quarter?" "No, Lord. Why one and a quarter? One and a half." (Research: "What do you mean? One and a half of these? Would one and a half of these rotis be enough?" "Yes, Lord.) That's how many rotis we've made." The omniscient one said, "Then we'll call you 'One-and-a-Half Man.'"

They ate their meal and left for their sleeping places. Upadhye stayed on. Baïse asked, "Why have you stayed here, Batika? You should go. Your companions are waiting for you." The omniscient one said, "Let him stay, my woman. He will sleep with Cango."

६६ लेणां छाया पुरूखु दाखवणें⁹⁵ :॥:

गोसावीयांसि उदयाचा पूजावसर जालेया नंतरें गोसावी
वीहरणा बीजें केलें : एका लेणेयांचां चौकीं आसन :
भक्तजन चौकावरि उभे ठाकले : तवं पुढीले भितिसी भव्य
पुरूखु : एकू कमळाची आंगी लेइलां असे : ऐसा देखीला :
चौका खालि उभे ठाकति आणि न देखति : भक्तजनीं
पुसिलें : हें काइ जी : सर्वज्ञें म्हणीतलें : आतां जा : पाहा :
शोधु : हे काइ गा पुरूषु जी :॥: छाया पुरूषु सीधाचां संकेतु :
शोधु :॥: हा सीधाचां आगम समो : जेणें केलें : तेणें
आपुलीया छाया ठेवीली असे : हीराइसा पाठ : छाया
पुरूषु : सकळा करितेनि पुरुखें एथ आपुली छाया निक्षेपीली
असे :॥:

६७ आगम समो कथन⁹⁶ :॥:

एकुदीस गोसावीयांसि उदेयाचा पूजावसर जालेया नंतरें
गोसावी वीहरणासि बीजें केलें : माणिकेश्वरीं : एका
लेणेयासि वीवरें बीजें केलें : पुढां गोसावी : मागां बाइसें :
सर्वज्ञें म्हणीतलें : बाइ : मागा धरा : मग यरा मागें यरातें
धरूनि : ऐसीं भक्तजनें आवघींचि कासें लावीली : वीवरें
वीवरें गोसावी बीजें करिताति : तवं एके ठाइं भगकरि उजेड

66 HE POINTS OUT A SHADOW
MAN IN A CAVE.

After his morning worship service, the Gosavi went out to wander. He was sitting in the central hall of a cave. When the devotees stood above the central hall, they saw on the front wall a huge man who was wearing a cloak made of lotuses. When they stood below the central hall, they did not see the man.

"What is this, Lord?" asked the devotees. "Go there now and take a look," said the omniscient one. (Research: "What kind of man is this, Lord?") "It is a shadow man, the mark of a perfected yogi." (Research: "The man who created the Siddhas' tantric rites has placed his shadow here." Hiraïsa version: "It is a shadow man. The man who made all this has deposited his shadow here.")

67 HE TELLS ABOUT TANTRIC RITES.

After his morning worship service one day, the Gosavi went wandering to the Manikeshvar cave-temple. He went through an underground passage to another cave. The Gosavi was in front, with Baïse behind him. The omniscient one said, "Hold on from behind, my woman." Then all the devotees held on to one another at the waist, one behind the other.

As the Gosavi went from one underground passage to another, suddenly there was light at one place. Up ahead a pot had been set up, and people were sitting all around

पडिला : तवं पुढां एकु घटु मांडीला असे : घटा भवंती
भवंती : डोइ गुंडु गुंडु : बैसलीं असति : बाइसीं पुसीलें :
बाबा : हें काइ : बाइ : हा आगम समो१७ : म्हणौनि पुढारें
बीजें केलें : ते वीवर इसाळुवाचिए लेणां उसासिलें : तेणें
ठायें गोसावी बीजें केलें : लेणा उभे ठेले : तवं यळापुर
देखीलें : बाइसीं पुसीलें :॥: बाबा हें कवण नगर : सर्वज्ञें
म्हणीतलें : बाइ : हें येळापुर : हें काइ बाबा : इतुकी भुई
आलों :॥: सर्वज्ञें म्हणीतलें : बाइ : हा अवघा डोंगरू पोकळ
असे : कोन्ही एथीचें रिगणें निगणें जाणे ना :॥:

६८ चांगदेवो भटा लेणा परिखु :॥:

गोसावीयांसि उदेयाचा पूजावसर जालेया नंतरें गोसावी
एका लेणेया बीजें केलें : तेथ आसन : चांगदेवो भटातें :
काट वसिये पाठवीले : पैला१८ लेणेयांकडे जा : गेले : तवं
आडवी तिडवी पडलीं देखिलीं : एकीकडे एकाचे पाय :
एकीकडे एकाचीया डोइया : ऐसी पासली पडलीं असति :
डोळे मिलमिलवीत : वोठ फुलफुलवीती : आणि : भीयाले :
गोसावीयांपासि आले : देडवतें घातलीं : श्रीचरणां लागले :
हीराइसा : सर्वज्ञें म्हणीतलें : कां गा : आलेति :॥छ॥: मागील
वृतांत आवघेंचि सांघीतलें : भियालां म्हणौनि आलां जी :
सर्वज्ञें म्हणीतलें : तुम्हीं बोलवितेति : तरि बोलतीं : पुसतेति
तरि मार्गु सांघति१९ :॥:

it, with cloths wrapped around their heads. "What is this, Baba?" asked Baïse.

"It is a tantric rite, my woman," he said, and continued on ahead. The passage opened out into the Jealous Man's cave.[94] The Gosavi passed into it.

When they stood up in the cave, they saw Yelapur. "What town is this, Baba?" asked Baïse. "This is Yelapur, my woman," replied the omniscient one. "What do you mean, Baba? Have we come that far under the ground?" The omniscient one said, "This whole hill is hollow, my woman. No one knows all the ways in and out of this place."

68 CANGDEVBHAT UNDERGOES AN ORDEAL IN A CAVE.

After his morning worship service one day, the Gosavi went and sat in a certain cave. He sent Cangdevbhat to the Katevasai cave, saying, "Go to that cave over there."[95]

When he went there, he saw a jumble of fallen figures. They were lying in disarray, with the legs of one on one side and the head of another on the other side. They were blinking their eyes and puckering their lips.

Cangdevbhat got frightened. He returned to the Gosavi, prostrated himself, and touched the holy feet. (According to Hiraïsa, the omniscient one said, "Why have you come back?") Cangdevbhat told him everything that had happened. "I got frightened, Lord, and so I came back."

The omniscient one said, "If you cause them to speak, they will speak. If you ask them, they will tell you the way."

६९ आपदेवो भटा : प्राल्हादवीद्या निरूपण :॥ः

एकु दीस गोसावीयांसि उदयाचा पूजावसर जालेया नंतरें
नागझरियें बीजें केलें : तथा लेणा एकासि बीजें केलें : तेथ
आसन : आपदेवों भटातें म्हणीतलें : जा गा : हीराइसा
पाठ : भटो तुम्हीं पैला लेणेया जा :॥छ॥ः हो कां जी :
म्हणौनि : गेले : बैसले : तवं भव्य पुरुष१०० : आंगी
कमळाची लेउनि ऐसा आला : हातीं सुवर्णाचें खर्ग : तो
खांडेवरि आपदेवोभटासि हाणे : तवं तवं सुखचि होए :
खांडें पाणियांतु घातले : तैसें तैसें निगौनि जाए : तवं तवं
सुखचि होए : ऐसी स्तीति केतुला काळ एकू भोगीली :
भंगली : तवं गोसावी पुढें मढासि बीजें केलें : मागिली
कडौनि आपदेवोभट वाडावेळा आले : दंडवतें घातलीं :
श्रीचरणां लागले : हीराइसा पाठ : उसीरू कां या लावी-
ला :॥छ॥ः मागील आवघेंचि सांघीतलें : तरि तें काइ जी :
सर्वज्ञें म्हणीतलें : ते प्राल्हादाची वीद्या : ते आम्हा जाली जी :
सर्वज्ञें म्हणीतलें : तें तुम्हां नव्हे : एथौनि दीसे१०१ :॥ः

69 HE TELLS APDEVBHAT
ABOUT THE SCIENCE OF PRALHAD.

After his morning worship service one day, the Gosavi went and sat at the winding stream. (Or, he went to a cave.) "Go," he said to Apdevbhat. (Hiraïsa version: "Go to that cave over there, Bhat.")

"All right, Lord," he said, and he went and sat there. Soon a huge man came along, wearing a cloak made of lotuses. He carried a golden sword in his hand, and he kept striking Apdevbhat with it. Every time the man struck him, Apdevbhat felt pure joy. The sword would go through him as if it were slicing through water, and he would feel pure joy each time. He experienced a trance this way for some time, and then it broke.

The Gosavi had gone on ahead to the hermitage, and Apdevbhat followed him there much later. Apdev prostrated himself to the Gosavi and touched his holy feet.

(Hiraïsa version: The Gosavi asked, "What took you so long?") He told him everything that had happened, then asked, "What was that, Lord?" "That was the science of Pralhad," replied the omniscient one.[96] "Do I have that, Lord?" "You do not have it," said the omniscient one. "You see it because of me."

७० तथा सप्तदशकळा नीक्षेदु¹⁰² :॥:

एकु दीस : गोसावी : उदेयाचा पूजावसर जालेया नंतरें
नागझरिएसि बीजें केलें : आसन : सर्वज्ञें म्हणीतलें : जा गा :
हीराइसा : भटो तुम्हीं पैला लेणेयां जा : आपदेवभट¹⁰³
गेले : बैसले¹⁰⁴ : तवं षोडशवरूषीं स्त्री : ते खळिचा
साउला : खळिची चोळी : हातीं सूवर्णाचा कळशु : तथा
करा : ते करेनि माथेयावरि उदकाची धार घाली : तवं तवं
सूखचि होए : ऐसी स्तिति केली : एकु काळु भोगिली : मग
भंगली : गोसावी पुढां बीजे केलें : ते मागीला कडौनि आले :
गोसावी पुसीलें : मागील सांघीतलें : तरि : तें काइ जी :
सर्वज्ञें म्हणीतलें : ते चंद्रींची सतरावी कळा गा : हीराइसा
पाठ : तुम्हावरि वीरखत होती :॥छ॥: जी जी : तरि ते आम्हा
जाली : सर्वज्ञें म्हणीतलें : तुम्हां नाहीं : ते एथौनि दीसे¹⁰⁵ :॥:

७१ सारंगपंडीता भेटी :॥:

सारंगपंडित देवगिरीसि कांहीं आपुलेनि कार्यें आले :
सरिसीं देमाइसें : मुकुंद असति : तवं गोसावीयांतें एळापुरीं
आइकीलें : मग दरिसना आले : मार्गीं येत असति : तवं

70 AND HE DENIES THAT APDEVBHAT HAS THE SEVENTEENTH DIGIT OF THE MOON.

One day, after his morning worship service, the Gosavi went and sat at the winding stream. "Go," said the omniscient one to Apdevbhat. (According to Hiraïsa, "Go to that cave over there, Bhat.")

Apdevbhat went there. While he was sitting there, a sixteen-year-old woman appeared. She had on a starched silk sari and a starched blouse. She was holding a golden water pot, and she was pouring water from the pitcher onto his head. Every time she poured some, he felt pure joy. She put him into a trance this way. He experienced it for some time, and then it broke.

The Gosavi went on ahead, and Apdevbhat followed him later. When the Gosavi asked, he told him what had happened. "What was that, Lord?" he asked. The omniscient one said, "That was the seventeenth digit of the moon."[97] (Hiraïsa version: "She was pouring nectar over you.") "So do I have that, Lord?" The omniscient one said, "You don't have it. You see it because of me."

71 HE MEETS SARANGPANDIT.

Sarangpandit came to Devgiri to conduct some business. Demaïse and Mukunda* were with him. They heard that the Gosavi was at Yelapur, and so they came for his *darśan*. On

---

* Mokananda.

माहादेवोपुर घाटीं आंबे वानिएचे वीकत असति : ते घेतले :
केलें घेतलीं : देउगीरीचीं पोफळें घेतलीं : नागझरीयें आले :
देमाइसातें म्हणीतलें : देमाइ एथ जेउं : मग जावों : देमाइसीं
म्हणीतलें : हें काइ पंडितो : इतुकेयांचि गोसावीयां न
भेटतां : कैसे जेउं : ना आमचेया गोसावीयाचां ठाइं तैसें
कांहीं नाहीं : तुम्हीं तवं सांघों नको पा : गोसावी काइ
नेणति : देमाइसीं म्हणीतलें : मुकुंदे म्हणीतलें : तथा
लखुबाइसीं म्हणीतलें : देमाइसें : पंडीत भुकेले असति :
जेउं दिया : मग रोटीया : परशरामबास :॥: सीळीया
जेविले : आवगु सरिसा केला१०६ : टोपरियाचिए बाले
दरिसनालागि आसू बांधली : निगाले : देमाइसें जेवितें
होतीं : केळांचिया साली : रोटीयाचीं शकळें तें चावति ना :
तेणें उशीरू लागला : सारंगपंडितीं म्हणीतलें : देमाये तुम्ही
मागीलाकडौनी या : आले : गोसावीयां भेटि जालीं :
दंडवतें घातलीं : श्रीचरणा लागले : बैसले : तवं मागील
कडौनि देमाइसें आलीं : दंडवतें घातलीं : श्रीचरणा लागली :
बैसली : सारंगपंडीतीं पोफळें केलें आंबे दर्शना केले : सर्वज्ञें
म्हणीतलें : देमती माघारे कां१०७ : जी जी : रोटीयाचीं शकले
चावति ना जी : तथा खपले : म्हणोनि : उशीरू लागला
जी : हीराइसा पाठ : रोटीया काइसेया : देमाये :॥छ॥: मग
देमाइसीं मागील आवघें वृतांत सांघीतले : ते सांगती :

their way there, there were excellent mangos for sale along the road at Mahadevpur Ghat. They bought some of them, and also some bananas and Devgiri betel nuts.

When they reached the winding stream, Sarangpandit said to Demaïse, "Demaï, let's eat here and then go on." "What do you mean, Pandit?" replied Demaïse. "We are so close. How can we eat without meeting the Gosavi?" "Our Gosavi doesn't care about things like that. Just don't tell him!" "Wouldn't the Gosavi know?" replied Demaïse. Mukunda said (or Lakhubaïse said), "Demaïse, Pandit is hungry. Let him eat." So they ate some rotis (according to Parasharambas, stale ones).

Sarangpandit straightened his clothes. He stuck a gold coin in the edge of his cap for an offering and then set out. Demaïse was still eating. She got slowed down trying to chew the banana skins and the hard pieces of roti. Sarangpandit said, "Demaï, you follow behind."

He arrived, and he met the Gosavi. He prostrated himself and touched the holy feet, then sat down. At that point, Demaïse caught up with him. She prostrated herself, touched the holy feet, and sat down. Sarangpandit offered the betel nuts, bananas, and mangos.

The omniscient one asked, "Why did you fall behind, Demati?" "I couldn't chew the hard pieces of roti, Lord. That slowed me down, Lord." (Hiraïsa version: "What rotis, Demaï?")

तेविचि सारंगपंडिताची वास पाहाति : ते गळेयाकडे
आंगुळीया दाखवीति : सर्वज्ञें म्हणीतलें : आणिका देवा
तीर्थिंचेया ठाया जाइजे : तिर्थ उपवासू कीजे : देवो पाहीजे :
मग जेवीजे : तेतुलें हीं पां एथ नाहीं : तरि सांघातधर्मा पुरतें
नाहीं : तथा सांघात धर्मू नाहीं¹⁰⁸ : एथही सांघात धर्मू एकु
आति : आधिं सांघातिया : म्हणौनि चौराची गोष्टि
सांघीतली : इतुलेनि सारंगपंडित दैनावले : आसू दरिसना
करावी : ते न करीतिचि : पुढां पोफळें ठेवीलीं होतीं तेयांतुल
एक पोफळ गोसावी श्रीकरीं घेतलें : सर्वज्ञें म्हणीतलें :
पांडेया : हें पोफळ कैसें असे गा¹⁰⁹ : सर्वज्ञें म्हणीतलें :
एथौनि चौखट नव्हे :॥: तथा निकें नाहीं : म्हणीजत असे :
होडु काइ : गोसावी दृष्टीचेया खूणा : आसू दाखवीली :
हीराइसा पाठ : आसू जाए :॥छ॥: हो कां जी : हे
गोसावीयाचे नव्हे : मग गोसावी¹¹⁰ फोडिलें : तवं वोखटें
निगालें : मागुतें मेळविलें : सर्वज्ञें म्हणीतलें : एथौनि : निकें :
तथा चोखट : ऐसें म्हणीजत असीजे : पाहीलें तवं चोखट :
आसू आसुडुनि घेतली : बाइसां कडे¹¹¹ घातलें : बाइ : एथ
एकू उपहारू करा : आंबे दरिसना ठेले होते : तेयांतु एकु
आंबा श्रीकरीं घेउनि अवग्रहण केला : बाइसें आंबे नेत
होती : सर्वज्ञें म्हणीतलें : बाइ एकु आंबा वेगळा ठेवा : कां
बाबा : एथौनि स्विकरिला असे : बाइसीं म्हणीतलें : कांहीं

Then Demaïse told him everything that had happened. As she told him, she kept looking at Sarangpandit, who was pointing a finger at his throat.*

The omniscient one said, "When you go to another god's holy place, you fast as part of the pilgrimage: you see the god, and then you eat. You don't have to do that much for me, but you have not fulfilled your duty toward your companions.[98] Even I have a duty toward my companions. 'First my companion,'" he said, and he told the story of the thief.[99]

That made Sarangpandit feel miserable. He completely forgot to present the gold coin that he had meant to give him as an offering.

The Gosavi picked up in his holy hand one of the betel nuts that had been placed in front of him. The omniscient one said, "Pande, is this betel nut good or bad?" "It is good, Lord." The omniscient one said, "I say it's not good." "What do you want to bet?" The Gosavi looked pointedly at the gold coin. (Hiraïsa version: "You'll lose the gold coin," he said.) "All right, Lord Gosavi. You won't win it."

Then the Gosavi cut open the betel nut. It was rotten. He put it back together, and then he said, "I say it is good."

When they looked at it, they saw that it was good. The Gosavi plucked the gold coin out of the cap and tossed it to Baïse, saying, "Prepare a meal for me, my woman."

With his holy hand he picked up one of the mangos that had been placed there as an offering. As Baïse was taking the mangos away, the omniscient one said, "My woman, put one

---

* To silence her.

देखीजे ना : बाबा : सर्वज्ञें म्हणीतलें : बाइ : वीषये^{११२} वीखो
ऐसा भोगीति^{११३} : बाइ : वीखो भोगुं कव्हणीचि नेणति :
का : निर्वधी वीखो : श्रीकृष्ण चक्रवर्ति जाणति : कली योगीं
वीखो असे : परि वीखवा : नाहीं : हे राये मंडलिका : द्वापरीं
श्रीकृष्णें वीखो भोगीला : हीराइसा पाठ : का इंद्रादीक
जाणति^{११४} :॥:

७२ तथा श्रीप्रभु दाखवणें :॥:

एकु दीस गोसावी श्रीप्रभुची महीमा निरोपीत होते :
सारंगपंडितीं म्हणीतलें : जी जी : मज श्रीप्रभुचें दर्शन
करावें : सर्वज्ञें म्हणीतलें : तेथ गेलेया होइल^{११५} : ना जी :
गोसावी करिति तरि काइ नव्हे : मग विळिचां वेळीं
आणिकैकडे बीजें केलें : मार्गीं सर्वज्ञें म्हणीतलें : पांडेया :
मागां काइ म्हणत होतेति : ना जी : एकु दीस ते गोसावी
एथचि दाखविती : तरि : काइ नव्हे : सर्वज्ञें म्हणीतलें : हें
पाहा चांग श्रीप्रभु^{११६} : तवं पैलाकडौनि नाभि चुंबित खाड :
मोकळें केसकळाप : मोकळा कासोटा : उतरासंगीं धोत्र :
हास्य करीत : टाळी वात : गगन अवलोकित : खाडवीं
चुरीत : श्याम श्रीमूर्ति ऐसे श्रीप्रभु माळिया वरौनि बीजें

mango aside." "Why, Baba?" "I have accepted it." Baïse said, "I can't see any difference, Baba."

The omniscient one said, "My woman, that is how true sensualists enjoy sense pleasure.[100] No one at all truly knows how to enjoy sense pleasure, my woman. Why? Sense pleasure is unlimited. Shri Krishna Chakravarti knew how, but in the Kali yuga, even though there is sense pleasure, there are no true sensualists. These kings and princes...[101] In the Dvapara yuga, Shri Krishna truly enjoyed sense pleasure." (Hiraïsa version: "Or Indra and the other gods know how to.")

72 AND HE SHOWS HIM SHRIPRABHU.

One day, when the Gosavi was extolling Shriprabhu, Sarangpandit said, "Lord, give me *darśan* of Shriprabhu." The omniscient one said, "If you go there,* that will happen." "But, Lord Gosavi, wouldn't it happen if you made it happen?"

That evening, the Gosavi went to the Anakai cave.[102] Along the way the omniscient one asked, "Pande, what were you saying earlier?" "Lord Gosavi," he replied, "wouldn't it be possible for you to show him to me right here someday?"

The omniscient one said, "Look carefully! Here is Shriprabhu." And there, coming toward them from up on the high grazing land, was Shriprabhu. His beard reached down to his navel. His hair hung free. The folds of his dhoti hung loose from his waist, and one end was slung over his shoulder. He

---

* To Riddhipur.

करिति : सारंगपंडिता गोसावी दाखविलें : सर्वज्ञें म्हणीतलें :
चांग पाहा¹¹⁷ : जी जी : समोर आले : मग सर्वज्ञें¹¹⁸
म्हणीतलें : घाला दंडवत : मग दंडवतें घातलीं :॥:

७३ साळिवाहाना¹¹⁹ हटु निरूपण :॥:

एकु दीस गोसावीयांसि उदयाचा पूजावसर जालेया नंतरें
बाइसीं पडिसाळेवरि आसन केलें : गोसावी आसनीं बैसले
असति : तवं माहादेवो रायाचा राउत साळीवाहानू आले :
दंडवतें घातलीं : श्रीचरणा लागले : बैसले : मग गोसावीयांतें
पुसिलें : हे कव्हणी¹²⁰ हटु जाणति¹²¹ : श्रीमुगुटें निरा-
करिलें : सर्वज्ञें म्हणितले : आपण जाणिजे : तीहीं
म्हणीतलें : तरि काइ जी¹²² : हटु तो आम्हींचि जाणों :
हीराइसा : पां बोला :॥छ॥: बोलों लगले : जारक : पुरक :
कुंभकू : त्राहीटकू : सर्वज्ञें म्हणीतलें : ऐसा तुम्ही हटु जाणा :
तरि हें काइ : म्हणौनि : आंगुलिया कानसूल दाखविलें :
तेयांचीं कानसुलें नावेक म्हांतारीं जालीं होतीं¹²³ : सर्वज्ञें
म्हणीतलें : हटीचीं कार्यें : तें ऐसीं होतीं : जी जी : हा
आमुचा अप्रेलु : सर्वज्ञें म्हणीतलें : हटीचीं कार्यें ऐसीं होति

was laughing, clapping his hands, looking at the sky, and pulling on the hairs of his beard. His holy body was dark. The Gosavi pointed him out to Sarangpandit. "Look carefully," said the omniscient one. "Yes, Lord."

He approached them, and the omniscient one said, "Prostrate yourself." So Sarangpandit prostrated himself.

73   HE TELLS SALIVAHAN ABOUT HATHA YOGA.

One day, after the Gosavi's morning worship service, Baïse prepared a seat on the veranda. While the Gosavi was sitting there, King Mahadev's cavalry officer Salivahan arrived. He prostrated himself, touched the holy feet, and sat down. Then he asked the Gosavi, "Do any of these people know hatha yoga?"[103] The omniscient one shook his holy head and asked, "Do you know it?" "Of course, Lord," he replied. "I know hatha yoga better than anyone else." (Hiraïsa: "Tell me about it.") He began to talk about it: "Jaraka, Puraka, Kumbhaka, Trahitaka."*

The omniscient one said, "If you know hatha yoga so well, then what is this?" And he pointed with his finger at the area around the man's ear. The hair near his ear had begun turning a bit white.[104] The omniscient one said, "Can hatha yoga have this effect?" "That is because I don't practice enough, Lord."

The omniscient one began to tell him about it. "These are the effects of hatha yoga. This is what hatha yoga is like,"

* Yogic practices.

कीं : हटु तो ऐसा कीं : म्हणौनि बोलों लागले : हीराइसा :॥:
हटें वय स्तंभे : अपमृत्यु जीके : वळित पळित लोपति : तेहीं
म्हणीतलें : जी जी : परिसों नेणो जी : मा : बौलोनि काइ : हें
गोसावीचि बोलावें : आणि : गोसावीचि परिसावें :॥:

७४ डखलेया सीक्षापण :॥:

एकुदीस डखले चरणवीहीरियां धोत्रें धों गेले : धुतलीं :
घडिया केलिया : वाळत घातली : मग म्हणीतलें : ये
चरणवीहीराचें उदक उपसिजे : परि : तेतुलेंचि असे :
ऐसें आइकीजे : तें काइ साचें कीं लटिकें : ऐसें पाहों पां :
म्हणौनि : पाणीं उपसों नीगाले : परि पाणी तेतुलेंचि : मग
धोत्रें धडिया केलिया : आले : सर्वझें म्हणीतलें : उसीरू कां
लाविला¹²⁴ : मागील वृतांत सांघीतलें : सर्वझें म्हणीतलें :
ऐसा अंतु न पाहिजे कीं :॥:

७५ सूकर रोखू हरणें :॥:

एकु दीस गोसावीयांसि उदेयाचा पूजावस्वर जालेया नंतरें
मग कान्हारळेया कडे वीहरणा बीजें केलें : ते माहादेनि
रायें तें रान राखीलें होतें : तेथौनि सोरू निगाला : मग तो
गोसावीयांसि उजू आला : भक्तजन भीयाले : ते पळाले :
सोरू गोसावीया जवळि आला : गोसावी अवलोकीला :

he said. (According to Hiraïsa, "Hatha yoga stops the aging process. It prevents untimely death. It makes wrinkles and gray hair disappear.")

Salivahan said, "Lord Gosavi, I don't know how to listen to this, so how could I possibly tell about it? You alone should tell about this, and you alone should listen to it."

74 HE CHIDES DAKHALE.

One day Dakhale went to the Charan Well to wash the dhotis.[105] After he had washed them, folded them, and set them out to dry, he said, "I have heard that if you draw water from this Charan Well, there is still just as much there. Let's see if that is true or false." So he drew some water from the well, but the level of the water remained just the same. Then he folded the dhotis and came back.

"What took so long, Dakhale?" asked the omniscient one. Dakhale told him what had happened. The omniscient one said, "Don't test the limits this way."[106]

75 HE PACIFIES A BOAR.

After his morning worship service one day, the Gosavi went wandering toward Kanharale.[107] The forest there was protected by King Mahadev. A wild boar emerged from it, running straight toward the Gosavi. The devotees got frightened and ran away. The wild boar approached the Gosavi. The Gosavi looked at it. Its anger subsided, and it left.

रोखू हरला : आणि तो तेथौनि गेला : मग भक्तजन आले :
गोसावी इखीत हास्य केलें : सर्वज्ञें म्हणीतलें : काइ गा :
भियालेति : ना जी : आम्हीं पापीये : आम्ही गोसावीयांतें
सांडौनि पळालों : गोसावीयां असतां आम्हांसि काइ होत
असे : मग कान्हराळा नावेक आसन : गोसावी बीढारा
बीजें केलें : भक्तजनीं बाइसां पूढें सांघीतलें : मग बाइसीं
म्हणीतलें : पोरें हो : बाबातें कैसें सांडौनि गेलेति :॥:

७६ अदंडीनाथा सामर्थ्य कथन :॥:

एकु दीस : उदेयाचा पूजावस्वर जालेया नंतरें गोसावी मग
मळेयासि बीजें केलें : सर्वज्ञें म्हणीतलें : हा अदंडीनाथाचा
मळा : हां जी : अदंडीनाथु म्हणीजे काइ : सर्वज्ञें म्हणीतलें :
अदंडीनाथु नावें महात्मे : ते मळा होते : ते आले : तीय
दीउनि अवकाळीं अवची फुलो फळो लागलीया१२५ :
रायाचिय राणीयचा मळा१२६ : माळिण सेव घालुं गेली :
राणीयां पूसिलें : हां गे : जीये नाही : जीये काळी : तीये फुले
फळे ये१२७ कैची गे : माळिणी म्हणीतलें : आमचिय मळां :
जे पुरूखु एक आले१२८ : ते आले तीय दीउनि अवकालिं
फुलें फुलेति असति : राणीयां म्हणीतलें : तेयांतें म्हणीजे :
रायाची राणी तुमचेया दरिसना यों१२९ : तेयां पुसिलें :
तेहीं म्हणीतलें : एती तरि१३० येतु कां : मग येकें परियळीं

Then the devotees came back. The Gosavi laughed gently and said, "What happened? Did you get frightened?" "We are sinners, Lord," they replied. "We ran away, abandoning the Gosavi. What harm could have come to us with the Gosavi there?"

Then, after sitting for a little while at Kanharale, the Gosavi went to their lodgings. The devotees told Baïse what had happened. Then Baïse said, "Children, how could you have gone away and left Baba behind?"

76   HE TELLS ABOUT
ADANDINATH'S POWERS.

After the morning worship service one day, the Gosavi went to a garden. "This is Adandinath's garden," said the omniscient one. "What does 'Adandinath' mean, Lord?" The omniscient one replied, "A Mahatma named Adandinath was in the garden. From the day he arrived, everything began to bear flowers and fruits out of season. It was the queen's garden. When the Gardener woman went to give the queen her regular allotment of produce, the queen asked, 'How can these flowers and fruits be growing at a time when they normally don't?'

"The Gardener woman said, 'A holy man has come to our garden.[108] From the day he arrived, the flowers have been blooming out of season.' The queen said, 'Ask him, "May the queen come for your *darśan?*"' The Gardener woman asked him. 'If she wants to, let her come,' he replied.

पूजाद्रव्यें : एकू अनाचा : आली : पुजा केली : जेंउ वाढिलें :
तांबूळ दीधलें : ऐसें प्रत्येहीं करीति : मग आपण जेविति :
रावो क्षेपणिकाचां सीरव्य : तो तैसाची भगती करी :
क्षेपणिकीं म्हणीतलें : राया तुं आमची सेवा करिसी : तरी
स्त्रीपुरूखा एकूचि धर्मू होआवा कीं : मग रायें पूसीलें : तुम्ही
म्हणे : पुरूखाचेया दरिसना जात असा : जावों : तरि आतां
न वचा : तेयां म्हणीतलें : आम्हां तेयांचें दरूसन घेतलेंया
वाचौनि जेवण नाहीं : तरि जा : आणि काइ : म्हणौनि
दारवंठेया पासौनि मळावेव्ही राखणे घातली१३१ : माळीणितें
पुसों धाडीलें : म्हणावें आजि रायें निर्वडि थोर केली असे :
एसें पुसावें : गेलीं : पुसीलें : तेंहीं म्हणीतलें : एती तरि एवों
एइल : गेली : दरिसन घेतलें : पुजा केली : आली : रायें
पुसीलें : दरिसना न वचाचि तें काइ : ना : गेलों होतों :
हें नव्हे : आतांचि आलों : राखत होते ते बोलावीलें : मग
तेयांसि कोपों लागला : एक म्हणति : आम्हीं देखोंचि ना :
एक म्हणति : देखों : परि : कांहीं करवेना : मग म्हणीतलें :
पुरुखु सामर्थ्यवंतु असति : तेणें क्षेपणीकापूढें सांघीतलें :
तेहीं म्हणीतलें : राणियतें पूसा : ते आम्हासि उघाणी
करीती : राणियेतें पुसीलें : तुमचे गुरु आमचीया गुरुसीं

"She came there then, with puja materials on one tray and food on another. She did puja to him, served him a meal, and gave him pan. She did this every day, and afterward she would have her own meal.

"The king was a devoted disciple of a certain Jain ascetic. The ascetic said, 'You serve me, oh King, but a husband and wife should have the same dharma.'

"So the king asked his wife, 'I've heard that you go for *darśan* of a holy man.' 'May I go there?' 'Stop going there now.' She said, 'I won't eat a meal unless I have had his *darśan.*' 'Go, then. Why not?' said the king.

"He stationed guards from the doorway all the way to the garden. The queen sent the Gardener woman to ask the holy man: 'Ask him by saying, "Today the king has taken great precautions."'

"The Gardener woman went and asked. The holy man said, 'If she wants to come, she will be able to get here.'

"The queen went there, took his *darśan,* and did puja to him. When she returned, the king asked, 'What happened about never going for *darśan?*' 'I went there,' she replied. 'Don't you see? I just got back.'

"The king summoned the men who had been standing guard, and he began to interrogate them angrily. Some of them said, 'We didn't see her at all.' Others said, 'We saw her, but we couldn't do anything about it.'

"So the king said, 'That holy man is powerful.' He told the Jain ascetic what had happened. The ascetic said, 'Ask the queen if he will have a debate with me.' The king asked the queen, 'Will your guru have a debate with my guru?' 'He'll be glad to do that, she said.'

उघाणी करीति ः तीया म्हणीतलें ः आधीं करीति ः
सभामंडपीं बैसों घातलें ः तेयांतें बोलाउं धाडीलें ः गेले ः रायें
तुमतें बोलाविलें असे ः न येतीचि ः तेहीं म्हणीतलें ः होए
भीयाले ः राणीये अभिमान पडीला ः जा ऐसें म्हणावें ः तुमतें
राणियां बोलावीलें असे ः ऐसे सांघीतलें ः आणि आले ः
पाइं पाउवा ऐसे आले ः मग उघाणीं प्रवर्तली ः अदंडीनाथीं
क्षेपणिक अडीले ः इतुलेनि तेहीं म्हणीतलें ः हें काइ ः हें
वाग्जाळ१३२ म्हणा ः आतां तुम्हीं आम्हीं सामर्थ्यें भांडो ः
हो कां ः आमची अमृत कूपीं स्वर्गींचें अमृत आणिल ः तेहीं
म्हणीतलें ः आम्हीं आणुं नेदुं ः हो कां ः कूपी अभिमंत्रुनि
परिहरिली ः गेली ः अमृत घेउनि येत होती ः अदंडीनाथीं
डावीये पाइंची पाउ भिड भिड म्हणौनि परिहरिली ः अमृत
कुंडीहुनि अमृत घेउनि येत होतीं ः पाउ तीसि ठुस ठुस करि
लागली ः आणि कुपी फुटली ः तिन कोरें जालीं ः तें तीं ठाइं
पडलीं ः ते तिन तीर्थें जाली ः चरण वीहीरा ः उपरकूंडी ः
सिवाळें ः सर्वज्ञें म्हणीतलें ः भटाचार्या मागां पुडती
अदंडीनाथें वेद प्रतिष्ठीले ः ते निर्वतले ः तेयाचें देउळ हें ः॥ः

"Seats were arranged in the assembly hall. The king sent men to invite Adandinath. They went there and said, 'The king has invited you,' but Adandinath would not come. The Jain ascetic said, 'That's right. He's afraid.'

"The queen was embarrassed. She said to them, 'Go to him and say, "The queen has invited you."' They said that, and he came there, wearing his wooden clogs.

"Then the debate got started. Adandinath defeated the Jain ascetic. Immediately the ascetic said, 'What is this but a web of words? Now let's you and I compete with our powers.' 'All right.' 'My nectar vial will bring nectar from heaven.' 'I will prevent it from bringing it,' said Adandinath. 'All right.'

"The ascetic said mantras over the vial and made it disappear. It went and got filled at the pool of nectar. As it was coming back filled with nectar, Adandinath made the clog from his left foot disappear, saying, 'Hit it! Hit it!' As the vial came back, the clog crashed into it, and the vial shattered. It broke into three pieces that fell in three different places and formed three *tīrthas:* Charan Well, Uparkundi, and Shivale."[109]

The omniscient one said: "Adandinath was the next one after Bhatacharya to support the Vedas. He departed, and this is his temple."

७७ तथा भिड शब्द कथन :॥:

अदंडीनाथाचें देउळ : पसिमामूखु : ते निवर्तले : मग राणियां
तेयाची प्रतीष्ठा केली : देउळ केलें१३३ : गोसावी तेथ बीजें
केलें : सर्वज्ञें म्हणीतलें : हे अदंडीनाथाची गुंफा गा : एथ
अद्यापि भिड भिड ऐसा शब्दु वर्ते : तेथ जोगी येति : भिड
भिड ऐसा पुरुखाचा शब्दु आंतुलि कडौनि होए : मग :
जाति: भक्तजनें आइकों ठाकलीं :॥:

७८ कुइ रामा सिधि निषेध :॥:

गोसावीयांसि दुपाहाराचा पूजावस्वर : आरोगणा : पहुड :
उपहुड : मग वीलिचां वेळीं मढावरि बीजें केलें : सरिसे
भक्तजन असति : गोसावी दीशा अवलोकिलीया : मग
म्हणीतलें : हां गा : भागेया : हें कोण कोण गांव : तेहीं
म्हणीतलें : हें इटखेडें१३४ : हें मातखेडें : हे सीउर : हें
लासौर : एथ कुइ राम नांवें पुरूखु असति : तेयासि अनंता
सीधि प्रगटति : सर्वज्ञें म्हणीतलें : रीधी सीधी : तीया
कैसीया गा : कांबळेयाची मोट बांधौनि पाणिया आंतु
घालिति आणि तरंगती जी : देउळा आंतु कोंडिजति :
आणि बाहिरि दीसति : हें चेटक कार्यें : पाणियांतु तरंगति
हें पवनकार्यें : हीराइसा : सरांडेयाचीए दांडीए केळाचीया

77   AND HE TELLS ABOUT
THE WORDS "HIT IT!"

Adandinath's temple faces west. After he departed, the
queen built the temple to memorialize him.[110]

The Gosavi went there and said, "This is Adandinath's cell.
Still today the words 'Hit it! Hit it!' can be heard here. Yogis
come here. They hear the holy man's words, 'Hit it! Hit it!'
coming from inside, and then they go away."

The devotees stayed there to listen.

78   HE REPUDIATES
KUÏRAM'S YOGIC POWERS.

After the Gosavi's midday worship service, he ate his meal,
went to sleep, and woke up. Then in the evening went up
on top of the hermitage. The devotees were with him. The
Gosavi looked around in all directions and said, "Hey, my
fellows, what villages are these?"

"This is Itkhede," they said. "This is Matkhede. This is
Siür. This is Lasaur.[111] There is a holy man there named
Kuïram. He exhibits limitless yogic powers." "What kind
of yogic powers are they?" asked the omniscient one. "When
people bundle him up in a blanket and throw him into water,
he floats, Lord. They lock him up in a temple and then see
him outside it." "These are magic tricks. He floats on the
water by controlling his breath."

(According to Hiraïsa, the devotees said: "He goes along on
a mat of banana leaves in a palanquin made of millet stalks,

267

पानाचा पुडवा : लेकुरुवांचीए खांदी जाति : हें पवन-
कार्य :॥छ॥: गोसावी म्हणीतलें : कलियोगीं कें असति :
विद्या : शोधु : कलियोगीं विद्या होवावीया : मा : तदजनिता
रिधि सीधि : तिया कैचीया : कलियुगीं वीद्या असे : तरि
पुरुखु सृष्टसंहारीं समर्थ नव्हे : तथा वीद्यावंत पुरुषु :॥छ॥:
उध्वरित चेति आणि बाहीरि सांडति : सर्वज़ें म्हणीतलें : ते
ऊध्वरिते ते ऐसे कीं : अर्धे उर्ध्व रिगों नेदीति : पवनें भीतरि
जारठ करीति : मग भीतरि आणिक देह होए : तेयसि
छेदभेद नाहीं¹³⁵ : जैसें नारिएळ : मुळें पाणी पीयें : तें वरूतें
जाए : भितरि पाणी : नारिएळ होए : बाहीरि करटें निबर
होए : तेया छेदभेद न प्रभवति¹³⁶ :॥:

७९ विद्यावंता भेटी :॥:

एकु दीस : गोसावीयांसि उदेयाचा पूजावसर जालेया
नंतरें मग गोसावी आसनीं उपविष्ट असति : वीद्यावंतु
जोगीयाचेनि वेखें दरिसना आले : गोसावी आदरू केला :
बैसौं घातलें : बाइ : तुमतें कांहीं भातुकें असे : ना : नाहीं :
बाबा : कवडे हाटवटीये पाठवीले : रांधवण हाटीचें खाजें
आणवीलें : तेयाचें पात्र भरिलें : आपूलेनि श्रीकरें टीळा

carried on children's shoulders." "This is done by breath control.") The Gosavi said, "Where is esoteric knowledge in the Kali yuga?"[112] (Research: "If esoteric knowledge is to come into existence in the Kali yuga, where are the yogic powers that give rise to it? In the Kali yuga there is esoteric knowledge, but no holy man—or, no holy man with esoteric knowledge—has the ability to destroy the world.")[113]

"He retains his semen and ejaculates it," said the devotees. The omniscient one replied, "What those men who retain their semen do is to prevent half of it from going up. They use their breath to dry it inside themselves. Then another body comes into being inside them, and it is indestructible.[114] It is like a coconut tree: it drinks water with its roots. The water goes upward on the inside and forms a coconut. Its outer shell gets so hard that it cannot be cut or broken."[115]

79   HE MEETS A MAN WHO HAS ESOTERIC KNOWLEDGE.

After his morning worship service one day, the Gosavi was sitting in his place. A man who had esoteric knowledge came for *darśan,* dressed as a yogi. The Gosavi treated him with respect. He put down something for him to sit on and asked Baïse, "My woman, is there any food?" "No, there isn't, Baba."

He sent someone to the market with some money to bring a snack from the prepared-food stalls. The man's plate was filled with food. The Gosavi put a mark on the man's

लाविला : तांबूळ देवविलें : मग गोसावी अनोझा दीधली :
गेले : मग बाइसीं पूसिलें : बाबा : हे कोण : बाइ : हे
द्वारावतीकार श्री चांगदेवो राउळाचे अनूग्रहीत : मग
हाटवटीये : सर्वें सिमोरी : हातीं सूनेयाचे जवट : बोर :
गाजर : उळि कांदे : ऐसे मांगतां डखलां देखिलें : बाइसीं
डखले तेलां धाडीले होते : ते हांसत हांसत आले : बाइ
ऐसे आमचे गोसावी जेयांसि मानु केला : ते हाटवटीये ऐसे
देखीले : म्हणौनि : अवघें सांघीतलें : सर्वज्ञें म्हणीतलें : ऐसें
न म्हणीजे ॥छ॥ तयावरि लुइपाईची गोष्टि सांघितली :॥:

८० ब्रह्मसानी विखस्तंबन :॥:

गोसावी अचाट वेधवती स्वीकरीली : राजीके तेतुके
गोसावीयांचेया दरिसना एति : साळिवाहान : पाल्हा डांगी-
या : हे मुख्य करूनि हे अवचे राजीके आणिकही लोकू ये :
एकू माहादेश्रमू आणि ब्रह्मसान हे वांचैनि येर आवघांचि
लोकू दरिसना येति : तेहीं म्हणीतलें : हे रायातेंहीं
आदिकरूनि वेधीति : मां च्यान्ही वीखें मेळउनि१३७ फोडी
केलिया : मग तीया फोडी : पुजा : आपूलीया सीष्या हातीं

forehead with his own holy hand, and he had someone give him pan. Then the Gosavi gave the man leave to go, and he left.

Afterward Baïse asked, "Who was that man, Baba?" "That was a disciple of Shri Cangdev Raül of Dvaravati, my woman."

Later Dakhale saw the man again, in the market. He had a snot-nosed girl with him. He was holding onto a pair of dogs and asking for jujube fruits, carrots, and green onions. Baïse had sent Dakhale to get some oil. He came back laughing and told her all about it. "My woman," he said, "that's what the man our Gosavi treated with respect is like. I saw that man in the market, looking like this."

The omniscient one said, "Don't talk that way."[116] On that subject, he told the story of Luïpaï.[117]

80 HE STOPS BRAHMASAN'S POISON.

The Gosavi took on an extraordinary power of attraction. All the courtiers, especially Salivahan and Palha Dangiya, were coming for his *darsan,* and other people came too. Everyone except Mahadashram and Brahmasan was coming for his *darsan.*[118] The two of them said, "He is even attracting royalty and people like that." So they cut bits of betel nut and mixed them with four kinds of poison, then sent the pieces of betel nut with their disciple as an offering.

When it was time for the Gosavi's morning worship service, Baïse prepared a seat for him on the veranda. The

धाडीलिया : गोसावीयांसि उदयाचा पूजावसर असे :
बाइसीं पटीसाळे आसन केलें : तेहीं पुजा केली : श्रीकरीं
फोडी दीधलिया : गोसावीया अवलोकीलीया : मग श्रीमुखीं
घातलीया : तेहीं वीडिया करूनि दीधलिया : मग ते नीघाले :
दीस दोनी : तथा तिन गेलेयां : मग तेंहीं सीरव्याते पुसीलें :
तुम्ही गेलेति : मां : काइ केलें : तेंहीं अवघें सांघीतलें : अया :
अया : ईश्वर पुरुषु होति : दृष्टी पूढां वीरव न व्हाये :॥ः

८१ तथा वीरवशक्तिस्वीकारू :॥ः

ब्रह्मसानी सीरव्यातें म्हणीतलें : आतां तुम्हीं जावें : मां :
आंधारीं आसन घालावें : आपुलेनि हातें फोडी श्रीमुखीं
घालाविया : गेले : गोसावीयांसि उदयाचां पूजावसर होता :
भितरि आसन रचिलें : मां : पूजा केली : मग आपुलेनि
हातें : श्रीमुखीं फोडी घातलिया : वीडिया करूनि दीधलिया :
हीराइसा : मग सर्वज्ञें म्हणीतलें : आतां तुमचें कार्ये जालें :
आतां तुम्हीं जा :॥छ॥ः मग ते गेले : मग तांबूळ प्रत्येजीलें :
भागवतीं मागीतलें : गोसावी नेदीतिचि : सर्वज्ञें म्हणीतलें :
बाइ : हे तांबूळ पुरा : हीराइसा : बाइ : हें एके ठाइं पुरा :
तथा : बाइ वाटें आणा :॥छ॥ः अवघा उगाळु हीरवा जाला :
तिन तांबुळें पुरवीलीं : तिसरेया तांबुळाची फोडी भागवतां

disciple did puja to him and handed him the pieces of betel nut. The Gosavi looked at them, then put them into his holy mouth. The disciple made rolls of pan and gave them to him, then left.

After two or three days had passed, Mahadashram and Brahmasan asked their disciple, "What did you do when you went there?" He told them everything. "Oh, no!" they said. "Oh, no! He is a divine holy man. Poison cannot survive his gaze."

81   AND HE ACCEPTS THE POWER OF POISON.

Brahmasan said to the disciple, "Go there now and arrange a seat for him in the dark. Put the pieces of betel nut into his holy mouth with your own hand."

The disciple went there while the Gosavi's morning worship service was going on. The disciple prepared a seat for him inside and then did puja to him. Then, with his own hand, the disciple put the pieces of betel nut into the Gosavi's holy mouth. He made rolls of pan and gave them to him. (According to Hiraïsa, then the omniscient one said, "You have done what you came to do now. Now go away.") He left.

Then the Gosavi spat out the pan. Bhagavat asked for it.[119] The Gosavi refused to give it to him. The omniscient one said to Baïse, "My woman, bury this pan somewhere." (Or, "Bring a bowl, my woman.") The whole mass that he had spat out turned green. He had her bury three rolls of pan. He gave

दीधली^{१३८} : तेंहीं तोंडीं घातलीं : तेयांसि हटाटुनि जरू
आला : बाइसीं एकांतीं पुसीलें : ते इषित कपोळीं स्वेदबींदु
आले : श्रीमूर्तीं घामैली : नेत्र आलोहीत जांले : वांति
स्वीकरीली : श्रीमूर्तींवरि अणिया अणिया ऐसिया आलिया :
सर्वज्ञें म्हणीतलें : बाइ : एथ वीषप्रळो जाला : ते दीसी
मल्हारवसीए अवस्थान माझारिले खणी : दीस तिन
जालें :॥: गोसावीयांसि दुधाची आरोगण होए : ऐसें गजबजों
लागलीं : काइ करूं : बाबा : सर्वज्ञें म्हणीतलें कांहीं करूं
नैए : एका एक विरोधियें : च्याऱ्ही वीखें मिळवीली असति :
बासनाग : काळकूट : मेणा : खडिया : तथा : रगतसिंगीं :
बाइ : प्राणिया बहुत दीस : सात : तथा दीस तिन : प्राणिया
जचतु असे : तरि आतां काइ करावें बाबा : बाइ हें ऐसेंचि
नव्हे : एकातें निमित्य करिल : राष्ट्रा बोलु लावील : मग :
जाइल^{१३९} : तरि तीन दी येकांतु देया : मग मल्हार वसैए
अवस्थान : दुधाची आरोगण : मागौतें गोसावीयांसि
चतुर्विधांचां मढीं अवस्थान जालें^{१४०} :॥:

८२ दखलेयां चांगदेवोभटातें
श्रीदत्तात्रयोप्रभूचेया दरीसना पाठवणें^{१४१} :॥:

एकु दीस : उदेयाचां पूजावसर जालेया नंतरें गोसावी
श्रीदत्तात्रय प्रभूची महीमा निरोपीत होते : डखला आणि
चांगदेवो भटीं म्हणीतलें : जी जी : आम्हां श्रीदत्तात्रय प्रभुचें

Bhagavat a piece of betel nut from the third pan roll. Bhagavat put it in his mouth and came down with a raging fever.

Baïse asked the Gosavi in private what was going on. A few beads of perspiration formed on his cheeks. His holy body became covered with sweat. His eyes turned red, he accepted vomiting, and a rash broke out on his holy body. The omniscient one said, "I have been poisoned, my woman." That day, the Gosavi went and stayed for three days in the middle section of the Malharvasai.[120] He drank milk for his meals.

Baïse became frightened. "What can we do, Baba?" she asked. The omniscient one said, "You can't do anything. They have mixed together four kinds of poison that work against one another: *bāsnāg*, *kāḷkūṭ*, *meṇā*, and *khaḍiyā* (or, *ragatsingī*). They torment a person for a long time, my woman—seven days (or, three days)." "So what is to be done now, Baba?" "My woman, this is not the end for me. I will make someone the excuse, I will blame the whole country, and then I will go away.[121] Just leave me alone for three days."

He stayed in the Malharvasai, drinking milk for his meals. Later the Gosavi returned to the Chaturvidh hermitage and stayed there.

82 HE SENDS DAKHALE AND CANGDEVBHAT FOR *DARŚAN* OF SHRI DATTATREYA PRABHU.

After his morning worship service one day, the Gosavi was extolling Shri Dattatreya Prabhu. Dakhale and Cangdevbhat said, "Lord, let us have *darśan* of Shri Dattatreya Prabhu."

दर्शन होआवें : तथा : जी जी : आम्हीं जाउनि : तरि :
भेटति : हीराइसा : सर्वज्ञें म्हणीतलें : जाल : तरि : होइल :
आतां ऐसेंचि निगा^{१९२} : सर्वज्ञें म्हणीतलें : ऐसेंयांचि निगावें :
गाउनि गावां जावें : उपेणें न करावें : संबंधियाचिया ठायां
न वचावें^{१९३} : एकी भिक्षा न करावी : घाटां खालि भेटति :
ते नव्हति : घाटां वरि भेटति ते हों म्हणति : परि ते नव्हति :
पर्वतावरि भेटति ते नव्हों म्हणति : परि ते होती^{१९४} : मग ते
नीगाले : देवगीरी गेले : चोलिया तोड घेउनि : डाउलवाडीये
गेले : संबंधीयासि भेटले : मग : निगाले : चांगदेवो भटीं
म्हणीतलें : हें काइ : डखले हो : गोसावी वारिलें तेंचि केलें :
आतां काइ दर्शन होइल : आतां चाला : माघौतें आले :
दंडवतें घातलीं : श्रीचरणा लागले : मागील सांघीतलें : सर्वज्ञें
म्हणीतलें : श्रीदत्तात्रय प्रभूचें दर्शन : कां गा होइल : हें
अमोघ दर्शन :॥:

८३ उपाधीया म्हणीयें :॥:

बाइसीं म्हणीतलें : बटीका जाए कां : पत्र शाक घेउनि ए :
आणि गेले : घेउनि आले : बटीका : जाए पां : तेल घेउनि
ए : गेले : आणिलें^{१९५} : कांहीं बटिका विसरलियें : सांबार
घेउनि ए : सर्वज्ञें म्हणीतलें : हां गा : म्हातारीएचें काइ : एका

(Or, "Lord, if we go where he is, will we meet him?)

(According to Hiraïsa, the omniscient one said, "If you go, that will happen. Just set out, right now.")[122] The omniscient one said, "Simply set out. Go from village to village. Do not stop anywhere for the night. Do not go to the homes of your relatives. Do not beg food from only one house.[123] The person you meet at the foot of the pass is not him.[124] The person you meet at the top of the pass claims to be him but is not. The person you meet at the top of the mountain claims not to be him but is."[125]

They set out and went to Devgiri. They got a sari blouse and a bracelet and proceeded to Daülvadi.[126] There they met one of their relatives and then left. Cangdevbhat said, "What is this, Dakhale? We have done exactly what the Gosavi forbade us to do. How will we get *darśan* now? Come on, now."

They came back. They prostrated themselves, touched the Gosavi's holy feet, and told him what had happened. The omniscient one said, "Why would you get to have *darśan* of Shri Dattatreya Prabhu? It is an unfailingly effective *darśan*."[127]

83   AN ERRAND FOR UPADHYE.

Baïse said, "Batika, will you go and get some leafy vegetables?" He went and got some. "Batika, go and get some oil." He went and brought it. "I've forgotten something, Batika. Go and get some spices."

वींचूकी आणा : मा यासि लावा : मा हा ऐसाचि असैल :
एके वेळ न पुरे : सर्वज्ञें म्हणितलें : बटिका : जाल : तरि :
काइ जीः बाइसाचें म्हणीये तें गोसावीयांचें कीं¹⁴⁶ : सर्वज्ञें
म्हणीतलें : कां गा जाल : जी जी : बाबा : बाइसें कोपती :॥:

८४ देवां होणें :॥:

एकू दीस : वीळींचां वेळीं : पाटाउ पाग : काळी धारी :
तथा लोहवी धारी : ते पाग पुढें धाटेया वेढिली : आंगणीं
भक्तजनांसि खेळु मांडीला : उघडी श्रीमूर्ति : एरातें
डवचीति : एरातें डवचिती : ऐसा खेळ सरे ना : वीळचेयां
पूजावस्वराची वेळ जाली : बाइसें पूजावसराची आइति
करिती : तेविचि म्हणति : पुरें कीजो बाबा :॥: गोसावी
उगेचि : नाइकतीया भाखा¹⁴⁷ : खेळतचि असति : मग
बाइसीं म्हणितलें : आरे बटिकुरें हो : पुरों दीया ना : बाबासि
उसीरू होतु असे : सर्वज्ञें म्हणीतलें : पुरे गा : बाइसें कोपती :
मग पटिसाळेवरि वोलणियेवरि बाहीरवासू होता : तो
गोसावी प्रावर्ण केला : आसनीं बैसले : सर्वज्ञें म्हणीतलें :
बाइ : या : आतां हें देवों जालें¹⁴⁸ : मग गोसावीयांसि
पूजावस्वर : वीळचा पूजावस्वर :॥:

The omniscient one said, "What is going on with the old lady? Bring a scorpion and put it on him, and he'll remain just the same. Isn't once enough?"

"Will you go, Batika?" the omniscient one asked him. "Why not, Lord? An errand for Baïse is one for the Gosavi!" "Why will you go?" asked the omniscient one. "Baïse will get angry if I don't, Baba."

84   HE BECOMES A GOD.

One evening he was wearing a silk turban with a black border (or, a red border) and a strip of cloth wrapped on the front of it. His holy body was bare. He was playing a game in the courtyard with the devotees. They were tickling one another again and again.

The game went on and on, until eventually it was time for the evening worship service. As Baïse made the preparations for it, she said, "Please stop, Baba."

The Gosavi made no reply. He kept on playing as if he had not heard. Then Baïse said, "Come on, boys! Won't you stop? It's getting late for Baba."

The omniscient one said, "That's enough! Baïse will get angry." Then the Gosavi put on his outer garment, which was hanging on the clothesline on the veranda. He sat down in his place and said to Baïse, "Come on, my woman. Now I have become a god."

Then the Gosavi's evening worship service took place.

८५ संतोषा भेटि : स्तीति :॥:

एकु दीस : गोसावीयांसि उदेयांचा पुजावस्वर जालेयानंतरें
अणकैचेया लेणेया बीजें केलें : अनकएपासीला लींगाचिए
देउळिए : तेथ संतोष¹⁴⁹ बैसले होते : सर्वज्ञें म्हणीतलें :
महात्मे हो : एथ असिजे : असों सुखें संतोखें : नगरीं भिक्षा
कीजे : कीजे सुखें संतोखें : हीराइसा : एथचि नींद्रा कीजे :
कीजे सुखें संतोखें :॥छ॥: सर्वज्ञें म्हणीतलें : तरि : तुम्हीं
संतोखु म्हणा : आणि स्तीति जाली : गोसावीयांसि अनेकैयें
आसन : मग बीढारा बीजें केलें : गोसावीयां सरिसे तेहीं
आले : मग गोसावीयांचां ठाइं असों लागले : एकाचेनि मतें :
पासवडी एथेंचि :॥:

८६ तथा अशसू करणें :॥:

गोसावीयां पासि असतां तेयाचे जोगी म्हणति : आम्हांपासि
ये ना : आम्हांसी अदेशू न करी : आम्हांसि सीख्या न करि :
भिक्षे गेले होते : तेंहीं काठी खापरी कंथा हीरतली : संतोखें
म्हणीतलें : मासीं अशसू घाला पां : तेंहीं म्हणीतलें : हो कां :
मग संतोषें अशसू घालुं आदरिला : तेयाची ते सोए नेणति :

85 HE MEETS SANTOSH,
WHO GOES INTO A TRANCE.

After his morning worship service one day, the Gosavi went
to Anakai's cave. Santosh was sitting in a linga shrine near
the cave. The omniscient one said, "When you stay here,
Mahatma, stay with happiness and satisfaction. When you
beg in the town for food, beg with happiness and satisfaction." (According to Hiraïsa, "When you sleep here, sleep
with happiness and satisfaction.") "Then," said the omniscient one, "you'll be called Santosh."* And Santosh went
into a trance.

After sitting for a while in the Anakai cave, the Gosavi went
to their lodgings. Santosh came too, along with the Gosavi.
Then he began to stay with the Gosavi.

(In the view of some, this is where the episode of the thick
shawl should be placed.[128])

86 AND SANTOSH DOES ASANAS.

While he was with the Gosavi, Santosh's yogi companions
would say, "You don't come to us. You don't salute us in the
manner of yogis. You don't perform *sikṣā* to us." Once, when
he went to beg for food, they snatched away his stick, his clay
begging bowl, and his patchwork quilt. Santosh said, "Do
some asanas with me!" "All right," they said.

Then Santosh started doing asanas. They did not know
how to do them the way he did. "What is going on?" they

---

* "Satisfaction."

तेहीं म्हणीतलें : हें काइ गा : हा साक्षात गोरक्षनाथु :
म्हणौनि : पुजा केली : चंदन लावीलें : टिळा केला : माळ :
तांबुल : खाजेया पात्र भरिलें : आलें : गोसावीया अनुकारें
पुसीलें : संतोषा हें काइ : जी जी : मीयां म्हणीतलें : मासीं
अशसू घाला : पां जी जी : जोगरुवें मातली होतीं : माझी
काठी खापरी हीरतली : मागिल सांघितलें : सर्वज्ञें
म्हणीतलें : संतोखा : आपुलें रहस्य आणिकां प्रति प्रगटीजे
ना कीं :॥:

८७ तथा सांडाक्रमुज्ञान१५० :॥:

गोसावीयांसि उदेयाचां पूजावस्वर जालेयानंतरें पटिसाळे
आसन : तवं इंद्राइ नाम माहात्मे : गोसावीयाचेया दरिसना
आले : आदेशू केला : सिक्षा केली : गोसावीयांतें पूसीलें :
हां जी : यांसि संतोखु ऐसें नांव काइसें : सर्वज्ञें म्हणीतलें :
संतोखा : जोगी काइ म्हणतु असे : हीराइसा : संतोखा :
काइ म्हणतु असति : इंद्राइ माहात्मे :॥छ॥: तेहीं म्हणीतलें :
जी जी : म्हणत असति : तरि : म्हणत असति : आणि काइ :
सर्वज्ञें म्हणीतलें : तुमतें धरिती : मारिती : काठी खापरी
हीरति : कंथा हीरति : जी जी : हीरति तरि हीरति : आणि

asked. "This is Gorakshanath himself, in person," they decided, and so they did puja to him. They anointed him with sandalwood paste. They put a mark on his forehead and a garland around his neck. They gave him pan to chew, and they filled a bowl with food for him.

When he returned, the Gosavi questioned him with a gesture. "What is going on, Santosh?" He told him what had happened. "I said, 'Do some asanas with me.' Those lousy yogis were insolent, Lord. They snatched away my stick and my begging bowl."

The omniscient one said, "Santosh, do not reveal your secret to others."[129]

87 AND HIS KNOWLEDGE OF PENETRATING THE CHAKRAS.

When the Gosavi was sitting on the veranda after his morning worship service, a Mahatma named Indraï came for his *darśan*.[130] He saluted the Gosavi in the manner of yogis and performed *sikṣā* to him. "Lord," he asked the Gosavi, "why is he named Santosh?"

The omniscient one said, "Santosh, what is the yogi saying?" (According to Hiraïsa, "Santosh, what is Indraï Mahatma saying?") "Lord," he replied, "if he is saying something, he is saying it. What of it?"

The omniscient one said, "They grabbed you. They beat you. They snatched away your stick and your begging bowl. They snatched away your patchwork quilt." "Lord, if they snatched them away, they snatched them away. What of it?"

काइ : सर्वज्ञें म्हणीतलें : तुम्ही तवं सांडाक्रमू जाणा ना१५१ :
हीराइसा : तथा ऐसें नव्हे कीं : तुमतें सांडाक्रमू पुसती : तो :
तरि : तुम्ही नेणा ॥छ॥: नेणों तरि नेणों : आणि काइ : सर्वज्ञें
म्हणीतलें : म्हणौनिचि संतोखू कीं :॥:

८८ शांतिबाइसा भेटी :॥: अस्तिति१५२ :॥:

शांति बाइसें तियें वसुमतिकारें : तेया नांव माइबाइसें : लेकु
फीटला : एकाइसे हातरितलें : जसमाइसां कावरें लागलें :
वरैता नावडति : सासुसासूरेया ना पढीयेति : तेंहीं दवडीली :
मग माइबाइसीं आपणेयांपासि आणिलीं : माइबाइसें थोर
दुखियें जालीं : द्वारावतिए लोकू निगाला : माइबाइसीं
म्हणीतलें : जाइन द्वारावतीएसि : एकी पाठीसीं बांधैन :
एकी पोटेसीं बांधैन : मा : रिगैन गोमतीए मध्यें : ऐसें
म्हणोनि निगालीं : पैठणसि आली : सारंगपंडित सोएरे :
भासे : तेयासि भेटलीं : मागील आवघें सांघीतलें : तेवींचि
दुख करिति : सारंगपंडितीं म्हणीतलें : तुम्ही द्वारावतिए
जाल : तरि : एळापुरा वरौनि जा : तेथ आमुचे गोसावी
असति : तयाचें दरिसन घेया : तुमचें दुख जाइल : आणि :
याचें कावरें जाइल : मग द्वारावतीये जा : निगाली : एळापुरां

The omniscient one said, "But you don't know how to penetrate all the chakras." (Or, according to Hiraïsa, "Isn't it like this: if they ask you how to penetrate all the chakras, you don't know?") "If I don't know, I don't know. What of it?" "*That's* why you are Santosh," said the omniscient one.

88 HE MEETS SHANTIBAÏSE, AND SHE GOES INTO A TRANCE.

Shantibaïse was from Vasumati.[131] Her original name was Maïbaïse. Her son died. Her daughter Ekaïse was widowed, and her daughter Jasamaïse went mad. Jasamaïse's husband did not like her, and her mother-in-law and father-in-law did not love her. They threw her out, and Maïbaïse took her in. Maïbaïse was desolate.

When a group of pilgrims was leaving for Dvaravati, Maïbaïse set out too, saying, "I'll go to Dvaravati. I'll tie one of them to my back and the other to my front, and I'll jump into the Gomati river."

Sarangpandit was a relative of hers, a nephew. When she reached Paithan,* she met him. Tearfully she told him everything that had happened.

Sarangpandit said, "If you are going to Dvaravati, go by way of Yelapur. Our Gosavi is there. If you take his *darsan,* your grief will come to an end and her madness will go away. Then go to Dvaravati after that." She set out and came to Yelapur.

---

* Pratishthan.

आली : गोसावी वीहरणाहुनि बीजें केलें : बाइसीं पटिसाळे
पाटसरेयावरि आसन केलें : गोसावी आसनीं बैसले :
शांतिबाइसें एकाइसें : जसमाइसें आलीं : शांतीबाइसीं
दंडवतें घातली : श्रीचरणा लागली : हीराइसा : नारीएळ
दरिसना केलें :॥छ॥ः मग मागें एकाइसें : पुढें जसमाइसें :
ऐसीं बैसली : जी जी : माझेया पुत्राचे ऐसेचि हात : ऐसेचि
डोळे : ऐसेंचि तोंड : दुख करूं लागली : मागील अवघी गोष्टि
सांघीतली : सांघति तवं तवं दुख करिति : सर्वज्ञें म्हणीतलें :
पांडेनि एथ धाडीलें : जी जी : माझेया पुत्राचे ऐसेचि
हात : ऐसेचि डोळे : ऐसेचि तोंड : सर्वज्ञें म्हणीतलें :
दुःख न करा : दुख म्हणजे पाप : दुखातवं नरक : होति :
सोनेयाची फळी : तथा : प्रतीमां पोटीं बांधौनि पुरांतु रीगों
नये कीं : जन्ही जाली सोनेयांची : तऱ्हीं बुडळील कीं : बाइ
दुख न करा : बाइसीं चरणक्षाळण केलें : तेयांसि चरणोदक
दीधलें : तेहीं आपुलें आणि तेयांचेंहीं जसमाइसांवरि घातलें :
मग : पूजावस्वर जाला : तोही पाहिला : मग ताट केलें :
आरोगणा जाली : तेयांसि प्रसादु दीधला : मग तियें बीढारा
गेलीं : वीळीचेया पुजावस्वरा आली : मागुतें चरणोदक :
जसमाइसातें पाजीलें : माथेयावरि घातलें : पुजावस्वर
पाहीला : मग बीढारा गेली : उदीयांचि आली : दंडवतें

When the Gosavi returned from wandering, Baïse prepared a seat for him on a stone block on the veranda. The Gosavi was sitting there when Shantibaïse, Ekaïse, and Jasamaïse arrived. Shantibaïse prostrated herself and touched his holy feet. (According to Hiraïsa, she gave him a coconut as an offering.) Then she sat down, with Ekaïse behind her and Jasamaïse in front. "Lord, my son's hands looked just like yours, his eyes looked just like yours, his mouth looked just like yours," she said, and she began to cry. She told him everything that had happened. All the while she was telling him, she kept on crying.

The omniscient one asked, "Did Pande send you here?" "Yes, Lord. My son's hands looked just like yours. His eyes looked just like yours. His mouth looked just like yours." "Do not cry," said the omniscient one. "Crying is a sin. Crying causes you to go to hell. If a plank (or, image) is made of gold, you cannot tie it to your stomach and enter a flood. It may be made of gold, but it will still sink. Do not cry, my woman."

Baïse washed his feet and gave her the foot water. She poured it over herself and over her Jasamaïse. When the Gosavi's worship service took place, they watched that as well. Then Baïse prepared a plate of food. The Gosavi ate his meal, and they were given *prasād*. Afterward they went to their lodgings.

They came back for the evening worship service. Again she gave Jasamaïse foot water to drink, and poured some over her head. They watched the worship service, then went to their lodgings.

287

घातलीं : श्रीचरणा लागली : गोसावी पुसीलें : एथौनि
गेलेयां रात्रीं आलें होतें : नाहीं जी : सर्वज्ञें म्हणीतलें : आतां
तें न ए : गेले हो१५३ : बाइ आतां द्वारावतीयें जा ना१५४ :
तेहीं म्हणीतलें : ना जी : आमची द्वारावती हेचि : आमचा
कान्हेया एथेंचि भेटला : सर्वज्ञें म्हणीतलें : यांतें सासूरेया
पाठवा ना : जी जी : हे सासुसासूरेया नावडे : वरिता नावडे :
तेहीं दवडीली जी : सर्वज्ञें म्हणीतलें : आतां आवडती :
हीराइसा : आतां तेयाची वाट पाहातें असति :॥छ॥: मग
बीढारा गेली : एकाइसातें म्हणीतलें : एकाइ तुं बोळवीत
जाये कां : तीयें म्हणति : मज न वचवे : उदीयाचि दरिसना
आलीं : सांघीतलें : जी जी : एइतें म्हणीतलें : तुं बोळवीत
जाए : ना : हे म्हणे : मज न वचवे : सर्वज्ञें म्हणीतलें : बाइ :
यांसि एथ असतां जें होइल : तेंचि तुम्हांतें तेथ असतां
होइल : जा : मग : निगाली : पैठणा गेली : सारंगपंडितीं :
चिरचोळी : तोडु : घोडें : जनु : दीधला : गेलीं : तवं तीयें
वाट पाहातें होतीं : हरखैली : आदरू केला : तेयांसि भांगार
केलें : असों लागलीं : तव गोसावीया जवळी शांतीबाइसा
स्तीती जाली१५५ : तीएचि दीसीं तेथ१५६ एकाइसें

Early the next morning they returned. They prostrated themselves and touched the Gosavi's holy feet. "Did it come on her at night, after you left here?" he asked. "No, Lord." The omniscient one said, "Now it won't come on her anymore. It is gone.[132] Go ahead and go to Dvaravati now, my woman."[133] "No, Lord," said Shantibaïse. "*This* is our Dvaravati. *This* is where we have met our Kanha."*

The omniscient one said, "Send her back to her in-laws' house." "But, Lord, her mother-in-law and father-in-law don't like her, and her husband doesn't like her either. They threw her out, Lord." The omniscient one said, "They will like her now." (According to Hiraïsa, "Now they are eagerly waiting for her.")

They returned to their lodgings. Shantibaïse asked Ekaïse, "Ekaï, will you take her there?" "I can't leave here," she said.

Early the next morning, they came for *darśan*. Shantibaïse told the Gosavi, "Lord, I asked Eï, 'You'll go with her, won't you?' and she said, 'I can't leave here.'" The omniscient one said to Ekaïse, "My woman, whatever happens to your mother here will happen to you there. Go."

So they left. When they reached Paithan, Sarangpandit gave them each a sari, a blouse, and a bracelet. He gave them horses, and also a man to accompany them. When they reached Jasamaïse's village, her in-laws were waiting for them, delighted. They treated them with respect and had gold jewelry made for them. They stayed on there.

One day Shantibaïse went into a trance in the Gosavi's presence. That same day Ekaïse went into a trance as she sat

---

* Krishna.

देव्हारेयावरि बैसलीं होतीं : स्तीति जाली : तियें म्हणति :
इचें पिसें गेलें : तें इस लागलें : मग : एकाइसें म्हणति :
मातें बोलावा : तियें म्हणति : सेतासीवाराचे दीस : आम्ही
आरावोंना : राहा साउला घेउनि : मग : बोळवीत येउनि :
न ह्यातींचि : निगाली : सर्वझें म्हणीतलें : बाइ : तुमची :
येई : येत असे : तेंहीं म्हणीतलें : जी जी : माझीं लेंकरूवें :
माझी काढीली रेघ नोलांडीति : पैठणा इतुकेयां आली :
बाइ : तुमची : एइ : आलीया : ना जी : मियां तेयांतें
म्हणीतलें असे : मि येइन : कां कोण्ही नीरोपू धाडीन : तेयां
वांचौनि न यावें : यळापुर पातली : दारवठां पातलीं :
बाइ : तुमची : येइ : आली : मां : मग दंडवतें घातलीं :
श्रीचरणा लागलीं : हें काइ गे येइ : मीं गोसावीयांसि ऐसें
म्हणें : तुं कैसी आलिसी : एकाइसीं मागील अवघें सांची-
तलें : शांतीबाइसीं म्हणीतलें : हो गे आइ : तीये दीसींचि
मज अस्तिति जाली : ऐसी सांगों लागलीं : गोसावी बाहिर
वीहरणा बीजें केलें : वीहीरीचिये कडे : बोरी बाबूळ होती :
सर्वझें म्हणीतलें : बाइ : मासू दीसू बोरी बाबूळ सींपा१५७ :
शांति नगरीचा पाटु दीजैल : शांतिबाइसें नांव ठैवीजैल :
सातां जन्मा१५८ : कर्माचें एथौनि१५९ हस्तोदक घेइजैल :
हो कां जी : उदयांसीचि उठीति : वोलिया पडदणिया बोरी

at the shrine in Jasamaïse's in-laws' house. They said, "That one's madness has gone away, and this one has caught it."

"Take me back there," said Ekaïse. "It is the harvest season," they replied. "We don't have time. Stay here. We'll give you a sari, and we'll take you back later." But she refused to stay. She left.

The omniscient one said to Shantibaïse, "My woman, your Eï is coming." Shantibaïse replied, "Lord, my children will not cross a line I have drawn."

When Ekaïse reached Paithan, he said, "My woman, your Eï is almost here." "No, Lord. I told her, 'Don't come back unless I come for you or send someone to get you.'"

Ekaïse reached Yelapur. She arrived at the doorway. "My woman, your Eï has arrived!" Ekaïse prostrated herself and touched his holy feet. Her mother said, "What is this, Eï? I was telling the Gosavi you wouldn't do this. How can you have come here?"

Ekaïse told her everything that had happened. Shantibaïse said, "That's right, my dear. I went into a trance that same day." And she began telling her about it.

The Gosavi went out to wander. Near the well, there were jujube and babul trees. The omniscient one said, "My woman, sprinkle water on the jujube and babul trees for a month or so. You will be given the throne of the city of peace. You will be given the name Shantibaïse.* I will take away seven lifetimes' worth of your karma."[134] "All right, Lord."

For a month or so, she got up very early in the morning and sprinkled the jujube and babul trees with a wet bathing

---

* "Shanti" means "peace."

बाबुळ सींपति : ऐसें मास दीसा केलें : सर्वज्ञें म्हणीतलें :
म्हातारीएचीं कर्में जाळीता१६० न जळति : तें एथौनि
नाशिलीं : मग सर्वज्ञें म्हणीतलें : बाइ : तुम्हीं परमेश्वरपुरा
जा : हो कां जी :॥: सर्वज्ञें म्हणीतलें : गाउनि गांवां जावें :
उपेणें न करावें : संबंधां न वचावें : नवें वस्त्र न नेसावें :॥:
येकि भीक्षा नेघावी१६१ : इंद्रीयार्थ रसू न सेवावा : श्रीप्रभूंचां
प्रसादु तीं बोटांतु सामाये : इतुला घेयावा : वायां जाइल तरि
देयावा : पर तेथचीं चीमुटी मिठा नेघावी१६२ : ऐसा वीधि
वीहीला : मग तेहीं म्हणीतलें : जी जी : माझी : एइ :
गोसावीयांसि लागे हो : सर्वज्ञें म्हणीतलें : बाइ : तुमचीयें
येइसि एथौनि तल्हातें सावली कीजैल१६३ : उगीचि ठेली :
सर्वज्ञें म्हणीतलें : तुमचीए एइसि तरि देमतीएचा सांघातु
हो : होकां जी : सर्वज्ञें म्हणीतलें : देमती या : आलीं :
देमती : तुम्ही यांसि सांघातु दीया : हो : हो कां जी : मग तेंहीं
सांघातु दीधला : दंडवतें घातलीं : श्रीचरणा लागली :
मग पुसीलें : पैठणेंहुनि जावों जी : सर्वज्ञें म्हणीतलें : जा :
पांडेयासि भेटा : तें तुमचें निमीत्य : निमीत्य मानिजे :॥:
निगाली : पैठणा गेलीं : सारंगपंडितांसी भेटलीं : गोष्टी
करितां वेळु गेला : मग भीक्षेसि नीगालीं : सारंगपंडित
राहावीत होते : पांडेया : एकी भिक्षा : गोसावी वारीली
असे : पाठीं जेउं बैसलीं : तुप वाढुं बैसलें : पांडेया : इंद्रियार्थ

cloth. The omniscient one said, "The old lady's karma could not be burned up, but I have destroyed it."

Later the omniscient one said, "Go to Parameshvarpur, my woman." "All right, Lord." The omniscient one said, "Go from village to village. Do not stay a second night in any one place. Do not go to the homes of your relatives. Do not wear new clothes. Do not beg food from only one house. Do not eat tasty foods for the sake of your senses.[135] Take as much of Shriprabhu's *prasād* as you can pick up with three fingers. If it is going to go to waste, give it away. But do not take a pinch of his salt."[136]

After he gave her these instructions, she said, "Lord Gosavi, my Eï is attached to you." The omniscient one said, "My woman, I will shade your Eï with the palm of my hand." She stood there silently. The omniscient one said, "Your Eï will have Demati for company." "All right, Lord."

"Demati," said the omniscient one, "come here." She came there. "Demati, keep her company." "Yes. All right, Lord." After that, she kept her company.

Shantibaïse prostrated herself and touched his holy feet. Then she asked, "May I go by way of Paithan, Lord?" The omniscient one said, "Go and meet Pande. He was the cause of your meeting me. You should respect the cause."[137]

She left. She went to Paithan and met Sarangpandit. They conversed for some time, and then she set out to go begging. Sarangpandit was trying to prevent her from going out. "Pande," she said, "the Gosavi has forbidden me to beg food from just one house." Afterward, when she sat down to eat her meal, he was about to serve her ghee. "Pande," she said, "I am forbidden to eat tasty foods for the sake of my senses."

रसू वारिला असे : नवें वस्त्र देवों आदरिलें : पांडेया : नवें
वस्त्र वारिलें असे : एरी दीसीं राहावीत होते : पांडेया : उपेणें
न करावें : म्हणीतलें असे : मग परमेश्वरपुरा गेलीं : बहुत दी :
श्रीप्रभुची सेवा केली :॥ः

८९ नाथोबा करवि टिळा जानिवें पुरवणें :॥ः

एकु दीस : गोसावीयांसि उदेयाचां पूजावसर जालेया नंतरें
गोसावी अनकैये कडे बीजें केलें : आसन : जवळी नाथोबा
होते१६४ : सर्वज्ञें म्हणीतलें : बटिका टिळा कां लावा : आणि
जानिवें कां घाला : तेहीं म्हणीतलें : जी जी : भिक्षा यावीया :
सर्वज्ञें म्हणीतलें : जा : टिळा : जानिवें : अनकेये पुरुनि
बैसा : गेले : टिळा : जानिवें पुरिलें : तेथ बैसीले : गोसावी
बीढारा बीजें केलें : हीराइसा : भटो तुम्ही एथचि राहा : मग
बैसले :॥छ॥ः नावेक जालें : आणि टिळा जानवें काढूं पाति :
ऐसें वेळा च्यारि गेले : मग काढीलें : टिळा लावीला : जानिवें
घातलें : तवं देवतेसि परियेलु आला : तेंहीं म्हणीतलें :

294

When he tried to give her new clothes, she said, "Pande, I am forbidden to wear new clothes." When he tried to prevent her from leaving the next day, she said, "Pande, he told me not to stay a second night in any one place."

She went to Parameshvarpur and served Shriprabhu for a long time.

89   HE HAS NATHOBA BURY
HIS FOREHEAD MARK
AND SHOULDER THREAD.

After his morning worship service one day, the Gosavi went and sat at the Anakai cave. Nathoba was nearby.[138] The omniscient one said, "Batika, why do you put a mark on your forehead? And why do you wear a thread over your shoulder?" "So that people will give me food when I go begging, Lord," he replied.

The omniscient one said, "Go and bury your forehead mark and shoulder thread near the Anakai cave, then sit there." He went there, buried his forehead mark and his shoulder thread, then sat there. The Gosavi returned to their lodgings. (According to Hiraïsa, he said, "You stay right here, Bhat." So he sat there.)

After a little while, he had the urge to dig up his forehead mark and his shoulder thread. He went there four times, and then finally he dug it up.

When he had put the mark on his forehead and the thread over his shoulder, some people came with a tray of food for the goddess. "Will you take some, Bhat?" they asked. "I will,"

भटो घेयाल : घेयाले : तांबटवटीए तुप : घेतलें : आले :
गोसावीयांसि दृष्टपूत केलें : सर्वज्ञें म्हणीतलें : पोरा :
वेळोवेळां टिळया जानिवेयापासि कां जासि :॥:

९० चांगदेवो भटा स्मरणें वंध्य दिवसु कथन१६५ :॥:

परमेश्वरपुरोनि आलेयां : चांगदेवो भटा गांवां जाणें नाहीं :
माहाजनीं विनवीलें : जी जी : चांगोसी बहुत दीस लागले :
यांची माता खंति करीत असे : सर्वज्ञें म्हणीतलें : बटिका :
जा : भेटौनि या : हो कां जी : निगाले : गोसावी अनुवर्जन
केलें१६६ : सर्वज्ञें म्हणीतलें : बटिका : हें परमेश्वरपुरा गेलें :
तै या१६७ सांघातें आलेति : तेथौनि मागौतें आलें : तै सवेंचि
आलेति : आतां गांवां जात असा : तरि हे तुम्हांसि आठवैल :
जी जी : सर्वज्ञें म्हणीतलें : बटिका : दीसामध्यें हें वेळा
दाहावीस आठवीजे : वेळा दाहावीस नाहीं : तरि : वेळा
सात पांच आठवीजे : सात पांच नाहीं तरि दोन च्यारि
वेळां आठवीजे : दोन च्यारि वेळ नाहीं तरि एक दोन तरि
वेळ आठवीजे : एकदोन वेळ नाहीं तरि एकु तरि वेळ
आठवीजे१६८ : परि दिवसु वंध्यू जावों नेदीजे :॥:

he said, and he took a copper bowl of ghee. He came back and had the Gosavi purify it with his glance.

The omniscient one said, "My child, why do you go back time and again to your forehead mark and shoulder thread?"[139]

90 HE TELLS CANGDEVBHAT THAT A DAY WITHOUT RECOLLECTION IS WASTED.

When they returned from Parameshvarpur, Cangdevbhat did not go home to his village. The leading citizens of the village appealed to the Gosavi: "Lord, Cango has been away for a long time. His mother is distressed." The omniscient one said, "Go there, Batika. Go and meet her, then come back." "All right, Lord," he said, and he set out.

The Gosavi went to see him off. "Batika," said the omniscient one, "when I went to Parameshvarpur, you came along with me. When I returned from there, you came along. Now that you are going to your village, will you think of me?" "Yes, Lord." The omniscient one said, "Think of me ten or twenty times a day, Batika. If not ten or twenty times, then think of me five or seven times. If not five or seven times, then think of me two or four times. If not two or four times, then think of me at least once or twice. If not once or twice, then think of me at least once. But do not let a day go to waste."[140]

९१ दायांबा भेटि : स्तीति :॥:

एकु दीस दायांबा गोसावीयांचेया दरिसनां आले : दंडवतें
घातलीं : श्रीचरणा लागले : बैसले : स्तिति जाली : मग
असंनिधानीं दायांबा : अखंड दुख करीतचि असति : दुखें
डोळे कुहीजले : एकु दीस दायांबाए स्वप्न देखीलें : गोसावी
स्वप्निं आले : ते रडों लागले : भोजेया : तुम्हीं दुख कां करीत
असा : पोरें हो : हें केंहीं गेलें असे : हे सर्वत्र असे : यळापुरीं
जालें : तें तुम्हां आठवत असे : हें वीसेखें यळापुरीं असे :॥:

९२ वीष्णूभटा परियेळु :॥:

वीष्णुभट ते भलेतेयाची अप्राप्ति भावीति : एकु दीस
गोसावीयांसि उदेयाचां पूजावस्वर जालेया नंतरें गोसावी
अनकै कडे बीजें केलें : नावेक आसन : मग बीढारा बीजें
केलें : वीष्णुभटातें राहाविलें : सर्वज्ञें म्हणीतलें : भटो : तुम्हीं
एथ राहा : हो कां जी : म्हणौनि राहिले : अणकैये बैसले
होते : तवं देवतेसि परियेळु आला : तेंहीं म्हणीतलें : भटो :
घेयाल : हो कां : घेतलें : तांबवटी तुप घेतलें : आले :
गोसावीयांसि दृष्टपूत केलें : सर्वज्ञें म्हणीतलें : तुम्हीं दीसवडी
अनकैये जा : तुम्हां परियेळु येइल१६९ :॥:

91 HE MEETS DAÏMBA,
WHO GOES INTO A TRANCE.

One day Daïmba came to have *darśan* of the Gosavi. He prostrated himself, touched the holy feet, and sat down. He went into a trance.

Later, in the Gosavi's absence, Daïmba was constantly crying.[141] His eyes got red from crying. One day the Gosavi appeared to him in a dream. Daïmba began to cry. "Why are you crying, Bhoja?"[142] asked the Gosavi. "I have not gone away somewhere, my child. I am everywhere. You are remembering what happened in Yelapur. I am especially present in Yelapur."

92 A TRAY OF FOOD
OFFERINGS FOR VISHNUBHAT.

Vishnubhat used to feel any deprivation intensely.

After the Gosavi's morning worship service one day, the Gosavi went to the Anakai cave. He sat there for a little while, then went to their lodgings. He told Vishnubhat to stay at the cave. "You stay here, Bhat," said the omniscient one. "All right, Lord," said Vishnubhat, and he stayed there.

While he was sitting at the Anakai cave, some people came with a tray of food offerings for the goddess.[143] "Will you take some, Bhat?" they asked. "All right."

He took some, and he took a copper bowl of ghee. He came back and had the Gosavi purify it with his glance. The omniscient one said, "Go to the Anakai cave every day, and you'll get a tray of food offerings."

९३ नागदेवो भटा वेददान :॥:

पदकर नागदेवो भट म्हणति : मज संध्यातुल्य तथा
गायत्रीतुल्य वेद होए : ऐसें मीं गोसावीयांसि मागैन :
दरिसना एति : आणि : वीसरति :॥छ॥: एकु दीस गोसावी
आसनीं उपवीष्ट असति : नागदेवो भट : पासीं बैसले
असति : सर्वज्ञें म्हणीतलें : भटो : एथ कांहीं मागा : जी जी :
संहिताक्रमु यावा : सर्वज्ञें म्हणीतलें : हें होइल : आणिक
कांहीं मागा : जी जी : मज हेंचि होआवें : सर्वज्ञें म्हणीतलें :
हें होइल हो : मग जालें : मग : ते वेद म्हणतचि असति : वेदु
तो तेयांसिचि निगे : मग पदकर नागदेवो भट ऐसें
नांव जालें१७० :॥:

९४ राकेयां लक्ष्मींद्रभटा गंडकोदक प्रसाद ग्रहण :॥:

एकु दीस गोसावीयांसि गुळळा : दंतधावन जालें : पासि
रांके लक्ष्मीधर भट बैसले असति : तेंहीं गंडकोदक भीतरि
घेतलें : सर्वज्ञें म्हणीतले : ऐसें उदक नेघीजे कीं : घृणा
नुपजैल :॥:

93   HE GIVES NAGDEVBHAT
THE ABILITY TO RECITE THE VEDAS.

Nagdevbhat the Reciter would say, "I will ask the Gosavi for
the ability to recite the Vedas as well as I recite the Gayatri
mantra in the *sandhyā* rite."[144] He would come for *darśan,*
but he would forget to ask.

One day the Gosavi was seated in his place, and Nagdevbhat
was sitting nearby. The omniscient one said, "Bhat, ask
me for something." "Lord, enable me to recite the Vedas
correctly." "That will happen," said the omniscient one. "Ask
for something else." "That is the only thing I want, Lord."
"That will happen," said the omniscient one.

It did happen, and then he was always reciting the Vedas.
He was the only one who could recite the Vedas properly, so
he got the name "Nagdevbhat the Reciter."[145]

94   RAKE LAKSHMINDRABHAT TAKES
SPAT-OUT WATER AS *PRASĀD.*

One day the Gosavi rinsed his mouth and cleaned his teeth.[146]
Rake Lakshmindrabhat was sitting nearby. He drank the
spat-out water.

The omniscient one said, "Don't drink such water! Then
you won't get disgusted."[147]

९५ सारंगपंडीती वीनती :॥:

गदोनायेक चहुं रायाचे भांडारी : ते कटकीं धरिले होते :
तेंहीं सारंगपंडितासि निरोपु पाठविला होता : पंडीतो : तुम्हीं
गोसावीयांचेया दरिसना जावें : मा : गोसावीयांतें माझीये
सूटकैयचें वीनवावें : मग सारंगपंडित वीनवावेया आले :
दंडवतें घातलीं : श्रीचरणा लागले : रित हस्त भेटले : बैसले :
मग : वीनवीलें : जी जी : गदोनाएक कटकीं धरिले असति :
मज निरोपु धाडीला : मागील आवघें सांघीतलें : तरि तेया
सूटि करावें जी : सर्वज्ञें म्हणीतलें : तुम्हीं रीतहस्त भेटलेति :
म्हणोनि वरवड जाइल : जीवें सूटति : तथा चुकति¹⁷¹ : हे
लीळा : रामेश्वरबास :॥: छीनपापी : सिंहस्थळीए वरि भेटी :॥:

९६ तथा रितुपें कथन :॥:

एकु दीस : सारंगपंडीत दरिसना नीगाले : तेव्हळि गदोनायकें
पुसिलें : सारंगपंडीतो : सीध जात असा : ना : एळापुरा :
गोसावीयांचेया दरिसना जात असों : मग गदोनाएकीं दोनि
फळें दीधलीं : यें गोसावीयांसि दरिसन करावीं : आणि याचें
नांव पुसावें : सारंगपंडित आले : दंडवतें घातलीं : श्रीचरणा
लागले : फळें दरिसना केलीं : बैसले : मागील वृतांत
सांघीतलें : गोसावी श्रीकरीं फळें घेतलीं : सर्वज्ञें म्हणीतलें :

302

95   SARANGPANDIT MAKES A REQUEST.

Gadonayak was the treasurer for four kings.[148] When he was detained in the capital, he sent a message to Sarangpandit: "Pandit, go for *darśan* of the Gosavi and ask him to get me released."

So Sarangpandit came to make the request. He prostrated himself and touched the holy feet, but he came empty-handed to meet him. Sarangpandit sat down and made the request: "Lord, Gadonayak has been detained in the capital. He sent me a message." He told him everything that had happened. "So please get him released, Lord." The omniscient one said, "You have come empty-handed to meet me, and so he will just barely escape. He will get out alive."[149]

According to Rameshvarbas, this *līlā* took place at Chhinnapap.[150] They met above Chhinnasthali.

96   AND HE TELLS
ABOUT *RITUPE* FRUITS.

One day when Sarangpandit set out to have *darśan,* Gadonayak asked him, "Sarangpandit, are you going straight there?" "Yes, I'm going to Yelapur to have *darśan* of the Gosavi."

Then Gadonayak gave him two pieces of fruit. "Give these to the Gosavi as an offering and ask him what their name is."

When Sarangpandit arrived, he prostrated himself and touched the holy feet. He gave the fruits as an offering, then sat down and told the Gosavi what had happened.

यें काइसेयाचीं फळें गा : कव्हणी काइसेयाची म्हणें :
कव्हणी काइसेयाची म्हणे : ऐसीं आपुलालिया परीं नांवें ठेउं
लागले : सर्वज्ञें म्हणीतलें : यें रितुपें :॥:

९७ तथा केलें रोटी दर्शन :॥:

दुसरा दीसीं सारंगपंडिती रोटीया केलिया : केलें आणिलीं :
तुप केलें : रोटिया जेविलें : उरलीं केलें रोटिया ते
गोसावीयांसि दरिसन केलें : सर्वज्ञें म्हणीतलें : पांडेया :
एथ उसीटें केलें रोटी : संपादीत असा : उगेचि राहिले :॥:

९८ गोपाळपंडीता पारधी नीरोपणें :॥:

गोसावीयांसि उदेयाचा पूजावस्वर जालेया नंतरें
पटिसाळेवरि बाइसीं आसन केलें : मग आसनीं बैसले
असति : गोपाळपंडित ते रायाचे वक्ते : बरवें बोलों
जाणति : गोसावीयाचेया दरिसना आले : सरिसे सारंगपंडित
आले असति : दंडवतें घातलीं : श्रीचरणा लागले : बैसले :
सर्वज्ञें म्हणीतलें : पांडेया : हे कोण : जी जी : माझे मैत्र : हे
शास्त्रवक्ते : हे बरवें बोलों जाणति : सर्वज्ञें म्हणीतलें ऐसें

The Gosavi took the fruits in his holy hand. "What kind of fruit are these?" asked the omniscient one. Some said one kind, some said another: they began naming them in their own ways. The omniscient one said, "These are *ritupe* fruits."

97 AND HE RECEIVES BANANAS AND ROTIS AS AN OFFERING.

The next day Sarangpandit made rotis, got some bananas, and made ghee. He ate some of the rotis and gave the rest of the bananas and rotis to the Gosavi as an offering. The omniscient one said, "Pande, are you giving me leftover bananas and rotis?"

Sarangpandit kept silent.

98 HE DESCRIBES HUNTING TO GOPALPANDIT.

After the Gosavi's morning worship service, Baïse prepared a seat on the veranda. The Gosavi was sitting on it.

Gopalpandit was the king's orator. He was an eloquent speaker. He came for *darśan* of the Gosavi, and Sarangpandit came with him. They prostrated themselves to the Gosavi and touched his holy feet, then sat down.

The omniscient one asked, "Who is this, Pande?" "This is my friend, Lord. He expounds the scriptures. He is an eloquent speaker." The omniscient one asked, "Does he do it from books, or extemporaneously?" "He speaks extemporaneously, Lord."[151] "Say something!"

कांहीं ग्रंथाधार : कीं : उबेणें : जी जी : उबेणें ऐसें
बोलति^{१७२} : बोला पां : जाड : वाड : कोड : कवतीक :
सावजाचा उठावा : धुरेचा लाठु : ऐसें बोलिलें : मग आपण
निरोपिले : सावजाचा यावा बोलिले : तेव्हळि राजकें मुख्य
करूनि जेतुलेही आले होते : तेतुकेयांसि लेणें फोडुनि
पळावें : ऐसा भयानकु अवतरवीला : भक्तजन भीयाले :
मग धुरेचा लाठु बोलतां : राजकेयांचिया कडीदबेया वरि
हात पडीले : बाइसें मुक्षकरूनि अवघेयां भगतिजनां लाठु
उपजला^{१७३} : ऐसा वीररसू अवतरवीला : तेहीं म्हणीतलें :
जी जी : हें परीसों नेणीजे : मा बोलौनि काइ :॥:

९९ राकेया लक्ष्मींद्र भटा
गंडशोदक प्रसाद नीराकरण^{१७४} :॥:

पस्यात पाहारीं गोसावी परिश्रया बीजें केलें : मा : आले :
आसनीं बैसलें : बाइसीं सीळीका वोळगवीलीया :
जिव्हामळ फेडिले : तें गंडकोदक लक्ष्मीधर भट सांडुं गेले :
तेथ तो प्रसाद घेतला : आले : सर्वज्ञें म्हणतीलें : ऐसे उदक
नेघीजे कीं : हीराइसा : जी जी : घेतलिया काइ होइल :

306

Gopalpandit spoke: "Hunting for elephants or wild boars; hunting for tigers; hunting for antelopes or deer; hunting for rabbits, partridges, or fish. The wild beast's attack. The hero's valor."

Then the Gosavi himself expounded on the subject. When he told about the attack of the wild beast, he evoked the sentiment of terror so vividly that everyone who had come, especially the royal servants, felt like bursting out of the cave and running away. The devotees were frightened too. Then, when he told about the hero's valor, he evoked the heroic sentiment so vividly that the royal servants' hands went to the weapons at their waists, and Baïse and all the other devotees felt courageous.

Gopalpandit said, "Lord, I don't know how to listen to this, so how could I possibly speak it?"

99 HE FORBIDS RAKE LAKSHMINDRABHAT TO TAKE SPAT-OUT WATER AS *PRASĀD*.

Before sunrise, the Gosavi went out to defecate. He came back and sat in his place. Baïse offered him twigs, and he scraped his tongue. Lakshmindrabhat went to toss out the water the Gosavi had spat out. Instead of throwing it out, he drank it as *prasād*.[152]

When Lakshmindrabhat returned, the Gosavi said, "Don't drink such water."

(According to Hiraïsa, Lakshmindrabhat asked: "Lord, what will happen if I drink it?" The omniscient one said,

सर्वज्ञें म्हणीतलें : हाड गदलेया पापा पुरश्ररण होए : ना हा :
घृणा जरि उपनली : तरि नाहीं : तेया परतें पाप होए :॥:

१०० शंकर लेणा बोनें कथन :॥:

एकु दीस : गोसावीयांसि उदयाचा पूजावस्वर जालेया नंतरें
शंकरलेणासि बीजें केलें : तेथ आसन : बाइसीं म्हणीतलें :
बाबा : हे केसना दारवठा : हें केसणें लेणें : सर्वज्ञें म्हणीतलें :
या देउळासि : तथा : देवतेसि : हातिवरि बोनें ये : अवचे-
यासि वीस्मो जाला :॥:

१०१ पेखणें कथन :॥:

एकु दीस : गोसावीयांसि उदयाचा पूजावस्वर जालेया नंतरें
गोसावी माणिकेश्वरा बीजें केलें : लेणेयाचां द्वारीं उभें
राहीले : तथा माणिकेश्वरीं चौकीं आसन : सर्वज्ञें म्हणीतलें :
एथ पेखणें होत होतें : तें चोरीं नेलें : नीवरें वीवरें नेलें :
अवचेयासि वीस्मयो जाला :॥:

१०२ माहादेवो राज्यप्रशंसा :॥:

एकु दीस : राज्यधर्मांचिया गोष्टी निगालीया : माहादेओ
राजा राज्यधर्म जाणे : कान्हर देवो आस्तिक : रामदेवो
निपरवस :॥:

"It will expiate sins that are nailed into your bones." "I see."
"But not if you get disgusted. That will cause a worse sin.")

100 HE TELLS ABOUT THE FOOD OFFERINGS AT THE SHANKAR CAVE.

After his morning worship service one day, the Gosavi went
and sat at Shankar cave.[153]

Baïse said, "Baba, what a big doorway this is! What a big
cave this is!" The omniscient one said, "Food offerings used
to come to this temple (or, to this god) on an elephant."

Everyone was amazed.

101 HE TELLS ABOUT DANCING.

After his morning worship service one day, the Gosavi went
to the Manikeshvar cave-temple. The Gosavi stood at the
door of the cave (or, he sat in the central hall of the Manikeshvar temple) and said, "Dancers used to perform here.
Thieves abducted them and carried them off through the
tunnels and underground passages."

Everyone was amazed.

102 HE PRAISES MAHADEV'S RULE.

One day the Gosavi talked about the duties of rulers: "King
Mahadev knows the duties of a ruler. Kanhardev was orthodox. Ramdev is harsh."

१०३ इंद्राइ सांडाक्रमु जाणति :॥:

एकु दीस : गोसावीयांसि उदयाचां पूजावस्वर जालेया नंतरें :
गोसावी आसनीं बैसले असति : तवं इंद्राइ माहात्मे आले :
आदेशू केला : सिक्षा केली : बैसले : नावेक होते : मग
नीगाले : भक्तजनीं म्हणीतलें : जी जी : हें काइ जाणति :
सर्वज्ञें म्हणीतलें : इंद्रा जोगी : सांडाक्रमु जाणे :॥:

१०४ राजादरिसन स्वीकार :॥:

राजके अवघेचि कटकौनि गोसावीयाचेया दरिसना एति :
माहादेवो रावो सभामंडपासि आला : तवं नावा रूपाचा
येकूही सभामंडपीं नाहीं : तेव्हळि कोपुनि माहादेनि रायें
पुसिले : हां गा : जो जीये वोळगीचा तो तीयें वोळगीं न
देखों : तुम्हीं अवघे के जातां : तेहीं म्हणीतलें : नाभियें देसी :
तरि सांधौनि : सांधा ना : यळापुरीं जे पुरूखु असति :
तेयाचेया दर्शना जात असों : तेयां नांव काइ : ना : श्री
चांगदेवो राउळ : गोसावी : इतुलेनि वेधु संचरला : तरि
आम्हांसि तेयांचें दरिसन कराल : हो कां : पाल्हा डांगिया
सांघों आला : जी जी : गोसावीयाचेया दरिसना रावो येत
असे : गोसावी स्विकरिलें :॥:

103 INDRAÏ KNOWS HOW TO PENETRATE ALL THE CHAKRAS.

After his morning worship service one day, the Gosavi was sitting in his place.[154] Indraï Mahatma arrived, saluted the Gosavi in the manner of yogis, and performed *sikṣā* to him. After sitting there for a little while, he left.

The devotees said, "What knowledge does he have, Lord?" The omniscient one said, "The yogi Indra knows how to penetrate all the chakras."

104 HE ALLOWS THE KING TO COME FOR *DARŚAN*.

All the royal servants were coming from the capital for *darśan* of the Gosavi. When King Mahadev came to the assembly hall, not a single member of the assembly was there.

King Mahadev got angry and asked, "Hey! Where do you all go? Not one of you has reported for duty." "If you promise us immunity, we will tell you," they replied. "Tell me." "We go for *darśan* of the holy man who is at Yelapur." "What is his name?" "Shri Cangdev Raül Gosavi."

With that, the king felt a powerful attraction. "Will you arrange for me to have his *darśan,* then?" "All right."

Palha Dangiya came to tell the Gosavi, "Lord, the king is coming for your *darśan.*"

The Gosavi agreed.

१०५ तथा गमन :॥:

एकु दीस रायें आइत केली : गोसावीयाचेया दरिसना
निगाला : तवं पाटाचा हाति पडिला१७५ : तो अपशकुन
जाला : म्हणौनि : परतला : तथा प्रतिविला : पाल्हा डांगीया
आला : तेणें सांघितलें : जी जी : रोवो येत होता : तवं
हाती पडिला : मग रावो परतला : एकु दीस : मागौता
रावो नीगाला : तवं पाउसू पडिला : मग मागौता परतला :
तिसरिये वेळे : रावो निगालाचि : सर्वज्ञें म्हणितलें : बाइ :
माहादेवो पात्र : एथीचेया दर्शना एइल : राज्य संपादील :
आपण सेवक होउनि वर्तैल : बाइसीं म्हणितलें : हो कां :
बाबा : सर्वज्ञें म्हणितलें : पोरें हो : तरि तुम्हीं रिगों नल्हा१७६ :
बाइसीं म्हणितलें : नको बाबा : सर्वज्ञें म्हणितलें : तो दीवसू
एथेंनि निल : तुम्हीं आपुली आइत करा : बाइसीं अवघीं
आइत केली : गोसावी निगालें :॥:

१०६ तथा वार्ताप्रसंगे :॥:

परशरामबास :॥: मातखेडा वसति : रामेश्वरबास :॥: इटखेडा
वसति जाली : गोसावी आसनीं बैसले असति : बाइसें
उदकपात्र भरूं गेली : दही दूध वीकूं गेलीया होतिया : तीया
लवकरि आलीया१७७ : तवं पाणिवथाचिया बाइया पुसों
लागलीया१७८ : हा वो : आजी लवचिकरी आलीयाति :

105 AND THE KING COMES.

One day the king made his preparations and set out for *darśan* of the Gosavi. But the lead elephant fell down.[155] Because of that bad omen, the king turned back.

Palha Dangiya came and told the Gosavi, "Lord, when the king was on his way here, an elephant fell down, and so the king turned back."

Another day, the king set out again. That time it rained, and so he turned back again. The third time, the king set out for real.

The omniscient one said to Baïse, "My woman, Mahadev is an estimable person. He will come for my *darśan,* he will hand over the kingdom to me, and he himself will become my servant." "Is that so, Baba?" asked Baïse. The omniscient one said, "Then, my children, there will be no place left for you." "Oh, no, Baba!" said Baïse. "I will prevent that day from coming," said the omniscient one. "Make preparations for us to leave."

Baïse made all the preparations, and the Gosavi left.

106 AND THEY GET THE NEWS.

(According to Parasharambas, the Gosavi stayed overnight in Matkhede. According to Rameshvarbas, he stayed overnight in Itkhede.)

While the Gosavi was sitting in his place, Baïse went to fill a pot with water. The dairy women who had gone to sell yogurt and milk had come back early. Other women at the

तें काइ : ना दीसवडी कटका जातां उसीरू लागे : तेहीं
म्हणीतलें : रावो येळपुरा पुरुखाचेया दरीसना आला : ते
दहिदुध तेथेंचि वीकलें : म्हणौनि लवकरि आलों : तें बाइसीं
आइकीलें : तें गोसावीयां पूढां सांघितलें : बाबा : पाणिवथा
बाइला गोष्टी करिती होतीया : मागील वृत्तांत सांघीतलें :
बाबायें म्हणीतलें : तें साच जालें : सर्वज्ञें म्हणीतलें : बाइ :
तुमतें म्हणीतलें कीं दीसु एथेंनि नील :॥:

१०७ रामेश्वरबास : लासौरी वसति :॥:

१०८ परशरामबास : घोगरगांवीं वसति :॥:

१०९ डोमेग्रामीं वसति :॥:

place to get water started asking them, "Why have you come back so early today? Other days, when you go to the capital, you come back later than this."

The dairy women replied, "The king came to Yelapur for *darśan* of a holy man. We sold our yogurt and milk right there, and so we came back early."

Baïse heard this. She told the Gosavi, "Baba, the women at the place to get water were talking..." She told him what they had said. "What you said would happen really did, Baba."

The omniscient one said, "I told you I would prevent that day from coming, my woman."

107   HE STAYS OVERNIGHT IN LASAUR (ACCORDING TO RAMESHVARBAS).

108   HE STAYS OVERNIGHT IN GHOGARGAV (ACCORDING TO PARASHARAMBAS).

109   HE STAYS OVERNIGHT IN DOMBEGRAM.[156]

११० मार्गीं डखलेया सुवर्णहाटि कथन :॥:

मार्गीं वेचु सरला : बाइसीं म्हणीतलें : बाबा वेचावेया नाहीं :
सर्वज्ञें म्हणीतलें : पोफळफोडना गाहाण ठेवा : बाइसीं
म्हणीतलें : ऐसें कीती दी कीजैल : बाबा : सर्वज्ञें म्हणीतलें :
बाइ एथ जरि प्रवृत्ति होए : तरि हे आवघी हाटी सोनेयाची
न किजे : पोरे हो : तुम्हीं नुरा :॥: बाइ : एथ तैसी प्रवृत्ति
नाहीं कीं¹⁷⁹ : मग पोफळफोडना गाहाण ठेवीला : वेचु
आणिला : उपाहारू निफजवीला : आरोगणा जाली : गोसावी
आसनीं बैसले असति : तवं तो वाणिया आला : गोसावीयांतें
देखीलें : दंडवतें घातलीं : श्रीचरणा लागले : मग म्हणीतलें :
पोफळफोडना तो या गोसावीयांचां नाहीं : गोसावीयांचा ठाइं
कांहीं वोळगवीलें : डखलेया या : मा : तो पोफळफोडना घेउनि
या : गेले : आणिला :॥:

१११ यरंडबन उपाहास :॥:

मार्गीं गोसावी बीजें करिताति : तवं पुढें एके वोस गांवीं
येरंडाचें बन देखीलें : मग बाइसीं म्हणीतलें : बाबा हें कवणें
गांवीचें बन : तथा बाबा कैसें बरवें आंबेयाचें बन दीसतु असे :
गोसावी उगोचि राहिले : गांवांपासि बीजें केलें : मग
म्हणीतलें : बाइसाचें बन तें येरंडाचें कीं¹⁸⁰ : इतुलेनि डखले

110   ALONG THE ROAD, HE TELLS
DAKHALE ABOUT A GOLDEN BAZAAR.

Along the road they ran out of provisions. "Baba," said Baïse, "there is no money to buy provisions." "Pawn the betel-nut cutter," replied the omniscient one.[157] "How long can we go on doing this, Baba?" asked Baïse. "My woman," said the omniscient one, "could I not turn this whole bazaar into gold, if I were so inclined? There would be nothing left of you, my children. But I am not so inclined."[158]

So they pawned the betel-nut cutter and got provisions. Baïse prepared some food, and the Gosavi ate his meal.

While the Gosavi was sitting in his place, the Grocer arrived. He saw the Gosavi, prostrated himself, and touched the holy feet. "Doesn't the betel-nut cutter belong to this Gosavi?" he asked.

He made an offering to the Gosavi, then said, "Come along, Dakhale. Come and get the betel-nut cutter."

Dakhale went and got it.

111   A JOKE ABOUT A GROVE
OF CASTOR-OIL PLANTS.

As the Gosavi was traveling along the road, they saw a grove of castor-oil plants in a deserted village up ahead. Baïse said, "Baba, what village's grove is this?" (Or, "Baba, what a lovely mango grove I see!")

The Gosavi kept silent. After they got closer to the village, he said, "Baïse's grove is full of castor-oil plants!"

हासों लागले : कैसें आंबेयाचें बन१९१ : ऐसे वीपलावो
लागले :॥:

११२ श्रीनगर दाखवणें१९२ :॥:

गोसावी श्रीनगरासि बीजें करित असति : तवं बाइसीं
अडवांगौनि बरवे वृक्ष : बरवीं देउळें देखीलीं : मग पुसीलें :
बाबा : हें कवण नगर : सर्वज्ञें म्हणीतलें : बाइ : हें श्रीनगर :॥:

११३ भीलमढीये अवस्थान :॥:

शोध : भीलमढीये आंतु देवतेपूर्वें उत्तरामूख आसन :॥:

११४ स्वयंनामगोपन :॥:

माहादेवो रावो ठाणेया कटकै गेला होता : तो सिंनरा आला :
तेणें म्हणीतलें : हें नगर बरवें : तरि एथ गोसावी असति :
म्हणौनि : पाल्हा डांगेयातें पाहों धाडीलें : ते अवघीं देउळें
पाहुनि : भिलमढीयेसि आला : एथें काइ असति : हा धाकुटा
मढू : म्हणौनि : आपण बाहीरि राहिला : जनु पाहों धाडीला :
दुपाहाराचां पूजावस्वर जालेया नंतरें आरोगण :

With that, Dakhale began to laugh. He began to ridicule her, saying, "What a mango grove!"[159]

112 HE POINTS OUT SHRINAGAR.

As the Gosavi was approaching Shrinagar, Baïse saw some beautiful trees and temples off to the side.[160] "What town is this, Baba?" she asked. "This is Shrinagar, my woman," said the omniscient one.

113 HE STAYS IN THE BHILMADH.

(Research: He sat in the Bhilmadh hermitage facing north, to the east of the god.)

114 HE CONCEALS HIS OWN NAME.

King Mahadev had gone to Thane on a military campaign.[161] He came to Sinnar. Thinking, "This is a beautiful town. Could the Gosavi be here?" he sent Palha Dangiya to take a look.

After looking in all the temples, Palha Dangiya came to the Bhilmadh. "How could he be here?" he thought. "This is a small hermitage." And so he himself stayed outside and sent a man in to look.

The Gosavi was standing next to the sculpted central part of a pillar. His afternoon worship service had been performed, and he had eaten his meal. He had rinsed his

गुळळा : वीडा : पहुड : उपहुड करूनि सोरठिए जाडीचें
प्रावर्ण करूनि : गोसावी मदळसेसीं उभे असति : तवं तेणें
पुसिलें : श्रीचांगदेवो राउळ : गोसावी : एथ असति कीं :
सर्वज्ञें म्हणीतलें : माति : मा इहां कोइ नथी : कांहीं
नथी१८३ : हीराइसा : चांगदेवो राउळ नेणों : बांगदेवो१८४
राउळ नेणों : मातारी एकी छे : ते गावमां हें भिक्षामागन गैइ
छे : हउ इहां अछों१८५ : मग गेला :॥ः

११५ माहादाइसां१८६ : उमाइसां भेटि :॥ः

आबाइसाचा वडिलु पुत्रु : सारंगपाणि होता : तो सरला :
तेणें दुखें रावसगांवीं भटोबासीं गुंफा केली : ते तेथ राहीली :
मग : तेथ दादोस आले : तवं तेथ भट पडिताळावेया
आले१८७ : दादोसातें भीतरि देखीलें : आणि तमले : दारीं
वाहाणा होतिया : तिया बाहीरि टाकीलिया : दादोसीं घोंगडें
घेतलें : जाउनि बाहिरिल वडाखालि बैसले : महदाइसें१८८
उमाइसें तेयातें देखौनि पळाली : भटीं म्हणीतलें१८९ :
निकें करीत असा हो आबै : याचि कारणें तुम्हीं येथें गुंफा
केली कीं : हें काइ नागदेया : दादोस निकें माहात्मे : या
पासौनि आनंदु होए : होइल मां काइ : रूपैयेसि उमैयेसि
होइल : हे तरूणेधारे : याही तरुणीया धारीया : अस्त्रीयेसि
पुरुषापासौनि होइल : आणि काइ : ऐसें कैसें म्हणत
अससि : तरि मज हो कां१९० : मग : जाणों : आबैसीं
म्हणीतलें : होइल :॥ः आतां बोलावीलेयां येती : नां हो :

mouth, chewed pan, gone to sleep, and waked up. A blanket from Saurashtra was draped over his shoulders.

"Is Shri Cangdev Raül Gosavi here?" asked the man. "No," replied the omniscient one,* "there's nobody here. There's nothing here." (According to Hiraïsa, he said: "I don't know about any Cangdev Raül. I don't know about any Bangdev Raül. There was an old woman. She has gone into the village to beg for food. I am here.")[162]

So the man left.

115 HE MEETS MAHADAÏSE AND UMAÏSE.

Abaïse's eldest son, Sarangpani, died. In her grief over that, she stayed in a hermit's cell that Bhatobas built at Ravasgav.

Later Dados came there. When Bhat came to comfort Abaïse, he saw Dados inside and got angry. Dados's sandals were at the door. Bhat threw them out of the compound.

Dados took a blanket and went and sat under a banyan tree outside the compound. Mahadaïse and Umaïse saw him and ran away. Bhat said, "Well done, Abai. That's why you had your hermit's cell built here!" "What do you mean, Nagdev? Dados is a good Mahatma. People get happiness from him." "So what if they do? Rupai† and Umai will. He is young and strong, and they are young and strong too. A woman gets happiness from a man. What of it?" "How can you say that?" "If it happens to me," said Bhat, "then we will know." Abaïse said, "It will happen."

_____

* Speaking in Gujarati.
† Mahadaïse.

एति : तरि : माहात्मे होती : जरि बोलाविलेया न येति तरि
नव्हेति : गेले : माहात्मे हो : तुमतें आबाइसें बोलावितें
असति : घोंगडें घेतलें : वाहाणा घेतलीया : आले : आबैसी
ठाये केले : दादोसाचिए पांती : भट : जेवीलें : मग :
दादोस गंगेकडे गेले : आबैसी म्हणीतलें : नागदेया : ऐसा
दादोसाकडे जाये : गेले : तवं ते बैसले असति : जाउनि
तेयाजवळि बैसले : मग भटी पुसीलें¹⁹¹ : म्हणें : तुम्हां
पासौनि आनंदु होए : ना : आम्हां पासौनि होए : ऐसेंहीं
आति : नव्हे : ऐसेंहीं आति : आमचेया गोसावीयां पासौनि
होएचि : आणि : स्तिति भोगीली : भंगली : मग दादोसाचें
घोंगडें घेतलें : दोचै बिढारा एत असति : तवं भटीं
पुसिलें¹⁹² : ते तुमचे गोसावी कव्हणीकडे असति : ना :
सीनगरीं असति : तेयाचेया दरिसना आमतें नेयाल : ना :
नेउनि : तुम्हीं कै जाल : ना : पर्वा लागौनि जाउनि :
आमचेयां गांवां या : मा : तेथौनि जावों : हो कां : कैं याल :
ना : अमुका दीसीं एउनि : ऐसा सीधु जाला : आबैसातें
घेउनि या : हो कां : मग आबैसें उमाइसें : महदाइसें :
दादोस : ऐसीं साडेगांवां आलीं : दादोसातें पाहुणेरालागि
म्हणीतलें : पाहुणरू केला : मग दादोस गंगे गेले :
वाहाळुवंटीं बैसले असति : भटोबास आले : पुढां बैसले :
आणि : स्तिति जाली¹⁹³ : मग दादोस बीढारी निगाले¹⁹⁴ :
भटोबासि हातीं करवंटी घेतली : घोंगडें घेतलें : उमैसीं
म्हणीतलें : रूपै : दादोसा पासौनि नागदेयासि कांहीं गोमटें
जालें : मग दादोस : आबैसें : उमाइसें : महदाइसें : भट¹⁹⁵ :

322

"If you invite him now, will he come?" "Yes." "If he comes, he is a Mahatma. If you invite him and he doesn't come, then he is not."

Bhat went and said to Dados, "Mahatma, Abaïse is inviting you." Dados took his blanket and his sandals, and he came there. Abaïse prepared a plate of food for Dados, and Nagdev ate in the same row with him.

Then Dados went to the river. Abaïse said, "Nagdev, go to Dados." Bhat went there. Dados was sitting down. Bhat went and sat down near Dados, then asked him, "Do people get happiness from you?" "There are some who get it from me," he replied, "and some who do not. Everyone gets happiness from our Gosavi." And Nagdev went into a trance.

After he experienced the trance for some time, it broke. He picked up Dados's blanket. As the two of them were returning to their lodgings, Bhat asked, "Where is that Gosavi of yours?" "He is at Sinnar," he replied. "Will you take me for his *darśan?*" "Yes, I'll take you." "When will you go there?" "I will go for the festival.[163] Come to my village, and we can leave from there." "All right." "When will you come?" "I'll come on such-and-such a day." They agreed on it. "Bring Abaïse along." "All right."

So Abaïse, Umaïse, Mahadaïse, and Dados came to Sadegav.[164] They asked Dados to give them hospitality, and he did so. Then he went to the river. While Dados was sitting on the sandy beach, Bhatobas came there, sat down in front of him, and went into a trance.[165] Afterward Dados set out for their lodgings. Bhatobas picked up the begging bowl and the blanket. Umaïse said, "Rupai, something good has happened to Nagdev because of Dados."

यल्हंभट : ऐसे गोसावीयाचेया दरिसना निगाली :
सिनरा आली : भिलमढीये सेजें बीढार केलें : उमाइसीं
म्हणीतलें : रूपै : दादोस नागदेव जवं पानें पोफळें घेउनि
येती तवं दादोसाचे गुरू पाहुनि येवों : हो कां : म्हणौनि
गेली : गोसावीयासि आरोगण : पहुड : उपहुड : मा आंगणीं
वेढें करित असति : गेलीं : देखीलें : गोसावीयांची श्रीमूर्ति
पाहातेंचि ठेली : सर्वज्ञें म्हणीतलें : बाइ : कवनीकडौनि एते
असा१९६ : तेंहीं म्हणीतलें : रावसगांवां कडौनि : कोणिकडे
जाणें : ना : त्रींयबकाकडे : रावसगांवींचे माहादेवो पाठक
ब्राह्मणु असे कीं : असे१९७ : बाइसीं पुसीलें : बाबा : आपण
केंवी जाणिजे : बाइ : एथ पाणिभातु : बाबूळसेंगा :
संपादिलीया : बाइ : एथींचे एजमान१९८ : मग तीयें बीढारा
गेलीं :॥:

११६ देवां भटां भेटी :॥:

मग दादोस पानें पोफळें घेउनि आले : मग आवघींचि
गोसावीयांचीया दरिसना आलीं : मग दादोसा मढीये आंतु
भेटी जाली : गोसावी दादोसांसि खेंव दीधलें : दादोसीं
दंडवतें घातलीं : श्रीचरणा लागले : येरीं अवघां दंडवतें
घातलीं : उमाइसें महदाइसें श्रीचरणा लागलीं : सर्वज्ञें
म्हणीतलें : त्रीयंबक बाइया एथींचेयाचि : मा : अवघीं
बैसलीं :॥:

Then Dados, Abaïse, Umaïse, Mahadaïse, Bhat, and Elhambhat set out to have *darśan* of the Gosavi. When they reached Sinnar, they arranged their lodgings near the Bhilmadh. Umaïse said, "Rupai, while Dados and Nagdev go and get betel leaves and betel nuts, let's go and see Dados's guru." "All right," said Mahadaïse, and they went there.

The Gosavi had eaten his meal, gone to sleep, and waked up. When they arrived, he was walking back and forth in the courtyard. They saw him and simply stood there, staring at the Gosavi's holy form.

The omniscient one asked, "My women, where are you coming from?" "From Ravasgav," they replied. "Where are you going?" "To Tryambak." "Is the Brahman Mahadev Pathak from Ravasgav still alive?" "He is."[166] Baïse asked, "Baba, how did you know about him?" "My woman, he gave me a meal of water-and-rice gruel and babul pods.[167] He was my patron, my woman."

Then they went to their lodgings.

116 HE MEETS DEV AND BHAT.

Then, after Dados returned with betel leaves and betel nuts, they all came for *darśan* of the Gosavi. The Gosavi met Dados inside the hermitage. He hugged Dados, and Dados prostrated himself and touched the holy feet. All the others prostrated themselves as well, and Umaïse and Mahadaïse touched the holy feet. The omniscient one said, "The Tryambak women belong to me alone."

Then everyone sat down.

११७ भटां तांबूळ ग्रहण :॥:

गोसावी तांबुळ परित्यजीलें : मग बाइसीं श्रीमुखींचे तांबुल
अवघेयांसि प्रसादु दीधला : दादोसीं मागांचि भटोबासातें
वारिलें होतें : नागदेया : गोसावी आमचे गुरु : म्हणौनी :
आम्हीं तांबोळ घेवौनि : तुवां नेघावें हो : तांबोळ दीधलें
तेव्हळि तेहीं वीचारिलें : जरि ईश्वरपुरुषु होती तरि आम्हांसि
गोमटें होइल : ना : तरि : आम्हीं थोडे याचें तांबुळें घेतलें
असे : म्हणौनि : घेतलें : आणि : स्तिति जाली :॥:

११८ तथा स्थित्यांतर :॥:

अस्तिति भोगीली : मग केतुलेया एका वेळां भंगली : मग
गोसावी भटोबासातें पुसीलें : महात्मेयां पासौनि सुखस्तीति
आतिꣻꣻꣻ : जी जी : सांपें कणु एकु अधिक : सर्वज्ञें म्हणी-
तलें : तें नव्हें : हें स्थीत्यांतर꣒꣐꣐ :॥:

११९ तथा श्लेष्मा हरणीं अभ्यासू नीराकरण :॥:

गोसावी बाहीरि बीजें केलें : तवं भटोबास पैलाकडौनि येत
होते : गोसावी पुसीलें : कें गेले होतेति : जी जी : श्लेष्मा
झाडुं गेलां होतां : सर्वज्ञें म्हणीतलें : महात्मेयांपासौनि

117 BHAT TAKES THE GOSAVI'S PAN.

The Gosavi spat out the pan from his holy mouth, and Baïse gave it to all of them as *prasād*. Dados had previously forbidden Bhatobas to take it: "Nagdev," he had said, "the Gosavi is *my* guru, so *I* will take his pan. You should not take it."

When Baïse gave Bhatobas the pan, he thought, "If he is a god-man, it will be good for me. If he is not, then I will have taken a little bit of his pan." So he ingested it. And he went into a trance.

118 AND HE EXPERIENCES A DIFFERENT KIND OF TRANCE.

After he experienced the trance for some time, it broke. The Gosavi asked Bhatobas, "Do you get a pleasant trance from the Mahatma?" "Yes, Lord. This one now is a bit better." The omniscient one said, "That's not right. This is a different kind of trance."[168]

119 AND WHEN BHATOBAS BLOWS HIS NOSE, THE GOSAVI FORBIDS HIM TO MAKE A HABIT OF IT.

As the Gosavi went out one time, Bhatobas was coming in from outside. "Where did you go?" asked the Gosavi. "I went to blow my nose, Lord." The omniscient one said, "What has

जालें²⁰¹ : तेणें सिंवनीं रांड नव्हे : तथा मुंगीं : मा : श्लेष्मा
काइ झडैल :॥:

१२० दमनिकारोपणीं डखलेया स्तीति :॥:

ऐसा एकू दीसु : पर्वाचा दीसु आला : अवघीं : पानें पोफळें
दवणा आणिला : अवघीं न्हाणिलीं : गोसावीयांसि बाइसीं
मादनें केलें : पुजा केली : तंव दादोस सीक्षांसी आले :
गोसावीयांसि दवणा वाइला : दंडवतें घातलीं : श्रीचरणा
लागले : बैसले : सर्वज्ञें म्हणीतलें : डखलेया :
येथ एहीं अवघां पर्व केलें : तुम्हीं न करा तें काइ : ना जी :
मातें दवणा नाहीं : यें दैवाचीं : यांतें करावीया असे :
मातें कांहींचि नाहीं : जी जी : सर्वज्ञें म्हणीतलें : बाइ : आणा
दवणा²⁰² : बाइसीं दवणा दीधला : माळ तांबुल²⁰³ :
डखला वाइला : गोसावीयांसि दवणा वाइला : वीडा
वोळगवीला : आणि स्तिति जाली : मग उगेचि बैसले :
सर्वज्ञें म्हणीतलें : हां गा : उगीयांचि असीजे : ऐसा एकु मार्गु
आति : शोध : मोक्ष मार्गु²⁰⁴ : तेहीं म्हणीतलें : जी जी :
आति : उघाणी प्रवर्तली : सर्वज्ञें म्हणीतलें : तरि तुम्हीं
माहात्मे ना²⁰⁵ : आणि स्तीति भंगली :॥:

happened to you because of the Mahatma has not widowed a sparrow (or, an ant).[169] So can it blow your nose for you?"

120 DAKHALE GOES INTO A TRANCE WHEN HE OFFERS SOUTHERNWOOD.

Eventually the day of the festival arrived.[170] Everyone got betel leaves, betel nuts, and southernwood. Everyone took a bath, and Baïse gave a bath to the Gosavi. She did puja to him. At that point, Dados arrived, along with his disciples. They offered southernwood to the Gosavi, prostrated themselves to him, touched his holy feet, and sat down.

"Dakhale," said the omniscient one, "all these people have made offerings to me to celebrate the festival. Why haven't you?" "Lord," he replied, "I don't have any southernwood. They are lucky: they have something to celebrate the festival with. I have nothing at all, Lord."

The omniscient one said to Baïse, "Bring him some southernwood, my woman." She gave Dakhale some southernwood, a garland, and some pan, and he offered them. He presented the southernwood to the Gosavi and gave him the pan. And then Dakhale went into a trance. He sat there, completely silent.

The omniscient one said, "All right. Keep silent. That is one path." (Research: "a path to liberation.") "Yes, Lord," he said. "It is." They started to debate.

The omniscient one said, "But you are Mahatmas, aren't you?" And Dakhale's trance broke.

१२१ डखलेयांसि खेळ :॥:

उदयाचां पूजावसर जालेया नंतरें गोसावी वीहरणा बीजें
केलें : विहरणी पाट होता : गोसावी पैलाडी बिजे केले²⁰⁶ :
डखले पाटु उडो बैसले : आणि गोसावीयांते बरखलिति :
उडों नेदीती : मागुतें उडों निगती : गोसावी तेयांतें परतेंचि
लोटिति : आवघी श्रीमूर्ति पाणियें सीतोडली : देव म्हणति :
मर मरा : डखलेया : जेणें जेणें नरका जा : तें तेंचि करीत
असा : गोसावी ईश्वरू : गोसावीयांसि खेळु काइसा : सर्वज्ञें
म्हणीतलें : यातें कां गा म्हणत असा : हीराइसा : कोपत
असा :॥छ॥: हें एथुनिचि करूं आवडत असे कीं :॥:

१२२   तथा पादव्यथा संबोखू :॥:

पाटु उडतां डखलेयाचा पावो अवटळला : तो रात्रीं दुखों
लागला : वीवळति : परुवति : उदीयांचि गोसावी परिश्रया
बीजें केलें : बाइसीं म्हणीतलें : डखले : सागळ घे :
बाबा सांघातें जाय²⁰⁷ : डखला म्हणीतलें : जी जी : मी
गोसावीयांसि रूसलां : सर्वज्ञें म्हणीतलें : कां गा : गोसावी
मातें पडिताळीतिचि ना : सर्वज्ञें म्हणीतलें : तुम्ही माहात्मे
कीं गा : तुम्हा सकळै²⁰⁸ भोगे नीमानावे कीं²⁰⁹ :॥:

121 HE PLAYS WITH DAKHALE.

After the morning worship service, the Gosavi went out to wander. As he wandered, he came to a stream. He crossed the stream. As Dakhale went to jump over it, he bumped into the Gosavi, who prevented him from jumping across. When he tried again to jump, the Gosavi pushed him back. Water splashed all over the Gosavi's holy body.

Dev said, "Die! Die, Dakhale! You are doing exactly the kind of thing that makes you go to hell. How can you play with the Gosavi? He is God."

The omniscient one said, "Why are you saying that to (Hiraïsa: angry with) him? I'm the one who is making him enjoy doing it!"

122 AND HE CONSOLES HIM
ABOUT HIS HURT FOOT.

As Dakhale was jumping over the stream, he twisted his foot. That night the foot began to hurt. He was whining and moaning.

Early the next morning the Gosavi went out to defecate. Baïse said, "Dakhale, take the water bag and go with Baba."[171]

Dakhale said, "Lord Gosavi, I am annoyed with you." "Why?" asked the omniscient one. "You haven't asked after me at all." The omniscient one said, "You are Mahatmas! You should endure everything!"[172]

१२३ माहादाइ राहावणें :॥ः

गोसावी महदाइसां म्हणीतलें : बाइ : एथ राहों आवडैल तरि
राहाना कां : तेहीं म्हणीतलें : जी जी : सांघातु नाहीं : सर्वज्ञें
म्हणीतलें : वृद्धाबाइसा : आणि : तुम्हां सांघातु²¹⁰ : एथौनि
कोण्ही येक : बोळवीत धाडीजैल : तें न ऱ्हातीचि :॥ः

१२४ अवडळ नाम करणें :॥ः

एकु दीस गोसावीयांपासि बैसली असति : गोसावी
एरातें अवलोकीति : ऐसीं गोसावी पृथकीकारें अवघींचि
अवलोकितिं : एक एल्हंभट वांचौनि यरा अवघेयां स्तीति
जालिया : सुख भोगीत होते : येल्हंभटीं म्हणीतलें : जी जी :
इतुकेया आंतु : मीचि एकु अवडळ : सर्वज्ञें म्हणीतलें : तरि
तुम्ही अवडळभट म्हणा : हीराइसा : ऐसे तरि तुम्ही :॥छ॥ः
आणि स्तीति जाली :॥ः

123   HE INVITES MAHADAÏ TO STAY.

The Gosavi said to Mahadaïse, "My woman, if you would like to stay here, why not stay?" "I would not have a companion, Lord," she replied. The omniscient one said, "Vriddhabaïse* and you will be companions for each other. I will send someone to accompany you when you leave."

But she refused to stay.

124   HE GIVES ELHAMBHAT
THE NAME "HARD-HEARTED."

One day when they were sitting with the Gosavi, he was looking at them one after another. Eventually the Gosavi had looked at each and every one of them. Each of them had gone into a trance and was enjoying bliss, except for Elhambhat.

"I am the only hard-hearted one among so many, Lord," he said. "So we'll call you 'Hard-Hearted Bhat,'" said the omniscient one. (Hiraïsa: "After all, that's how you are.") And Elhambhat went into a trance.

---

* Abaïse.

१२५ गोंदेश्वरा पुढें पद्मेश्वरू कथन :॥:

एकु दीस : गोसावी उदेयाचां पूजावस्वर जालेया नंतरें
वीहरणा बीजें केलें : गोंदेश्वराचा देउळीं : बाळाणेयावरि
आसन : बाइसीं पुसीलें : बाबा : देउळापुढें देउळ काइसें :
सर्वज्ञें म्हणीतलें : बाइ : मागां गोवींद नामें वेव्हारा : तेणें
केलें : म्हातारी एकीचा पुत्र : तेया नांव पद्मा : तो न्हातु
होता : तो हाटा जावेयाचिया लवड सवडा : लवकरि पाणीं
सारविलें : माया म्हणीतलें : हो हो : जासी : मां : जोडुनि
घेउनि एसी : ऐसा वेगु करीतोसि२११ : काइ : गोंदेश्वरा पुढें
पद्मेश्वरू करीसी२१२ : तैसाचि तो नीगाला : पैन्हां न्हाला :
तेलंग देशा गेला : द्रव्य जोडीलें : मग देउळ करविलें :
देउळासि उद्यापन जालें : मग आपण आला : मायेतें पुसों
धाडीलें : गोंदेश्वरापुढें पद्मेश्वरू केला : आतां मी येवों२१३ : हें
अभिमान कार्यें : ते दोघैं भाचे मेहुणें : एके म्हणति : मामे
भाचे :॥:

125 HE TELLS ABOUT PADMESHVAR BEING IN FRONT OF GONDESHVAR.

After the morning worship service one day, the Gosavi went out to wander. He sat on the balcony in the temple of Gondeshvar.* Baïse asked, "Baba, why is there one temple in front of another?"

The omniscient one said, "My woman, in the past, a moneylender named Govinda built the Gondeshvar temple.

"Later, a certain old woman had a son named Padma. He was taking a bath, and he was in a hurry to go to the market, so he wanted the water to be poured quickly. His mother said, 'Yes, yes. You're in such a hurry, it's as if you're going to go and earn lots of money. What are you going to do? Build Padmeshvar† in front of Gondeshvar?'

"He left right away and took a bath somewhere else. He went to the Telugu land and made a great deal of money, then had a temple built.[173] After the temple was inaugurated, he came back and sent someone to ask his mother, 'I have built Padmeshvar in front of Gondeshvar. May I come back now?'[174]

"This is a work of pride. The two of them were nephew and brother-in-law." (Some say, "maternal uncle and nephew.")

---

* "Lord of Govinda," a Shiva temple.
† "Lord of Padma," a Shiva temple.

१२६ नासीकीं पंचवटीये गुंफे अवस्थान ः
दीस दहा ः।ः उदास्य स्वीकारू ः॥ः

शोध ः आरतिये नंतरे गोसावीयांसि रामाचां देउळीं आसन ः
परशरामबास ः पंचायातनाचा देउळीं आसन ः रामेश्वरबास ः
गोसावी भक्तजनातें म्हणीतलें ः तुम्ही एथौनि अवघे जा
गा ः हें एकाकी असैल ः तुम्ही एथींचिये प्रवृत्ति विखो हो
जाणाना ः तुम्हा एथ असतां अनिष्टचि होत असे ः तुम्ही एथ
काइसेया असा ः ते उगेचि होते ः सर्वज्ञें म्हणीतलें ः तुम्ही न
वचा ः तरि ः हेंचि जाईल ः मग उदकामध्यें रिगाले ः सवेंचि
बाइसें रीगालीं ः बाइसां पाणी बहुत आलें ः आणि ः बाबा ः
म्हणौनि बोबाइली ः सर्वज्ञें म्हणीतलें ः बाइसां हातीं केहींचि
जावों न लभे ः मग कपाळेश्वरीं आसन ः तिमलीं वस्त्रें
फेडिलीं ः आणि आणिकें वेढीलीं ः मग अवघीं भक्तजने
उगीचि बैसलीं होतीं ः गोसावीयाचां ठाइं उदास्य देखीलें ः
पुढां रिगवेना ः मग बाइसीं आरोगणा लागि वीनवीलें ः
हीराइसा ः गोसावींचि म्हणीतलें ः बाइ एथ पूजावस्वरू कां
न करा ः हो कां बाबा ः॥छ॥ः मग कपाळेश्वरा अडवांगीं गुंफा
होती ः तेथ पूजा ः आरोगणा ः रामेश्वरबास ः तेथ उदास्य
परिहरलें ः परशरामबास ः॥छ॥ः

126 IN NASIK HE STAYS TEN DAYS IN A HERMIT'S CELL AT PANCHAVATI.[175] HE TAKES ON INDIFFERENCE.

(Research: According to Parasharambas, after *āratī* had been performed, the Gosavi was sitting in the temple of Ram. According to Rameshvarbas, he was sitting in a *pañcāyatan* temple.)[176] The Gosavi said to his devotees, "Go away, all of you. I want to be alone. You do not know how to please me. When you are here, only bad things happen. Why are you here?"[177]

They kept silent. The omniscient one said, "If you do not leave, then I myself will go away." And he jumped into the water.

Baïse went right in with him. The water was too deep for her. "Baba!" she shouted. The omniscient one said, "I will never be able to escape Baïse's clutches."

After that, he took off his wet clothes, put on dry ones, and sat in the Kapaleshvar temple.* All the devotees sat there in silence. They saw that the Gosavi was indifferent to them, and they could not come forward.

Then Baïse offered to prepare him a meal. (According to Hiraïsa, the Gosavi himself said, "My woman, why don't you do my worship service?" "All right, Baba.")

Then, according to Rameshvarbas, his puja was performed and he ate his meal at a hermit's cell off to the side of the Kapaleshvar temple. According to Parasharambas, that is where his indifference was dispelled.

———

* A Shiva temple at Panchavati, Nasik.

१२७ गोवर्धनीं वसति :॥:

१२८ त्रीयंबकीं अवस्थान :॥:

गोसावी त्रीयंबका बीजें केलें : त्रीयंबका वीडा वोळगवीला :
जगती आंतु गुंफे अवस्थान जालें : दीस तीन :॥:

१२९ गंगाद्वारीं बडुवा संबोखू :॥:

गोसावी गंगाद्वारा बीजें केलें : तेथ आसन जालें : तवं
कोळाइचां बोंबींहुनि पाणी निगत असे : तेथ डखलां आगुळी
सूदली : उभे गंगातीरें गांवों नेसी आतां माझी आंगुळी ने
पां : सर्वज्ञें म्हणीतलें : डखलेया ऐसें न म्हणिजे कीं :
देवतेसि :॥: खालि पाणिया आडी²¹⁴ भरें : ते पाणी डखला
अवघें सांडीलें²¹⁵ : तवं बडुवा गाऱ्हाणेनसीं आला : देखीलें
जी : येइं अवघें पाणी सांडिलें : एथ आम्हा कांहीं मिळे :
सर्वज्ञें म्हणीतलें : भटो : तुम्हां दीसवडी काइ मिळे : जी
जी : दामू एकु : रुवे तीन : मिळति : सर्वज्ञें म्हणीतलें :
बाइ : येकु दामू वोपा : डखला म्हणीतलें : हां जी : हें काइ
गोतमाचे दाइ : मग एकु दामू वोपवीला :॥छ॥:

127 HE STAYS OVERNIGHT
AT GOVARDHAN.[178]

128 HE STAYS AT TRYAMBAK.

The Gosavi went to Tryambak. He offered pan to Tryambak.* He stayed three days in a hermit's cell in the temple courtyard.

129 AT GANGADVAR, HE PACIFIES
THE TEMPLE PRIEST.

The Gosavi went and sat at Gangadvar.[179] Water was coming out of Kolaï's navel. Dakhale stuck his finger into it and said, "Now carry off my finger the way you carry off villages all along the banks of the Ganga." The omniscient one said, "Don't talk that way to a deity, Dakhale."[180]

Dakhale spilled out all the water that had flowed into the cistern below the goddess.[181] The priest came to complain to the Gosavi. "Did you see what he did, Lord?" he asked. "He spilled out all the water. Will I get some compensation for this?" The omniscient one asked, "How much do you make each day, Bhat?" "I get a copper coin or so, Lord. Three pennies." The omniscient one said to Baïse, "My woman, give him a copper coin."

Dakhale said, "Hey, Lord! Is he Gautam's heir?"[182] Even so, the Gosavi had her give the man a copper coin.

* The name of Shiva at Tryambakeshvar.

१३० ब्रह्मगिरीवरि गोटेमाळां उदंबरें आरोगण :॥ः

मग गोसावी ब्रह्मगीरीवरि गोटुमाळेया बीजें केलें : पाळीवरि
उंबरू पीकला होता : तेथ आसन : उंदबऱ्हें पीकलीं होतीं :
सर्वज्ञें म्हणीतलें : कां गा : पींड प्रदान वर्तेना²⁹⁶ :॥ः हो कां
जी : मग अवघां भक्तजनीं उदंबराचिया रासी केलिया :
गोसावी श्रीकरीं उदंबर घेतलें : आरोगीलें²⁹⁷ : आणि अवघां
भक्तजनीं धाएवरी उदंबरें खादलीं : सर्वज्ञें म्हणीतलें : या
गौतमाचीया भातवडीया गा : हीराइसा : हा सीतेचा कोथळा
गा²⁹⁸ :॥छ॥ः ब्रह्मगिरीवरौनि बीजें केलें :॥ः

१३१ आंजनीये वसति :॥ः

१३२ नासीकीं नगरांतु वसति :॥ः

340

130 HE EATS CLUSTER FIGS AT GAUTAM'S LAKE ATOP BRAHMAGIRI.

Then the Gosavi went to Gautam's Lake on top of Brahmagiri.[183] He was sitting near a cluster-fig tree on the embankment. The fruit was ripe, and the omniscient one said, "Why not offer these as balls of rice to the ancestors?"

"All right, Lord," said the devotees, and they all made heaps of figs. The Gosavi took a fig in his holy hand and ate it.[184] Then all the devotees ate figs until they were full.

The omniscient one said, "These are Gautam's heaps of rice." (According to Hiraïsa, he said, "This is Sita's store of grain."[185])

He came down from Brahmagiri.

131 HE STAYS OVERNIGHT AT ANJANIYA.[186]

132 HE STAYS OVERNIGHT IN THE TOWN AT NASIK.

१३३ उदास्य स्वीकारे चांगदेवोभटा पाठवणी२१९ :॥:

पंचवटिके गुंफे अवस्थान :॥: दिस ती :॥: गोसावीयासि
उदयांचां पूजावस्वर जालेया नंतरें : रामाचेया देउळां बीजें
केलें : तेथ आसन : सर्वज्ञें म्हणीतलें : आवघें तुम्ही एथौनि
जा गा : हें एकाकी असैल : तुम्ही एथीचीये प्रवृत्ति वीखो
हों जाणाना : तुमचा एथु निरोधु कीं : तुम्हां एथ असतां :
अवीधु होत असे : तुम्ही एथ असतां अनिष्टिचि होत असे :
तुम्हीं एथ काइसेया असा : तुम्हीं जा : ते आवचे उगेचि
राहीले : सर्वज्ञें म्हणीतलें : चांगो : हे कव्हणी न वचति :
तुं जाए : तुम्ही आदि होए : हो कां जी : म्हणौनी चांगदेवो
भट नीगालें : बाइसीं म्हणीतलें : तें कव्हणी न वचतीचि :
तरि यातें कां पाठवीजत असीजे : बाबा : गोसावी उगेचि :
दुसरा दीसीं सर्वज्ञें म्हणीतलें : तुम्हीं कव्हणी न वचा : तरि :
चांगोयेंचि२२० काइ केले : डखलेया जा : चांगोतें बोलावा :
हो का जी : म्हणौनि डखला दंडवत केले : निगाले : गोसावी
सरीसी जाडी दिधली :॥ शोध ॥: सर्वज्ञें म्हणीतले : हे जाडी
घेया : जेथ राहाल तेथ आडवी बांधावी : होकाजी : तव२२१
बाइसीं म्हणीतलें : तो काइ एइल : बाबा : यासी काइ भेटत
असे : सर्वज्ञें म्हणीतलें : बाइ : याची यात्रा काइ निर्फळ
जाइल२२२ : बाइ बापुडीं बटीकें डोंगरें डोंगर गीवसीतें
असति२२३ : येथचें दर्शन घेयावीया : मग गावां जावें ऐसा
परिछेदु केला असे : बाइ२२४ :॥:

342

133 HE TAKES ON INDIFFERENCE AND SENDS CANGDEVBHAT AWAY.

The Gosavi stayed for three days in a hermit's cell at Panchavati. After his morning worship service, he went and sat at the temple of Ram. The omniscient one said, "Go away, all of you. I want to be alone. You do not know how to please me. You are an obstacle for me. When you are here, offenses occur. When you are here, only bad things happen. Why are you here? Go away!"[187]

They all kept silent. The omniscient one said, "Cango, none of them is leaving. You go away. You be the first." "All right, Lord," said Cangdevbhat, and he left.

Baïse said, "Not a single one of them is leaving, Baba, so why are you sending *him* away?" The Gosavi kept silent.

The next day the omniscient one said, "If none of you is leaving, what has Cango done that's different from anyone else? Dakhale, go and invite Cango back." "All right, Lord," said Dakhale, and he prostrated himself and left.

The Gosavi gave him a blanket to take with him. (Research: The omniscient one said, "Take this blanket. Hang it up wherever you stay." "All right, Lord.")

Baïse asked, "Will he come back, Baba? Will Dakhale find him?" The omniscient one said, "Can his pilgrimage be fruitless, my woman?[188] Some poor boys* are searching all over the hills in order to get my *darśan*. They have cut off any chance of going home, my woman."[189]

---

* Upadhye and Nathoba.

१३४ उपाध्या नाथोबा भेटि :॥:

डखले गेले : चांदोरी अग्नीष्टीके जाडि आड बांधली : मग
तेथ पाठी घातली : उपाध्ये नाथोबा पर्वाकारणें न टकेचि :
मा : गोसावीयातें गीवसत एतें असति : सिनरा आले :
भिलमढीये संन्यासी होते : तेयातें पुसीलें : एथ आमुचे
गोसावी होते कीं : काइ कराल गोसावी : ब्रह्मवीद्या तरि
आम्ही सांघौनि : तेंहीं म्हणीतलें : आम्हीं काइ तुमतें
ब्रह्मवीद्या पुसत असों : आम्ही आपुलेया गोसावीयांतें पुसत
असों : ऐसीं गा बटीकुरें चाळवीली असति : तरि : आम्हासि
दंडवत करा : मां सांघौनि : तेंहीं म्हणीतलें : आधीं सांगा :
मग दंडवत करूनि : कैसीं गा बटकुरें आग्रहाचीं :
मग : दंडवत केलें : जा तुमते गोसावी सत्रसिंगा गेले
असति : निगाले : मग वीचारीलें : डोंगरा आंतु जावों नये :
तरि चांदोरीं पांगुरणें ठेउं : मग जावों : म्हणौनि चांदोरीं
आले : तवं गोसावीयाची जाडि देखीली : मग म्हणीतलें :
हे जाडि गोसावीयांची नव्हे : म्हणौनि : आले : हें काइ
डखलेया : गोसावी कव्हणें ठाइं असति : तेंहीं म्हणीतलें :
गोसावी नासिकीं असति : गोसावी तुमतें बोलाउं पाठवीलें
असे : मग : डखला : म्हणीतलें : ऐसें गा आमचे गोसावी

134   HE MEETS UPADHYE AND NATHOBA.

Dakhale left. When he reached Chandori, he hung up the blanket at a brick fire pit and lay down there.

Upadhye and Nathoba did not arrive in time for the festival.* As they came along searching for the Gosavi, they reached Sinnar. They asked an ascetic who was in the Bhilmadh, "Was our Gosavi here?" "Why do you need the Gosavi? *I* will tell you about ultimate truth." "Are we asking you about ultimate truth?" they replied. "We are asking about our Gosavi." "How deluded you poor boys are! At least prostrate yourselves to me, and then I will tell you." "First tell us," they replied, "and then we will prostrate ourselves." "How insistent you poor boys are!" Then they prostrated themselves to him. "Go to Satrasinga," he said. "That is where your Gosavi has gone."

They set out. Then it occurred to them, "We shouldn't go straight into the hills. Instead, let's leave our shawls at Chandori and then go."[190]

So they came to Chandori. When they saw the Gosavi's blanket there, they said to each other, "Isn't this blanket the Gosavi's?" and they came toward it. "What is going on, Dakhale?" they asked. "Where is the Gosavi?" "The Gosavi is at Nasik," he replied. "The Gosavi sent me to invite you."[191] Then Dakhale said, "This is how our Gosavi hides his divinity."[192]

---

* The Southernwood festival.

आपुलें ऐश्वर्य लोपीती : मग नासीकासि आले : उपाध्या :
नाथोबा : भेटी जाली : दंडवतें घातलीं : श्रीचरणा लागले :
मग मागील अवघें वृत्तांत सांघीतलें : सर्वज्ञें म्हणीतलें :
कैसें म्हणे : भगवा : शोधु : वेळां तिन पुसीलें : हीराइसा :
मग बटिका काइ म्हणे : भगवा ॥छ॥: माघौतें सांघीतलें :
सर्वज्ञें म्हणीतलें : कैसें जाले : ब्रह्मवीद्या सुपीं सूनि वीकीजत
असीजे२२५ : देखीलें बाइ : बटिकुरें पुसति : यातें : ते यांसि
ब्रह्मवीद्या सांघे :॥:

१३५ नाथोबा केसदर्शनीं वीस्मयो :॥:

चांगदेवो भट भीक्षे गेले : तेयांतें बाइलीं देखिलें होतें : मग
नाथोबा गाउनि आले :॥: गोसावीयांसि उदयाचां पूजावसर
जालेया नंतरें गोसावी वीहरणा बीजें केलें : सरिसे नाथोबा
असत२२६ : पाणीवथा बाइलीं देखीलें२२७ : आवो आवो
माए : कालिचा बटिकू बोडीका कीं : आजिचि येवढें केस
कैचे२२८ : मग गोसावी उभें राहुनि उत्तर दीधलें : बाइ : हा तो
नव्हे : ते याचा भाऊ : हे दोचै जावळाचे : तो गांवा गेला२२९ :
हा आजि गाउनि आला :॥:

Then they all came to Nasik. Upadhye and Nathoba met the Gosavi. They prostrated themselves and touched his holy feet, then told him everything that had happened. The omniscient one said, "How could that ascetic say such a thing?" (Research: "We asked him three times," they replied. According to Hiraïsa, the Gosavi asked, "What did the ascetic say then, Batika?") They told him again.

The omniscient one said, "How could that happen? He is making a business out of ultimate truth.[193] Do you see, my woman? The poor boys ask him a question, and he tells them about ultimate truth."

135 WOMEN ARE AMAZED TO SEE NATHOBA'S HAIR.

The women there had seen Cangdevbhat when he went to beg for food. Then Nathoba arrived.

After his morning worship service, the Gosavi went out to wander. Nathoba was with him. Women at the place to get water saw them.[194] "Oh!" said the women. "Oh, mother! Yesterday the boy's head was shaven. How did he come to have so much hair already today?"

The Gosavi stopped there and told them, "My woman, this is not the same man. That one was this one's brother. The two of them are identical twins. That one has gone away, and this one arrived here today."

१३६ मार्गीं चौरंगीवीद्या नीरूपण :॥:

गोसावी मार्गीं बीजें करीत असति : नासीकीहुनि नीगी-
लीया : वृक्षातळीं आसन : बाइसीं म्हणीतलें : बाबा :
एथ आसन किजत असिजे : परि एथ उदक नाहीं : मग
गोसावी[२३०] उपाध्यातें म्हणीतलें : ऐसें ऐसें जा पां[२३१] :
शोध : तथा बटिका : पाहा पां : उपाध्ये गेले : तिकडे
पाहीलें : तवं उदक देखीलें : सागळ भरीली : मग म्हणीतलें :
ऐसे गा आमचे गोसावी : कीं अमूकीकडे उदक असे : ऐसें
सांघती ना कां : परि आपुलें ईश्वर्य लोपती कीं : मग उदक
घेउनि आले : गोसावीयांसि आरोगण : ऐसें अवलोकिलें :
तवं पळसाचा वृक्ष तोडिला असे[२३२] : मग भवंते भवंते :
बरवे कोंभ निगाले : असति : सर्वज्ञें म्हणीतलें : देखिलें
गा : याचा तरि स्वभावो : ऐसें माणुसाचां ठाइं दीसे : तरि
चौरंगीचि वीद्या जाली : म्हणिजे[२३३] :॥:

१३७ अडगांवीं वसतीं :॥:

136 ALONG THE ROAD, HE EXPLAINS ABOUT THE SCIENCE OF CAURANGI.

The Gosavi set out from Nasik and was traveling along the road. He sat down at the foot of a tree. Baïse said, "Baba, you're sitting down here, but there is no water at this place." The Gosavi said to Upadhye, "Go over there! Over there!" (Or, research: "Take a look, Batika!")

Upadhye went and looked there, and he saw water. He filled the water bag, and then he said, "That's what our Gosavi is like. He doesn't say, 'There is water in such-and-such a place.' Instead he hides his divinity." Upadhye brought the water, and the Gosavi ate his meal.

When the Gosavi looked around, he saw a flame-of-the-forest tree whose branches had been hacked away. Healthy shoots had sprouted all over it. The omniscient one said, "Do you see? That is its nature. If you see a human doing this, people say he has mastered the science of Caurangi."[195]

137 HE STAYS OVERNIGHT IN ADGAV.[196]

१३८ मार्गीं उपासनीया स्तीति :॥:

मग गोसावी : उपाध्यें : आणि : उपासनीये : पूढें पाठवीलें :
हीराइसा : सर्वज्ञें म्हणीतलें : बटिका : तुम्ही पुढीलेया गावा
जा : तेथ भीक्षा करा : मा : हे तुम्हां उदीया दरिसन
देइल :॥छ॥: ते निगाले : गोसावीयांसि अडगांवीं वसति
जाली :॥: उदयाचा पूजावस्वर जालेया नंतरें मग तेथौनि
बीजें केलें : उपाध्ये : उपासनीये : साउमे आले : मार्गीं भेटि
जाली : गोसावीयांतें देखीलें : आणि उपासनीया स्तिति
जाली : वस्त्रें सांडिलीं : मार्गीं पुढें चालतां मागुतें पाहाति :
गोसावी श्रीमुगुटें चाला म्हणति : आणि मागौतें गोसावीया
वरि चालौनि एति : आणि : गोसावी श्रीमुगुटें निराकरीति :
श्रीमुगुटें चालवीति : वाटेकडे दाखवीति : आणि पुढें
चालती : मग बाइसीं पुसीलें : बाबा : हें काइ सांभवीचि
विद्या : सर्वज्ञें म्हणीतलें : बाइ : सांभवीचा रश्मि : तरि
शाक्तेयाचा : नव्हे : तरि आणव : सर्वज्ञें म्हणीतलें :
आणवहि नव्हे : तरि काइ बाबा : आणवीचा रश्मि : एकू :॥:

१३९ सुकीयाना²³⁴ वसति :॥:

138 ALONG THE ROAD, UPASANIYE GOES INTO A TRANCE.

The Gosavi sent Upadhye and Upasaniye on ahead. (According to Hiraïsa, the omniscient one said, "Batika, you go to the next village and beg for food there. I will give you *darśan* tomorrow.") They left.

The Gosavi spent the night in Adgav. He left there after the morning worship service. Upadhye and Upasaniye came back toward him and met him on the road. When they saw the Gosavi, Upasaniye went into a trance. He took off his clothes and dropped them on the ground.

As they went along the road, he walked ahead and kept looking back at the Gosavi. The Gosavi would nod his holy head to tell him to go on, but he would walk back toward the Gosavi. The Gosavi would move his holy head to stop him and nod his holy head to keep him walking forward. The Gosavi would point him toward the road ahead, and Upasaniye would walk on.

Finally Baïse asked, "Is this the Shambhava science, Baba?"[197] The omniscient one said, "It is a ray of the Shambhava, my woman." "So then is it the Shakteya?" "No." "Then is it the Anava?" The omniscient one said, "It is not the Anava either." "What is it then, Baba?" "It is a single ray of the Anava."

139 HE STAYS OVERNIGHT IN SUKIYANA.[198]

१४० निफाडें अवस्थान :॥:

गोसावी निफाडेसी मढा बीजें केलें²³⁵ : माहात्मे होते :
तेंही म्हणीतलें : या पापीयाचां गांवां कां आलेति : म्हणौनि
आरोळीया देवों लागले : गोसावीयांसि पटिसाळे :
मढाचिये : आसन : गोसावी बाइसातें पुसीलें : बाइ : हें
कवण : बाबा : हे वामदेवाचे प्रथम सिष्य : आत्माराम :
गोसावी परिश्रया बीजें केलें : सरिसे डखले असति : तैसेचि
गोसावी कोंकणाये बीजें केलें : डखले जाडि आणावेया
धाडीले²³⁶ : गोसावी पुसीलें : डखलेया : माहात्मेयासि
पयोवर्त जालें : ना जी : ते आत्मारामू बोबात असति :
या पापियाचीया गावां कां आलेति : मिं तिन दी : भुका
आरोळिया देतु असें : सर्वज्ञें म्हणीतलें : हां गा : डखलेया :
आत्मारामू ऐसें नांव : आणि भुकीं आळुकीळु देती : हें
अतिविरोध कीं : मग बाइसां करवि दुगाणिचें तुप देववा :
यऱ्हवी बाइसां नीरोध कीं गा : हीराइसा : तथा दुध
दुगाणिचें²³⁷ :॥छ॥: बाइसीं दीधलें : गोसावी मढासि बीजें
केलें : तेथ अवस्थान :॥:

१४१ मार्गीं गोसावीयांसि आरोगण :॥:

गोसावी निफाडेहुनि बीजें केलें : मार्गीं कांटिये तळीं आसन :
पुजा जाली : आरोगणा जाली :॥: हीराइसा : मार्गीं सर्वज्ञें

140   HE STAYS IN NIPHAD.

The Gosavi went to a hermitage in Niphad.[199] A Mahatma who was there began to cry out, "Why have you come to this sinners' village?"

The Gosavi was sitting on the veranda of the hermitage. He asked Baïse, "Who is this, my woman?" "Baba, it's Atmaram, the first disciple of Vamdev."

The Gosavi went to defecate. Dakhale was with him. Then the Gosavi went straight to the temple of Konkanaï,* and he sent Dakhale to get a blanket.[200]

The Gosavi asked, "Dakhale, has the Mahatma gotten his milk products to eat?"[201] "No, Lord. Atmaram is shouting, 'Why have you come to this sinners' village? I have been crying out from hunger for three days.'" The omniscient one said, "That's funny, Dakhale. His name is Atmaram,† and he is crying out from hunger? What a total contradiction! Have Baïse give him a penny's worth of ghee then. (Or, Hiraïsa: of milk.) She will object to giving him more than that."

Baïse gave it to him. The Gosavi went to the hermitage and stayed there.

141   THE GOSAVI HAS A MEAL
ALONG THE ROAD.

The Gosavi set out from Niphad. Along the road, he sat under a thorn tree. His puja took place, and he ate a meal.

(According to Hiraïsa: Along the road, the omniscient

* A goddess.
† "He who delights in the Self."

म्हणीतलें : एथ आसन करा : बाइसीं म्हणीतलें : बाबा :
अरण्य : एथ पाणी नसे : गावां जवळि चालिजो का : बाबा :
सर्वज्ञें म्हणीतलें : बाइ : एथिचिये प्रवृत्ति वीखो हो जाणा
ना : तरि यथ कां असा : बाइसीं आसन केलें : गोसावी
आसनीं बैसले : गोसावी उपाध्यातें म्हणीतलें : बटिका : ऐसें
एसें हाण : उदक नसैल : गेले तवं सरे भरलिया असति : ऐसें
आमचे गोसावी ईश्वर्ये लोपीति : उदक आणीलें : मग बाइसीं
पुजा केली : आरोगण दीधली : पहुड : उपहुड²³⁸ :॥:

१४२   नांदौरीं²³⁹ जळक्रिडा :॥:
मध्येमेश्वरीं वीडा वाणें :॥:²⁴⁰

तेथौनि गोसावी नांदोरासि बीजें केलें : गोसावीयासि
जळक्रिडेची प्रवृति : सर्वज्ञें म्हणीतलें : बाइ : हें आतां नये :
हें ऐसेंचि जाइल :॥: हां गा : डखलेया : गोसावी जाती :
भिक्षा मागती : भिक्षा मागौनि मध्यें पुजा आरोगण : मग
दों पाहारा : गंगे बीजें केलें : पांगुरणें कडे ठेवीलीं : गंगे
आंतु रिगाले : गोसावी : उपाध्ये : नाथोबा : डखले²⁴¹ :
यरातें डोंचळिति : यरातें डोंचळिति : ऐसा खेळु केला : मग
पव्हत पव्हत²⁴² थडीया थडीया बीजें केलें : बाइसें यरी
थडीया थडीया बोबाति : पुरे कीजो बाबा : सर्वज्ञें म्हणीतलें :
डखलेया पुरे करा गा : बाइसें श्रमती²⁴³ : दोही गंगेचा फाटां

one said, "Prepare a seat for me here." Baïse said, "Baba, it's wilderness here. There's no water. Let's go closer to a village, Baba." The omniscient one said, "You do not know how to please me. So why are you here?"[202]

Baïse prepared a seat, and the Gosavi sat on it. The Gosavi said to Upadhye, "Batika, if you strike the ground like this, won't you find water?"

When Upadhye went to fetch water, the streams were full. "This is how our Gosavi hides his divinity," he said.[203]

He brought back some water, and then Baïse did puja. She gave the Gosavi his meal, he went to sleep, and he woke up.)

142 HE PLAYS IN THE WATER
AT NANDAUR. HE OFFERS A ROLL
OF PAN AT MADHYAMESHVAR.

From there the Gosavi went to Nandaur.[204] Inclined to play in water, he said, "I'm not coming with you now, my woman. I'll go on my own. Come on, Dakhale."

The Gosavi went and begged for food. After he begged, in between, his puja was done and he ate his meal. Then at midday he went to the river, set aside his shawl, and entered the water. The Gosavi, Upadhye, Nathoba, and Dakhale were dunking one another. After playing this way, he swam alongside the bank of the river. Baïse ran along the other bank, shouting, "Please stop, Baba!" The omniscient one said, "Stop now, Dakhale. Baïse is getting upset."

संगमीं सीळातळ : तेयावरि आसन : गोसावी : नाथोबातें
म्हणीतलें : मंडळिका बल्हेग्रामीं ग्रहो बहुत : आपुलीया
पितेयाचिए वारिची येकी बुडी अधीक दीया²⁹⁴ :
उपाध्यी²⁹⁵ म्हणीतलें : पोराचा पूरुखोत्तमु ग्रहो जाला असे :
मग नाथोबायें स्नान केलें : मग मध्यमेश्वरा बीजें केलें :
मध्यमेश्वरा वीडा वाइला : तथा वाववीला : चौकीं आसन :
आदीत्यीं वसति :॥:

१४३ कानळदीं लींगाचां देउळीं वसति :॥:

१४४ चासीं आसन :॥: माणिकेश्वरीं आसन :॥:
जगतीं आंतु लिंगाचां देउळीं वसति :॥:

गोसावी चासांसि बीजें केलें : चास अवलोकीलें : मग
आसन : माणिकेश्वरीं जगती आंतु वसति जाली :॥:

The Gosavi sat down on a flat slab of rock at the confluence of two rivers. He said to Nathoba, "Mandalik, there are many ghosts in Balhegram.[205] Take one more dip in the water on behalf of your father." Upadhye said, "The poor boy's father has become a ghost."[206]

After Nathoba took a bath, the Gosavi went to the Madhyameshvar temple. He offered (or, had them offer) a roll of pan to Madhyameshvar and sat in the central hall of the temple.

He stayed overnight in the Aditya temple.

143 HE STAYS OVERNIGHT IN A LINGA TEMPLE AT KANALADE.[207]

144 HE SITS ON A CLIFF ON THE RIVERBANK. HE SITS IN THE MANIKESHVAR TEMPLE. HE STAYS OVERNIGHT IN A LINGA TEMPLE IN THE COURTYARD.

The Gosavi went to a cliff on the riverbank. He looked at the cliff, then sat down there. He stayed overnight in the courtyard of the Manikeshvar temple.

१४५ सुरेगांवीं आदीतीं वसति :॥ः

सोधु : सुरेगांवा पुर्वे कुंभारवाडा : आदीत्यीं वसति :॥ः

१४६ सोणारीयें आदीतीं वसति :॥ः

१४७ सवसरीं सिंगेश्वरीं आसन : आदीतीं वसति :॥ः

१४८ कुंकुमठाणीं आग्रिष्टीकें वसति :॥ः

गोसावी दामोधरा बीजें केलें : माड अवलोकीलें : जळसेना
बीजें केलें : हें रामेश्वरबास :॥ः सींगेश्वरीं आसन हें
परशरामबास :॥ः

१४९ पुणितांबा पाताळ गुंफे वसति :॥ः

145 HE STAYS OVERNIGHT IN THE ADITYA TEMPLE IN SUREGAV.

(Research: He stayed overnight in the Aditya temple in the Potters' quarter to the east of Suregav.)[208]

146 HE STAYS OVERNIGHT IN THE ADITYA TEMPLE IN SONARI.[209]

147 HE SITS IN THE SINGESHVAR TEMPLE IN SAMVATSAR.[210] HE STAYS OVERNIGHT IN THE ADITYA TEMPLE.

148 HE STAYS OVERNIGHT AT A BRICK FIRE PIT AT KUMKUMTHAN.

The Gosavi went to the Damodar temple.[211] He looked at the wooden handle of the oil lamp. (According to Rameshvarbas, he went to the Jalsen* temple. According to Parasharambas, he sat in the Singeshvar temple.)

149 HE STAYS OVERNIGHT IN AN UNDERGROUND CELL AT PUNATAMBE.[212]

* Vishnu (lying on the serpent Shesha).

१५० नायगांवीं दायंबा भेटी :॥:

१५१ नाउरीं कंटकेश्वरीं वसति :
अग्रिष्टिके क्षेउर :॥:

१५२ पुनरपि पुणतांबां पाताळगुंफे अवस्थान²⁴⁶ :॥:

गोसावी पुणेतांबेया बीजें केलें : पाताळ गुंफे अवस्थान :
दीस पांच : तीन²⁴⁷ :॥: सोधु : वीळीचां परिश्रया बीजें केलें :
तवं ठाकूरू उपद्रवीला देखवीला : बाइसातें तेथौनिचि बोलाउं
पाठविलें : आलीं : बाइसीं म्हणीतलें : येवढेया वेळां काइ :
बाबा : गोसावी ठाकूराचा उपद्रो दाखविला : एथ एसणी
हींसा वर्तली²⁴⁸ : मग हींगुणीये बीजें केलें : तेथ वसति :॥:

१५३ पुर्णगावी वसती²⁴⁹ :॥:

सोधु : दक्षीणे पुर्णगांवा उत्तरे देउळ : तेथ वसती
जाली²⁵⁰ :॥:

150 HE MEETS DAÏMBA IN NAYGAV.[213]

151 IN NAÜR, HE STAYS OVERNIGHT IN
THE KANTAKESHVAR TEMPLE
AND HAS HIS HEAD SHAVED
AT A BRICK FIRE PIT.[214]

152 HE STAYS AGAIN IN THE
UNDERGROUND CELL AT PUNATAMBE.

The Gosavi went to Punatambe and stayed in the under-ground cell there for five (or, three) days. (Research: In the evening, when he went to defecate, he saw a Thakur who had been killed. He immediately sent for Baïse. She came there.

"Why have you sent for me at such an hour, Baba?" asked Baïse. The Gosavi showed her the murdered Thakur. "Such great violence has happened here.")[215]

Then he left for Hinguni and stayed there overnight.[216]

153 HE STAYS OVERNIGHT
AT PURNAGAV.

He stayed in a temple to the north (Research: to the south) of Purnagav.[217]

१५४ सांगवरखेडां सिधनाथीं आसन :॥:

१५५ वांजरगांवीं मढीं वसति :॥:

१५६ जूना नागमठाणीं वसति :॥:

नागमठाणीं : सोधु : जूना नागमठाणीं आदित्यीं : पूर्वामुख :
दारवठा उत्तरामूख :॥:

१५७ तपोवनीं माणिकेश्वरीं आसन :॥:

१५८ खातेगावीं आदीत्यीं वसति : वामाचा उपाहारू :॥:

१५९ रामनाथीं आसन :॥:

154 HE SITS IN THE SIDDHANATH TEMPLE IN SANGAVKHEDE.[218]

155 HE STAYS OVERNIGHT IN A HERMITAGE IN VANJARGAV.[219]

156 HE STAYS OVERNIGHT IN OLD NAGAMTHAN.

He stayed in the Aditya temple in Nagamthan (Research: in Old Nagamthan).[220] The temple faces east; its gate faces north.

157 HE SITS IN THE MANIKESHVAR TEMPLE IN TAPOVAN.[221]

158 HE STAYS OVERNIGHT IN THE ADITYA TEMPLE IN KHATEGAV.[222] HE EATS VAM'S* FOOD.

159 HE SITS IN THE RAMNATH† TEMPLE.

---

* Vamdev.
† "Lord of Ram," a name of Shiva.

१६० डोंबेग्रामीं अवस्थान : दीस सात :॥ः

मढीं दाइंभागवतासी ज्वरू आला : तेहीं वीनवीलें : जी जी :
माझा ज्वरू फेडावा जी : सर्वज्ञें म्हणीतलें : एथ आधीं वोटा
करा : मग फेडीजैल : हो कां जी : केला : मग जरू फीटला :
हें लिळा रामेश्वरबास : उत्तरार्धी अवस्थान२५१ :॥ः

१६१ दाइंबा डखलेया पाठवणीं :॥ः

१६२ बीडीं अटवेलिये गुंफे अवस्थान :॥ः

गोसावी बीडीं बीढार पाहात होते : माहालक्ष्मीचें देउळ
पाहिलें : देउळा दक्षीणे पटीसाळा : पांत पांत देउळां नैऋत्ये
गुंफा : तेथ बीजें केलें : दोन्ही दारसंका धरूनि भितरि
अवलोकीलें : प्रसनायक वोटेयावरि बैसले असति :
तेहीं म्हणीतलें : येईजो जी : म्हणौनि : भीतरि बोलावीलें :
एथ बीढार कीजो जी : आपुला परिग्रहो परता ठेउनि
गोसावीयासी वोटा संपादीला : बाइसीं आसन केलें :
गोसावी आसनीं उपविष्ट जाले : मास च्यारि अवस्थान :॥ः

160 HE STAYS IN DOMBEGRAM FOR SEVEN DAYS.

In the hermitage, Daï Bhagavat got a fever. "Lord," he pleaded, "please make my fever go away." The omniscient one said, "First make a pedestal here; then the fever will go away." "All right, Lord."

He made the pedestal, and then his fever went away.

(According to Rameshvarbas, this *līlā* belongs during the Gosavi's stay there in "The Second Half.")

161 HE SENDS OFF DAÏMBA AND DAKHALE.

162 HE STAYS IN A HERMIT'S CELL ON THE RIVERBANK IN BID.

The Gosavi was searching for a place to stay in Bid. He looked at Mahalakshmi's temple, with a veranda to the south of the temple. Searching, he went to a hermit's cell to the southwest of the temple. He held onto both doorjambs and looked inside.

Parasnayak was there, sitting on a pedestal. He invited him in, saying, "Please come in, Lord. Please stay here, Lord." Moving his belongings aside, he offered the pedestal to the Gosavi.

Baïse prepared a seat on it, and the Gosavi sat on the seat. He stayed there for four months.

१६३ प्रसनाएका स्तीति :॥:

प्रसनाएक पुढां बैसले : तेयां स्तिति जाली : मग : प्रसनाएक
म्हणती : गोसावीया पासौनि आम्हांसि ब्रह्मवीत्पति जाली :
चातुरमासीची पासोडी आली होती : ते धूनि ठेवीली
होती²⁵² : ते गोसावीयासि वोळगवीली :॥:

१६४ पद्मनाभि स्तीति :॥:

सारस्वत भटां : भोगनारायेणाचां देउळी दरिसन जालें होतें :
म्हणौनि : ते गोसावीयाचेया दरिसना येति : तेया सरिसे
पद्मनाभिदेव येति : ते नावेक चळवळे : बाइसां कांहीं
म्हणीयें करूं लागती : बाइसें म्हणति : बटिका : येइजे हो :
बाबा निके : आणि येकलेयांचि येवों जावों लागले : मग
सारस्वत भट : देहा एका आड येति : मग दीसां आठां
येति : मग म्हणति : मि अमूकेया तमूकेया गेलां होतां : तो
आरायेंचि ना : मग गोसावीया पासौनि पद्मनाभिदेवा²⁵³
स्तीति जाली : मग ते गोसावीयापासि आसेति : मग
सारस्वतभट न एती²⁵⁴ : गोसावीयासि उदयाचां पूजावस्वर
जालेया नंतरें मग गोसावी दक्षिणेश्वर वीहरणा बीजें
करीती²⁵⁵ : मागौतें बीढारा बीजें करीती : ऐसा एकदीस²⁵⁶
गोसावी दक्षिणेश्वराकडे बीजें केलें : बनीं आसन : पासि
पद्मनाभिदेव बैसले असति : तेया वरौनि : सारस्वतदेव

163 PARASNAYAK GOES INTO A TRANCE.

Parasnayak sat in front of the Gosavi and went into a trance. Then he said, "Through the Gosavi I have received knowledge of the Absolute."

He had washed and set aside a thick shawl that he had received for the four-month rainy-season retreat. He offered the shawl to the Gosavi.

164 PADMANABHI GOES INTO A TRANCE.

Sarasvatbhat had had *darśan* of the Gosavi in the Bhognarayan temple, and so he would come for the Gosavi's *darśan*. Padmanabhidev would come with him. For a little while, Padmanabhidev would be restless, but then he would begin doing some tasks for Baïse. Baïse would say, "Batika, you should keep on coming here. Baba is good." And he began to come and go all by himself.

After some time, Sarasvatbhat started coming only every other day, and then he was coming once a week. Then he would say, "I went to such-and-such a place, and so I didn't have time." Eventually, after Padmanabhidev went into a trance caused by the Gosavi and stayed on with him, Sarasvatbhat stopped coming.

When the Gosavi's morning puja service was over, the Gosavi would go wandering to the Dakshineshvar temple and then return to their lodgings. One day he went to the Dakshineshvar temple and sat in the grove. Padmanabhidev was sitting with him. Sarasvatdev went past them, holding the end of his garment in front of his face.

आडपालौ वोडउनि गेले : तवं बाइसी म्हणीतलें : बाबा
पैल सारस्वतभट नव्हति : सर्वज्ञें म्हणीतलें : होति : हो :
बाबातें देखौनि आडवे आडवे कां जात असेति : गोसावी
पद्मनाभितें दाखवीलें : हा एथ असे : म्हणौनि२५७ : तवं
बाइसीं म्हणीतलें : बाबा : हा एथ असे : तरि यासि आडवेया
जावेया काइ कारण : सर्वज्ञें म्हणीतलें : बाइ : सिक्षाचां
अभिमान :॥: या उपरि पंचकौळाचार्याची गोष्टि सांगीतली :
मग बाइसी म्हणीतलें : बटिका : तरि तुं न ये एथ :॥:

१६५ रेमनायकां अवसरू :॥:

एकवेळ पद्मनाभि देवी : रेमनायेका पुढें गोसावीयाची प्रशंसा
केली : रेमनायेकू : गोसावीयाचेया दरीसना आले : तवं :
गोसावीयासि मर्दना होति असे२५८ : एकें म्हणति : पद्मनाभि
देव मर्दना देत होते : तवं रेमनायक आले : गोसावीयां पुढें
जाणवीलें : जी जी : रेमनायक आले : गोसावीयासि जाडी
आसना घातली होती : तेची२५९ ऐकूनि जाडी पांगरौनि
गोसावी बाहीरि बीजें केलें : गोसावी पटिसाळेवरि उभे
राहीलें२६० : तथा कोंगटें : रेमनायकें पुसीलें : श्री चांगदेवो
राउळां : गोसावीयासि कैसा अवसरू असे : सर्वज्ञें म्हणी-
तलें : ऐसा असे : म्हणौनि : जाडि फेडुनि दाखवीलें : मग
आसन : गोसावीयांसि गोष्टी करीति : तेवीचि पस्यातापु
करिति : जी जी : अवसरू नेणेंचि जी : एकाचेनि मतें :
नायको : तुम्हां अवस्वरू अनवस्वरू नाहीं कीं :॥:

Baïse asked, "Baba, wasn't that Sarasvatbhat over there?" "Yes, it was," replied the omniscient one. "Why was he hiding his face when he saw you, Baba?" The Gosavi gestured toward Padmanabhi. "Because *he* is here." "Even if he is here, Baba," asked Baïse, "why should Sarasvatbhat go by hiding his face?" The omniscient one said, "My woman, pride in one's disciples..."[223] And then he told the story of Panchakaulacharya.[224]

Then Baïse said, "So you shouldn't come here, Batika."

165 THE RIGHT TIME FOR REMNAYAK.

Once Padmanabhidev praised the Gosavi to Remnayak, so Remnayak came for *darśan* of the Gosavi. The Gosavi was having a massage at the time. (Some say Padmanabhidev was giving him a massage when Remnayak arrived.) "Lord," someone told the Gosavi, "Remnayak has come."

Hearing that, the Gosavi picked up the blanket (or, cloak) that had been put down for him to sit on. He wrapped it around his shoulders, went outside, and stood on the veranda. Remnayak asked, "What is Shri Cangdev Raül Gosavi doing now?" "This," said the omniscient one, and he took off the blanket and showed him. Then the Gosavi sat down.

Remnayak was conversing with the Gosavi, but at the same time he was feeling remorseful. "I have no idea of the right time to come, Lord," he said. (In the view of some, the omniscient one replied, "Nayak, for you there is no right or wrong time.")

१६६ कोले घायखंडी दाखववणें :॥:

एकुदीस उदयाचा पूजावस्वर जालेया नंतरें गोसावी वीहरणा
बीजे करिति : बनाकडे जातां : तवं राजगुरु एकू : आपुलिया
सिरव्यांसि सराउं देवों गेला होता : बना आंतु गोसावीयाचें
दर्शन जालें : आपुलिए हातींचा कोलु : गोसावियाचिये
श्रीकरीं वोळगवीला : मग मागौता सरला : सिरव्यांचिए
हातींचा कोलु आपणें घेतला : गोसावी बद करूनि घावो
लावीला : तेणें म्हणीतलें : जी जी : एकू वेळ घाएखंडी
दाखवीजो जी : म्हणौनि : श्रीचरणा लागला : सर्वज्ञें
म्हणीतलें : न दाखवीजे : भक्तजनीं म्हणीतलें : हीराइसा :
तथा : बाइसीं म्हणीतलें : कां न दाखवीजे जी : सर्वज्ञें
म्हणीतलें : घाया घाया प्राणियातें ठेवील : तथा हिराइसा :
बाइ : पोरू प्राजू असे : एकू वेळ दाखवीजतें आणि कळौनि
घेता : प्राणियातें घतता : तथा मारिता :॥:

१६७ सुकीया जोगनाएका दुखापनौति :॥:

एकुदीस गोसावीयांसि उदयाचा पूजावस्वर जालेया नतरें
गोसावी वीहरणा बीजें केलें : यानंतरें भीतरि वोटेयावरि
आसन²⁶¹ : बाइसें चरणक्षाळण करितें असति : तवं सूकीये
जोगनाएक आले : हीराइसा : सर्वज्ञें म्हणीतलें : नायेको
या :॥छ॥: दंडवतें घातलीं : श्रीचरणा लागले : बैसले :

370

166 HE DEMONSTRATES HOW
TO FIGHT WITH A CUDGEL.

After the morning worship service one day, the Gosavi was going out to wander. As he went toward the grove, a royal guru had gone there to give his students a practice session. He had *darśan* of the Gosavi in the grove. He handed his cudgel to the Gosavi, then stepped back and took a cudgel from one of his students. The Gosavi thumped him hard.

He touched the Gosavi's holy feet and said, "Show me once how to fight, Lord." "I won't show you," said the omniscient one. The devotees said (or, according to Hiraïsa, Baïse said), "Why won't you show him, Lord?" The omniscient one said, "He will batter living beings." (Or, according to Hiraïsa, "My woman, the child is intelligent. If I show him once, he will learn the lesson, and he will kill living beings.")

167 JOGNAYAK THE TAX
COLLECTOR'S TALE OF WOE.

One day, after the Gosavi's morning worship service, he went out to wander. Later he was sitting indoors on the pedestal.[225] As Baïse was washing his feet, Jognayak the tax collector arrived. (According to Hiraïsa, the omniscient one said, "Come in, Nayak.") Jognayak prostrated himself, touched the holy feet, and sat down. He was given the Gosavi's foot

चरणोदक प्रसाददान होए : ताप गेले : जी : निवाला जी :
ताप काइसे : नाएको²⁶² : जी जी : मीं मिरजेकडील : उभे
मार्गिंचा सूंकिया : तेलंगदेशासि गेलो : द्रव्य जोडिलें : बैलु
भरुनि²⁶³ घेउनि एत होतों : तो बडुवे बैलु फांकीला : तें द्रव्य
गेलें : मग गांवा आलों : घरिचा वेलुवाकू वीकूनि वडिलु पुत्रु
सोवनीं हाती बैसवीला : तो मेला : मग धाकुटा बैसवीला :
तोही मेला : ब्राह्मणि मेली : ऐसा दुखीया जालां जी :कव्हणे
ठाइं सुखासि नये : एथ आलां : आणि ताप जात देखत असें
जी : सर्वज्ञें म्हणीतलें²⁶⁴ : पुरुखासि घरभंगु पुत्र सोखू द्रव्य
सोखू : ये तिन्हीं असाहे : नावेक होते : गोसावी पाठवणी
दीधली : निगतां सर्वज्ञें म्हणीतलें : नायेको : यथ येवों
आवडे : तेधवां येइजे हो : मग निगाले :॥:

१६८ बाइसीं माहात्मेयाची वाट पाहाणें :॥:

बाइसीं म्हणीतलें : बाबा : सापें माहात्मे कोण्हीं न यति : तथा
बाबाचीं भक्तें कोन्हीं न येति : कीं अळसु लागतु असे :
बाबा : सर्वज्ञें म्हणीतलें : हें एथ असे : ऐसें कोण्ही जाणेना :
हीराइसा : बाइ : एथही आळसू लागत असे : एती : बाइ :
पाणीभातु सांचा : अभ्यागतें एतें असति : काइ गा :॥:

water as *prasād*. "My anguish has gone away, Lord," he said. "I have calmed down, Lord."

"Why were you in anguish, Nayak?" "I am from Miraj, Lord, and I collect the tolls all along the road.[226] I went to the Telugu land and made some money. When I was coming back with it loaded it on a bullock, some temple priests drove away the bullock. I lost the money. Then I returned to my village, sold all the jewelry in the house, and set up my elder son in a goldsmiths' shop. That son died, so I set up my younger son in the shop. He died too, and my wife died as well. I was grief-stricken, Lord. I could not find happiness anywhere. Now I have come here, and I see my anguish going away."

The omniscient one said, "Grief over three things is unbearable for a man: losing his wife, losing his sons, and losing his money."

Jognayak stayed there for a little while, and then the Gosavi gave him leave to go. As he left, the omniscient one said, "Come here whenever you like, Nayak." Then he set out.

168 BAÏSE WAITS EXPECTANTLY FOR MAHATMAS.

Baïse said, "Baba, these days none of the Mahatmas (or, your devotees) is coming to visit. I'm getting bored, Baba." The omniscient one replied, "No one knows that I am here." (According to Hiraïsa, "My woman, I am getting bored too. But they are coming, my woman, so stock up on water-and-rice gruel. Guests are coming, all right?")

१६९ देवां भटां भेटि :॥:

देव : भट : कांबखेडाहुनि बीडासि२६५ आले : हाटवटिया
जात असति : विळिचां गोदरी भरली असे : दोहीं सूरकौनि
दीवे लागले असति : ऐसें जात असति : तवं भटोबासीं
म्हणीतलें : कैसीं बरवीं चोखें पानें फुलें : गोसावीया जोगीं
वीकतें असति : देवीं म्हणीतलें : हो नागदेया : गोसावी
कवणें ठाइ असति : ऐसें नेणिजे : यन्हवी घेवौनि जातों :
गेले : एकाचां घरीं वसीले : उदीयांचि आटवलीये२६६ धोत्रें
धोंआवेंया आले : देव बैसले : भटोबास धोत्रें धुत असति :
गोसावीयांसि उदयाचा पूजावसर जालेया नंतरें गोसावी
मा आसनीं उपविष्ट असति : तवं देवीं उजाइ केली : सर्वज्ञें
म्हणीतलें : बाइ : उजाइ माहात्मेया सारिखी : माहात्मा
आला असे : गोसावी उठीले : दोन्हीं दारसंका धरूनि
अवलोकीलें : तवं देवां भटातें देखीलें : आणि खांकरिले :
भटीं मागौतें पाहीलें : गोसावीयांतें देखीलें : मग म्हणीतलें :
दादो दादो गोसावी कीं असति : ना कें असति२६७ : हे
नव्हति : ऐसें म्हणति : गोसावी खालि उतरले : आणि
दादोसावरि साइली पडली : मागुतें पाहीलें तवं गोसावी :
नागदेया गोसावी : गोसावी देवासि क्षेवं दीधलें : भटोसि
मागिला कडौनि खेवं दीधलें : गोसावी मागौता ऐसा श्रीकरू
केला : करूनि पूढें आणिले : मग गोसावी क्षेमालिंगन

169   HE MEETS DEV AND BHAT.

Dev and Bhat came from Kambkhed to Bid to go to the market.[227] In the evening the marketplace was full of people, and lamps were lit on both rows of stalls. As they went along, Bhatobas said, "What nice, fresh leaves and flowers they are selling! They would be fit for the Gosavi!" "Yes, Nagdev," replied Dev. "We don't know where the Gosavi is. Otherwise we would get some and take them to him."

They went and stayed at someone's house. Early the next morning they came to the riverbank to wash their dhotis. Dev sat there while Bhatobas washed the dhotis.

After the Gosavi's morning worship service, when he was sitting in his place, Dev made a yogic breathing sound. The omniscient one said, "My woman, that breathing sound is like the Mahatma's. The Mahatma has come here." The Gosavi got up. He held onto both doorjambs and looked out. He saw Dev and Bhat, and he cleared his throat.

Bhat looked back and saw the Gosavi. "Dado! Dado!" he said. "It's the Gosavi!" "No! Where is he?" "Isn't that he?" As they were talking that way, the Gosavi came down to where they were, and his shadow fell on Dados. Dados looked back and saw the Gosavi. "It is the Gosavi, Nagdev," he said.

The Gosavi embraced Dev, and he embraced Bhat from behind. He placed his holy hand on Bhat, pulled him forward, and then embraced him again. Then the Gosavi went to his cell.

दीधलें : मग गुंफे बीजें केलें : दादोसीं भटोबासाकरवि पुजा
द्रव्यें आणवीलीं : पुजा केली२६८ : मग दादोसीं वीनवीलें :
जी जी : अवघी भक्तजनें गोसावीयाची वाट पाहातें
असति : जी : गोसावी कवणी ठाइ राज्य करीताति : ऐसें
नेणिजे : तरि नागदेवातें बोलावु धाडू२६९ : गोसावी मानिलें :
हीराइसा : धाडा : मग भटोबास बोलाउं धाडिलें :॥:

१७० पर्वि पुजा :॥:

भटोबास साडेगावां गेले : दोनि वस्तें विणविलीं : एक
आपणेया लागौनि : एक दोदोसां लागौनि : आपणेयाते२७०
दामें हीन : एकें म्हणति : कांबरखेडां वीणवीलें : मग
भटोबास : आबैसें : उमाइसें : सौभागें : महदाइसें : ऐसीं
आलीं : दादोसांचेया बीढारा : दादोसांसीं भेटी जाली : ते
दीसीं पर्वाचां चातुर्दशू : बल्हेग्रामकार द्रिढपुरुषु आले :
उपाधीं सीदोरी दादोसांचिये बीढारीं ठेवीली होती : ते घेउनि
आले : तव२७१ बाइसीं : उपाध्यातें पुसीलें : बटिका :
माहात्म्येयाचां ठांइं : पर्व वर्तत असे : तथा होत असे : हो
बाइ : वर्तत असे : तरि तुम्हीं आलेति : सर्वज्ञें म्हणीतलें :
बाइ : चांगो आणि हे एथीचेचि कीं२७२ : भटोबासि
दादोसांसि पुजा केली : अवघा पंवंती वाइलीं : भटोबासि :
हीन वस्त्र तें दादोसांसि वाइलें : मग गोसावीयांसि पर्वींतें
वाविया दादोस सिक्षासहीत निगाले : भटोबासि वस्त्र

Dados had Bhatobas go and get materials for puja, and then he performed puja to the Gosavi.[228] Then Dados made a request: "Lord Gosavi, all the devotees are waiting to meet you. They don't know where you are, Lord. May I send Nagdev to invite them?"

The Gosavi agreed to this. (Hiraïsa: "Send him.") Then Dados sent Bhatobas to invite them.

170 WORSHIP ON A FESTIVAL DAY.

Bhatobas went to Sadegav.[229] He had two garments woven, one for himself and one for Dados. The one for himself cost one copper coin less than the other one. (Some say he had them woven in Kambkhed.) Then Bhatobas, Abaïse, Umaïse, Sobhage, and Mahadaïse came to Dados's lodgings. They met Dados on the fourteenth day of the festival fortnight. One-and-a-Half Man from Balhegram came too.[230]

Upadhye went and got his lunch packet, which he had left in Dados's lodgings. Baïse asked Upadhye, "Batika, do the Mahatma's disciples celebrate the festival in his honor?" "Yes they do, my woman." "But even so you have come here?" The omniscient one said, "My woman, he and Cango belong to me alone!"[231]

Meanwhile, Bhatobas performed puja to Dados, he offered shoulder threads to everyone, and he offered the cheaper garment to Dados. Then Dados set out with his disciples to offer a shoulder thread to the Gosavi. Bhatobas had stuck the other garment under his arm, to offer to the Gosavi.

वावीया खाके सुदलें असें : दादोसीं पुसीलें : नागदेया :
कारखे काइ : ना वस्त्र : काइसें : ना : गोसावीयांसि वावीया :
तुज गोसावी काइ होति : गोसावी आमचे गुरू : आम्हीं
गोसावीयांसि वावें : तुवां आम्हांसि वावें : घेउनि ये आरूतें :
मा : वाय आम्हासि : वाइलें : मग गोसावीयांसि पवीतें
वावेयालागि आले : गोसावीयासि मर्दना जाली : माजनें
जालें : पुजा जाली : अवघा पवीतें वाइलें : मग देव आलें :
गोसावीयासि पवीतें वाइलें : पुजा केली : वस्त्र वोळगवीलें :
गोसावी श्रीचरणीचेनि आंगुठेनि करूनि वस्त्र परूतें केलें :
दादोस : बाइसां : पवींतें वावीया गेले : वाइलें : मां : बिढारा
गेले : हीराइसा पाठ : सर्वज्ञें म्हणीतलें : जाणा पा गा : हा
बाइसासि पवीतें वावीयां कां गेला : जी जी : बाइसी वडिलें
म्हणौनि : आणि काइ : ऐसें नव्हें कीं गा : एणें बाइसाचां
ठाइं वावें : मा : तुम्ही अवघी याचां ठाइं वावें : पोरू कवण
वडिल : ऐसेंहीं : तथा इतुलेंही नेणे : बाइसांपासौनि मिचि
वडिल ॥छ॥ः मग गोसावी वस्त्र धुववीलें२७३ : बाइसीं
म्हणीतलें : काइसेया धुवावें बाबा : एक दोनि दीस तऱ्हीं
नवें वस्त्र पंगुरिजो कां बाबा : सर्वज्ञें म्हणीतलें : बाइ :
प्राणियांसि आपुलीं आंगसीकें एथ वाउं एति कीं न एति :
इतुलेंही प्राणियांसि आपुलीया विधी अविधिचें ज्ञान
नाहीं२७४ : हीराइसा पाठ : बाइ : पोरें आपुलें वोवळें वस्त्र
वोळगवीलें म्हणौनि : मागिल वृतांत सांघीतलें : प्राणियांसि
आपुलिया वीधि अवीधीचें ज्ञान नाहीं : काइ करीतां काइ
होइल : ऐसेंहीं नेणे :॥:

Dados asked him, "What is that under your arm, Nagdev?"
"A garment." "What is it for?" "To offer to the Gosavi." "Is
the Gosavi yours? The Gosavi is *my* guru. *I* should make
offerings to the Gosavi, and *you* should make offerings to
me. Bring it here and offer it to me." He offered it to him.

When they arrived to offer shoulder threads to the Gosavi,
he had had a massage and a bath, his puja had been done,
and everyone had offered him shoulder threads. Then Dev
arrived, offered a thread to the Gosavi, did puja to him, and
offered him the garment. With the big toe of his holy foot,
the Gosavi pushed the garment away. Dados went to offer
a shoulder thread to Baïse, and after he offered it to her he
went to his lodgings.

(Hiraïsa version: The omniscient one said, "Look at that!
Why did he go to offer a shoulder thread to Baïse?" "Because
Baïse is senior to him, Lord. Why else?" "That's not why.
If he offers one to Baïse, then all of you have to offer one to
him. The child doesn't even know who is senior to whom. I
am the only one who is senior to Baïse.")

Then the Gosavi had the garment washed. "Why should
you have it washed, Baba?" asked Baïse. "When a garment
is new, you should wear it for at least a day or two, Baba."

The omniscient one replied, "My woman, that person
knows so little about right and wrong that he can't tell
whether he may or may not offer his own garment to me."[232]
(Hiraïsa version: "My woman, the child has offered me a
garment that he has used. That's why." He told her what had
happened. "That person does not know right from wrong,
nor does he know what actions have what effects.")

१७१ सोभाग नामकरण :॥:

सोभाग बाइसां नाम माइबाइसें : गोसावी आसनीं बैसले
असति : पुढां तियें बैसलीं असति : प्रभुत : फाळएसणे
दांत : गोसावीयांची श्रीमूर्ति अवलोकीतें : सर्वज्ञें म्हणीतलें :
बाइ : तुम्हीं वरैता पढीया : तेहीं म्हणीतलें : तरि काइ
जी२७५ : मि वरैतासि जीउ ऐसी पढीयें : तीं आपण कोरडें
खाये ते तुप मज सुति : तथा वाढीति : सर्वज्ञें म्हणीतलें : तरि
तुम्हीं सोभाग म्हणा : हीराइसा पाठ : मां रे अपुर सोभाग
मा :॥छ॥: तेविचि गाये दुभे : गाडुगाभरि दुध होए : आपण
ताक जेवी : मज गाडुगाभरि दुध रिचविति : तें : सोभागाचा
गाडुगा मां२७६ :॥:

१७२ तथा एकादशीं केळें खाववणें :॥:

एकुदीसीं गोसावीयांसि दुपाहाराचा पुजावस्वर : आरोगणा :
पहुड : उपहुड : जालेयानंतरें गोसावी आसनीं उपविष्ट
असति : बाइसीं म्हणीतलें : बाबा : केळें बहुत साचलीं
असति : नासती : वेचिजतु कां : आनवीलीं : हीराइसापाठ :
बाइ : घेउनि या :॥छ॥: आणिलीं : मग वांटे केलें : गोसावी
आबैसासि केळें देत होते : हीराइसापाठ : बाइ केळें
खा :॥छ॥: जी जी : आजि एकादशी : आम्हा बारमासीया
एकादशी : गोसावी आबाइसातें२७७ म्हणीतलें : यें तवं

171 HE GIVES SOBHAGE HER NAME.

Sobhagbaïse's name was Maïbaïse. The Gosavi was sitting in his place, and she was sitting in front of him, looking at the Gosavi's holy form. Her teeth were large, as big as plowshares.

The omniscient one asked, "My woman, does your husband love you?" "Of course, Lord," she replied. "My husband loves me like his own soul. He eats his own food dry and serves me ghee." The omniscient one said, "So you are Sobhage,* I tell you."[233]

"Besides, when the cow gives milk, there is a potful of it. He drinks buttermilk himself and serves the whole potful of milk to me." "That is a potful of marital bliss!"

172 AND HE FEEDS HER BANANAS
ON THE EKADASHI DAY.

After the Gosavi's midday worship service one day, he ate his meal, went to sleep, woke up, and was seated in his place. Baïse said, "Baba, we have accumulated so many bananas that they are going bad. Can we use them up?" He told her to bring them to him. (Hiraïsa version: "Bring them here, my woman.") She brought them, and then he handed them out.

The Gosavi was giving a banana to Abaïse. (Hiraïsa version: "Eat a banana, my woman.") "Lord," she said, "today is the Ekadashi.[234] We observe the Ekadashi every month of the year." The Gosavi said to Abaïse, "But these are women who fast for a month at a time." ____

* "Marital Bliss."

मासोपासियें²⁷⁸ : मग सोभागातें म्हणीतलें : सोभागें हो या :
हे केलें तुम्हां देइल : पासि बैसलीं : मांडियेवरि मान
घातली : आं करा : चांग : आं करा : तें आं करिति : केलें
सोलीति : वाटां साकर असे : तेथ घांसू माखीति : तेयाचेया
तोंडाकडे दाखवीति : आणि : आपुलीए²⁷⁹ श्रीमूखीं
घालिति : आणि तें म्हणति : हें काइ : बाइ : कीं ये
चाळवीजत असीजे : मागुतें म्हणति : वेळां दोनि च्यारि
केलें : पुडती म्हणीतलें : आं करा : चांग आं करा : ना
चाळवीजताये : बाइ : की यें : आतां या : सर्वझें म्हणीतलें :
न खेलों : बाइ : की यें : आतां न चाळवीजे : ना बाइ की ये
चाळवीजत असीजे : आतां चाळविजे : तरि माल्हबाइचि
आण : मग धायवरि केलें खाववीलीं :॥ः

१७३ आबैसां आपदे धर्मू निरूपण :॥ः

आबैसें : उमाइसें : रात्रीं निद्रास्थाना गेलीं : तेयांचां घरीं
अवघेया उपवासू : तेहीं रांधिलें : प्रधिलें : दादलें जागरणा
गेले : घरिचीं आवघीं निजैलीं तें : भानवसीं निजैलीं : पाहारू
दीढू रात्रि भरली : आणि आबैसा पीडा उठीली : उमाइ :
उमाइ : मज थोर पीडा उठिली : बारमासिया एकादशी

Then he said to Sobhage, "Come here, Sobhage. I will give you a banana." She sat down near him, and he put her head on his lap. "Open your mouth. Open it wide!" he would say, and she would open her mouth. He would peel a banana and coat a piece of it in a bowl of sugar that was there. He would move the piece toward her mouth. And then he would pop it into his own holy mouth. She would say, "What is going on? Come here, my woman! He is teasing me."

Again he would tell her to open her mouth. He did this a few times, then he told her once again, "Open your mouth. Open it wide!" "No!" she replied. "You are teasing me. Come here, my woman! Come now!" The omniscient one said, "Let's not play games." "Come here, my woman!" "I won't tease you now." "No! Come here, my woman! He is teasing me." "I swear by Malhabai* that I will not tease you now."

Then he fed her bananas until she was full.

173 HE TEACHES ABAÏSE THE RULES FOR EMERGENCIES.

At night, Abaïse and Umaïse went to the house where they were sleeping. Everyone in the household was fasting. The women had cooked some food and left it there, while the men had gone out for a vigil. Everyone in the house was asleep.

Abaïse and Umaïse were sleeping in the kitchen. In the middle of the night, Abaïse got a stomachache. "Umaï! Umaï! I have a terrible stomachache. I fast every Ekadashi all year long, but I have never had a stomachache like this."

---

* His mother.

करीं : परि ऐसी पीडा नाहीं कहीं : ते उगीचि होति : मग :
कोपौनि म्हणति : उमाइए कां मज थोर पीडा होत असे :
मग तियें उठिलीं : डेरींचा भातु काढिला२८० : आणि
आणासिचां कांजि घेतला : भातु सिंपीला : मूठीकळा वळुनि
दीधला : पाणियाचां चूळ भारिला : इतुकेनि तेयाची पीडा
समली : नावेक गेलें इतुकेनि उमाइसां तैसीचि पीडा
उठीली : आबैये : आबैये : मजही तैसीची पीडा उठीली :
इतुके मास उपवास केले : परि मज ऐसी पीडा कहींचि
जाली नाहीं : तेहीं तैसेंचि केलें : उदीयांचि दरिसना आलीं :
सर्वज्ञें म्हणीतलें : पारणाइती बाइया सवीया श्रमलिया :
नां२८१ : वासना : पारणाइती बाइया आलिया : मां : भिक्षा
अवसरु जाला : मां :॥छ॥: तेहीं म्हणीतलें : काइसा भीक्षा
अवसरु जी : म्हणौनि : मागिल आवघें सांगितलें : जी जी :
अपुसीं आम्हीं तेयांचें घेतलें२८२ : तरि काइ दोषू जाला जी :
सर्वज्ञें म्हणीतलें : तेतुलें घेतलेयां तैसा दोषू नाहीं२८३ :॥:

१७४ उमाई निरे निरूपण :॥:

उमाई अवकासां गेलीं होतीं : मानुस अवकासां बैसलें होतें :
तेयसि कींव पडिली : वरि पाउस पडिला : कशमळ वाहुनि
गेलें : कीवीयाचां पुंजा उरला : तेयातें मुंगिया तोडतोडुं नेतीं
होतीया : मग : कांटाळौनि नर्क नर्क ऐसें म्हणिजति : तें :

Umaïse didn't say anything, so Abaïse got angry and said, "Umaï! Why am I having this terrible stomachache?"

Umaïse got up. She took some cooked rice from its earthen pot, and she took gruel from another clay pot. She sprinkled water on the rice, scooped out a bit, and gave it to Abaïse, along with a sip of water. Abaïse's stomachache quickly subsided.

Soon Umaïse got the same kind of stomachache. "Abai! Abai! Now I have a stomachache just like yours. I have fasted for many months, but I've never had pain like this." Abaïse did the same thing for Umaïse that Umaïse had done for her.

Early the next morning they came for *darśan*. The omniscient one said, "Of course the women who have broken their fast are tired, aren't they?" (Another version: "The women who have broken their fast have arrived! It is time to go begging!")

"How can it be the time to go begging, Lord?" they asked, and they told him everything that had happened. "We took their food without asking permission, Lord. Was that wrong?" The omniscient one replied, "It is not really wrong to take such a little bit."[235]

174 HE TELLS UMAÏ ABOUT HELL.

Umaï had gone to defecate. A man who had worms had squatted to defecate near the place where she went, and afterward it had rained. The man's feces had gotten washed away, and what was left was a heap of worms. Ants were breaking them up and carrying them off. Disgusted, Umaï

एथचि मां : आणि आबैसां पुढें सांघीतलें : सांघतां गोसावी
आइकीलें : तथा आबैसीं सांघीतलें : सर्वज्ञें म्हणीतलें :
बाइ : मास उपवासीयें काइ म्हणतें असति : मग आबैसीं
सांघीतलें : सर्वज्ञें म्हणीतलें : बाई : जाणतेया एथचि
नरक२८४ :॥छ॥:

१७५ आबैसा अनंत नीरोपणे :॥:

आनंतचां चतुर्दशीं आबैसीं भटोबासा करवि : पाटसूवाचा
अनंतु करवीला : गोसावीयालागि उपाहारू निफजवीला :
आपणेया लागि हविक्षान्न करवीलें : गोसावीयासि मर्दना
दीधली : मादनें जालें : पुजा जाली : आबैसी श्रीचरणावरि
अनंत ठेवीला : मग श्रीचरणावरौनि अनंतु घेतला : हीराइसा
पाठ : मग दोहीं श्रीकरीं दोनि सेवट धरिले :॥छ॥: गोसावी
पुसिलें : हें काइ : जी हा अनंतु : सर्वज्ञें म्हणीतलें : अनंतु तो
काइ सुताचा : बाइ : अनंत तो काइ एवढा : तथा बाइ :
अनंतु तो अनंत कीं ॥ गोसावीयांसि ताट जालें : गोसावी
आरोगण करीतां आबैसाचें अवीक्षान्न पुसिलें : बाइ हें काइ :
जी हें अवीक्षान्न : आणां आरूतें : आणिलें : मग प्रसाद
केला : मग आरोगणा : गुळळा : वीडा :॥:

386

said, "Hell! What they call hell is right here!" And she told Abaïse about it.

The Gosavi overheard her telling Abaïse. (Or, Abaïse told him about it.) The omniscient one asked, "My woman, what is the woman who fasts for a month saying?" Abaïse told him. "My woman," said the omniscient one, "for one who knows, hell is right here."

175   HE TELLS ABAÏSE ABOUT ANANTA.

On Ananta Chaturdashi, Abaïse had Bhatobas make an Ananta out of silk.[236] She prepared some food for the Gosavi and had a special festival meal made for herself. She gave the Gosavi a massage, he had a bath, and his puja was performed. Abaïse placed the Ananta on his holy feet, then she took it off his holy feet. (Hiraïsa version: Then he picked it up, one end in each of his holy hands.)

"What is this?" asked the Gosavi. "It is Ananta, Lord." The omniscient one said, "Is the Infinite One made of cloth? Is the Infinite One this small, my woman?" (Or, "My woman, the Infinite One is infinite!"[237])

A plate of food was prepared for the Gosavi. As he ate his meal, he asked about Abaïse's special festival food. "What is this, my woman?" "It is special festival food, Lord." "Bring it here."

She brought it to him, and he made *prasād* of it. Then he ate his meal, rinsed his mouth, and chewed pan.

१७६ प्रसनायका चांदोवां ब्रह्मकथन :॥:

एकुदीसु गोसावी महालक्ष्मिचेया देउळा बीजें केलें : सवें
बाइसें : भटोबास : प्रसनायक : असति : चौकीं चांदोवा
केला होता : एकें म्हणति श्रीमुगुटीं चांदोवा लागला :
गोसावी वरती वास पाहीली : तवं सेण : माती : लादि :
हरियाळु : आणिकीही वर्त : ऐसीयांचीं फळें केलीं होतीं :
सर्वज्ञें म्हणीतलें : प्रसेया : घेया गा तुमचीं ब्रह्में : जी जी :
बाइसीं पुसीलें : तें कैसी बाबा²⁸⁵ : बाइ : आंबेया सारिखी
दीसत असे कीं : तोंडीं घातलेया : तोंड सेणामातीया भरे :
दृष्टांतु नीरोपीला :॥:

१७७ चांगदेवोभटां धोत्रें :॥:

एकुदीसु चांगदेवोभट गोसावीयांचीं²⁸⁶ धोत्रें धों गेले होते :
धोत्रें धुतलीं : घडीया करीत होते : तवं चाटे धोत्रे धों आले :
तेहीं म्हणीतलें : आरे यां श्रीचांगदेवो राउळाची आण घाला :
आणि आमचीहीं धोत्रें धुतीं : एतुलेनि एक चाटा आला²⁸⁷ :
म्हणे : चांगदेवो राउळाची आण : जर हे धोत्र धुवाना²⁸⁸ :
ते धुति : तव आनीक ए²⁸⁹ : तोहीं तैसेंचि म्हणे : तेयाचिंहीं
धुतलीं : ऐसीं अवघेयाचीं धुतलीं : मग आले : गोसावी

176 HE TELLS PARASNAYAK ABOUT
THE ABSOLUTE BY MEANS OF
A CANOPY OF FRUITS AND FLOWERS.

One day the Gosavi went to Mahalakshmi's temple. Baïse, Bhatobas, and Parasnayak were with him. A canopy festooned with fruits had been set up in the central hall of the temple. (Some say his holy head touched the canopy.) The Gosavi looked up.

The fruits had been fashioned out of dung, mud, stones, grass, and rope. The omniscient one said, "Hey, Praseya! Take your Brahmas."[238] "Yes, Lord."

Baïse asked, "What do you mean, Baba?"[239] "They look like mangos, my woman, but when you put them in your mouth it gets filled with dung and mud." He told the parable.[240]

177 DHOTIS FOR CANGDEVBHAT.

One day Cangdevbhat had gone to wash the Gosavi's dhotis. When he had washed the dhotis and was folding them, some students came to wash theirs. They said to one another, "Hey! Swear by Shri Cangdev Raül to him, and he will wash our dhotis too."

Right away, one of the students approached him and said, "I swear by Cangdev Raül that you must wash this dhoti." As Cangdevbhat was washing it, another of them approached him and said the same thing. Cangdevbhat washed his as well. Eventually he washed all of their dhotis.

पुसिलें : बटिका उसिरू कां लावीला : अवघें सांघितलें :
सर्वज्ञें म्हणीतलें : तुम्हीं एथ यावें कीं : हीराइसा पाठ : तुम्हीं
तेयातें एथ घेउनि यावें कीं :॥छ॥: जी जी : आण देती :
सर्वज्ञें म्हणीतलें : एथींचिये आणे हें समर्थ कीं :॥:

१७८ आपदेवोभटा निंब माधुर्यें :॥:

एकु वेळु : गोसावी पटिसाळेवरि बीजें केलें : सरीसे
आपदेवोभट मुख्य अवघीं भक्तजने असति : पौळिसीं
निंब होता : अर्ध बाहींरि : अर्ध आंतु : गोसावी निंबाचें पान
तोडिलें : आपदेओ भटासि दिधलें : हीराइसापाठ : घेया गा :
भागेया :॥छ॥: तेहीं चारखीलें : सर्वज्ञें म्हणीतलें : भागेया कैसें
असे गा : जी जी : कडु असे : अवळोकौनि दुसरें दीधलें :
तें चारखीलें : भागेया कैसें असे गा : जी जी : हें गोड असे :
मग गोसावी अवळोकुनि खांदीचि गोड केली : मग खांदींचि
वोरपौनि खादली : हीराइसापाठ : पोरां काइ२९० खांदीया
सकट खासी :॥:

When he came back, the Gosavi asked, "What took you so long, Batika?" He told him everything that had happened. "You should have come back here," said the omniscient one. (Hiraïsa version: "You should have brought them back here.") "But, Lord, they were swearing by you." The omniscient one said, "I am capable of dealing with oaths taken in my name."[241]

178 THE SWEETNESS OF NEEM FOR APDEVBHAT.

Once when the Gosavi went out onto the veranda, Apdevbhat and all the other devotees were with him. There was a neem tree next to the compound wall, with half its branches outside and the other half inside. The Gosavi broke off a neem leaf and gave it to Apdevbhat. (Hiraïsa version: "Take this, my friend.") Apdevbhat tasted it, and the omniscient one asked, "How does it taste, my friend?" "It's bitter, Lord."

The Gosavi took another one, looked at it, and gave it to him. Apdevbhat tasted that one. "How does it taste, my friend?" "This one is sweet, Lord."

Then the Gosavi looked at a whole branch and made all the leaves on it sweet. Apdevbhat stripped all the leaves off the branch and ate them.

(Hiraïsa version: "Will you eat the branch as well, my child?")

१७९ विद्यावंता भेटि :॥:

गोसावीयांसि उदेयाचा पुजावसर जालेया नंतरें गोसावी
आसनीं उपवीष्ट असति : विद्यावंतु एकू : ब्राह्मणाचां वेखू
धरूनि आला : आंगीं लेइले असति : गोसावीयांसि दरिसन
जालें : तेयांसि गोसावीयां आदरू केला : गोसावी उभे
ठाकले : अर्धासनीं बैसवीलें : येक म्हणति : बाइसां करवि
पाये धुवविले : गंधाक्षेत करवीले : भातुकें वाटां घातलें :
तेंहीं खादलें : गुळळा केला : तांबुळ दीधले : मग ते निगाले :
मग उभे ठाकौनि अनुकरण केलें : बाइसीं पुसीलें : बाबा
हे कवण पुरुष : हे चांगदेवो राउळाचे अनुग्रहीत : बाबा :
हे ऐसेंचि कीं²⁹¹ : सर्वज्ञें म्हणितलें : बाइ : तेथौनि ऐसेयां
बावनां पुरूखां वीद्यादान²⁹² :॥:

१८० दाइंबा सोभागातें हसणें :॥:

दायांबा सोभागतें हासों लागले : माझेगा सोभागा : माझेगा
सोभुगया : ऐसे हांसति : सोभागीं म्हणितलें : जी जी :
हा भोजा : मातें हांसतु असे : सर्वज्ञें म्हणीतलें : भोजेया
सोभागतें हासाना गा²⁹³ : ना जी हें आम्हां सक्ष नव्हे :
सर्वज्ञें म्हणितलें : तरि तुम्ही एथौनि जा : हो कां जी : हें वर
होववैल : परि : ना हासणें असक्ष : सर्वज्ञें म्हणीतलें :
जा पडो वाट : सोभागा हांसों दीया : हां गा : तुम्हीं
सोभागातें हांसत असा : तरि मेलेया काइ कराल : जी जी :

179 HE MEETS A MAN WHO HAS ESOTERIC KNOWLEDGE.

After the Gosavi's morning worship service, he was seated in his place. A man who had esoteric knowledge came and had *darśan* of the Gosavi. The man was dressed like a Brahman and was wearing a cloak. The Gosavi treated him with respect, standing up and sharing his seat with him. (Some say he had Baïse wash the man's feet and put sandalwood paste and grains of rice on his forehead.)

Baïse put some food into a bowl. The man ate it and rinsed his mouth, and she gave him pan. Then, when he left, the Gosavi stood up to see him off.

"Who is that holy man, Baba?" asked Baïse. "He is a disciple of Cangdev Raül." "He is just like that other one, Baba."[242] "My woman," replied the omniscient one, "Cangdev Raül gave esoteric knowledge to fifty-two men."[243]

180 DAÏMBA MAKES FUN OF SOBHAGE.

Daïmba began to make fun of Sobhage, laughing at her and saying, "My Sobhage! My Sobhugaye!"

"Lord," said Sobhage, "Bhoja is making fun of me." "Bhoja," said the omniscient one, "stop making fun of Sobhage." "No, Lord. I can't stop." The omniscient one said, "Then leave here." "All right, Lord. That I can do, but I cannot stop making fun of her." The omniscient one said, "Go on! Get going." "Please let me make fun of Sobhage."

"Listen! You are making fun of Sobhage, but what will you do if she dies?" "I will do what it's appropriate for a son to

पुत्रा वोजे तें मि करीन : जी जी : गोसावी काइ करीती :
सर्वज्ञें म्हणीतलें : मायाबहीणी वोजे तें हें करील : जी जी :
सोभागा मरेल : तरि : मि सोभागाचे आंगठे बांधैन : कीडडी
करीन : खांदी रीगैन : चडा फोडीन : सोभागाचा संसकारू
करीन : जी तर आताची करु२९४ : सोभाग न मरे : सर्वज्ञें
म्हणीतलें : पोरा : आतांचि मारों पांतु असिसि : हीराइसा-
पाठ : म्हातारीएतें ॥छ॥ म्हणौनि हास्य केलें :॥:

१८१ गोंदो माळ देणें :॥:

गोंदो म्हणति : गोसावी : आपुली गळाची माळ मज देतु
कां : ऐसा मनोर्थु करीति : उदयाचा पूजावसर जालेया नंतरें
आंगणीं आसन असे : श्रीकंठीं माळ होती : गोसावी गोंदोचां
गळां माळ घातली : हीराइसापाठ : गोंदो माळ घीया : हो कां
जी :॥छ॥ मग ते आवचेया माळा दाखवीति : मज गोसावी
माळ दीधली :॥:

१८२   आबैसीं दीठी उतरणें :॥:

माहालक्ष्मियेसी पर्वणी एकी आली : तो लोकू अपार :
देवतादर्शना आला : तेवींचि गोसावीयांची प्रसिध आइकीली
होती : तो गोसावीयांचें दर्शन सकळ लोकां जालें : गोसावी
दीठिची प्रवृत्ति स्विकरिली : श्रीमूर्ति आलोहित : नेत्र
आलोहित जाले : श्रीमूख कोमाइलें : बाइसें चिंता करूं

394

do, Lord. What will you do, Lord Gosavi?" The omniscient one said, "I will do what it's appropriate for a mother and sisters to do." "Lord, when Sobhage dies, I will tie her big toes together. I will make a bier and carry it on my shoulder, and I will break the clay pot. I will perform Sobhage's funeral rites. So, Lord, may I do that now? Sobhage isn't dying."

The omniscient one said, "You are trying to kill her off right now, my child!"[244] And he laughed.

181   HE GIVES A GARLAND TO GONDO.

Gondo used to make a wish. He would say to himself, "Will the Gosavi give me the garland from around his neck?"

After the morning worship service, the Gosavi would sit in the courtyard with a garland around his holy neck. One day he put the garland around Gondo's neck. (Hiraïsa version: "Take this garland, Gondo." "All right, Lord.")

After that Gondo was showing the garland to everyone. "The Gosavi gave me his garland!" he would say.

182   ABAÏSE REMOVES THE EVIL EYE.

When there was a festival at the Mahalakshmi temple, a large crowd of people came for *darśan* of the goddess. At the same time, because they had heard about the Gosavi, everyone had his *darśan*.

The Gosavi allowed himself to be given the evil eye. His holy body turned red. His eyes turned red and his holy face

लागली : आबैसीं बाइसातें म्हणीतलें : गोसावीयांसि दीठि
जाली : बाइसीं विनविलें : बाबा : वृधाबाइसाकरवि दिठि
उतरउं²⁹⁵ : सर्वज्ञें म्हणीतलें : बाइ : जनुपदु बहुत कीं :
आणि ए लेकाची माये म्हणौनि ए दीठि उतरु जाणति²⁹⁶ :
मग आबैसीं हळदीची दीठि उतरली : परशरामबास : सातां
घरीचि कुहीट आणिली : रामेश्वरबास : मग गोसावीयांसि
समाधानाची प्रवृत्ति जाली :॥:

१८३ देवांप्रति गिरिकपाट प्रशंसा :॥:

पर्व जालें : बाइसें वाढावाढि करितें असति : पुजा
जालेयानंतरें गोसावी निंबातळि आंगणीं आसनीं बैसले
असति : चांदीणें पडत असे : देवीं सेंभरि दंडवतें घातलीं :
पुढां पोफळ ठेवीलें : मग गोसावी पुसीलें : माहात्मेया प्रभाते
काइ गतु कामू :॥: जी जी : ऐसें घाटावरि कीं गंगातिरें :
जी जी : गंगातिरें : सर्वज्ञें म्हणीतलें : ऐसें होए : घाटु तो
कोणासि : जेयाचां हृदै परमेश्वरु वसे तेया घाटु कीं : नवीं
नवीं अग्राहारें : श्रधाधान लोक : सवें सातपांच भातवे-
ळितीं : सरवळेयां नाखवळेयांचिया क्षीरी : वरि वाटेयाभर
तुप : गंगातीर तुम्हांसीचि होए : घाटु कोणा : जयाचां हृदै

wilted. Baïse began to get worried. Abaïse said to her, "The Gosavi has been given the evil eye."

Baïse appealed to him: "Baba, may Vriddhabaïse remove the evil eye from you?" "My woman," replied the omniscient one, "there are many people here.[245] And, as the mother of children, she knows how to remove the evil eye."[246]

Then Abaïse removed the evil eye with turmeric. (This is according to Parasharambas. According to Rameshvarbas, she brought rotten food from seven houses.) After that the Gosavi was inclined to be pleased.

183 HE PRAISES MOUNTAIN CAVES TO DEV.

The day of the festival came. Baïse was serving food. After puja had been done to him, the Gosavi was sitting in his place at the foot of the neem tree in the courtyard. The moon was shining.

Dev prostrated himself a hundred times and placed a betel nut in front of the Gosavi. The Gosavi asked, "Do you want to leave at dawn, Mahatma?" "Yes, Lord." "Will you be going to the mountains, or to the Godavari valley?" "To the Godavari valley, Lord."

The omniscient one said, "That is right. Who are the mountains for? The mountains are for one in whose heart the supreme God resides. The Godavari valley is just the place for you: one new Brahman village after another, people of faith, plenty of freshly cooked rice, twists of wheat dough in sweetened milk, and a cupful of ghee as well.

परमेश्वरु वसे तेयासि²⁹⁷ : गहीवरीं कपाटीं निभरें उदकें :
परशरामबास : वृक्षाचे मांदाडे : मंजीष्ठा छाया : सचरते
चंद्ररश्मी : यें सुखें कवणासि : जेयाचां हृदै : परमेश्वरु वसे
तेयासि कीं :॥ः

१८४ दायांबा सरावीं चुकि :॥ः

गोसांवी उदयाचां पूजावसर जालेया नंतरें वीहरणा बीजें
केलें : गरुडी आसन : गोसांवी दायांबातें म्हणीतलें : भोजेया
तुम्ही सराउं करूं जाणा गा : जी जी : जाणे : हें काइ जाणावें
असे : जी जी : काइ ब्रह्मविद्या²⁹⁸ : सर्वज्ञें म्हणीतलें : एथें
करूनि दाखवा पा : मग सराडेयाचा कोळु केला : परवडी
दोनिच्यारि एकी दाखवीलीया²⁹⁹ : आले : श्रीचरणा लागले :
एक चुकलेति : तें काइ जी : गरूडा नमस्कारू : जी जी³⁰⁰ :
रामेश्वरबास : हे लीळा बीडीं : परशरामबास :
अज्ञातस्थान :॥ः

"Who are the mountains for? For one in whose heart the supreme God resides. Caves and caverns, abundant water." (According to Parasharambas: "Groves of trees. Dappled shade. Moonbeams streaming down. Who gets these delights? One in whose heart the supreme God resides!")

184 DAÏMBA MAKES A MISTAKE AT GYMNASTICS.

After his morning worship service, the Gosavi went out to wander. He was sitting at the gymnasium.

The Gosavi asked Daïmba, "Bhoja, do you know how to do gymnastics?" "Yes, Lord, I do know. What is there to know about it? Is it ultimate truth, Lord?" "Show me," said the omniscient one.

So Daïmba made a baton out of a millet stalk. He showed him a few exercises, then came over and touched his holy feet. "You made one mistake," said the omniscient one. "What was it, Lord?" "Do reverence to the Garuda."[247] "Yes, Lord."[248]

(According to Rameshvarbas, this *līlā* took place in Bid. According to Parasharambas, no one knows where it happened.)

१८५ दायांबा वखरीं चुकि :॥:

उदयाचा पूजावसर जालेया नंतरें : गोसावी वीहरणा बीजें
केलें : तवं कूणबी आउत वाहात असे : सर्वज्ञें म्हणीतलें :
भोजेया हें कांहीं तुम्ही जाणा : तरि : काइ जी : हें आम्हींचि
जाणों कीं : सर्वज्ञें म्हणीतलें : दाखवा : मग सराडेयाचे
आउत केलें : दोरीयाचे नाडे केले : मा : दाखविलें : सर्वज्ञें
म्हणीतलें : भोजेया : एक वीसरलेति गा : काइ जी : वोसान
फेडु वीसरलेति : जी जी : रामेश्वरबास : हे लीळा बीडीं :
परशरामबास : अज्ञातस्थान :॥:

१८६ पालीं मैराळीं वसति :॥:

१८७ निंबा बाहिरिले देउळीं वसति :॥:

185 DAÏMBA MAKES A MISTAKE AT PLOWING.

When the Gosavi went out to wander after the morning worship service, there was a farmer who was plowing. The omniscient one asked, "Bhoja, do you know how to do this?" "Of course, Lord! I know it better than anyone else." "Show me," said the omniscient one.

So Bhoja made a plow out of a millet stalk and a rope out of string and showed him.

The omniscient one said, "Bhoja, you have forgotten something." "What, Lord?" "You have forgotten to knock the mud off the plowshare." "Yes, Lord."

(According to Rameshvarbas, this *līḷā* took place in Bid. According to Parasharambas, no one knows where it happened.)

186 HE STAYS OVERNIGHT IN THE MAIRAL TEMPLE IN PALI.[249]

187 HE STAYS OVERNIGHT IN THE OUTER TEMPLE AT NIMBA.[250]

१८८ पाटवधां केदारीं गुंफे अवस्थान ॥

पाखु एकु उणा :॥:

गोसावी पाटवधेया केदारचेया देउळा बीजें केलें : देउळा
पुर्वें गुंफा उत्तरामूख : गोसावीयांसि पसिमिले भिंतीकडे
पटीसाळे आसन : बाइसीं चरणक्षाळण केलें : भीतरि पहुड
केला : बाइसीं उपहारू निफजवीला : गोसावीयांसि उपहुड :
आरोगण : गुळळा : वीडा : माघौता पहुड : ऐसें पक्षा आरुतें
अवस्थान :॥:

१८९ राहीया भेटी :॥:

पटिसाळेवरि बाइसीं आसन केलें : गोसावी आसनीं उपविष्ट
असति : राहीनायकासि केदाराची भक्ति : तो केदारासि
आला : तवं गोसावीयातें देखीले : आणि गोसावीयाकडे
जाले आणि उभेया भेटि जाली : दंडवतें घातलीं : श्रीचरणा
लागले : पुढें बैसले : मग गोसावीयातें म्हणीतलें : आंग उघडें
घालि गा जी : डोलेयां हों देइजो पारणें : नावेक गोसावी
आंग उघडें घातलें : आणि विचारिलें : गोसावी रावो होति :
कां देवो होति : मग पूसिलें : हां जी : गोसावी रावो कीं
देवो : सर्वज्ञें म्हणीतलें : हें रावो नव्हे : हें देवो नव्हे : हें
महात्में[३०१] : हीराइसा : हें भिक्षु :॥छ॥: ना जी : मियां महात्में

402

188   HE STAYS IN A CELL IN THE KEDAR TEMPLE IN PATAVADHE FOR LESS THAN A FORTNIGHT.

The Gosavi went to the temple of Kedar* in Patavadhe. To the east of the temple was a hermit's cell that faced north. The Gosavi sat on a veranda at the western wall. Baïse washed his feet there, and then she prepared some food while he slept inside. The Gosavi woke up, ate his meal, rinsed his mouth, chewed pan, and went back to sleep.

He stayed there this way for less than a fortnight.

189   HE MEETS RAHIYA.

Baïse had prepared a seat on the veranda of the Kedar temple, and the Gosavi was sitting there. Rahinayak was a devotee of Kedar. When he came to the temple, he saw the Gosavi and went over to him. Rahinayak greeted the Gosavi standing up, then prostrated himself, touched the holy feet, and sat down in front of him. Then he said to the Gosavi, "Uncover your body, Lord. Let my eyes break their fast."

The Gosavi uncovered his body briefly. And Rahinayak thought to himself, "Is the Gosavi a king, or is he a god?" Then he asked, "Lord Gosavi, are you a king, or are you a god?" The omniscient one said, "I am not a king. I am not a god. I am a Mahatma." (According to Hiraïsa he said, "I am a mendicant.")

---

* Shiva.

बहुत देखीले होते : वामदेव : गुणाकारदेव : त्या मज बहुत
दी सन्नेधि : मातें गौतमारी नांवें जाळ होतें : तें तेंहीं सगडी
आंतु घालुनि जाळवीलें : तेयांचीं आंगे भैडीं पाणिभातांचीं :
गोसावीयाचें आंग सराउवाचें : गोसावी रावो कां देवो : हां
जी : गोसावीयांतें कव्हणी असे : सर्वज्ञें म्हणीतलें : यातें
कव्हणी नसे :॥:

१९०   भटां : महादाइसां : भेटि :॥:

पटिसाळे आसन : तवं भटोबास : महादाइसें : बिडींहुनि :
देहें आलीं : भेटि जाली : गोसावी क्षेमालिंगन दीधलें :
दंडवतें घातलीं : श्रीचरणा लागले : महादाइसें दुख करूं
लागली : मग म्हणीतलें : हां होयें कीं मीं राहीया : म्हणौनि :
बाहे आफळिली : गोसावीयाची लेकी होइल : कां बहिण
होइल : मग पुसीलें : हां जी : यें गोसावीयां काइ होति :
सर्वज्ञें म्हणीतलें : हें : कांहीं नव्हति३०२ : तरि यें रडतें
असति : सर्वज्ञें म्हणीतलें : तुम्हीं हीं दीस दोनि च्यारी :
असों लागाल : आणि हें निगे : आणि तुम्हींही भेंकों
लागाल३०३ :॥:

"No, Lord. I have seen many Mahatmas. I spent a long time in the presence of Vamdev and Gunakardev. I had a special fishing net. They made me put it in a stove and burn it. Their bodies were flabby, nourished on water-and-rice gruel. Your body is fit, Lord Gosavi, because you get exercise. Are you a king or a god? Do you have any relatives, Lord Gosavi?"

The omniscient one said, "I have no one."

190 HE MEETS BHAT AND MAHADAÏSE.

When the Gosavi was sitting on the veranda one day, Bhatobas and Mahadaïse arrived from Bid. The Gosavi embraced them, and they prostrated themselves and touched his holy feet. Mahadaïse began to cry.

Then Rahinayak said, "See? I was right! I am Rahiya," and he slapped his upper arms to congratulate himself. "This must be the Gosavi's daughter, or else his sister."

Then he asked, "Who is she to you, Lord Gosavi?" The omniscient one said, "She is no relation of mine." "But she is crying." The omniscient one said, "It will be the same with you. You'll stay with me for a few days, and then when I leave you too will start to cry."

१९१ महादाइसाचें आंग चुरवणें :॥:

पस्यात पाहारीं गोसावीयांसि उपहुड³⁰⁴ : केदाराचेया देउळा
बीजें केलें : महादाइसें पालथी नीजैली होती : गोसावी
पाठीवरि श्रीचरणू ठेवीला : महदाइसीं म्हणीतलें : एथेंचि
वो : एथेंचि वो : कवणी दैवाचें भाग्याचें : पाहाती तवं
गोसावी : हें काइ जी : नागदेया उठी : उठि : गोसावी बीजें
केलें : गोसावी आसनीं बैसलें : दीवा आणवीला : मग
भटोबासा करवि पायेवरि श्रमनिवृत्ति करवीली :॥:

१९२   तथा उपाहारू :॥:

मग महादाइसीं³⁰⁵ म्हणीतलें : राही नायको : एका दामाचें
आम्हांलागि दुध आणावें : माहादाइसें राहीयाचां हातीं एका
दामाचें कवडे देत होतीं³⁰⁶ : तेहीं म्हणीतलें : मा : दुध
माझें : येर तुमचें : तें निराकरिति : सर्वज्ञें म्हणीतलें : यें
म्हणतें असति तेंचि कां न करा : सोधु : तुमचें कंहीं गेलें
असे³⁰⁷ : हो कां जी : मातें साकरी नांवें म्हैसीं असे जी :
तीयेचां तांबीयाभरूनि दुध मी गोसावीयांलागि व्यालिये
आणिन : गोसावी मानीलें : मग रात्रीं दुध आणिलें : बाइसीं
उपाहारू निफजवीला : आरोगणा : पहुड : भटोबास :
महदाइसें : केदाराचा देउळीं निजैली :॥:

406

191 HE GIVES MAHADAÏSE A MASSAGE.

The Gosavi woke up before dawn and went to the temple of Kedar. Mahadaïse was there, sleeping on her stomach. The Gosavi placed his holy foot on her back. Mahadaïse said, "Oh! That's the spot! That's the spot! Who is this? I am so lucky, so fortunate!"

Then she looked up, and she saw the Gosavi. "What is going on, Lord? Get up, Nagdev! Get up!"

The Gosavi went and sat in his place. He had them bring a lamp, and then he had Bhatobas massage her with his feet.

192 AND SOME FOOD.

Then Mahadaïse said, "Rahinayak, bring a copper coin's worth of milk for us." She was handing Rahiya a copper coin. He refused the money. "No," he said. "I'll provide the milk. You pay for everything else."

The omniscient one said to her, "Why not do what he is saying?" (Research: "What do you stand to lose?") "All right, Lord."

"I have a water-buffalo cow named Sakari," said Rahiya. "I will bring a copper pot full of her milk for your evening meal, Lord Gosavi." The Gosavi agreed.

That night Rahinayak brought the milk. Baïse prepared some food, and the Gosavi ate his meal and went to sleep. Bhatobas and Mahadaïse slept in the Kedar temple.

१९३ तथा उपाहारू स्विकारू :॥:

महादाइसी उपाहारा लागि आणिलें : तें बाइसीं हातीं
दीधलें : बाइ : भक्तजनासहीत गोसावीयासि उपाहारू
करावा : गुळा मिरीयाचिया आंगारिका : तांदुल वेलावे :
सरवळेयाची खीरि करावी : बाइसीं म्हणीतलें : तांदुलाची
खीरि : सरवळीं वेळु : महदाइसें म्हणति : ना : तांदुल
वेळु : बाइसें म्हणति : बाबासि तांदुलाची खीरि आवडे :
महदाइसी म्हणीतलें : गोसावी ईश्वरू : ईश्वरीं काइ आवडि
नावडि असे : सर्वज्ञें म्हणीतलें : बाइ : यें म्हणतें असति तेंचि
कां न करा[३०८] : आणि महदाइसीं जाणीतलें : गोसावी :
बाइसीं म्हणीतलें तैसेंचि केलें : उपाहारू निफजवीला :
वडाखाली गोसावी आसनीं बैसले आसति : बाइसीं
वीनवीलें : बाबा : उपाहारू जाला असे : बीजें कीजो : सर्वज्ञें
म्हणीतलें : बाइ : एथचि कां न वर्तें : पूजा : हीराइसापाठ :
बाइ : एथेंचि घेउनि या :॥छ॥: मग तेथेंचि पुजा जाली :
बाइसीं ताट केलें : भक्तजना ठायें केलें : सर्वज्ञें म्हणीतलें :
हें काइ बाइ : तांदूळांची खीरि केली : जी जी[३०९] : यें
म्हणतें होती तेंचि कां न कराचि :॥छ॥: जी जी : मीं काइ
गोसावीयांची प्रवृत्ति जाणत असें : बाइसें प्रवृत्ति जाणति :
तें कीरु तैसेंचि : एथ काइ आवडी नावडि असे : परि एथची
प्रवृत्ति बाइसें जाणति[३१०] : मग आरोगणा : भक्तजन
जेवीलें : गुळळा : वीडा वोळगवीला : पहुड : उपहुड :॥:

193   AND HE ACCEPTS A MEAL.

Mahadaïse brought the ingredients for a meal and handed them over to Baïse. "My woman, let's make a meal for the Gosavi and the devotees. Let's make chapatis with jaggery and black pepper, boil some rice, and make twists of wheat dough in sweetened milk." Baïse said, "Let's make rice pudding and boil the twists of wheat dough." Mahadaïse said, "No, let's boil the rice." Baïse said, "Baba likes rice pudding." Mahadaïse said, "The Gosavi is God. Does God have likes and dislikes?"

The omniscient one said, "My woman, why not do what she is saying?"[251] And Mahadaïse understood.

They made exactly what the Gosavi and Baïse had said. When they finished cooking, the Gosavi was sitting beneath a banyan tree. Baïse went and invited him: "Baba, the meal is ready," she said. "Please come." The omniscient one replied, "Why can't the puja be done right here, my woman?" (Hiraïsa version: "Bring it here, my woman.") So the puja took place right there. Baïse prepared a plate for the Gosavi and leaf plates for the disciples.

The omniscient one said to Baïse, "What is this, my woman? You made rice pudding?" "Yes, Lord." "Why didn't you make what Mahadaïse was saying?" Mahadaïse said, "Lord Gosavi, do I understand your inclination? Baïse understands your inclination." "Yes, that is exactly right. I don't have likes or dislikes, but Baïse understands my inclination."[252]

Then the Gosavi ate his meal, and the devotees ate theirs. He rinsed his mouth and was offered pan, then he went to sleep and woke up.

१९४ तथा मास उपवास प्रश्रू :॥:

महदाइसीं प्रश्रू केला : जी जी : मास उपवास केलेयां काइ
होए : सर्वज्ञें म्हणीतलें : कीजे : तरि दोन्हीं होति : न कीजे
तरि दोन्हीं नव्हति : सोधु : बाइ : पाप होए : पुण्य होए :
तें कैसें होए : जी : बाइ : वात्मा पीडे : तेणें पाप होए : व्रत
कीजे तेणें पुण्य होए : न कीजे तरि काइ : तरि : पापही
नाहीं : पुण्यही नाहीं :॥:

१९५ तथा एकादशीं प्रश्रू :॥:

महदाइसीं पुसीलें : जी जी : एकादशी केलेयां काइ होए :
सर्वज्ञें म्हणीतलें : दोन्हीं होती : महादाइसीं म्हणीतलें : जी
जी : व्रत केलेयां कां पाप होए : सर्वज्ञें म्हणीतलें : जीवासि
पीडा होए : जीउ पळभरि मांस भोजन करी म्हणौनि पाप
होए³¹¹ :॥:

१९६ तथा एकादशी :॥:

महदाइसीं पूसिलें : हां जी : आम्ही येकादशी करु : न
करु³¹² : ऐसें कोण्हीहिंचि नेणति : आणि येन्हवीं तरि म्हणति :
एकादशि न करीति : सर्वज्ञें म्हणीतलें : एथार्थु तो प्रकटे :

410

194   AND HE ANSWERS A QUESTION ABOUT FASTING FOR A MONTH.

Mahadaïse asked a question: "Lord, what happens when you fast every day for a month?" The omniscient one replied, "If you do that, you get both. If you don't do it, you get neither." (Research: "My woman, you get sin and you get merit.") "How so, Lord?" "My woman, you get sin from causing yourself pain. You get merit from performing a vow."

"What happens if you don't do the fast?" "Then you get no sin, and you get no merit."

195   AND HE ANSWERS A QUESTION ABOUT THE EKADASHI.

Mahadaïse asked, "Lord, what happens when you observe the Ekadashi?" The omniscient one replied, "You get both sin and merit." "How can performing a vow cause sin?" asked Mahadaïse. The omniscient one replied, "A living being suffers pain; a living being eats a bit of flesh, and that causes sin."[253]

196   MORE ABOUT THE EKADASHI.

Mahadaïse asked, "Lord, no one knows whether we observe the Ekadashi or not. And even so people say, 'They don't observe the Ekadashi.'" The omniscient one said, "The truth shines forth."[254]

तथा सत्य अर्थु ॥ हां जी : भिक्षा कां न किजे : तथा प्रगट
कां जेवीजेना : सर्वज्ञें म्हणीतलें स्त्री पुरुषाचा वेवहारू : जग
वीश्व जाणे : तरि : काइ चोहटां बाज घालूं एइल : ते घराचां
माजिघरींचि घालावी कीं एरवीं लोकु सेणवरि घे : हे लिळा
आज्ञातस्थानीं :॥:

१९७ दायांबा जावाइ निराकरण³¹³ :॥:

दायांबा भीक्षेसि गेले होते : ते एका ब्राह्मणाचेया आवारासि
गेले होते : तयाचा जावाइ तयांचीए लेकीतें सांडुनि गेला
होता : तो दायांबाचि सारिखा : तवं तेहीं म्हणीतलें :
आमचे जावाइ नव्हति : दाइंबाएं म्हणीतलें : मी नव्हें :
ते म्हणती : होए : ते म्हणति : नव्हें : मग तेहीं म्हणीतलें :
आगा याची ब्राह्मणि बोलावा : मग ते ओळखैल : मग तेहीं
बाइल बोलाविली : हां ओ : हा तुझा पति होए : तवं तीया
म्हणीतलें : ना होए : तुम्हीं इतुले दीस आपुलीए ब्राह्मणितें
सांडुनि गेले होतेति : तरि आतां इतें घेउनि जा : आम्ही
कीती दीस संवसाळुनि : इतुकेनि दायांबा उगेचि राहिले :
तैसेंचि ते एन्हएन्हीं गोसावीयांपासि आले : जी जी : हे
आमचे जावाइ : इतुके दीस ब्राह्मणितें सांडूनि गेले होते :
आतां नव्हों म्हणताति : सर्वज्ञें म्हणीतलें : तुमची कोणि
साखा : जी जी : माध्यांजन : सर्वज्ञें म्हणीतलें : हे कन्हाडे :

412

"But, Lord, why should we not beg for food on that day?" (Or, "Why should we not eat in the open?") The omniscient one replied, "The whole world knows what happens between a woman and a man. Even so, can you put their bed in the public square? It can only be put in the inner room of the house! Otherwise people will pick up wet cow dung to throw at them."

It is not known where this *līḷā* took place.

197 HE DENIES THAT DAÏMBA IS A MAN'S SON-IN-LAW.

When Daïmba was out begging for food, he went to the compound of Brahmans whose son-in-law had abandoned their daughter. The son-in-law looked just like Daïmba.

The man said, "Aren't you our son-in-law?" Daïmba said, "No, I'm not." The man said, "Yes, you are." Daïmba said, "No, I'm not." Then the man said to his wife, "Call his wife here. She will recognize him." So they called their daughter there. "Is this your husband?" "Yes, it is," she replied.

"You have abandoned your wife for a long time," said the man, "but you must take her with you now. How long are we supposed to support her?" At that, Daïmba kept silent.

Immediately they all came to the Gosavi. "Lord, this is our son-in-law. He has abandoned his wife for a long time. Now he denies it." The omniscient one said, "What school of the Vedas do you belong to?" "Madhyandin, Lord." The omniscient one said, "This man is a Karhade. His father-in-

यांचे सासुरे पैठणीं असति : चांगदेविचे भोपे : म्हणौनि
हे तुमचे जावाइ नव्हति : मग ते उगेचि नीगाले : सर्वज्ञें
म्हणीतलें : पोरा : नीराकारिसीचि ना कैसा : गळां लोढणें
बांधते तरि काइ करितासि : दाइंबाएं म्हणीतलें : जी मीं
काइ जी : हे असती आणि काइ जी : गोसावीं म्हणीतलें :
पोरू यासीचि टेकला मां :॥:

१९८ पाटवधा भटा घोंगडे पतन :॥:

पूर्वीले पाइरी उभे असति : तथा देउळीये आसनीं असति :
तवं चांगदेवोभट इकडे तिकडे पाहों लागले : सर्वज्ञें
म्हणीतलें : बटिका : काइ पाहात असा : जी जी : घोंगडें :
काइ पडिलें : ना जी : तरि काइ विसरलेति : ना जी :
विसरलें³¹⁴ : गोसावी इखीत हास्य केलें : जा : तेथेंचि असे :
हीराइसा पाठ : पैले घाटीं असे :॥छ॥: गेले तवं होतें :॥:

१९९ दायांबा आसन निषेधु :॥:

दाइंबासि स्तीति जाली होती : ते पुढां गेले : गोसावीयांसि
जेथ आसन रचावें तेथ जाऊनि³¹⁵ घोंगडेयाची चौघडी
घालुनि बैसले : बाइसीं म्हणीतलें : बटिका : उठि : यथ

law is a priest at the Cangdev temple in Paithan. So he is not your son-in-law." They left in complete silence.

The omniscient one said, "My child, why did you not deny it? What would you have done if they had tied that clog to your neck?" Daïmba said, "Why me, Lord? With you there, what problem could there have been?"

The Gosavi said, "The child depends on me!"

198 BHAT'S BLANKET
FALLS DOWN AT PATAVADHE.

The Gosavi was standing on the eastern steps (or, sitting in his place in the temple) when Cangdevbhat began looking around for something.

"Batika," asked the omniscient one, "what are you looking for?" "My blanket, Lord." "Did it fall down?" "No, Lord." "Did you lose it somewhere, then?" "Yes, Lord. I lost it."

The Gosavi smiled gently. "Go to where you left it. It's still there." (Hiraïsa version: "It's on that ghat over there.") He went there and found it.

199 DAÏMBA IS FORBIDDEN
TO SIT IN A CERTAIN PLACE.

Daïmba had gone into a trance. He went on ahead. Going to the place where a seat was to be prepared for the Gosavi, he folded his blanket and sat down on it. Baïse said, "Get

बाबासि^{३१६} आसन घालुं दे : ऐसे पैन्हां घाला ना : बाइसीं
घागरा बांधला : सर्वज्ञें म्हणीतलें : बाइ : आणिकाचें तरि
टाकौनि घालीता : एथचें म्हणौनि : आडुळिचि ना^{३१७} :
आणि तेयाची स्थिति भंगली : गोसावीयासि तेथ आसन
घातलें : चरणक्षाळन जालें : पूजावस्वर जाला : आरोगणा :
पहुड :॥:

२०० नदीधारे प्रदक्षेणा :॥:

एकुदीसीं गोसावी धारेचिया कुंडासि बीजें केलें :
सिळातळांवरि आसन : सर्वज्ञें म्हणीतलें : धारे प्रदक्षणा
करा^{३१८} : ऐसीं अवघींची गेलीं : एका एका मागें प्रदक्षणे
रिंगाली : पडति : निसरति : गोसावी ईखीत हास्य करीति :
श्रीमूर्तिवरि तुषार पडति : ते सुवर्णाचे कणकण ऐसे दीसती :
प्रदक्षेणा करूनि आलीं : मग गोसावी गुंफेसि बीजें केलें :॥:

२०१ मग प्रसनायका भिक्षास्वीकर्य :॥:

भक्तजन दीसवडि भीक्षे जाति : एक मात्रकवळियें : एक
संवतडेया : दायांबा : प्रसनाएक : जांबखेडेया भिक्षे गेले :
प्रसनायेकें म्हणीतलें : दायां आम्हीं एथ राहुनि : गोसावी

up, Batika. Let me put something down here for Baba to sit on." "Why not put it over there?" he asked, and Baïse upbraided him.

The omniscient one said, "My woman, you make other people go somewhere else, but you don't move my place, because it's mine." And Daïmba's trance broke.

She put down a cloth there for the Gosavi to sit on. His feet were washed, and his worship service took place. He ate his meal and went to sleep.

200 CIRCUMAMBULATING A WATERFALL.

One day the Gosavi went and sat on a flat rock near a pool of water at a waterfall. "Circumambulate the waterfall," said the omniscient one. All of them went to do that. They set out circumambulating it one behind the other. They were falling down, they were slipping, and the Gosavi was smiling gently. Spray fell on his holy body, looking like bits of gold.

After they finished their circumambulation and came back, the Gosavi went to his cell.

201 THEN PARASNAYAK ACCEPTS ALMS.

Every day the devotees went to beg for food. Some would go to Matrakavali, some to Samvatada.[255] Daïmba and Parasnayak went to Jambkhede to beg.[256] Parasnayak said, "Daya, I'm going to stay here. If the Gosavi asks, what should

पुसती तरि कैसें सांघावें : भिक्षा सौकर्यें : मढु सौकर्य असे :
उदक सौकर्य : गोसावी बीजें करीति : ते दीसीं मज
जाणवा : मग : मी एइन : एरी दिसीं दायांबा आले :
गोसावीया पुढें सांघीतलें³¹⁹ : सर्वज्ञें म्हणीतलें : पोरू गेला
आपूलीया अंगा : सर्वज्ञें म्हणीतलें : संन्यासियाचा शिष्य :
एके गावीं राहे : मढूसौकर्य : पाणीसौकर्य : भिक्षासौकर्य :
ऐसें सांघोनि धाडी : पोरू आपुलेया भगवेपणाचेया अंगा
गेला³²⁰ : मग दायांबा गेले : प्रसनायेको तुमतें गोसावी
बोलाउं धाडिले असे : वासुदेवो म्हणौनि निगाले :
गोसावीयांपासि आले :॥:

२०२ मार्गीं बाइसा आग्रहो निरूपण :॥:

गोसावी तेथौनि बीजें केलें : मात्रकवळियें बीजें करितां :
मध्यें बाइसीं आग्रहो केला : बाबा: जांबखेडेयासि बीजें
कीजो : सर्वज्ञें म्हणीतलें : बाइ एथ प्रवृति नाहीं : नको
म्हणों : बाबा : या वाटा जावें : तेया वाटा जावें : आणि
काइ : सर्वज्ञें म्हणीतलें : बाइ : एथ प्रवृति नाहीं : आग्रहो
न करा : बाइ : हें हरिण देखीलें : यामध्यें एकाधें हरिण
होइजैल : कोण हरिण होए : कोणा पाठीं धावाल³²¹ :
आणि बाइसे भीयाली : मग उगीचि राहीली³²² :॥:

you tell him? That the begging is easy here, the hermitage is convenient, and water is readily available. Send word to me on the day the Gosavi is leaving, and I will come there."

The next day Daïmba came and told this to the Gosavi. The omniscient one said, "The child has taken his own path," and then he said, "The disciple of an ascetic stays in a certain village. He sends word that the hermitage is convenient, that water is readily available, that the begging is easy. The child has taken his own path as an ascetic."

So Daïmba went there and said, "Parasnayak, the Gosavi has sent me to summon you." "Vasudev!"* said Parasnayak, and he left there and came to where the Gosavi was.

202   ALONG THE ROAD, HE TEACHES BAÏSE ABOUT STUBBORNNESS.

The Gosavi left there and went toward Matrakavali. When they were halfway there, Baïse said insistently, "Let's go to Jambkhede, Baba." The omniscient one said, "My woman, I am not inclined to do that. Don't tell me to." "Baba, what difference does it make if we go by this road or that one?"

The omniscient one said, "My woman, I am not inclined to do that. Don't insist on it. Do you see these deer, my woman? I will become one of the deer. Which deer will I become? Which one will you run after?"

And Baïse got frightened. She kept silent.

———

* Krishna.

२०३ मात्रकवळियें ग्रहीं पूजा आरोगण :॥:

गोसावी मात्रकवळियें बीजें केलें : भक्तांचिया काठिया :
भाले ऐसे दीसति : गोसावी प्रसनायकाची दुटी प्रावर्ण
केली होती : ते सुर्याचा रश्मिकरूनि सेंदुरें वोडणें ऐसी दीसों
लागली : सेतकरीं देखिलें : गावीचीं मनुष्यें भीयालीं : वेसि
घातली : आले आले वोरपेकार³२३ : ऐसें म्हणति : मग
गोसावी सामोरें बीजें केलें : गोसावीयातें देखिलें : आरे हे
गोसावी : मां : गोसावीयासि पटिसाळे देउळाचिये बाहिरिली
आसन : सोवणी एकू ब्राह्मणु : तेयासि तेथ भेटि जाली :
तेणें वीनवीलें : घरीं नेलें : पुजा केली : आरोगणा : मग
वसती जाली :॥:

२०४ आसुटीए हरिचंद्रीं वसति :॥:

गोसावी उदीयांचि असूटियें बीजें केलें : हरिचंद्रीं वसति
जाली : एरी दी वीनायेकीं क्षेउर जालें : एकें म्हणति : गांवांतु
माजणें जालें : वसति :॥:

203 AT A HOUSE IN MATRAKAVALI, HIS PUJA IS PERFORMED AND HE EATS A MEAL.

As the Gosavi approached Matrakavali, the devotees' staffs looked like spears. In the bright sunlight, Parasnayak's shawl, which the Gosavi had draped over his own shoulders, looked like a bright-orange shield. People working in the fields saw this. The villagers got frightened and shut the village gate, saying, "Robbers! A band of robbers has come!"

The Gosavi went straight up to the village gate. When the people saw the Gosavi, they said, "Hey! It's the Gosavi!" They prepared a seat for the Gosavi on the outer veranda of the temple.

A Brahman goldsmith met the Gosavi there and invited him to his home. He took him there and did puja to him. The Gosavi ate his meal there and stayed there overnight.

204 HE STAYS OVERNIGHT IN THE HARICHANDRA TEMPLE IN ASUTI.

Early the next morning, the Gosavi went to Asuti.[257] He stayed overnight in the Harichandra* temple. The next day his head was shaved in the Vinayak temple. Some say he had a bath in the village. He stayed there overnight.

---

* Probably Harishchandra, a saintly Puranic king.

२०५ सिराळां वसति :॥:

२०६ वांकिये मठीं अवस्थान : मासू एकू :॥:

२०७ चोरकुमति हरण :॥:

गोसावी मढाचिये पटिसाळे विळीचा आसन३२४ : भक्तजनें
भिक्षें गेली होती : तें आलीं : तेंहीं झाडांतु चोर देखीलें :
तवं चोर आले : शोधु : बाइसीं म्हणीतलें : बाबा : चोरू :
बाबा : सर्वज्ञें म्हणीतलें : बाइ : भीयाना : भितरि जा : चोरीं
म्हणीतलें : जी जी : वोखटें हुनि आलों : सर्वज्ञें म्हणीतलें :
कां गा : माहात्मे हो : वोखटेयां कां होवावें :॥छ॥: जी जी :
हें रान : एथ नसावें : सर्वज्ञें म्हणीतलें : एथ काइ नसे : मां :
काइसेया नसावें : फाळुकीं दोनि एकें असति : ते तुम्ही
नेया : यासि आणिक कव्हणीं देइल३२५ : इतुलेनी तयाची
कुमती हरली : मग ते निगाले३२६ :॥:

205 HE STAYS OVERNIGHT IN SHIRALA.[258]

206 HE STAYS FOR A MONTH IN A HERMITAGE AT VANKI.[259]

207 HE DOES AWAY WITH ROBBERS' EVIL INTENTIONS.

One evening the Gosavi was sitting on the veranda while the devotees went to beg for food. When they came back, they saw robbers in among the trees.

The robbers approached the hermitage. (Research: Baïse said, "Baba! Robbers, Baba!") The omniscient one said, "Don't be afraid, my woman. Go inside."

The robbers said, "We came out of evil motives, Lord." The omniscient one said, "Why, Mahatmas? Why should you do evil?" "This is a wilderness, Lord. You should not be here." The omniscient one said, "I don't have anything worth stealing, so why should I not be here? Take the few clothes I have. Someone will give me more."

With that, their evil intentions went away, and they left.

२०८ जोगनायका विज्ञापणें :॥: पद्मनाभी पाठवणी :॥:

जोगनायक पद्मनाभितें नेयावीया आले : पाइक निवडिलें :
तुम्हीं पुढें जावें : गोसावीयांसि पटिसाळे आसन : वीळिचां
भक्तजनें भिक्षा करूं करूं आलीं : भक्तजनीं म्हणीतलें : जी
जी : पाइक आले : तथा बाइसीं म्हणीतलें : सर्वज्ञें
म्हणीतलें : भीया ना : याचा भाउ यातें नेयावेया येत असे :
आले : तेहीं गोसावीयांतें देखिलें³²⁷ : पूढां वोडणें घालुनि :
वरि हातियेर ठेउनि बैसले : पापीयें लिंगभेदु करवीला गा :
तवं जोगनायकु आले : दंडवत घातलें : श्रीचरणा लागले :
बैसले : जी जी : पद्मनाभितें पाठवावें : सर्वज्ञें म्हणीतलें :
हा एथौनि बोलावीला : ना जी : तरि काइ एथिचां कोण्हीं
बोलाविला : ना जी : यथ याची काइ चाड पडिली असे :
नेयाना कां आपुला पद्मनाभि : तेहीं म्हणीतलें : ना जी :
गोसावीयांपासि असे : म्हणौनि आणि काइ : सर्वज्ञें
म्हणीतलें : जाए गा : पद्मनाभी : पद्मनाभीदेवीं म्हणीतलें :
हा मातें नेइल कैसा : ऐसें याचें बळ पाहों या : सर्वज्ञें
म्हणीतलें : आतां तवं जाएपा : हो कां जी : म्हणौनि
निगाले :॥:

208   AT JOGNAYAK'S REQUEST, HE
ALLOWS PADMANABHI TO LEAVE.

Jognayak came to take Padmanabhi away. He picked out some soldiers and commanded them, "You go on ahead."

The Gosavi was sitting on the veranda that evening when the devotees returned from their begging rounds. "Soldiers are coming, Lord!" said the devotees. (Or Baïse said it.) The omniscient one said, "Don't be afraid. It is his brother coming to take him away."

The soldiers arrived. When they saw the Gosavi, they put down their shields in front of him, placed their weapons on top of them, and sat down. "That sinner has caused us to commit a sacrilege," they said.

At that point, Jognayak arrived. He prostrated himself, touched the holy feet, and sat down. "Lord," he said, "send Padmanabhi home." "Did I invite him to come here?" asked the omniscient one. "No, Lord." "Well, then, did any of my people invite him?" "No, Lord." "Do I have any particular desire for him to be here? Why don't you take your Padmanabhi with you?" "Because he is with you, Lord Gosavi," said Jognayak. "Why else?"

"Go with him, Padmanabhi," said the omniscient one. Padmanabhidev said, "Let's see if he has the strength to take me away." "Go with him, for now at least," said the omniscient one. "All right, Lord," he said, and he set out.

२०९ उपासनियां स्थीति :॥:

एकु दीसीं उपासनिया स्तिति जाली : मग रातांजना भिक्षे
गेले : एकाची वाठि उचलौनि घेउनि आले : नागीवेचि भीक्षा
करीति : एकांचि वेसि उचलिली : यकांचिय चुली वरिल
रांधणें घेउनि कुंपावरि घातलें : तो कुपु जळिवला : मग
बाइला भीक्षा घालू भीति३२८ : दादुले भिक्षा घालीति : लोकु
म्हणे : गावां पांडवें आलीं : ऐसी सात दी स्तिति होती : मग
भंगली : मग गोसावी तेथौनि बीजें केलें :॥:

२१० डाको भेटि :॥:

डाको गोसावीयांचेया दरिसना आले : गोसावीयासि भेटि
जाली : दंडवतें घातलीं : श्रीचरणा लागला : बैसला : मग
पाठवणी दीधली :॥:

२११ मिरडां वसति :॥:

२१२ घोगरगांवीं वसति :॥:

209   UPASANI GOES INTO A TRANCE.

One day Upasani went into a trance, and he went to Ratanjan to beg for food.[260] He begged stark naked. He stole some-one's water-buffalo calf. He stole the gate from some people's house. He took a burning ember from someone's stove and tossed it onto a hedge, setting the hedge on fire. That made the women afraid to give him food, so the men were giving it to him. "The Pandavas have come to our village," said the people.[261]

He stayed in the trance for seven days, and then it broke. Then the Gosavi left that place.

210   HE MEETS DAKO.

Dako came for *darśan* of the Gosavi.[262] He met the Gosavi, prostrated himself to him, touched his holy feet, and sat down. Then the Gosavi gave him leave to go.

211   HE STAYS OVERNIGHT IN MIRADE.[263]

212   HE STAYS OVERNIGHT IN GHOGARGAV.

२१३ मांडवगणीं सिधनाथीं वसति :॥:

२१४ अरणग्रामीं अवस्थान :॥:

गोसावी अरणग्रामासि बीजें केलें : गुंफे अवस्थान : दीस
पांच : तथा पक्षु एकु :॥:

२१५ देमती आग्रकत्वचाग्रहणीं दोखू कथन :॥:

बाइसीं म्हणीतलें : देमाइसें : हें आलें धुनि आणा कां : बाबा
लागौनि साकवटी करिन : गेलीं : धुतलें : कोंडा निगाला : तो
वायां जाइल : तरि काइसेयां जावों : पाणीभातेसीं खावेया
होइल : म्हणौनि : गाठीं बांधला : आलीं : गोसावीयां पासि
बैसलीं : गोसावी पुसिलें : देमती गाठीं काइ : शोधु : पालवीं
काइ : ना जी : हा कोंडा : आणि मागिल सांघितलें :
सर्वज्ञें म्हणीतलें : बाइसातें पुसिलें : नाहीं जी : तथा ना जी :
कोंडेयासीचि काइ पुसावें असे जी : सर्वज्ञें म्हणीतलें :
आणिका देवाचें देवस्व होए : मा एथ नव्हे : शोधु : तथा
आणिका देवाचें :॥: मा एथचें नव्हें : वर वायां जावों : परि :
अनोज्ञात : एथचें कांहींचि घेवों नये³²⁹ :॥:

213 HE STAYS OVERNIGHT IN THE SIDDHANATH TEMPLE AT MANDAVGAN. [264]

214 HE STAYS IN ARANGRAM.

The Gosavi went to Arangram and stayed in a cell there for five days (or, for a fortnight). [265]

215 HE TELLS DEMATI THAT SHE WAS WRONG TO TAKE GINGER SKIN.

Baïse said, "Demaïse, will you go and wash this ginger? I'm going to make a vegetable dish for Baba."

When Demaïse went and washed it, the skin came off. "Why should it go to waste?" she thought. "We can eat it with water-and-rice gruel." And she tied it in a knot in the end of her sari.

She came back and sat down near the Gosavi. He asked her, "Demati, what is in the knot in the end of your sari?" "Ginger skin, Lord," she replied, and she told him what had happened.

The omniscient one said, "Did you ask Baïse?" "No, Lord. Do I have to ask, if it is just ginger skin?" The omniscient one said, "Other gods have property, so why can't I? Better let it go to waste, but don't take anything at all of mine without permission." [266]

२१६ उपासनी लाठि :॥:

गोसावीयांसि उदयाचा पूजावस्वर जालेया नंतरें आरोगण :
पहुड : तवं उपासनिया स्तिति जाली : ते तेलियाची लाठी
घेउनि आले : गोसावीयांवरि चालूं आदरिली : ते बाइसीं
बरखिलें : पोरा : बाबावरि वो लाठि चालूं आला : देखिलें :
बाबा : ऐसें काइ : बाबा : सर्वज्ञें म्हणीतलें : बाइ : ऐसिया
एकी तामसा विद्या आति : जेया पासौनि होए : तेयासिचि
वोखटें कीजे : ऐसीं बुधि उपजे : शोधु : ऐसेयाही : सर्वज्ञें
म्हणीतलें : आदी माहादेवो³³० नावें पुरुषु : हीराइसा पाठ :
माहात्मे :॥छ॥: तेयां पासौनि विद्या होति : तेयाचीया स्त्रीया
म्हणीतलें : तुम्हापासौनि आवघीया विद्या होति : तरि : मज
होआवी : तेहीं म्हणीतलें आम्हीं तुम्हांसि विद्या देउनि : तरी
तुम्हीं आमतें भक्षाल : नको : ना : देयावीचि विद्या :
दीधली : ते वीदेहीं पुरूखु : देहापासौनि वेगळे हों जाणति :
तेयातें खादलें : स्तीति भंगली : मग प्रीया प्रीया करूनि
करूणां अळापीं रडों लागली : अंतरक्षवाचा बोलों लागले :
अस्ती³³¹ माघौतीया मेळवा³³² : ऐसीया एकी तामसा
विद्या :॥:

216 UPASANI AND THE PESTLE.

After his morning worship service, the Gosavi ate his meal and went to sleep. Meanwhile Upasani went into a trance. He brought the Oil Presser's wooden pestle and was about to attack the Gosavi with it, but Baïse drove him away. "The child came to attack you with a pestle, Baba," she said. "Did you see that, Baba? How could that happen, Baba?"

The omniscient one said, "My woman, there are some dark forms of esoteric knowledge like that, ones that even inspire you to harm the very person from whom you got them."[267] The omniscient one said, "There was a holy man (Hiraïsa version: a Mahatma) named Adi Mahadev* from whom people used to get esoteric knowledge. His wife said, 'Everyone gets esoteric knowledge from you, so let me have some too.' He said, 'If I give you that esoteric knowledge, you will eat me. No, thanks!' 'But you *must* give me the knowledge.'

"He gave it to her. He was a disembodied holy man; he knew how to separate himself from his body. She ate him, and then, after her trance broke, she began to wail piteously, crying, 'My beloved! My beloved!' A voice from the sky began to say, 'Put the bones back together.'

"Some forms of esoteric knowledge are dark like that."

---

* "The Primordial Great God."

431

२१७ भिंगारीं आदितीं अवस्थान :॥:

गोसावी भिंगारा बीजें केलें : आदित्याचा देउळीं अवस्थान :
दीस पंधरा :॥:

२१८ लक्षेमीदेव ग्रहवसें असंनिधान :॥:

गोसावीयांसि चौकीं आसन : तवं लक्षमीदेवा भाइदेवाची
माता : ते दोघातें घेउनि देउळासि आली : तवं गोसावीयांतें
देखीलें : दंडवतें घातलीं : श्रीचरणां लागली : बैसलीं :
विनवीलें : जी जी : याचा ग्रहो जावा जी : हीराइसा पाठ :
सर्वज्ञें म्हणीतलें : एथीचीए दृष्टी समोर : होइल : तरि
जाइल :॥छ॥: गेली : तेयातें प्रार्थुनि घेउनि आली : दारा
आलें : सर्वज्ञें म्हणीतलें : लक्ष्मिदया : या गा : या गा
लक्ष्मिदेया : आरूते : गोसावीयातें देखीलें : आणि पळालें :
नारायणाचेया देउळा आंतु रिगाले : गोसावी पाहावेया
आलें : ते नारायणाचेया देउळावरि वळघले : गोसावीहीं
वळघले : तेहीं नासी आंतु तोंड घातलें : हीराइसापाठ : तुं
कवण : तो म्हणे : तुम्ही कवण :॥छ॥: मग गोसावी खालि
उतरले :॥:

217 HE STAYS IN THE ADITYA TEMPLE IN BHINGAR.

The Gosavi went to Bhingar.[268] He stayed in the temple of Aditya for fifteen days.

218 GHOST POSSESSION CAUSES LAKSHMIDEV TO AVOID HIM.

The Gosavi was sitting in the central hall of the temple when the mother of Lakshmidev and Bhaïdev brought the two of them there.[269] She saw the Gosavi, prostrated herself, and touched his holy feet. Then she sat down and made a request: "Lord, please make the ghost that is possessing Lakshmidev go away." (Hiraïsa version: The omniscient one said, "If my gaze falls on him, the ghost will go away.")

She went and begged him to come, then brought him back with her. He came as far as the doorway. The omniscient one said, "Lakshmidev, come here. Come here, Lakshmidev. Over here."

When he saw the Gosavi, he ran away and went into the temple of Narayan. When the Gosavi came there to look for him, he climbed up on top of the temple. The Gosavi climbed up too. Then Lakshmidev stuck his face in a drain.

(Hiraïsa version: "Who are you?" asked the Gosavi. "Who are *you*?" Lakshmidev replied.)

Then the Gosavi climbed down.

२१९ भाइदेवातें लघुनिती बोलावणें :॥:

भाइदेव ते गोसावीयांचा संनिधानीं असति : बाइसापुढें
निजत : गोसावीयांसी म्हणति : जी मुतों : बाइसें म्हणति :
उठी बटिका तुते मी घेउनि जाइन : हु हु म्हणौन नुठीति³³³ :
तरि : मग गोसावी उठवीति : हीराइसा पाठ : उठा गा
भागोया :॥छ॥: मग उठीति : गोसावी तेयातें लघुनिती घेउनि
जाति : दोन्हीं श्रीचरण धरूनि मूतिति : श्रीचरण सींतोडति :
मग बाइसें धुति :॥:

२२० तथा बदरीफळें आरोगण :॥:

भाइदेव³³⁴ बोरि खालि जाति : गोडें गोडें बोरें चाख
चाखोंनिये ओटीए³³⁵ घालिति : मग घेउनि येति :
गोसावीयांसि वोळगवीति : जी जी : घेया : तथा देवहो :
मियां तुम्हालागि बोरें आणिलीं : वोळगवीलीं : गोसावी
एकदोनि आरोगिलीं : एरें बाइसा हातीं दीधलीं : हिराइसा
पाठ : बाइ घेया : एथचेया उपयोगा निया :॥छ॥: बाइसीं
म्हणीतलें : बाबा : यें उसटीं बोरें : सर्वज्ञें म्हणीतलें : बाइ
उसीटी ऐसीं यासि काइ भावो असे :॥:

219 HE ACCOMPANIES BHAÏDEV WHEN HE GOES TO URINATE.

Bhaïdev was staying with the Gosavi, sleeping in front of Baïse. He would say to the Gosavi, "Lord, I have to urinate." Baïse would say, "Get up, Batika. I will take you."

He would grunt, but he would not get up. Then the Gosavi would tell him to get up (Hiraïsa version: "Get up, my friend."), and he would get up. The Gosavi would take him to urinate.

As he urinated, he would hold onto the Gosavi's holy feet. The holy feet would get splashed on, and afterward Baïse would wash them off.

220 AND HE EATS JUJUBE FRUITS.

Bhaïdev went beneath a jujube tree. He tasted the sweet jujubes and put them in a fold in his garment, then brought them and offered them to the Gosavi. "Take them, Lord" (Or, "God, I have brought jujubes for you"), he said, and he offered them.

The Gosavi ate a couple of them and handed the rest to Baïse. (Hiraïsa version: "Take them, my woman. Put them to use for me.") Baïse said, "Baba, these jujubes are polluted leavings." The omniscient one said, "My woman, do I care about anything like leavings?"

२२१ तथा चणक आरोगण :॥:

चणेयांची पेवें काढित असति : तेथ गेले : पांढरे पांढरे चणे
वेंचुनि वोटां भरूनि घेउनि आले : देवहो : मियां तुम्हांलागि
चणे आणिले : पुढां पुजा करूनि वोळगवीलें : सर्वज्ञें
म्हणीतलें : बाइ : घेया : एथचेया उपयोगा निया : मग बाइसें
बरवी साकवति करिति : गोसावी आरोगीति :॥:

२२२ उपाध्या विष्णूभटा भेटि :॥:

एकु दीसीं गोसावीयांसि दुपाहाराचा पुजावस्वर जाला :
भिंगाये देवीचिया देउळा बीजें केले : वीहरणा बीजें केलें :
तेथ उपाध्या विष्णुभटां भेटि जाली : दंडवतें घातलीं :
श्रीचरणां लागले : बैसले : मग गोसावीं विष्णुभटाते पुसीले :
तुमचा कुटुंब परीवार निकेन असे : जी असे : आन तया
स्तीती जाली३३६ : तेथौनि गोसावी बीजें करीत असति :
ते टेकावरुनि उतरतां गाढउ भुंकिनलें : आणि विष्णुभट
भुंकिनले : सर्वज्ञें म्हणीतलें : हें काइ गा : जी जी : हा
पंचम वेद : सर्वज्ञें म्हणीतलें : पंचम वेदु तो काइ गा ऐसा :
गाढवाचिया सारिखें भुंकिजे : ऐसा : आणि स्तीति भंगली :
बीढारा बीजें केलें :॥:

436

221 AND HE EATS CHICKPEAS.

Some people were digging a grain cellar for chickpeas. Bhaïdev went there. He collected fine, white chickpeas, put them in the fold of his garment, and brought them back. "I have brought you some chickpeas, oh God," he said. He performed puja to the Gosavi and placed the chickpeas in front of him.

"Take them, my woman," said the omniscient one. "Put them to use for me." Baïse made a tasty dish with them, and the Gosavi ate it for his meal.

222 HE MEETS UPADHYE
AND VISHNUBHAT.

One day, after the Gosavi's afternoon worship service, he went wandering to the temple of the goddess Bhingai.* Upadhye and Vishnubhat met him there. They prostrated themselves, touched his holy feet, and sat down. Then the Gosavi asked Vishnubhat, "Are your relatives and friends doing well?" "Yes, Lord, they are." And he went into a trance.

As the Gosavi was leaving, going down the hill, a donkey brayed. Vishnubhat brayed as well. "What is going on?" asked the omniscient one. "This is the fifth Veda, Lord."

The omniscient one said, "Is that what the fifth Veda is like? Does it get brayed the way a donkey brays?" And Vishnubhat's trance broke.

The Gosavi went back to his lodgings.

* The village goddess of Bhingar.

२२३ देमती प्रति : प्रतितपंथु निरूपणें :॥:

देमाइसें स्नाना जातें असति : तवं दोघी बाइया स्नान करूनि
येति असति : एकी एकींतें म्हणितलें : बाइ : पुराणा गेलीयें :
तेथ ऐसें निगालें : जें गुरुवीण संसारू न तरिजे : तरि आतां
स्वर्गा जाइजो : अथवा नरका जाइजो : तें येउनि देमाइसीं
गोसावियांपुढें सांघीतलें : सर्वज्ञें म्हणीतलें : देमती एकू
प्रतीतिपंथ : एकू वीश्वास पंथु :॥छ॥: हा प्रतीतपंथु
देमति^{३३७} :॥: तो कैसा जी : सर्वज्ञें म्हणीतलें : तुम्हीं स्त्री
असा : तुमतें एथैनि म्हणितलें : जा : तुम्ही पुरुषू : तें
ऐसेंचि घेउनि ठाकाल : तैसा हा वीस्वास पंथू नव्हे^{३३८} :
हा प्रतीतिपंथु^{३३९} : जी जी : विश्वासपंथु तो कैसा : सर्वज्ञें
म्हणीतलें : देमती : माहात्मेया एकातें एकू : उपदेशू मागे :
तेणें म्हणितलें : जाय : तुं म्हैसा : अभ्यासू वाढवीला : एकू
दी जेउं गेला : वाकुडी मान करूनि भितरि रिगाला : तेंहीं
पुसीलें : ऐसें कां केलें : सांगितलें : हा वीश्वासपंथु :
देमती^{३४०} : रामेश्वरबास : हे लिळा पैठणीं नागनाथीं :॥:

223   HE EXPLAINS TO DEMATI
THAT HIS IS A RELIGIOUS WAY
BASED ON DIRECT EXPERIENCE.

As Demaïse was on her way to take a bath, two women were returning from taking theirs. One of the women said to the other, "My woman, when I went to a Purana recital, I learned that without a guru one cannot escape the cycle of birth and death. So, now, will we go to heaven, or will we go to hell?"

Demaïse came and told the Gosavi about this. The omniscient one said, "Demati, some religious ways are based on direct experience, and others are based on faith. This is a religious way based on direct experience, Demati."[270]

"What is that other kind of way like, Lord?" The omniscient one said, "You are a woman. If I said to you, 'Go ahead; you are a man,' that is what you would accept. My way is not one based on faith like that. This is a way based on direct experience."[271]

"Lord, what is a way based on faith like?" The omniscient one said, "Demati, someone asked a certain Mahatma to give him instruction. The teacher said, 'Go away! You are a water buffalo!' He told him to practice more. One day when the student went in to eat a meal, he bent his neck as he went through the doorway.[272] The Mahatma asked him, 'Why did you do that?' and the student told him. That is a religious path based on faith, Demati."[273]

(According to Rameshvarbas, this *līḷā* took place at the Nagnath temple in Paithan.)

२२४ तथा ज्ञान भक्ति निरूपण :॥ः

एकुदीसीं गोसावीचि नीरूपिलें : एकें म्हणति : देमाइसे
पुराणा आइकौनि एति : मग तेथींचें पुसीलें : सर्वज्ञें
म्हणीतलें : एक ज्ञान भक्ति वैराग्य मोचक : एक अमोचक :
देमती३४१ :॥ः

२२५ मार्गीं बाइसा आग्रहें स्वरुप अदृश्य :॥ः

भिंगारुनि बीजें केलें : मार्गीं वाट फाकली : एकी वाट
पापविनाशना जाये : एकि जेउरा जाये : सर्वज्ञें म्हणीतलें :
एणें मार्गें जाणे : तें ऐणेंचि कां न वचावें : बाइसीं म्हणीतलें :
बाबा : जेउरा चालिजो कां : सर्वज्ञें म्हणीतलें : बाइ : एथ
प्रवृत्ति नाहीं : शोधु : बाइ ऐसें कां करितें असा : न करा :
मग अदृश्ये जाले : आणि बाबा म्हणौनि बाइसें पडलीं :
आन गोसावी प्रगट जाले३४२ : हनवटिये धरिली : मग
सर्वज्ञें म्हणीतलें : हें काइ बाइ : हें काइ बाइ : थोरलेनि
शब्दें म्हणीतलें : डोळे प्रमार्जिले : मग बाइसें उठिलीं : बाबा
आपण कें गेलें होती : सर्वज्ञें म्हणीतलें : बाइ : हें एथ होतें :
हीराइसापाठ : रिंगणिचेंया झाडा तलि होतें : गोसावी
पापविनाशनाकडे बीजें केलें :॥ः

224 AND HE TEACHES HER ABOUT KNOWLEDGE AND DEVOTION.

One day the Gosavi taught her of his own accord. (Some say that Demaïse came back after listening to a Purana recital and asked him about what she had heard there.) The omniscient one said, "Some knowledge, devotion, and dispassion bring about liberation. Some do not bring about liberation, Demati."[274]

225 ALONG THE ROAD, HE BECOMES INVISIBLE BECAUSE OF BAÏSE'S STUBBORNNESS.

He set out from Bhingar. Along the way, there was a fork in the road, with one road going to Papvinashan and the other to Jeür.[275] The omniscient one said, "Instead of taking this road, why shouldn't we just take this other one?" Baïse said, "Can we go to Jeür, Baba?" The omniscient one replied, "I am not inclined to do that, my woman." (Research: "My woman, why are you doing this? Don't do it.") Then he disappeared, and Baïse fell to the ground, crying, "Baba!"

The Gosavi reappeared. He held her by the chin and said, "What is this, my woman? What is this, my woman?" He said it loudly and wiped her eyes.

Then Baïse stood up. "Where did you go, Baba?" she asked. "I was right here, my woman," said the omniscient one. (Hiraïsa version: "I was at the foot of that thorny bush.")

Then the Gosavi proceeded toward Papvinashan.

२२६ पींपळगांवीं घोलाणा : आरोगण :॥:

गोसावीयांसि पींपळगांवीं मळा आसन³⁴³ : बाइसें
पींपळगावां भिक्षे गेली : उपाध्यीं चणा आणीला³⁴⁴ : मग
गोसावी उपाध्यातें म्हणीतलें : बटिका : पैले बोरीचीं बोरें
गोडें : घेया : बाइसें भीक्षा करूनि आली : घोलाणा केला :
पुजा जाली : गोसावियांसि घोलाणा प्रधान आरोगण :॥:

२२७ पापविनाशनी आसन :॥:

पापविनाशना बीजें केलें : चोकी आसन : मग धार
अवलोकीली :॥:

२२८ कपाटीं माहात्मेयातें बोलावणें :॥:

गोसावी कपाटासि बीजें केलें : तेथ महात्में एक बैसले
असति : गोसावी पुसीलें : माहात्मा एथ असीजे : या नगरा
भीक्षा कीजे³⁴⁵ : टकमका पाहति : परि बोलति नां : सर्वज्ञें
म्हणीतलें : देखलें गा कें रिगौनि ठाकला असे : ऐसा जरि
एथीचा होए : तरि : आन एक लाहे : दात असति : तेथ चणे
नाहीं³⁴⁶ :॥:

226 AT PIMPALGAV, HE EATS
A MEAL OF CHICKPEA STEW.

The Gosavi was sitting in an orchard at Pimpalgav.[276] Baïse went to Pimpalgav to beg for food. Upadhye brought some chickpeas.[277] Then the Gosavi said to him, "Batika, the jujubes on that tree over there are sweet. Go get some." When Baïse returned from begging, she made the chickpeas into a stew. Puja was done to the Gosavi, and he ate a meal consisting primarily of the stew.

227 HE SITS AT PAPVINASHAN.

He went to Papvinashan and sat in the central hall of the temple. Then he looked at the waterfall.

228 HE URGES A MAHATMA
IN A CAVE TO SPEAK.

The Gosavi went to a cave where a certain Mahatma was sitting. The Gosavi asked him, "Is this where you stay, Mahatma? Do you beg for food in this town?" The man stared at him intently but did not speak.

The omniscient one said, "Do you see how far gone he is? If a man like that belonged to me, he would get something different. Where there are teeth, there are no chickpeas..."[278]

२२९ गोसावीया वामोरी दक्षीणेश्वरीं अवस्थान :॥ः

वामोरी दक्षीणेश्वरीं चौकीं आसन जालें : तवं मशक खावों
लागले : गोसावी बाहिरी बीजें केलें : पींपळा तळिं आसन :
भक्तजनांकरवीं निंबाचिया काडीया वेचवीलीया : देउळा
आंतु धुप करवीला : दोन्हीं कवाडें घातलीं : मग मशक
गेलेयां मग भितरि अवस्थान :॥ः

२३० मळे संदीं माहात्मेया वैराग्य निरूपण :॥ः

गोसावीयांसि उदयाचा पूजावस्वर जालेया नंतरें मग
वीहरणा बीजें करित असति : दोहीं मळेयाचीया संदीं
माहात्मे एक उघडे देखीलें : भक्तजनीं म्हणीतलें : कैसा
विरक्त : सर्वज्ञें म्हणीतलें : बटिका काइ म्हणत असा : जी
जी : कैसा विरक्त : सर्वज्ञें म्हणीतलें : याचि लागि : जी
याचि लागि : म्हणीतलें : काइ जी : सर्वज्ञें म्हणीतलें : तुम्हीं
म्हणत असा तेयांचि लागि : यक कीर्ति लागौनि वैराग्य :
यक वीखयालागि : एक सतेव : सतेव वैराग्य : तें निके :
हां जी : यांसि काइ वीखो असे जी : सर्वज्ञें म्हणीतलें : यातें
वीखो : लोकु आपुलेया घरा ने : शोधु : हे ऐसे उघडे :

229   THE GOSAVI STAYS IN THE DAKSHINESHVAR TEMPLE AT VAMORI.

While the Gosavi was sitting in the central hall of the Dakshineshvar temple at Vamori, mosquitoes began to bite him.[279] He moved outside and sat at the foot of a pipal tree. He had the devotees collect neem twigs and burn them as incense inside the temple. They closed both the doors. Then, after the mosquitoes went away, he went and stayed in the temple.

230   IN A BOUNDARY BETWEEN ORCHARDS, HE EXPLAINS ABOUT A MAHATMA'S DISPASSION.

After his morning worship service, the Gosavi had gone out to wander. In the boundary between two orchards, they saw a Mahatma who was naked. "How dispassionate he is!" said the devotees.

The omniscient one asked, "What are you saying, Batika?" "How dispassionate he is, Lord." The omniscient one said, "That's exactly why." "Lord, what do you mean by 'That's exactly why'?" The omniscient one replied, "He does this so that you will say exactly what you are saying. Some dispassion is for the sake of fame. Some is for the sake of sense pleasure. Some is for its own sake. Dispassion for its own sake is good."[280]

"Yes, Lord. How does such a person get sense pleasure, Lord?" The omniscient one replied, "He gets sense pleasure when people take him to their home." (Research: "They seat

बाजसूपवतियांवरि बैसवीजति : आंग उटिति : न्हाणिति :
सर्वांगीं चंदन लावीति : माळा घालीति : आड वाटीया
ठाणवैया तुपें भातु जेउं सुति : पाटाउवें सूटाउवें देति : हे
पुरीं पाटणीं : हातें हातु न पवति : ज्ञानेंवीण वैराग्य : तें काइ
करावें बापीया३४७ :॥

२३१ सोनये वनदेवीं वसति :॥:

२३२: हरिणेश्वरीं वसति :॥:

२३३ कानडि गांवीं सिधनाथीं त्रीरात्रि अवस्थान :॥:

गोसावी कानडगांवां बीजें केलें : रामेश्वरबास : हरिणेश्वरीं
वसति जाली : यरी दीसीं सिधनाथा बीजें केलें : सिधनाथीं :
परशरामबास : गुंफे अवस्थान : रामेश्वरबास :॥:

446

him, naked like this, on a bed with a mattress. They anoint him and bathe him. They rub sandalwood paste all over his body and put garlands around his neck. They place a lighted lampstand in front of him and serve him a meal of rice with ghee. They give him silk and cotton garments. You can't find this in cities or towns. What use is dispassion without knowledge, my fellow?")[281]

231 HE STAYS OVERNIGHT IN THE VANDEV TEMPLE AT SONAI.[282]

232 HE STAYS OVERNIGHT IN THE HARINESHVAR* TEMPLE.

233 HE STAYS THREE NIGHTS IN THE SIDDHANATH TEMPLE AT KANADGAV.

The Gosavi went to Kanadgav (according to Rameshvarbas).[283] He stayed overnight in the Harineshvar temple. The next day he went to the Siddhanath temple. According to Parasharambas, he stayed in the Siddhanath temple; according to Rameshvarbas, he stayed in a hermit's cell.

---

* "Lord of Deer," Shiva.

२३४ गांगापुरीं वसति :॥:

गोसावी गांगापुरा बीजें केलें : तवं मार्गीं पद्मनाभिदेव
भेटले : दंडवतें घातलीं : श्रीचरणा लागले : गोसावीयापुढें
सांगितलें : हीराइसापाठ : गोसावी पुसिलें : बटिका कैसेन
आलेति ॥छ॥: जी जी : दुर्गासि सोल लावीली : वोहणिचिये
पाठीवरि पाये देउनि चढलां : मग सोळा सोला उतरलां जी :
मग गोसावीयां तेथ वसति जाली :॥:

२३५ मार्गीं पद्मनाभि मनोर्थ : धांदलमोक्षकथन :॥:

मार्गीं पद्मनाभदेवीं मनोर्थु केला : घरीचां आवघिंचि
गोसावीयांचीं होतु कां तरि मीं गोसावीयापासि असों
लाहातां : सर्वज्ञें म्हणीतलें : बाइ : या पासिल जाडि
चेया³⁴⁸ : बाइसीं म्हणीतलें : कां बाबा : सर्वज्ञें म्हणीतलें :
तेयां अवचेयां यथीची बुधि होए कां³⁴⁹ : हा दोखू : मग
मी एथ असों लाहीन : ऐसें म्हणत असे : तेयां बूधि काइ
याचेनि होइल : तया बूधि काइसी : तेयां इतुलियां ऐसीया
आसू होआवीया : आणि हा होआवा : तेयां एथीचेया बुधी
काइ करीति : बाइ : धांदुलाचिया परीं : पोरु सकुटुंबी मोक्षा
जावों पातु असे : हीराइसापाठ : बाइसीं म्हणीतलें :

234   HE STAYS OVERNIGHT IN
GANGAPUR.

As the Gosavi went to Gangapur, he met Padmanabhidev along the road.[284] Padmanabhidev prostrated himself to the Gosavi and touched his holy feet. He told the Gosavi what had happened.[285] (Hiraïsa version: The Gosavi asked, "How did you get here, Batika?") "A rope got tied to the parapet, Lord. I stood on my sister-in-law's back and climbed up the wall. Then I held onto the rope and climbed down the other side, Lord."

The Gosavi stayed there overnight.

235   ALONG THE ROAD, PADMANABHI
MAKES A WISH AND THE GOSAVI TELLS
ABOUT DHANDAL'S LIBERATION.

Along the road, Padmanabhidev made a wish: "If everyone in my family would come to belong to the Gosavi, then I would get to stay with him."

The omniscient one said, "My woman, take his blanket."[286] "Why, Baba?" asked Baïse. The omniscient one said, "Can all of them come to have faith in me? This is the flaw. 'Then I will get to stay here,' he says. But can he cause them to have faith? How will they come to have faith? They must have some degree of desire for it, and they must have him. What use is faith in me to them? My woman, the poor child is trying to reach liberation along with his family, like Dhandal."

(Hiraïsa version: Baïse said, "What do you mean, Baba?") "My woman, there was a farmer named Dhandal. Indra's

449

तें कैसें बाबा : बाइ : धांदुल नावें कूणबी : तेयांचें पल्हें
इंद्राचा ऐरावतु चरौनि जाए : दीसवडि पल्हें चरौनि कोणाचें
ढोर जात असे पां : म्हणौनि : राखों ठेला : तवं तो चरों
आला : हें जेयाचें म्हैसरू तेयाचीया घरा नेवों : पुंस धरिलें :
तो उत्पवला : वरि गेला : तवं सभा बैसली असे : हें म्हैसरूं
विकाना कां : चोरां कां दीयाना : माझें अवघें सेत खादलें :
आतां मीं सी दावो काइसेनि फेडी : तुझिए सेतीं काइ होए :
बीटी दोनि होति : तेणें सी दावो फेडी : ना : तुझेनि नेववेल
तेतुके चे : गेला : रगटें पसरिलें : आसु भरिलिया : घेउनि
आला : मि कैसेनि जावों : याचें पुंस धरूनि जाय : घेवुनी
आला : खावेया जाले³⁵⁰ : मागौतें खेत पीकलें : पल्हें
वेचावेया जालें : मोलकीयें बोलावीलीं : पल्हें वेचितां
पुसिलें : हांगा : धांदला दादो : तुज खावेया कैसेनि जाले :
तेणें मागिल आवघें सांघीतलें : तें आतां येताये : हो हो :
तरि : आमुतें ने कां : हो कां : यैरावत आला : पुंस धरिलें :
येकमेकां मागें लागलीं : उत्पवला : हां गा : धांदल दादो :
तेथ³⁵¹ : मजलागि अमुकें जोडे : तेथ कापुसु जोडे : जोडे :
दामांचा कीती : ना इतुका : म्हणौनि : दोन्ही हात सोडुनि
दाखवीलें : अवघींचि रीचवलीं :॥ः

elephant, Airavat, would come to graze on his cotton crop. When Dhandal realized that someone's large animal was grazing on his cotton crop every day, he stood guard. Airavat came to graze, and Dhandal thought to himself, 'Let this lousy water buffalo take me home to its owner.' He grabbed Airavat's tail, flew up into the air, and went to heaven.

"Indra's court was in session. Dhandal asked, 'Why don't you sell off this lousy water buffalo? Why don't you give it to robbers? It has eaten up my whole crop. How am I going to pay back the seed loan now?' 'What crop was in your field?' asked Indra. 'There was two gold coins' worth of it. I was going to use it to pay off the loan.' 'Take as much money as you can carry.'

"He went and spread out a piece of rough cloth, filled it with gold coins, and brought it back. 'How can I go back?' he asked. 'Hold onto his tail and go.'

"He brought it back with him, and he prospered. Another crop grew in his field. When the cotton was ready to be picked, he recruited laborers. As they were picking the cotton, they asked, 'Hey, Dhandal Dada, how did you get to be so prosperous?' He told them everything that had happened. 'Does he come here now?' 'Yes. He does.' 'Will you take us there, then?' 'All right.'

"Airavat came there. Dhandal took hold of his tail. They hung on behind him, one after the other, and flew up into the air. 'Hey, Dhandal Dada!' they asked. 'Can I get such-and-such there? Can you get cotton there?' 'Yes, you can.' 'How much do you get for a copper coin?' 'This much,' he said, and he let go to show them with both hands.

"One and all, they fell to the ground."

२३६ फुलसरा वसति ः॥ः

२३७ एलापुरीं चतुर्विधा मढीं अवस्थान ः॥ः

गोसावी येलापुरीं बीजें केलें ः चतुर्विधाचां मढीं ः अवस्थान दीस ॥१५॥ ः॥ः

२३८ परमाणुभव नामखंडनीं पद्मनाभी सीक्षापण ः॥ः

एलापुर परमाणुभव देव ः ते उपाधीस्थुळ ः एकी आसूचें तांबुल एका वीडेयासि लागे ः तेयाचेया बीढारासि पद्मनाभिदेव गेले ः तेंहीं मानु केला ः बैसों घातलें ः तेयातें पुसिलें ः तुम्हां नांव काइ ः नां ः आम्हां नाव प्रमाणुभवदेव ः मग व्याकरणाचेनि सुत्रें ः नकारा नकारा३५२ भेदु नाहीं ः म्हणौनि तेयाचें नांव खडिलें ः तुमचा अनुभवो काइ परमानु इतुका३५३ ः तेंहीं म्हणीतलें ः घाला घाला ः बाहीरि ः मग बिढारा३५४ आले ः सर्वज्ञें म्हणीतलें ः बाइ ः यांसि भितरि रिगों नेदा ः कां ः बाबा ः बाइ ः हा प्राणियाचें चैतन्य पोळुनि आला असे ः आतां ः बाहीरि घाला ः॥ः बाइ ः प्रमाणुभव

452

236   HE STAYS OVERNIGHT
IN PHULSARA.[287]

237   HE STAYS IN THE CHATURVIDH
HERMITAGE IN YELAPUR.

The Gosavi went to Yelapur and stayed fifteen days in the hermitage of Chaturvidh.

238   HE REBUKES PADMANABHI
FOR MAKING FUN OF
PARAMANUBHAV'S NAME.

Paramanubhavdev was a prominent citizen of Yelapur. He used to need a gold coin's worth of betel nut for a single pan.

Padmanabhidev went to his home. Paramanubhavdev treated him with respect and put down something for him to sit on. Padmanabhidev asked him, "What is your name?" "My name is Paramanubhavdev."

Then, relying on the grammatical aphorism "There is no difference between *na* and *ṇa*," Padmanabhidev analyzed his name. "Is your experience infinitesimally small?" he asked.[288] "Throw him out!" said Paramanubhavdev. "Throw him out!"

Then Padmanabhidev came back to their lodgings. The omniscient one said to Baïse, "My woman, do not let him come in." "Why, Baba?" "My woman, he has burned a person's spirit.[289] Throw him out now. He went to Paramanubhav-

देवाचेया ठाया गेला : तेहीं एथींचा म्हणौनि मानु केला :
तेयांतें म्हणीतलें : प्रमाणु यतुका अनुभवू म्हणौनि प्रमाणुभव
म्हणीतलें : तेहीं बाहीरि घातला : मग ते पद्मनाभिदेव दुख
करूं लागलें : सर्वज्ञें म्हणीतलें : बाइ : यांतें परतें धाडा : याचें
शब्द एथींचां कानीं पडती तरि यासि महंत अनिष्ट होइल :
बाइसीं विनविलें : बाबा : बापूडा दुख करीतु असे : यवों
द्यावा : बाबा : सर्वज्ञें म्हणीतलें : बाइ : तेयाचेया ठाया
जावों : सेणें मातीया आंग माखौनि तेया आड पडो : तेयांतें
म्हणों : आमचा होता : आपणेयापासि असों दीयावा : तरि :
असों दीजैल : गेले : तेयांसि : सेणें मातीया आंग माखौनि
आड पडिलें : तेहीं म्हणीतलें : ऐसेगा ते श्री चांगदेवो राउळ
निके : तेथींचां ठाइं ऐसें असे : तेयातें धुतलें : घेउनि आले :
तेहीं निरोवीलें : जी जी : आमचे होते : असों दीयावें : सर्वज्ञें
म्हणीतलें : हा तुमचा होता : येथौनि स्वीकरीजत असीजे :
हो कां : जी३५५ :॥:

२३९ हातनौरि वसति :॥:

सोधु : हातनौरांतु वाव्ये नरसींहू पूर्वामूखू : तेथ वसती
जाली३५६ :॥:

454

dev's place, my woman. Paramanubhavdev treated him respectfully, because he is my disciple. Padmanabhidev said to him, 'You have an infinitesimally small amount of experience and so you are called Paramanubhav.'"

She threw Padmanabhidev out, and he began to cry. The omniscient one said, "Send him farther away, my woman. If I hear his voice, something very bad will happen to him." Baïse pleaded, "Baba! The poor fellow is crying. Let him come back, Baba." The omniscient one said, "My woman, he must go to Paramanubhavdev, smear cow dung and mud on himself, and prostrate himself to him. If *he* says, 'He used to be mine; now let him stay with you,' then I will let him stay."

Padmanabhidev went there, smeared cow dung and mud on himself, and prostrated himself to Paramanubhavdev. Paramanubhavdev said, "That is how good that Shri Cangdev Raül is. It is like that with him." He washed him off, brought him to the Gosavi, and entrusted him to him, saying, "Lord, he used to be mine; now let him stay with you." The omniscient one said, "He was yours. I accept him now." "All right, Lord."

239 HE STAYS OVERNIGHT IN HATNAUR.

(Research: He stayed overnight in the northwestern part of Hatnaur, in a Narasimha temple that faces east.)[290]

२४० कनरडे वसति :॥:

कनरडे : गोसावी ब्राह्मण एकाचेया घरा बीजें केले : पुजा
जाली : आरोगणा जाली : वसति जाली : रात्रीं चांदीणें
पडीलें होतें : दारीं द्राक्षाचा मांडउ होता : द्राक्षाचे घड लोंबत
होतें : रात्रीं वेढें करीतां द्राक्षघडु स्परिसीला :॥:

२४१ साएगव्हाणीं वसति :॥:

२४२ वागुळीए वसति :॥:

२४३ कानसे मळां देवांसीक्षां भेटि :॥:

दादोसीं श्रीप्रभूतें वीनवीलें : गोसावी कवणे ठाइं भेटती :
जी : सर्वज्ञें म्हणीतलें : मेला जाए कानडगावां जाए म्हणे :
भलुगावां जाए म्हणे : निगाले : चारठाणेया आले : तेथ
महदाइसें : साधें होतीं : तेयाचीये वोसरीये वरि बैसले :
श्रीप्रभुचीं महिमा नीरोपुं लागले : साधीं म्हणीतलें : पीसे
पीसे राउळ ते : होवो होवो पींसे पींसे राउळ ते : तैसीचि

456

240 HE STAYS OVERNIGHT IN KANARADE.

In Kanarade, the Gosavi went to the home of a certain Brahman.[291] The Gosavi's puja was performed there, and he ate his meal. He stayed there overnight.

The moon was shining that night. There was a grape arbor at the door, with bunches of grapes hanging down from it. As the Gosavi walked back and forth that night, he touched a bunch of grapes.

241 HE STAYS OVERNIGHT IN SAEGAVHAN.[292]

242 HE STAYS OVERNIGHT IN VAGULI.[293]

243 HE MEETS DEV'S DISCIPLES IN AN ORCHARD AT KANASE.[294]

Dados asked Shriprabhu, "Where can I meet the Gosavi, Lord?" "Drop dead!" replied the omniscient one. "Go to Kanadgav, I say. Go to Bhalugav, I say."[295]

Dados set out. When he reached Charthane, Mahadaïse and Sadhe were there.[296] He sat on their veranda and began to extol Shriprabhu. Sadhe said, "That Raül* is very crazy." "Yes, yes. That Raül is very crazy."

---

* Shriprabhu, also called Gundam Raül.

अस्तीति जाली : एकी वासना३५७ : साधें डेरा खरवडितें
होतीं : दादोसासीं भेटि जाली : साधीं पुसीलें : रामा कवणी
कडौनि येत असिस : ना रिध्दपुरौनि : काइ करूं गेला
होतासि : श्रीगुंडम राउळां गोसावीयांचेया दरिसना : गुंडम
राउळ गुंडम राउळ ते कवण : लेंकरूवांपाठीं धावति :
पीसे पीसे ते : होए वो ते : आणि डेरेयांत तोंड सूनि : होबो
होबो ते : म्हणौनि स्तीति जाली : मग महदाइसीं करविं
खांद चुरविलें : आणि स्तीति भंगली : मग साधीं पुसीलें :
रामा कवणीकडे जात असिस : नां : श्रीचांगदेवो राउळा
गोसावीयांचेया दरिसना : तरि मिहीं येइन : या : सरवळेयां
पोतें भरिलें : साधें काकोसयें तेथौनि निगालीं : साडेगांवां
आले : तेथौनि आबैसें : उमाइसें : महदाइसें : सामकोसें :
सोभागे : इंद्रोबा : गौराइसे : ऐसीं नीगालीं : रावसगांउनि :
सांढगावीहुनि : भालुगाउनि कनरडें आली : तवं तेथौनिहीं
गोसावी बीजें केलें : मग कनरडें वसीनली : तेथ ब्राह्मणीं
सांघीतलें : पर्वां एथौनि बीजें केलें : दादोसीं म्हणीतलें :
जेयासि टाकैल तें यावें : न टके तेहीं हळु हळु यावें : मि
आजि गोसावीयांतें देखैन : तेव्हळी चुल पाणिया भरीन :
ऐसा परिछेद केला : गांवें च्यारि आले : तवं गोसावी कानस
पावले : गांवां नृत्य विभागें मळा : मळेयांतु बीजें केलें :
सर्वझें म्हणीतलें : बाइ : घाला जाडि : हीराइसापाठ : एथ
आसन करा :॥छ॥: बाइसीं म्हणीतलें : बाबा : उदीयांचि

Immediately Sadhe went into a trance. (Another version: Sadhe was scrubbing out a large earthen pot. She greeted Dados. "Ram," asked Sadhe, "where are you coming from?" "From Riddhipur." "What did you go there to do?" "To have *darśan* of Shri Gundam Raül Gosavi." "Gundam Raül? What Gundam Raül? The one who runs after children? The one who is very crazy?" "Yes, that one." And she stuck her face in the pot, said, "Yes! Yes, that one!" and went into a trance.) Then he had Mahadaïse squeeze her shoulder, and the trance broke.

Then Sadhe asked, "Where are you going, Ram?" "For *darśan* of Shri Cangdev Raül Gosavi," he replied. "Then I want to come along." "Come on."

Sadhe filled a sack with twisted bits of wheat dough, and she and Kakos set out and came to Sadegav. From there, Abaïse, Umaïse, Mahadaïse, Samakose, Sobhage, Indroba, and Gauraïse joined them. By the time they reached Kanarade, via Ravasgav, Sandhgav, and Bhalugav, the Gosavi had left that place too, so they spent the night in Kanarade. The Brahman there told them, "He left here the day before yesterday."[297]

The next morning, Dados said, "Those who can travel fast should come along with me, and those who can't manage may follow more slowly. I will see the Gosavi this day," he resolved, "and until then I will not take a sip of water."

By the time Dados had come a distance of four villages, the Gosavi had reached Kanase and entered an orchard in the southwestern part of the village. The omniscient one said to Baïse, "My woman, put down a blanket on the ground." (Hiraïsa version: "Prepare a seat for me here.") "Baba, why

कैसे : आसन : गाउ साना : दीसीकडा पुढारें चालिजो :
बाबा : सर्वज्ञें म्हणीतलें : पानरटें ऐसीं उडतें एतें असति :
घाला जाडि : बाइसीं आसन केलें : गोसावी आसनीं
उपवीष्ट जालें : तेथ जोगी आणि जोगीण बैसलीं होतीं :
तेंहीं गोसावीयांतें देखीलें : अया : कैसें सौंदर पुरुषु : साक्षांत
गोरक्षनाथु : होए देवी : ऐसीया गोष्टी करीतें मार्गें जात
असति : तवं दादोस : महदाइसें यतें असेति : महदाइसीं
आइकीलें : तेयांतें पुसिलें : तेंहीं सांघीतलें : तेयांतें
म्हणीतलें : आमचीं मागा एतें असति : तेयापुढें सांघावें :
तुमचे गोसावी पुढीले गावीं मळां असति : देव : महदाइसें :
उमाइसें टाकौनि आलीं : आहा : माहात्मे आले : मा नावेक
साउमे बीजें केलें : देव दंडवती आले : गोसावी खेवं दीधले :
मग मागिला कडौनि अवघीं आलीं : दंडवतें घातलीं :
श्रीचरणा लागलीं : आवघीं बैसलीं : गोसावी पूसिलें : तुमचीं
अवघीं आलीं कीं : कीं कोण्हीं मागें असति : जी जी :
सोभागें मागें असति : सर्वज्ञें म्हणीतलें : ऐसें सोभाग आलें :
गोसावी हरिखू स्वीकरीला : सर्वज्ञें म्हणीतलें : मार्तंडा
सोभागातें पाटकूळीये घालुनि आणा३५८ : मार्तंड गेले :
आणिलें : सोभागासीं भेटि जाली : हीराइसापाठ : सोभाग

do you want to sit down so early in the morning?" asked Baïse. "This is a small village. We should walk on farther while it is daylight, Baba." The omniscient one said, "They are coming like dry leaves blown by the wind. Put down the blanket." Baïse prepared a seat, and the Gosavi sat down on it.

A yogi and yogini who were sitting there saw the Gosavi. "What a beautiful holy man! He is Gorakshanath himself," said the yogini. "That is true, my Goddess," replied the yogi. They kept saying things like that to each other as they went along the road.

As Dados and Mahadaïse came near them, Mahadaïse heard what they were saying. She asked them what they were talking about, and they told her. She said to them, "More of our people are coming along behind us. Please tell them, 'Your Gosavi is in an orchard in the next village.'"

Dev, Mahadaïse, and Umaïse reached the orchard. "Hey! The Mahatmas have arrived," said the Gosavi, and he went a short distance toward them. Dev came to him prostrating himself again and again, and the Gosavi embraced him. Then the others arrived, catching up with them. They prostrated themselves and touched his holy feet. Everyone sat down.

The Gosavi asked, "Have all your people arrived? Or are some lagging behind?" "Sobhage is lagging behind, Lord." The omniscient one said, "So Sobhage is coming!" and the Gosavi accepted joy.

The omniscient one said, "Martanda, put Sobhage on your back and bring her here." Martanda went and brought Sobhage there. The Gosavi greeted her (Hiraïsa version: "Sobhage has come!" he said), and she sat down.

आलें मां : तथा सोभागा आलीति :॥छ॥: बैसली : बाइसीं
श्रीचरणक्षाळण केलें : अवघेया तांबूल : प्रसाददान केलें :
साधीं तांबोळ हातीं घेतलें : साधीं म्हणीतलें काको घेइल
तरि मी घेइन : काकोसीं भितरि घेतलें : मग साधीं घेतलें :
साधें गोसावीयाची श्रीमूर्ति अवलोकीतें उभींचि असति :
डोइयेचें पोतें गळेयासि आलें : दादोसीं म्हणीतलें : येल्होचीए
गळाचें पोतें घेया : यल्हो गोसाविया नमस्कारू करील :
सर्वज्ञें म्हणीतलें : माहात्मे हो : यें तुम्हांसि काइ होति : जी
जी : संबंधीयें : तथा चुलती³⁵⁹ : सर्वज्ञें म्हणीतलें :
तिर्थ : देवता : पुरुषु :॥: तिर्थ जैसी वाराणसि : देवता
जेसी शारंगधरू : आणि पुरुषू जैसें हें³⁶⁰ : आणि काइ :
साधें दंडवत न करीतिचि : श्रीचरणू साउमा नेउनि आंगुठा
लावीला : निडळीं लाविला : गोसावी आबैसातें पुसीलें :
बाइ : यें कवणें³⁶¹ : जी : यें अवडलाची माता : हे
अवडलाची लेकि : हा अवडलाचा जावाइ : ऐसीयें अवघीं
अवडळीं लावीलीं : शोधु : बाइ : वाराना : एथींचेया दरिसना
येतें असति : माथां जाजारू वाळेना : एथें पीसें येक आति :
तें लागतें तरि काइ : सामकोसीं म्हणीतलें : ऐसें लागो कां
जी : सर्वज्ञें म्हणीतलें : तरि : तुम्हीं मदळसा म्हणा : मग
देवीं साधें आंघोळी धाडीली : देवीं वीहीरी दाखवीली :

Baïse washed his holy feet and gave everyone his pan as *prasād*. Sadhe held the pan in her hand, saying to herself, "If Kako puts it in his mouth, I will put it in mine."[298] Kakos put it into his mouth, and then Sadhe put it into hers.

Sadhe was just standing there, staring at the Gosavi's holy form. The sack she was carrying on her head sagged down to her neck. Dados said, "Take the sack from Elho's* neck, and she will bow to the Gosavi."

The omniscient one said, "Who is she to you, Mahatma?" "My relative, Lord." (Or, "My paternal uncle's wife.")[299] The omniscient one said, "Holy places, deities, and holy men...[300] Holy places like Varanasi,† deities like Sharngadhar,‡ and holy men like me. Why not?"

Still Sadhe did not prostrate herself. He brought his holy foot in front of her and placed his big toe on her forehead.

The Gosavi asked Abaïse, "Who are these people, my woman?" She connected all of them with Hard-Hearted, saying, "Lord, this is Hard-Hearted's mother, this is his daughter, and this is his son-in-law."[301]

(Research: "Warn them off, my woman. They are coming for my *darśan,* but the soft spot on their heads has not yet hardened.[302] There is a kind of madness here. If it afflicts them, what will happen?" Samakose said, "Why should it afflict us?" The omniscient one said, "Then we will call you Madalsa.")[303]

Then Dev sent Sadhe to take a bath. He showed her the well and said, "Go take a bath, Elho." She went and bathed,

* Sadhe's.
† Banaras.
‡ Vishnu, "bearer of the Sharnga bow."

येल्हो : स्नान करि जाए : गेली : आंघोळि केली : माळियातें
म्हणीतलें : आलेया कांहीं वावेयातें दे कां : तथा दवणा दे
कां : तंव कांहीं नाहीं : दवणेयांचे वाफे पाणियें भरले
असति : घेया जा : घेतला : तेथेंचि वोहळिला : घेउनि
आलीं : गोसावी आसनीं उपविष्ट असति : दवणा गळतु
समुळीं वाइला : पूजा केलीं : पुढां उभीं राहिलीं : दोन्हि हात
जोडुनि मग म्हणीतलें : जी जी : संसारीं जन्मलेयाचें फळ
आजि जालें : सर्वज्ञें म्हणीतलें : साधे होः तें कैसें³⁶² : जैसें
तुम्हीं देखिलेति : सर्वज्ञें म्हणीतलें : ऐसें होए : बाइसें आलीं :
तंव श्रीमूर्तिवरि दवणा थीबतु असते : ऐसें कोणें वो केलें :
बाइसीं सवीया दीधलीया : सर्वज्ञें म्हणीतलें : बाइ : यांसि
कां कोपतें असा : यें वराडीची साधें कीं : एथ गोसावीं साधें
नावं ठेविलें³⁶³ :॥:

२४४ इंद्रोबातें सूखस्वास्ति पुसणें :॥:

गोसावी इंद्रोबातें म्हणीतलें : माहात्मेया पासौनि तुम्हां
सूखस्वास्ति आति : ना जी : तरि : एथीचेया दरिसना
यावेया काइ कारण : जी जी : दादोस म्हणति : मागां
श्रीकृष्ण चक्रवर्ति पासौनि : अकृतम्य आनंदु आति : आतां
गोसावीयांपासौनि आति :ः शोधु : तथा जी जी : श्रीकृष्ण

then said to a Gardener, "My friend, will you give me something to offer?" (Or, "will you give me southernwood?") "No problem," he replied. "The southernwood bed is filled with water. Go ahead and take some."

She took some, washed it right there in running water, and brought it to where the Gosavi was seated. She offered him the southernwood dripping wet, roots and all. She performed puja, then stood before him, folded her hands, and said, "Lord, today I have received my reward for having been reborn in this world." "What do you mean, Sadhe?" asked the omniscient one. "For one thing, I have seen you." "That is true," said the omniscient one.

When Baïse came there, the water from the southernwood was dripping onto his holy body. "Who did this?" Baïse asked, cursing. The omniscient one said, "Why are you getting angry with her, my woman? She is a simple woman, a Sadhe, from Varad." This is when the Gosavi gave her the name Sadhe.

244 HE ASKS INDROBA
IF HE IS PEACEFUL AND HAPPY.

The Gosavi said to Indroba, "Do you get peace and happiness from the Mahatma?" "Yes, Lord." "So why should you come for my *darśan?*" "Lord, Dados says, 'In the past people got genuine joy from Shri Krishna Chakravarti. Now they get it from the Gosavi.' (Or, research: "Lord, we have come out of a desire for the genuine joy that men, beasts, and animals

चक्रवर्ति पासौनि : नरां³⁶⁴ : पशूवां : त्रीयंचा : अक्रतुम्य
आनंदु आति : तेयाची आम्हा चाड : तेया चाडां आलों जी :
आनंदु तो ब्रह्म नीरूपीना : गोसावी गोराइसाकडे दाखवीलें :
तरि : हें काइ³⁶⁵ : तेही म्हणीतलें : धर्मेंचि अर्थेंचि कामेंचि
नातिचरितव्या : नातिचरामि : ऐसें म्हणीतलें असे³⁶⁶ कीं :
सर्वज्ञें म्हणीतलें : तरि मोक्षेंचि नाहीं कीं : हो जी : तरि
यें आपुलिया भलेयाचिया चाडा आलीं : यासि यावेयाची
उतकंठा :॥:

२४५ ब्राह्मणा वीज्ञापनें : भृत्यातें जेउं पाठवणें :॥:

गोसावीयांतें ब्राह्मणें वीनवीलें : जी जी : माझेया घरा
गोसावी बीजें करावें : सर्वज्ञें म्हणीतलें : देखीलें : रंधन
वर्तत असे : हीराइसापाठ : आतां हे न ए : मग एइल :॥छ॥:
जी जी : तरि महात्मेयांतें धाडावें : सर्वज्ञें म्हणीतलें : जा
गा³⁶⁷ : मग अवडळ : मार्तंड : काको : इंद्रोबा नीगाले :
महदाइसीं गोसावीया लागि उपाहारू नीफजवीला : पोटीं
गोसावी दादोसातें राहवावे³⁶⁸ ऐसें : महदाइसा : परि
बोलों न शकति : सर्वज्ञें म्हणीतलें : काइ बाइ लुखलुखीतें :
म्हणौनि : श्रीकर ऐसें केलें³⁶⁹ : सर्वज्ञें म्हणीतलें : माहात्मे हो

get from Shri Krishna Chakravarti. Not even Brahma can describe that joy.")

The Gosavi gestured toward Gauraïse.* "What is this, then?" Indroba said, "It is said, 'One should not go to extremes with respect to duty, profit, or pleasure.' I am not going to extremes."[304] "But not with respect to moksha!" said the omniscient one. "That's right, Lord. She has come out of a desire to promote her own welfare. She was eager to come."

245 WHEN A BRAHMAN INVITES HIM FOR A MEAL, HE SENDS HIS SERVANTS TO EAT THERE.

A Brahman invited the Gosavi for a meal. "Lord Gosavi," he said, "please come to my house." The omniscient one said, "Don't you see? Cooking is going on here." (Hiraïsa version: "I won't come now. I will come later.") "All right, Lord. But please send the Mahatmas." "Go on," said the omniscient one.[305] Hard-Hearted, Martanda, Kako, and Indroba set out.

Mahadaïse prepared food for the Gosavi. In her heart, Mahadaïse hoped that the Gosavi would have Dados stay back, but she couldn't bring herself to say that out loud. "What are you muttering, my woman?" asked the omniscient one, and he gestured with his holy hand. "You stay here, Mahatma," said the omniscient one. So Dev stayed there.[306]

* Indroba's wife.

राहा : मग देव राहीले३७० : मग गोसावीयांसि पुजा जाली :
आरोगण : देवांसी पांती जाली : पहुड : उपहुड : आंगीटोपरें
केलें : मग वीळिचां वेळीं ब्राह्मणाचेया घरां बीजें केलें :
ब्राह्मणें सडासंमार्जन केलें : चौक रंगमाळिका भरिलीया :
ओसरीयेवर बाज सुपवती घातली३७१ : तेथ गोसावीयांसि
आसन जाले३७२ : बाइसें चरणक्षाळण करावेया आलीं :
सर्वज्ञें म्हणीतलें : बाइ : तुम्हीं राहा : एथचीं एजमानें धुती :
हीराइसापाठ : एथचेया यजमाना करूं दीया : मग ब्राह्मणें
चरणक्षाळण केलें : चरणोदकें घर सींपीलें : कोठा सींपीला :
बाइसीं म्हणीतलें : रुपै : बाबांसि बहुत दीस मादनें नाहीं :
पाणि ठेवीलें होतें : तेथेंचि आणिक रिचवीलें : पाणी ठेवीतां
वीनवीलें : बाबा मादनें बहुत दीस नाहीं : कीजो : गोसावी
मानिलें : बाइसें करूं रिगाली : मग गोसावी पद्मनाभि३७३
करवि करविलें : हीराइसा पाठ : बाइ : पद्मनाभि देइल :॥:
मा गोसावीयांतें वोलणी दीधली : पद्मनाभिदेव मर्दना देत
असति : तवं दादोसीं साधें धाडीलीं : यल्हो : जाय पां :
गोसावीयांसि अवस्वरू कीं अनवस्वरू : ऐसें पाहुनि ए :
आलिं : तवं बाइसें गोसावीयांचें अंगीं टोपरें : घेउनि आंगणीं
उभीं असति : गोसावी म्हणौनि३७४ : साधें बाइसाकडे
आलीं : बाइसीं म्हणीतलें : येल्हो बाबा पैन्हां असति :

The Gosavi's puja took place, and he ate his meal. Dev was served in the same row with him. The Gosavi went to sleep and woke up. He put on a cloak and a cap, and then, in the evening, he went to the Brahman's house.

The Brahman's home had been smeared with cow dung, and designs had been drawn on the ground with colored powder. A bed and mattress had been set out on the veranda.[307] The Gosavi sat there.

As Baïse came to wash his feet, the omniscient one said, "Wait a minute, my woman. My host will wash them." (Hiraïsa version: "Let my host wash them.") Then the Brahman did the foot washing, and he sprinkled the house and the cattle shed with the foot water.

Baïse said, "Rupai, it has been a long time since Baba had a proper bath." They added more water to the pot that had been put on to heat. As they were heating the water, they made a request: "Baba, you have not had a proper bath for a long time. May we give you one?" The Gosavi agreed.

Baïse was about to give it to him, but then he said to have Padmanabhi do it. (Hiraïsa version: "Padmanabhi will give it to me," he said.) They gave the Gosavi a cloth to wear while bathing.

While Padmanabhidev was giving him a massage, Dados sent Sadhe there. "Elho," he said, "go there and find out if it is a good time or a bad time to visit the Gosavi."

When she arrived, Baïse was standing in the courtyard holding the Gosavi's cloak and cap. Sadhe came over to Baïse, thinking that she was the Gosavi. "Elho," said Baïse, "Baba is over there."

साधीं लवणे उघडौनि पाहिलें : सर्वज्ञें म्हणींतलें : देवो एथ
असे^{३७५} : आलीं : दंडवतें घातलीं : श्रीचरणा लागलीं :
सर्वज्ञें म्हणीतलें : साधे व्हो : तुम्हीं मर्दना देवो जाणा : साधीं
म्हणीतलें : ना जी : मर्दना देओं नेणें : सर्वज्ञें म्हणीतलें :
तरि वैरातें कोण उटी : ना जी : आमतें चाटे बहुत
असति : ते आंगें उटिति^{३७६} : सर्वज्ञें म्हणीतलें : लेंकरूवें
न्हाणा^{३७७} : जी जी : तें ऐसी परवसीजति : सर्वज्ञें
म्हणी-तलें : तें एथ दाखवा^{३७८} : सर्वज्ञें म्हणीतलें : कासोटा
दीया : तेहीं कासोटा दीधला : मांडीया उघडीया घातलीया :
सर्वज्ञें म्हणीतलें : ऐसा नको : ऐसा देया : हीराइसापाठ :
गोसावी आपुलेनि श्रीकरें कासोटा दीधला :॥छ॥: तेहीं
पालौ खोवीला : सर्वज्ञें म्हणीतलें : पालौ ऐसा खोवा :
हीराइसापाठ : आपुलेनि श्रीकरें पालो खोविला :॥छ॥: सर्वज्ञें
म्हणीतलें : साधे व्हो : आपुली मांडी पर पुरुषा दाखउं
नए :॥: सरा गा : पद्मनाभि : मांडिया चीकसा लावीला :
सर्वज्ञें म्हणीतलें : साधें व्हो : तुमतें बळ असे : तेतुलेंहीं एथ
दाखवा : एन्हवीं एथौनि जाणिजत असीजे^{३७९} : एकू चरण
उटीला : मग गोसावी पूरें केलें : हीराइसापाठ : साधे व्हो :
पूरें आतां तुमची होती : पद्मनाभि करील :॥छ॥: यगा
पद्मनाभि : मग पदमुनाभि मर्दना दीधली : साधें प्रसाद
म्हणौनि मळीया^{३८०} घेति : मग पाणी सारिलें : गाडु ढाळीतां

Sadhe opened the curtain and looked. "God is in here," said the omniscient one. [308] She came in, prostrated herself, and touched his holy feet.

"Sadhe," asked the omniscient one, "do you know how to give a massage?" "No, Lord," replied Sadhe. "I don't know how to give a massage." The omniscient one asked, "Then who massages your husband?" "We have a lot of servants, Lord," she replied. "They give the massages." The omniscient one asked, "Do you bathe the children?" "They just get a rub-down, Lord." The omniscient one said, "Show me what that is like."

"Tuck up your sari," said the omniscient one. When she tucked up her sari, that exposed her thighs. The omniscient one said, "Not that way. Tuck it up like this." (Hiraïsa version: The Gosavi tucked up her sari with his own holy hands.) She tucked in the end of her sari at her waist. The omniscient one said, "Tuck in the end of your sari this way." (Hiraïsa version: He tucked in the end of her sari with his own holy hands.) The omniscient one said, "Sadhe, you may not show your thigh to any man other than your husband. [309] Move aside, Padmanabhi."

She put fragrant ointment on the Gosavi's thigh. The omniscient one said, "Sadhe, show me every bit of your strength. In any case, I already know." She anointed one of the Gosavi's feet, and then he made her stop. (Hiraïsa version: "You've done enough now. Padmanabhi will do the rest.") "Come on, Padmanabhi," he said. Then Padmanabhi massaged him, and Sadhe took the scurf as *prasād*.

Then the bath water was drawn. As Padmanabhi poured water from the bathing cup, she cupped her hands and took

श्रीमूर्तिंचेया पाणीयांचे चुळ घेति : पाणी पीति : पाठीमोरीं
ठाकौनि : बाइसें वस्त्र आणुं गेलीं : सर्वज्ञें म्हणीतलें : साधे
व्हो : बाइसें देखती तरी काइ करा : हीराइसापाठ : तथा
साधे व्हो : बाइसां भीयाना :॥छ॥: जी जी पाणीयांसीचि
काइ भियावें जी : बाइसें वस्तें घेउनि आलीं : आणि
पाणीयां आजूळि भरूनि पैन्हां गेली : बाइसीं वस्त्र
वोळगवीलें : मग पुजा जाली : सर्वज्ञें म्हणीतलें : साधे व्हो :
आतां जा ना बिढारा : हो कां : जी³⁹¹ : मग गेली : मग
आरोगणा : पहुड : देवीं साधातें म्हणीतलें : एल्हो : सांघों
न यसीचि : तेंही म्हणीतलें : तुम्हीं कां न याचि : म्हणौनि
मागिल सांघीतलें :॥:

२४६ मार्गीं अनुवर्जनीं ब्राह्मणा वरप्रदान :॥:

उद्याचा पूजावस्वर जालेया नंतरें : मग गोसावी बीजें केलें :
ब्राह्मणु अनुवर्जित आला : जी जी : या माझिया पाटिया :
सेतें दाइं हीरतलीं जी : सर्वज्ञें म्हणीतलें : भटो एथ कांहीं
मागा : काइ मागों जी : कोठेयां कोणीं : ताक आंबिल
सुनाचेनि हातें : हें दीयावें जी³⁹² : सर्वज्ञें म्हणीतलें : हें
होइल कीं : तथा भटो हें होइल कीं : आणिक कांहीं मागा :

water as it flowed off the holy body. She was turning her back and drinking the water. Baïse had gone to get his clothes. The omniscient one said, "Sadhe, if Baïse sees you, what will you do?" (Or, Hiraïsa version: "Sadhe, aren't you afraid of Baïse?") "What is there to be afraid of, Lord? It's just water."

When Baïse brought the clothes, Sadhe filled her cupped hands with water and went off to the side. Baïse offered him the clothes, and then his puja took place. The omniscient one said, "Sadhe, go to your lodgings now." "All right, Lord."[310] After she left, he ate his meal and went to sleep.

When Sadhe returned to their lodgings, Dev said to her, "Elho, you didn't come back to tell me." "Why didn't you simply come there?" she said, and she told him what had happened.

246 ALONG THE ROAD, HE GIVES THE BRAHMAN A BOON WHEN HE COMES ALONG TO SEE HIM OFF.

After the morning worship service the next day, the Gosavi left. The Brahman came along to see him off. "These are my fields, Lord. My relatives have grabbed my land." The omniscient one said, "Ask me for something, Bhat." "What can I ask for, Lord? Give me this: let my daughter-in-law serve me buttermilk gruel in a corner of the cattle shed." "This will happen, Bhat," said the omniscient one. "Ask for something else." "That is all I want, Lord." The omniscient

जी जी : तेंचि होआवें जी : सर्वज्ञें म्हणीतलें : हें होइल हो :
हीराइसापाठ : हें कर्मवशें होइल : आणिक मागा : तेंचि
मागीतलें : यावरि वेवाचा दृष्टांत नीरूपिला^{३८३} :॥:

२४७ मार्गीं कामधेनु नामकरण :॥:

मार्गीं बीजें करीतां नदी होती : तेथ गोसावीयांसि आसन :
ऐलाडि पैलाडि गांव : पैलाडिला गावां : महदाइसें : उमाइसें
भिक्षे गेली : ते दीसीं बारसि : मुंजी घरा एका भीक्षे गेलीं :
तेयांतें आधीले दीसीं : मुंजि जाली होती : तेहीं मांडें :
पुरीया : घारिया : अमृतफळें : भातु : रोवै : सरवळे : वेळुनि
सुदलीं : लाडु : तिळोवे : शाकवटी : रांधौनि सूदलि :
जेतुकें वन्हाडीचें तेतुकेंही सूदलें : घेउनि आलीं : सर्वज्ञें
म्हणीतलें : माहात्मेयांचीया कामधेनू पातलिया गा^{३८४} : मग
गोसावीयांसि पुजा आरोगण भक्तजनासहीत जालीं :॥:

one said, "It will happen." (Hiraïsa version: "This will happen by the power of karma. Ask for something else." He asked for the very same thing.)

Thereupon the omniscient one told the parable of the spindle.[311]

247 ALONG THE ROAD, HE CALLS MAHADAÏSE AND UMAÏSE "WISH-GRANTING COWS."

As he went along the road, the Gosavi came to a river and sat down there. There were villages on both sides of the river. Mahadaïse and Umaïse went to beg for food in the village on the far side. It was the twelfth day of the lunar fortnight.[312] They went to beg at a home where a thread ceremony had been performed the previous day.[313] The people there had prepared wheat pastries, puris, stuffed fried wheat cakes, filled sweets, rice, vermicelli, and bits of twisted wheat dough, and they put them into the women's begging bags. They had also cooked lentil sweet balls, sesame sweet balls, and vegetables, and they put those into the bags as well. They put in enough for everyone in the group.

When Mahadaïse and Umaïse came back with the food, the omniscient one said, "The Mahatma's Wish-Granting Cows have arrived." Then the Gosavi's puja was performed, and he ate his meal along with the devotees.

२४८ भडेगांवीं सीवाळा अवस्थान³⁸⁵ :॥:

गोसावी भडेगावां बीजें केलें : विळीचां वेळीं सीवाळां
अवस्थानें : दीस तीन :॥:

२४९ अनंताचा सूड :॥:

गोसावीयांसि पटिसाळे आसन : विष्णुदेव आले : तेहीं
गोसावीयाचां ठाइं अवसरु केला : अनंताचे दोनि सूड
आइकीलें : मग तेयासि पाठवणी दीधली : एकू दामु देव-
वीला : हीराइसापाठ : दोनि दाम : इंद्रंभटाकरवि देववीलें :॥:

२५० वसैए अवस्थान :॥:

सीवाळें रचमचेचें स्थान म्हणौनि गोसावी वसैए बीजें करूं
आदरीलें : सीमुगेयाचीया पाडवेयाचां दीसीं उदीयांचि
कासारवाडेयाहुनि बीजें केलें : मार्गीं होळी होती : तेथ
गोसावी उभे राहिले : श्रीचरणिचेनि आंगुठेनि राख
उधळिली : शोध : हो जैरे : म्हणैनि : अवघेयाचां निडळी :
रेघ उठीली : मग नावेक सींपणें जालें : मग वसए अवस्थान
दीस सात : सोधु दीस वीस :॥:

248 HE STAYS IN A SHIVA TEMPLE AT BHADEGAV.

The Gosavi reached Bhadegav in the evening.[314] He stayed in a Shiva temple there for three days.

249 SONGS ABOUT THE INFINITE ONE.

The Gosavi was sitting on the veranda. Vishnudev came there and spent some time with the Gosavi. The Gosavi listened to two songs about the Infinite One, then gave Vishnudev leave to go. He had them give him a copper coin. (Hiraïsa version: He had Indrabhat give him two copper coins.)

250 HE STAYS IN A JAIN TEMPLE.

Because the Shiva temple was crowded, the Gosavi decided to go to a Jain temple. Early in the morning on the first day after the Holi festival, he went through the Braziers' quarter.[315] Along the way, he came to a place where there had been a Holi fire. The Gosavi stopped there, and, with the big toe of his holy foot, he flipped some of the ashes up into the air. (Research: "Hey! Victory!" he said.) A line of ash appeared on everyone's forehead. Then they sprinkled one another for a little while.

Afterward he stayed in the Jain temple for seven days. (Research: for twenty days.)

२५१ गारि बूजवणें :॥:

गोसावीयां बीजे करितां मार्गींचि गारि होती : तेथ येतां
जातां अवघड : गोसावी ते गारिपासीं उभे ठाकले : सर्वज्ञें
म्हणितलें : रामाचें वानरसैन्य रिगे : तरि गारि बूजे :
हीराइसापाठ : ऐसें रामाचें सैन्य :॥छ॥: एकें म्हणति :
देवीं आइकिलें : एके म्हणति : बाइसीं आइकीलें : बाइसीं
म्हणितलें : रामां रामां : ऐसें म्हणतें असति : देवीं म्हणितलें :
या गा : या गा : म्हणौनि : अवघां गारि बूजविली : एकें
म्हणति : दीसां दो चौ उपरि बूजीली :॥:

२५२ इंद्रंभटां स्तीति : नामकरण :॥:

गोसावीयांतें इंद्रंभटीं उपहारलागि वीनवीलें : मग गोसावी
वीहरणासि सीवाळेयासि बीजें केलें : तेथ आसनापासि
इंद्रंभट असति : इंद्रंभटा स्तिति जाली : गोसावी बीढारा
बीजें केलें : तेथेंचि होते : महदाइसीं पुसिलें : जी जी :
नागदेवो भट कें : सर्वज्ञें म्हणितलें : बाइ : तो तेथचि असे :
तेयासी इंद्राची आंकुशमूद्रा घातली असे३८६ : म्हणौनि :
श्रीकराचेनि अनुकारें : दाखवीलें :॥छ॥: महदाइसीं
म्हणीतलें : जी जी : बोलाउं जावो : सर्वज्ञें म्हणीतलें : जा :

251   FILLING IN A POTHOLE.

As the Gosavi went along, he came to a large pothole right in the middle of the road. It was hard to get past the pothole, either coming or going. Stopping at the pothole, the omniscient one said, "If Ram's army of monkeys came here, they would fill in this hole."[316] (Hiraïsa version: "That's what Ram's army is like." Some say Dev heard this, while others say Baïse heard it.)

"Ram! Ram!" said Baïse. "Listen to what he is saying!" Dev said, "Come here! Come here!" And so they all filled in the hole. (Some say they filled it in a few days later.)

252   INDRABHAT GOES INTO A TRANCE, AND THE GOSAVI GIVES HIM HIS NAME.

Indrabhat* had invited the Gosavi for a meal. Then, when the Gosavi went wandering to the Shiva temple, Indrabhat was there, near the Gosavi's seat. Indrabhat went into a trance. The Gosavi returned to their lodgings, but Indrabhat stayed right where he was.

Mahadaïse asked, "Where is Nagdevbhat, Lord?" "He is still there, my woman," said the omniscient one. "He is under the influence of Indra's *aṅkuśmudrā*."[317] And he gestured with his holy hand to show what he meant. "Lord," asked Mahadaïse, "may I go to get him?" "Go ahead," said the omniscient one.

* Nagdevbhat, Indroba.

मग तीयें आलीं : हे काइ नागदेवोभटो : गोसावीयासि
आरोगणे उसीरू जाला : तुम्हीं आझुइं कैसे : बैसलेति : काइ
करू रूपाबाई : पायेंचि गेले : उठों जातों : आणि : उठवेंचि
ना : मग तेहीं आंगेसीं धरूनि उठवीलें : खांदीं वाउनि
आणिलें : गोसावीयांतें देखवीलें : आणि स्तीति भंगली :
शोधु : एथचें एजमान आले मा : मग भंगली : हीराइसा-
पाठ : सर्वज्ञें म्हणीतलें : काइ गा : इंद्रेया३८७ : इंद्राची
आंकुशमूद्रा वर्तत होती : जी : आणि स्तीति भंगली : एकें
म्हणति : इंद्रेया : मग भंगली :॥छ॥: मग दंडवतें घातलीं :
श्रीचरणा लागले : मग गोसावीयांसि पूजा जाली : धुपार्ति
मंगळार्ति जाली : आरोगणा : गोसावीयांचिये पांती
भक्तजना जेवणें जाली :॥:

२५३ तथा वसै निक्षेदु :॥:

एकुदीसीं गोसावीयांसि वसैए अवस्थान : इंद्रभटीं दंडवतें
घातलीं : श्रीचरणा लागले : बैसले : सर्वज्ञें म्हणीतलें :
इंद्रेया : ब्राह्मणासि वसैए आंतु रिगों नैए : तुम्हीं रिगालेति
कैसे : जी जी : आम्हीं आपुलेया गोसावीया सरिसे आलों :
हाती वेंझ देवों ए तऱ्हीं वसैए आंतु रिगों नैए३८८ : हां गा :

So she went there and asked, "What is going on, Nagdevbhat? It's past the time for the Gosavi's meal. How can you still be sitting here?" "What can I do, Rupabai? My legs have stopped working. I try to get up, but I simply can't stand."

So she put her arms around him and lifted him up. She put him on her shoulders and carried him back. When he saw the Gosavi, his trance broke. (Research: The omniscient one said, "My host has arrived!" and then it broke. Hiraïsa version: The omniscient one said, "What is going on, Indra?" "I was under the influence of Indra's *aṅkuśmudrā*, Lord," he replied, and his trance broke. Some say: the omniscient one said, "Indra," and then it broke.) Then he prostrated himself to the Gosavi and touched his holy feet. Then the Gosavi's puja took place, and *āratī* was performed with incense and with lighted lamps. As the Gosavi ate his meal, the devotees dined in the same row with him.

253   AND THE PROHIBITION ON ENTERING JAIN TEMPLES.

One day while the Gosavi was staying in the Jain temple, Indrabhat prostrated himself to him, touched his holy feet, and sat down. The omniscient one said, "Indra, a Brahman may not enter a Jain temple. Why did you come into this one?" "I came in along with my Gosavi, Lord." "'Even if an elephant attacks you, you may not enter a Jain temple.'"[318] "Yes, Lord." "But this is one of the deities among the ten avatars."[319] "Yes, Lord."[320]

दश अवतारांमध्यें हे एकि देवता कीं : जी^{३८९} : भटाचार्ये
आपूलेनि शास्त्रीचेनि बळें देवते आंबुखा घातला : वैरीयाचा
देवो जाला तरि काइ दगडें फोडावा^{३९०} : इंद्रभटीं म्हणितलें :
जी जी : तो भटाचार्या नव्हे : सूणा होए : जेउतें तेउतें
भुंकतचि गेला :॥:

२५४ तथा तांबोळग्रहण :॥:

एकुदीसीं गोसावी आसनीं उपविष्ट आसति : इंद्रंभट आले :
दंडवत घातलें : श्रीचरणा लागले : बैसले : गोसावी तांबोळ
परित्येजीतां तेंहीं श्रीमुखींचेया तांबोळा आंजुळि वोडवीली :
सर्वज्ञें म्हणितलें : इंद्रेया : एथींचें तांबोळ घेयावें : ऐसा काइ
वीधि नेणिजे : तरि : काइ शास्त्र नेणिजे तरि कां घेत असा :
जी जी भाओ : सर्वज्ञें म्हणीतलें : भावासि काइ रावो राणा
असे : मग गोसावी तेयासि तांबुळ दीधलें :॥:

२५५ तथा तुळसी वाणें :॥:

एकुदीसीं गोसावीयांसि उदेयाचां पूजावस्वर जालेयानंतरें
गोसावी आसनीं उपवीष्ट असति : सोभागें भिक्षा करूनि
आली : गोसावीयांसि दृष्टपूत झोळी केली : गोसावी डावा
श्रीकरू झोळिये तळि घातला : कृपादृष्टी अवलोकिलें :
गोसावी प्रसादु करीत असति : तवं इंद्रोबा गोसावीयाचीया

"On the strength of his knowledge of scriptures, Bhatacharya demolished the deity. Even if it is the enemy's god,
should he break it with a rock?"[321] "He was not a Bhatacharya, Lord," said Indrabhat. "He was a dog. He went
anywhere and everywhere, just barking."

254 AND INDRABHAT TAKES HIS PAN.

While the Gosavi was sitting in his place one day, Indrabhat
arrived. He prostrated himself to the Gosavi, touched his
holy feet, and sat down. As the Gosavi spat out the pan from
his holy mouth, Indrabhat stretched out his cupped hands
for it.

The omniscient one said, "Indra, there is no known rule
that you must take my pan. So if no scriptural source is
known, why are you taking it?" "Loving faith, Lord." The
omniscient one said, "For loving faith there is no king or
prince."[322]

Then the Gosavi gave him the pan.

255 AND INDRABHAT OFFERS TULSI.

After his morning worship service one day, the Gosavi was
seated in his place. Sobhage returned from begging for food
and had the Gosavi purify her begging bag with his glance.
The Gosavi put his left holy hand beneath the begging bag
and looked into it with his merciful glance.

As the Gosavi was making *prasād* of it, Indroba came to

श्रीचरणा तुळसी वावेया आले : सर्वज्ञें म्हणीतलें : इंद्रेया :
देवो ऐसा असे गा^{३९१} : जी : जी : देवो ऐसाचि बरवा कीं :
मग गोसावी श्रीकरिचिया आंगुळीया झोळियेसी पुसीलिया :
मग तीयें परतीं गेलीं : मग इंदोबेनि : गोसावीयांचें श्रीचरण
उदकें सींचिलें : श्रीचरणा तुळसी वाइलिया : साष्टांगीं
वाइलिया : हीराइसापाठ : श्रीचरणा लागले : मग गेले : तवं
सोभागै दुख करूं लागलीं : हीराइसापाठ : सर्वज्ञें म्हणीतलें :
सौभागा : जेवा ना कां : जी जी : जेवीन आणि काइ : सर्वज्ञें
म्हणीतलें : आणा झोळी : माचौता प्रसादु केला : सर्वज्ञें
म्हणीतलें : चेया : आतां जेवा : मग तीयें जेवीली :॥:

२५६ गौराइ दर्शना ज्ञान करणे^{३९२} :॥:

एकुदीसीं : गोसावीयांसि आरोगण : पहुड : उपहुड : मग
शयनासनीं असति : गौराइसें गोसावीयांचेया : दरिसना
आली : दारंवठेसीं उभी असति : सर्वज्ञें म्हणीतलें : बाइ :
बाहिर पाहा पां : कोण आलें : बाइसीं पाहीलें : बाबा :
कोणी नाहीं : सर्वज्ञें म्हणीतलें : बाई : पंचराणेयाचा मुख्य
नायकू आला असे : मग बाइसें गेलीं : तवं गौराइसें बाहिरी
उभी असति : बाइसीं म्हणीतलें : बटिकी : भीतरि ये :
बाबासि दंडवत करि : तीये आलीं : गोसावीयांसि दंडवतें
घातलीं : श्रीचरणा लागली : गोसावीयांपासि बैसली :
सर्वज्ञें म्हणीतलें : बाइ : तीयें अवघीं एथींचेया : दर्शना : तथा

offer sprigs of tulsi to the Gosavi's holy feet. The omniscient one said, "Indra, this is what God is like." "Yes, Lord. God is fine just like this!"

Then the Gosavi wiped the fingers of his holy hands on the begging bag. Then Sobhage moved aside, and Indroba sprinkled water on the Gosavi's holy feet. He offered sprigs of tulsi to the holy feet and prostrated himself completely. (Hiraïsa version: He touched the holy feet.) Then he left.

Sobhage began to cry. (Hiraïsa version: The omniscient one said, "Sobhage, why aren't you eating your food?" "Of course I will eat it, Lord." The omniscient one said, "Bring the begging bag here." He made *prasād* of it again, then said, "Take it. Eat it now." Then she ate her meal.)

256 HE ENLIGHTENS GAURAÏ ABOUT COMING FOR *DARŚAN*.

One day, after the Gosavi had eaten his meal and gone to sleep, when he had waked up and was lying on his bed, Gauraïse came for his *darśan*. As she stood at the door, the omniscient one said to Baïse, "Take a look outside, my woman, to see who has come." Baïse looked. "There's no one there, Baba," she said. The omniscient one said, "My woman, the general-in-chief of the five princes has come."

So Baïse went to the door and found Gauraïse standing outside. Baïse said, "Come in, my dear. Prostrate yourself to Baba." She came in, prostrated herself to the Gosavi, and touched his holy feet. She sat down near the Gosavi.

अवसरा : आलीं होतीं : तुम्हीं न याचि तें काइ³⁹³ : ना जी :
मातें बीढारीं राखण ठेवीति : मग आपण गोसावीयांचेया
दर्शना एति : सर्वज्ञें म्हणीतलें : देखीलें बाइ : एथीचेया
दर्शनाचेया चाडा : वाहानाचें वर्त : न्हाणाचें आदि करूनि
वर्त : बाइ : माथाचा जाजारू वाळेना : ए दशे एहीं काइ
हें करावें : ए दशे एहीं खावें : जेवावें : लेयावें : नेसावें :
ऐसेयाकरवि बिढार राखवीति : मग आपण एथ एति :
हीराइसापाठ : बाइ तुम्हीं एथचेया दर्शना आलींति : कीं
बीढार राखों आलीति : देखीलें बाइ :॥छ॥: सर्वज्ञें म्हणीतलें :
बाइ : तीए नीगती : तवं आपण पुढें एउनि उभेयां ठाकीजे :
मग तीयें आपुलेया बीढारा भलेतें करूत : आपण एथीचेया
अवसरा न चुकीजे हो :॥: मग तीये गोसावीयांचेया तीहीं
अवसरां एति :॥:

२५७ तथा नीद्रा प्रसंगें इंद्रोबा सीष्यापने³⁹⁴ :॥:

एकू दीसू : गौराइसे³⁹⁵ गोसावीयांचेया वीळीचीया अवसरां
आलीं : खांबा आड बैसलीं : गोसावीयांसि पूजावस्वर : मग
पाहारू एकू निरूपण जालें : गौराइसा निद्रा आली : गोसावी

"My woman," said the omniscient one, "all the others have come for my *darśan* (or, for my worship service), but you don't ever come. Why is that?"[323] "Lord Gosavi," she replied, "they leave me to guard our lodgings while they come for your *darśan.*"

The omniscient one said to Baïse, "Do you see that, my woman? Out of a desire for my *darśan,* they are scrupulously careful about their shoes, scrupulously careful about bathing and so on. The soft spot on their heads has not yet hardened, my woman.[324] When they are in such an immature state, what do they do? In this state, they eat some food, they have their meal, they get dressed up. They make someone like her guard their lodgings, and then they themselves come here."

(Hiraïsa version: To Gauraïse he said, "My woman, have you come to have my *darśan,* or have you come to guard the lodgings? Do you see, my woman?") Then the omniscient one said, "When they set out, my woman, you come on ahead and stand here. Then let them do whatever they want with their lodgings, but don't you skip my worship service."

After that she came to all three of the Gosavi's worship services every day.

257 AND WHEN SHE FALLS ASLEEP, HE UPBRAIDS INDROBA.

One day when Gauraïse came for the Gosavi's evening worship service, she was sitting behind a pillar. After the Gosavi's worship service, he taught them for three hours, and Gauraïse fell asleep.

भक्तजना पाठवणी दीधली : तीएं आवघीं गेलीं : मग
गोसावियांसि व्याळी जाली : गुळळा जाला : बाइसीं
फोडी वोळगवीलीया : वीडीया करूनि देतें असति : सर्वज्ञें
म्हणीतलें : बाइ : भीतरि पाहा पां : कोण असे : बाइसीं
पाहीलें : तवं न देखतीचि : बाइसीं म्हणीतलें : बाबा :
कोण्ही नसे : सर्वज्ञें म्हणीतलें : बाइ : इंद्रीयाची जाया असे :
बाइसें गेलीं : तंव खांबा आड गौराइसें निजलीं असति :
बाइसी म्हणीतलें : बटीकी उठि : तुझीं अवघीं बीढारा गेलीं :
तु निजैलीसि कैसी : उठिलीं : गोसावीयां दंडवतें घातलीं :
श्रीचरणा लागलीं : पद्मनाभि३९६ बोलवीत दीधला३९७ : रात्रीं
गौराइसांसि इंद्रभट कोपों लागले : चीमोरे चेति : इसाळु
करीति : उदीयांचि गोसावीयांचे पुजावस्वरासि भक्तजन
अवघेचि आले : आणि गैराइसें आलीं : कोमाइलीं :
उमाइलीं : ऐसीं गोसावी देखीलीं : गोसावी इंद्रभटातें
म्हणीतलें : हांगा मुक्तीचीया चाडां आणि खुंटदावें
सांभाळणें : ऐसें कोपले : गौराइसासि ऐसें जालें :
जें गोसावीं माझा कैवारू घेतला : आणि इंद्रभटासि ऐसें
जालें३९८ : जें गोसावी माझें अनुचित सांडवीले :॥:

The Gosavi gave the devotees leave to go, and they all left. Then the Gosavi had his evening meal. He rinsed his mouth, and Baïse offered him pieces of betel nut. As she was making rolls of pan and giving them to him, the omniscient one said, "Look inside, my woman. Who is there?" When Baïse looked, she simply did not see Gauraïse. "There's no one there, Baba," said Baïse. The omniscient one said, "Indra's Jaya* is there, my woman."

When Baïse went there again, she saw Gauraïse asleep behind the pillar. Baïse said, "Get up, my dear. All your people have gone back to your lodgings. Why are you sleeping here?"

She got up. She prostrated herself to the Gosavi and touched his holy feet. He gave her Padmanabhi to accompany her.[325]

That night Indrabhat got angry with Gauraïse. He was pinching her and acting jealous. Early the next morning, when all the devotees came for the Gosavi's worship service, Gauraïse came too. The Gosavi saw her looking wan and wilted, and he said angrily to Indrabhat, "How can you come here out of a desire for liberation and still attend to your domestic fetters?"[326]

Gauraïse felt, "The Gosavi has taken my side," and Indrabhat felt, "The Gosavi has caused me to stop behaving improperly."

---

* "Victory," the god Indra's wife.

489

२५८ स्त्री सूळवेथा निवृत्ति :॥:

ब्राह्मणा एकाची स्त्री : ते वसैए पुढील पींपळ सींपों येति :
तेव्हळि गोसावीयांतें देखति : वीहरणा बीजें करिति तेव्हळि
झळकतां देखति : तेयांसि गोसावीयांचेया दर्शनाची
अवस्था : महदाइसें तेयाचेया घरासि भिक्षेसि जाती : बैसों
घालीति : सोपस्कर भीक्षा देति :॥: एकूदीस तयांसि सूळ
उठिला : महदाइसें भीक्षें गेलीं : तवं तीएसि उठवेना :
म्हणीतलें : तुं ऐसी कां : ना मज सूळ उठिलास : तुझा सूळ
आमचेया गोसावीयांचेनि दर्शनें जाइल : वसैए असति : ते :
गोसावी : नां हो : तयाचेया दरिसना मि आधींचि जावों
पातु असे : परि माझा वैरतु दुरळु : महदाइसीं म्हणीतलें तुं
पडि घे : तेया पडि घेतली : हीराइसा पाठ : गोसावीयांचेया
दरिसनाचि तीसि चाड उपनली : तीया महदाइसातें
म्हणीतलें : बाइ तुमचेया गोसावीयांचें मज दरिसन कैसेनि
होईल : माझा वैरतु दुरळु : महदाइसीं पुसिलें : तुज कांहीं
रूजा असे : तेहीं म्हणीतलें मज सूळ वेथेची सवे असे :
तरि तेयाचा बाहाणा घे : मग तेहीं सूळ वेथेचा : बाहाणा
घेतला :॥छ॥: तेयांसि ते धावणी करूं लागले : तवं ते
काइसेनहीं शमेना : मग तेहीं म्हणीतलें : माझा सूळ तै
जाइल : वसैए जे गोसावी असति : तेयांचेया दरिसना नेयाल
तरि माझा सूळ जाइल : वैरतें म्हणीतलें : हो कां : मग तो
हाटवटीए गेला : पाने पोफळें घेतलीं : नारीएळ आणिएलें :

258 HE REMOVES THE PAIN OF A WOMAN'S CRAMPS.

The wife of a certain Brahman used to come to water the pipal tree in front of the Jain temple. She would see the Gosavi then, and she would get a glimpse of him when he went out to wander. She was yearning for the Gosavi's *darśan*.

Mahadaïse used to go to that woman's house to beg for food. The woman would put down something for Mahadaïse to sit on, and she would give her plenty of good food as alms.

One day the woman got stomach cramps. When Mahadaïse went there to beg for food, the woman was not able to stand up. Mahadaïse asked her, "What has happened to you?" "I've got cramps in my stomach." "Having *darśan* of our Gosavi will make your cramps go away." "The Gosavi who is in the Jain temple?" "Yes, that's right." "I have already been wanting to go for his *darśan,* but my husband is strict." Mahadaïse said, "You must insist." So she became insistent.

(Hiraïsa version: She came to desire nothing but *darśan* of the Gosavi. She said to Mahadaïse, "My woman, how can I get *darśan* of your Gosavi? My husband is strict." Mahadaïse asked, "Do you have any illness?" She said, "I often get cramps." "Then pretend to have that." So she pretended to have cramps.)

Her husband began trying various remedies on her, but none of them made the pain subside. Then she said to him, "What will make my cramps go away is for you to take me for *darśan* of the Gosavi who is in the Jain temple. Then my cramps will go away." "All right," said her husband.

मग दरिसना निगाले : तेहीं तें नारिएळ सूपवतीएचां दुनवंगीं
ठेवीलें : अधीएक वाट पातली : आणि म्हणीतलें : पाहा
कां³⁹⁹ : मी नारिएळ वीसरलीयें : तो नारेळ आणुं गेला :
तवं ते वहीली गोसावीयांचेया दरिसना गेली : गोसावीयांसि
पडिसाळेवरि उजवेयाकडे आसन : गोसावीयांसि तेहीं
बाहीया पसरूनि क्षेमलिंगन दीधलें : दंडवतें घातलीं :
श्रीचरणा लागली : गोसावीयांपासि बैसलीं⁴⁰⁰ : तवं ते
नारिएळ घेउनि आले : पानें पोफळें नारिएळ गोसावीयांसि
दर्शन केलें : मग तेहीं दंडवतें घातलीं श्रीचरणा लागले :
गोसावीयांजवळि बैसले : गोसावीयां पुढें सांघों लागला :
वोषदें केली : बहुत धावणी केली : परि सूळ काइसेनहीं न
ऱ्हाएचि जी : गोसावी आइकतचि होते : मग दंडवतें करूनि
निगाली : तो पूढारा गेला : आणि तें गोसावीयांपासि आलीं :
श्रीमुखीचीया तांबुळा आंजूळि वोडवीली : गोसावी तांबोळ
दीधलें : तें तोंडीं घातलें : आणि दंडवत करूनि निगालीं :
सर्वज्ञें म्हणीतलें : बाइ : आद्यप्रवृति तुमतें सूळ न बंधी
हो⁴⁰¹ : तेहीं महदाइसातें म्हणतीलें : नीच माझें एक पक्कान्न
गोसावीयां लागि नियावें : मग महदाइसें नीच भीक्षें जाति :
एक पक्कान घेउनि एति :॥:

He went to the bazaar and got betel leaves and betel nuts, and he brought home a coconut. Then they set out for *darśan.*

She put the coconut in a fold of the mattress. When they were halfway to the temple, she said, "Take a look, will you? I forgot the coconut." He went to get the coconut, and so she arrived first for the Gosavi's *darśan.*

The Gosavi was sitting on the right side of the veranda. She spread her arms and embraced the Gosavi. She prostrated herself and touched his holy feet, then sat down near the Gosavi. When her husband arrived, bringing the coconut, he presented the betel leaves and betel nuts and the coconut to the Gosavi. Then he prostrated himself to the Gosavi and touched his holy feet. He sat down close to the Gosavi and began to tell him, "We have tried medicines, we have tried lots of remedies, but nothing makes her cramps stop, Lord." The Gosavi simply listened.

Then they prostrated themselves and left. He went on ahead, while she came back to the Gosavi. She stretched out her cupped hands for the pan in his holy mouth. The Gosavi gave her the pan, and she put it in her mouth. And she prostrated herself to him and left. "My woman," said the omniscient one, "from this day on you will not be troubled by cramps."

The woman said to Mahadaïse, "You must take a sweet dish from me for the Gosavi every day." So every day Mahadaïse would go begging there and bring back a sweet dish.

२५९ देव निवारित महदाइसा वस्त्रपूजा स्वीकारू :॥:

महदाइसासि गोसावीयांचां ठाइं एक वस्त्र वोळगवावें
ऐसी वासना जाली : नागदेओ भटातें म्हणीतलें : मज एक
वस्त्र घेउनि देया कां : तेहीं म्हणीतलें : मातें काइ म्हणत
असा : दादोसांतेंचि म्हणा : मग दादोसातें म्हणीतलें : दादो
मज एक वस्त्र घेउनि देया कां : काइ कराल वस्त्र : ना :
गोसावीयां लागि : केतुलेयाकाचें वस्त्र : ना : मातें : सोळा
दाम असति : तेयांचें घेउनि दीया : इसि काइसे सोळा दाम :
मां : तेयां सोळा दामांचे वस्त्र काइ एइल : तें काइ : गोसावी
पांगरों जावें असति : दीस च्यारि पांगुरती आणि भलेतेया
देउनि फेडीति : उपाहारू कां न करा : उपाहारूचि करा :
महदाइसीं विचारीलें : आतां तें गोसावीयांसिचि वीनउं : तवं
गोसावीयांचि बोलावीलें : बाइ : या आरूती : काइ म्हणतें
असा : जी जी : मियां गोसावीयाचां ठाइं वस्त्र वोळगवावें
ऐसा मनोर्थ जाला : तैं नागदेवो भटातें म्हणीतलें : मागील
शब्द सांघीतले : दादोसाचें सांघीतलें : सर्वज्ञें म्हणीतलें :
माहात्मां म्हणतु असे : तैसें कां न कीजे⁴⁰² : हीराइसापाठ :
दीस च्यारि पांगुरिजैल : आणि भलेतेयासि देउनि फेडीजैल :
माहात्मा म्हणतु असे : तेंचि कां न कीजे : ना : मिं :
गोसावीयाचां ठाइं वोळगवीन : मग : गोसावी दीस च्यारि
पांगुरत : मग भलेतेया देउनि फेडीत :॥छ॥: सर्वज्ञें

259 HE ACCEPTS A GARMENT THAT MAHADAÏSE OFFERS HIM DESPITE DEV'S DISCOURAGING HER.

Mahadaïse wanted to offer the Gosavi a garment. She said to Nagdevbhat, "Will you get a garment for me?" "Why are you saying this to me?" he asked. "Dados is the one you should say it to."

So she asked Dados, "Dado, will you get a garment for me?" "What will you do with the garment?" "It is for the Gosavi," she replied. "How expensive should the garment be?" "I have sixteen copper coins," she said. "Get me one worth that much." "How can sixteen copper coins be enough for something like that? Can you get a garment for sixteen copper coins? Is the Gosavi supposed to go around wearing it? He will wear it for a few days and then give it away to someone or other. Why don't you make some food for him? Just make him some food."

As Mahadaïse was thinking, "Now I should ask the Gosavi directly about that," the Gosavi himself called to her. "Come here, my woman. What are you saying?" "Lord Gosavi, I wanted to offer you a garment, so I said to Nagdevbhat..." She told him what they had said to each other, and she told him what Dados had said.

The omniscient one said, "Why don't you do what the Mahatma says?" (Hiraïsa version: "I will wear it for a few days, and I will give it away to someone or other. Why don't you do what the Mahatma says?" "No, I want to offer it to you, Gosavi. Then you may wear it for a few days, and after that give it away to anyone you want.") The omniscient one

म्हणीतलें : हें एतुलें : तुम्हांचियास्तव नव्हवे : ऐसी ऐसी
जा पां : कव्हणि एक साह्यातें करील :॥छ॥ः मग तेयांसि
आठवलें : मग तीए बाइएचीया घरा गेलीं : हांवों : तुझा
भाउ दुसी : तरि आम्हांसि एक वस्त्र देइल घेउनि : आइ :
तो एवों दीया : मग पुसैन : तवं तो आला : हा रे बा : तुतें
जें गाहाणवस्त्र असें : तें आइसांसि वोपि कां : तेणें तें वस्त्र
सोडीलें : महदाइसासि दीधलें : तेहीं तेयासि सोळा दाम
दीधलें : एकें आसूचें वस्त्र : पूण तेणें सोळा दामीं दीधलें :
वस्त्र घेउनि आली : गोसावीयांचि पुरता उपहारू केला :
गोसावीयांसि पुजा केली : धुपार्ति मंगळार्ति केली : वस्त्र
वोळगवीलें : गोसावीयांसि आरोगण : गुळळा : वीडा :
पहुड : उपहुड : गोसावी आसनीं उपविष्ट असति : दादोस
गोसावीयांचे वोळगे आले : गोसावी फूटेयाचा पदरू तेयांकडे
घातला : सर्वज्ञें म्हणीतलें : माहात्मे हो : हें वस्त्र काइ लाहे :
जी जी : दामु सोळा एक लाहे : आणुनि दीयाल : जी जी :
दामु आठरा एक लाहे : ऐसे अठरें आणुनि दीयाल : जी
जी : दाम वीस लाहे : वीसें आणुनि दीयाल : हो जी : बाइ
दीया दाम[४०३] : महदाइसें वास पाहाति[४०४] : मग गोसावी
फुटीयाचा पालौ आसूडीला : सर्वज्ञें म्हणीतलें : हें वस्त्र

said, "Won't you be able to get such a small thing to happen? Keep going the way you are, and someone will come to your aid."

Then she remembered something, and she went to that woman's house and said to her, "Your brother is a cloth merchant. Will he bring me a garment?"[327] "When he comes here, Mother, I will ask him."

He came there, and she said, "Hey! Will you give this woman that garment you've received as security for a loan?" He handed over the garment to her, and she gave it to Mahadaïse. Mahadaïse paid her the sixteen copper coins. The garment was worth one gold coin, but he let her have it for sixteen copper coins.

Mahadaïse brought back the garment and prepared enough food for just the Gosavi. She did puja to the Gosavi, performed *āratī* with incense and with lighted lamps, then offered him the garment. The Gosavi ate the meal, rinsed his mouth, and chewed pan. He went to sleep and woke up.

Later, when the Gosavi was seated in his place, Dados came to serve him. The Gosavi tossed the end of the garment toward him. "Mahatma," asked the omniscient one, "how much is this garment worth?" "It's worth about sixteen copper coins, Lord." "Will you get one for that price and give it to me?" "It's worth about eighteen copper coins, Lord." "Will you get me one like it for eighteen?" "It's worth twenty copper coins, Lord." "Will you get me one for twenty?" "Yes, Lord." "Give him the copper coins, my woman," said the omniscient one to Baïse.

Mahadaïse was watching. The omniscient one jerked back the end of the garment and said, "This garment is worth a

आन लेख लाहे : यासि कव्हणी मोल करूं नेणे : तें गोसावी
सामास पांगुरलें :॥ः

२६० साधां पुजाअज्ञान कथन :॥ः

एकु दीसीं साधें स्नाना गेलीं : त्रींसंदीचीं फुलें देखीलीं : तें
चेउनि आलीं : गोसावीयांसि आरोगण होउनि पहुड असे :
साधें आलीं : गोसावीयांचेया श्रीचरणा फुलें वाइलीं :
वक्षेस्थळावरि वाइलीं : श्रीमुगुट उघडुनि मुगुटावरि वाइलीं :
तवं बाइसें बाहिरिली कडुनि आलीं : तेहीं देखीलें :
ऐसी कवणें वो पुजा केलीं : म्हणौनि घागरा बांधला :
श्रीचरणाकडे देवो नव्हे : मग श्रीमुगुटाकडे देवो होए : तवं
गोसावी उपहुडले असति : सर्वज्ञें म्हणीतलें : साधें जाणति
ना कीं : जाणतीं तरि ऐसें काइसेया करीतीं : हीराइसापाठ :
बाइ : यांसि कां कोपतें असा : एं काइ जाणतें असति :
यें जरि जाणतीं तरि ऐसें न करितीं : आणि अनवसरीं कां
एतीं :॥छ॥ः तवं तवं साधासि अधीक दुख होए : मग सर्वज्ञें
म्हणीतलें : साधें व्हो : भेवों नको : तुम्हीं जाणानां कीं :
जाणां तरि : काइसेया कराल : तथा जाणतीति तरि ऐसें कां
करीतीति : वेळा दोनि च्यारी : हीराइसापाठ : साधें व्हो :
दुख न करा : तुम्हीं काइ जाणतें असा : जरि जाणाल तरि
ऐसें कां कराल : आणि अन्नवसरीं कां याल :॥छ॥ः मग ऐसें

different kind of price. No one can estimate its value."
The Gosavi wore it for six months.

260 HE TELLS ABOUT SADHE'S IGNORANCE ABOUT DOING PUJA.

One day when Sadhe went to take a bath, she saw some mallow flowers and brought them back. The Gosavi had eaten his meal and was sleeping when Sadhe arrived. She placed some of the flowers at the Gosavi's holy feet, put some on his chest, and uncovered his holy head and put some on the top of his head.

At that point, Baïse came in from outside. When she saw what Sadhe had done, she upbraided her, saying, "Who has done puja this way? Is God not in his holy feet? Is God in his holy head?"

By that time, the Gosavi had waked up. The omniscient one said, "Sadhe doesn't know any better. If she knew better, why would she have done this?" (Hiraïsa version: "My woman, why are you angry with her? Does she know any better? If she knew better, she would not do this, and why would she come at the wrong time?")

Sadhe was feeling worse and worse. The omniscient one said to her, "Don't be afraid, Sadhe. You don't know any better! If you knew better, why would you do this?" He said this a few times. (Hiraïsa version: "Oh, Sadhe, don't be sad. Do you know any better? If you knew better, why would you do this? And why would you come at the wrong time?")

साधीं आपुलें अनुचीत देखीलें : मीं अन्नवसरीं आलींए नां :
मग गोसावी तेयाचें दुख दो चौ वेळीं संभाषुन फेडीलें :॥:

२६१ महदाइसें द्वारावतीए जाणें :॥:

पव्हा द्वारावतीए निगाला : दादोसीं महदाइसां उस्तभवीलें :
द्वारावतीए जावें ऐसें : मग महदाइसें द्वारावतीए जावेया
गोसावीयांतें पुसों आलीं : जी जी : मीं द्वारावतीएसि जाइन :
गोसावी आज्ञा दिधली : हीराइसापाठ : सर्वज्ञें म्हणीतलें :
बाइ : तीर्थ क्षेत्र अमोचक : सन्निधान मोचक : तवं ते न
ह्वातीचि : निगाली :॥छ॥: सर्वज्ञें म्हणीतलें : बाइ : कोणहीं
कोण्हा स्थाना जाए : तथा ठाया : तुम्हीं द्वारावतीकारां
श्रीचांगदेवो राउळाचीया गुंफा स्थाना जाइजे हो⁴⁰⁵ : जी
जी : मग तेहीं दंडवतें घातलीं : श्रीचरणा लागलीं : आणि
निगालीं :॥:

२६२ उमाइसातें सवें पाठवणें :॥:

रामेश्वरबास :॥: सर्वज्ञें म्हणीतलें : मासोंपवासीयें हो :
द्वारावतीए न वचा : ना जी : मीं न वचें : सर्वज्ञें म्हणीतलें :
आतांचि पाठवीतां न वचा : पाठीं रडतें जाल⁴⁰⁶ : मग तीयें

Then Sadhe saw her mistake. "I came at the wrong time, didn't I?" she said. Then the Gosavi said comforting words to her a few more times and made her feel better.

261 MAHADAÏSE GOES TO DVARAVATI.

A group of pilgrims was setting out for Dvaravati. Dados encouraged Mahadaïse to go to Dvaravati, so she came to ask the Gosavi about going there. "I want to go to Dvaravati, Lord," she said.

The Gosavi gave her leave to go. (Hiraïsa version: The omniscient one said, "My woman, pilgrimage places do not give liberation. The divine presence gives liberation." Still, she did not stay. She set out.)

The omniscient one said, "My woman, people go to various places there. You should visit the hermit's cell where Shri Cangdev Raül of Dvaravati stayed."[328] "Yes, Lord," she said. Then she prostrated herself to the Gosavi, touched his holy feet, and left.[329]

262 HE SENDS UMAÏSE ALONG.

According to Rameshvarbas, the omniscient one asked, "Oh woman who fasts for a month,* aren't you going to Dvaravati?" "No, Lord. I'm not going." The omniscient one said, "If I send you there right now and you don't go, you'll go there later crying." She did not go.

---

* Umaïse.

राहीलीं : पाठीं निद्रा स्थानासि गेलीं : रात्रीं रडों लागलीं :
दोघी मासउपवास करों : दोघी भीक्षा करों : ऐसें म्हणौनि
रडों लागलीं : उदीयांचि एउनि गोसावीयां पुढें सांघीतलें :
शोधु : मासोपवासीए हो : आतां एथौनि तुमतें पाठवीजत
असीजे : हो कां जी : मग गोसावी तेयांसि सांघातु लावीला :
मग निगालीं :॥ः

२६३ द्वारावती निषेध पुर्वक काको स्तीति :॥ः

काकोस द्वारावतिये जावेया लागि आले : जी जी : मी
द्वारावतीए जाइल : गोसावी ऐसें तेयातें अवलोकीलें : सर्वज्ञें
म्हणीतलें : आजीचा दीसू राहा पां म्हणौनि हातीं धरूनि
बैसवीलें[४०७] : आणि स्तीति जाली : आणि देखों लागले :
सूवर्णाची द्वारका : गोसावी यादवासहीत सिंहासनीं
उपवीष्ट : आवघें ऐसें देखीलें : स्तीति : भोगुं सरली :
श्रीकृष्ण ऐसी प्रतीति बैसली : सर्वज्ञें म्हणीतलें : आतां
द्वारावतीए जा ना[४०८] : तेहीं म्हणीतलें : जी जी : आतां कें
जावों : साचोकारी द्वारावती ते मीयां एथचि देखीली :
मग तेहीं आपुली मात्रा गोसावीयां पुढें ठेवीली : देव
गांठीया ब्राह्मणां एका दीधलीया : हिराइसापाठ : पाणीयांतु
घातलीया :॥छ॥ः नक्षेत्रमाळा उपक्रणें होतीं तींए वीकुनि :
गोसावी आपुलां ठाइं उपाहारू करविला : मग गोसावीयांचां
ठाइं राहीले :॥ः

Later she went to her sleeping place. At night she began to cry, saying, "The two of us used to fast together for a month. The two of us used to go begging for food together."

Early the next morning, she came and told the Gosavi. (Research: "Oh woman who fasts for a month, I am sending you now," he said. "All right, Lord.")

The Gosavi gave her someone to travel with, and she set out.

263 FORBIDDEN TO TRAVEL TO DVARAVATI, KAKO GOES INTO A TRANCE.

Kakos came to speak to the Gosavi about going to Dvaravati. "I want to go to Dvaravati, Lord," he said. The Gosavi gave him a look, took him by the hand, and sat him down. "Stay here for today," said the omniscient one.

And Kakos went into a trance. He began to see a golden Dvarka, the Gosavi seated on a throne, and the Yadavas with him.[330] When the trance came to an end, he realized clearly that the Gosavi was Shri Krishna.

The omniscient one said, "Go on, now. Go to Dvaravati."[331] "Lord," he said, "where do I need to go now? I have seen the true Dvaravati right here."

Then he placed his belongings before the Gosavi. His bundles of gods were given to a Brahman. (Hiraïsa version: They were immersed in water.) His constellation necklace and his materials for worship were sold, and the Gosavi had food prepared at his own place with the proceeds.[332] From then on Kakos stayed with the Gosavi.

२६४ साधें द्वारावतीए पाठविणें :॥:

गोसावी साधातें म्हणीतलें : साधें व्हो : द्वारावतीए जा ना :
तथा तुम्ही :॥: ना जी : मातें संबळ नाहीं : सर्वज्ञें म्हणीतलें :
संबळ दीजैल : जी जी : पाए नाहीं : सर्वज्ञें म्हणीतलें : पाए
दीजैल[४०९] : मग म्हणीतलें : जी जी : मीं न वचे : गोसावी
उगेचि राहिले :॥:

२६५ साधां मोदक विपलावणें :॥:

एकुदिसीं इंद्रभटीं साधातें म्हणीतलें : एल्हो : मज लाडु
करूनि दे कां : मां : मीं गोसावीयांसि वोळगवीन : तेंहीं
म्हणीतलें : हो कां : मग तेंहीं गुळ : गहु : मीरीयें : तेल : ऐसें
आवघेंचि आणुनि दीधलें : मग साधीं सोजी काढीली :
शेव केली : तळीली : चुल्हीवरि पाकू ठेवीला : तवं भीक्षा
अवस्वरू लोटला : तेंहीं म्हणीतलें : पांकू होइल : तवं मी
चौघरीं भीक्षा करूनि येइन : तवं तेयासि उसीरू लागला :
पांकू लंघला : आलिं : मग लाडु बांधलें : मग दुरडीए भरूनि
इंद्रभटीं गोसावीयां लागौनि आणिले : वोळगवीले : रात्रीं
बाइसें गोसावीयालागिं फोडुं बैसली तवं फुटेना : ऐरे दीसीं
उदयाचा पुजावस्वर जाला : साधें आलीं : सर्वज्ञें म्हणीतलें :

264   HE SENDS SADHE TO DVARAVATI.

The Gosavi said to Sadhe, "Go on, Sadhe, go to Dvaravati." "But, Lord, I have no provisions for the journey." "I will give you provisions," said the omniscient one. "Lord, my legs aren't good enough." "I will give you good legs," said the omniscient one. Then she said, "Lord, I am not going."

The Gosavi kept silent.

265   HE MAKES FUN OF SADHE'S SWEET BALLS.

One day Indrabhat said to Sadhe, "Elho, will you make some sweet balls and give them to me? I want to offer them to the Gosavi." "All right," she replied.

He brought all the ingredients—jaggery, wheat, black peppers, and oil—and gave them to her. Then Sadhe ground the wheat into semolina, rolled tiny bits of dough and fried them, and put a mixture of jaggery and water on the stove.

By that time, it was getting late to go begging for food. "While the jaggery water is cooking," she said, "I will go and beg at a few houses." But she got delayed, and the jaggery water coagulated.

She came back and formed the sweet balls. Indrabhat filled a basket with them, brought it, and offered them to the Gosavi. That night, when Baïse tried to crumble one for the Gosavi, it would not break. The next day, when Sadhe came for the morning worship service, the omniscient one said, "I have seen many good cooks, but never a good cook

505

बहुती सुगरणी देखीलीया : परि : कोंही सूगरणीचे लाडू
सात पांच मूसळें मेळऊनि फोडीले नाहींति४१० : तवं साधीं
म्हणीतलें : ना जी : तें जालें ऐसें : चुल्हीवरि पाकू ठेवीला :
भीक्षे उशीरू जाला : म्हणौनि : चौ घरांसि भीक्षेसि गेलीए :
तवं उसीरू जाला : जी जी : तेणें पाकू लंघला : म्हणौनि :
कठीण जाले कीं : सर्वज्ञें म्हणीतलें : तरि : सवीया वीशेषू :
बहुती सूगरणी देखीलीया परि चुल्हीवरि पाकू ठेउनि भीक्षें
कोण्ही गेलीया नाहीं : गोसावी हास्ये केलें : मग इंद्रभट आनू
आन रांधवीति : गोसावीयांसि वोळगवीति :॥:

२६६ माहात्मा नाम कुमारी खाजें :॥:

एकुदीसी वीळीचां वेळीं : वसैएचां आंगणीं आसन४११ :
गोसावी खाजें वाटीत होते : कीं : साधीं वाटीलें होतें तें
नेणीजे : बाहुल्यें प्रस्तुतींचि कुमारी एकी करा घेउनि पाणी
वाहे : वसैएचें द्वार पावें : आणि उभी ठाकौनि गोसावीयांतें
पाहे : हीराइसापाठ : आणि गोसावी म्हणति : उंहु : आणि
आपेआप खेवं देति : ऐसें वेळा दोनि तीन केलें :॥छ॥:
माघौतीं आलीं : वसैयेचेया द्वारापासि उभी ठेली :
गोसावीयांतें पाहुं लागली : सर्वज्ञें म्हणीतलें : माहात्मां
एइजे : क्षेवं देइजे४१२ : म्हणौनि गोसावी आपणयां आपण
खेवं दीधलें : मग गोसावी आपणेयापासि बौसवीली : मग

whose sweet balls can't be broken by the combined force of half a dozen pestles!"

Sadhe replied, "This is what happened, Lord. I put the jaggery water on the stove. It was getting late to go begging, so I went begging at a few houses. I got delayed, Lord, and so the jaggery water coagulated. That's why the sweet balls got hard." The omniscient one said, "That is even more special then. I have seen many good cooks, but none who puts jaggery water on the stove and goes out begging." The Gosavi laughed.

After that, Indrabhat used to have her make sweet balls over and over again, and he would offer them to the Gosavi.

266   HE CALLS A GIRL "MAHATMA" AND HAS HER GIVEN A SNACK.

One evening he was sitting in the courtyard of the Jain temple.[333] It is not known whether the Gosavi was handing out a snack or Sadhe had handed it out. A young girl— probably the one in this episode—was serving water from a pitcher. When she reached the temple door, she would stand there looking at the Gosavi. (Hiraïsa version: And the Gosavi would say, "Hey, there!" and hug himself. This happened two or three times.)

Again she came and stood near the temple door and began looking at the Gosavi. The omniscient one said, "Come here, Mahatma. Give me a hug." And the Gosavi hugged himself. Then the Gosavi had her sit down near him, and he said to Baïse, "My woman, bring her a snack."

म्हणीतलें : बाइ : खाजें आणा४१३ : बाइसें गेलीं : थोडेंचि
ऐसें घेउनि आलीं : सर्वज्ञें म्हणीतलें४१४ : तुम्हां आवघेया हें
काइ होए : यां काइ हें नव्हें : अवचेया सरीसा भागु
आणां ॥छ॥ः हीराइसापाठ : माहात्मेया सरीसा भागु
आणा : बाइसीं म्हणीतलें : बाबा : माहात्मेयां सरीसें कैसें :
सर्वज्ञें म्हणीतलें : बाइ : एथ तुम्हीं काइ होआ : मां : एं :
यथ काइ नव्हति ॥छ॥ः मग बाइसीं अवघेया सरीसें :
खाजें आणीलें : मग गोसावी आपुलेनि श्रीकरें जेनेसी जे
ते तीयेसी४१५ दीधलें : तेंहीं भातुकें खादलें : मग पाणि पेवों
सूदलें : तांबोळ दीधलें : मग सर्वज्ञें म्हणीतलें : माहात्मेंहो :
आतां जाइजो : मग तीए गेलीं : शोधु : एकोबा : खूडडी :
गुळ : उततीया : साकर : फुटाणें : सोले : गळदंडा :
टीळा ॥छ॥ः

२६७ पद्मनाभि क्षोर नीराकरण४१६ :॥ः

एकुदीसीं गोसावीयांचें क्षौर होत होतें : तवं पद्मनाभिदेव
गोसावीयांतें वीनउं लागले : जी जी : मी क्षौर करीन :
म्हणौनि चौंडका उडे ऐसें उडों लागले : आणि गौराइसें
भीतरि दुख करीतें असति : क्षोर कीजे : मग गोसावीयाचां
ठाइं अनुसरिजे : ऐसें म्हणौनि दुख करीतें होतीं : मग
गोसावीयांतें बाइसीं विनवीलें : बाबा : बटीकु क्षौर करीन

Baïse went and brought back just a small amount. The omniscient one said, "Is this what all of you get? Doesn't she get as much as the others? Bring her as much as everyone else gets." (Hiraïsa version: "Bring her as much as the Mahatmas get." Baïse said, "Baba, why should she get as much as the Mahatmas?" The omniscient one replied, "My woman, are you here and she is not here?")

So Baïse brought as much of the snack as everyone else had gotten. Then, with his own hand, the Gosavi gave her the proper amount. The girl ate the food, she was served water to drink, and she was given pan. Then the omniscient one said, "Go now, Mahatma," and she left.

(Research: According to Ekoba, each one received fresh chickpeas, jaggery, dried dates, sugar, parched chickpeas, shelled peas, a necklace of flowers, and a forehead mark.)

267 HE FORBIDS PADMANABHI TO HAVE HIS HEAD SHAVED.

One day when the Gosavi's head was being shaved, Padmanabhidev began to entreat him, "I want to get my head shaved, Lord."[334] As he said this, he started jumping up and down like a drummer. Inside, Gauraïse was crying. "You'll have your head shaved, and then you will become a disciple of the Gosavi," she said, crying.

Then Baïse requested the Gosavi, "Since Batika is saying he wants to have his head shaved, may we let him do it, Baba?"

म्हणतु असे : तरि करूं देइजो कां : सर्वझें म्हणीतलें : बाइ :
पोरू पोकळु : घाला बाहिरी : भीतर वर्तत असे तें साच :
हा कां क्षौर करील : बाइ : दांडीए बैसौनि आडवा पावो⁴¹⁷
घालुनि : पुढां आसुचि वाखारी झेलावी असे : मग तयांसि
क्षौर करूं नेदींतिचि :॥:

२६८ सेंदुरणीं गोपाळीं अवस्थान :॥:

सेंदुरणीं पूर्वामुख गोपाळाचें देउळ : तेथ अवस्थान दीस १० :
१२ :॥:

२६९ पद्मनाभि चणकयाचनीं उपाहारू :॥:

एकुदीसीं गोसावी वीहरणा बीजें केलें : मग बीढारा बीजें
करितां मार्गीं पद्मनाभि देवातें म्हणीतलें : पद्मनाभि जा :
चणा मागा⁴¹⁸ : जी जी म्हणौनि : नीगाले : सेतकरीया
पासि गेले : तेयांतें म्हणीतलें : आम्हांसि काइ चणा दीया :
निका संभावनीक देखौनि तेणें म्हणीतलें : लागे तो घेया
जा : गेले : चणा वोली घालौनि घेउनि आणिला :॥:

The omniscient one said, "My woman, the child is empty. Throw him out. What is inside a person is true. Why does he want to have his head shaved, my woman? He wants to sit in a palanquin with his legs crossed, catching a bagful of gold coins."

He completely refused to let Padmanabhi have his head shaved.

268   HE STAYS IN THE GOPAL TEMPLE IN SENDURANI.

In Sendurani he stayed ten days (or, twelve) in the temple of Gopal, which faces east.[335]

269   WHEN PADMANABHI ASKS A FARMER FOR CHICKPEAS, THE GOSAVI HAS A MEAL OF THEM.

One day the Gosavi went out to wander. As he was returning to their lodgings, along the way he said to Padmanabhidev, "Go and ask for some chickpeas, Padmanabhi." "Yes, Lord," he said, and he set out.

He went up to a farmer and said to him, "Give us some chickpeas." Seeing that he was a good, respectable person, the farmer said, "Take whatever you need."

Padmanabhidev went and got some chickpeas. He put them in a fine cloth and brought them back. He had them pounded and winnowed.[336]

रगडवीला : उपणवीला^{४१९} : सर्वेझें म्हणीतलें : तुम्हीं एथ
आपुलेनि हातें धीडरीं करा^{४२०} : हीराइसापाठ : अर्ध चणे
वीका : वीकूनि तूप घेया : अर्धयाची धीडरी करा : मग तेहीं
तैसेंचि केलें :॥: मग तेंहीं डाळि दळुनि भीजत घातली^{४२१} :
मग तेहींचि चणे सोंडीएवरि भरडीलें : आपणचि अवघें
केलें : तवं बाइसें आलीं : तेहीं म्हणीतलें : बटिका : ऐसें
काइ करित असिस : बाइसीं गोसावीयांतें वीनवीलें : मीं
बाबा पुरती आजूळिभरि दाळिचीं धीडरीं वेगळीं करूं :
मानिलें : बाइसीं गोसावीयांलागि धीडरीं केलीं : पद्मनाभिदेव
बाइसातें पुसत जाति : तियें सांघति : तैसें करित जाति :
बाइसातें अवघा वेसरू मागीतला : मिठ मागीतलें : मग
केलीं : काइसेयावरि केली ते नेणीजे :॥छ॥: एकी
वासना^{४२२} : वाटित होते : ते देमाइसीं देखीलें : देमाइसीं
म्हणीतलें : दे मी करीन : मग देमाइसीं धीडरीं केलीं : थोडे
ऐसे चणे वीकीले : तांदुळ घेतले : तुप घेतले : उपाहारू
निफजवीला : मग गोसावीयांसि पुजा केली : आरोगण :
गोसावीयांसि सहपंक्ति भोजनें जालीं : गोसावीयांसि
गुळळा : वीडा :॥:

The omniscient one said, "Make me some gram pancakes. Make them yourself." (Hiraïsa version: "Sell half the chickpeas and buy ghee. Make gram pancakes with the other half."

So that is what he did.) He split the chickpeas and put them to soak.[337] Then he ground the chickpeas himself, on the elephant-trunk-shaped parapet. He did everything himself.

At that point, Baïse came along. "Batika," she said, "what are you doing?" Baïse requested the Gosavi, "Baba, may I make some other gram pancakes just for you, out of a handful of the split chickpeas?" He agreed, and Baïse made some gram pancakes for the Gosavi.

Padmanabhidev kept asking Baïse questions as he went along. She would tell him what to do, and he would do what she said. He asked Baïse for all the ingredients, including salt. Then he made the pancakes. It is not known what he cooked them on.

(One version: Demaïse saw him grinding the chickpeas. "Here," she said. "I will make them." Then Demaïse made the pancakes. She sold some of the chickpeas and got rice and ghee. She prepared a meal.)

Then they did puja to the Gosavi, and he ate his meal. The disciples ate in the same row with him. The Gosavi rinsed his mouth and chewed pan.

२७० तथा पाठवणी :॥:

माता गौराइसें पद्मनाभिदेवातें नेयावेया आली : दांडीये
बैसौनि : गोसावियांसि दर्शन केलें : परि : काइ दर्शन केलें
तें नेणिजे : आलीं : दंडवतें घातलीं : श्रीचरणा लागली⁴²³ :
उपाहारू केला : मग वीनवीलें : जी जी : रेमनायक सरलें :
जोगनाएकासि कुळवाडी सांवरेना : तरि गोसावी पद्मनाभीतें
पाठवावें : सर्वज्ञें म्हणीतलें : तुमचा पद्मनाभि : एथौनि
बोलावीला : ना जी : नेया ना कां आपुला पद्मनाभि : हा एथ
असावा : ऐसी काइ एथ चाड पडली असे : ना जी :
गोसावीयां पासि असे : म्हणौनि : आणि काइ : सर्वज्ञें
म्हणीतलें : जाए गा : पद्मनाभि : पद्मनाभिदेवीं म्हणीतलें :
यें मातें कैसी नेती : ऐसें याचें बळ पाहों पां : सर्वज्ञें
म्हणीतलें : आतां तवं जाए पां : मग निगाले :॥:

२७१ उपाध्या वीष्णुभटां भेटि :॥:

उपाधीं वीष्णुभटीं एरंडवलीकडे आइकीलें : हीराइसापाठ :
करंजखेडाकडे आइकीलें :॥छ॥: मग वीष्णुभट उपाध्ये :
दवने⁴²⁴ पर्वालागि टाकौनि येत असति : सेंदुरणासि आले :
वीष्णूभट बीढारासि गेले : उपाधिये हाटवटीये कणीक घेवों
गेले : तवं तेथ⁴²⁵ म्हणीतलें : तुम्हीं काइ गोसावीयांचें :
तेहीं म्हणीतलें : गोसावी कोण⁴²⁶ : ना एथ गोसावी एक

270 AND HE SENDS HIM OFF.

Padmanabhidev's mother, Gauraïse, came in a palanquin to take him away. She made an offering to the Gosavi, but it is not known what she gave him. When she arrived, she prostrated herself and touched his holy feet. She prepared some food for him, and then she made her request: "Lord, Remnayak has died, and Jognayak can't manage all the farm work alone. So please send Padmanabhi home, Gosavi."

The omniscient one said, "Did I invite your Padmanabhi to come here?" "No, Lord." "Is there any reason you should not take your Padmanabhi away? Do I want him to be here?" "No, Lord. I'm asking because he is with you, Gosavi. That's all."

The omniscient one said, "Go with her, Padmanabhi." Padmanabhidev said, "How can she take me away? Let's see if she has the strength to do that!" "Go for now," said the omniscient one, and Padmanabhidev left.

271 HE MEETS UPADHYE AND VISHNUBHAT.

Upadhye and Vishnubhat heard that the Gosavi was in Erandavali (Hiraïsa version: They heard that he was in Karanjkhed), so they were coming there for the Southern-wood festival.[338] When they reached Sendurani, Vishnubhat went to their lodgings, and Upadhye went to the market to get wheat flour. Someone there said, "Do you belong to the Gosavi?" "What Gosavi?" asked Upadhye. "There's a Gosavi who has come to the temple of Gopal here. That one."

गोपाळाचेया देउळा आले असति : एकी बीढारीं आइकिलें :
एकी हाटवटी आइकिलें : तैसेंचि ते गोसावीयांचेया दरिसना
निगाले : बिढारीं निरोपु ठेवीला : आमचे कोण्ही येती : तरि :
गोसावीयाचेया दरिसना गेले ऐसें सांघावें : तैसेंचि तेहीं
निगाले : दोघां दारवठां भेटि जाली : सांघातें गोसावीयांचेया
दरिसनासि आले : दंडवतें घातलीं : श्रीचरणा लागले :
बैसले : हीराइसापाठ : सर्वज्ञें म्हणीतलें : हें एथ असे :
ऐसें काइ आइकिलें : उपाधीं म्हणीतलें : जी जी : मीयां
हाटवटिएसी आइकिलें : विष्णुभटातें पुसिलें : तुम्हीं कोणे
ठाई आइकिलें : जी जी : मियां बीढारीं आइकिलें : ऐसें
येन्हयेन्हीं आवघें गोसावीयां पुढें सांघीतलें :॥:

२७२   तथा प्रसनाएक उपाध्ये रिधपुरा पाठवणें :॥:

एकुदीसीं गोसावी श्रीप्रभुची महीमा निरोपीत होतें :
परसनाएकासि ऐसें उपनलें : जे श्रीप्रभुचेया दरिसनासि
जावों : उपाध्ये आणि परसनाएक बाहीरि निगाले :
प्रसनाएकें म्हणीतलें : जानो : मीं श्रीप्रभुचेया दरिसनासि
जाइन : तरि : तुं एसी : जावों : तुज श्रीप्रभुचें दर्शन नाहीं :
तेहीं म्हणीतलें : गोसावीयांतें पुसा : गोसावी पाठवीति तरि
जाइन : मग दोचै गोसावीयांचेया दरिसनासि आलें :
मग गोसावीयांसि प्रसनायेकीं पुसिलें : जी जी : मीयां
जानोतें एसे म्हणीतलें : मीं श्रीप्रभुचेयां दरिसना जाइन : तरि

One of them heard this at their lodgings, and the other heard it in the market. Immediately they set out for *darśan* of the Gosavi. Vishnubhat left a message at their lodgings: "If any of our people come here, tell them I have gone for *darśan* of the Gosavi." He set out right away.

The two of them met at the doorway, so they arrived together for the Gosavi's *darśan*. They prostrated themselves, touched his holy feet, and sat down.

(Hiraïsa version: The omniscient one asked, "How did you hear that I was here?" "I heard it in the market, Lord," said Upadhye. He asked Vishnubhat, "Where did you hear?" "I heard it at our lodgings, Lord." In this way, each of them told the Gosavi everything that had happened.)

272 AND HE SENDS PARASNAYAK AND UPADHYE TO RIDDHIPUR.

One day when the Gosavi was praising Shriprabhu, Parasnayak got the idea of going for Shriprabhu's *darśan*. As Upadhye and Parasnayak went outside, Parasnayak said, "Jano, I want to go for *darśan* of Shriprabhu. So will you come along? Let's go. You haven't had *darśan* of Shriprabhu." Upadhye replied, "Ask the Gosavi. If the Gosavi says to go, I will go with you."

Then, when the two of them came for *darśan* of the Gosavi, Parasnayak asked him. "Lord," he said, "I said to Jano, 'I want to go for *darśan* of Shriprabhu. So will you come along? Let's go.' Jano said, 'Ask the Gosavi. If the Gosavi says to go, I will come along.'"

तुं एसी : जावों : जानो एसें म्हणें : गोसावीयांतें पुसा :
गोसावी पाठविति तरि मी एइन : सर्वज्ञें म्हणीतलें : ऐसें हा
बटीका : हो जी : तुम्हीं परमेश्वरपुरा जाल आणि एथौनि
वारिजैल : परमेश्वरपुरा जावों म्हणे : तेणें मार्गे निगे : एक
एक पाउल घाली : तेयाचें केसणें गोमटें : तुम्हीं तेथें जाल :
आणि एथौनि वारिजैल४२७ : मग सर्वज्ञें म्हणीतलें : बटीका :
तुमतें परमेश्वरपुरां जाणें काइ४२८ : तेहीं म्हणीतलें : जी जी :
गोसावीयांचां ठाइं पर्व करूनि मग जाउनि : गोसावीयांचां
ठाइं दवने पर्व केलें : उपाधीं गोसावीयांतें जावयाचें४२९
पुसीलें : सर्वज्ञें म्हणीतलें : ऐसेयांचि निगावें : पेणोवेणां
जावें : उपेणें न करावें : श्रीप्रभुचें दर्शन घेयावें : समोर न
बैसावें : वाडवेळु श्रीचरणावरि माथा ठेउनि नमस्कारू न
करावा : देवतेसि निरोधू होए४३० : मग तेहीं दोघीं पैन्हां
विचारीलें : प्रसनायक म्हणति : लोणारावरौनि जावों :
वर्जेचें स्नान होइल : तेथौनि मेहकरीं४३१ सारंगधराचें दर्शन
होइल : मग श्रीप्रभुचेया दर्शना जावें : उपाध्ये म्हणति :
उजुचि चांगदेवेंहुनि श्रीप्रभुचेया दर्शना जावों : ऐसे दोघै
विचारीत गोसावीयांपासि आले : सर्वज्ञें म्हणीतलें : तरि
सांघातियां सवादु असे म्हणा४३२ : उपाधीं गोसावीयां पुढें
सांघीतलें : मागील आवघेंचि : सर्वज्ञें म्हणीतलें : वर्जेचें
स्नान : सारंगधराचें दर्शन : नेणोंकोण आलें : कीर्तितें करूनि
गेलें : आतां तेथ काइ असे४३३ : मग निगाले : चांगदेवासि

The omniscient one said, "Is that so, Batika?" "Yes, Lord." "If you want to go to Parameshvarpur, how could I prevent you? How blessed is someone who says, 'Let's go to Parameshvarpur,' who sets out on the road and takes one step after another! If you want to go there, how could I prevent you?"

Then the omniscient one asked, "Batika, will you go to Parameshvarpur?"[339] "Lord Gosavi," he said, "we will celebrate the festival with you, and then we will go."

They celebrated the Southernwood festival with the Gosavi. Upadhye asked the Gosavi about how to go. The omniscient one said, "Simply set off. Go straight there without staying anywhere overnight. When you take *darśan* of Shriprabhu, do not sit facing him. Do not put your head on his holy feet for a long time when you do reverence to him. That would cause difficulties for the god."[340]

Then the two of them went some distance away and had a discussion. Parasnayak said, "Let's go via Lonar. We can have a ritual bath there. From there we can go for *darśan* of Sharngadhar in Mehkar, and then we can go for *darśan* of Shriprabhu." Upadhye said, "Let's go straight from Cangdev to *darśan* of Shriprabhu."

Discussing this way, the two of them came to the Gosavi. The omniscient one said, "I see there is a disagreement between the traveling companions."[341] Upadhye told the Gosavi everything that had happened. The omniscient one said, "Some unknown person came and made the ritual bath and *darśan* of Sharngadhar famous. What is there in that place now?"[342]

Then they set out. When they reached Cangdev, a meal

गेले : तवं तेथ संन्यासियांसि परिक्षा निमंत्रण आंबेभोजन
मांडलें असे : यऱ्हायऱ्हासि निमंत्रण दीधलें : जेवीले : जेउं
सरलें : आणि उदीयां आखत लाविलीं : आणि उपाध्यें म्हणों
लागलें : हें काइ : प्रसनाएको : सर्वज्ञें म्हणीतलें : पेणोवेणां
जावें : उपेणें न करावें : तरि तुम्ही राहात असा : प्रसनाएकीं
म्हणीतलें : राहे : आंबेयाची सराय तवं घेवों : मग श्रीप्रभुचें
दर्शन तें काइ केंहीं जात असे : मग तोहीं दीस राहीले :
जेवण जालें : आणि येरी दीसीचें माघौतें निमंत्रण दीधलें :
उपाधीं म्हणीतलें : तुम्ही राहाल तरि राहा : मि जाइन :
प्रसनायक राहीले : उपाध्ये निगाले : ते अळजपुरासि आले :
दामाचें पांच आंबे घेतलें⁴³⁴ : देहें श्रीप्रभुचेया दर्शनासि
आले : श्रीप्रभु टीकोउपाध्याचिए वोसरीय वरि आसन :
उपाध्ये आले : श्रीप्रभु पुढां आंबे ठेवीले : दंडवतें घातलीं :
श्रीचरणा लागले : श्रीप्रभुपुढें उभे होते : श्रीप्रभु करीं आंबे
घेति : आणि मध्यें‍चि आरोगण : आंबा गोड आहे म्हणे :
खावा म्हणे : आडवा आंबा आरोगण : ऐसे पांच आंबे :
कणु कणु चाखीले : मेला जाए : चे ना : म्हणे : आरे घे घे
म्हणे : म्हणौनि श्रीचरणें तेयाकडे लोंटिले : उपाधीं ते आंबे
घेतलें⁴³⁵ : मग वीळींचां वेळीं : उपाध्ये माघौतें दर्शना
आले : मेला जाए : ऐसा एइल : खाइल म्हणे : न खाय

520

of mangos had been arranged there, and all the sannyasis had been invited. They were both given an invitation, and they ate the meal. As soon as they finished eating, they were invited for the next day.

Upadhye began to say, "What is this, Parasnayak? The omniscient one told us, 'Go straight there without staying anywhere overnight.' But you are staying here?" Parasnayak said, "If we stay, we'll get plenty of mangos. And we can go for *darśan* of Shriprabhu anytime."

So they stayed that day as well. They ate the meal, and again they were given an invitation for the following day. Upadhye said, "If you want to stay, then stay. I am leaving."

Parasnayak stayed there. Upadhye left. When he reached Alajpur, he bought five mangos for one copper coin.[343] He arrived during the daytime for *darśan* of Shriprabhu.

Shriprabhu was sitting on Tikopadhye's veranda when Upadhye arrived. He placed the mangos before Shriprabhu, prostrated himself, and touched the holy feet. Then he stood in front of Shriprabhu.

Shriprabhu was picking up the mangos and biting right into the middle of them. "This mango is sweet, I say. I should eat it, I tell you." He was taking one bite out of each of the five mangos, biting sideways into each one. "Drop dead! Take them, I say. Hey, take them! Take them, I tell you." And he pushed them toward Upadhye with his holy foot. Upadhye took the mangos.

Then in the evening Upadhye came again for *darśan*. "Drop dead!" said Shriprabhu. "It will come here. It will

म्हणे : आरे साळे जाए : साळे : हीराइसापाठ : तथा
दोंदावरि रसू गळे : खाड मारवे : तें पूसीति : ऐसे आंबे
आरोगिले : मग श्रीचरणीचेनि आंगुठेनि करूनि उपाध्या देवों
आदरिलें : मेला जाए : घे घे म्हणे : आरे चेना म्हणे : आरे
घे घे म्हणे : तें उपाध्यां उमटेना : टिकोपाध्याचिया कन्यां
म्हणीतलें : भटो तुम्हांसि राउळ प्रसादु देतु असति : मग
उपाधीं माहाप्रसाद म्हणौनि घेतला : श्रीप्रभु म्हणीतलें : मेला
जाए : साळे जाए ना म्हणे : ऐसाचि ऐइल : तो खाइल
म्हणे ॥छ॥: तें उपाध्यासि उमटेंचि ना : तवं सर्पू आला :
तेयांतें देखौनि वासरूं बूजालें : मेला जाये : परि खायेचि ना
म्हणे : आतां एइल : तो खाइल म्हणे : साळे जाए ना म्हणे :
तवं टिकोपाध्याचियां कन्यां म्हणीतलें : भटो : गोसावी
तुमतें साळेंसिं पाठवीत असति : मग उपाध्यें साळेसि गेले :
त्री रात्र होते : मग दंडवत घालौनि निगाले :॥:

२७३ लखुमबाइसा देमाइसा भेटि :॥:

देमाइसें : लखूबाइसें गोसावीयाचेया दरिसनां येतें होतीं :
गोसावी कोणे ठाइं राज्य करीत असति : ऐसें नेणति :
सेंदुरणांसि आलीं : पैले थडीए भिक्षा केली : नदी जेवीली :

bite, I say. It won't bite, I tell you. Hey! Go to the rest house.*
The rest house!" (Or, Hiraïsa version: As he ate the mangos,
the juice dripped onto his belly and his beard got smeared
with it. He would wipe it off. Then he tried to give them to
Upadhye with the big toe of his holy foot. "Drop dead! Take
them! Take them, I say. Hey! Take them, I say. Hey, take
them! Take them, I tell you."

Upadhye did not understand that. Tikopadhye's daughter
said, "The Raül is giving you *prasād,* Bhat." Then Upadhye
took them, considering them great *prasād.*

"Drop dead!" said Shriprabhu. "Go to the rest house, I tell
you. It will come just like this. It will bite, I tell you.")

Upadhye did not understand that at all. But then a snake
came along. The calf saw it and got frightened. "Drop dead!"
said Shriprabhu. "But it surely won't bite, I say. It will come
now. It will bite, I tell you. Go to the rest house, I tell you."
Tikopadhye's daughter said, "Bhat, the Gosavi is telling you
to go to the rest house."

So Upadhye went to the rest house. He spent three nights
there, then prostrated himself and left.

273   HE MEETS LAKHUBAÏSE
AND DEMAÏSE.

Demaïse and Lakhubaïse were coming for *darśan* of the
Gosavi, but they did not know where he was living. When
they reached Sendurani, they begged for food on the far side

---

* A particular place in Riddhipur.

एरी थडीएचिये आळीए निद्रा करूं आलीं : गोसावीयांसि
वीळीचां पुजा अवस्वरू जाला : व्याळी जाली : बाइसीं
फोडी वोळगवीलीया : वीडीया करूनि देतें असति : सर्वज्ञें
म्हणीतलें : मार्तंडा या आरूतें : ऐसे ऐसे जा : दुध जोडे :
दुध वो : ऐसें फोकरा⁴³⁶ : जी जी : म्हणौनि : निगाले : मग
म्हणों लागले : गोसावीयांसि तरि व्याळी जाली : आतां दुध
काइसेया लागि : ऐसें वीचारित गेले : कवडां दुध जोडे वो :
म्हणौनि फोकरूं लागले : तवं देमाइसीं म्हणीतलें :
लखुबाइ : मार्तंडाचेया ऐसा शब्द : म्हणौनि : साउमीं गेलीं :
हें कोण : मार्कंडा : ना वो : हें कोण देमाइसें : ना वो : चाला
चाला : तुमतें गोसावी बोलाउं पाठविलें असे : ऐसे गा
आमचे गोसावी : आपूलें ईश्वर्यें जाणों नेदीति : ऐसें म्हणौनि
येन्हें येन्हें गोसावीयांचेयां दरिसनां आलीं : दंडवतें घातलीं :
श्रीचरणा लागलीं : गोसावीयांपूढें अवघें सांघों लागलीं : जी
जी : आम्ही पैलाडिले थडीए भिक्षा केली : नदी जेवीलों :
ऐलाडिले थडीए नीद्रा करावेया आलों : तवं मार्तंडु आला :
भेटला : आलों : ऐसें आवघें सांघीतलें :॥छ॥ः

of the river and ate their meal at the river. They came to a lane on the near side of the river to sleep.

After the Gosavi's evening worship service and meal, Baïse offered him bits of betel nut. As she was making rolls of pan and giving them to him, the omniscient one said, "Come here, Martanda. Take such-and-such a route, get some milk, and cry out, 'Hey! Milk!'"[344] "Yes, Lord," he said, and he set out.

Then he began to say to himself, "The Gosavi has already had his evening meal. Why does he need milk now?" As he went along thinking that, he began to cry out, "Milk for a cowrie shell!"

Demaïse said, "Lakhubaï, that sounds like Martanda's voice." So they approached him. "Who is this?[345] Martanda?" "Yes, it is. Who is this? Demaïse?" "Yes, it is." "Come on, come on. The Gosavi has sent me to invite you."

Saying, "That is what our Gosavi is like: he does not reveal his divinity," the two of them came for *darśan* of the Gosavi. They prostrated themselves, touched his holy feet, and began to tell the Gosavi everything that had happened. "We went begging on the opposite side of the river, Lord," they told him, "and we ate at the river. When we came to this side of the river to sleep, Martanda came along. We met him and came here."

525

२७४ प्रथम वसति : लखुबाइसां भेटि :॥:

लखुबाइसें : देमाइसें सेंदुर्णीसि सन्निधानीं होतीं : तेथ
तयांसि आणि बाइसांसि काहीं तुडपुड जाली होती : मग
गोसावी सेंदर्णीहुनि बीजें करूं आदरिलें : तेव्हळीं आधी^{४३७}
गोसावी : लखूबाइसें देमाइसें गावां पाठवीली : मागीली
कडौनि त्याचि गावा गोसावी बीजें केलें : एका वृक्षाखालि
आसन : लखुबाइसीं गोसावीयांतें देखिलें : देमाइ देमाइ :
गोसावी बीजें केलें : चाल जावों : गोसावीयाचेया दरिसनां :
आइ मीं न ए : तूं जाए : जाइजैल आणि बाइसें वीसारूंचि
लागति : लखुबाइसीं म्हणीतलें : तुम्हीं न या : तरि न या : मी
जाइन : तें गोसावीयापासि आलीं : दंडवतें घातलीं : श्री-
चरणा लागलीं : बैसली : आणि बाइसें वीसारूंचि लागलीं :
आणि तीयें तैसीचि नीगालीं : देमाइसा पुढें सांघों लागलीं :
तुवा म्हणीतलें : तेंचि जालें : गेलीं आणि बाइसें वीसारूंचि
लागलीं : तुम्हीं न याचि तें बरवें केलें : मग बाइसाचि दृष्टि
चुकूनि : गोसावी तेयाचेया बीढारा बीजें केलें : गोसावीयांसि
आसन घातलें : आसनीं उपविष्ट जाले : दंडवतें घातलीं :
श्रीचरणा लागले : गोसावीयांजवळि बैसलीं : सर्वज्ञें
म्हणीतलें : देमती : तुम्हीं एथीचेया दर्शना न याचि तें
काइ^{४३८} : जी बाइसा हातीं एवों नैए : सर्वज्ञें म्हणीतलें :
देमती : वोढळा गोरूवाची परि तुम्हां होआवी : माळीयावरि
जो असे तो थै थै म्हणे : तवं तें एकू घासूं घे : तो तवं फळे
कीं : तैसें होआवें देमती^{४३९} : मग गोसावी तयांतें बीढारा

274 THE FIRST OVERNIGHT STAY.
HE MEETS LAKHUBAÏSE.

While Lakhubaïse and Demaïse were staying in Sendurani in the presence of the Gosavi, they got into a quarrel with Baïse. After that, the Gosavi decided to leave Sendurani, and he sent Lakhubaïse and Demaïse ahead to another village.

Later the Gosavi went to that other village. He was sitting under a tree. Lakhubaïse saw him and said, "Demaï! Demaï! The Gosavi has come here. Come on! Let's go have *darśan* of the Gosavi." "I'm not coming, Mother. You go. What if we go there and Baïse starts insulting us?" Lakhubaïse said, "If you aren't coming, then don't come. I'm going." She approached the Gosavi, prostrated herself, touched his holy feet, and sat down. And Baïse began insulting her right away.

So she left immediately. She started telling Demaïse, "It happened exactly the way you said it would. When I reached there, Baïse began insulting me right away. You were right not to come."

Then the Gosavi came to their lodgings without letting Baïse see him go. They put down something for the Gosavi to sit on, and he sat down on it. They prostrated themselves, touched his holy feet, and sat down near the Gosavi.

The omniscient one said, "Demati, why won't you come for my *darśan?*"[346] "In order to avoid Baïse, Lord." The omniscient one said, "Demati, you should be like a wild bull. When the man in the pasture says, 'Shoo! Shoo!' it takes one bite and runs away. You should be like that, Demati."[347] Then the Gosavi brought them to his lodgings.

527

घेउनि आले : मग बाइसीं म्हणीतलें : बाबायें यांसि राहों
दीधलें : आतां कांहीं म्हणोंचि नए : म्हणौनि : स्नेहचि
करिति :॥ः

२७५ पाचोरा वसति :॥छ॥ः

२७६ चांगदेवो पुरीए अवस्थान^{८८०} :॥ः

मग गोसावी चांगदेवासि बीजें केलें : चांगदेवीं जगती आंतु
मठीं अवस्थान : दीस सात : कीं : पांच :॥छ॥ः

२७७ चींचखेडकर रामदेवाचा अवसरू :
आइकणें^{८८१} :॥ः

एकुदीसीं : गोसावी : उदयाचा पूजावसर जालेयानंतरें
वीहरणा बीजें केलें : स्याळीएचे आंगीं टोपरें लेउनि :
चांगदेवाचिए दक्षीणीला दारवठां पूर्विलें सोंडीवरि
दक्षीणामूखु गोसावी उभे असति : कवडिंब रामदेव
गंगेकडौनि हाटवटियेहुनि गावांतु येत असति : तवं
गोसावीयांतें सोंडीयेवरि उभेयां देखीले : धावत पुढें आले :
हातीं चित्रीव काठी होती : ते गोसावीयाचां श्रीकरीं
वोळगवीली : दंडवतें घातलीं : श्रीचरणा लागले : मग

Baïse said to herself, "Baba has allowed them to stay, so now I can't say a thing." So she treated them with loving kindness.

275 HE STAYS OVERNIGHT IN PACHOR.[348]

276 HE STAYS IN CANGDEV PURI.

Then the Gosavi went to Cangdev.[349] He stayed for five or seven days in a hermitage within the compound wall of the Cangdev temple.

277 HE LISTENS TO CHINCHKHEDKAR RAMDEV'S SONG.

After his morning worship service one day, the Gosavi went out to wander wearing a winter cloak and cap. The Gosavi was standing on the eastern elephant-trunk-shaped parapet at the southern doorway of the Cangdev temple, facing south. As Kavadimba Ramdev came from the river through the market into the village, he saw the Gosavi standing on the elephant-trunk-shaped parapet. He came running up to the Gosavi and offered him a decorated stick that he was

गोसावी ते काठी श्रीकरीं घेउनि त्रीभंगी ठाण मांडौनि : उभे
असति : तेहीं जति केली :

शंकचक्र सांडौनि हातीं डांग चेतली :
        हातियरू गोवळेया ॥
ऐसा गोवळु गोसावी माझा गोरूवें राखे :
        गोपाळवेरखें ॥
आलीएं परि गोवळु ऐसा नावडे :
        माया मानवीया जाले ॥
रामेयांसि स्वामी नोळखे कव्हणी :
        आलीएं॑४४२ ॥

हे जति वोळगवीली : सर्वज्ञें म्हणीतलें : आतां पुरे : वारिले :
मग गोसावी पुडवाटुवा झाडौनि तांबूल दीधलें : पीवळी
आंगीं टोपरें : गळदंडा दीधला : तें टोपरें डोइए चालुनि
नावेक नाचीनले : मग गोसावी तेयासि पाठवणी दीधली :
ते निगाले : मग बाइसीं पुसीलें : बाबा : हा कवणु : सर्वज्ञें
म्हणीतलें : रामदेवो कवडींबू : बाबा : भगतु कैसा निका :
सर्वज्ञें म्हणीतलें : हा आणिका भक्तासारिखा : कोरडा
नव्हे॑४४३ : मग गोसावी तेथौनि बीजें केलें :॥ः

530

holding. He prostrated himself and touched the holy feet. The Gosavi took the stick and held it in his holy hand. Then he stood there in the three-bend pose.[*]

Kavadimba Ramdev composed a song of praise:

> Dropping his conch and discus, he took a staff in his
> hand, the weapon of a cowherd.
> My cowherd Gosavi protects the cows this way,
> in the garb of a cowherd.
> But my women friends don't like such a cowherd,
> so he became a human mother.
> Ram recognizes no master,
> my friends.

After he had performed this song, the omniscient one stopped him, saying, "That's enough now." The Gosavi shook out his partitioned pouch and gave him some pan. He gave him a yellow cloak and a cap, and a garland for around his neck. Putting the cap on his head, Ramdev danced for a moment. Then the Gosavi gave him leave to go.

After he left, Baïse asked, "Who was that, Baba?" The omniscient one said, "Ramdev Kavadimba." "What a good devotee he is, Baba!" The omniscient one said, "He is not dried out like other devotees."[350]

After that the Gosavi left.

---

[*] A pose typical of Krishna.

२७८ तापीं तटीं मार्तंडा देवता दर्शन :॥:

एकुदीसीं गोसावी वीळीचां वेळीं वीहरणा बीजें केलें :
गोसावीयां जवळि बाइसें मार्तंड बैसलीं असति : मार्तंडा
स्तीति जाली : पुढां देखों लागले : गोसावी पाणीयां आंतु
बीजें केलें : हातीं मार्तंडातें धरीलें : दोनि देवता साउमीया
आलीया : दंडवतें घातलीं : श्रीचरणा लागलीया : सोनीयाचा
मांचा पासौडिला : तेथ आसन : सोनियाचे परियेळ : रत्नाचे
दीप : दोघी स्त्री : गोसावीया वोवाळणि केली : माथाचां
केशीं श्रीचरण झाडीले : ऐसें मार्तंडें देखीलें : मग बाइसां पुढें
सांघीतलें : बाइसीं म्हणीतलें : बाबा : मार्तंडु काइ म्हणतु
असे : सर्वज्ञें म्हणीतलें : बाइ : यातेंचि पुसा : बाबा आपण
के गेलीयां होतीयां : बाइ हें कें गेलें होतें : हें एथेंचि होतें
नव्हे : सर्वज्ञें म्हणीतलें : बाइ : यासि ऐसी बूधि॥४ : म्हणौनि
गोसावी मढासि बीजें केलें :॥:

२७९ मार्गीं व्याघ्रू पाठी येणें :॥:

गोसावी चांगदेवीहुनि सांवळदेवाकडें बीजें करितां व्याघ्रें
गोसावीयांतें देखीलें : आणि स्तीति जाली : आणि साउमा
आला : बाइसीं म्हणीतलें : बाबा बाबा : वाघू : म्हणौनि
भीयालीं॥५ : सर्वज्ञें म्हणीतलें : भीयाना : पाठीं पाठीं

278   ON THE BANK OF THE TAPI,*
MARTANDA HAS *DARŚAN* OF A DEITY.

One evening the Gosavi went out to wander. As Baïse and Martanda were sitting near him, Martanda went into a trance. He began staring straight ahead. He saw the Gosavi go into the water, taking him by the hand. Two goddesses approached the Gosavi, prostrated themselves, and touched his holy feet. They spread a cloth over a golden bedstead, and the Gosavi sat on it. The two women waved a golden tray with jeweled lamps in front of him and wiped his holy feet with their hair.

When Martanda told Baïse what he had seen, Baïse asked, "Baba, what is Martanda saying?" The omniscient one said, "Ask *him,* my woman." "Where did you go, Baba?" "Where did I go, my woman? Wasn't I right here?" The omniscient one said, "My woman, that is what he believed he saw."[351] And, with that, the Gosavi went back to the hermitage.

279   ALONG THE ROAD,
A TIGER FOLLOWS HIM.

As the Gosavi was going from Cangdev to Savaldev, a tiger saw him.[352] It went into a trance and approached him. Baïse was frightened. "Baba!" she cried. "Baba! A tiger!" "Don't be afraid," said the omniscient one.

It followed along behind them. At the edge of a certain

---

* The main river at Cangdev.

आला : गावां एकाचां आखरीं : सर्वज्ञें म्हणीतलें : माहात्मां :
आतां राहीजो^{४७६} : बाइसीं म्हणीतलें : बाबा : हा कोण्हाचें
कांहीं न करी : तरि : एवों कां दीजेना : सर्वज्ञें म्हणीतलें :
बाइ : हा आतां कोण्हांसि उपद्रो न करी : यासि लोकु उपद्रो
करील^{४७७} : माहात्मां आतां जा :॥छ॥: तो निगाला :॥

२८० देमती तुरंगम आरोहणी :॥:

गोसावी एरी दीसीं सावळदेवा बीजें करीती : ऐसें आधींलें
दीसीं बाइसीं मार्तंडातें म्हणीतलें : मार्तंडा तुं सावळदेवासि
जाए : दाया पुढें सांघावें : बाबा एत असति : अवघी आइति
करावी : आणि घोडेनिसीं बाबासि साउमेया यावें : मार्तंड
सावळदेवासि गेले : तेथ बाइसाचे भाचे दाएनाएकू होते :
तेयापूढें सांघीतलें : मग तेहीं सडासंमार्जन करवीलें : चौक
रंगमाळीका भरवीलीया : गुढी उभविली : उपहाराची आइति
करविली : आपण घोडें घेउनि साउमे आले : मार्गीं भेट
जाली : गोसावीयांसि दंडवतें घातलीं : श्रीचरणा लागले :
मग गोसावीयांतें वीनवीलें : घोडेयावरि बैसावें जी : वीनती
स्वीकरिली : घोडेयावरि आरोहण केलें : पुढें भक्तिजन
चालति : गोसावीयांचें घोडें वारिकें : गोसावी मागील
वास पाहीली : तवं मागीली कडे देमाइसें एतें असति : ते
गोसावीयां टाकौनि आली : सर्वज्ञें म्हणीतलें : देमती या :
घोडेया बैसा : म्हणौनि : पासाडाचा अनुकारू दाखवीला :

534

village, the omniscient one said, "Mahatma, you must stay here now."[353]

Baïse said, "Baba, he isn't going to hurt anyone, so why not let him come along?" The omniscient one said, "He won't harm anyone now, my woman, but people will harm him. Go away now, Mahatma."

The tiger left.

280   DEMATI MOUNTS A HORSE.

Because the Gosavi was going to Savaldev the next day, Baïse said to Martanda, "Go to Savaldev, Martanda. Tell Daya that Baba is coming, so he should get everything ready and come toward Baba with a horse."

Martanda went to Savaldev and gave the message to Baïse's nephew Dayanayak, who lived there. So Dayanayak had cow-dung wash smeared on the ground and designs drawn on it with colored powder. He had a decorated pole erected, and he had preparations made for a meal. He himself took a horse and went toward the Gosavi.

They met on the road. He prostrated himself to the Gosavi and touched his holy feet. Then he requested the Gosavi, "Please sit on the horse, Lord." The Gosavi acceded to the request and mounted the horse.

The devotees were walking ahead of the Gosavi. The horse was small. The Gosavi looked back and saw Demaïse lagging behind. When she caught up with the Gosavi, the omniscient one said, "Come on, Demati. Sit on the horse,"

देमाइसीं म्हणीतलें : हो कां : जी : तथा जालें नव्हे जी :
म्हणौनि : पासाडावरि हातु ठेविला : यावरि गोसावी
कुबजका भवनीं बीजें केलें : ते गोष्टि सांघीतली : तैसें तुम्हीं
केलें देमती : तुम्हीं एथीचे प्रवृत्ति वीखो जालीति :॥ः

२८१ सावळदेवीं अवस्थान :॥ः

शोधु : सावळदेवा दारवंठे दोनि : पूर्वामूखु : मग गोसावी
सावळदेवा बीजें केलें : सावळदेवा दक्षीणे : भीतरीलीकडे
जगतीसीं पूर्वपश्चिमी पटिसाळ होती : पश्चीमीले सीरां एका
खणाची गुंफा पूर्वाभिमूखु : तेथ अवस्थान : शोधु : देउळा
पोळि बाहीरि : उत्तरे ग्रह : वाव्ये दाए नाएकाचा आवारू :
तेथ गोसावी प्रतदीनीं पूजा : आरोगण : तथा मादनें होए :
आंबेयातळीं वीहरण : शोधु : गावां अग्रे बदरिखा एकू
आंबा : सावळदेवीं वीहरण : प्रत्तदीनीं दाएनाएकाचें ताट
ए : एकुदीसीं दाएनाएकीं गोसावीयांसि वस्त्रपुजा केली :॥ः

and he gestured toward the back of the horse. Demaïse said, "All right, Lord" (or, "Hasn't this happened before, Lord?"[354]), and she placed her hand on the horse's back.

At this, the Gosavi told the story of going to the home of Kubjaka.[355] "You've acted the same way, Demati. You have pleased me."

281 HE STAYS AT SAVALDEV.

(Research: The Savaldev temple had two doorways. It faced east.) The Gosavi reached Savaldev. To the south of the Savaldev temple, on the inner side of the compound wall, was a veranda that was oriented east-west. He stayed at the western end, in a hermit's cell that faced east and took up one section of the veranda. (Research: To the north, outside the temple's compound wall, was a house. To the northwest of that was Dayanayak's compound. The Gosavi's puja was done there, and he had his meal—or a bath—there every day.)

(Research: There was a large, shady mango tree to the southeast of the village.) He would wander to the foot of the mango tree, and he would wander to the Savaldev temple. Every day a plate of food would come from Dayanayak. One day Dayanayak did puja to the Gosavi by offering him a garment.

———

* A goddess.

२८२ वालसेंग वसति :॥:

तेथौनि वालसेंगेसि बीजें केलें४५८ : गावां नृत्ये म्हाळसेचें
देउळ : पूर्वामूखु : तेथ वसति जाली : हीराइसापाठ :
गोसावी आंगी टोपरें लेउनि आंगणीं उभे ठाकले :
मग तपोवन अवलोकीलें : हीराइसापाठ : पैला देउळा
जाइजैल :॥छ॥: तैसेंचि गोसावी बीजें केलें ॥ शोधु :
वालसेंगे अग्रे तपोवन :॥:

२८३ तपोवनीं साइदेवां भेटि :॥:

तपोवनासि बीजें केलें : देउळांत बीजें केलें : हीराइसापाठ :
नावेक आसन जालें४५९ :॥छ॥: अडवांगीं देउळीए बीजें
केलें : सीधनाथाचें रचमचेचें देउळ : म्हणौनि तेथ आसन :
तवं साइदेवो दांडीए बैसौनि देउळा आले : चौकीं आपुलीं
वस्त्रें ठेविलीं : कुपीनु केला : घागरि घेउनि पाणि वाहीलें :
सडा घातला : देवतासि अस्तर्पण केलें : पुजा केली : मग
प्रदक्षीणा करावेया आला : तवं गोसावीयांतें देखीलें : दंडबत
घातलें : श्रीचरणा लागले : भेटि जाली : मग गोसावीयांतें
विनविलें : वीनवणि स्विकरीली : गोसावीयांसि आंगणि
दांडिएवरि आसन केलें : ते वोडण खांडें घेउनि पुढां खोलति

282   HE SPENDS THE NIGHT AT VALSENG.

From there he went to Valseng.[356] He stayed overnight to the southwest of the village, in a temple of Mhalsa* that faced east. (Hiraïsa version: The Gosavi put on a cloak and a cap and stood in the courtyard.)

Then the Gosavi went to look at Tapovan.[357] (Hiraïsa version: "I'm going to go to that temple over there," he said.) He set out immediately.

(Research: Tapovan was to the southeast of Valseng.)

283   HE MEETS SAÏDEV IN TAPOVAN.

When he reached Tapovan, he went into the temple there. (Hiraïsa version: He sat there for a little while.) Then, because the temple of Siddhanath was crowded, he went and sat in a shrine that was off to the side.

While he was sitting there, Saïdev* came to the temple, seated in a palanquin. He placed his clothes in the temple hall, put on a loincloth, took a pot, and offered water. He smeared the floor with cow-dung wash, made a water offering to the deity, and performed puja. Then, as he was circumambulating the deity, he saw the Gosavi. He prostrated himself and touched the holy feet. They greeted each other. Then he invited the Gosavi to his home, and the Gosavi accepted the invitation.

In the courtyard, Saïdev prepared a seat for the Gosavi in the palanquin. Taking a shield and sword, he set off, leading

---

* A prominent citizen of Masraul.

निगाले : मग घोडेयावरि बैसवीलें : हीराइसापाठ : सर्वझें
म्हणीतलें : तुम्ही घोडेयावरि बसा : तेंही म्हणीतलें : जी जी :
मीं गोसावीयांपुढें चालैन : सर्वझें म्हणीतलें : तरि हें उतरैल :
मग ते घोडेयावरि बैसले :॥:

२८४ मासरौळीं अवस्थान :॥:

मग गोसावी मासरौळांसि बीजें केलें : देव्हारचौकीए
अवस्थान दीस तीन : तथा मासू एकू :॥छ॥: तेयांतें एक
ब्राह्मणाचें भानवस होतें : तेथ भक्तजनलागि अन्न निफजे :
गोसावीयां लागि ताट ए : पुर्वे विहीरिचीये पालि : आंबा :
तेथ विरहण होए :॥:

२८५ पींपळगांवीं वसति :॥:

२८६ भोगवर्धनीं रामीं वसति :॥:

२८७ शेलवडे बामेश्वरीं वसति :॥:

the way. Then the Gosavi had him sit on a horse. (Hiraïsa version: The omniscient one said, "You sit on the horse." Saïdev replied, "Lord, I will walk in front of the Gosavi." The omniscient one said, "Then I will get out of the palanquin." So Saïdev sat on the horse.)

284 HE STAYS IN MASRAUL.

Then the Gosavi went to Masraul.[358] He stayed in the central shrine there for three days (or, for a month). They had the use of a Brahman's kitchen, where the devotees' food was cooked. A plate of food would come for the Gosavi.

There was a mango tree to the east, at the wall of a well, where he used to go to wander.

285 HE STAYS OVERNIGHT IN PIMPALGAV.[359]

286 HE STAYS OVERNIGHT IN THE RAM TEMPLE AT BHOGVARDHAN.[360]

287 HE STAYS OVERNIGHT IN THE BAMESHVAR TEMPLE AT SHELAVADE.[361]

२८८ आनवां बनि अवस्थान :॥:

गावां उत्तरे बन : तेथ गुढरू आंबा होता : तेयातळि
गोसावीयांसि अवस्थान : दीस वीस : तथा पाखू : उदयाची
बनकर हात पावो धुवावेया एति : हातुपाए धुति : पांच
पांच आंबे : एकी वासना : दाहा दाहा बारा बारा⁴⁵⁰ : आंबे
प्रतदीनी गोसावीयांसि दर्शन करिती :॥:

२८९ देमती अंबग्रासू कथन⁴⁵¹ :॥:

गोसावीयांसि आंबेयातळि आसन : गुढरू आंबा : तेयाचे
आंबे खाली लोंबति : गोसावी देमाइसातें म्हणीतलें : देमती :
ऐसेया निजावें : आं करावा : लवकरि आंबा तोंडी
रीगैल⁴⁵² : ऐसें गोसावी दाखविलें :॥:

२९० तथा भिक्षान्न प्रशंसा :॥:

एकुदीसीं देमाइसें झोळीया धुवावीया पाटासि गेलीं : अन्न
उरलें होतें : तें पाटीं पुंजा केलें : मागील कडुनि गोसावी
तेथेंचि बीजें केलें : सर्वज्ञें म्हणीतलें : हें कोणे गा : केलें⁴⁵³ :
हीराइसापाठ : देमती हें अन्न कोणें सांडीलें : जी जी : उरलें
होतें : मीयां पुंजा केलें :॥छ॥: जी⁴⁵⁴ : सर्वज्ञें म्हणीतलें :

288   HE STAYS IN A GROVE AT ANAVE.[362]

The grove was north of the village. For twenty days (or, for a fortnight), the Gosavi stayed at the foot of a mango tree there that formed a canopy. Early in the morning the orchardist would come to wash his hands and feet.

After washing his hands and feet, he would offer the Gosavi five mangos (one version: ten or twelve mangos) each day.

289   HE TELLS DEMATI HOW TO EAT A MANGO.

The Gosavi was sitting at the foot of the mango tree that formed a canopy. Mangos were hanging down from it.

The Gosavi said to Demaïse, "Demati, lie on your back and say 'Aah.' Soon a mango will drop into your mouth." The Gosavi showed her how to do it.

290   AND HE PRAISES FOOD OBTAINED AS ALMS.

One day Demaïse went to the stream to wash her begging bag. There was some food left in the bag, and she made a pile of it in the stream. Later the Gosavi came to that place. "Who did this?" asked the omniscient one. (Hiraïsa version: "Demati, who has thrown away this food?" "I made a pile of what was left over, Lord.")

देमती ऐसें कां केलें : जी जी : खाती बापूडे मासे : सर्वज्ञें
म्हणीतलें : देमती जैसे मासे तैसीं तुम्हीं पोरें⁴⁵⁵ : हे तुमची
महीमा : ऐसें गोसावी सीक्षापण केलें :॥:

२९१ तथा राहावणें :॥:

एकूदीसा बाइसां आणि देमाइसा भांडण जालें : मग
बाइसीं म्हणीतलें : बाबा : दवडावीया : भांडती असति :
मग उदियांचि देमाइसें गोसावीयांचेया पुजावसरा आलीं :
पुजावसर जाला : मग देमाइसातें गोसावी पाठौं आदरिलें :॥:
हीराइसापाठ : देमती तुम्ही एथौनि जा :॥छ॥: देमाइसीं
वोवीया तीन⁴⁵⁶ म्हणीतलीया :॥:

पाउलें म्हणीतलें : न करीती हरी :
कवणें परी : जावों आम्ही ॥१॥

तुझां चरणीं : रंगलें मन :
काइसीया कान्हा : पाठविसी ॥२॥

तुझेनि वेधें : असो संभ्रमीतें :
निर्वीकारा जोगीयाचें : चीत कैसें निष्ठुर ॥३॥

मग सर्वज्ञें म्हणीतलें : देमती : तुम्हां मासु दीसु असों
देइजैल : शोधु : तथा देमती एथ तुम्हां असों आवडैल
तवं असो दीजैल⁴⁵⁷ : रामेश्वरबास :॥: हे लीळा एथ :॥:
परशारामबास : गणपतिमढीं :॥:

The omniscient one asked, "Why did you do that, Demati?" "The poor fish will eat it, Lord." The omniscient one said, "Demati, you children are like fish. If I extol your greatness…"[363] The Gosavi chided her this way.

291 AND HE LETS HER STAY.

One day Baïse and Demaïse had a quarrel. Afterward Baïse said, "You should throw her out, Baba. She keeps on quarreling."

Then, early the next morning, Demaïse came for the Gosavi's worship service. When the worship service was over, the Gosavi tried to send Demaïse away. (Hiraïsa version: "Leave here, Demati.")

Demaïse sang three verses:

1 My feet said they won't do it, Hari.
   "How can we go?"
2 My mind is engrossed in your feet.
   How can you send me away, Kanha?
3 Let me be entranced by your power of attraction.
   How can a dispassionate yogi's mind be so cruel?

Then the omniscient one said, "Demati, you may stay another month or so" (or, research: "Demati, you may stay as long as you would like").

(According to Rameshvarbas, this *līlā* belongs here. According to Parasharambas, it took place at Ganapati Madh.[364])

२९२ द्रीढ पुरुखु आयागमनीं आंब्रवेचानुवाद :॥:

आंबे बहुत सांचले : बाइसीं पुसीलें : बाबा : आंबे बहुत
साचले : काइ करूं : सर्वज्ञें म्हणीतलें : बाइ : द्रीढपूरुखु जरी
येती : तथा एत : तरि आंबेया वेचु होए⁴⁵⁸ :॥:

२९३ उपाध्या भेटि :॥:

तवं उपाधे परमेश्वरपुरूनि आले : गोसावी क्षेमालिंगन
दीधलें : तेहीं दंडवतें घातलीं : श्रीचरणा लागले : पुढां
बैसले : मग गोसावीयां पूढें सांघों आदरीलें : निगाले :
तेथौनि : श्रीप्रभुचे भेटीवरि सांघीतलें : श्रीप्रभु आंबेयाचा
प्रसादु दीधला : या उपरि सर्वज्ञें म्हणीतलें : नेणिजे श्रीप्रभुची
लीळा :॥: मग गोसावी आपुलीए पांती रसू चालविति :
प्रसादु देति : मध्यें बाइसांकरवि आंबे देवविति : मागुतां
विलीचां रसू वाढविति : ऐसें गोसावी तृप्तपर्यंत आंबे
खावविले : सराए केली :॥:

292 HE SAYS THAT WHEN ONE-AND-A-HALF MAN COMES, THE MANGOS WILL GET EATEN.

They had stored up a large number of mangos. Baïse asked, "We have a lot of mangos, Baba. What should we do with them?"

The omniscient one said, "My woman, if One-and-a-Half Man comes here, the mangos will get eaten up."[365]

293 HE MEETS UPADHYE.

At that point, Upadhye returned from Parameshvarpur. The Gosavi embraced him. He prostrated himself, touched the holy feet, and sat in front of the Gosavi. Then he began to tell the Gosavi what had happened from the time he left until he met Shriprabhu.[366] "Shriprabhu gave me mangos as *prasād*," he said. After that, the omniscient one said, "No one understands Shriprabhu's *līlā*."[367]

Then the Gosavi had mango pulp served as *prasād* to his own row of diners. In between he had Baïse hand out mangos. In the evening he had mango pulp served again. In this way the Gosavi fed them their fill of mangos. He satiated them.

२९४ संसारू मोचकू आंब्र कथन⁴⁵⁹ :॥:

एकू दीसीं गोसावी वीहरणा बीजें करीत असति : सवें
भक्तजनें असति : तवं एका आंबेयाचे आंबे : व्रि तैसेचि
असति : आणि : ख्रालि तैसेचि असति : ते देखोंनि
भक्तजनीं पूसीलें : जी जी : हे आंबे : अवघे काढीत
असति : तरि : या आंबेयाचे आंबे कोण्हीं काढीति ना :
नेति ना : सर्वज्ञें म्हणीतलें : हा आंबा संसारू मोचकू :
तथा मोचकू गा : संसारमोचकू म्हणीजे : काइ जी :
सर्वज्ञें म्हणीतलें : आंबा खाइजे : आणि : संसारापासौनि
मूचीजे⁴⁶⁰ : मग भक्तजनीं बनकरातें पूसीलें : हां गा : हे
आंबे अवघे उतरिता : तरि : या आंबेयाचे आंबे नूतरा तें
काइ : तेहीं म्हणीतलें : हे आंबे ख्राए तेयासि ज्वरू ए : याचे
आंबे पाख्रीरूवेंहीं न ख्राती : तरि : हे काइ कीजति : ना : हे
मीठ मोहरीयांतु दाटीजति : मग : एरे वरीख्रीचे : एरें वरीख्रें
ख्रावों एति : मग तेयां साच मानलें :॥:

294 HE TELLS ABOUT MANGOS THAT CAUSE LIBERATION FROM WORLDLY LIFE.

One day the devotees were with the Gosavi as he went out to wander. There was one mango tree with mangos still left on it, both at the top of the tree and on the lower branches. Seeing them, the devotees asked, "Lord, people are picking all the mangos on the other trees, but no one is picking the mangos on this tree, and no one is taking them." The omniscient one said, "This mango tree causes liberation from worldly life." "What does 'causes liberation from worldly life' mean, Lord?" The omniscient one said, "You eat a mango and get liberation from worldly life."[368]

Then the devotees asked the orchardist, "People pick the mangos from all the other trees, but no one picks the mangos from this tree. Why is that?" The man replied, "Anyone who eats a mango from this tree gets a fever. Not even birds eat the mangos from this tree." "Then what do people do with them?" "They pickle them with salt and mustard seeds. Then one year's crop can be eaten the following year."

After that, they considered it true.

२९५ देमाइसा करवी वाटी धुववणे४६१ :॥:

गोसावी चारनेरा बीजें करीत असति : ऐसां मार्गी कव्हणे
एके ठाइं : गोसावी आसनीं उपविष्ट असति : देमाइसें
लखुबाइसें जेवीली४६२ : लखुमबाइसें : देमाइसें वरि
वाटी सांडौनि गेलीं : देमाइसें तेयाची वाटी घेउनि निगों
बैसलीं : सर्वज्ञें म्हणीतलें : देमती : हे वाटी ठेवा : गोसावी
लखुबाइसातें म्हणीतलें : बाइ : वाटी धुवा : हीराइसापाठ :
बाइ या : आपुली वाटी धुवा : तुमचा ताटकाढा बाहीरि
गेला : मग तीयें आपुली वाटी घेउनि गेली : तीयें दीउनि :
लखुबाइसें देमाइसासि आपुली वाटी धों नेदीति :॥:

२९६ देमाइसांसि जाडी ठेंववणें :॥:

एकुदीसीं गोसावी मार्गी बीजें करीत असति : तवं
देमाइसाचे डोइए लखुबाइसाची जाडी देखवीली४६३ :
सर्वज्ञें म्हणीतलें : देमती : हे जाडि कवणाची : जी जी : हे
लखुबाइसांची : सर्वज्ञें म्हणीतलें : ठेवा : हीराइसापाठ :
तुम्ही चाला :॥छ॥: तवं मागीला कडौनि लखुबाइसें४६४
आलीं : सर्वज्ञें म्हणीतलें : बाइ : जाडि वाहावेना : तरि :
एकू कडीवळ कां खडाना : हीराइसापाठ : बाइ : आपुली
जाडि घेया : तुमचा कडिवळु तो पुढां गेला असे :॥छ॥: मग

295 LAKHUBAÏSE HAS DEMAÏSE
WASH HER BOWL.[369]

The Gosavi was seated somewhere along the road to Charner.[370] After Demaïse and Lakhubaïse ate a meal, Lakhubaïse went off, leaving her bowl for Demaïse to wash. As Demaïse had picked up Lakhubaïse's bowl and was about to go off with it, the omniscient one said, "Put down that bowl, Demati."

To Lakhubaïse the Gosavi said, "Wash the bowl, my woman." (Hiraïsa version: "Come here, my woman. Wash your bowl. Your server has gone outside.") So she picked up her bowl and left.

From that day on, Lakhubaïse did not have Demaïse wash her bowl.

296 HE HAS DEMAÏSE
PUT DOWN A BLANKET.

As the Gosavi was going along the road one day, he saw Demaïse carrying Lakhubaïse's blanket on her head. The omniscient one said, "Demati, whose blanket is this?" "It's Lakhubaïse's, Lord." "Put it down," said the omniscient one. (Hiraïsa version: "Keep on walking.")

At that point, Lakhubaïse caught up with them. The omniscient one said, "My woman, if you can't carry your blanket, why don't you hire a porter?" (Hiraïsa version: "Take your own blanket, my woman. Your porter has gone on ahead.")

तेंहीं आपुली जाडि घेतली : तीयें दीउनि आपुली जाडि :
देमाइसां : वाहों⁴⁶⁵ नेदीति :॥: रामेश्वरबास : हे लिळा एथें :
परशरामबास : अज्ञात :॥छ॥:

२९७ चारनेरीं वसति : मार्तंड रोगा उपावो :॥:

मग गोसावी चारनेरा बीजें केलें : पूर्वाभिमूर्खू लिंगाचें
देउळ : तेयाचां आंगणीं : पींपळु : तेथ गोसावीयांसि
आसन : बाइसा गोसावीयांसि अखंड वीनवीति :
अवचेयांसि : बाबा : कांही करीति : परि या मार्तंडासि
कांहींचि न करीति : ते अखंड घोकीतें⁴⁶⁶ असति : तीये
दीसीं सर्वज्ञें म्हणीतलें : मार्तंडा जा : शोधु : मार्तंडा गावांतु
जा : भिक्षा करूनि या : एथ अठरा घास संपादा⁴⁶⁷ : भिक्षा
संपादा : तुमचे अठरा रोग धाडीजति⁴⁶⁸ : तेहीं म्हणीतलें :
हो कां जी : म्हणौनि तेहीं दंडवतें घातलीं : श्रीचरणा लागले :
शोधु : आपुलेनि श्रीकरें : गोसावी झोळीयेसि गांठी
घातलीया : झोळि दीधली :॥छ॥: मग गावांतु गेले : ते
आपुलिए मामिचिया घरा गेले : तेहीं पाय धुतलें : उटिलें :
न्हाणीलें : उन्हतिन जेउं सूदलें : मग निजैले : भिक्षा अवसरीं
उठीले : मामी तुमतें कांहीं भातु असे : तरि : घेउनि या :

So she took her own blanket.

From that day on, she did not have Demaïse carry her blanket.

(According to Rameshvarbas, this *līlā* belongs here. According to Parasharambas, it is an unknown *līlā*.)[371]

297 HE STAYS OVERNIGHT IN CHARNER. HE OFFERS A TREATMENT FOR MARTANDA'S DISEASES.

Then, after the Gosavi reached Charner, he was sitting beneath a pipal tree in the courtyard of a linga temple that faced east.

Baïse used to entreat the Gosavi constantly, "Baba, you do things for everyone else, but you don't do anything at all for Martanda." She kept repeating this all the time.

That day the omniscient one said, "Go, Martanda." (Research: "Martanda, go into the village and beg for food. Come back and give me eighteen mouthfuls of food. If you give me food you've gotten as alms, your eighteen diseases will be done away with."[372]) "All right, Lord," he said, and he prostrated himself to the Gosavi and touched his holy feet. (Research: The Gosavi knotted the begging bag with his own holy hands and gave it to him.)

Martanda went into the village. He went to his maternal uncle's home. They washed his feet, anointed him, gave him a bath, and served him a piping hot meal. Then he went to sleep.

भातु काइ कराल : तुम्हां काइ तेणें : आणां पां : सांघा ना
का : काइ : गोसावी बीजें केलें असे : ना हो : कटकट
गा भास्करा : सांघतेति कां : तरि : मीं गोसावीयां कारणें
उपाहारू निफजवीतीयें : ना तें कांहीं न लगे : भातु आणां :
तेंहीं भातु रांधीला : झोळी भरिली : हीराइसापाठ : सिळेया
भाताचिया ढेंपा तेयाचिये झोळिये घातलीया :॥छ॥ः
गोसावीयापासि घेउनि आले : गोसावीयांसि झोलि दृष्टपूत
केली : मग सर्वज्ञें म्हणीतलें : मार्तंडा हें अन्न : एकें घरिचें :
ऐसें दीसत असे४६९ : ना जी गावीं एकचि पेव काढीलें :
सारिखेंचि जोन्हळे : अवघां घरिं सारिखाचि भातु : याउपरीं
बाइसीं म्हणीतलें : काइ बाबा : एथ काइ याची मायबहिण
असे : मा : ते घालिल : बापुडें उदास भीक्षा करूनि आलें :
गोसावी उगेंचि राहीले : तवं ते मागील कडौनि : ताक मिठ :
भाजी : ऐसें घेउनि आलीं : गोसावीयांसि दंडवतें घातलीं :
श्रीचरणा लागलीं : बैसलीं : सर्वज्ञें म्हणीतलें : बाइ : अन्न
अपार धाडीलें४७० : तेंहीं म्हणीतलें : जी जी : काइसा
भातु४७१ : मागील अवघेंचि सांघीतलें : गोसावी बाइसाची
वास पाहीली : सर्वज्ञें म्हणीतलें : बाइ : ऐसा असे : शोधु :
मुर्ख तुमचा मार्तंडु : मग बाइसीं घागरा बांधला : पोरा : तुज

When it was time to go begging, he got up. "Aunt," he said, "if you have any cooked rice, bring me some." "What will you do with the rice?" "What difference does it make to you? Just bring it!" "Tell me! Has the Gosavi come here?" "Yes." "Oh, no, Bhaskar!* If you had told me, I would have cooked food for the Gosavi." "No, that's not necessary. Bring some rice."

She cooked some rice and put it into the begging bag. (Hiraïsa version: She put lumps of stale rice into his begging bag.) He brought it to the Gosavi and had him purify it with his glance. The omniscient one said, "Martanda, it looks as if this food is all from one house."[373] "Lord, they have only one grain cellar in the village. Everyone's millet is the same, and they have the same rice in all the houses."

At that, Baïse said, "Do you know what, Baba? Doesn't his maternal aunt live here? She must have put it in the bag. The poor fellow has begged lazily." The Gosavi kept silent.

At that point, Martanda's aunt came there, following him, bringing buttermilk, salt, and cooked vegetables. She prostrated herself to the Gosavi, touched his holy feet, and sat down.

"My woman," said the omniscient one, "you've sent a vast amount of food!"[374] "Lord," she replied, "it was just a little rice."[375] She told him everything that had happened.

The Gosavi was looking at Baïse. "My woman," said the omniscient one to her, "that is what he is like." (Research: "Your Martanda is a fool.") Then Baïse upbraided Martanda, saying, "My child, I criticized Baba on account of you."

———

* Martanda; both are names for the Sun.

कारणें बाबातें उरोधिलें : सर्वज्ञें म्हणींतलें : एथौनि म्हणितलें
तें करीतेति तरि तुमचे रोग धाडिजेति : मार्तंडा इतुले दीस
आपुले हीताहीत नेणा : परि : ऐसें कां होइल : पसेयाचें
पाइलियें कां एइल४७२ : गोसावीयांसि तेथ वसति जाली :॥ः

२९८ करंजखेडीं पानुनाएका हाटग्रहीं अवस्थान :॥ः

तेथौनि गोसावी करंजखेडा बीजें केलें : मग नगरापुर्वें वृक्षा
एका खालि आसन : पाउसु थोरू येत होता : बाइसें नगरांतु
बीढार पाहावेया गेलीं : कव्हणीं एकीं म्हणीतलें :
पानुनायकाचें हाटग्रह असे तें मागा : बाइसें तेयाचीया
घरासि गेलीं : म्हणीतलें : बाइ : तुमचें हाटग्रह असे : तें
आमचेया बाबासि दीया : तेहीं म्हणीतलें : बाइ : तथा आइ :
तेथ देवता असे : ते वसों नेंदी : तुम्हीं दीया पां : आमचेया
बाबाचां ठाइ तैसें कांहीं नाहीं : तेहीं बीढार दीधलें : बाइसें
गोसावीयांपासि आलीं : अवघें सांघितलें : मग गोसावी
हाटग्रहा बीजें केलें : पुर्वपसिम हातवटी : हाटवटीचां
पसिमिली शिरां उत्तरिले वोळीं घर : तेथ गोसावीयासि
अवस्थान : मास दोनि : दक्षिणिल हाटदार : गोसावी
बुजवीलें : उत्तरीलेनि दारेंहूनि४७३ राज्य करिति :॥छ॥ः

The omniscient one said to him, "If you had done what I said, your diseases would have been done away with. For a long time, Martanda, you have not known what is good for you and what is bad. But how could that happen? Can you get a bushel's worth for a handful?"[376]

The Gosavi stayed there overnight.

298 IN KARANJKHED HE STAYS IN PANUNAYAK'S HOUSE IN THE BAZAAR.

From there the Gosavi went to Karanjkhed. He was sitting under a tree to the east of the town. Rain was falling heavily. When Baïse went into the town to look for lodgings, someone told her, "Panunayak has a house in the bazaar. Ask for that."

Baïse went to his house and said, "My woman, give our Baba your house in the bazaar." She replied, "There's a deity in that house, my woman." (Or, "Mother.") "It doesn't let anyone stay there." "Our Baba doesn't care about anything like that. Give him the house!"

She let them use it as their lodgings. Baïse came back to the Gosavi and told him everything that had happened, and then the Gosavi went to the house in the bazaar.

The bazaar was arranged from east to west. The house was at the western end, in the northern row. The Gosavi stayed there for two months. He had them block the southern door, the one that opened onto the market, and he went in and out by the northern door.

२९९ पानुनायका वातापनौति ः॥ः

बाइसें प्रतदिनीं पानुनायकाचेया घरा भिक्षे जाति ः गोसावी
तिये बीढारीं राहीले ः तेणें तेयासि थोर आश्चर्य जालें ः बाइसें
जाति ः तेव्हळि पाट बैसों घालीति ः सोपस्कार भिक्षा देति ः
एकुदिसीं बाइसीं पुसीलें ः हावो घरधनी दीसेति ना ः
ते वातें तीन वरीखें मोडीखोडी करूनि घातले असति ः
बाइसीं म्हणीतलें ः आमचे गोसावी रोग धाडीति ः आमचेया
बाबाचेया दरिसना येतुका ः आणि ः वातु जाइल ः
तेयाचिया ब्राह्मणीं म्हणीतलें ः हाट घरीचे पुरुषु असति ः
तेयांची येकें आईसें आलीं ः तेही म्हणीतलें ः आमचेया
बाबाचेया दरिसना एतु कां ः आणि ः तेयांचा वातु जाइल ः
मग गोसावीयाचेया दरिसनासि आले ः दोनी आंगीया ः
माथां ः दौडि ः तेयावरि पासौडी पांगुरले ः वरि जाडीचे
कोंगटें ः ऐस गोसावीयांचेया दरिसनासि आले ः
गोसावीयांसि दंडवतें घातलीं ः श्रीचरणा लागले ः मग जवळि
बैसले ः सर्वज्ञें म्हणीतलें ः तुमचा देहीं कांहीं रूजा असे ः हो
जी ः कांहीं असे ः जी जी ः वातु असे[४७४] ः इतुलाही वारा न
साहे जी ः एकी उसीसां सगडी ः एकि पाइतां सगडी ः दोनि
आंगिया ः दोनि पासोडिया ः दोनि पागा ः एकि जाडि[४७५] ः
इतुकें असे जी ः परि वायो जाए ना ः सर्वज्ञें म्हणीतलें ः

299   HE CURES PANUNAYAK'S
RHEUMATISM.

Every day Baïse would go to beg at Panunayak's house. The people of his household were amazed that the Gosavi had stayed in those lodgings. When Baïse went to Panunayak's house, they would set out a low wooden seat for her, and they would give her delicious food as alms.

One day Baïse asked, "Why do I never see the master of the house?" "He has been crippled by rheumatism for the past three years." "Our Gosavi cures diseases," said Baïse. "If Panunayak comes for our Baba's *darśan,* his rheumatism will go away."

Panunayak's wife told him, "A woman disciple of the holy man who is staying in our house in the bazaar came here. She said, 'If he comes for our Baba's *darśan,* his rheumatism will go away.'"

So he came for *darśan* of the Gosavi. He came for *darśan* wearing two cloaks, a turban on his head, a thick shawl wrapped over that, and a blanket draped on top. He prostrated himself to the Gosavi and touched his holy feet, then sat down nearby.

The omniscient one asked him, "Are you ill?" "Yes, Lord, I am. I have rheumatism, Lord.[377] I can't stand even a light breeze, Lord. Even with a stove at my side, a stove at my feet, even though I wear two cloaks, two thick shawls, two turbans, and a blanket, Lord, the rheumatism won't go away."

The omniscient one said, "Don't light the stoves today."[378] "I can't manage that, Lord," he said. The omniscient one said,

आजी सगडीया नको घालुं४७६ : तेहीं म्हणीतलें : जी जी :
मज : न गमे जी : सर्वज़ें म्हणीतलें : उपद्रो उपजैल : तरि :
मग घाला४७७ : मग तेहीं सगडीया फेडीलीया४७८ : मग
बीढारासि गेले : च्यारि पाहार सूखेंचि निद्रा केली : उदीयांचि
गोसावीयांचेया दरिसना आले : दंडवतें घातलीं : श्रीचरणा
लागले : बैसले : मग गोसावी पुसिलें : काली सगडीया न
घलाचि तरि उपद्रो उपनला४७९ : जी जी कांहींचि नाहीं :
सूखेंचि नीद्रा आली जी : सर्वज़ें म्हणीतलें : आजि आतां
जाडि नको पांगरो४८० : जी जी : जाडि वीण न गमे जी :
सर्वज़ें म्हणीतलें : उपद्रो उपजैल तरि काइ घेवों नैये : मग ते
घरासि आले : जाडि फेडीली : च्यारी पाहार सूखें निजैले :
एरी दीसीं उदीयांचि आले : दंडवतें घातलीं : श्रीचरणा
लागले : बैसले : गोसावी पुसिलें : जाडि न पांगुराचि : तरि
काइ उपद्रो : उपनला४८१ : जी जी : कांहींचि नाहीं : सूखें
निद्रा आलि जी : सर्वज़ें म्हणीतलें : आजि पासोडी एकी
नको पांगरों४८२ : पासोडीविण न गमे जी : सर्वज़ें म्हणीतलें :
उपद्रो उठिल : तरि : मग पांगुरा : हो कां जी : मग घरा गेले :
निद्रा केली : उदियांचि गोसावीयांचेया दरिसना आले :
दंडवतें घातलीं : श्रीचरणा लागले : बैसले : सर्वज़ें म्हणीतलें :
पासौडी न पांगराचि : तरि : कांहीं उपद्रो उपनला :॥छ॥: ना
जी च्यारी पहार स्वस्त गेले४८३ : सर्वज़ें म्हणीतलें : आजि
एकि आंगी : एक पांगुरण नको : होकां जी : मग ते पासोडी
न पांगुरति : पाग बांधति : कदाचित आंगी लेति : मग
गोसावीयाचेया दरिसना एति : नगरांतु हींडति : हाटवटिये

"If you start to suffer, then light them."[379] So he dispensed with the stoves.[380] He went home and slept soundly for twelve hours.

Early the next morning he came for *darsan* of the Gosavi. He prostrated himself, touched the holy feet, and sat down. The Gosavi asked him, "Did you suffer yesterday from not lighting the stoves?" "Not at all, Lord. I slept soundly."

The omniscient one said, "Now today don't sleep under the blanket."[381] "I can't manage without the blanket, Lord." The omniscient one said, "If you start to suffer, can't you take it back?" So he came home, took off the blanket, and slept soundly for twelve hours.

Early the next morning, he came to the Gosavi, prostrated himself, touched the holy feet, and sat down. The Gosavi asked, "Did you suffer by not sleeping under the blanket?" "No, Lord. Not at all. I slept soundly, Lord."

The omniscient one said, "Today leave off one of the thick shawls."[382] "I can't manage without that shawl, Lord." The omniscient one said, "If you start to suffer, put it on later." "All right, Lord." So he went home and slept.

Early the next morning he came for *darsan* of the Gosavi. He prostrated himself, touched the holy feet, and sat down. The omniscient one asked, "Did you suffer by not sleeping under the thick shawl?" "No, Lord. I slept peacefully for twelve hours." The omniscient one said, "Today leave off one cloak and one more cover." "All right, Lord."

So he stopped covering himself with a thick shawl. He would wear a turban, and sometimes he wore a cloak. He would come for *darsan* of the Gosavi. He would wander around in the town. He would go to the market. The towns-

जाति : नगरीचा लोकू म्हणे : हाटघरा पुरुषु आले असति :
तेंहीं कैसा पाननायकु उजरिला : कांमठ पडितालुं जाति :
मग तेयांचे दाइ म्हणति : हा कोणे गा उपचारिला : या हातीं
खावों न ल्हावों : ऐसा गोसावी तेयाचा वातु फेडीला⁴⁸⁴ :॥:

३०० तथा उपाहारा दीपनशक्ति देणें :॥:

एकुदीसु : गोसावीयांतें पानुनायकें वीनवीलें जी जी : वायो
गेला : पर दीपन नाहीं : हीराइसापाठ : गोसावी पुसीलें :
तुम्हांसि पुर्वीं कवण अन्न रूचे : तेहीं म्हणितलें : जी जी :
मज उडीदान्न रूचे जी : सर्वज्ञें म्हणीतलें : वडे प्रधान
करूनि एथ एकू उपाहारु करा :॥: सर्वज्ञें म्हणीतलें : एथ
उपाहारु करा : मग होईल : मग तेहीं उपाहारु केला : वडे
प्रधान करूनि : कोरडे वडे : आंबिचे वडे : मुख्य करूनि :
उपाहारु निफजविला : पुजाद्रव्यें मेळविलीं : मग उपाहारु
घेउनि आले : मग गोसावीयांसि पुजा केली : बाइसीं ताट
केलें : भक्तजना : ठाये केले : तेयां लागौनि ती वरिसां
तांदळाचे सीत आणिलें : तें तेयांसि वाढिलें : सर्वज्ञें म्हणीतलें
बाइ अवघेयां सरिसें वाढा⁴⁸⁵ : बाइसीं म्हणीतलें : बाबा
बाधिल : सर्वज्ञें म्हणीतलें : न बधी : मग भक्तजना सहीत
वाढिलें : मग गोसावियांसि आरोगणा : भक्तजना जेवणें
जालीं : पानुनायेक तृप्त परियंत अवघीं अन्नें जेवीलें : मग

people said, "See how the holy man who has come to the house in the market has cured Panunayak!"

He would go to check on his fields, and his relatives would say, "Who has cured him? He used not to be able to eat with those hands of his."

In this way, the Gosavi cured his rheumatism.

300   AND HE GIVES HIM
A GOOD APPETITE.

One day Panunayak appealed to the Gosavi: "My rheumatism is gone, Lord, but I have lost my appetite." (Hiraïsa version: The Gosavi asked, "What food did you used to like?" "I liked food made with *uḍīd* dal, Lord," he replied. The omniscient one said, "Eat a meal of mostly *vaḍās* here.)[383] Eat the food here," said the omniscient one, "and then you will get better."

So he had a meal prepared that consisted mostly of *vaḍās:* primarily dry *vaḍās* and *vaḍās* in sour broth. After he had had the food prepared and had gathered the materials for puja, he brought the food and did puja to the Gosavi.

Baïse served the food on a plate for the Gosavi, and on leaf plates for the devotees. She served Panunayak rice made with three-year-old grains that she got for him.

"Serve everyone the same thing, my woman," said the omniscient one.[384] "It will upset his stomach, Baba," replied Baïse. "It will not upset it," said the omniscient one.

So she served Panunayak along with the devotees. The Gosavi ate his meal and the devotees ate theirs. Panunayak

गोसावीयांसि गुळळा विडा जाला⁴⁸⁶ : ते बीढारासि गेले :
रात्रीं म्हणीतलें : अजि आम्हीं सदन्न जेवीलें : असों : रात्रीं
कांहीं उपद्रो होइल : तरि वीसदेवो दडपौनि ठेवा हो : मग
तेहीं निद्रा केली : मध्यान्हे एके रात्रीं : तेया भुक लागली :
आणि ते उठिले : ब्राह्मणितें म्हणीतलें : वाति लावी हो : ते
भियाली : वाति लावीली : मग पुसिलें : कांहीं उपद्रो जाला :
तेहीं म्हणीतलें : मज थोर क्षुधा लागली असे : पीडा होति
असे : कांहीं अन्न असे : तेहीं म्हणीतलें : अन्न अवघें पाळलें :
वडे आणि तुप असे : हो कां : घेउनि या : मग ते वडे तुप
जेवीलें : आंचवलो : तांबूळ घेतलें : माघौतें निजैले :
उदीयांचि गोसावीयांचीया दर्शना आले : दंडवतें घातलीं :
श्रीचरणा लागले : बैसले : सर्वज्ञें म्हणीतलें : रात्रीं तुमतें
बाधीना कीं⁴⁸⁷ : जी जी : तें जालें ऐसें : रात्रीं थोर भुक
लागली : अवघें अन्न पाळलें : वडे होते : ते आठ वडे तुपेंसि
जेवीलों : मग निजैलों : ऐसा गोसावी तेयासि दीपनशक्ति
दीधली :॥:

३०१ तथा सितळानंद नामकरण :॥:

एकुदीसीं : उदयाचा पूजावसर जालेया नंतरें : गोसावी
वीहरणा सेंदुराळेया बीजें केलें : तळेयाचिये नृत्यकोणी
पाळीवरि आसन : पानुनायक⁴⁸⁸ कामठु पडीताळावेया
आले होते : तेहीं तेथ⁴⁸⁹ आइकीलें : सेतकरी सांघीतलें :

ate his fill of all the foods. Then the Gosavi rinsed his mouth and chewed pan.

Panunayak went home. At night he said, "I ate good food today. So be it. I'll have some trouble tonight, so keep the fire banked." Then he went to sleep.

In the middle of the night he got hungry. He got up and said to his wife, "Light the lamp." She got frightened. She lit the lamp, then asked, "Are you having some trouble?" "I am very hungry," he said. "I'm starving. Is there any food?"[385] "All the regular food is gone," she said. "There are *vaḍās* and ghee." "All right. Bring that." Then he ate *vaḍās* and ghee. He rinsed his mouth, chewed pan, and went back to sleep.

Early the next morning he came for *darśan* of the Gosavi. He prostrated himself, touched the holy feet, and sat down. The omniscient one asked him, "Your stomach wasn't upset last night, was it?"[386] "What happened, Lord, is that I got very hungry last night. All the regular food was gone, but there were some *vaḍās*. I ate eight *vaḍās* with ghee, and then I went to sleep."

In this way, the Gosavi gave him a good appetite.

301 AND HE GIVES HIM THE NAME SITALANANDA.

After the morning worship service one day, the Gosavi went wandering to the Sendurale reservoir. He was sitting on the embankment at the southwest corner of the reservoir. Panunayak heard about this when he came to check on his fields: a farmer told him that the Gosavi had gone to

जें : गोसावी सेंदुराळेंया बीजें केलें असे : आले : दंडवतें
घातलीं : श्रीचरणा लागले : मग गोसावीयां पुढां पालखति
घालूनि बैसले : भटोबासि गोसावीयांसि कमळाची पुजा
करावी ऐसें म्हणौनि कमळें तोडावेया रिगत होते : गोसावी
भटोबासातें डोळा घातला : भटोबासीं पानुनाएकातें धरिलें :
पालवीं धरूनि वोढिलें : ते बोबाइलें : जी जी : मज
सीतोळोदक न साहे : भटोबासीं उदकामध्यें नेले : आणि
पव्हों लागले : जवं जवं पव्हति तवं सूखानंदचि होए :
गोसावी बोलावीति : परि : न येति : मग वाडुवेळां निगाले :
गोसावीयां पूढां सांघितले : हीराइसापाठ : सर्वज्ञें
म्हणीतलें : नायेको : एथौनि बोलाविंतां न या तें काइ :॥छ॥:
जी जी : जवं जवं : हीव ऐसें पाणी लागे : तवं तवं
सुखानंदुचि होए : जी : सर्वज्ञें म्हणीतलें : तरि तुम्हांसि
सितळानंदु म्हणा४९० : मग बाइसीं कमळीं पुजा केली :
गोसावीयांसि आरोगण जाली : मग वीळीचां गोसावी
बिढारा बीजें केलें :॥:

३०२ आबाइसां : महदाइसां भेटि :॥:

देव : भट : आबाइसें : महदाइसें : गोसावीयांचिया दरिसना
आलीं : दंडवतें घातलीं : श्रीचरणा लागलीं : भेटि जाली :॥:

Sendurale. Panunayak came there. He prostrated himself to the Gosavi, touched the holy feet, and then sat cross-legged in front of him.

Bhatobas was getting into the water to pick lotuses in order to do a lotus puja to the Gosavi. The Gosavi winked at Bhatobas. Bhatobas grabbed Panunayak, took hold of the end of his garment, and pulled. Panunayak shouted, "Oh, Lord! I can't stand cold water!"

Bhatobas pulled him into the water. He began to swim. The more he swam, the more he felt pure bliss. The Gosavi called to him, but he did not come.

Eventually, after a long time, he came out. He told the Gosavi what had happened. (Hiraïsa version: The omniscient one asked, "Why didn't you come when I called you, Nayak?") "Lord, as long as I felt the cold water, I felt pure bliss." The omniscient one said, "So we'll call you Sitalananda."*

Then Baïse performed puja with the lotuses, and the Gosavi ate his meal. Then, in the evening, the Gosavi went back to his lodgings.

302 HE MEETS ABAÏSE AND MAHADAÏSE.

Dev, Bhat, Abaïse, and Mahadaïse came for *darśan* of the Gosavi. They greeted him, prostrating themselves and touching his holy feet.

---

* "One for whom cold is bliss."

३०३ माहादाइ वस्त्राची आंगी भटोबासा देणें :॥:

गोसावी महादाइसातें पुसीलें : बाइ : हें तुमचें वस्त्रा कीतुलें
एकु दी पांगुरलें : आणि : आंगीं सिवीली : मग आंगीं लेइलें :
आतां ते आंगी वानरेसासि दीजो⁴⁹¹ : महदाइसीं म्हणीतलें :
हो कां : जी : दीजो कां जी : महदाइसां सूख जालें : सर्वज्ञें
म्हणीतलें : घेया गा वानरेया : भटोबासीं आंगी घेतली :
लेइले : श्रीचरणा लागले : हे लीळा : हीराइसापाठ
हीवरळिये : मग रिधपुरासि निगाले :॥:

३०४ आबैसां मयोररेखीं म्हणीये :॥:

गोसावी आबैसातें म्हणीतलें⁴⁹² : बाइ : एथ तुम्ही दीसवडि
दोनि मोरें लेहा : मासा दीसा⁴⁹³ : मग तेहीं वान मेळवीले :
दीसवडि दो दो मोरें लेखति : गोसावी वीहरणाहुनि बीजें
करिति : मोरें पाहाति : निकी नव्हति तरि चुकि ठेविति :
हीराइसापाठ : याचा पाख⁴⁹⁴ निका नव्हेचि : याचि चांचु
निकी नव्हेचि : याचा पावो निका नव्हेचि : ऐसें चुकि
दाखविति : मग तियें एरि दीसीं बरवें लीहीति :॥छ॥: एकाधें

303 HE GIVES BHATOBAS THE CLOAK MADE FROM THE GARMENT MAHADAÏ GAVE HIM.

The Gosavi asked Mahadaïse, "My woman, I wore this garment you gave me draped over my shoulders for a long time.[387] Then it was made into a cloak, and I have been wearing the cloak. Now may I give the cloak to Lord Monkey?" That pleased Mahadaïse. "All right, Lord," she said. "Please give it to him, Lord."

"Take it, Lord Monkey," said the omniscient one. Bhatobas took the cloak. He put it on and touched the Gosavi's holy feet.

(According to Hiraïsa's version, this *līḷā* took place at Hivarali.[388]) Afterward they set out for Riddhipur.

304 ABAÏSE GETS THE TASK OF DRAWING PEACOCKS.

The Gosavi said to Abaïse, "My woman, draw two peacocks here every day for a month."[389]

So she got some paint, and she drew two peacocks every day. When the Gosavi returned from wandering, he would look at the peacocks. If they were not right, he would point out the mistakes. (Hiraïsa version: "This one's wing is all wrong. This one's beak is all wrong. This one's foot is all wrong." After he pointed out the mistakes this way, the next day she would draw them right.)

दीसीं एक उणें लीहीति : मग गोसावी म्हणति : बाइ : एक
मोर एथीचें लागा : अधीक लीहीति तरि म्हणति : हें तुमचें
लागे⁴⁹⁵ : ऐसीया परी च्यान्हीं भीती मोरें भरीलीया⁴⁹⁶ :॥:

३०५ भट होडे⁴⁹⁷ अद्दश्य होणें :॥:

एकुदीसीं गोसावी रामतीर्थाकडे बीजें केलें : भट⁴⁹⁸ : बाइसें
सरीसीं असति : वीहरण सारूनि बीढारा बीजें करीतां :
मार्गी चालतां : गोसावी म्हणीतलें : हां गा : हें उठिताए :
उठीता : हें बैसताए : बैसतां : हें धावैल तरि टाकाल⁴⁹⁹ :
भटीं म्हणीतलें : हो जी : सर्वज्ञें म्हणीतलें : वानरेश चळवळे
दीसताति : हे टाकीति⁵⁰⁰ : मग गोसावी बहीरवासू
खोवीला : आंगीं खोवीली : आंगीचीया बाहीया वरतीया
केलीया : गोसावी गजगति बीजें केलें : भटीं वोली
काखे सूदलीं : गोसावीयां पाठीं धांवत जाति : गोसावी
हातावीहाती पूढें जाति : भट गोसावीयांतें टाकीत जाति :
परि टाकतिना : वोहळापासि गोसावीयांतें सीओं गेले :
आणि : अद्दश्ये जाले : भट गोसावीयांतें पाहो लागले : तवं
न देखति : आणि : बाइसें पडिलीं : मग प्रगट जालें : तवं
बाइसें पडीलीं देखीलीं : गोसावी बाइसातें हातीं धरीलीं :
उठवीलें : सावधें जाली : मग पुसीलें : बाबा : आपण के

Some days she would draw one too few. Then the Gosavi would say, "My woman, you owe me one peacock." If she drew too many, he would say, "I owe you one."

In this way, all four walls got filled with peacocks.

305   HE DISAPPEARS AFTER CHALLENGING BHAT.

One day the Gosavi went to Ramtirtha with Bhat and Baïse.[390] He had finished wandering and was returning to their lodgings. As he walked along the road, the Gosavi said, "When I stand up, you stand up. When I sit down, you sit down. If I run, can you catch up with me?" "Yes, Lord," said Bhat. The omniscient one said, "Lord Monkey looks energetic. He'll catch up with me."

Then the Gosavi tucked up his dhoti. He tucked in his cloak and pushed up the sleeves. The Gosavi set out at a stately gait. Bhat stuck his fine silk shawl under his arms and went running after the Gosavi.

The Gosavi would stay an arm's length ahead of him. Bhat would almost catch up to the Gosavi but would not quite reach him. When they got close to a stream, he reached out to touch the Gosavi. And the Gosavi disappeared. Bhat began to look for him, but he was not to be seen. Baïse collapsed on the ground.

When the Gosavi finally reappeared, he saw Baïse lying on the ground. He took her by the hand and got her up. She came to and asked, "Where were you, Baba?" "My woman,"

होतेयां : सर्वज्ञें म्हणीतलें : बाइ : हें ए रींगणीए तळि
होतें ॥छ॥ः मग बाइसां : भटां आश्चर्यें जालें : मग गोसावी
बीढारा बीजें केलें ॥ः

३०६ प्रकाशदेवां गुंफे गमन ॥ः

एकूदीसीं गोसावी प्रकाश देवांचिए गुंफेसि बीजें केलें :
सरीसे भट असति : गावां उत्तरे पैलाडि गुंफा होति॥५०१ :
प्रकाशदेवो आपूलेयां सिक्षांसीं नगरामध्यें गेले होते :
गोसावी गुंफा उघडवीली : भीतरिला वोटेयावरि आसन :
चरणक्षाळण करवीलें : साहाणेवरि चंदन होतें : तेयाचा
आपणेयांसि आडा रेखविला : सुकली ऐसी माळ होती :
ते श्रीकंठीं घातलि : अक्षेता लाविलीया : पाणिभातु
पाहाविला॥५०२ : गोसावीयांसि पाणिभाताची आरोगणा
दीधली : सूकलीं ऐसीं पानें : घोटीं येसी फोडि होति : तेयाचा
गोसावी विडा घेतला : मग गोसावी गुंफेचें कवाड
बांधविलें : गोसावी बीजें केलें : तवं मार्गीं प्रकाशदेव एत
देखीलें : गोसावी भटोबासातें म्हणीतलें : तुम्हीं यांसि
नमस्कारू कराेगा : तेहीं म्हणीतलें : यांचे जरि आम्हांसि
करीती : तरि : आम्हीं यांसि करूनि॥५०३ : सर्वज्ञें म्हणीतलें :
या अभिमानु मां : एथ काइ तैसे असे ॥छ॥ः सर्वज्ञें
म्हणीतलें : उपाधि मानिजे : तवं ते आले : गोसावीयांचें

replied the omniscient one, "I was at the foot of this thorny bush." Baïse and Bhat were amazed.

Then the Gosavi went to their lodgings.

306 HE GOES TO PRAKASHDEV'S CELL.

Prakashdev's hermit's cell was to the north of the village, across the river. One day the Gosavi went there, with Bhat accompanying him. Prakashdev had gone with his disciples into the town.

The Gosavi had his own disciples open the cell, and he sat inside on the pedestal. He had them wash his feet and draw a horizontal line on his forehead with sandalwood paste from the grindstone. They put a dried-up garland that was there around his holy neck, and they put some unbroken grains of rice on his head. He had them look for water-and-rice gruel.[391] They gave the Gosavi a meal of it, and he chewed pan made of some dried-up betel leaves and pebble-like pieces of betel nut that were there. Then the Gosavi had them fasten the door of the cell.

As the Gosavi was leaving, they saw Prakashdev coming along the road. The Gosavi said to Bhatobas, "Greet him reverently." "If his people do that to us," replied Bhatobas, "then we will do it to him."[392] The omniscient one said, "That would be arrogant! Am I like that?" The omniscient one said, "Respect the conventions."[393]

दर्शन जालें : प्रकाशदेवीं दंडवतें घातलीं : भटीं प्रकाशदेवां
नमस्कारू केला : तथा भक्तजनीं : गोसावीयां अवघें
सांघीतलें : खुंटिएची माळ पुजा करवीली : पाणीभातु
आरोगीले : हीराइसापाठ : हें तुमचीए गुंफेसि गेलें होतें :
गुंफा उघडवीली : भीतरि वोटेयावरि आसन : चरण
क्षाळण५०४ जालें : तुमचें चंदन लाविलें : हा नव्हे टीळा : या
नव्हति अक्षता : लाविलीया : पाणिभातु आरोगण केला :
हा नव्हे विडा घेतला : ऐसें गोसावी प्रकाशदेवां पूढें सांघति
असति :॥छ॥: प्रकाशदेव तोखों लागले : जी जी : दैवाचा :
भाग्याचा : मीं : कृत्याकृत्य केला : सूखीया केलां : ऐसे
शब्दाप्रति तोखति जाति : मग प्रकाशदेवीं सीक्षांतें
म्हणीतलें : देखीलें गा कैसी निराभिमानिनि वस्तु : मग :
गोसावी बीढारासि बीजें केलें :॥:

३०७ तथा गर्वानुवाद :॥:

भट : नदीं धोत्रें धुआवेआ गेलें होतें : तेथ प्रकाशदेव भेटले :
गुंफे घेउनि गेलें : मग भटातें म्हणीतलें : नागदेया तुवां
संसारू सांडीला : निकें केलें : तरि : पुस : कांहीं : बोलता
असे : परि : पुसता नाहीं : एन्हविं आचार्या नावें कांकण
बांधीलें असे : मग गोसावीयांपासी आलें : सर्वज्ञें म्हणीतलें :
केउते गेले होतेति : जी जी : प्रकाशदेवाचीए गुंफेते : ऐसें

With that, Prakashdev arrived. He had *darśan* of the Gosavi and prostrated himself. Bhat (or, the devotees) greeted him reverently. The Gosavi told him everything that had happened: "I had them do my puja with the garland that was hanging on the peg on the wall. I ate some water-and-rice gruel." (Hiraïsa version: The Gosavi told him, "I went to your cell. I had them open the cell, and I sat inside on the pedestal. They washed my feet and put some of your sandalwood paste on me. See this forehead mark? See these unbroken grains of rice that have been put on me? I ate a meal of water-and-rice gruel. I took some pan. See?")

Prakashdev was delighted to hear this. In his delight, he said things like, "I am lucky, Lord; I am fortunate. You've made me satisfied; you've made me happy." Then Prakashdev said to his disciples, "Do you see what a humble Absolute being he is?"

After that, the Gosavi went back to their lodgings.

307 AND HE TELLS ABOUT PRIDE.

When Bhat had gone to the river to wash dhotis, he met Prakashdev there. Prakashdev took him to his cell, then said to him, "Nagdev, it's good that you have given up worldly life. But you should ask me something. You are telling me things, but you are not asking me any questions. If you don't ask me anything, you are claiming the title of Acharya."*

Then Bhat came to the Gosavi. The omniscient one asked him, "Where did you go?" "To Prakashdev's cell, Lord. He

* Teacher.

म्हणति : जी जी : आचार्या नावें कांकण बांधलें असे : ब्रह्म
सांघता असे परि पूसता नाहीं : म्हणौनि आवघें सांघीतलें :
सर्वज्ञें म्हणीतलें : आज्ञानाचेनि प्रसादें :॥: तेहींचि कां न
म्हणावें५०५ : सर्वज्ञें म्हणीतलें : आज्ञानाचेनि प्रसादें हा जनू
सुखीया होउनि असे५०६ :॥:

३०८ वानरा नामकरण :॥:

एकुदीसीं : गोसावी रामतीर्थासि बीजें केलें : गोसावीयांसि
गुंफा करावेयाचि प्रवृत्ति जाली : रामनाथा वाव्ये पौळी
भितरि गुंफा करविली : भिंती घालविलिया : धाबे
करावेया : भट पींपळावरि फाटे मोडावेया वळघले :
तेयाचि पींपळातलि गोसावीयांसि आसन : भट एकू फाटा
धरिति : आणि : खालिल कोरडा फाटा पाएं मोडिति : ऐसे
डाहळिएहुनि डाहाळिएसि जाति : तें गोसावी देखीलें :
मग म्हणीतलें : कैसें वानर ऐसें दीसत असे : एरिहुनि एरि
डाहाळिए जात असे : हा वानरा होए५०७ : ते दीउनि गोसावी
वानरा ऐसें म्हणति : मग ते गुंफा गोसावी करविली :॥:

was saying, 'You are claiming the title of Acharya. You are telling me about the Absolute, but you are not asking me any questions.'" And he told the Gosavi everything that had happened.

The omniscient one said, "By the grace of ignorance, why shouldn't he say this?" The omniscient one said, "By the grace of ignorance, such people are happy."[394]

308 HE GIVES BHATOBAS THE NAME MONKEY.

One day the Gosavi went to Ramtirtha. He was inclined to build a hermit's cell there. He had them build the cell to the northwest of the Ramnath temple, inside the compound wall.

After they had built the walls, Bhat climbed up into a pipal tree to break off branches for the roof. The Gosavi was sitting at the foot of that same tree. Bhat was moving from branch to branch, holding onto one branch and breaking off a lower, dry one with his feet.

When the Gosavi saw this, he said, "How much he looks like a monkey, going from one branch to another! He is a monkey!"[395] From that day on, the Gosavi called him Monkey.

Then the Gosavi had them complete the hermit's cell.

३०९ देवाकरवि जाडि तुणवणें :॥:

एकुदीसीं गोसावीयांतें देवीं वीनवीलें : जी जी : सापें माझी
विद्या पातळ जाली : गोसावीयांची जाडि उदै खादली कां
उंदरीं खादली होती तें नेणिजे : सर्वज्ञें म्हणीतलें : हे जाडि
सांदाल : तवं तवं तुमची वीद्या साधैल : मासू दी जा : भीक्षा
करा : गंगातटीं भोजन करा : देउळीं निद्रा करा : वृक्षमूळीं
बैसौनि जाडि तुणा : तुमची वीद्या सांधैल५०८ : जी जी :
म्हणौनि : जाडि हातीं घेतली : श्रीचरणा लागले : मग
नीगाले : ते सागवखेडेयांसि गेले : एल्हंभटाचेया
डोल्हारेयावरि जाडि तुणिति : ते उटिति : न्हाणिति :
ताटीं ठाणवै : तुपीं भातीं जेउं सुति : बाजेसूपवतियांवरि
नीजविति : ऐसी मासूदीसावरि जाडि तुणीली :॥: मग
गोसावीयांचेया दरिसना आले : मग गोसावीयांसि
क्षेमालिंगन दीधलें : तेहीं दंडवतें घातलीं : श्रीचरणा लागले :
बैसले : जाडि पुढां ठेवीली : बाइसीं जाडि हातीं घेउनि
पाहीली : बाबा : जाडि कैसी बरवी सांदीली : जैसी सांदीली
जाणवेना५०९ : सर्वज्ञें म्हणीतलें : बाइ : जाडि सांधीली परि
वीद्या न संदेचि : तेंहीं म्हणीतलें : हो जी : सर्वज्ञें म्हणीतलें :
एथौनि म्हणीतलें तें काइ तुम्ही केलें : एथौनि तुमतें
सांगवखेडेयां धाडीलें : एल्हंभटांचां घरीं उष्णोदकें स्नान :
आडवाटीं ठाणवै जेवण : डोल्हारेयावरि बैसौनि जाडि
तुणा : एथौनि काइ तुमतें हें म्हणीतलें : तुमतें एथौनि
म्हणीतलें : भीक्षा करा : गंगातटीं भोजन करा : देउळीं निद्रा

309   HE HAS DEV MEND A BLANKET.

One day Dev appealed to the Gosavi. "Lord," he said, "these days my knowledge has grown thin."

Something had eaten holes in the Gosavi's blanket, whether termites or mice no one knows. The omniscient one said, "Mend this blanket. As you do so, your knowledge will improve. Go away for a month or so, beg for food, eat your meals on the riverbank, and sleep in a temple. Sit at the foot of a tree and mend the blanket. Your knowledge will improve."[396] "Yes, Lord," he said, and he picked up the blanket. He touched the holy feet and left.

He went to Sangavkhede, where he mended the blanket sitting on Elhambhat's swing. They would anoint him and bathe him. They fed him ghee and rice, served on a plate with a lampstand, and they gave him a bed with a mattress to sleep on. After he had spent a month this way, mending the blanket, he came for *darśan* of the Gosavi. He embraced the Gosavi, prostrated himself, touched the holy feet, and sat down. He placed the blanket in front of the Gosavi.

Baïse picked up the blanket and inspected it. "Baba, see how well he has repaired the blanket! You can't even tell it has been repaired." The omniscient one said, "My woman, he has repaired the blanket, but his knowledge has not improved." "Yes, Lord," she said.

To Dev the omniscient one said, "Did you do what I told you? Did I send you to Sangavkhede? Did I tell you to take hot-water baths in Elhambhat's house? To eat your meals on a large plate with a lampstand? To mend the blanket sitting on a swing? What I told you was, 'Beg for food, eat your meals

करा : वृक्ष मूळीं बैसौनि जाडि तुणा : हें काइ तुम्हीं केलें :
एथौनि तुमतें म्हणीतलें तें करीतेति तरि तुमची विद्या
सांधति : सहस्रवरुखें आयुष्य होतें : परि ऐसें कां होइल :
पसेयाचे पाइलिए कां एइल : आपणेयाचां परिवरि पाय
पसरूनि मरावें : तें कां चुकैल : आझूनीं तरि करा५१० :॥:

३१० पाठक त्यागु परिहासु५११ :॥:

एकुदिसीं गोसावी रामनाथासि वीहरणा बीजें केलें :
रामनाथीं उत्तरे पौळी बाहीरि आंबा होता : तेथ गोसावीयांसि
आसन असे : पाठक गोसावीयांचेया दरिसनां आले : दंडवतें
घातलीं : श्रीचरणा लागले : मग वीनवीलें : जी जी : न्यायें
कीं ऐसें म्हणीतलें असे : जें : सकळै गुरुसि आर्पावें : चित :
वीत : काया : तीन्हीं : इश्वरासि आर्पावि : ऐसें म्हणौनि :
गोसावीयांजवळि आपुली ब्राह्मणि : जवळि बैसवीली :
जवळि कांठाळ ठेवीली : बैलु बांधला : गोसावीयांसि दंडवतें
घातलीं : श्रीचरणा लागले : मग सर्वज्ञें म्हणीतलें : आतां
एथीचें होतें तुम्ही घेया : जी जी : न्याये कीं ऐसेंचि म्हणीतलें
असे : गुरु म्हणति तें कीजे : माहा प्रसादु जी : म्हणौनि :
माघौतें घेतले : या उपरि सर्वज्ञें म्हणीतलें : तल्हातिचेया

at the riverbank, sleep in a temple, and mend the blanket sitting at the foot of a tree.' Did you do this? If you had done what I said, your knowledge would have improved and you would have lived for a thousand years. But why should that happen? Can you get a bushel's worth for a handful? You must spread out your legs and die at your own home. Why should you escape doing that? Still now, do what I said."[397]

310 HE RIDICULES PATHAK'S RENUNCIATION.

One day the Gosavi went wandering to the Ramnath temple.[398] To the north of the Ramnath temple, outside the compound wall, there was a mango tree. The Gosavi was sitting there when Pathak came for his *darśan*. Pathak prostrated himself, touched the Gosavi's holy feet, and then appealed to him: "Lord, Nyaya philosophy says that one should offer everything to one's guru and that one should offer three things to God: one's mind, one's wealth, and one's body." Saying this, he had his wife sit near the Gosavi, placed a bundle of belongings near him, and tied his bull there. He prostrated himself to the Gosavi and touched his holy feet.

The omniscient one said, "Now you take back what has become mine." "Lord, that is exactly what Nyaya philosophy says! One should do what one's guru says. It is great *prasād*, Lord," he said, and took it all back.

After that, the omniscient one said, "Pathak's renunciation is like fathoming with your finger the water in the palm

पाणियांतु बोटें ठाउं : तैसा पाठकाचा त्याग : इतुकेनि ते
घेउनि गेले : गोसावी बीढारासि बीजें केलें :॥:

३११ भट : इंद्रभट : कटका पाठवणें :॥:

एकुदिसीं : इंद्रभट : कटकीं माहादेवरायाचें श्राध : ब्रम्ह
दानासी५१२ निगाले : गोसावी भटा : इंद्रभटातें५१३
म्हणीतलें : वानरेया : इंद्रया : कटका जा : महादेरायाचें
श्राध५१४ : तुमतें मुख्य पितरीया करिती :॥छ॥: जी जी :
आम्हीं मूख्य सूट देवो : कांहीं शास्त्र नेनें : सर्वज्ञें म्हणीतलें :
एथौनि धाडिजत असीजे कीं : मग भट : इंद्रभट : कटकासि
गेले : माहादेरायाचें श्राध होत होतें : भट : इंद्रभट : मुख्य
पीतरीया केले : तिस तिस आसू दानासि आलिया :॥:

३१२   भटां लखुबाइसां भांडण :॥:

एकुदिसीं लखुबाइसें झाडीतें होतीं : दादोसावरि रज गेले :
भटीं म्हणीतलें : हें काइ लखुबाइ : दादोसांवरि रज गेलें :
काइ डोळां देखाना : लखुबाइसीं म्हणीतलें : आधीं तुं काइ :
मग तुझे दादोस काइ : कैसे माझे दादोस काइ : माझेया
दादोसाचे केसु पडे : तेथ मि सीर लोटींना : तेंहीं म्हणीतलें :|

of your hand."[399] With that, Pathak took his belongings and left.

The Gosavi went to their lodgings.

311 HE SENDS BHAT AND INDRABHAT TO THE CAPITAL.

Donations were being made to Brahmans at King Mahadev's ancestor rite. One day Indrabhat set out for the capital to get a donation. The Gosavi said to Bhat and Indrabhat, "Monkey and Indra, go to the capital for King Mahadev's ancestor rite.[400] They will make you the principal ancestors." "We are the principal dolts, Lord. We don't know any scriptures." The omniscient one said, "I am sending you!"

So Bhat and Indrabhat went to the capital. King Mahadev's ancestor rite was under way. Bhat and Indrabhat were made the principal ancestors, and they each received a donation of thirty gold coins.

312 BHAT AND LAKHUBAÏSE QUARREL.

One day when Lakhubaïse was sweeping, dust got onto Dados. "What is this, Lakhubaï?" asked Bhat. "Dust has gotten onto Dados. Are you blind?" Lakhubaïse said, "To begin with, what are you? And then, what is your Dados?" "What do you mean, 'What is my Dados'? If one hair of my Dados's falls to the ground, I will cut off my head there." "Go ahead," she said. "Why don't you do that?"

जाये ऐसा पडसिनां कां : ऐसें गोसावी आइकीलें : मग
म्हणीतलें : जऱ्ही नावडतीचा जाला : तऱ्हीं बोटें कोण्हांसि
दाखउं नये : आणिकीं जयजय शब्दें बोलवावा कीं : कां :
रायाचां जांघीवां जाला कीं⁵¹⁵ : ऐसें गोसावी भटांसि कोपलें :॥:

३१३ इंद्रभटा पवीतें देणें :॥:

एकुदिसीं आबैसें : गौराइसें : इंद्रोबाये : गोसावीयाचां ठाइं
पवीतें पर्व केलें⁵¹⁶ : गोसावी पाठवणी दीधली : मग गावांसि
निगाले : वाटें गौराइसाचें पोट उठिलें : आबैसी म्हणीतलें :
इंद्रभटो : गोसावीयांपासि जा : पोट दुखत असे : ऐसें सांघा :
गोसावीयांते कांहीं मागा : मग ते गोसावीयांपासि आले :
दंडवतें घातलीं : श्रीचरणा लागले : कां गा : माधौतें
आलेति⁵¹⁷ : इंद्रभटीं म्हणीतलें : जी जी :
पोट दुखत असे : म्हणौनि : आबाइसिं मातें पाठविलें : मग
गोसावी कंठीचें पवीतें दीधलें : सर्वज्ञें म्हणीतलें : जा : उदरीं
बांधा : घरां जातुखेवों सोडा⁵¹⁸ : मग तैसेंचि तेहीं केलें :
गौराइसाचां पोटीं पवीतें बांधीलें : गाउं पावलीं आणि
सोडीलें : आणि तेयांसि प्रसूति जाली :॥:

When the Gosavi heard this, he spoke angrily to Bhat. "Don't point your finger at anyone, even if you don't like them," he said. "And cheer them to victory, as if they had become the king's son!"

313 HE GIVES INDRABHAT HIS SHOULDER THREAD.

One day Abaïse, Gauraïse, and Indroba celebrated the thread festival with the Gosavi.[401] After the Gosavi gave them leave to go, they set out for their village. Along the way, Gauraïse's stomach began to hurt.[402] Abaïse said, "Indrabhat, go to the Gosavi and tell him that her stomach is hurting. Ask the Gosavi for help."

So he came to the Gosavi, prostrated himself, and touched the holy feet. "Why have you come back?" asked the Gosavi.[403] Indrabhat said, "Gauraïse's stomach is hurting, Lord, so Abaïse sent me."

Then the Gosavi gave him the thread that was at his neck. The omniscient one said, "Go and tie this around her stomach. As soon as you get home, untie it."

That is exactly what he did: he tied the thread around Gauraïse's stomach, and he untied it when they reached the village. And then she gave birth.

३१४ दायांबा : पाटणीं सरिखे वाटणी :॥:

पूर्वीं भोगनारायणीं अवस्थान : तै⁵¹⁹ गोसावी चांगदेवीं
वीहरणा बीजें केलें : दायांबा गोसावीयांतें देखति आणि
आडवे जाति : एकाधा वेळु वीडीया मोडित मोडित जाति :
एकाधा वेळां सुरंगु मिरवित मिरवित जाति : एलापुरीं स्तिति
जाली होती : मग : ते करंजखेडीं गोसावीयाचेया दरिसना
आले होते : मग गोसावी तेयाचे मागील काढीति : काइ
काइ भोजा : भोजा यांतें देखौनि आडवा आडवा जाय :
दायांबा म्हणति : जी जी : हें तै कीं : एकाधा वेळु गोसावी
माघौतें म्हणति : भोजा : काइ : भोजा यांतें देखौनि सुरंगु
मीरवी : जी जी : हें तै कीं⁵²⁰ : मागुतें गोसावी एकाधा वेळु
म्हणति : भोजा काइ : भोजा यांतें देखौनि वीडिया मोडीत
मोडीत जाये : जी जी : हें तै कीं : एकुदीसीं दायांबा स्तीति
जाली : होती : तें पैलाकडौनि झुलत एतु असति : सर्वज्ञें
म्हणीतलें : भोजा काइ भोजा : भोजेयासि आजी कालि
माथां ब्रह्मांड⁵²¹ लागत असे : तेहीं म्हणीतलें : जी जी :
गोसावीयाचेनि प्रसादें : सर्वज्ञें म्हणीतलें : तैसे नव्हे कीं :
एकी पाटणीया : एकी सारिखे वांटणियां :॥: दुधही पांढरें
आणि ताकही पांढरें : सोनेंहीं पीवळें आणि बेगडहीं
पीवळी : दायांबा म्हणीतलें : जी जी : तरि होए तें

314 HE TELLS DAÏMBA THAT THE PLANKS IN A CEILING ARE ALL THE SAME SIZE.

Earlier, when the Gosavi was staying in the Bhognarayan temple, he would go wandering to the Cangdev temple.[404] Daïmba would see the Gosavi and walk right past him. Sometimes he would go along chewing pan, and other times he would swagger along arrogantly.

Daïmba had gone into a trance at Yelapur.[405] Then, when he came for *darśan* of the Gosavi in Karanjkhed, the Gosavi would bring up his previous behavior. "What is this, Bhoja? When Bhoja saw me, he would walk right past me." Daïmba would say, "That was then, Lord!"

Sometimes the Gosavi would say again, "What is this, Bhoja? When Bhoja saw me he would swagger arrogantly." "That was then, Lord!"

Sometimes the Gosavi would say again, "What is this, Bhoja? When Bhoja saw me, he would go along chewing pan." "That was then, Lord!"

One day Daïmba went into a trance and came sauntering along toward the Gosavi. The omniscient one said, "Bhoja! What is this, Bhoja? These days the weight of the universe is resting on Bhoja's head." "Yes, Lord," he said, "by the grace of the Gosavi." The omniscient one said, "That's not right! The planks in a ceiling are all the same size. Milk is white and buttermilk is white too. Gold is yellow and tinsel is yellow too." "Then, Lord," said Daïmba, "please tell me what is right."

निरोपीजो : सर्वज्ञें म्हणीतलें : बाइ : पोरु बहुतां दीसां
लाधला : मग गोसावीयां दायांबासि अन्यव्यावृत्ति
निरूपीली : यावरि बहुत निरोपण जालें : मग दायांबासि
बोधु जाला : मियांबा : गोसावी यावरि हीरडेया बेहाडेयाचा
दृष्टांत निरोपिला⁵²² :॥: रामेश्वरबास : ढोरेश्वरीं :॥:

३१५ माहात्मेया सींके उपहासू⁵²³ :॥:

एकुदीसीं गोसावीयाचेया दरिसना माहात्मे एक आले :
नावेक बैसले होते : मग ते परते गेले : आणि : गोसावीयांसि
सींक आली : सर्वज्ञें म्हणीतलें : मा रे : घायेंचि माहात्मेपण :
गेलें होतें : मां⁵²⁴ :॥:

३१६ रामतीर्थीं वसति :॥:

३१७ दाभाडीये वसति :॥:

The omniscient one said, "My woman, the poor child has had to wait for a long time." Then the Gosavi expounded "Exclusion of Others" to Daïmba, explaining it in great detail.[406] Daïmba became enlightened. (According to Miyamba: On this subject, the Gosavi told the parable of the myrobalan fruit.)[407]

(According to Rameshvarbas, this *līlā* took place in the Dhoreshvar temple.[408])

315   HE MAKES A JOKE ABOUT MAHATMAS WHEN HE SNEEZES.

One day a certain Mahatma came for *darśan* of the Gosavi. After sitting there for a little while, he went away. And then the Gosavi sneezed.

The omniscient one said, "Hey! In one stroke I would have lost my status as a Mahatma!"[409]

316   HE STAYS OVERNIGHT AT RAMTIRTHA.

317   HE STAYS OVERNIGHT IN DABHADI.[410]

३१८ हीवरळीये राजमठीं वसति :॥ः

तेथौनि गोसावी हीरवळीयेसि बीजें केलें : राजमठीं वसति
जाली : येरि दीसीं गोसावी उदीयांचि वनदेवाचेया देउळासि
बीजें केलें : शोधु : गावां पसिमे वन देवाचें : उतरामूखु
देउळाचा दारवठा : उपरि तिन : तेथें उतरे देउळी :
पसिमामूख : बीजें करीतां मार्गीं दादोसीं वीनवीलें : जी जी :
मीं गावांतु वाहाणा सांदु जाइन५२५ : एक म्हणति५२६ :
जी जी गावांतु सीदोरी आणूं जाइन : सर्वज्ञें म्हणितलें :
माहात्मे हो गावांतु जात असा : हें आलें ऐसें : कव्हणाइ
सांघों नको५२७ : दादोस तिकवनाएकाचेया घरासि आलें :
तवं आबाइसें उमाइसें आलीं होतीं : तेयांसि खेवं दीधलें :
दादोसां बैसों घातलें : तेयांचे पाए धुतलें : मग पुसिलें :
दादो तुम्ही आलेति : तरि काइ गोसावी बीजें केलें असे : तें
हांसति : माघौतें म्हणति : दादो सांघाना कां : परि सांघति
ना : मग आबैसीं म्हणितलें : उमै हे जाति : आणि या मागा :
मागा : आम्हीं जावों : गोसावी बीजें केलें असे : मग दादोसीं
उमाइसातें म्हणीतलें : उमै तुमतें कांहीं : सीदोरी असे : तरि :
सूआ : मग तेहीं दधीभातु सीदोरी सूदला : लोणिचें घातलें :
ते घेउनि गोसावीयांपासि दर्शनासि आले : गोसावी आधीं
वनदेवासि बीजें केलें : मग मढावरि बीजें केलें : देव :
आबाइसें : उमाइसें : आलीं : गोसावी मढावरि उभे होते :
देखीलें : उतरले : भेटि जाली : दंडवतें घातली : श्रीचरणा

318 HE STAYS OVERNIGHT
IN THE RAJMATH AT HIVARALI.

From there the Gosavi went to Hivarali and stayed overnight in the Rajmath.[411] Early the next morning he went to
Vandev's temple. (Research: Vandev's temple was to the
west of the village. The temple had a doorway that faced
north, and three upper stories. To the north was a shrine
that faced west.)

As the Gosavi was on his way there, Dados appealed to
him: "Lord, I want to go into the village to get my sandals
repaired." (Some say, "Lord, I want to go into the village to
get a packed lunch.") The omniscient one said, "Mahatma,
when you go into the village, don't tell anyone that I have
come here."

When Dados reached Tikavnayak's house, Abaïse and
Umaïse were there. They embraced Dados, put down something for him to sit on, and washed his feet. Then they asked,
"Dado, if you have come here, has the Gosavi come too?" He
laughed. Again they asked, "Won't you tell us, Dado?" But
he wouldn't tell them.

Then Abaïse said, "Umai, when he leaves, let's follow him.
The Gosavi has come here."

Then Dados said to Umaïse, "Umai, if you have any food
for a packed lunch, give me some." So she packed a meal of
yogurt and rice and gave it to him. She put in some pickle.
He took it, and they came to the Gosavi for *darśan.*

The Gosavi went first to the Vandev temple and then to the
hermitage. When Dev, Abaïse, and Umaïse arrived, he was

GOD AT PLAY

लागले : हीराइसापाठ : गोसावी पुसीलें : बाइ : हें आलें :
ऐसें काइ माहात्मेनि सांघीतलें : जी जी : दादोसातें पुसीलें :
ना दादो : तुम्हीं आलेति : तरि : गोसावी : म्हणौनि अवधें
सांघीतलें : सर्वज्ञें म्हणीतलें : हांसणें हेंहीं एक सांगणेंचि
कीं :॥छ॥: गोसावी लींगाचीये पसीमे मूर्खे देउळीये बीजें
केलें : आसन : गोसावीयांसि पुजा जाली : दधी भाताची
आरोगण जाली : पहुड जाला : एकें म्हणति : वसति जाली :
सर्वज्ञें म्हणीतलें : एथें अभ्यागतें आलीं : आतां ग्रामांतर न
कीजे : मग वीळींचां वेळीं गोसावी राजमठासि५२८ बीजें
केलें : तेथ अवस्थान : मास दोनि : शोधु : पसिमीलीकडे :
आंत उतरिलें भिंतीसी५२९ : पूर्वपसीम वोटा : तेथ अवस्थान
जाले५३० :॥:

३१९ बलिपा भक्तिकथन :॥:

गोसावी वनदेवासि बीजें केलें : नासी उतरीली गोसावी उभे
राहीले : लींग अवलोकीत होते५३१ : बाइसीं पुसीलें : बाबा :
ये तिन लिंगें काइसीं : सर्वज्ञें म्हणीतलें : बाइ : एकू हींवंजू
कोली : एकू बळीपू गौळी : हींवजू कोली : तो माहादेवाचा
अवताऱू : ते दोघे मैत्र : तें दोघे पारधी जाति : पारधि करूनि

592

standing on top of the hermitage. He saw them, and he came down and greeted them. They prostrated themselves and touched his holy feet. (Hiraïsa version: The Gosavi asked, "My woman, did the Mahatma tell you that I had come here?" "Lord, we asked Dados, 'Dado, if you have come here, is the Gosavi here too?'" and they told him everything that had happened. The omniscient one said, "Laughing too is a kind of telling.")

The Gosavi went and sat in a linga temple that faced west. His puja was performed there, he had the meal of the yogurt and rice, and he went to sleep. (Some say he stayed overnight there.)

The omniscient one said, "Guests have come here, so now we should not go to another village." So, in the evening, the Gosavi went to the Rajmath. He stayed there for two months. (Research: He stayed inside, on the western side, on an east-west pedestal against the northern wall.)

319 HE TELLS OF BALIPU'S DEVOTION.

The Gosavi went to the Vandev temple. He stood at the northern drain there, looking at the lingas.

Baïse asked, "Why are there these three lingas, Baba?" The omniscient one said, "My woman, one is Hivaju Koli,* and another is Balipu Gauli.† Hivaju Koli was an incarnation of Mahadev. The two of them were friends, and they would go

---

* Hivaju the Fisherman.
† Balipu the Cowherd.

येति : मग जेवीति : एकुदीस पारधी गेले : पारधि करूनि
आले : बळिपें म्हणीतलें : हीवजां मी तुजसरीसा जेवीन :
तेणें म्हणीतलें : मजसरीसा कैसा जेवीसी : मीं कोळी :
तूं गोळी : मज सरिसा कैसा जेवीसी : तेणें म्हणीतलें :
मी तुजसरीसा जेवीन : हीवजें म्हणीतलें : माझा शब्द
उरोधिसिना : तरि : मज सरिसा जेवि : तेणें मानिलें : दोघै
एकत्र जेवीलें : एकुदीसीं पारधी गेले : पारधि करूनि आले :
हीवजें तिन भाग केलें : तेथ गुपित वेखें पार्वती होती : हा
तुज : हा मज : हा आपणेयांसि : तो कोणा : मागौतें तेणें
म्हणीतलें हा मज : हा तुज : हा तो कोणा : मागौतें तेणें
म्हणीतलें : हा मज : हा तुज : हा आपणेयांसि : तो कोणा :
जाये कोळी तें कोळीचि कीं : मासाकारणें आळुकेंचि : ऐसें
म्हणीतलें : आणि तो अदृश्य जाला : आणि : बळीयांसि
अवस्था प्रगटली : हीवजां कोळीया दागटा कोळीया : ऐसें
म्हणौनि ५२ झाडा खेवें दे : ऐसीया नव अवस्था प्रगटलिया :
झाडा एका तळि निजैला : डोळेयांचे वाट भवों लागले :
दाहावी अवस्था प्रगटली : तवं देवता प्रत्यक्ष जाली :
बळियेपा : वळियेपा : हें काइ : तेणें म्हणीतलें : तूं कोण :
ना मीं हीवजुं कोळी : मग तेणें खांदावरि हात घातले : मग
प्रसन जाला : तेणें म्हणीतलें : मीयां आणि तुवां ऐसेयांचि

hunting together. When they returned from hunting, they would eat their meals.

"One day when they went hunting, after they came back Balipu said, 'Hivaju, I want to eat my meal with you.' 'How can you eat with me?' he replied. 'I am a Koli, and you are a Gauli. How can you eat with me?' Balipu said, 'I want to eat my meal with you.' Hivaju said, 'If you won't go against what I say, then eat with me.' Balipu agreed, and the two of them dined together.

"One day when they went hunting, after they came back Hivaju divided the meat into three portions. Parvati was there in invisible form. 'This one is yours. This one is mine. This one is ours.' 'Who is that one for?' Again Hivaju said, 'This one is mine. This one is yours.' 'Who is that one for?' Again he said, 'This one is mine. This one is yours. This one is ours.' 'Who is that one for? Go away! A Koli is always a Koli! Always craving for meat.'

"When Balipu said this, Hivaju disappeared. And Balipu went mad with longing for him. Saying, 'Hivaju Koli! You big, strong Koli!' he would hug a tree. He exhibited nine of the signs of longing: he slept under a tree, his eyes started rolling, and so on. When the tenth sign* began to manifest itself, the god appeared to him, saying, 'Balipu! Balipu! What is going on?' 'Who are you?' Balipu asked. 'I am Hivaju Koli,' he said, and he placed his hand on Balipu's shoulder. The god was pleased with Balipu. 'You and I should remain just like this,' he said."

---

* Death.

असावें : सर्वज्ञें म्हणीतलें : बाइ तो भक्तू होए : परि : ते
देवता नव्हे :॥ः

३२० वायनायका भेटि : नामकरण :॥ः

वायनायक उमाइसांसि भेटाविया आले : एकु पाबो धुतला :
एकू धुवावा असे : उमाइसीं म्हणीतलें : रूपैचें गुरू :
श्रीचांगदेवो राउळ : आले असति : तैसीचि स्तिति जाली :
पाबो आसूडिला : आणि वेगें निगाले : हाटवटिएसि गेले :
पानें : पोफळें : माळ घेतली : गोसावीयांचेया दरिसनासि येत
असति : धोत्रीं अवघें चेतलें असे : तवं लोकू पूसे : हें काइ
नायको : ना रूपैचे गुरु : श्रीचांगदेवो राउळ आले असति :
तेयांसि भेटों जात असों : संभ्रमें धोत्र वरतें करिति : तैसेचि
गोसावीयाचेया दरिसना आले : गोसावीयांसि पटिसाळे
पूर्विलीकडे पाटसरेयावरि आसन : ते संभ्रमें आडचि :
गोसावीयां उजुचि एत होते : सर्वज्ञें म्हणीतलें : ऐसे या :
ऐसे या५३३ : मग पाइरियावरौनि आले : पानें पोफळें :
दरिसना केलीं : फुलें : माळ : वोळगवीली : दंडवतें घातलीं :
श्रीचरणा लागले : मग गोसावीयांपासि बैसले : पालखति
घातली : आणि स्तीति जाली : भोगीली : मग म्हणों लागले :
जी जी : रूपै गोसावीयांचें गुण सांघती असे : ते थोडे :

The omniscient one said, "My woman, that one is a devotee, but the other one is not a deity."

320 HE MEETS VAYANAYAK
AND GIVES HIM A NAME.

Vayanayak* came to meet Umaïse. When she had washed one of his feet and the other was yet to be washed, Umaïse said, "Rupai's guru, Shri Cangdev Raül, has come here."

Immediately Vayanayak went into a trance. He drew back his foot and set out swiftly. He went to the market and got betel leaves, betel nuts, and a garland. He was coming for *darśan* of the Gosavi, carrying everything in his dhoti. People were asking him, "What is going on, Nayak?" "Rupai's guru, Shri Cangdev Raül, has come here," he replied. "I am going to meet him." In his excitement, he was lifting up his dhoti.

He arrived this way for *darśan* of the Gosavi. The Gosavi was sitting on a stone block on the eastern side of the veranda. In his excitement, Vayanayak was coming straight toward the Gosavi, climbing over the obstacles. "Come this way. Come this way," said the omniscient one.

Then Vayanayak came up by way of the steps. He offered the Gosavi the betel leaves and betel nuts. He gave him flowers and the garland, prostrated himself, touched the holy feet, and then sat down cross-legged near the Gosavi. And he went into a trance. After experiencing it for a while, he began to say, "Lord Gosavi, Rupai extols your virtues, but

* Mahadaïse's father.

597

गोसावीयाचां ठाइ दीसत असेति ते बहुत : जी : ते सांघों
नेणें५३४ : मा : गोसावी तेयांतें पूसीलें : आपणेयां नांव काइ :
जी जी : मातें वामनायेक ऐसें म्हणति५३५ : सर्वज्ञें म्हणीतलें :
तरि : वामनाचार्य म्हणा५३६ : जी जी : रूपै : अखंड :
गोसावीयांची वाट पाहे : गोसावी कव्हणे ठाइं राज्य करीत
असति : ऐसें जाणे ना : तरि : तियेतें बोलाउं धाडुं : सर्वज्ञें
म्हणीतलें : तुम्हां दरिसन जालें : तरि : तुमचीए लेकींसि
होआवें कीं५३७ : हीराइसापाठ : तथा धाडा :॥छ॥: मग तेहीं
एकु मोलकै करूनि धाडिला :॥:

३२१ महदाइसां भेटि :॥: उपाहारू स्वीकारू :॥:

मग तेहीं मोलकै करूनि पाठवीला : तो मोलकै महदाइसां
वाटेसि भेटला : महदाइसें द्वारावतीयेहुनि पाडलीयेसि
आली : परि गोसावी कवणे ठाइं राज्य करीत असति ऐसें
चोजवलें नाहीं : मग आइकीलें : जें गोसावी हीवरळाये
राज्य करीत असति५३८ : मग ते मोलकै करूनि येते होतीं :
येन्ह येन्हा भेटि जाली : महदाइसीं पूसीलें : आलेया तुं कें
जात असति : तेणें म्हणीतलें : पाडली गाउं : तेथ जात
असे : कां जात असति : ना : वाय नायकु : तेयाची लेंकी
रूपाइसें : तेयांतें बोलाउं जात असे : कां कां : ना : तेयांचे
गुरु आले असति : तेहीं म्हणीतलें : चाला : तें आम्हींचि :
येरू मोलकै मागौता पाठवीला : तेयाचां हातीं पोतें दीधलें :

her description is inadequate. There's a great deal more to be seen in you, Lord Gosavi. I don't know how to express it."[412] Then the Gosavi asked him, "What is your name?" "They call me Vamanayak, Lord."[413] The omniscient one said, "So let's call you Vamanacharya."[414]

"Lord Gosavi, Rupai is continually waiting for you. She doesn't know where you are living. So may I send for her?" The omniscient one said, "You have had *darśan,* so your daughter should have it too." (Or, Hiraïsa version: "Send for her.")

So he sent a servant for her.

321 HE MEETS MAHADAÏSE AND ACCEPTS FOOD FROM HER.

The servant he sent for Mahadaïse met her along the road. Mahadaïse had returned from Dvaravati to Padali, but she had not found out where the Gosavi was living.[415] Then she heard that the Gosavi was living in Hivarali, and so she was coming there with a servant.

When Mahadaïse met the servant Vayanayak had sent, she asked, "Where are you going, my friend?" "I am going to the village of Padali," he replied. "Why are you going there?" "I am going to summon Vayanayak's daughter Rupaïse." "Why? Why?" "Her guru has come." "Come on," she said. "Let's go. That's me." She sent her own servant back, handed the other one her bag, and set out.

When Mahadaïse arrived for *darśan* of the Gosavi, he was sitting on the stone block on the veranda. Mahadaïse hugged

आणि निगालीं : महदाइसें गोसावीयाचेया दरिसना आलीं :
गोसावायांसि पटिसाळे पाटसरेयावरि आसन : महदाइसीं
गोसावीयांसि बैसलेया : क्षेमालिंगन दीधलें : मग दंडवतें
घातलीं : श्रीचरणा लागले : मग गोसावीयां जवळि बैसलीं :
गोसावीयां पूढें : वाटे मोलकै भेटला : तें सांघीतलें५३९ : मग
महदाइसी गोसावीयांलागि उपाहाराते वीनवीलें : गोसावी
वीनवणी स्वीकारिली : महदाइसीं वडे प्रधान करूनि
उपहारू निफजवीला : गोसावीयांसि पुजावसरू केला : ताट
केलें : भक्तजनां आवघीयां ठायें केलें : गोसावी
अवघेयाचीया ठायाकडे अवलोकीलें : महदाइसीं अवघां
ठाइं वडे वाढीले : आपुला ठाइं न वाढतिचि : सर्वज्ञें
म्हणीतलें : बाइ : या अवघेयाचां ठाइं वडा असे : एथ नाहीं :
तें काइ : महदाइसी म्हणीतलें : जी जी : द्वारावतीये गेलीयें
होतीयें : तेथ मज शूळ उपनला : ते दीउनि मज उडीदान न
साहे : मग गोसावी आपुलीये ताटीचा वडा तेयासि
वाढवीला : मग गोसावीयांसि आरोगण : अवघेया जेवणें
जालीं : गुळळा जाला : वीडा वोळगवीला : मग वडा
साहे५४० :॥छ॥: एकी वासना५४१ : महदाइसीं गोसावीयाते
वीनवीले : जी जी मज मांद्यें असे : दीपन नाहीं : सर्वज्ञे
म्हणीतले : एथ उपहार करा मग होइल५४२ : मग वडेप्रधान
उपाहारू केला : महदाइसें पांतीं बसली : गोसावी
महदाइसातें अवलोकीलें : मग म्हणीतलें : बाइ : यांसि कांहीं

the Gosavi as he sat there. Then she prostrated herself, touched his holy feet, and sat down near him. She told the Gosavi about meeting the servant along the road.

Then Mahadaïse offered to prepare some food for the Gosavi, and the Gosavi accepted her offer. Mahadaïse prepared a meal with fried lentil cakes as the main dish. She performed the Gosavi's worship service, and she prepared a plate for him and leaf plates for all the devotees.

The Gosavi looked at everyone's plate. Mahadaïse had served lentil cakes to everyone else, but she had not served herself any. The omniscient one said, "My woman, they all have lentil cakes, but you don't have any. Why is that?" "Lord," replied Mahadaïse, "while I was in Dvaravati I got a sharp pain in my stomach. Since then I can't digest foods made with *uḍīd* dal."

The Gosavi had a lentil cake from his own plate served to her. Then he ate his meal, and everyone else ate theirs. He rinsed his mouth and was offered pan. After that she could digest lentil cakes.[416]

(One version: Mahadaïse appealed to the Gosavi: "Lord, I have lost my appetite. I have no appetite for food." The omniscient one said, "Prepare some food here, then you'll get your appetite back."[417]

Then she prepared a meal with fried lentil cakes as the main dish. Mahadaïse sat in the row of eaters. The Gosavi looked at her, then said to the server, "Serve some to her, my woman."[418]

वाढाना⁵⁴³ : गोसावीयांसि आरोगण : गुळळा : वीडा :
तीये दीउनि : महदाइसासि उडीदान साहे : भलेते न साहे :
दीपन जालें :॥:

३२२   तथा श्राध :॥:

एकुदीसीं गोसावीयांसि वृंदावन करावयाची प्रवृति जाली :
सर्वज्ञें म्हणीतलें : एथ वृंदावन करावें : जी जी तुळसीया :
वृंदावन करूं जाणे : ऐसें गोसावीयां पूढें सांघीतलें : तो
टेंभूरणीए असे : मग भट बोलाइं धाडीले : हीराइसापाठ :
वानरेया : तेयातें बोलाउं जा :॥छ॥: मग भटोबास तेयातें
बोलवावेया टेंभुरणीसि गेले : तुलसीयातें म्हणीतलें : तुमतें
गोसावी वृंदावन करावीयां बोलाविलें असे : तेहीं म्हणीतलें :
आमचां घरीं आजि श्राध : आजीचा दीसू राहा : मग जाउं :
भटीं म्हणीतलें : तुम्हीं पाहे या : मि आजि जाइन : तैसेचि
भट : देहाचेया देहा : विळौनि आले : दंडवतें घातलीं :
श्रीचरणा लागले : उठीतां म्हणीतलें : जी जी : ते उदीयां
येती : तैसेचि भट : नारायणाचेया देउळा गेले : तेथ पाठि
घातली : महदाइसें गेली : तेयांचीए पाठिवरि पाए देतें
असति : तवं गोसावी लघू परिहारासि बीजें केलें : तैसेंचि
तेथ बीजें केलें : महदाइसीं गोसावीयांतें देखीलें : आणि
भीयालीं : गोसावीयाचेया श्रीचरणा लागली : महदाइसीं
गोसावीयांतें पुसीलें : जी जी : नागदेवो भागला असे : मग

The Gosavi ate his meal, rinsed his mouth, and chewed pan. From that day on, Mahadaïse could digest food made with *uḍīd*. Her appetite came back, and there was nothing she could not digest.)

322   AND THERE IS
AN ANCESTOR RITE.

One day the Gosavi was inclined to build a *vṛndāvan*. "We should build a *vṛndāvan* here," said the omniscient one. "Lord," they told the Gosavi, "Tulsiya knows how to make a *vṛndāvan*." He lived in Tembhurni, and so Bhat was sent to invite him.[419] (Hiraïsa version: "Go there to invite him, Monkey.")

When Bhatobas went to Tembhurni to invite Tulsiya, Bhatobas said to him, "The Gosavi has invited you to come and make a *vṛndāvan*." "There is an ancestor rite at our house today," he replied. "Stay here tonight, and then we can go." Bhat said, "You come tomorrow morning. I'll go back today."

Bhat returned right away, that same day, in the evening. He prostrated himself to the Gosavi and touched his holy feet. As he stood up, he said, "He is coming tomorrow, Lord."

Bhat went straight to the temple of Narayan and lay down there. Mahadaïse went there. The Gosavi went out to urinate and then came straight there. When he arrived, she was massaging Bhat's back with her foot.

When Mahadaïse saw the Gosavi, she got frightened. She touched the Gosavi's holy feet and asked him, "Lord, Nagdev

याचिये पाठीं मज रगडुं येइल : तथा जी ऐसे करु ए५४ :
सर्वेझें म्हणीतलें : बाइ : श्रमलेयाचें करूं ये५४५ :
मग गोसावीयांसि तेथ आसन : दीवा लावीला : मग
महदाइसांकरवि भटांची श्रमनिवृति करवीली :॥:

३२३ तुळसीया आंगुळींव्येथा हरण :॥:

मग यरी दीसीं तुळसीया आले : ते वृंदावन करूं लागले :
चिरा उचलीतां५४६ बोटावरि पडीला : तेणें आंगुळी रगडीली :
तेणें तेयांसि मूर्छा आली : तुळसीयासि मूर्छा आली :
म्हणौनि : भक्तजनें बोबाइलीं : पडीले : सरला व्यापारु :
गोसावीयांसि पटीसारेयावरि आसन : गोसावी तेथ बीजें
केलें : पीक घातली : हीराइसापाठ : श्रीकरें स्परिसीलें :॥छ॥:
सावदु जाले : सर्वेझें म्हणीतलें : आतां व्यापरु पुरा दीया गा :
मग गोसावीयांसि पटिसालेवरि आसन : भक्त बैसले :
तुळसीए वृंदावनाचे तीन खण ती दीसीं निर्वाळीले :
पाहारूचि दी व्यापारू करिति : मग वृंदावन केले :॥:

is tired out. So is it all right for me to massage his back?"
(Or, "Is it all right to do this, Lord?") "My woman," said the
omniscient one, "you can do it for someone who is weary."[420]

The Gosavi sat there then. He lit a lamp and had Mahadaïse ease Bhat's weariness.

323 HE TAKES AWAY THE PAIN
IN TULSIYA'S FINGER.

The next day, Tulsiya arrived and began to build the *vṛndāvan*.
As he lifted a dressed stone, it fell on his finger, crushing it.
That made him faint. The devotees shouted, "Tulsiya has
fainted! He has fallen down! He has stopped working!"

The Gosavi was sitting on the stone block on the veranda.
He went over to Tulsiya and put spittle on his finger. (Hiraïsa
version: He touched it with his holy hand.) Tulsiya regained
consciousness. "Now finish the job!" said the omniscient
one. Then the Gosavi sat back down on the veranda. The
devotees were sitting there too.

Tulsiya built the three sections of the *vṛndāvan* in three
days. He worked on the *vṛndāvan* for a few hours each day.
Finally he finished it.

३२४ आपलें भेटि :॥:

एकूदीसीं आपलोयें जू हारवीलें : जुवारीं बोकणा बांधला :
मग ते घरासि आले : तेयांचीया माता म्हणीतलें : जाए कां
ऐसा : जैसी रूपै गेली श्रीचांगदेवो राउळा पाठीं : तैसा तुं
जाए कां : तेयांसि स्तीति जाली : आणि ते तैसेचि नीगाले :
ते अहोरात्रें गोसावीयांचेया दरिसनासि आले : गोसावीयांसि
उदयाचा पुजावसर असे : सर्वांगीं चंदन : चंदनाचा
आडा⁵⁴⁷ : गोसावी पूर्वीले सोंडीयेवरि उभे
असति : आपलोये गोसावी देखीले : दंडवतें घातलीं :
श्रीचरणा लागले : महदाइसीं काउरवाउरें देखौनि पुसों
आदिरिलें : करीं बा : ऐसा : सर्वज्ञें म्हणीतलें : बाइ : हा जू
खेळिनला : जू हारविलें : याची माता कोपली : महदाइसें
भीयालीं : सर्वज्ञें म्हणीतलें : तैसें कांहीं नाहीं : हा तान्हैला
असे : भुकैला असे : पाणी पेवों सूआ : जेउं सूआ :
पाठी गोष्टी पुसा⁵⁴⁸ : बाइ : पूर्वीं हें जु खेळे : हे जुं जींके
परि हारवीना : मग या उपरि गोसावी जुतक्रीडेची गोष्टि
सांघीतली⁵⁴⁹ :॥छ॥: मग महदाइसीं उदक आणिलें : ते न
पीयतीचि : ते म्हणति : मीं गोसावीयांचें चरणउदक वांचौनि
न पीयें : मग गोसावीयांसि सोंडीयेवरि आसन : महदाइसीं
श्रीचरणक्षाळण केलें : मग चरणोदक पीयाले : मग तेहीं
महदाइसा पुढें अवघें सांधीतलें :॥:

324   HE MEETS APLO.

One day Aplo lost at gambling, and the gamblers tied a gag on him.[421] When he came home, his mother said, "Why don't you just leave? Why don't you go away the way Rupai did, following Shri Cangdev Raül?" He went into a trance, and he set out immediately. Traveling day and night, he arrived for *darśan* of the Gosavi.

The Gosavi's morning worship service was going on. He was standing on the elephant-trunk-shaped parapet at the eastern side of the steps. His whole body was covered with sandalwood paste, and there was a horizontal line of it on his forehead. Aplo saw the Gosavi, prostrated himself, and touched the holy feet.

Flustered at seeing Aplo, Mahadaïse began to ask, "Why are you like this?" The omniscient one said, "My woman, he was gambling, and he lost. His mother got angry." That frightened Mahadaïse. The omniscient one said, "It's not that bad. He is thirsty and hungry. Give him some water to drink and serve him a meal. Ask him about it afterward.

"My woman, in the past I used to gamble. I would win at dice, but I did not lose." Then the Gosavi told the story of his own gambling.[422]

Mahadaïse brought Aplo some water, but he refused to drink it. "I won't drink anything," he said, "but water that has washed the Gosavi's feet." So the Gosavi sat on the elephant-trunk-shaped parapet, and Mahadaïse washed his holy feet. Then Aplo drank the water, and after that he told Mahadaïse everything that had happened.

३२५ उमाइ उपाहारू स्विकारू :॥:

उमाइसें मास उपवास करावेयाची आइत करितें असति :
सर्वज्ञें म्हणीतलें : मास उपवासी बैसतां ब्राह्मणातें५५०
जेउं सूइजे : मग उमाइसीं गोसावीयांसि उपाहारालागि
विनवीलें : दशमीचां दीसीं रात्रीं स्परिसें जाली : उदीयाचि
गोसावीयांचेया दरिसना आलीं : अळगौनि गोसावीयांसि
दंडवतें घातलीं : आबैसांपुढें दुख करूं लागलीं : गोसावी
आबैसातें बोलाविलें : बाई : मासउपवासीयें काइ म्हणतें
असति : मग उमाइसें गोसावीयां पुढें साघों लागलीं : जी
जी : मीयां गोसावीयांलागि उपाहारू आपूलां हातीं
निफजवावा : मग गोसावीयांसि पुजा करावी : तें मज दैव
नाहीं : जी : ऐसें म्हणौनि दुख करूं लागलीं : सर्वज्ञें
म्हणीतलें : मास उपवासीए हो : पैन्हाचें पैन्हा असीजे :
याची शूधि वार्ता नेणिजे : धुवा५५१ डोळें भरावें : तथा
भरिजति : हें निकें : या जवळिकें असीजे : तें वोखटें५५२ :
वृधाबाइसें उपाहारू करीती : नागदेवो तुमचिया वारिया
पुरोहीत द्वारे५५३ : पुजा करीती : दुख न करा५५४ : हो
कां : जी : मग गोसावीयांसि वीहरणा जावेयाची प्रवृति
होती : मग ते भंगली : मग न वचतिचि : मग उमाइसें
प्रधान करूनि गोसावी निरूपण केलें : तवं आबाइसीं
उपाहारू निफजविला : भटोबासीं गोसावीयांसि पुजा
केली : गोसावीयांसि ताट केलें : भक्तजनां ठाय केलें :
गोसावीयांसि आरोगण : भक्तजनां जेवणें जालीं : उमाइसां
पांतीं जेवण जालें : गोसावीयांसि गुळळा : वीडा : गोसावी

325 HE ACCEPTS UMAÏ'S FOOD.

Umaïse was preparing to fast for a month. The omniscient one said, "Someone embarking on a month-long fast should serve a meal to a Brahman." So Umaïse invited the Gosavi for a meal.

On the night of the tenth day of the fortnight, her menstrual period started.[423] Early the next morning she came for *darśan* of the Gosavi. She prostrated herself to him from a distance and began to express her sorrow to Abaïse.

The Gosavi called Abaïse over and asked, "My woman, what is the woman who fasts for a month saying?" Then Umaïse began to tell the Gosavi, "I do not have the good fortune of cooking for you myself, Lord Gosavi, and then performing puja to you." And she began to cry.

The omniscient one said, "Oh woman who fasts for a month! Is it better to be far, far away, not to know where I am, and to have your eyes filled with smoke?* Is it worse to be close to me?[424] Vriddhabaïse will prepare the food. Nagdev will have a priest do the puja on your behalf. Don't cry."[425] "All right, Lord."

The Gosavi had been inclined to go out wandering, but he changed his mind and didn't go at all. Then, while the Gosavi was teaching Umaïse and the others, Abaïse prepared the food. Bhatobas did puja to the Gosavi. A plate was prepared for the Gosavi, and leaf plates for the devotees. The Gosavi ate his meal, and the devotees had theirs. Umaïse ate in the same row as the others.[426]

---

* In the kitchen.

आसनीं उपवीष्ट असति : उमाइसीं श्रीमूर्वीचें तांबूल
मागीतलें : सर्वज्ञें म्हणीतलें : हें काम्यव्रत : एथचा विधि
ऐसा नव्हे५५५ : मग भटोबासा करवि उमाइसासि वीडा
देववीला : मग उमाइसीं चुळीं पाणी घेतलें५५६ : मग
म्हणीतलें : जी जी : मी येकू मास उपवासू : गोसावीयाचां
ठाइं करीन : तथा मास उपवासी बैसेन : तवं बाइसें
कोपलीं : हें काइ वो जालें : पुहीयांनि घाणातेनि तोंडेंसीं५५७
बाबापासि उपवास सातरिया काइसिया : पैन्हा जा : मग
उपवास करा : सर्वज्ञें म्हणीतलें : बाइ : रावसगांवा जा : हें
तेथेंचि येइल५५८ : मग तीयें एकादशीसि नीगालीं :॥:

३२६ जोगीवेर्खें मनभुलि क्रीडा :॥:

एकुदीस गोसावीयांसि उदयाचा पुजावसर जालेयानंतरें :
मळेयांआंतु माहालक्ष्मीचेया देउळांतु वीहरणा बीजें
केलें५५९ : गोसावीयांसि चौकीं आसन : तेथ जोगीयाची गळ
कंथा खापरी काठी आंधारी होती : ते देखीलीं : गोसावी
चौकीं वस्तें ठेवीलीं : वीभुती श्रीमूर्ख माखीलें : भस्म आंगी
लाविलें : गळ कंथा घातली : एके श्रीकरी खापरी : एके
काठी घेतली : आणि गोसावी उभे ठेले : मग म्हणीतलें : कर
धरि खपर : भिक्षापात्र : भस्म वीधुळीत : वीगळित गात्र :
नित्य चळ चित : मंद मंद मनसो : वीगळित गात्र :
परमानंद : परमानंद : मन भुलि रे : मन भुलि रे : सर्वज्ञें

The Gosavi rinsed his mouth and chewed pan, seated in his place. Umaïse asked for the pan from his holy mouth. The omniscient one said, "That is an optional practice. My rules don't require that."[427] Then the Gosavi had Bhatobas give Umaïse some pan.

Umaïse took water in her cupped hand* and said, "Lord, I intend to fast for a month in the Gosavi's presence."

At that, Baïse got angry. "What is going on? How can you put your fasting mat near Baba when your face is stinking with pus? Go far away and do your fast there."

"Go to Ravasgav, my woman," said the omniscient one. "I will come there."[428] So Umaïse set out on the Ekadashi day.

326 IN THE GARB OF A YOGI, HE PLAYS AT LURING THE MIND.

After his morning worship service one day, the Gosavi went wandering to a temple of Mahalakshmi in an orchard.[429]

The Gosavi was sitting in the central hall of the temple. He saw a yogi's cloak, clay begging bowl, and staff that were in a dark corner there. He left his own clothes in the central hall, smeared his holy face with holy ashes, and rubbed ashes on his body. The Gosavi put on the cloak and stood there, holding the begging bowl in one holy hand and the staff in the other. Then he said, "The hand holds a clay pot, a begging bowl. Dusted with ashes. Limbs fallen apart. Intellect constantly moving. Mind going slowly. Limbs fallen

---

* To express a ritual intention.

म्हणीतलें : बाइ : मागील सीध एणें वचनें भिक्षा
करिति५६० : मग बाइसें भेवों लागलीं : फेडीजो जी बाबा :
फेडीजो जी बाबा : म्हणीतलें : मग तें गोसावी फेडीलें मग
आपुलीं वस्तें प्रावर्ण केलीं : मग बीढारा बीजें केलें :॥:

३२७ महदाइसीं वेवादें तिकवनाएका जैत्य :॥:

एकु दीस तीकवनाएकाचां घरीं श्राध जालें : गोसावीयांतें
उपहारालागि वीनवीलें : गोसावी वीनती स्विकरीली :
दुपाहारिचा : वीळिचांचा गोसावीयांसि पुजावसर :
आरोगणें उसीरू जाला : म्हणौनि महदाइसें आलीं : हें काइ
तीकवनाएको : गोसावीयांसि आरोगणे उशीरू जाला :
आझूइं कैसें ताट नेयाना : तीकवनाएकें म्हणीतलें :
ब्रांम्हणांसी संकल्पु देवों : मग नेवों : महदाइसीं म्हणीतलें :
आधीं तुमचे ब्राह्मण जेवीती : मग गोसावीयांसि ताट नेसी :
म्हणौनि महदाइसें भीतरि गेलीं : गोसावीयांलागि ताट
वोगरीलें : घेउनि आलीं : गोसावीयांसि आरोगण : मग
ताट घेउनि आली : तिकवनायेकें म्हणीतलें : रूपै : टाटा
सतसारिलें कीं नाहीं : तेंहीं म्हणीतलें : सतसारीलें म्हणीजे
काइ : ना : गोसावीयांसि आरोगण म्हणौनि : मा गोसावी

apart. Supreme joy. Supreme joy. Lure the mind! Lure the mind!" The omniscient one said, "My woman, Siddhas in the past would use these words to beg for food."[430]

Baïse got frightened. "Take it off, Baba!" she said. "Take it off!" So the Gosavi took off the yogi's garb and put on his own clothes. Then he went to their lodgings.

327 TIKAVNAYAK WINS A DISPUTE WITH MAHADAÏSE.

One day an ancestor rite was to be performed at Tikav-nayak's house.[431] He offered to bring the Gosavi food from the meal, and the Gosavi accepted the offer.

The Gosavi's afternoon and evening worship services took place. It was past the time for his meal, so Mahadaïse came to Tikavnayak's house and asked him, "What is going on, Tikav-nayak? It's past the time for the Gosavi's meal. Why haven't you brought his plate of food yet?" Tikavnayak said, "After the Brahmans have made the ritual expression of intention, I will bring the food."

"First your Brahmans will eat," said Mahadaïse, "and *then* you will bring the plate of food for the Gosavi?" She went inside the house, put food on a plate for the Gosavi, and brought it to him. After the Gosavi ate his meal, she brought the plate back.

"Rupai," asked Tikavnayak, "has the plate been purified or not?" "What do you mean, 'purified'?" she asked. "Because the Gosavi ate off it." "Why does it have to be purified if the Gosavi ate off it?" "Because the devotees do not know

आरोगणा केली : तरि सतसारावें कां : भक्तजना गोसावी
काइ ऐसें : म्हणौनि : नेणिजे : महदाहसीं म्हणीतलें : कैसें
काइ गोसावी : ईश्वरू : आणि : काइ : होए होए : घीया :
गोसावी ईश्वरू होति : परि : काइ म्हणौनि नेणिजेति :
ऐसें वेळां दोनि उरोधीलें : मग महदाइसें ताट घेउनि
निगालीं : उदीयांचि ते गोसावीयांचेया दरिसना आलें :
भावें दंडवतें घातलीं : श्रीचरणा लागों बैसले : हळुचि
महदाइसी म्हणीतलें : घेइ : काइ घेवों तुझेया भावाचें : मग
तिकवनाएकें गोसावीयां पुढें मागिल आवघे सांधीतलें : मग
यावरि सर्वज्ञें म्हणीतलें : बाइ : नायक म्हणत असति : तें
साचचि : बाइ५६१ : हें काइ ब्राह्मण : कीं : क्षेत्री : कीं वैश्य :
कीं शूद्र : हें नेणिजे कीं बाइ : नायक म्हणत असति तें
साच५६२ : ऐसें गोसावी म्हणीतलें : आणि तीकवनाएकासि
जैत्य जालें :॥:

३२८ भट वेवादें तीकवनाएका जैत्य :॥:

भटोबासीं : तीकवनाएकें नदीसि धोत्रें धुतलीं : सीधनाथा-
कडे निगाले : तिकवनायेकें म्हणीतलें : नागदेया नागदेया :
आमचे गोसावी साक्षातु सीधनाथू : भटोबासीं म्हणी-
तलें५६३ : बह्मादीकां नीसरबोडी : तुझा सीधनाथु कोणे ठाइं

what the Gosavi is." Mahadaïse said, "How can you ask what the Gosavi is? He is God. What else?" "Yes, yes. Listen: the Gosavi is God, but no one knows what he is."

After he had argued with her twice this way, Mahadaïse took the plate and left. Early the next morning Tikavnayak came for *darśan* of the Gosavi. As he prostrated himself reverently and was about to touch the holy feet, Mahadaïse said very quietly, "Take whatever you can get from your reverence."

Then Tikavnayak told the Gosavi everything that had happened. Thereupon the omniscient one said, "What the Nayak is saying is completely true, my woman. No one knows if I am a Brahman or a Kshatriya or a Vaishya or a Shudra.[432] What the Nayak says is true." When the Gosavi said this, it was a victory for Tikavnayak.

328 TIKAVNAYAK WINS A DISPUTE WITH BHAT.

Bhatobas and Tikavnayak washed their dhotis at the river, then set out for the Siddhanath temple. "Nagdev, Nagdev!" said Tikavnayak, "our Gosavi is Siddhanath himself." Bhatobas said, "How can your Siddhanath reach a place that is hard for Brahma and the other gods to reach?" Tikavnayak

लागें : तीहीं म्हणीतलें : हें तुं म्हणत असिस : कीं : गोसावी
म्हणत असति : भटीं म्हणीतलें : गोसावी : तीहीं म्हणीतलें :
गोसावी जरि ऐसें म्हणती : तरि मी डोई बोडुनि धोत्र फाडुनि
उतरापंथें जाएं : तैसेंचि गोसावीयांपासि आले :
दंडवतें घातलीं : श्रीचरणा लागले : मग तिकवनाएकें
गोसावीयांपासि सांघों लागले : जी जी : मीयां आणि
नागदेनि : ऐसें आवघें सांघीतलें : जी जी : तरि : गोसावी
काइ ऐसें सांघावें : गोसावी तिकवनायकाचें मानिलें :
हीराइसापाठ : तुम्हीं म्हणत असा तेंचि :॥छ॥: यावरि
तीकवनायकें बाहे आफळीली : हा होएं मी तीकव देवो :
दंडवतें घातलीं : श्रीचरणा लागले : मग निगालें : मग
भटीं म्हणीतलें : जी जी : गोसावी कैसे सीधनाथु : सर्वज्ञें
म्हणीतलें : हा गा : हा उत्तरापंथें धोत्र फाडुनि डोइ बोडुनि
जाये तें निकें कीं हें सीधनाथु होए तें निकें५६४ :॥:

३२९ माहादाइ अवतारू प्रतिभिज्ञा :॥:

पूर्वीं महादाइसीं पुसीलें होतें : हा जी : गोसावी कवणाचे
पुत्र : सर्वज्ञें म्हणीतलें : हें गुजराथेचेया प्रधानाचें कूमर :
मग द्वारावतिए जाउनि आलीं : मग एकुदीसीं पुसीलें :

asked, "Is that what you say, or is it what the Gosavi says?"
"The Gosavi," replied Bhat. "If the Gosavi says that," said
Tikavnayak, "then I will shave my head, rip up my dhoti, and
take the road to the north."[433]

Immediately the two of them came to the Gosavi. They
prostrated themselves and touched his holy feet. Then,
starting with, "Lord, Nagdev and I...," Tikavnayak told the
Gosavi everything that had happened. "So, Lord Gosavi,
would you say that?"

The Gosavi said that Tikavnayak was right. (Hiraïsa
version: "What you are saying is true.") At that, Tikavnayak
slapped himself on his upper arms.* "I am the great Tikavdev!" He prostrated himself, touched the holy feet, and left.

Then Bhat asked, "Lord Gosavi, how can you be Siddhanath?" The omniscient one said, "Hey, is it better for him
to rip up his dhoti, shave his head, and take the road to the
north, or is it better for me to be Siddhanath?"[434]

329   MAHADAÏ RECOGNIZES
HIM AS AN AVATAR.

Earlier Mahadaïse had asked, "Lord Gosavi, whose son are
you?" The omniscient one said, "I am the son of a minister
in Gujarat."

Then one day, after she had gone to Dvaravati and come
back, she asked the omniscient one, "Lord, because you said
that I should look at Shri Cangdev Raül's hermit's cell, I went

* A gesture of self-congratulation.

जी जी : सर्वज्ञें म्हणीतलें होतें : श्रीचांगदेवो राउळाचीं
गुंफास्थानें पाहावीं : तरि : मी तेथ गेलीयें होतीयें : तेथें
पुरूखु येक बैसले होते : जी जी : तेयाचीये तोंडींहुनि कीं
रूपेचीया सरिया सरीया ऐसीया निगति : हां जी : तरि तें
काइ : सर्वज्ञें म्हणीतलें : बाइ : ते तेयांचि लाळ : जी : मग
मीयां तेयांतें पुसीलें : आपणेयां नांव काइ : तीहीं म्हणीतलें :
आम्हां नांव माहादमूनि : आपण कवणाचे अनुग्रहीत :
ना : आम्हीं अनंतमूनिचे : ते कवणाचे अनुग्रहीत : ना :
ते श्रीचांगदेवो राउळा गोसावीयांचें : श्रीचांगदेवो राउळीं
कवणेपरी बीजें केलें : तें तुम्ही जाणां : ना : ते आम्हीं नेणों :
तरि : तुमचे अनंतमुनि काइ म्हणति : ना : माहाराष्ट्रीं : पुरुषु
आणि विद्या असे : ऐसें म्हणति : तुम्हीं काइ म्हणा :
ना : आम्ही अनंतु अनंतु ऐसें म्हणों : याउपरि सर्वज्ञें
म्हणीतलें : हें कोण्हीहिच नेणें : तें तो तऱ्हीं केवि जाणे : तें
एथौनि सांघीजैल५६५ : या उपरि गोसावी कामाक्षेची गोष्टि
सांघीतली : मग पूर्वील गोष्टि : तवं महादाइसां ऐसें उमटलें :
जे : द्वारावतीकार तेचि आमचे गोसावी : मग रात्रीं नीद्रा
करावेयां गेली : वृंदावनावरि बैसली : आबैसातें म्हणीतलें :
आबै : आबै : द्वारावतीकार तोचि आमचे गोसावी : ऐसी
अवघी गोष्टि सांघीतली : तेया सूख जालें : मग उदीयांचि
गोसावीयांचेया दरिसनां आलीं : तेयांतें देखौनि : सर्वज्ञें
म्हणीतलें : बाइ : तैशा स्थानीं तैसीया तैसीया गोष्टी न
कीजति कीं : महादाइसीं म्हणीतलें : हां जी : गोसावी केवि

there. There was a holy man sitting there, Lord, with silver threads coming out of his mouth. What was that, Lord?"[435] "My woman," said the omniscient one, "that was his saliva." "Then I asked him, Lord, 'What is your name?' 'My name is Mahadev Muni,' he said. 'Whose disciple are you?' 'Ananta Muni's.' 'Whose disciple is he?' 'He is Shri Cangdev Raül Gosavi's.'

"'Do you know how Shri Cangdev Raül left the world?' 'No, I do not know that.' 'Then what does your Ananta Muni say?' 'He says that the holy man and his knowledge are in Maharashtra.' 'What do you say?' 'I say, "Ananta! Ananta!"'"

After that the omniscient one said, "No one at all knows that, so how could he know it? I will tell you what happened." Thereupon the Gosavi told the story of Kamakhya. When Mahadaïse heard the story about what had happened in the past, she realized this: "Our Gosavi is the one from Dvaravati."

That night, when she went to their sleeping place, she sat on the *vrndāvan* and said to Abaïse, "Abai! Abai! Our Gosavi is the one from Dvaravati," and she told her the whole story. She was delighted.

Early the next morning, Mahadaïse and Abaïse came for *darsan* of the Gosavi. When he saw them, the omniscient one said, "My woman, do not talk about such things in such a place."[436] "Yes, Lord," said Mahadaïse. "How did you know,

जाणीतलें : सर्वज़ें म्हणीतलें : जाणिजे हेतु धातु करूनि : हां
जी : हेतु धातुतें कैसेनि जाणिजे : सर्वज़ें म्हणीतलें : जाणिजे
तुम्हां उठीतां बैसतां^{५६६} : मग महदाइसां विस्मयो जाला :
महदाइसीं म्हणीतलें : आबै जे आम्हीं रात्रीं बोलिलों : तें
गोसावी जाणीतलें : मग आबैसा विस्मो जाला :॥:

Gosavi?" The omniscient one said, "I can tell from your intentions and actions." "Yes, Lord. How can you tell from my intentions and actions?" The omniscient one said, "I can tell from the way you stand up and sit down."

Mahadaïse was amazed. "Abai," she said, "the Gosavi knew what we were talking about last night." And then Abaïse was amazed.

ABBREVIATIONS

A	*Ajñāt Līḷā* section of the *Līḷācaritra*
DGR	Mhaïmbhat 1984
E	*Ekāṅka* section of the *Līḷācaritra*
FH	"The First Half" (*Pūrvārdha*) section of *God at Play*
K	Kolte edition of the *Līḷācaritra*
K(n)	footnote in Kolte's edition
MCLI	Murty Classical Library of India
Na	Nagpure edition of the *Līḷācaritra*
Na(n)	footnote in Nagpure's edition
Ne	Nene edition of the *Līḷācaritra*
P	*Pūrvārdha* section of the *Līḷācaritra*
Pa	Panjabi edition of the *Līḷācaritra*
S	Solapure edition of the *Līḷācaritra*
SH	"The Second Half" (*Uttarārdha*) section of *God at Play*
SP	"The Solitary Period" (*Ekāṅka*) section of *God at Play*
T	Tulpule edition of the *Līḷācaritra*
T(n)	footnote in Tulpule's edition
U	*Uttarārdha* section of the *Līḷācaritra*

NOTES TO THE TEXT

एकांक

१ तेव्हळि गोसावी बिजें करिती] K, Na, Pa, S; तेव्हळि Ne, T.

२ गोसावीं दादोसांतें म्हणीतलें] K; सर्वज्ञें म्हणीतलें Na; lacking in Ne, T, Pa, and S.

३ गोसावी] Na; lacking in Ne and T; sentence lacking in K, Pa, and S.

४ Ne adds चेया चेया : माझे बापे : दुसरी वासना.

५ पव्हेसि गोसावियांसि आसन जालें] K, T; तथा मार्गीं गावीं एकी गोसावीयास पव्हेसी आसन असे Pa; गांवीं एकीं पव्हे Ne; Na begins the chapter with गोसावीयांसि गावी एकी पव्हेसि आसन असे.

६ पुडवाटवा सोडीला] Pa, S, Na; पुडवांटुवा काढिला K; तथा पुडु वाटुवा सोडिला Ne, T.

७ गोसावीं तांबूळ प्रतेजीता तेणे हात ओडविला : तो प्रसादु घेतला] Pa, S, Na; गोसावीं तांबूळ परित्यजीलें : तवं तेणें हातु वोडिवला : तो प्रसादु घेतला T; गोसावीं तांबोळ प्रत्यजुं आदरिलें : आणि तेणहें दोन्ही हात ओडविले : श्रीमुखीचें तांबोळ घेतलें : तांबोळाचा प्रसादु घेतला K; lacking in Ne.

८ पोटकुळिया देति होती] S; पोटकुळीया देत होती : तथा थापटीत होती Pa; थापटीति होती Na; पोटकुळीया दे : थापनीती होती Ne, T; lacking in K.

९ Ne adds दुसरी वासना : गोसावी पहुडले असति : ते बाइ : चरणसंवाहन करीति होती : तैसेचि निद्रा आली.

१० जातिशुद्ध तो बहुतांमध्यें एकु खडेन हाणें : तो घोडा तयाची वास रोखें पहातुचि असे] S, Pa, T; जातिसुधू घोडा एकु आति : तेयातें एकाधा एकु सभेआंतुनि मागिलीकडुनि पासाळवरि हरळेंकरूनि ऐसा हाणे : आणि ऐसा रोहके दृष्टी तेयांकडे पाहे K, Na; जाति सुवास रोषें पाहातचि असे Ne.

११ गोसावीयांते] K, Na, Pa, S; म्हणीतलें Ne, T.

१२ गोसावी घोडेयाची जाति जीवन बोलेति] Pa; घोडे विजाती जीवन बोलति S; घोडे वीजाति जीवन बोलति Ne, T; lacking in K and Na.

१३ Ne adds दुसरी वासना : आसनि बैसले असति : तीयें आउसें वारा घालितें असति.

१४ Ne adds एकी वासना : तेल वीकीत होती.

१५ Ne adds एकी वासना : आगा ए बरवेया देवा : पालवी धरूनि घरा.

१६ सर्वज्ञें म्हणीतले] Pa, S; lacking in K, Na, Ne, and T.

१७ शिष्या अभिमानू : म्हैळीचेयापसि अधीकू] Na; शिष्याभिमानु तो म्हैळियेपसि अधिक T; म्हेळीचेयापस्य सीक्षाचा अभिमानु थोरू K; सीष्याभिमानु म्हैळीयाचा Ne; lacking in Pa.

१८ बाईसीं] Na, T; आउसीं Ne; sentence lacking in K, Pa, and S.

625

१९ एकु दीं] S, Pa, Na, K, T; आणि Ne.

२० भूत हिंसा जाली] Na; भूतहींसा केली तथा जाली Pa, S, T; भूतहींसा केली K; भूतहींसा केली : जाली Ne.

२१ माहादाइसे] Na, K; वींझी भक्तजनें Ne, T; lacking in Pa and S.

२२ डांबीर चालीति] Na, Pa, K, S; डांबीर देति : चालीति Ne, T.

२३ Ne adds एकी वासना : काल लागैल जी : ससा सोडीजो जी.

२४ Ne adds रामेश्वरबास : हें दृष्ट कीं श्रुत.

२५ Ne adds एकी वासना.

२६ श्रीमूर्ति अवलोकीत] S, T; श्रीमुर्ति अवळोकीति K; मुर्तीं अवलोकींत Pa; श्रीमूर्ति Ne; lacking in Na.

२७ शोधु :॥: मग रावो नीगाला : गोसावी ते परित्यजुनि बीजें केलें] S, Pa; lacking in K, Na, Ne and T.

२८ मग गोसावी] Pa, S; lacking in Ne and T; sentence lacking in Na and K.

२९ पाठी येरांचें पाय धूतले : आधी गोसावीयांसि विडा ओळगविला] S, Pa; lacking in K, Na, Ne and T.

३० Ne adds सोधु : तरि कां बोलावा ना.

३१ चुर्णजाति निरुपण] S; चुनेजाति नीपरोपण K, Pa; चुणे जाति निरूपणे Na; घोडेया स्थीति : चूर्ण जाति निरूपण Ne, T.

३२ गोसावी वडनेरेया बीजें केलें] S, Pa; lacking in Ne, T, K, and Na.

३३ मागौतें वडनेरेया] Pa, S; मग मोगौतें वडसावीं तेथौनि वडणेरेयासि K; मग गोसावी मागौतें वडनेरेयासि Na; तेथौनि Ne, T.

३४ रात्रीं चोरु विद्रावन]; S, Pa; गुंफे चोरविद्रावण K; गुंफे चोरू विद्रावणे Na; बाणेश्वरीं चोरविद्रावण Ne, T.

३५ रीगाला] K, Na, Pa, S; नीगाला Ne, T.

३६ Ne adds दुसरी वासना : तरि कवणे कवणु नागवीला : बाइ.

३७ पुडती तीयां तैसेंचि म्हणीतलें : एरीं तैसेंचि नीराकरीलें] T, Pa, S; पुडती तीयां ऐसेंचि नीराकरीलें Ne; lacking in K and Na.

३८ मग सर्वज्ञें म्हणीतलें] K, Na; सर्वज्ञें म्हणीतलें Pa, S; महदाईसांप्रति सर्वज्ञें म्हणीतलें Ne, T.

३९ गोसावी अवळा वेळीं कैसें बीजें केलें] K; गोसावी अवळा वेळी केली Na; गोसावी अवेळ केली Pa, S; lacking in Ne and T.

४० वाटें मिळेल] S, Pa; वाटेसि मीळैल K; मार्गीं काइ मीळैल : वाटे मीळैल Ne, T; lacking in Na.

४१ श्रीचरणीं उपानहौ नाहीं] S, Pa; गोसावियांचां स्रीचरणीं उपान्हौ नाहीं K; उपाहानौ न देखतिचि Ne, T; lacking in Na.

४२ Ne adds दुसरी वासना तियाचि आणिलिया.

४३ देउळी कां पडवीए] T, S, Pa; कापडवीये Ne; गावांबाहिरि देउळीं K, Na(n); lacking in Na.

४४ बीढारां जावों या कां] S, Pa; बीढारां या कां जावों Ne, T; lacking in K and Na.

४५ गोसावी देउळीं असति कां नदी असति] S, Pa; गोसावी असति कां नदी Ne, T; lacking in T, K, and Na.

पूर्वार्ध

१ त्रीएंबका न वचणें] K, Na, Pa; (प्रतिष्ठानीं अवस्थान) T; lacking in Ne.

२ नैएतीचि] K; एथ न एति कीं Ne, T; एथ न येतीची Pa; चुकले Na.

३ हे ऐसेची आले] Pa; हें ऐसेंचि आलें : मग : ऐसेंचि आलें Ne, T; हें एथ असे K; sentence lacking in Na.

४ हे माहात्मे] Pa; वो माहात्मे Ne, T; lacking in K and Na.

५ बाइसां स्तीति] K, Na; (बाइसां प्रेमदान) T; बाइसा मुर्ती नीरक्षनी प्रेमदान Pa; lacking in Ne.

६ सांडूनी] Pa; नासिला K, Na; lacking in Ne and T.

७ Ne adds परशरामबास : वामदेवाचीए गुंफें जाति.

८ आओ नागुबाइ] K; आवो Na; जी Pa; lacking in Ne and T.

९ Ne adds तथा हीराइसा पाठ : पटीसाळें आसन.

१० तव लेकी म्हणीतले] Pa; तवं लेंकीं गोसावीयांतें देखिलें : आणि माएतें म्हणीतलें K; तवं लेंकीं म्हणीतलें Na; lacking in Ne and T.

११ मार्जने जाले : पुजा केली] Pa; भक्तजनें पुजा केली Ne, T; मादणें जालें : पुजा जाली K, Na.

१२ ग्रहेसारंगपाणिभट ते बव्ल्हेग्रामिचे] K; ग्रह सारंग पाणी ते बळहे ग्रामीचे Pa; ते बव्ल्हे-ग्रामीचे Na; lacking in Ne and T.

१३ Ne adds परशरामपाठ :॥: वामदेवाचीए गुंफें देखीले : मग चासी भेटि जाली.

१४ Ne adds परशरामबास :॥: मागां पुरुषाचां ठाइं आकृत्रिम्य आनंदु आति : तैसा अन्येत्र आति : जेतुलेंही पाहीजे : तेतुकेंही एथ आति : आणि स्तीति जाली.

१५ Ne adds सोधु : देव्हार चौकीये : मर्दना : माळवधावरि मादनें : सकृत.

१६ Ne adds हीराइसा पाठ :॥: कटका गेले : शासन घातलें : मग आले : न्हाले : जेवीले : मग दरीसना आले.

१७ Ne adds सोध : तेव्हळीसीचि सारंगपंडीता ज्वरू : सर्वज्ञें म्हणीतलें : आतां कैसें असे : न्हां : जेवों जा : सूखें असा : दीस सतरा जरू :॥: जाला.

१८ आरोगणा जाली] Pa, K; गोसावीयांसि आरोगणा जाली Na; lacking in Ne and T.

१९ नागदेवोभटीं] K, Na, Pa; चांगदेवो भटीं Ne, T.

२० नागदेवोभटीं] K, Pa; चांगदेवोभटीं Ne, T; lacking in Na.

२१ गोसावीयास उपहुड जाला] Pa; गोसावीयांसि पजाअवस्वरू जाला K; गोसावीयांसि उदयेचा पुजावसर Ne, T; lacking in Na.

२२ तीथी श्रवण] Pa; तीथिश्रवण K(n); तीर्थ श्रवण Ne, T; lacking in K, Na.

२३ Ne adds तथा नरवीर म्हणा.

२४ Ne adds सोधु : बटीका : एथीचें उसीटें तांबूळ घेत असा : तें काइ.

627

२५ मग गोसावी तांबुळ दीधले] Pa; मां गोसावीं तेयांसि तांबोल दीधलें K; मग गोसावी
श्रीमुखीचे तांबूळ दीधले Na; lacking in Ne and T.

२६ Ne adds सोधु :॥: लोकु तुमतें नष्टभ्रष्टां म्हणतील कीं : गोत्रा कुटुंबा वेगळेयां करीति :
थाळां वाटिया जेऊं न सुती : पाटी तींवै जेवु सुती : धायरी सोएरी तुमतें वर्जीती : ऐसेयां :
मग म्हणीतलें : बटिका तुमतें कव्हणी कांहीं न म्हणे हो :॥: सोधु : बटिका : हें कांहीं :
ऐसें कांहीं तवं जाणीजैना : एथींचें उसीतें तांबूळ काइ : म्हणौनि : घेत असा : जी जी :
आपुलेया भलेया :॥: मा : तुमतें नष्टभ्रष्ट न म्हणती कीं : जी जी : म्हणती तरि म्हणती :
सोयरीं धायरीं थाळां वाटियां जेऊं न सुती : न सुती तरि (न) सुती : आणि काइ : तुमतें
वर्जिती : वर्जिति तरि वर्जिति : आणि काइ : तरि कां घेयावें : जी जी : आपुलेया भलेया :
सर्वज्ञें म्हणीतलें : बटिका : तुमतें कव्हणी कांहीं न म्हणे हो.

२७ गोपाळमंत्रभेद नीरोपण] K, Na; गोपाळ मंत्र भेद निरोपणे Pa; भेटी T; lacking in
Ne.

२८ जालेया नंतरे] Pa; जाला K; lacking in Ne and T; clause lacking in Na.

२९ जालेया नंतरे] Na; जालेया Pa; lacking in Ne and T; clause lacking in K.

३० म्हणतु असे] K, Na, Pa; lacking in Ne and T.

३१ जालेयानंतरें] K, Na, Pa; lacking in Ne and T.

३२ Ne adds हीराइसा पाठ :॥: बाइ : पुरूखाचिए भेटि जाइजे : तरि : समूखा बैसीजे :
राजागुरूदेवता यांसि पाठि देवों नये.

३३ जालेयानंतरें] K, Pa; जाला Ne, T; clause lacking in Na.

३४ Ne adds सोध :॥: येसणें जन्म.

३५ Ne adds हीराइसा पाठ :॥: पुरूखाकारणें.

३६ जालेया नंतरे] Pa; lacking in Ne, T, K, and Na.

३७ Ne adds एकें म्हणति : देउळामागें नृत्य कोणीं आसन : तवं गोसावीयांतें देखीलें.

३८ Ne adds सोधु : तथा हेचि तेथ येइल : हीराइसा पाठ :॥: तेथचि जा : मा : हे तेथचि
येइल.

३९ Ne adds हीराईसा पाठ :॥: निमंत्रीलें असे.

४० Ne adds हीराइसा पाठ :॥: हा बटिका परमेश्वरपुरा येता : कां : वारिजैल : गावां जा : पुसा :
मग : या.

४१ असे : हा ना] K, Pa; असे हा Ne; असे हो T; असे : हे ना? Na.

४२ सेंदुर्जनीं ब्राह्मणां स्तीति] K, Na; सेंदुर्जनीं ब्राह्मणा भेटि T; सेंदुर जनी वसेती :
ब्राम्हणा भेटी : स्तीती आरोगणा Pa; lacking in Ne.

४३ स्तीति जाली] Pa; तेयांसि गोसावीयांपासौनि स्तीति जाली K, Na; lacking in Ne
and T.

४४ Ne adds सोधु : सर्वज्ञें म्हणीतलें : भटो : घरा जाना : मग वीनवीलें.

४५ मर्दनामादणें जालें] K; मर्दना दीधली : मार्जने जाले Pa; मर्दना दीधलें Ne, T; lacking
in Na.

४६ मेघंकरीं बाइसें हाटा गमन] K, Na; (बाणेश्वरीं वाणियाचा आदरु) T; मेघंकरी बानेश्वरी
वसेती Pa; lacking in Ne.

४७ Ne adds तथा दाखवीति :॥: परशरामबास :॥: सोधु :॥: आतांचें : सोधु : देशकाळींचे

आचार्यें इतुलेया एकामध्यें ऐसे करीति : सारीति : हे दुसरी वासना :॥: सोधु : संकलीति : संकलौनि देति : सारिति : ऐसे तिन शब्द

४८ भेटी] T, K; स्तीति Na; भेटी : स्तीती Pa; lacking in Ne.

४९ विळचा मागुती तया स्तीती] Pa; विळिवाचा वसती Ne, T; lacking in K and Na; वीळचां हरिभटां स्तीति K(n).

५० Ne adds हीराइसा पाठ : मर्दना मादनें जालें : भक्तजना सहीत आरोगणा जाली.

५१ Ne adds (हिराइसा पाठ) : बाइ : आजी वाकीयेचा हाटु : श्रीप्रभुलागि वस्त्र घेया : तुम्ही हंसराजु पुढां जा.

५२ Ne adds हीराइसा पाठ : सर्वज्ञें म्हणीतलें : बटिका : काइ गा खडखांबुलां खेळतु असा : आणि स्तीति भंगली.

५३ Ne adds हीराइसा पाठ : बटिका या : म्हणौनि सेवटिले घरीं एकाधा एकू ठावो आपजवीजे.

५४ Ne adds : सर्वज्ञें भणीतलें : बटिका : हें काइ : आपजेवणेयाचे शब्द.

५५ Ne adds सोध : बटिका आरुतें सरा.

५६ खेळो पाठविणे] Pa, Na; खेळावया परीखू K; खेळो Ne and T.

५७ गोसावी] K, Pa, Na(n); गोसावीयांसि Ne, T; lacking in Na.

५८ बीजें करिति : आसन होए] K, Pa, Na(n); बीजें होए Ne, T; lacking in Na.

५९ खैराळां उपान्हौत्यागु] K, Na; खैराळा उपान्हौ त्याज्य Pa; lacking in Ne and T.

६० दोन्ही श्रीकर जोडूनि जय केलें] K; गोसावी जए केले Na; दोहीं श्रीकरीं नमस्करीलें Ne, T, Pa.

६१ Ne adds हीराइसा : बटिका : हें देखिलें परमेश्वरपुर : शाळेचां कळसु दीसतु असे : म्हणौनि : तेही जय केलें : एथौनि : श्रीप्रभुची महिमा : ऐसें : गा : ते श्रीप्रभु : ऐसें नीरूपण करीत.

६२ मेला जाए : जेवावें म्हणें : नेजवावें म्हणें : मेला जाए : जेवील म्हणें] K; जेवावें म्हणे : मेला जाए : जेवावे म्हणे Ne, T; आवो मेला जाए : जेवील म्हणे : नेजवी म्हणे : मेला जाए : जेवील म्हणे Na; जेवावे म्हणे : न जेवावे म्हणे : मेला जाए जेवावे म्हणे Pa.

६३ Ne adds परशरामबास : या श्रीप्रभु योग्य नव्हे : होए : या योग्य हें : होए : असों दीया.

६४ Ne adds सोधु : बाइ : उगी असा : हीराइसा पाठ : हे श्रीप्रभुची प्रवृती.

६५ Ne adds रामदेवमुनि : येया आतां माझा होए : मारूं दीधले म्हणे.

६६ एरीकडे आवारी] Pa; मग Ne, T; lacking in K, Na.

६७ उदयाची पुजा] Pa; उपहुड Ne, T; lacking in K, Na.

६८ तथा उपहार करवणे] Pa; lacking in Ne, T, K, and Na.

६९ आन आन आन्न] Pa, K; आन आन Ne, T; lacking in Na.

७० Ne adds सोध : वस्त्रपुजा करितां : हें काइ बाइ : हें काइ जालें : काइ करितें असा.

७१ नीडळावरि ठेवीति] K; lacking in Ne, T, and Pa; sentence lacking in Na.

७२ हंसराज श्रीप्रभू सेवे राहावणे] Pa; lacking in Ne, T, K, and Na.

७३ सोळें दामीं] K, Na; lacking in Ne, T, and Pa.

७४ वाणीयांपासि] K; lacking in Ne, T, Na, and Pa.

७५ आठ दाम रोकडे आणिला] K, Na; lacking in Ne, T, and Pa.

७६ Ne adds सोध : तैसें तैसें होइल : मग : हें काइ बाबा.

७७ मांगळौरीं वऱ्हारदेवीं वस्ति : चांगदेवोभटां खेळा अनुमोदन] K; मांगळौरी वस्ती Na; (बटिका खेळु) T; मांगरौळी वराह देवी वसेती and चांगदेव भटा खेळप्रसंगे स्मरणविधी निरुपण (two separate chapters) Pa; lacking in Ne.

७८ ब्राह्मणा आभासु] K, Na, Pa; ब्राह्मण अभ्यासु Ne, T.

७९ सर्वज्ञें म्हणीतलें : हें नव्हे आलें] K, Na; lacking in Ne, T, and Pa.

८० Ne adds हीराईपाठ : बाइ भीति असा : हो बाबा.

८१ Ne adds परशरामबास :॥छ॥: बाइ : चांगो सरिसा बटिकु आला : तेयासारिखा वाटतु असे : रामेश्वरबास.

८२ Ne adds शोधु : बाइ : अभ्यागतें आलीं.

८३ Ne adds दुसरी वासना : ईश्वरू काइ गा अन्यप्रकाशकू : तो स्वयंप्रकाशू कीं.

८४ Ne adds सोधु : बटिका : तुंचि आलासि : जी जी.

८५ Ne adds एकी वासना : हें श्रीकृष्णचक्रवर्ति होए : कां : जें होए तें होए.

८६ सीक्षासुत्र] K; सीक्षा शास्त्र Ne, T, Pa; lacking in Na.

८७ तेथ] K; lacking in Ne and T; sentence lacking in Na and Pa.

८८ मसणाचें] K, Pa; मशकाचें Ne, T; lacking in Na.

८९ Ne adds दुसरी वासना :॥: देव काइ सारिखे असति.

९० Ne adds शोधु : पंचाळेश्वरा गेला होतासि : पूसीलें : हें ते स्थानीं होतें : तेथ जाइजे हो.

९१ Ne adds शोधु : उपाधीं पासोडी बैसों घातली : बटिका : मळे ना : ना जी : तवं बाइसीं जाडी आणिली : आसन केलें.

९२ Ne adds परशरामबास : भागवत धाडिले : रामेश्वरबास.

९३ Ne adds हीराइपाठ : सर्वज्ञें म्हणीतलें : हा मढु रिता असे : एथ बीढार घेउनि या : यरी दीसीं पूजावस्वरा आले : गोसावीयांसि पूजावस्वर : देवीं बीढार आणविलें : मग रोटी.

९४ Ne adds शोधु : मारि : हे काइ गा : एसनीं रोटी टाके.

९५ दाखवणें] K, Na, Pa; lacking in Ne and T.

९६ कथन] K, Na, Pa; lacking in Ne and T.

९७ Ne adds शोधु : बाइ आगमीकाचा आगम समो वर्तत असे.

९८ पैला] K; lacking in Ne, T, and Na; passage lacking in Pa.

९९ Ne adds तथा मार्गु देति.

१०० भव्य पुरुष] Pa; पुरुखु एकु K, Na; भवीख पुरुषु Ne, T.

१०१ Ne adds तथा किजैल : हीराइसापाठ : तें तुम्हा कां गा होइल : ते तुम्हां एथौनि दीसे ऐसें.

१०२ नीक्षेदु] K, Na; निषेध Pa; निस्यंद Ne, T.

१०३ आपदेवभट] K(n), Pa; lacking in Ne and T; passage lacking in Na.

१०४ बैसले] Pa; नागझरिये बैसले Ne, T; lacking in K and Na.

१०५ Ne adds तथा दीजैल : हीराइस पाठ : ते तुम्हां कां गा होइल : ते तुम्हां एथौनि कीं गा.

१०६ आवगु सरिसा केला] K; आंगीया केलीया Ne, T, K(n)१, Pa; आंगीया सरिसीया केलीया K(n)२; lacking in Na.

१०७ Ne adds तथा मागां कां : हीराइसा पाठ : हे काइ देमती : तुम्हीं माघारे ते काइ.

१०८ Ne adds हीराइसा पाठ : हां गा : आणिक जडा पार्थिवा तीर्था जाइजे : तरि : ने जवीत जाइजे : तीर्थ उपवासू कीजे : तीर्थ देवता न पाहात न जेवीजे : मा : तेतुलेंहीं नाहीं.

१०९ Ne adds हीराइसा पाठ : पांडेया : आतां जाणा पां गा : हें पोफळ कैसें असे : चोखट असे जी.

११० हे गोसावीयाचे नव्हे : मग गोसावी] Pa; हें गोसावीयांचिंचि नव्हे K; मग गोसावी Na; हो : गोसावीयांची नव्हे Ne, T.

१११ Ne adds तथा श्रीकरींचेया आंगुळीया करूनि टोपरें काढुनि बाइसां कडे.

११२ वीषये] Pa; वीषय Ne, T; वीखया K; वीषया Na.

११३ Ne adds हीराइसा पाठ : तथा सेवीति : बाइ ऐसा एक वीखो भोगणें आति.

११४ का इंद्रादीक जाणेती] Pa; काइ हा दीक जाणति Ne; काहीं काहीं इंद्रादिकांचां ठाई असे K(n); sentence lacking in T and Na.

११५ Ne adds हीराइसा पाठ : ते तेथ कीं गा.

११६ Ne adds हीराइसा पाठ : हे चेया गा श्रीप्रभु.

११७ Ne adds हीराइसा : चांग पाहा : नीकें पाहा.

११८ सर्वज्ञें] K, Na; lacking in Ne, T, and Pa.

११९ साळिवाहाना] K, Na; साळीवाहानु Ne, T; साळी वाहान Pa.

१२० कव्हणी] K(n); काही Na; lacking in Ne, T, and Pa; sentence lacking in K.

१२१ Ne adds तथाः जी जी : हटु जाणा.

१२२ तीहीं म्हणीतलें : तरि काइ जी] K, Na; Pa; हो जी : निराकरीलें Ne, T.

१२३ तेयांचीं कानसुलें नावेक म्हांतारीं जालीं होतीं K; lacking in Ne, T, Na, and Pa. Ne adds हीराइसा : ऐसें जरि तुम्हीं हटु जाणा : तरि ऐसें काइ : मग कानसूल.

१२४ Ne adds हीराइसा : डखलेया उसीरू कां लाविला.

१२५ अवची फुलो फळो लागलीया] Na; अवघी फळो लागलीया Pa; फळांफूलांसि आलीया K; अवची फुलें फुलों लागलिया Ne, T.

१२६ Ne adds तथा अदंडीनाथु मळां राहीले : आनिकाळींची आनीं काळीं फुलें फुलों लागलीं.

१२७ जीये नाही : जीये काळी : तीये फुले फळे ये] Pa; अवकाळीं अवची कैची या Na; जें नाहीं जीए काळीं तीएं फूलें : जें नाहीं जीए काळीं तीएं फळें K; जें नाहीं जे जे काळीं : ते फुलें जीयें नाहीं जीये काळीं : तें फुलें तें Ne, T.

१२८ Ne adds तथा माहात्मे एक आले.

१२९ Ne adds शोधु : तेयांतें पुसा पां : मीं तेयाचेया दरिसना येवों.

१३० एती तरि] K, Na, Pa; lacking in Ne and T.

१३१ म्हणौनि दारवंठेया पासौनि मळावेन्ही राखणे घातली] Na; म्हणौनि दारवठेयापासौनि दोहीं सुरूकणी मळावरि राउत पाइक खेडेभालेयांसीं मारावेया राहाविले : ठाइं ठाइं राखणें घातलीं : चांगि नीर्वडि केली K; lacking in Ne, T, and Pa.

१३२ वाग्जाळ] K; वाघजाळ Na; वाकजाळ Pa; वागैल Ne, T.

१३३ Ne adds हीराइसा : तथा : मग ते तेथें पाताळ गुंफेसि साधनिं रिगाले.

१३४ हें इटखेडें] K, Pa; इटखेडें Ne, T; हा आमुका Na.

१३५ Ne adds हीराइसा : उर्ध्विरेते होति : ते बिंदुतें बिंदुचि जारणा जाणति : उर्ध्व रेत घेति :
ते भितरिचिया भितरि जारिति : भीतरि एक देह होए : वरिल देहा छेदभेद न प्रभवति.

१३६ Ne adds एके म्हणति : उर्ध्विरेता तो गोरक्ष : कर्म करितां न दीसे : जैसें नारियेळीं पाणि
पैसे : मग नारियेलाचें सांघीतलें.

१३७ वीखें मेळउनि फोडी] K, Pa; वीखें मीळोनि फोडी Ne, T; वीषे फोडी घोळुनि Na.

१३८ Ne adds तथा चांगदेवो भटीं.

१३९ Ne adds हीराइसा : हें काइ बाबा : तथा बाइ याचें काइ : इतुलेंचि स्विकरिजे ना : काइ
बाबा : बाइ हें हळाहळ : काळकूट : रगत सिंगीं : एकसि एक विरोधीयें : एकासि उपावो
कीजे : तवं एक चढे : च्यान्ही मेळवीली असति : तें आतां काइ करावें : बाबा : बाइ हें
काइ ऐसेंचि जाइल : एथौनि एकातें निमित्य करिल : आणि या राष्ट्रा बोलूं लावीजैल :
मग जाइजैल कीं : बाइ : एक म्हणति : बाइ : भियाना : हें राळे मवणें कीं : बाइ : खांबीं
पुजा ते होआविचि असे : एथौनि एकांतें निमित्य कीजैल : बाइ : प्राणिया : बहुत दीस
जाचतु होता : तरि तेयाचा काइ उदीमू वायांचि जावों : ना : बाबा.

१४० मागौतें गोसावीयांसि चतुर्वीधांचां मढीं अवस्थान जालें] K; मागुतें चतुर्वीधाचां मढीं
अवस्थान : दीस Ne; मागुतें चतुर्वीधाचां मढीं अवस्थान T; मग मढासी बिजे केले Pa;
मग गोसावी मागौते मढासी बीजें केलें Na.

१४१ दखलेयां चांगदेवोभटातें श्रीदत्तात्रयोप्रभूचेया दरीसना पाठवणें] K, Na; दखलें चांगदेव
भट श्रीदत्तात्रय प्रभूचेया दर्शना पाठवणे Pa; दखले चांगदेवो भट Ne; (डरखलेया चांगदेवो
भटा निराकरण) T.

१४२ Ne adds शोध : तथा तें कां गा होइल : तें नव्हें कीं : ना जी : गोसावी करीती : तरि :
होइल.

१४३ Ne adds तथा शोधु : सोइरेयाचिया गांवां न वचावें.

१४४ Ne adds परशरामबास : घाटांखालि भेटती : ते नव्हति : घाटावरि संन्यासि वेखें भेटति
ते नव्हति : मेरुवाळियाचिये पाळीं पारधीयाचेनि वेखें भेटति : ते नव्हों म्हणति : ते होति :
रामेश्वरबास.

१४५ घेउनि आले : बटिका : जाए पां : तेल घेउनि ए : गेले : आणिलें] K; lacking in Na,
Ne, T, and Pa.

१४६ Ne adds हीराइसा : सर्वज्ञें म्हणितलें : काइ जालें : एं म्हातारिएसि : एक वेळ न पुरे :
दोनी वेळ न पुरे : ऐसी वीचुकी लावा :॥: मां : उभाचि असैल : तथा उभाचि राहील :
सर्वज्ञें म्हणितलें : कां : बटिका : जाल : तरि काइ जी : बाइसाचें म्हणियें तें गोसावीयांचे :
एकें म्हणति : बाइ : एकी वीचूकी आणा : मां : एथें टेका : मां : ऐसाचि असैल : एकें
वेळें सांघों न ए.

१४७ भाखा] K; भरवा Ne, T; भाका Na.

१४८ Ne adds हीराइसा : बाइ : या : आतां याचा देवो केला असे : तथा बाइ या : आतां
तुमचेया देवा होआवें.

१४९ तेथ संतोष] Na; तेथ जोगी माहात्मा एक K, Pa; lacking in Ne and T.

१५० सांडाक्रमुज्ञान] K; सांडाक्रमु नीरुपणे Na; सांडाक्रमु Ne, T; सांडा क्रमु नीराकरणी
संतोष नाम प्रसंसा Pa.

१५१ जाणा ना] T, Pa; जाणावा Ne; जाणा गा Na; lacking in K.

१५२ Ne adds शांतिबाइसीं अवघी वेवस्था सांघीतली : मग चरणक्षाळण जालें.

१५३ Ne adds हीराइसा : रात्रीं कांहीं उपद्रो जाला : ना : जी : दीहांतु वीस वेळ ये : तिस वेळ ये : तें न ये जी : बाइ आतां तें न ये हो :॥: तथा तें आतां गेलें हो.

१५४ Ne adds हीराइसा : तथा : बाइ : तेयांचें दुख गेलें : येराचें कावरें गेलें : मग : सर्वज्ञें म्हणीतलें : बाइ : द्वारावतिए पव्हा नीगाला : तरि : आतां द्वारावतीए जाना.

१५५ तव गोसावीया जवळी शांतिबाइसीं स्तीति जाली] Pa; मग एकु दीसु माइंबाइसांसि गोसावीयांपासौनि स्तीति जाली K; जीए दिसी सांतिबाइसा गोसावीयांपासौनि स्तीति जाली Na; शांतिबाइसां स्तीति जाली Ne, T.

१५६ तीएचि दीसीं तेथ] K, Na; एकू दीस Ne, T; तव तेथ Pa.

१५७ Ne adds हीराइसा : मग वोलिया पडदणिया.

१५८ Ne adds रामेश्वरबास :॥: तीं जन्मा : परशरामबास.

१५९ कर्मांचें एथौनि] K; Na; lacking in Ne, T, and Pa.

१६० जाळीता] Pa; जाळीतांहीं परी K; एथौनि जाळीतां Ne, T; sentence lacking in Na.

१६१ नेघावीं] K, Pa; न करावी Na; घावी Ne; घ्यावीं T.

१६२ Ne adds शोधु : तेथ लागे तें बोणें करावें : तेथीचा पदार्थु घेझेना : ऐसांहीं उरे : तरि उरों दीजे : तेथचेयाचें असणें तो काशिएचा वासू : श्रीप्रभु जै लागे बोणें : ऐसा जें उरे : ती बोटीं.

१६३ Ne adds शोधु : बाइ : तुमचि एइ : एथ लागे : तल्हातें साउली कीजैल.

१६४ Ne adds परशरामबास : चांगदेवो भट : रामेश्वरबास.

१६५ स्मरणे वंध्य दिवसू कथन] Pa; स्मरण वीधान कथन K; अवांझ दिसू करणे Na; स्मरणें Ne, T.

१६६ गोसावी अनुवर्जन केले] Pa; गोसावी बोळवीत नीगाले K; गोसावी बोळवीत बीजें केलें Na; lacking in Ne and T.

१६७ तै या] Pa; तेया Ne, T; lacking in K and Na.

१६८ तरि एक दोन तरि वेळ आठवीजे : एकदोन वेळ नाहीं तरि एकु तरि वेळ आठवीजे] T; तर एक दोन वेळ तरी आठबिजे : एक दोन वेळ नाही तर एक वेळ आठविजे Pa; एकु तरि वेळ आठवीजे : एक दोन वेळ तरि एकु तरि दोनि एकुवेळ आठवीजे Ne; तरी एक दोनि वेळ तन्ही आठवीजे Na, K.

१६९ Ne adds : हीराइसा : तुमचें भविख : ऐसें दीसवडी बैसाल : तरि दीसवडि ऐसेंचि होइल : ना जी.

१७० Ne adds शोधु : पदकर नागदेवो भटां भेटी : सर्वज्ञें म्हणीतलें : भटो : कांहीं एक मागा : पुढारले : हो कां जी : न टके : मग अस्तीति पोखली : बोलति ना : कुटुंबीचीं म्हणति : पीसें लागलें : वोखद :|: भिक्षुकांसि एकाधां शब्द बोलति.

१७१ Ne adds परशरामबास : रिक्तहस्तेन न पश्येत् | राजानं देवतां गुरुं ॥ रामेश्वरबास :॥: हीराइसा : सूटती परि वरवड जाइल : गोसावी आपणचि म्हणीतलें : तें कां पा : जें तुम्हीं रिक्तहस्त भेटलेति.

१७२ Ne adds शोधु : सर्वज्ञें म्हणीतलें : ग्रंथवक्ते कीं उबेणें बोलति : सारंगपंडितीं म्हणीतलें : जी जी : स्थानीवक्ते.

१७३ बाइसें मुक्षकरूनि अवघेयां भगतिजनां लाठु उपजला] K, Na; भक्तजन सन्मुख जाले
Ne, T; आन सन्मुख जाले Pa.

१७४ राकेया लक्ष्मींद्र भटा गंडशोदक प्रसाद नीराकरण] Pa; लक्ष्मीधरभटा गंडको-
दकीं निराकरण T; title lacking in Ne; chapter lacking here in K
and Na.

१७५ Ne adds तथा मेला.

१७६ Ne adds तथा हीराइसा : पोरें हो : मग तुम्हीं कडै पडाल कीं.

१७७ दही दूध वीकू गेलीया होतिया : तीया लवकरि आलीया] Na; दहींकिरणीं दहीएं दूधें तुपें
वीकावेया गेलीया होतीया : तै ती लवकरि आलीया K, Na(n); lacking in Ne, T,
and Pa.

१७८ पुसों लागलीया] K, Na(n); गोष्टी करूं लागलीया Ne, T, and Pa.

१७९ Ne adds परशरामबास :॥: डखला पोटी ऐसें केलें : जें गांवा जाइन : मग कांहीं
गोसावीयांलागि वेचावेया आणिन : सर्वझें म्हणीतलें : काई गा डखलेया : मनोर्थु राज्य
कीजत असीजे : जी जी : सर्वझें म्हणीतलें : एथ तैसी प्रवृति नाहीं कीं : एथ जरि प्रवृति
होए : तरि हे अवची राहाटि सुवर्णाची न कीजे : पोरें हो : तुम्हीं नासाल : रामेश्वरबास :॥:
शोध : पोरें हो तुमतें कांहीं नुरें.

१८० Ne adds परशरामबास : हें चेया गा डखलेया : बाइसाचें येरंडबन : रामेश्वरबास.

१८१ Ne adds : शोध : बन काइ गा : कैसें आंबेयाचे घड लागले असति.

१८२ श्रीनगर दाखवणें] K, Na; तथा श्रीनगर सांगणे Pa; भगतां श्रीनगर दाखवणें Ne, T.

१८३ Ne adds कमलाइ : शोधु : उंहुं नाहीं : बाइ एकी थी : भिक्षा हउ इहांछों.

१८४ बांगदेवो K, Na, Pa; बागदेवो Ne, T.

१८५ Ne adds तथा : माहातुमे बाहातुमे कांहीं नथी : हउ इहां छों.

१८६ माहादाइसां] K, Na, Pa; lacking in Ne and T.

१८७ तवं तेथ भट पडितालावेया आले] K; तवं भट पडितालावेया आले Na; तव भट आले
Pa; lacking in Ne and T.

१८८ महदाइसें] K; lacking in Ne, T, and Pa; sentence lacking in Na.

१८९ भटीं म्हणीतलें] K; lacking in Ne, T, Na, and Pa.

१९० हो कां] K(n); होका Pa; हो पां Ne, T; lacking in K and Na.

१९१ जाउनि तेयाजवळि बैसले : मग भटीं पुसिलें] K; जावुनी तया जवळे बैसले : पुसीलें Pa;
जावों : तेयां जवळि पुसीलें Ne, T; lacking in Na.

१९२ तवं भटीं पुसिलें] K(n); lacking in Ne, T, Pa, K, and Na.

१९३ Ne adds एकांचेनि मतें : राउसगांवींचि.

१९४ मग दादोस बीढारी निगाले] Pa; मग दादोस बीढारा गेले K(n); दादोस बीढार निगाले
Ne, T; lacking in K and Na.

१९५ भट] Pa, K; lacking in Ne and T; list of names lacking in Na.

१९६ बाइ : कवनीकडौनि एते असा] Na; बाइ : कवणीकडौनि येतीया असति K; बाइया
कोनी कडौनी एती असत P; बाइ : या कोणी कडौनि येति असती Ne; बाइ : या : कोणी
कडौनि येति असती T.

१९७ Ne adds हीराइसा : जाल तैं ऐसे म्हणावें : हें तुमतें पुसत होतें.

१९८ Ne adds हिराइसा : बाइ : तो एथीचा एजमान : एथ पाणिभातु बाबूळसेंगा आरोगणा दीधली.

१९९ Ne adds हीराइसा : तथा भटो : तुम्हां माहात्मेयां पासौनि सूखस्वास्थ्ये आति.

२०० Ne adds हीराइसा : एथौनि तुम्हां स्थित्यांतर : गा.

२०१ माहात्मेयांपासौनि जालें] K; तुम्हा जाले असे Na; तुम्हा जे जाले असे P; जें तुम्हां जालें असें Ne, T.

२०२ Ne adds शोधु : वोपा.

२०३ Ne adds हीराइसा : तथा हें देइल : बाइ : यांसि दवणा वोपा : आणि वीडा वोपा : दीधला.

२०४ Ne adds हीराइसा : हां गा उगीयांचि असीजे : ऐसा कोणु मार्गु.

२०५ Ne adds हीराइसा : ऐसें म्हणे : तरि तुम्हीं माहात्मे म्हणा : तथा तुम्हीं माहात्मे कीं गा.

२०६ विहरणी पाट होता : गोसावी पैलाडी बिजे केले] Pa; गांवां पश्चीमे पाटु असे : तेथ गोसावीं बीजें केलें K; गोसावी पाट उडाले Na; lacking in Ne and T.

२०७ Ne adds हीराइसा : सर्वज्ञें म्हणीतलें : डखलेया : सागळ घेया.

२०८ Ne adds तथा माहात्मेनि सकळै.

२०९ Ne adds हीराइसा : कां गा रूसलेति : तेहीं म्हणीतलें : गोसावी सांभाळीतिचि ना : तुम्ही माहात्मे कीं गा.

२१० Ne adds हीराइसा : म्हणीतलें : तथा बाइ तुम्ही राहा : जरि तुम्ही राहाल तरि तुम्हा सांघातें वृधाबाइसें : रावावीजति.

२११ करितोसि] Pa; करुतोये Ne, T; करितासि K; करीता Na.

२१२ करीसी] Pa, K; करील Ne, T; कराल Na.

२१३ Ne adds हीराइसा : तथा गोदेश्वरीं गोसावीयांसि आसन : सर्वज्ञें म्हणीतलें : जा ना पा गा : हें देउळ काइसें : कव्हणी कांहीं म्हणे : कव्हणी कांहीं म्हणे : सर्वज्ञें म्हणीतलें : अभिमानकार्ये गा : पद्या नावें बटिकु : तो आपुला घरीं न्हातु होता : तो डोइए चोखणी लावीली होती : पाणिया कारणें बोबावों लागला : माया म्हणीतलें : ऐसा लवडसवडी करीतु जसिस : काइ गोदेश्वरापुढें पद्येश्वरू करिसि : तैसाचि डोइचा जुडा बांधला : बांधौनि निगाला : तो तेलंगदेशासि गेला : तेथ अपार द्रव्यें जोडीलें : आला : मग : गोदेश्वरापुढें पद्येश्वरू केला : मायेसि म्हणितलें : आइ मियां गोदेश्वरापुढें पद्येश्वरू केला : आतां मातें न्हाणि.

२१४ आडी] Pa; अंडीं Ne, T; sentence lacking in K and Na.

२१५ Ne adds हीराइसा : नरसींहाचां देउळीं : आसन : वासना : मठाचां द्वारीं : गोसावी वेढे करीत असति.

२१६ Ne adds हीराइसा : हांगा माहात्मे हो : पींड.

२१७ Ne adds शोधु : कानडी लुखाइसें : सर्वज्ञें म्हणीतलें : ब्रह्म गोळकु ऐसा असे : हीराइसा : सर्वज्ञें म्हणीतलें : अफोडी उदंबरू खाइजे : तें ऐसें : म्हणौनि : श्रीमुखीं उदंबर घातलें.

२१८ Ne adds एकाचेनि मतें : गुपीत त्रीयंबकीं आसन.

२१९ उदास्य स्वीकारे चांगदेवोभटा पाठवणी] Na, Pa; नासिकीं पंचवटिये अवस्थान : दीस पांच : चांगदेवोभटां पाठवणी K; (एकाकी वृत्ती स्वीकरणें) T; title lacking in Ne.

२२० चांगोयेंचि] K, Pa; चांगोसेंचि Ne, T; sentence lacking in Na.

२२१ हो का जी : म्हणौनि डखला दंडवत केले : निगाले : गोसावी सरीसी जाडी दिधली :॥ शोध ॥:
सर्वज्ञें म्हणीतले हे जाडी घेया : जेथ राहाल तेथ आडवी बांधावी : होकाजी : तव] Pa;
जी जी : सर्वज्ञें म्हणीतलें : हे जाडि घेया : जेथ राहाल तेथ जाडी बांधावी : तवं K; मग ते
निगाले : सर्वज्ञें म्हणीतलें : राहाल तेथ आड जाडि बांधावी : मग तेही गोसावीयांसि दंडवते
घातली : श्रीचरणां लागलें : आणि निगाले Na; lacking in Ne and T.

२२२ Ne adds हीराइसा : जावो कीं बाइ याची यात्रा.

२२३ Ne adds शोधु : लंघीतें एतें असति.

२२४ Ne adds तथा : बापुडीं झाडा खेवें देतें एतें असति : एथचें दर्शन घेयावें : ऐसें केलें
असे.

२२५ Ne adds हीराइसा : तथा : कैसी बापुडी ब्रह्मविद्या.

२२६ सरिसे नाथोबा असत] Pa; गोसावीयांसि आंबेया तळि आसन : नाथोबा गोसावीयांज-
वळि बैसले होते K; नाथोबा गोसावीयाजवळी बैसले होते Na(n); lacking in Ne
and T.

२२७ Ne adds परशरामबास : परिश्रया बीजें केलें [तेथ Pa] : रामेश्वरबास.

२२८ केस कैचे] K; केस Na, Pa; कैसे Ne, T.

२२९ Ne adds हीराइसा : हे दोचै सारिखेचि : जावळाचे : तो गांवा गेला.

२३० गोसावी] Na, Pa; lacking in Ne and T; sentence lacking in K.

२३१ Ne adds परशरामबास : बटिका : इकडे : इकडे : हा नसैल : रामेश्वरबास.

२३२ Ne adds एके म्हणति : सालेचा.

२३३ Ne adds हीराइसा : देखिलें गा चौरंगीचि वीद्या : तरि सतसीद्ध स्वभाविक गुण पुरुखाचां
ठाईं तरि आश्चर्यासि कारण होए.

२३४ सुकीयाना] Pa; सुकियाणां K; सुक्याना Na; सुकेणां T; सुवियाणा Ne.

२३५ Ne adds तथा नारायणाचां देउळीं.

२३६ Ne adds रामेश्वरबास : एतांचि कोंकणाये आसन : डखले पुडवाटुवा आणुं गेले : घेउनि
आले : डखलां सांचीतलें : परशरामबास.

२३७ Ne adds कां गा : डखलेया विरोधु : ऐसें नांव आत्मारामू : आणि भुका आरोळिया : हें
अतिविरोध : मा : बाइसातें म्हणा : एका दामाचें दुध घेया : माहात्मेया पयोर्वत दीया :
यऱ्हवीं बाईसा नीरोध कीं गा.

२३८ हीराइसा ... उपहुड] Ne (a separate chapter, without a title, preceding
the present chapter), T(n); lacking in Pa, K, and Na.

२३९ नांदौरीं] K, Na; चासी Ne, T, Pa.

२४० Ne adds सोधु : मध्येमेश्वरा आग्रे चास.

२४१ गोसावी : उपाध्ये : नाथोबा : डखले] K; गोसावी डखले उपाध्ये नाथोबा Na; lacking
in Ne, T, and Pa.

२४२ पव्हत पव्हत] K; पव्हत Pa; lacking in Ne and T; sentence lacking in
Na.

२४३ Ne adds सोधु : बाइ : याना का : आतां पुरें : गा.

२४४ Ne adds हीराइसा : तथा एथ एक स्नान करा गा : बल्हेग्रामीं ग्रह बहुत असती कीं गा.

२४५ उपध्यी] Na, K, Pa; दायांबायें Ne, T.

२४६ पुनरपि पुणतांबां पाताळगुंफे अवस्थान] K; पुणतांबा पाताळ गुंफे अवस्थान Pa; पूनीवतांबा पाताळ गुंफे अवस्थान Na; (सोपद्रवस्थान त्याग) T; lacking in Ne.

२४७ Ne adds पुनीतांबा पाताळ गुंफे अवस्थान.

२४८ Ne adds सोधु : आतां एथौनि हें स्थान सोपद्रव जालें : हींसा वर्ते.

२४९ वसती] Pa, Na; सोमनाथीं आसन : मढीं वस्ति K; lacking in Ne and T.

२५० तेथ वसती जाली] Pa; lacking in Ne and T; passage lacking in K and Na.

२५१ उत्तरार्धी अवस्थान] Pa; उत्तरार्ध स्थानीं Ne, T(n); lacking in K; chapter lacking in Na.

२५२ ते धूनि ठेवीली होती] K; तेथ उलाउनि ठेवीली होती Ne, T; ते धौ लावुनि ठेविली होती Pa; धौ दीघली होती Na.

२५३ पद्मनाभिदेवा K, Pa; पद्मनाभिदेव ... त्यासी Na; ब्रह्मनाभिदेवा Ne, T.

२५४ न एती] Pa; म्हणति Ne; sentence lacking in K, Na, and T.

२५५ करीती] Pa; केलें Ne, T; passage lacking in K and Na.

२५६ करीती : ऐसा एकदीस] Pa; केलें Ne, T; passage lacking in K and Na.

२५७ Ne adds सोधु : हा एथ असे.

२५८ होति असे] K; होत होती Na; जाली असे Pa; जाली Ne, T.

२५९ तेची] Pa; तेथ Ne, T; lacking in K and Na.

२६० उभे राहीले] Pa; उभे ठेले K; lacking in Ne, T, and Na. Ne adds तथा कोंगटें.

२६१ Ne adds सोधु पटिसाळे आसन असे.

२६२ Ne adds सोधु : ऐसे काइसेन श्रमलेति : नाएको.

२६३ बैलु भरूनि] K; बैलू भरि द्रव्ये Na; lacking in Ne, T, and Pa.

२६४ सर्वज्ञें म्हणीतलें] K, Na, Pa; सोधु Ne, T.

२६५ बीडासि] K, Na; lacking in Ne, T, and Pa.

२६६ आटवलीये] Pa; अटवेदीये Ne, T; घाटासि K, Na.

२६७ ना कें असति] K; क्ये असत Pa; lacking in Na, Ne, and T.

२६८ Ne adds एकें म्हणति : केलें आणवीलीं होतीं ते गोसावी एकदोनी आरोगण केली : गुळळा : वीडा.

२६९ बोलावु धाडूं] Pa; पर्वाकारणें तीएं एथचि बोलाउं K; नागदेवातें बोलाउं धाडि देया Ne, T; lacking in Na.

२७० आपणेयाते] Pa; एक Ne, T; sentence lacking in K and Na.

२७१ ते घेउनि आले : तव] Pa; ते घेउनि गेले Ne, T; ते आणावेया गेले : सीदौरी घेउनि आले K; ते आणावेया गेले होते : ते आले : तवं Na.

२७२ बाइ : चांगो आणि हे एथीचेचि कीं] K; बाइ चांगो अन् हा एथीचे कीं Na; बाइ हा हन चांगो हन येथचेकी Pa; हा हानु चांगो हन : एथचें कीं Ne, T. Ne adds एकी वासना ॥ याचां ठाई ऐसिया चेष्टा नाहीं कीं.

२७३ Ne adds हीराइसा पाठ : बटिका हें धुनि या गा.

२७४ Ne adds परशरामबास : आपुलें वोवळें एथ वाउं ये कीं न ये : इतुलेंहीं प्राणियांसि ज्ञान नाहीं : हे रामेश्वरबास वासना : शोधु : बाइ वोवळें एथ संपादिलें.

२७५ तेहीं म्हणीतलें : तरि काइ जी] K, Na; तर काइजी Pa; शोधु : सोभागा तरि काइ जी Ne, T.

२७६ Ne adds हीराइसापाठ : मा रे तरि तुम्हीं सोभागाचा गाडुगा मां :॥: हीराइसापाठ : मा रे तरि तुम्हीं सोभागाचा गाडुवा म्हणा.

२७७ आबाइसाते] Pa; उमाइसातें Ne, T; lacking in K and Na.

२७८ Ne adds हीराइसापाठ : यथ तवं कांहीचि म्हणावेंचि न लगे.

२७९ आपुलीए] K; आपूला Na; lacking in Ne, T, and Pa.

२८० काढिला] Pa; काढिली Na; कढिला Ne, T; lacking in K.

२८१ Ne adds परशरामबासपाठ : पारणाइती बाइया : सवीया उसीरू जाला : रामेश्वरबास : सोधु : पारणाइती बाइया भीक्षां वेळ जाली.

२८२ जी जी : अपुसीं आम्हीं तेयांचें चेतलें] K, Na; मग निद्रा आलि : तैसेंचि उमाइ जालें जी : जी जी Ne, T; मग निद्रा आली जी : तैसेची उमाइसा जाले जी : जी Pa.

२८३ Ne adds रामेश्वरबास : हीराइसापाठ : तैंसा अवसरीं एतुलेया आंतु तेतुकें तेतुके घेतलेयां तैसा दोषु नाहीं.

२८४ Ne adds हीराइसापाठ : एकां एथचि नरक.

२८५ Ne adds तथा भटोबासीं पुसीलें : तें कैसें जी.

२८६ गोसावीयांचीं K, Na; lacking in Ne, T, and Pa.

२८७ एतुलेनि एक चाटा आला] K, Na; इतुलेनि एक आला Pa; येरू आणि Ne, T.

२८८ जर हे धोत्र धुवाना] Pa; माझे धोत्रे धुवावें : धूआ नां तरि K; माझे धोत्रे धू आणा : तरि Na; जरि धोत्रें धों आणा Ne, T.

२८९ तव आनीक ए] Pa; तवं दूसरा आला K, Na; आणिक धुति Ne, T.

२९० काइ] Pa; lacking in Ne and T; sentence lacking in K and Na.

२९१ Ne adds एकें म्हणति : बाबा : यक येळापुरा आला होते : एक एथ आले.

२९२ तेथूनि ऐसेया बावनां पुरुखां वीद्यादान] K; तेथौनि ऐसेया बावन्न पुरुषू वीद्यादान Na; हे एथ बावन विद्यावंत असत Pa; हे एथीचे बावन वीद्यावंत Ne, T.

२९३ Ne adds हीराइसापाठ : तुम्हीं यातें कांहीं सांगा.

२९४ जी तर आताची करु] Pa; जी जी : तरि आतांचि करूं? K; जी जी : करु आताचि? Na; जरि करि ना Ne, T.

२९५ Ne adds हीराइसापाठ : उतरवा.

२९६ आणि ए लेकाची माये म्हणौनि ए दीठि उतरु जाणति] Na; बाइ : ए पुत्राची माता : एं दीठि उतरूं जाणति K; रामेश्वरबास Ne, T; हे प्रश्रा [= परशरामबास] Pa.

२९७ Ne adds सोध : तथा घाटु तो कोणांसि : परमेश्वरपराएण तयांसि कीं.

२९८ काइ ब्रह्मविद्या] K, Na, Pa; काइ ब्रह्मविद्या : हें काइ जाणावें असे Ne, T.

२९९ परवडी दोनि च्यारि दाखवीलीया] Na; परवडी दोनिच्यारि एकी दाखवीलीया K; दाखवीले Ne, T, Pa.

३०० Ne adds हीराइसापाठ : वेताळा : पुढें कोलु ठेउनि वेताळा नमस्कारू वीसरलेति : होकां जी.

३०१ Ne adds रामेश्वरबास : हें महात्में : परशरामबास.

३०२ Ne adds हीराइसापाठ : तुम्ही काइ होआ : हां जी : जैसे आम्ही तैसी यें : तैसींचि.

३०३ Ne adds परशरामबास : एक दोनि वेळ एथें याल : तरि तुम्ही भेकों लागाल : रामेश्वरबास : सोधु : तुम्ही जरि दीन दोनि : हीराइसा पाठ : सांत पांच दीस असाल : आणि : ऐसेंचि रडाल.

३०४ Ne adds सोधु : उदीयांचि उपहुड.

३०५ महादाइसीं] K, Na(n), Pa; बाइसीं Ne, T.

३०६ माहादाइसें राहीयाचां हातीं एका दामाचें कवडे देत होतीं] K; माहादाइसी राहीनाएकाचा हाती दामाचे कवडे दीधले Na; lacking in Ne, T, and Pa.

३०७ Ne adds हीराइसापाठ : यें ऐसें कांगा करीतीं : आतां तवं हें म्हणतें असति : तैसेंचि करा : एकें म्हणति : तुमचें केंहीं गेलें असे.

३०८ Ne adds हीराइसापाठ : बाइ : आतां तवं यें म्हणतें असति : तेंचि करा : मग तुमचें तें केंहीं गेलें असे.

३०९ हें काइ बाइ : तांदूळांची खीरि केली : जी जी :] K; हे काइ : तांदूळाची क्षीरी केली : मा Na; बाइ Ne, T, Pa.

३१० Ne adds हीराइसापाठ : बाइ तुम्हीं म्हणतें होतीति : तें तैसेंचि : ईश्वरीं आवडि नावडि असे : परि ईश्वरीची प्रवृत्ति बाइसेंचि जाणति.

३११ Ne adds परशरामबास : पापही होए : पुण्यही होए : रामेश्वरबास.

३१२ करु : न करु] Pa, K(n); करूं Ne, T; न करु Na; lacking in K.

३१३ Ne gives only the title of this chapter. T leaves it out entirely. K, Na, and Pa give the title and various versions of the story. The version here comes from K, where it is *Pūrvārdha* 332.

३१४ Ne adds हीराइसा पाठ : तरि काइ जालें : ना जी : विसरलें.

३१५ दाइंबासि स्तीति जाली होती : ते पुढां गेले : गोसावीयांसि जेथ आसन रचावें तेथ जाऊनि] K(n), Pa; नाराएणाचा देउळीं चौकी दाइंबा बैसले होते : बाइसे तेथ आली : तवं तया स्तीति भरली होती Na; गुंफा जवं झाडिजे तवं बाइसें चौकी आसन घालुं गेलीं : तवं दायांबा स्तीतिवंत : चौकीं बैसले असति K; दायांबा गेले Ne, T.

३१६ बाबासि] K, Na, Pa; बाइसासि Ne, T.

३१७ Ne adds हीराइसापाठ : बाइ : हा ऐथचें म्हणौनि राहीला : आणिकाचें तरि टाकौनि घालीता.

३१८ Ne adds तथा : बाइ.

३१९ Ne adds हीराइसापाठ : मग पुसीलें : तो कें गा : जी जी : तो तेथ राहीला : सांगितले.

३२० Ne adds हीराइसा पाठ : आम्हांपरि होइल : पोरू गेला अंगा : तेथौनि निगा गा.

३२१ Ne adds हीराइसापाठ : बाइ : या पैला हरिणामध्यें हें एका हरिणा होइजैल : मग काइ कराल : कवणापाठीं धावाल.

३२२ आणि बाइसे भीयाली : मग उगीचि राहीली] Na; तवं दायंबायें म्हणीतलें : बाइ : अवघेयांची सीसें कां नीवटाल : आणि बाइसें गजबजिलीं K; तव दायंबाये म्हणीतले : बाइ अवघेयाची सीसे का लावाल : तथा निवटाल : मग बाइसै नावेक गज बजीली Pa; दायांबायें म्हणीतलें : बाइ : गजबज जाली Ne, T.

३२३ Ne adds तथा : पारिकें.

३२४ Ne adds तथा मदळसेसी उभे असति.

३२५ Ne adds हीराइसापाठ : तैसें कांहीं असे : तरि : कांगा ये स्थानीं असिजैल : तैसें एथ
कांहीं नाहीं.

३२६ इतुलेनी तयाची कुमती हरली : मग ते निगाले Pa; जुहारू केला आणि नीगाले K; तेही
म्हणीतलें : हे काइ जी : गोसावीयांचे ते गोसावीयांसिचि : हे आरण्ये म्हणौनि म्हणीतले
Na; lacking in Ne and T.

३२७ तेहीं गोसावीयांतें देखिलें K; शोध ॥ गोसावीयाते देखाले आन तयाची कुमती गेली :
दंडवते कर करु Pa; गोसावीयांसि दंडवते घातली : आणि श्रीमुर्ति देखौनि क्षोभले Na;
lacking in Ne and T.

३२८ मग बाइला भीक्षा चालू भीति] Na; एतुकेनि गाविचा लोकु भेओं लागला : भेणेंचि भीक्षा
चालिति K; नागिवे देखौनि Ne, T; lines missing in Pa.

३२९ Ne adds हीराइसा पाठ : येथचे तें बाइसातें पुसौनि घेयावें : जा : बाइसातें पुसा : माः
घेया.

३३० आदी महादेवो] Pa, K(n), Na; आदि माहादेवी Ne, T, K.

३३१ अस्ति] Pa; स्तिति Ne, T; lacking in K and Na.

३३२ Ne adds हीराइसा पाठ : तेयां पासौनि दोघां चौघां गोमटें : तेयाची स्त्री म्हणे : तुम्हां
पासौनि दोघांचौघां गोमटें : तरि मज नाहीं : तुम्हां पासौनि मज कांहीं गोमटें होआवें : तेहीं
म्हणीतलें : आम्हां पासौनि गोमटें होइल : आणि आम्हांसिचि वोखटें करावें ऐसी बूधि
उपजैल : ना : तुम्हां पासौनि मज कांहीं गोमटें होआवेंचि : आणि जाली : आणि आवेश
उठिला : काठी घेउनि पाठीं लागली : तेहीं देह सांडिलें : आणि तेया विशिर्ण केल [केलें] :
ते विदेहीए पुरुषु : देहा वेगळे हों जाणति : आणि स्तिति भंगली : आणि रडों लागली :
माझेया प्रिया : मज प्रियेवीण नसवे : तवं आसरणी जाली : तुमतें म्हणीतलें कीं आम्हां
पासौनि गोमटें होइल : आणि : आम्हांसिचि वोखटें करावें ऐसी बूधि उपजैल : ना : आतां
मज नसवे : हो कां : अवघें एकवट मेळवा : मेळवीले तेहीं स्किकरीलें

३३३ हु हु म्हणौन नुठीति] Pa; उंहुं नुठी Ne, T; ते नुठीति K; lacking in Na.

३३४ भाइदेव] Pa, K, Na; lacking in Ne and T.

३३५ ओटीए] Pa, K(n); आंगीचीया बाहीया K; आंगीचा वारखोरा Na, K(n); lacking
in Ne and T.

३३६ मग गोसावी विष्णुभटाते पुसीले : तुमचा कुटुंब परीवार निकेन असे : जी असे : आन
तया स्तीती जाली] Pa; सर्वझें म्हणीतलें : तुमचें कुटंबपरिवारू नीकेनि असे : जी जी :
मग गोसावीं तेयांतें कृपाद्दष्टि अवळोकिलें : आणि तेयां स्तीति जाली K; lacking in
Ne, T, and Na.

३३७ Ne adds हीराइसापाठ : देमती हा प्रतीतपंथु : एकू वीश्वासपंथु.

३३८ तैसा हा वीस्वास पंथू नव्हे] Na; lacking in Ne, T, K, and Pa.

३३९ Ne adds हीराइसापाठ : तथा तथ्ये नसें घेउनि ठाकाल : ऐसें म्हणति : जैसी पासवाणिची
रेघ.

३४० Ne adds हीराइसापाठ : माहात्मे एक : ते आपणिया सीक्षा घोकवीति : ते न ये : तेहीं
म्हणीतलें जाय तरि तुं म्हैसा : ऐसा मी म्हैसा : आणि काइ : म्हणौनि आपणेयासि सिंगें
केलीं : मग पैन्हां गेला : आले : तेहीं म्हणीतलें साउमा ये : तेहीं म्हणीतलें सींगें अडति ना :
ऐसी कानवडी मानु करूनि ये : हो का : म्हणौनि : आला : मग : तेहीं माथां हातु ठेवीला :

आतां तुं म्हैसा नव्हसि : हो : हो कां.

३४१ Ne adds हीराइसापाठ : एक ज्ञान मोचक : एक अमोचक : एक भक्ति मोचक : एकी अमोचक : एक वैराग्य मोचक : एक अमोचक.

३४२ आन गोसावी प्रगट जाले] Pa; मग गोसावी प्रगट जाले Na; तैसेंचि गोसावी दृष्ट जाले K; lacking in Ne and T.

३४३ Ne adds हीराइसा पाठ : पींपळगावां सरिया गव्हाण : ते गव्हाणि आसन.

३४४ Ne adds हीराइसा पाठ : चांगदेवो भटातें म्हणीतलें : बटिका : चणा घेया : खुडाना : घेतला : बटिका बोरें घेउनि या : बोरें एथ कांहीं देखों ना जी : ऐसें ऐसें जा पा : जाति : तवं बोरें खाली श्रवण पडीलें असें : ऐसे गा आमचे गोसावी : उजु म्हणतु कां पैले बोरीचीं बोरें आणा.

३४५ या नगरा भीक्षा कीजे] K, Na; माहात्मा या नगरीं असीजे Ne, T, P.

३४६ Ne adds हीराइसापाठ : लेख लाहे.

३४७ Ne adds हीराइसापाठ : काइसेया कारणें : जी जी : तुम्हीं म्हणत असा : तेयाचि लागि : तऱ्हीं नुमटे :॥: एक सतेव वैराग्य : एक वीखया कारणें वैराग्य : एक कीर्तिपर : ए ऐसीं उघडीं नागीवीं नगरीं पाटणीं : हातें हातु न पवीजे : घरा नेति : उटीति : न्हाणिति : ताटीं ठाणवै : जेउं वाडीति : बाजेसूपवटी निजवीति : एरीं दीसीं तैसेंचि तथा.

३४८ Ne adds सोधु : बाइसीं म्हणीतलें : काइसें मनोर्थे : बाइ : या पासिल जाडि मात्रा घेया.

३४९ Ne adds सोधु : तेयांही आवडि हो कां.

३५० घेवुनी आला : खावेया जाले] Pa; आलेखावीया जाले Ne, T; तें तो द्रव्य घेउनि आला : मग तेयाचां घरीं संपति जाली K; मग तो त्याते घेऊनि आला : घरांतु ते रोविले : इतुकेन तो सुखे असो लागला Na.

३५१ Ne adds शोधु : दादला.

३५२ नकारा णकारा] नकारा नकारा Ne, T; नकारा नुकारा Pa, K(n); lacking in K and Na.

३५३ परमानु इतुका] Pa; प्रमाणुचि इतुका K; प्रमाणु इतुला Na; प्रमाणु यतुका Ne, T.

३५४ बिढारा] Pa, Na; बीढारासि K; lacking in Ne and T.

३५५ Ne adds शोधु : ऐसें न कीजे.

३५६ तेथ वसती जाली] Pa; वस्ती जाली Na; lacking in Ne and T; passage lacking in K.

३५७ एकी वासना] Pa; lacking in K, Na, Ne and T.

३५८ Ne adds हीराइसापाठ : वाउनि घेउनि या.

३५९ Ne adds शोधु : एथ नांवें ठेवीलीं : यें साधें वराडीची कीं.

३६० जैसें हें] K, Na; lacking in Ne and T; sentence lacking in Pa.

३६१ Ne adds शोधु : ये कां अपूर्व.

३६२ Ne adds हीराइसापाठ : तें कैसें साधे हो.

३६३ यांसि कां कोपतें असा : यें वराडीची साधें कीं : एथ गोसावीं साधें नावं ठेविलें] K; तुम्ही यासि का कोपते असा : ए काइ जानते असति : ए वराडीची साधे Na; ए साधे वराडीचीकी : तथा बाइ यासी का कोपते असा : ये वराडीची साधेकी : एथ गोसावी साधे नाम ठेवीले Pa; साधें वराडीची Ne, T.

३६४ नरां] K(n), Pa; रांरां Ne, T; lacking in K and Na.

३६५ Ne adds हीराइसापाठ : तथा आनंदाचेया चाडा आलेति : तरि हें काइ.

३६६ असें K(n); ऐसें Ne, T, Pa; lacking in K and Na.

३६७ Ne adds हीराइसापाठ : बाइ : या एकादशि : दादोसातें नेया.

३६८ गोसावी दादोसाते राहवावे] Pa; गोसावी दादोसाते राहावीतु का K, Na; दादोस गोसावी राहावें Ne, T.

३६९ Ne adds हीराइसापाठ : तथा काइ बाइ लुखलुखीतें.

३७० Ne adds हीराइसापाठ : तरि कवण कवण पां धाडीजे : पद्मनाभि तरि तुम्हीं जा.

३७१ ओसरीयेवर बाज सुपवती घातली] Pa; आंगणीं बाजसुपवती घातली K, Na; lacking in Ne and T. Ne adds रामेश्वरबास : नसूधी सूपवतीचि : परशरामबास.

३७२ तेथ गोसावीयास आसन जाले] Pa; गोसावीयांसि तेथ आसन जाले Na; तेथ गोसावीयांसि आसन घातलें Ne, T; तेयावरि बाइसीं आसन रचिलें K.

३७३ पद्मनाभि] Pa; ब्रह्मनाभि Ne, T; lacking in K and Na.

३७४ गोसावी म्हणौनि K, Na, Pa; गोसावी Ne; lacking in T.

३७५ Ne adds हीराइसापाठ : काइ पाहातें असा : साधें हो : साधें व्हो देवो पातें असा : या : देवो एथें असे.

३७६ साधीं म्हणीतलें : ना जी : मर्दना देओं नेणें : सर्वज्ञें म्हणीतलें : तरि वैरातें कोण उटी : ना जी : आमतें चाटे बहुत असति : ते आंगें उटिति] K; साधी म्हणीतलें : ना जी : मी मर्दना देवो नेणे : सर्वज्ञें म्हणीतलें : तरि भातारासि कोण उटी : ना जी : आमते नाइ कवडी चाटे बहूत असति : ते आंगे उटिति Na; जी जी : आमतें नायकावांगडु : आमतें चाटे बडुवे मर्दना देति Ne, T; जी आम्हा ना इकावा गुंडू आमते चाटे बडुवे मर्दना देती P.

३७७ Ne adds हीराइसापाठ : तरि लेंकरूवां काइ करा.

३७८ Ne adds तथा ऐसें एथ दाखवा : हीराइसापाठः परसवणें एथें दाखवा.

३७९ Ne adds हीराइसापाठ : साधें व्हो जेतुलें बळ असे : तेतुले एथ दाखवा : यऱ्हवीं एथौंनि जाणीजत असीजे.

३८० मळीया] Pa, K, Na; साळिया, Ne, T.

३८१ Ne adds हीराइसापाठ : आरोगण जालेया उपरिं म्हणीतलें : बिढारा जा ना : रात्री वडिल जाली : बाइ : साधा प्रसादु देया : पद्मनाभी साधातें बोलवीत जा.

३८२ Ne adds हीराइसापाठ : धुइं पुर्ती कोठीयां कोणीं सुनाचेनि हातें ताक आंबील दीयावी जी.

३८३ Ne adds वासना.

३८४ Ne adds शोधु : सर्वज्ञें म्हणीतलें : अन्नराशि एक आलें : तथा [आलेमा Pa].

३८५ अवस्थान] K, Na, Pa; lacking in Ne and T.

३८६ Ne adds हीराइसापाठ : तथा बाइ : इंद्राचीं इंद्रीयद्वारें : नावें आंकुश शक्ति संचार.

३८७ इंद्रेया] K, Na, Pa; lacking in Ne and T.

३८८ Ne adds हीराइसापाठ : हां गा : हस्ति वेंझ देवों आलेयांहीं परि ब्राह्मणांसि वसैए आंतु रिगों नये : ऐसें तुमचें शास्त्र बोले : जी जी : तरि तुम्हीं कैसे आलेति : ना : जी : आम्ही आपुलेया गोसावीयां सरिसे आलों.

३८९ Ne adds हीराइसापाठ : देवता होए नव्हे.

३९० Ne adds हीरीइसापाठ : ऐसा गा : भटाचार्या : आपूलेनि आभिमानें देवता दुषिली : वैरीयाचा देवो जाला : तरि : काइ दगडें हाणौनि फोडावा : हां गा : देवतेसि [आणि K] आबूखा [घालिजे K].

३९१ Ne adds हीराइसा पाठ : तथा काइ गा इंद्रेया : देवो पाहिजतु असिजे : जी जी : देवो ऐसा असे.

३९२ गौराइ दर्शना ज्ञान करणे] Pa; गौराइ पंचराणेयांचा मुक्ष नाएकु म्हणणें K; गौराइ पंचराणेयाचा मुख्ये नाएकू कथन Na; तथा गौराइ नीद्राप्रसंगीं सीक्षापण Ne, T.

३९३ Ne adds हीराइसा पाठ : सर्वज्ञें म्हणीतलें : बाइ : तुम्हीं एथीचेया दर्शना आलींति : तरि एथीचेया अवसरा केधवांहीं न या : तें काइ.

३९४ तथा नीद्रा प्रसंगें इंद्रोबा सीष्यापने] Pa; गौराइनीद्राप्रसंगें इंद्रभटां सीक्षापण K; गौराइ नीद्रा प्रसंगी इन्द्रभटा कोपणे Na; lacking in Ne and T.

३९५ गौराइसे] Pa; lacking in Ne, T, K, and Na.

३९६ पद्मनाभि] Pa; ब्रह्मनाभि Ne, T; sentence lacking in K and Na.

३९७ Ne adds हीराइसापाठ : सर्वज्ञें म्हणीतलें : बाइ : यांतें बोळवीतें जा : सांघातें पद्मनाभि देव पाठविलें : बाइसें बोळवीतें गेलीं : तयांसि निरोवीली.

३९८ जें गोसावीं माझा कैवारु चेतला : आणि इंद्रभटासि ऐसें जालें] K; गोसावी माझा कैवारु चेतला : इंद्रभटी ऐसे जाले Pa; जे गोसावी माझा कैवारु चेतला : इन्द्रबासि ऐसे जाले Na; lacking in Ne and T.

३९९ पाहा] K, Pa; आम्हा Ne, T; lacking in Na.

४०० Ne adds एक म्हणति : दंडवत केलें : श्रीचरणा लागली.

४०१ Ne adds शोधु : एथौनि आद्यप्रवृति : हीराइसापाठ : आतां तुमतें हें न बंधी हो.

४०२ Ne adds शोधु : साच कीं : बाइ : हें काइ पांगुरूजावें असे : माहात्मा म्हणतु असे तैसें कां न कीजे : शोधु : ना जी.

४०३ Ne adds शोधु : दाम सोळा : वीस : बावीस : पाउनि : दोनि.

४०४ Ne adds हीराइसापाठ : सोळें दामीं ऐसें वस्त्र आणुनि दीयाल : बाइ दीया सोळा दाम : जी जी : पाउण आसु लाहे : पाउण आसूं आणुनि दीयाल : बाइ : दीया आसू.

४०५ Ne adds हीराइसापाठ : बाइ तेथें जातें असा : तरी तेथें श्रीचांगदेवो राउळांचेया पाताळ गुंफा असति तेया पाहा हो.

४०६ Ne adds हीराइसापाठ : मासोपवासीए हो : तुमचीं सांघातीएं द्वारावतीए जातें असति : तरि तुम्हीं कां न वचा : जी जी : मी न वचें : एथौनि पाठवीतां न वचा : पाठीं रडतें जाल.

४०७ Ne adds हीराइसापाठ : उभे ठाकले : हाती धरीले : ते प्रमाण म्हणौनि बैसले.

४०८ Ne adds हीराइसापाठ : भटो आतां सांघात दुर जाइल.

४०९ Ne adds हीराइसापाठ : एथौनि संबळ दीजैल : एथौनि पाए देइजति.

४१० Ne adds हीराइसापाठः बहुती सूगरणी देखीलीया : परि : सात पांच मूसळें मेळउनि लाडु फेडिजति ऐसी कव्हणी सूगरणी नाहीं देखीली.

४११ Ne adds हीराइसापाठ : पटिसाळे उजवेयाकडें : आसन.

४१२ Ne adds हीराइसापाठ : माहात्मेया एथ खेवं देया.

४१३ Ne adds हीराइसापाठ : बाइ : तुमतें खाजें असे तें आणा.

४१४ सर्वज्ञें म्हणीतले] Na, Pa; मग सर्वज्ञें म्हणीतलें K; lacking in Ne and T.

४१५ जेनेसी जे ते तीयेसी] Pa; जेयांसि दीजे तेयांसि K; जेनेसी जेन ते तयासि Na; जेणें
कीजे तें तेयांसि Ne, T.

४१६ नीराकरण] K, Pa, Na; lacking in Ne and T.

४१७ पावो] Pa, K, Na; पालो Ne, T.

४१८ Ne adds हीराइसा पाठ : बटिका : चणा आपजवाजा.

४१९ Ne adds हीराइसापाठ : कूणबीयें चणा रगडीला : उपणीला : मग मोट बांधौनि :
गोसावीयांपासि घेउनि आले.

४२० Ne adds शोधु : धीडरीं रांधावीं.

४२१ Ne adds हीराइसापाठ : आपणचि डालि करावी : आपणचि वाटावी : आपणचि धीडरीं
करावी : पुसों लाभे : परि : करूं न लभे.

४२२ एकी वासना] Pa; lacking in Ne and T; passage lacking in K and Na.

४२३ लागली] Pa, K, Na; lacking in Ne and T.

४२४ दवने] Pa, K(n); lacking in K, Na, Ne, and T.

४२५ तेथ] K, Na; तेथे Pa; तेणें Ne, T.

४२६ गोसावी कोण] Na, Pa; गोसावी कोण हो K; कोण Ne, T.

४२७ Ne adds हीराइसापाठ : हां बटिका : जी जी : सर्वेझें म्हणीतलें : श्रीप्रभुचेया दर्शना जातां
एथौनि कां गा वारिजैल : परमेश्वरपुरा जावों म्हणें : तें केसणें गोमटें : मा : तेया मोहरा :
पाउल घाली : तेथ केसणें गोमटें : मा : परमेश्वरपुरा जातां : पाउल पाउलां गोमटें कीं गा.

४२८ Ne adds हीराइसापाठ : कै जाल : मग पुसीलें.

४२९ जावयाचे] Pa; lacking in Ne and T; sentence lacking in K and Na.

४३० Ne adds हीराइसापाठ : वीधि वीहीला : पेणोवेणा जावें : उपेणें न करावें : वाडवेळ
श्रीप्रभुचेया श्रीचरणावरि माथा न ठेवावा : समूखां न बैसावें : श्रीप्रभु निरोधू न करावा :
पाठवीती तेव्हळिसीचि जावें : देवतेसि निरोधु कीं गा.

४३१ तेथौनि मेहकरीं] K; lacking in Ne, T, Na, and P.

४३२ Ne adds हीराइसापाठ : सांघातीयां एथचि संवाद मा.

४३३ Ne adds हीराइसापाठ : कव्हणी एक आलें : तें कीर्तितें करूनि गेलें : आतां तेथ काइ
असे : कें वर्जेंचें स्नान : शारंगधराचें दर्शन : आणि : कें श्रीप्रभुचें दर्शन : कें ल्यें : कें हें.

४३४ Ne adds एकी वासना : दाहा घेतले.

४३५ Ne adds शोधु : दोनि वेळ : वास पाहीली : श्रीचरणें घे घे : आवो मेला जायें म्हणे.

४३६ Ne adds हीराइसापाठ : मार्तंडा जा : कवडां दुध फोकरा.

४३७ लखुबाइसें : देमाइसें सेंदुर्णिसि सन्निधानीं होतीं : तेथ तयांसि आणि बाइसांसि काहीं
तुडपुड जाली होती : मग गोसावीं सेंदर्णीहुनि बीजें करूं आदरीलें : तेव्हळीं आधीं] K,
Na(n), Pa; lacking in Ne, T, and Na.

४३८ Ne adds हीराइसापाठ : बाइ : यें येथीचेया दरीसना आलीं : तुम्हीं न याचि तें काइ : ना
जी : एइजे आणि बाइसें वीसारुंचि लागति.

४३९ Ne adds हीराइसापाठ : देमती तुम्हा होआवी वोढाळा गोरुवाची वाणी : कव्हणी एकू
सेतकरी असे : तो आपुलें वल्हाटें राखत असे : वोढाळ गुरूं असे : तें थैक म्हणतां घांसू
घेउनि जाए : तेयांसि घांसू तवं फळें कीं.

४४० चांगदेवो पुरीये अवस्थान] Pa, K(n); चांदेवीं आवस्थान K, Na; चांगदेवो पुरीए

अवस्थान :॥: चींचखेडकर रामदेवाचा अवसरू : आइकणें Ne; चींचखेडकर रामदेवाचा अवसरू आइकणें T.

४४१ चींचखेडकरां रामदेवाचा अवसरू आइकणें] K; कविडींभ रामदेव गायन श्रवणे आंगी : टोपरे : माळ प्रदान Pa; चींचखेडकर रामदेव Ne, T; title lacking in Na.

४४२ ऐसा गोवळु गोसावी माझा गोरूवें राखे : गोपाळवेखें ॥ आलीएं परि गोवळु ऐसा नावडे : माया मानवीया जाले ॥ रामेयांसि स्वामी नोळखे कव्हणी : आलीएं K; गोसावी माझा गोरुवे राखे : गोपाळ वेखे आलीए : परि गोवळु ऐसा न वरे : माया मानवीया जाले : रामयास्वामि कव्हनी नोळखे कव्हणी आलीए Na; lacking in Ne, T, and Pa.

४४३ Ne adds हीराइसापाठ : बाइ हा आणिका भगता सारिखा नव्हे : हा सलोल.

४४४ Ne adds हीराइसा पाठ : बाइ : हा स्तीतितवं देखतु असे :॥छ॥: गोपाळबा : गोसावी साचचि: उदकांत बीजें केलें : बाइसीं देखीलें : तो आभासु पालुखा केला.

४४५ Ne adds तथा जी जी : वाघु आला.

४४६ Ne adds शोधु : लोकु देखैल : आतां राहीजो माहात्मा.

४४७ Ne adds हीराइसापाठ : बाइ हा कोण्हाचें कांहीं न करी : परि : लोकू यासि उपद्रो करील कीं.

४४८ वालसेंगेसि बीजें केलें] K, Na; वालसेंगे बीजे केले Pa; वालसेंगे Ne, T.

४४९ आसन जाले] K, Na, Pa; अवस्थान Ne; sentence lacking in T.

४५० दाहा दाहा बारा बारा] Pa; दाहा बारा बारा Ne; lacking in T, K, and Na.

४५१ कथन] Pa, Na; दरीसन K; lacking in Ne and T.

४५२ Ne adds हीराइसापाठ : देमती ऐसीयांचि निजावें : आणि : ऐसाचि आंबा : तोंडीं घालावा.

४५३ Ne adds शोधु : हें कोणें केलें : देमती : ऐसें.

४५४ जी] Pa; जी जी : देमाइसीं झोळी धुतली Ne, T; lacking in K and Na.

४५५ जैसे मासे तैसीं तुम्हीं पोरे] K, Na; जैसीं तुम्हीं तैसे पोरे Ne, T; जैसी तुम्ही तैसे : पोरे हो Pa.

४५६ तीन] Pa; दोनी Ne, T; lacking in K; chapter lacking in Na.

४५७ Ne adds हीराइसापाठ : देमती आतां तुम्हां सवइछा असावयां आज्ञा हो.

४५८ Ne adds हीराइसापाठ : बाइ : द्रीढपुरुषु एति आणि आंबेया वेचु होइल.

४५९ आंब्र कथन] Pa, K, Na; lacking in Ne and T.

४६० Ne adds हीरीइसापाठ : हा आंबा खाए : तेयासि : ज्वरू ए.

४६१ देमाइसा करवी वाटी धुववणें] Na; एकाइसांकरवि वाटी धूववणें K; लखुबाइसां Ne; (लखुबाइसाते 'आपुली वाटी धुवा' म्हणणें) T; chapter lacking in Pa. Ne adds शोधु : लखुबाइसें जेवीति : देमाइसां करवि वाटी धुवविति : एकुदीसीं लखुबाइसें जेविली : गोसावीयां देखीलें : सर्वज्ञें म्हणीतलें : बाइ : वाटी धुआ : तुमचा ताटकाढा : बाहीरि गेला असे : ऐसें रामेश्वरबास : परशरामबास : अज्ञातलीळा.

४६२ Ne adds तथा एकाइसें.

४६३ Ne adds हीराइसापाठ एकाइसाची.

४६४ लखुबाइसें] K(n); एकाइसें Ne, T, K, Na, Pa.

४६५ वाहों] K, Na, Pa; चेओं T; धों Ne.

४६६ घोकीते] Na; नोकीतु K; म्हणतेची Pa; खोवीतेंचि Ne, T.

४६७ संपादा] K, Na; मग Ne; lacking in T and Pa. Ne adds शोधु.

४६८ Ne adds परशरामबास : तुमचे आठरा रोग ये पींपळीं बांधीजति : रामेश्वरबास.

४६९ Ne adds हीराइसापाठ : मार्तंडा भातु एकें घरीचा.

४७० Ne adds परशरामबास :॥: शोधु : अन्न राशी एक धाडीलें : बाइ तुमचें अन्न निकें वेळें पातलें : रामेश्वर.

४७१ Ne adds हीराइसापाठः मार्तंडु सांघेचिना.

४७२ Ne adds हीराइसापाठ : बाइ यांसि कां कोपतें असा : याचे रोग न वचावें असति : ते कां जाति : आवेयाचे दीवेया कां येइल : प्राणिया आपुलें हीताहीत नेणे.

४७३ उत्तरीलेनि दारेंहूनि] K; उत्तरीले द्वारे Pa; मग गोसावी तेथ Na; उत्तरील हातद्वारें Ne, T.

४७४ Ne adds हीराइसापाठ : काइ नायको : वातें कष्टलेति : ना : जी : तिन वरिखें वाये कोडिमोडि करूनि घातलें असें जी.

४७५ एकि जाडि] Pa; एकि जाडि : दोनि सगडीया Ne, T; lacking in K and Na.

४७६ Ne adds हीराइसापाठ : नायेको एकि आंगीं फेडा : आणि जाडि फेडा : जी जी : जाडि वीण न गमे : जी जी : ऐसांहीं गोसावी फेडवीति : तरि : आंगीं फेडवीजे.

४७७ Ne adds तथा उठिल : हीराइसापाठ : आतां तंव फेडा होए : मग न गमे : तरी : चीया आणि काइ.

४७८ Ne adds हीराइसापाठ : जाडि आंगीं फेडीली.

४७९ Ne adds तथा : नायेको : रात्रीं कांहीं उपद्रो जाला.

४८० Ne adds हीराइसापाठ : दुसरी आंगी फेडवीली आणि दुसरी सगडी फेडविली : तेहीं म्हणीतलें : जी जी : आंगी फेडवीजैल : तरि : फेडवीजो : परि सगडीया वीण न गमे : आतां तवं फेडा होए : न गमे तरि घालुं येइल : फेडिली.

४८१ Ne adds हीराइसापाठ : नायेको : रात्रीं कांहीं उपद्रो जाला.

४८२ Ne adds हिराइसापाठ : दुसरी सगडी : आणि : दौंडि : फेडविली : तेहीं म्हणीतलें : जी जी : दौंडि फेडवीजैल : तरि : फेडवीजो : परि सगडी नको जी : सर्वज्ञें म्हणीतलें : आतां तवं फेडा होए : न गमें तरि घालुं एइल.

४८३ नाजी च्यारी पहार स्वस्त गेले] Pa; जी जी : काही नाही : च्यान्ही पाहार सुखे गेले Na; जी जी : काहीं उपद्रो नाही : च्यान्ही पाहार सुखें नीद्रा आली K; lacking in Ne and T.

४८४ Ne adds शोधु : आजि रात्रीं जाडी नका पांगरों : बाधील तरि काइ घेवों नये : पासवडि जाडि :॥: ती दीसीं :॥: आजि कैसें : आतां जे रूचैल : उपद्रो नुपजे.

४८५ Ne adds हीराइसापाठ : हें काइ बाइ : जी जी : हें नायेकालागीं सीत आणिलें : बाइ हें असों दीया : भक्तजना सरिसें वाढा.

४८६ विडा जाला] Pa, K, Na; वोळगवीला Ne, T.

४८७ Ne adds हीराइसापाठ : नायेको : रात्रीं कांहीं उपद्रो जाला : तेहीं म्हणीतलें : काइ सांघों : मग तेंहीं अवघेचि सांघितलें : मग सर्वज्ञें म्हणीतलें : आतां कैसें असे : ना जी : आतां जेवावें जेवावें ऐसें होत असे : सर्वज्ञें म्हणीतलें : तरि : आतां ऐसें किजे.

४८८ पानुनायक] Pa, K, N; lacking in Ne and T.

४८९ तेथ] K; lacking in Ne, T, Pa, and Na.

४९० Ne adds हीराइसापाठ : ऐसें तरि तुम्हां नांव सितळानंदु म्हणा.

४९१ Ne adds हीराइसापाठ : बाइ हें तुमचें वस्त्र सा मास पांगरलें : मग आंगी सीवीली : मग आंगी लेइलें : आतां हे आंगी वानरेसासि दीजो.

४९२ म्हणीतलें] K, Na, Pa; पुसिलें Ne, T.

४९३ Ne adds हीराइसापाठ : बाइ तुम्हीं चित्र पाडु जाणा : जी जी : मीं चित्र पाडु नेणें : मोरें लेहों जाणें : तरि : दीसवडीचीं दो दो मोरें लेहा.

४९४ पाख] Pa, K, Na; पावो Ne, T.

४९५ Ne adds हीराइसापाठ : बाइ तुम्ही एथींचें एक मोर लागा : बाइ हें एक मोर तुमचें लागे.

४९६ Ne and T add उमाइसा : महादाइसा : भेटि; lacking in all other versions.

४९७ होडे] Pa, K, Na; हटें Ne, T.

४९८ भट] Pa; मग Ne, T; lacking in K and Na.

४९९ Ne adds हीराइसापाठ : हां गा : हें जैसे उठिते : तैसे उठीता : हें जैसें बैसतें तैसें बैसतां : हें ऐसें निगैल तरि यातें तुम्हीं टाका.

५०० Ne adds हीराइसापाठ : टाकाल : कीरू : चळवळे ऐसे दीसतां.

५०१ Ne adds प्रकाश होती.

५०२ Ne adds हीराइसापाठ : सर्वज्ञें म्हणीतलें : पाहा पां : बाइ : काहीं पाणिभातु असे.

५०३ Ne adds हीराइसापाठ : जी जी : हे आमचेया गोसावीयांसि करिति : तरि : यांसि करूनि.

५०४ चरणक्षाळण] K, Na, Pa; प्रक्षाळण Ne, T.

५०५ Ne adds हीराइसापाठ : आज्ञानाचेनि प्रसादें तेंहीं काइएक न बोलावें.

५०६ असे] K, Na; lacking in Ne and T; phrase lacking in Pa.

५०७ Ne adds हीराइसापाठ : बाइसीं म्हणीतलें : बाबा : नागदेवो डाहाळीहुनि डाहाळिए कैसा जात असे : परि : पडेना : सर्वज्ञें म्हणीतलें : बाइ : कैसा वानरू ऐसा दीसत असे.

५०८ Ne adds शोधु : आतां ऐसेंचि नीगा : मासू दी जा :॥छ॥: वीजन :॥छ॥: भोजन :॥छ॥: सहस्रा वरिखें :॥छ॥: हीराइसापाठ : बाइसां करवि जाडि आणवीली : श्रीकरीं घेतली : माहात्मे हो : हे जाडि मासू दीसा वृक्षमूळीं तीनी पाहार तुणावि : तीं पाहारीं भीक्षा करावी : नदीं जेवावें : देउळीं निद्रा करावी : जव जव हे जाडि सांदेल तवं तवं तुमची वीद्या सांधैल.

५०९ जैसी सांदीली जाणवेना] Pa; जैसी जाणवे ना K; जैसा जानवेना Na; जैसी सांदीली नवेना Ne, T.

५१० Ne adds हीराइसापाठ : हांगा : तुमतें ऐसें म्हणीतलें : येल्हंभटाचां घरीं डोल्हारेयावरि बैसौनि जाडि तुणावी : ताटीं ठाणवै : तूपीं भातीं जेवावें : बाज सूपवतीवरि निजावे : ऐसें तुमतें म्हणीतलें होतें : एथौनि तुमतें ऐसें म्हणीतलें कीं : तीन पाहार वृक्षमूळीं : जाडि : सांदावी : तिसरा पाहारी भीक्षा करावी : नदीं जेवावें : देउळीं निद्रा करावी : ऐसें तुमतें म्हणीतलें : कीं : आझूइं जरि करीतेति तरि राये तिसरे ईश्वरवें मानिते : तवं ते उगेचि होते : मग : सर्वज्ञें म्हणीतलें : ऐसें कां होइल : पोरेयांसि आपेयाचां परीवरीं पाये पसरौनि मरावें : तें चुकैल : पसेयांचे पाइलिये कां येइल : ऐसें म्हणति : निचाचें तें पसेया कां एइल.

५११ Ne and T(n) add हें चरित्र दूसरीए प्रतिचें : मूळपोथीचें नव्हे : तें एथें फुटि आहे; lacking in all other versions.

५१२ ब्रम्ह दानासी] Pa; ब्राह्मण दानासि K(n); दांनासि K, Na(n); ब्रम्हणासि Ne, T; गोदानासि Na.

५१३ भटा : इंद्र भटाते] Pa; भटांतें K, Na; इंद्रभट Ne, T.

५१४ Ne adds हीराइसापाठ : इंद्रभट कटका दानासि निगाले : गोसावी भटांतें म्हणीतलें : वानरेया : तुम्हीही जा : मीं जाउनि काइ करूं : जी जी : मीं नसूधा सूटदेवो : कांहीं शास्त्र नेणे : सर्वज्ञें म्हणीतलें : जा : जेंचि यांसि तेंचि तुम्हांसि.

५१५ Ne adds शोधु : हां गा रायाचा : परशरामबास : रायाचां जांघी मांडी जाला : कीं : रामेश्वरबास.

५१६ पवीतें पर्व केलें] K; पर्व केले Na; पर्व करुनी Pa; पवीतें केलें Ne, T.

५१७ Ne adds हीराइसापाठ : कें गा आलेति : ते लाजीले : गोसावी ईखित हास्य केले.

५१८ Ne adds हीराइसापाठ : पवीतें बांधावें : गाउं पावति तवं असों दीयावें : मग सोडावें.

५१९ तैं] Pa; lacking in Ne, T, K, and Na.

५२० Ne adds बास : भोजा काइ.

५२१ ब्रह्मांड] K; ब्रह्म Ne, T, Pa, Na.

५२२ Ne adds यातें लेखीही ना : सुरंग मीरवी : यांतें देखौनि वीडीया मोडीतें :॥: चांगदेवीचेया बंधुआचा जावइं होता.

५२३ उपहासू] Na, Pa; उपहारू Ne, T; वीस्मो K.

५२४ Ne adds हीराइसापाठ : बाइसां : महात्स्पेपण गेलेंचि होतें.

५२५ Ne adds हीराइसापाठ : वनदेवा बीजें केलें : तेथ विनवीलें : वाहाणा सांदु जाइन.

५२६ एक म्हणति] Pa; (एकी वासना) Na; ऐसें म्हणति Ne; ऐसें म्हणसि T; lacking in K.

५२७ Ne adds हीराइसापाठ : हें आलें ऐसें कव्हणा पुढें न संगावें.

५२८ राजमठासि] Na, Pa; राजमढासि K; मढासि Ne, T.

५२९ भिंतीसी] Pa; भिंती Ne, T; sentence lacking in K and Na.

५३० तेथ अवस्थान जाले] Pa; lacking in Ne and T; sentence lacking in K and Na.

५३१ लींग अवलोकीत होते] Pa, Na; तेथ तिनि लींगें होतीं : तीएं अवलोकीत होते K; अवलोकीत होते Ne, T.

५३२ ऐसें म्हणौनि] K; lacking in Na, Pa, Ne, and T.

५३३ Ne adds तथा नायेको : ऐसे या : ऐसें या.

५३४ Ne adds हीराइसापाठ : तथा सांघति ते सांघों नेणति : जी जी : सांचौनि : नाशीति.

५३५ Ne adds हीराइसापाठ : नायेको : तुम्हां नांव काइ : जी जी : मातें वामनु वामनु ऐसें म्हणति : तथा वाया वाया ऐसें म्हणति.

५३६ Ne adds हीराइसापाठ : ऐसे तरि तुम्हां नांव वामनाचार्यें म्हणा.

५३७ Ne adds शोधु : नायेको : तुम्हांसि दरिसन जालें.

५३८ महदाइसें द्रारावतीयेहुनि पाडळीयेसि आली : परि गोसावी कवणे ठाइ राज्य करीत असति ऐसें चाजवलें नाहीं : मग आइकीलें : जें गोसावी हीवरळाये राज्य करीत असति] K(n); महदाइसे द्रारावतीहुनि पाडळीसी आली : पर गोसावी कवणी ठाइ राज्य करीत असत : ऐसे चोजवले नाही : मग गोसावी हीवरळीये राज्य करीत असत Pa; महदाइसीं

648

गोसावीयांतें आइकीलें Ne, T, Na.

५३९ Ne adds हीराइसापाठ : बाइ : तें तुम्हांसि कैसेनि स्फुरलें.

५४० Ne adds शोधु : [आली Pa] तीएची दीसी उपाहारू केला.

५४१ एकी वासना] Pa; lacking in Ne and T; passage lacking in K and Na.

५४२ सर्वज्ञे म्हणीतले एथ उपहार करा मग होइल] Pa; सर्वज्ञे मग होइल Ne; सर्वज्ञें म्हणीतलें T; passage lacking in K and Na. Ne adds परशरामबास : एथ मारखण करा : मग होइल : रामेश्वरबास.

५४३ Ne adds शोधु : थाळचें फेडीलें : बाइ : वाढाना : दोनि वेळ.

५४४ तथा जी ऐसे करु ए] Pa; तथा जी जी : ऐसें करूं ये Ne and T, placed at the end of the chapter; lacking in K and Na.

५४५ Ne adds परशरामबास : आपुलेया सीणलेया भागलेयाचें करूं ये : रामेश्वरबास : श्रम-णीबृत्ति कीजे : हीराइसापाठ : आपुलेया भागलेयाची श्रमनिवृत्ति कीजे.

५४६ उचलीतां] K, Pa; उखलीतां Ne, T; lacking in Na.

५४७ सर्वांगीं चंदन : चंदनाचा आडा] K, Na, Pa; सर्वांगीं चंदनाची भोरि आडा Ne, T.

५४८ पाठी गोष्टी पुसा] Pa; मग पुसा K, Na; पाठी गोष्टि सांघा Ne, T.

५४९ Ne adds हीराइसापाठ : पाणी पेवों सूवा : हे नइ वोलांडीति : परि पाणी न पियति.

५५० ब्राह्मणातें] K(n), Na(n); ब्राह्मण Pa; ब्राह्मणी Ne, T; sentence lacking in K and N.

५५१ धुवा] Pa; धूआं K, Na; धोयें Ne, T.

५५२ Ne adds शोधु : आराइजे : या जवळें असीजे तें वोखटें.

५५३ पुरोहीत द्वारे] Pa, Na; प्रोहीतद्वारें K; गृहीत द्वारें Ne, T.

५५४ Ne adds तथा दुख कां करीतें असा : शोधु : तथा : शुधि वार्ता : एथें असेंचि हें देखे :॥छ॥: हीराइसापाठ : बाइ : पैन्हाचें पैन्हा असीजे : धुवां डोळे भरीजति : तेयांपासि ऐसीया असीजे तें वोखटें : वृधाबाइसें उपाहारू निफजवीती : वानरेश एथ पुजा करीति : एथौनि तुमची पूजा स्विकरीजैल.

५५५ Ne adds हीराइसापाठ : तुम्हां उचिष्ट तांबोळ घेवों नये.

५५६ मग उमाइसीं चुळीं पाणी चेतलें] K, Na; मग बाइसी चुळी पाणी चेतले Pa; भट : उमाइसीं : चुळी पाणि घातलें Ne, T.

५५७ पुहीयांनि घाणातेनि तोंडेंसीं] K; पोहानी घाणाती तोंडेसी Na; पोहा निघाना ते नीतोडें Pa; पोहा न धूणातें न तोंडें [?] Ne; पोहा न धूणातें न तोंडें T.

५५८ Ne adds हीराइसापाठ : बाइ : तुम्हीं रावसगांवा जा : मग हें तुम्हां दर्शन देइल.

५५९ Ne adds रामेश्वरबास : मढा दखीणें बीजें केलें होतें :॥छ॥: परशरामबास : मढापूर्वें होतें.

५६० Ne adds हीराइसापाठ : आधिल माहात्में एणें वचनें भीक्षा.

५६१ Ne adds शोधु : हें म्हणत असति : हें काइ : ऐसें हें काइ जाणति : हें ब्राह्मण : हें काइ ऐसे : कांही जाणिजत असीजे.

५६२ Ne adds हीराइसापाठ : बाइ : नाएक म्हणत असति तें तैसेंचि : काइ हें : ऐसें काइ जाणीजत असीजे : काइ हें ब्राह्मण : कीं क्षेत्री : कीं वैश्य : कीं शूद्र : कीं काइ : ऐसें कवण जाणो.

५६३ नागदेया नागदेया : आमचे गोसावी साक्षातु सीधनाथू : भटोबासीं म्हणीतलें] K; नागदेया

649

नागदेया : गोसावी साक्षात सीधनाथु : भटी म्हणीतलें Na; नागदेया नागदेया : आमचे
गोसावी साक्षातु सीधनाथ : भटी म्हणीतले Pa; lacking in Ne and T.

५६४ Ne adds रामेश्वरबास : हा धोत्र फाडुनि उत्तरापंथे जाये हें नीके : परशरामबास :
हीराइसापाठ : ब्राह्मणु साभीमानीया असे : डोइ बोडुनि धोत्र फाडुनि उत्तरापंथे जाएं तें
निकें कीं हे नावेक सीधनाथु.

५६५ Ne adds शोधु : बाइ : द्वारावतिए श्रीचांगदेवराउळीं पुर कवणेपरीं त्येजीलें :॥: श्रीप्रभुची
अज्ञा लंघुनि :॥: बाइ तैशां स्थानीं : हें तुमचे वीषै :॥छ॥: हीराइसापाठ : बाइ : श्रीचांगदेवो
राउळीं कवणेपरीं बीजे केलें : तें तो केवि जाणे : तें कव्हणीचि नेणे : तें तुम्हां एथौनि
सांधीजैल : हे रामेश्वरबास : बाइ : श्रीचांगदेवो राउळीं : पूर त्येजीलें : तें कव्हणीचि नेणें :॥:
तें तुम्हां पूढां एथौनि.

५६६ Ne adds हीराइसापाठ : जाणिजे ऐसें हेतु धातु तवं :॥: जाणिजे ऐसें तुम्हां : उठीतां
बैसतां.

NOTES TO THE TRANSLATION

The Solitary Period

1 Karhade (*karhāḍe*): a member of a subgroup of Brahmans named for the town of Karhad in Satara District, Maharashtra. Phalethan (*phaleṭhāna*), now called Phaltan (*phalaṭaṇa*), is the headquarters of a taluka (a division of a district) in present-day Satara District.

2 Matapur (*mātāpura*) is Mahur (*māhūra*), a pilgrimage place and taluka headquarters in present-day Nanded District.

3 Devgiri (*devagirī*, Skt. *devagiri;* "god's mountain"), here, is the principal mountain at Matapur. Shri Dattatreya Prabhu (*śrī dattātreya prabhu*) is, for Mahanubhavs, Cangdev Raül's predecessor as an incarnation of the supreme God in human form.

4 This way of referring to Cangdev Raül's head is the first example of the hieratic language discussed in the Note on the Text and Translation.

5 Dvaravati (*dvārāvatī*), also called Dvarka (*dvārkā*), is a pilgrimage place on the west coast of India associated with the god Krishna and, for Mahanubhavs, with Cangdev Raül.

6 This is *Sūtrapāṭh*, "Vicār Mālikā" 51.

7 Riddhipur (*r̥ddhipura, ridhapura, rīdhapura, rīdhapūra;* "town of prosperity"), also called Parameshvarpur ("God's town"), now a village in Morshi Taluka, Amravati District, was Shriprabhu's hometown.

8 The mention of Hivarali and Mahadaïse here frames the episode as one that Chakradhar told his disciples about long after it happened, when he was staying with Mahadaïse and others in Hivarali (*hīvaraḷī, hīravaḷī;* present-day Jalna, now the headquarters of a district) late in "The First Half." This frame story is also found in FH329.

9 Kamakhya (*kāmākhyā*) was a female ascetic whose very name incorporates a term for desire (*kāma*). Kaürali (*kāüraḷī*) is Assam, a region also called Kamarup (*kāmarūpa*).

10 Ram (*rāma*) is Ramtek (*rāmaṭeka*, "Ram's hill"), a pilgrimage place of the god Ram that is now a taluka headquarters in Nagpur District. For the story, see SP7.

11 This is *Sūtrapāṭh*, "Ācār" 154.

12 Gopal mantra: recited syllables consisting of names of the god Gopal Krishna. Gopal oath: the regular practice of swearing by the god Gopal Krishna.

13 This is another example of hieratic language. As a divine incarnation, the Gosavi *could* win all the time; if he loses, it is because he himself decides to do so.

14 In Kolte's edition (*Pūrvārdha* 20), the king explains that "there is enmity between the Gujars and the Yadavas," the rulers of, respectively, the Gujarati- and Marathi-language regions.

15 "The Mountain" here is either the one at Salbardi, near the Maharashtra border in present-day Madhya Pradesh, or Shrishailam, a pilgrimage place of the god Shiva in Kurnool District, Andhra Pradesh (Dhere 1977: 122–123).

16 Chakradhar asks this framing question at a later period of his life, giving rise to the recollection from the earlier part of his life that constitutes the rest of this chapter. Kanti (*kāntī*), now called Katol, is a taluka headquarters in present-day Nagpur District.

17 The Andhra land is modern Andhra Pradesh, now comprising the states of Telangana and Seemandhra. Panchaleshvar (*pañcāḷeśvara*) is a village on the Godavari River in present-day Gevrai Taluka, Bid District. See FH397 for another iteration of the frame story in its proper geographical and chronological context.

18 Apegav (*āpegāva*) is a village in present-day Gangapur Taluka, Aurangabad District, across the Godavari River from Panchaleshvar.

19 See the Note on the Text and Translation for a discussion of Rameshvarbas's and other versions of the *Līḷācaritra* and my way of handling variants like this one that are included in the Marathi text.

20 The fact that the Oil Presser swears by the aniconic form of the god Shiva and shows respect for him (under the names Somnath and Malinath) suggests that the man was a Shaiva—even perhaps, as Tulpule suggests (1972: 49), a Virashaiva.

21 Literally, "was inclined to be thirsty," another example of pious language.

22 He made no attempt to swim or to steer himself to safety.

23 Kholnayak (*kholanāyaka*) was a Yadava general. Ambe (*āmbe*) is Ambejogai (*āmbejogāī*), a taluka headquarters in present-day Bid

District that in modern times has also been called Mominabad (*mominābād*).

24 The word "later" here refers to the time of the frame story, after the Gosavi has narrated this *līlā* to Mahadaïse.

25 See FH324 for the frame story here, about Mahadaïse's brother Aplo's gambling.

26 Orangal (*orangala*), now called Varangal (*varangaḷa*, often written Warangal), is a district headquarters in what is today Telangana state.

27 Another version: The Gosavi was lying down, and the woman was massaging his feet. She fell asleep doing that.

28 This is *Sūtrapāṭh*, "Ācār" 231.

29 This comment belongs to the frame story.

30 Aüse was a female yogi who became an important disciple of Chakradhar in a later period of his life. Nayaka (*nāyaka, nāeka,* "Lady"?) was Chakradhar's nickname for her. Her yogi's scarf appears in SH140.

31 A Gondhal (*gondhaḷa*) is a type of musical and dramatic performance in honor of goddesses, often performed as part of wedding festivities.

32 Another version: He was sitting in his place, and she was fanning him.

33 Mahadaïse's question and the answer to it belong to the frame story.

34 Dakaram (*ḍākarāma, ḍānkarāma*) is a village in present-day Tirora Taluka, Gondia District. Bhiveshvar (*bhiveśvara,* "Lord of Bhiva") is a name of the god Shiva.

35 Sesame-seed Oil Presser: a member of a subcaste of Oil Pressers (*telīs*). One version: She was selling oil.

36 The frame story of this chapter is also found in FH164. There we learn that Padmanabhi, or Padmanabhidev, was a former disciple of Sarasvatbhat. Bid (*bīḍa;* often written Beed) is a town in central Maharashtra that is now the headquarters of a district.

37 This is *Sūtrapāṭh*, "Vicār" 273.

38 Kishkinda (*khīkhīnda;* Sanskrit, *kiṣkindha*) is a mountain in Karnataka associated with the Ramayana story.

39 Dabhvihir (*dābhvihīr*) is a village southeast of Riddhipur. The two salt ponds were located outside Riddhipur, in the direction of Dabhvihir.

40 This mild curse is Shriprabhu's favorite expression (Mhaïmbhat 1984).
41 This sentence is part of the frame story of the Rupanayak episode. According to the editions by Kolte (Mhaïmbhat 1982, *Pūrvārdha* 40) and Nagpure (Mhaïmbhat 2004, *Pūrvārdha* 36), Chakradhar narrated the episode to his female disciple Sadhe at Jogeshvari, a place where he stayed at the end of "The First Half."
42 This is *Sūtrapāṭh,* "Ācār" 216.
43 According to Panjabi (n.d.[a], 820), fasting every day for a month is a vow that was typically undertaken by women who were widowed as children. As with other fasts, a person undertaking this one would be permitted to eat fruit and certain other foods. Sendurjan (*sendurajana, sendurjana*) is a village in present-day Sindkhed Raja Taluka, Buldhana District.
44 She was unaware that time had passed.
45 This frame story is also found in FH330 and SH19. Bhogaram (*bhogarām, bhogārām*) is the name of a temple at Ramtek whose principal deity is Vishnu portrayed as lying on the serpent (*bhoga*) Shesha in the cosmic milk-ocean. Lakhudevoba was a maternal cousin of Nagdev who became a follower of Chakradhar. "The capital" (*kaṭaka*) is Devgiri (*devagirī,* "god's [or gods'] mountain"), now Daulatabad (*daulatābād,* "city of wealth"), in Aurangabad Taluka, Aurangabad District.
46 Karanjale (*karañjāḷe*) is a village in present-day Ambad Taluka, Jalna District.
47 Mansil (*manasīla*) is present-day Mansar (*manasara*), a village in Ramtek Taluka, Nagpur District.
48 This is *Sūtrapāṭh,* "Vicār" 262.
49 Bhandara (*bhāṇḍārā,* now *bhaṇḍārā*) is a town in far-northeastern Maharashtra that is now the headquarters of a district. Bhandarekar's name indicates that he came from there.
50 This frame story is also found in FH482 during Chakradhar's extended stay later in his life in Belopur, a village in present-day Shrirampur Taluka, Ahmadnagar District. Alajpur (*aḷajapūra*), now called Achalpur, is a taluka headquarters in modern Amravati District that was called Ellichpur in British times.
51 This is *Sūtrapāṭh,* "Ācār Mālikā" 30, and *Sūtrapāṭh,* "Ācār" 62.
52 *Sannidhān,* the presence of a divine incarnation, is a necessary element of the path to liberation for Mahanubhavs.

53   Nanded (*nāndeḍa, nāndiyeḍa*), now the headquarters of a district, is a town on the Godavari River in central India. Bhavatirtha (*bhāvatīrtha*) is a holy place on the river there.

54   This is *Sūtrapāṭh,* "Ācār" 171.

55   This is an appropriate way of handling the corpse of a sannyasi.

56   In Mahanubhav theology, the cosmic power named here, *avagaḷā,* is a particular part of the creative principle maya (*māyā*) (Kolte 1975: 177n, 182–183, 248–249).

57   Ghogargav (*ghogaragāva*) is a village in present-day Nevase Taluka, Ahmadnagar District.

58   See FH93 for a fuller version of this frame story.

59   The man means that the Gosavi should do some simple kind of work, rather than begging for his food.

60   Lonar (*loṇāra*), a place of pilgrimage at the time of the *Līḷācaritra,* is the site of a lake formed in a large meteor crater, surrounded by elaborate stone temples; it is now a taluka headquarters in Buldhana District.

61   Research (*sodhu, sodh;* Sanskrit *śodha*), a term found throughout the text, introduces variants added by a premodern editor. See the Note on the Text and Translation.

62   Rayer (*rāer, rāyer*) is a village in present-day Biloli Taluka, Nanded District.

63   See SH369 for the story of Chardobā, who became habituated to sitting under a particular tree.

64   The Forest Region (*jhāḍī*) is the thickly forested area in eastern Maharashtra, comprising roughly the present-day districts of Gadchiroli, Chandrapur, Gondia, and Bhandara.

65   See SP28.

66   This remark is part of the frame story, something the Gosavi said as he told his disciples about these events, later in his life.

67   Vadner (*vaḍanera, baḍanera*) is a village in present-day Amravati District.

68   Vasani (*vāsanī*) is a village in present-day Achalpur Taluka, Amravati District.

69   If the Gosavi observed the rules about death pollution, he would not have accepted food from someone whose father had recently died.

70   See SP61.

71   Paturadi (*pāturaḍī*), now called Patur, is a taluka headquarters in

present-day Akola District. Valukeshvar (*vāḷukeśvara*) is a name of Shiva. Alegav (*ālegāva*) is a village in Patur Taluka.

72 A Mahar (*mahāra*) is a member of a very low caste formerly considered "untouchable." An Untouchable would have had the right to keep the cloth or clothes used to cover a corpse and then discarded at the cremation ground.

73 Anjani (*āñjanī*) is a village in present-day Mehkar Taluka, Buldhana District.

74 Vishaye (*viṣaye, vīsaye*) is a village in present-day Mehkar Taluka, Buldhana District.

75 Pratishthan (*pratiṣṭhāna*), now called Paithan, is a religiously important town on the Godavari River where Chakradhar eventually spent a good deal of time; it is now a taluka headquarters in Aurangabad District. In FH6, Dados sends some of his relatives to meet the Gosavi in Pratishthan. He himself next meets the Gosavi in FH31.

76 Baneshvar is a name of Shiva. Mehkar (*mehakara*) is a taluka headquarters in present-day Buldhana District.

77 Water-and-rice gruel: for the recipe for this staple food for ascetics, see FH435.

78 Another version: "Then who has robbed whom, my woman?"

79 Gokul Ashtami, the birthday of the god Krishna, falls on the eighth (*aṣṭamī*) day of the dark half of the month of Shravan (July–August). Gokul is the cowherd settlement where Krishna grew up.

80 A no-moon day that falls on a Monday is an important day for pilgrimage to certain holy places.

81 Some pilgrimage places have eight holy places (*tīrthas*) located at least notionally in the four cardinal and four intermediate directions around a central place. At Lonar, the eight are positioned around the lake that fills the large meteor crater.

82 The waterfall is at the place called Taratirtha in SP39.

83 Daityasudan (*daityasūdana*, "demon killer") is a name of Vishnu (or Shiva).

84 Where the Sondara meets another river.

85 The Simhastha (*siṃhastha*) is the thirteen-month period, occurring once every twelve years, during which the planet Jupiter is in the constellation Virgo; it is one of the four principal events in the twelve-year cycle of pilgrimages called the Kumbha Mela. Tryambak

(*tryambaka, trīyambaka, trimbaka*), also called Tryambakeshvar (*tryambakeśvara*), is a major pilgrimage place at the source of the Godavari River that serves as a taluka headquarters in present-day Nasik District. Bathing at Tryambak during the Simhastha is a major event in the Kumbha Mela cycle.

86 Another version: She went and got those same ones.

87 Ravasgav (*rāvasagāva*) is a village on the Godavari River in present-day Ghansavangi Taluka, Jalna District.

88 Named for an underground river understood to meet the Godavari River there, Bhogavati (*bhogāvatī*) was the easternmost of the four main gates of Pratishthan, as well as a bathing place (*tīrtha*) on the Godavari nearby. According to Nene (1954: 78), the cremation ground of Pratishthan was located on the riverbank there.

89 Bhognarayan (*bhoganārāyaṇa*) is the god Vishnu portrayed as lying on the serpent (*bhoga*) Shesha; this temple was Chakradhar's principal residence in Pratishthan during his initial stay there.

The First Half

1 Lonar (*loṇāra*) was the name of the southernmost of the four main gates of Pratishthan and of a bathing place (*tīrtha*) on the Godavari River nearby.

2 This is *Sūtrapāṭh,* "Vicār Mālikā" 136.

3 Nagubaï and her companions followed a religious path (*mārg*) whose typical ascetic practice was to take only milk as nourishment.

4 According to Parasharambas, he would go to Vamdev's cell.

5 This echoes *Sūtrapāṭh,* "Vicār Mālikā" 136, in which Chakradhar says something similar about Baïse (Nagubaï). See FH2.

6 Named for the confluence of the Ganga and Yamuna rivers at Allahabad in north India, Prayag (*prayāga*) was the westernmost of the four main gates of Pratishthan, as well as a bathing place (*tīrtha*) on the Godavari River nearby.

7 Pimpaleshvar (*pīpaḷeśvara*), meaning "Lord of the pipal tree," is a name of the god Shiva.

8 Or, Hiraïsa version: He was sitting on the veranda.

9 Balhegram (*balhegrāma*) is a village in present-day Ambad Taluka, Jalna District, that was home to several important followers of Chakradhar.

10 Hiraïsa version: the version of the *Līḷācaritra* memorized and then

657

recited by a disciple named Hiraïsa. See the Note on the Text and Translation.

11   The Maharvada (*mahāravāḍā*) was a neighborhood where "Untouchables" lived. It would have been to the east of the town, downstream and downwind from the main settlement.

12   Parasharam version: He looked in Vamdev's cell. Then they met on the high riverbank.

13   Research: He was given a massage in the household shrine and a brief bath in the loft.

14   Mokananda was either the brother of Sarangpandit's first wife (Kolte 1982: 804) or Sarangpandit's son by that first wife (Panjabi n.d.[a]: 755).

15   Queen Vaijaï was the wife of Mahadev Yadava (r. 1260–1270). Vaijanath is a name of Shiva.

16   Hiraïsa version: He went to the capital, got the grant deed, and came back. He took a bath, ate a meal, and then came for *darśan*.

17   "Thousand-headed" is the beginning of the *Puruṣasūkta* hymn from the *Ṛg Veda* (10.90).

18   This is the beginning of *Sūtrapāṭh*, "Vicār" 228. The sutra continues, "but he does not worship God at all." Baïse's reply refers to worshiping the supreme God, a being of a different category from *jīvas*.

19   The point of this warning is unclear. Perhaps a three-legged stand is one that is missing one leg?

20   In the view of Rameshvarbas, this episode should be included with the others that took place at the Ganapati Madh hermitage in Pratishthan, late in "The Second Half" section of the text. As the Concordance shows, Kolte (Mhaïmbhat 1982) places the episode in the *Ajñāt Līḷā* section of his edition, the section containing *līḷās* whose location is unknown (*ajñāta*).

21   Kavadimba (*kavaḍīmba, kavaḍimba;* Sanskrit *kaviḍimba;* "child poet") is a title given to several poets, including Chinchkhedkar Ramdev (in FH277) and two later poets named Krishnamuni (Raeside 1960: 506).

22   This is *Sūtrapāṭh*, "Vicār" 234.

23   This is the beginning of *Sūtrapāṭh*, "Vicār" 235. The sutra continues, "Some people live by them."

24   Hiraïsa version: "My woman, if you go to meet a holy man, you

should sit facing him. You should not turn your back to a king, a guru, or a god."

25 Some say the Gosavi was sitting at the southwest corner, behind the temple, when she saw him.

26 Dhanaï is hinting at her desire to marry the Gosavi. A common prenuptial ceremony involves smearing the bride and the groom with turmeric paste.

27 Hiraïsa version: "All right, Batika. If you want to come to Parameshvarpur, why would I forbid you? Go to your village, ask them, and then come."

28 Upadhye's mother and brother appear in FH10. In FH90 we learn that Cangdevbhat has a mother (who is distressed at his absence), and in FH136 we learn that he has a twin brother, Nathoba.

29 Rahatgav (*rāhāṭagāva*) is a village in present-day Paithan Taluka, Aurangabad District.

30 Kadethan (*kaḍeṭhāṇa*) is a village in present-day Paithan Taluka, Aurangabad District.

31 Rajaur (*rājaura*) is a village in present-day Bhokardan Taluka, Jalna District. Its name is now linked with the god Ganesh (*rājaura-gaṇapatīce*), rather than with Bhivandaüva (*bhivāṇḍ̣āüva*), who must have been a prominent citizen of the place in or before Chakradhar's time.

32 Research: The omniscient one said, "Go home, Bhat." Then he invited him.

33 Meghankar is Mehkar, a taluka headquarters in present-day Buldhana District.

34 Hiraïsa version: a pipal tree. "Another reservoir" may refer to one besides the reservoir next to the temple.

35 "When I am explaining the *devatācakra*..." *Sūtrapāṭh*, "Vicār" 270. The sutra continues, "... a slate the size of the earth and a piece of chalk the size of Mount Meru will not suffice."

36 Patauri (*pātaurī*, also written *pāturaḍī*), now called Patur (*pātura*), is a taluka headquarters in present-day Akola District.

37 Takli (*ṭākaḷī*) is a village in present-day Barshitakli Taluka, Akola District.

38 Lakshaneshvar (*lakṣaneśvara*) is a name of the god Shiva. Lakhepuri (*lākhepurī*) is a village in present-day Barshitakli Taluka, Akola District.

39 Kodeshvar is a name of the god Shiva. According to the *Sthānpothī* (1976: 21), this temple was in Kholapur, eighteen miles west of Amravati (Kolte 1976: 110).

40 Hiraïsa version: The Gosavi had a massage and a bath. He ate his meal along with the devotees.

41 Padmeshvar is a name of the god Shiva. According to the *Sthānpothī* (1976: 21), this temple was in Singnapur, five miles west of Kholapur (Kolte 1976: 123).

42 This Vanki (*vāṅkī*) is a village in present-day Bhatkuli Taluka, Amravati District.

43 Hiraïsa version: "My woman, today is the bazaar in Vanki. Get a garment for Shriprabhu there. You and Hamsaraj go on ahead."

44 The pillar game (*khaḍakhāmbul, khaḍakhāmbulī*): a game involving running around pillars. Hiraïsa version: The omniscient one said, "Batika, what are you doing, playing the pillar game?" And his trance broke.

45 Hiraïsa version: "Come here, Batika. And so you should get something at the last house you beg from."

46 That is, it should be placed in or before FH34.

47 Urveshvar (*urveśvar*) is a name of the god Shiva. Thugav (*tugāv, thūgāv*) is a village in present-day Chandurbazar Taluka, Amravati District.

48 Talvel (*taḷavela*) is a village in present-day Chandurbazar Taluka, Amravati District.

49 Khairala (*khairāḷā*) is a village in present-day Chandurbazar Taluka, Amravati District.

50 According to Hiraïsa, he said, "Batika, do you see this place, Parameshvarpur? You can see the pinnacle on the rest house roof." And he gave a cry of victory.

51 In Mahanubhav usage, the term "tradition" (*mārgarūḍhī*) refers to those traditions that stem from the third generation of leaders after Chakradhar, the second generation after Nagdev.

52 "The water-storage jars" (*āḷandī*) is the name of a particular place on the western edge of Riddhipur.

53 This hermitage (*maṭh*) is the Rajmath, the Narasimha temple where Shriprabhu lived.

54 The Tall Hermitage (*uñcamaḍh*) was next door to the Rajmath in Riddhipur.

55 The Tripurush (*tripurukha*) Hermitage, named for the three (*trī*) gods Brahma, Vishnu, and Shiva, was a third temple-monastery clustered with the Rajmath and the Tall Hermitage.

56 According to Parasharambas: "This is not appropriate for Shriprabhu?" "Right." "It is appropriate for me?" "Yes." "All right, give it to me."

57 Research: "My woman, be quiet." Hiraïsa version: "This is Shriprabhu's inclination."

58 According to Ramdevmuni: "Now he is mine. He let me hit him, I tell you."

59 This is the garment that Baïse bought in FH37.

60 This is similar to *Sūtrapāṭh,* "Ācār Mālikā" 224.

61 Keshav (*keśava*) is a name of Vishnu, who is for Mahanubhavs a mere deity (*devatā*), not the supreme God.

62 Shankanath (*saṅkanātha, śaṅkanātha,* "Lord of the Conch Shell"), Sangameshvar (*saṅgameśvara,* "Lord of the Confluence"), and Bhiveshvar are names of the god Shiva. Belor (*belora*) is a village in present-day Morshi Taluka, Amravati District.

63 Nagnath (*nāganātha,* "Lord of Cobras") is a name of the god Shiva. This Shirala (*sīrāḷā, śīrāḷā*) is a village in present-day Amravati Taluka, Amravati District.

64 This Asuti (*āsutī, āsaṭī*), now called Ashti (*āṣṭī*), is a village in present-day Amravati Taluka, Amravati District.

65 Compare FH110.

66 Research: The omniscient one said, "Things will not go well for him." Then Baïse said, "What do you mean, Baba?"

67 Vathavada (*vāṭhavaḍā*) is a village in present-day Chandurbazar Taluka, Amravati District.

68 Varhaddev (*varhāḍadeva;* "the god of Vidarbha") is a local deity. Mangrul (*māṅgarūḷa,* also written *māṅgaḷaura*) is a village, now a taluka headquarters, in present-day Akola District.

69 The last two sentences here are *Sūtrapāṭh,* "Ācār" 31.

70 The one in FH29.

71 In his trance state.

72 Dodvihir (*ḍoḍavīhīra*) is a village in present-day Deulgav Raja Taluka, Buldhana District.

73 Although absent from Nene's edition, on which this one is based, the episode referred to appears as *Pūrvārdha* 129 in Kolte's edition (Mhaïmbhat 1982): "Raghavdev came from

Dodvihir to Paithan. He met the Gosavi. He prostrated himself. Then he left."

74 In Kolte's edition (Mhaïmbhat 1982, *Pūrvārdha* 15), Dundi Raül (*duṇḍī rāüḷ*) accompanied Shriprabhu to Dvaravati. According to Panjabi's version of the present chapter (*Pūrvārdha* 59), Dundi Raül was also called Shuklabhat and was Shriprabhu's guru. In Dvaravati, he went into a trance, which was broken when Cangdev Raül hit him with a winnowing fan (compare SP3). After that he learned all mantras and threw his basket of gods into the Gomati River.

75 Phulambari (*phulambarī*) is a taluka headquarters in present-day Aurangabad District.

76 Gavan (*gavāṇa*), now called Gadana (*gadānā*), is a village in present-day Khuldabad Taluka, Aurangabad District.

77 Yelapur (*yeḷāpur, yaḷāpur, eḷāpur*), now called Verul (*verūḷa*) in Marathi and Ellora in English, is a major site of ancient Buddhist, Hindu, and Jain caves in present-day Khuldabad Taluka, Aurangabad District.

78 The Rajvihar cave is Cave 12 at Ellora.

79 Chaturvidh means "fourfold." In the next chapter, the hermitage is named Chaturvidya, "fourfold knowledge." The Gosavi is still staying here in FH81, and he stays here again, for two weeks, in FH237. According to Ranade (1988: 112), the place "may be identified with the site where an *īdagāh* [an open-air mosque] stands today adjacent to the *Śivālaya tirtha*," called Shivale (*śivāḷe*) in Marathi.

80 Devgiri (*devagirī*, "god's/gods' mountain"; also called *kaṭaka*, "the Capital") was the Yadava kings' capital; now called Daulatabad, it is the site of a fort and village in Aurangabad Taluka, Aurangabad District, less than ten miles from Ellora (Yelapur).

81 Another version: "Does God need another source of light? He is self-illuminating!"

82 See FH10–11.

83 See FH12.

84 One version: "I am Shri Krishna Chakravarti, or I am what I am."

85 A tuft of hair and a shoulder thread are marks of an orthodox Brahman man.

86 Dados first meets the Gosavi in E58–59, but there is no mention there of such a request.

87 He is not God, as I am.

88 These two sentences are *Sūtrapāṭh*, "Vicār" 225. Another version: "Are all gods alike?"

89 Atmatirtha (*ātmatirtha, ātmatīrtha*) is a holy place in the bed of the Godavari River near Panchaleshvar.

90 Research: "Have you gone to Panchaleshvar?" he asked. "I was in that place. You should go there." For Chakradhar's visit to Panchaleshvar, see SP11.

91 Research: Upadhye put down a thick shawl for him to sit on. The Gosavi said, "Won't it get soiled, Batika?" "No, Lord." At that point, Baïse brought a thick blanket and made a seat for the Gosavi.

92 This is according to Parasharambas. According to Rameshvarbas, she sent Bhagavat to get water. Ravalo (*ravaḷo*) is one of the men from Balhegram listed in the previous chapter.

93 Hiraï version: The omniscient one said, "This hermitage is empty. Bring your household here." The next day Dev came to the Gosavi's worship service, and, after the worship service, he had his lodgings moved there. Then came the episode with the rotis.

94 The Jealous Man's cave (*isāḷuvāce leṇe*) is high on the northern end of the hill full of caves at Ellora.

95 Katevasai (*kāṭevasai*) is a Jain cave at the northern end of the hill full of caves at Ellora, probably Cave 32 (Ranade 1988: 112).

96 The science of Pralhad is a type of esoteric knowledge (*vidyā*) that enables a person to cause joy in others.

97 The moon has sixteen digits, waxing and then waning by one digit each day of the lunar month. The seventeenth digit is nectar, the drink of immortality.

98 Hiraïsa version: "When you go to other holy places, which are lifeless matter, you go without eating. You do a pilgrimage fast. You do not eat until you have seen the god of the holy place. But you haven't done even that much!"

99 See SP36.

100 Or, Hiraïsa version: "... use it [sense pleasure]. My woman, that is one way to enjoy sense pleasure."

101 This passage combines *Sūtrapāṭh*, "Vicār" 79 ("Shri Krishna Chakravarti knew how to enjoy sense pleasure") and "Vicār" 97 ("In the Kali yuga, there are sense pleasures, but no one who knows how to enjoy them. All these kings and princes and so on enjoy only to relieve their tension").

102 Anakai (*aṇakai*) is a small cave at the foot of the northern end of the hill full of caves at Ellora; it housed a shrine of the goddess Anakai (cf. Ranade 1988:112).

103 Or, "Lord, do you know hatha yoga?"

104 If Salivahan were truly adept at hatha yoga, his body would not show signs of aging.

105 For a story about the origin of this well, see FH76.

106 This is *Sūtrapāṭh*, "Ācār" 236. There is a pun here: *antapāhaṇe* can mean to plumb the depths of a body of water or to test the limits of someone's patience or endurance.

107 Kanharale (*kānharāḷe*) was a water tank or artificial lake at Yelapur, possibly named for the Yadava king Krishnadev/Kanhardev.

108 Or, a Mahatma has come.

109 Charan (*caraṇa*, "foot") Well is the name of the well in FH74. It may be named for the sandal that hit the vial of nectar. Uparkundi (*uparakūṇḍī*) means "Upper Pool." According to Kolte's edition (Mhaïmbhat 1982, *Pūrvārdha* 198), it came from the uppermost of the three pieces into which the vial broke. Shivale (*sivāḷe/śivāḷe*) is the temple tank near the Ghrishneshvar temple at Ellora.

110 Or, according to Hiraïsa, then he entered an underground cell there to practice yoga.

111 All four of these villages are in present-day Aurangabad District.

112 Compare *Sūtrapāṭh*, "Vicār" 94: "In the Kali yuga, there is no one who has esoteric knowledge (*vidyā*)."

113 Compare *Sūtrapāṭh*, "Vicār Mālikā" 57: "A man may have esoteric knowledge (*vidyā*), but he is unable to destroy the world."

114 Hiraïsa: "Those men who retain their semen know how to absorb a drop within a drop. They hold their semen upward and dry it inside themselves, so that a body forms inside them. Their outer body cannot be destroyed."

115 According to some, he said: "The one who can really retain his semen is Goraksha. What he does is invisible, the way water spreads out in a coconut." Then he told them about the coconut.

116 This is the beginning of *Sūtrapāṭh*, "Ācār" 230. The full sutra reads, "Don't talk that way, Dakhale. What will you do when the man gets angry?"

117 Luïpaï was a guru who lived in a garbage heap. The story is about what happened to a king who laughed at him. See *Pūrvārdha* 202

in Kolte's edition (Mhaïmbhat 1982) and *Ajñāt Līlā* 5 in Nagpure's (Mhaïmbhat 2004).

118 According to Nagpure's edition (Mhaïmbhat 2004, *Pūrvārdha* 191), Brahmasan was the king's guru. He was worried that the king would reject him and follow Chakradhar instead. Mahadashram was an ascetic from Paithan who plays an important role much later in the text.

119 This Bhagavat may be Apdevbhat (Panjabi n.d.[a]: 745).

120 Malharvasai is a Jain cave at the northern end of the row of caves at Ellora (Ranade 1988: 112).

121 According to Hiraïsa, Baïse said, "What is this, Baba?" (Or, he said, "My woman, what of it? Shouldn't I accept such a little bit?" "What is it, Baba?") "My woman, it is *halāhal, kālkūṭ,* and *ragatsingī.* They work against one another. When you take the antidote for one of them, another gets stronger. All four of them have been combined." "What can be done about it now, Baba?" "Would I go this easily, my woman? I will make someone the excuse, and I will blame this land. Then I will go away, my woman." (Some say: "My woman, do not be afraid. This is as easy as counting panic-grass seeds. The harvest ritual is yet to come, my woman. I will make someone the excuse. My woman, if a living being has been suffering torment for a long time, should his efforts simply go to waste?" "No, Baba.") The Gosavi is hinting at the tragic events toward the end of the text.

122 Or, research: "Why would that happen? It won't." "Lord Gosavi," they replied, "if you make it happen, it will happen."

123 These commands include or resemble *Sūtrapāṭh,* "Ācār Mālikā" 41, "Ācār Mālikā" 55, and "Ācār" 83. Compare FH88.

124 The pass is the one leading up Devgiri mountain at Matapur.

125 This is according to Parasharambas. According to Rameshvarbas: "The one you meet at the foot of the pass is not him. The one in the garb of a renouncer whom you meet at the top of the pass is not him. The one in the garb of a hunter whom you meet on the embankment of Meruvale claims not to be him but is." Meruvale (*meruvāḷe*) is a reservoir or artificial lake at Matapur, named for the cosmic mountain Meru.

126 Daülvadi (*ḍāülavāḍī*) is a village in present-day Paithan Taluka, Aurangabad District.

127 This is *Sūtrapāṭh,* "Vicār" 284.

128 For the episode of the thick shawl, see SH207, in a subsequent volume.

129 This is the last part of *Sūtrapāṭh*, "Ācār" 155.

130 Compare FH103.

131 Vasumati (*vasumati*), now called Basmat, is a taluka headquarters in Hingoli District. Nene's edition begins this *līḷā* with two sentences that appear to belong later in the chapter: Shantibaïse reported all this. Then his feet were washed.

132 According to Hiraïsa: "Was there any trouble at night?" "No, Lord. It was coming on her twenty or thirty times a day. It has stopped now, Lord." "It won't come anymore now, my woman." (Or, "It is gone now.")

133 Or, according to Hiraïsa: "My woman, this one's grief is gone. The other one's madness is gone." Then the omniscient one said, "My woman, a group of pilgrims is setting out for Dvaravati. So go ahead and go to Dvaravati now."

134 This is according to Rameshvarbas. According to Parasharambas, three lifetimes' worth.

135 These commands include *Sūtrapāṭh*, "Ācār Mālikā" 41, "Ācār Mālikā" 73, "Ācār Mālikā" 55, and "Ācār" 98. Compare FH82.

136 Research: "Make whatever food offerings he requires. Do not take his food. Even if some is left over, let it be left over. To be there is to live in Kashi." Kashi (*kāśī*) is Banaras.

137 This is *Sūtrapāṭh*, "Ācār" 184.

138 This is according to Parasharambas. According to Rameshvarbas, it was Cangdevbhat.

139 This is the first sentence of *Sūtrapāṭh*, "Ācār" 93. The sutra continues: "Have you been fasting for a day, or fasting for two days? So wait at least a little while."

140 This is similar to *Sūtrapāṭh*, "Ācār" 32.

141 The period of the Gosavi's "absence" here is probably the time after his departure for the north, narrated at the end of the text.

142 The Gosavi gives Daïmba this nickname in SH399.

143 Compare FH89, where this same thing happens in the same place to Nathoba (or Cangdevbhat). In Kolte's edition (Mhaïmbhat 1982, *Pūrvārdha* 220), the disciple in this *līḷā* is Apdevbhat, not Vishnubhat.

144 The Gayatri mantra (*gāyatrī mantra*) is a verse recited as part of the daily *sandhyā* rites.

145 Research: He meets Nagdevbhat the Reciter. The omniscient one encouraged him, saying, "Ask for something, Bhat." "All right, Lord," he said, but he was not able to. Then his trance deepened, and he did not speak. His family said that he had gone mad, and they gave him medicine. He would speak a word or two to the mendicants.

146 Compare FH99.

147 This echoes *Sūtrapāṭh*, "Ācār Mālikā" 62.

148 Presumably these four Yadava kings were Krishna (r. 1246–1260 C.E.), Mahadev (r. 1260–1270 C.E.), Ammana (r. 1270 C.E.), and Ramchandra (r. 1271–1311 C.E.). See Altekar 1982, 2:543–549.

149 This is according to Parasharambas. According to Rameshvarbas, the omniscient one said: "One should not look empty-handed / at a king, a god, or a guru." According to Hiraïsa, the Gosavi himself said, "He will escape, but just barely." "Why is that?" "Because you came empty-handed to meet me." The verse in the Rameshvarbas version is in Sanskrit.

150 Chhinnapap (*chinnapāpa*), also called Chhinnasthali (*chinnasthaḷī*), is a place on the bank of the Godavari River at Dombegram. In the view of Rameshvarbas, the present *līlā* took place during one of the Gosavi's stays there: that is, either later in the present volume or (more likely) at some point during "The Second Half."

151 Research: The omniscient one asked, "Does he speak from books, or extemporaneously?" Sarangpandit replied, "He speaks in the assembly, Lord."

152 Compare FH94. As the Concordance shows, some *Līḷācaritra* editions include one or the other of these *līḷās,* but not both. Nene's edition, on which this one is based, includes both.

153 Shankar cave is Cave 29 at Ellora.

154 Compare FH87.

155 Or, died.

156 Dombegram (*ḍombegrāma, ḍomegrāma*), now called Kamalpur (*kamālapūra*), is a village on the Godavari River in Shrirampur Taluka, Ahmadnagar District. Chakradhar stayed here longer at a later period in his life.

157 Compare FH55.

158 This is according to Parasharambas. According to Rameshvarbas, Dakhale decided in his heart, "When I go home to my village, I

will bring some money to buy provisions for the Gosavi." The omniscient one said, "Dakhale, are you succumbing to wishful thinking?" "Yes, Lord." The omniscient one said, "I am not so inclined! If I were so inclined, could I not turn all of this into gold? You would be ruined, my children." Research: "There would be nothing left for you, my children."

159 Research: "What a grove! What great clusters of mangos are growing there!"

160 Shrinagar (*śrīnagara*) is Sinnar (*sinnara*), a taluka headquarters in present-day Nasik District that is home to the remains of many old temples.

161 Thane (*ṭhāṇe*) is a town on the west coast of India that is now the headquarters of a district.

162 Or, "There aren't any Mahatmas or Bahatmas. I am here."

163 This is the Southernwood festival. See FH120.

164 Sadegav (*sāḍegāva*) is a village on the Godavari River in present-day Ambad Taluka, Jalna District.

165 In the view of some, this happened in Ravasgav itself.

166 According to Hiraïsa, he said: "When you go there, say that I was asking you about him."

167 In SP73.

168 According to Hiraïsa, "What you get from me is a different kind of trance."

169 That is, what Dados has caused to happen to you has not had any great effect.

170 This is the Southernwood festival (*davaṇā/davaneparva*), which is celebrated at the full moon of the month of Caitra (March–April) by offering sprigs of the fragrant southernwood (*davaṇā*) plant. Compare Mhaïmbhat 1984, ch. 117.

171 According to Hiraïsa, the omniscient one said, "Get the water bag, Dakhale."

172 This is *Sūtrapāṭh*, "Ācār" 192.

173 The Telugu land is roughly the present-day state of Telangana.

174 Or, according to Hiraïsa: When the Gosavi was sitting in the Gondeshvar temple, he said, "Go and take a look. How is this temple constructed?" Some of them said one thing, and others said something else. The omniscient one said, "It is a work of pride.

"There was a Brahman boy named Padma who was taking a

bath at home. He had put scented paste on his head, and he began shouting for water. His mother said, 'What a hurry you are in! It's as if you are going to build Padmeshvar in front of Gondeshvar.'

"Immediately he tied his hair in a knot and set out. He went to the Telugu land, and there he acquired a vast amount of wealth. He came back and built Padmeshvar in front of Gondeshvar. He said to his mother, 'Mother, I have built Padmeshvar in front of Gondeshvar. Now give me a bath.'"

175 Nasik (*nāsika, nāsīka*), now the headquarters of a district, is a pilgrimage town on the upper reaches of the Godavari River. Panchavati (*pañcavaṭī, pañcavaṭikā*), a pilgrimage place associated with the *Rāmāyaṇa* story, is also on the river, next to Nasik.

176 A *pañcāyatan* temple is one with shrines of five gods.

177 Compare FH133. Also compare SH310, where something similar happens but with more dramatic consequences.

178 Govardhan (*govardhana*) is a village on the Godavari River between Nasik and Tryambakeshvar.

179 Gangadvar (*gaṅgādvāra*, "doorway of Ganga") is a cave partway up the mountain at Tryambakeshvar, with a pool of Godavari River water and a shrine to the goddess Kolaï. The Godavari is called "Ganga" because it is held to be identical in substance with the Ganges River (*gaṅgā*) of northern India.

180 This is close to *Sūtrapāṭha*, "Ācār" 229.

181 According to Hiraïsa, the Gosavi was sitting in the temple of Narasimha. According to another version, the Gosavi was walking back and forth at the doorway of the hermitage.

182 Dakhale means, "Does he have a right to be compensated for the water?" Gautam is the ancient sage understood to have brought the Ganges to earth as the Godavari River at Tryambakeshvar.

183 Brahmagiri is the mountain at Tryambakeshvar from the top of which the Godavari River is understood to originate.

184 Research: According to Kanadi Lukhaïse, the omniscient one said, "The universe is like this." According to Hiraïsa, he said, "Here is how to eat figs without breaking them," and he popped a fig into his mouth.

185 In the view of some, he sat at Hidden Tryambak.

186 Anjaniya (*āñjanīya*, "son of Anjana," a name of the god Hanuman), now Anjaneri (*añjanerī*), is the name of a mountain and a village near Tryambakeshvar.

187 Compare FH126.
188 According to Hiraïsa, he said, "He must go, my woman, on his pilgrimage." Although Cangdevbhat disappears from the story until FH177, in the next chapter here (FH134), Dakhale does meet two other disciples, one of them Cangdevbhat's twin brother, Nathoba.
189 Or, "The poor fellows are coming along hugging trees in order to get my *darśan*."
190 Chandori, in present-day Niphad Taluka, Nasik District, lies on the direct route north from Sinnar to the mountain place of the goddess Saptashringi (here called Satrasinga) in Dindori Taluka, Nasik District.
191 But see the previous chapter, where it is Cangdevbhat, not Upadhye and Nathoba, whom the Gosavi sends Dakhale to invite. In FH135 we learn that Nathoba is Cangdevbhat's twin brother.
192 The Gosavi arranged Dakhale's meeting with Nathoba and Upadhye without telling any of them in advance.
193 Or, according to Hiraïsa, "How sad for ultimate truth!"
194 This is according to Parasharambas. According to Rameshvarbas, it was at the place where the Gosavi went to defecate.
195 The science of Caurangi is the ability to restore one's own limbs, a power associated with a yogi named Cauranginath.
196 Adgav (*aḍagāva*) is a village in present-day Nasik Taluka, Nasik District.
197 Shambhava (*śāmbhava*), Shakteya (*śākteya*), and Anava (*āṇava*) are types of esoteric knowledge (*vidyā*, here translated "science") obtained from three different categories of deities in the *devatācakra*, the Mahanubhav system for classifying deities. See Feldhaus 1980: 106.
198 Sukiyana (*sukīyānā*) is a village in present-day Niphad Taluka, Nasik District.
199 Or, to a temple of Narayan. Niphad (*niphāḍa*) is a taluka headquarters in present-day Nasik District.
200 This is according to Rameshvarbas. According to Parasharambas, the Gosavi sat down in the Konkanaï temple as soon as he arrived. Dakhale went to get the partitioned pouch, and when he came back with it, he told the Gosavi about the Mahatma.
201 Milk products: As a disciple of Vamdev, Atmaram would have

followed the "milk-drinkers' way," including a diet consisting only of dairy products. See FH3 and FH4.

202 Compare FH126, FH133, and SH310.

203 Compare FH134 and FH136, in which Dakhale and Upadhye, respectively, make the same comment.

204 Madhyameshvar (*madhyameśvara;* "Lord of the Middle") is a name of the god Shiva. Nandaur (*nāndaura*) is a village in present-day Niphad Taluka, Nasik District. Before this sentence, Nene inserts the following comment, which appears to pertain to FH144: Research: The cliff on the riverbank was southeast of the Madhyameshvar temple.

205 For one (or three) of these ghosts, see FH6.

206 Kolte's edition (Mhaïmbhat 1982, *Pūrvārdha* 268) has Upadhye explain to Nathoba: "Your father was a most excellent man [*purūkhotamu*], but he has become a ghost. The Gosavi is trying to release him from being a ghost."

207 Kanalade (*kānaḷade*) is a village in present-day Niphad Taluka, Nasik District.

208 Suregav (*suregāva*) is a village in present-day Kopargav Taluka, Ahmadnagar District.

209 Sonari (*soṇārī*) is a village in present-day Kopargav Taluka, Ahmadnagar District.

210 Singeshvar (*siṅgeśvara*) is a name of the god Shiva. Samvatsar (*sāvatsara, savasara*) is a village in present-day Kopargav Taluka, Ahmadnagar District.

211 Kumkumthan (*kūkumaṭhāṇa*) is a village in present-day Kopargav Taluka, Ahmadnagar District. Damodar (*dāmodara*) is a name of Krishna.

212 Punatambe (*puṇatāmbe*) is a village in present-day Rahata Taluka, Ahmadnagar District.

213 Naygav (*nāyagāva*) is a village in present-day Kopargav Taluka, Ahmadnagar District.

214 Naür (*nāür*) is a village in present-day Kopargav Taluka, Ahmadnagar District. Kantakeshvar (*kaṇṭakeśvar*) is a name of the god Shiva.

215 Research: "Now this place has become dangerous because of me. Violence takes place here."

216 Hinguni (*hiṅguṇī*) is a village in present-day Vaijapur Taluka, Aurangabad District.

217 Purnagav (*purṇagāva*) is a village in present-day Vaijapur Taluka, Aurangabad District.
218 Sangavkhede (*sāṅgavakheḍe, sāgavakheḍe*) is a village in present-day Gangapur Taluka, Aurangabad District.
219 Vanjargav (*vāñjaragāva*) is a village in present-day Vaijapur Taluka, Aurangabad District.
220 Nagamthan, or Old Nagamthan (*jūnā nāgamaṭhāṇa*) is a village in present-day Vaijapur Taluka, Aurangabad District.
221 This Tapovan (*tapovana*, "ascetic grove") is in present-day Vaijapur Taluka, Aurangabad District.
222 Khategav (*khātegāva*) is a village in present-day Vaijapur Taluka, Aurangabad District.
223 This is the beginning of *Sūtrapāṭh*, "Vicār" 273. The full sutra reads, "Pride in one's disciples is greater than that of a woman in her man."
224 See SP19. The episode in the present chapter serves as the frame story there.
225 Research: He was sitting on the veranda.
226 Miraj (*miraja*) is a taluka headquarters in present-day Sangli District, in southern Maharashtra.
227 Kambkhed (*kāmbakheḍa*) is a village in present-day Bid Taluka, Bid District.
228 Some say the Gosavi ate one or two of the bananas that Dados had had Bhatobas bring, then rinsed his mouth and chewed pan.
229 The festival seems to be the one at the full moon of the month of Shravan, when Brahman men renew the loop of thread that hangs from their left shoulder to below the waist on the right side of their body.
230 One-and-a-Half Man is Upadhye. See FH65.
231 One version: "He doesn't do those kinds of antics." "Antics" (*ceṣṭā*) is a term Chakradhar uses elsewhere to describe the behavior of Dados. See FH442.
232 This is according to Parasharambas. According to Rameshvarbas, he said, "That person does not even know enough to tell whether he may or may not offer me something he has already used." Research: "My woman, he has given me something used."
233 Hiraïsa version: "So you are not lacking in marital bliss."
234 Although people observing a fast are now allowed to eat bananas, Abaïse's objection suggests that such people may earlier have been

forbidden to eat them.

235 This is according to Rameshvarbas. Hiraïsa version: "It's not really wrong to take such a little bit at such a time."

236 Ananta Chaturdashi (*ananta caturdaśī*) is a festival celebrated on the fourteenth day of the "bright" (waxing-moon) fortnight of the month of Bhadrapad (August–September) in honor of Ananta ("the infinite one"), the serpent upon whom the god Vishnu reclines.

237 This is *Sūtrapāṭh,* "Vicār" 226.

238 "Brahmas" is a playful pluralization of Brahma(n), the term for the impersonal Absolute being.

239 Or, Bhatobas asked, "What do you mean, Lord?"

240 The parable here is *Dṛṣṭāntapāṭh* 42: "A hungry person came to a temple. On a canopy decorated with fruits, he saw mangos that looked like real mangos. He saw bananas that looked like real bananas. He saw coconuts that looked like real coconuts (Rameshvarbas). He saw Java plums that looked like real Java plums. He started to pick them and eat them. His mouth got filled with dung and mud." The point of this parable is to contrast the lower forms of knowledge (*vidyā*) given by nontranscendent deities (*devatās*) with the *brahmavidyā* (knowledge of Brahman, the Absolute) that is given only by the one supreme God.

241 This is *Sūtrapāṭh,* "Vicār" 276.

242 Some say, "Baba, one such man came to Yelapur. Another has come here." For the similar man who came to Yelapur, see FH79.

243 This is *Sūtrapāṭh,* "Vicār Mālikā" 54.

244 Hiraïsa version: "trying to kill off the old lady."

245 Any one of the many people could have given me the evil eye.

246 A mother must regularly ward off and remove the evil eye from her children.

247 Garuda is Vishnu's eagle mount. There would have been an image of him in a gymnasium, which is, here and elsewhere, named for him.

248 Hiraïsa version: "... to Vetal. You forgot to place the baton in front of Vetal and do reverence to him." "All right, Lord." Vetal (*vetāla*) is the king of ghosts.

249 Mairal (*mairāḷa*) is a Shaiva deity. Pali (*pālī*) is a village in present-day Bid Taluka, Bid District.

250 Nimba (*nimbā*), now called Limba Ganesh (*limbā gaṇeśa*), is a village in present-day Bid Taluka, Bid District.

251 Hiraïsa version: "For now, my woman, do what she is saying. What do you stand to lose?"

252 Hiraïsa version: "My woman, what you were saying is true. God doesn't have likes or dislikes, but Baïse understands God's inclination."

253 This is according to Parasharambas. According to Rameshvarbas, he said, "You get sin, and you also get merit."

254 This is *Sūtrapāṭh*, "Ācār" 225. The two terms *ethārthu* and *satya arthu* are synonymous.

255 Matrakavali (*mātrakavaḷī*) is a village in present-day Ashti Taluka, Bid District. Samvatada (*sāvataḍā*), now called Sautada (*sautāḍā*), is a village in present-day Patoda Taluka, Bid District.

256 Jambkhede (*jāmbakheḍe*) is present-day Jamkhed (*jāmakheḍa*), a taluka headquarters in Ahmadnagar District.

257 This Asuti (*āsuṭī*), now called Ashti (*āṣṭī*), is a taluka headquarters in present-day Bid District.

258 This Shirala (*sīrāḷā*) is a village in present-day Ashti Taluka, Bid District.

259 This Vanki (*vāṅkī*) is a village in present-day Ashti Taluka, Bid District.

260 Ratanjan (*rātāñjana*) is a village in present-day Karjat Taluka, Ahmadnagar District.

261 The Pandavas are the heroes of the Mahabharata, the epic of tragedy and strife.

262 According to *Uttarārdha* 149 in Kolte's edition (Mhaïmbhat 1982), Dako was a Blacksmith.

263 Mirade (*miraḍe*), now called Mirajgav (*mirajagāva*), is a village in present-day Karjat Taluka, Ahmadnagar District.

264 Mandavgan (*māṇḍavagaṇa*) is a village in present-day Shrigonda Taluka, Ahmadnagar District.

265 Arangram (*araṇagrāma*) is a village in present-day Nagar Taluka, Ahmadnagar District.

266 Hiraïsa version: "Ask Baïse before you take anything of mine. Go and ask Baïse, then take it."

267 This is similar to *Sūtrapāṭh*, "Vicār Mālikā" 60.

268 Bhingar (*bhiṅgāra*) is a large village two miles east of present-day Ahmadnagar.

269 Lakshmidev and Bhaïdev: Kolte's edition (Mhaïmbhat 1982, *Pūrvārdha* 355) explains that Bhaïdev was mad (*veḍā*) and

Lakshmidev was possessed (*pīsā*), while Nagpure's edition (Mhaïmbhat 2004, *Pūrvārdha* 325) adds that Lakshmidev was the older of the brothers.

270 This last sentence is *Sūtrapāṭh*, "Vicar" 275.

271 Hiraïsa version: Or, "They say that you would accept something that is not true. Like a line inscribed on stone."

272 He bent his neck so that his horns would not get stuck.

273 Hiraïsa version: "A certain Mahatma was making his disciple memorize something. The disciple could not learn it. The Mahatma said, 'Go away! You are a water buffalo!' 'So I am a water buffalo. Why not?' And he made horns for himself, then went away. When he came back, the Mahatma said, 'Come straight ahead.' The disciple said, 'Won't the horns get in the way?' 'Turn your neck to the side this way and come in.' 'All right,' he said, and came in. Then the Mahatma put his hand on the disciple's head. 'Now you are not a water buffalo.' 'Yes. All right.'"

274 This is *Sūtrapāṭh*, "Vicār Mālikā" 31.

275 Kolte's and Nagpure's versions of this passage (Mhaïmbhat 1982 and Mhaïmbhat 2004) indicate that Baïse had relatives in Jeür, a village in present-day Nagar Taluka, Ahmadnagar District. Papvinashan (*pāpavināśana;* "destruction of sins") is a holy place with a waterfall near the village of Dongargan (*ḍoṅgaragaṇa*) in present-day Nagar Taluka, Ahmadnagar District.

276 This Pimpalgav (*pīpaḷagāva;* "pipal-tree village") is a village in present-day Nagar Taluka, Ahmadnagar District. Hiraïsa version: There was a hamlet by a stream at Pimpalgav. He was sitting in that hamlet.

277 Hiraïsa version: The Gosavi said to Cangdevbhat, "Get some chickpeas, Batika." He got some ripe ones. "Batika, go get some jujubes." "I don't see any jujubes here, Lord." "Go such-and-such a way." He went there and found fallen jujubes covering the ground. "That's what our Gosavi is like," he said. "Does he say directly, 'Bring jujubes from that jujube tree over there'?"

278 This is the beginning of *Sūtrapāṭh*, "Ācār" 220. The sutra continues, "Where there are chickpeas, there are no teeth."

279 Vamori (*vāmorī*), now called Vambori (*vāmborī*), is a village in present-day Rahuri Taluka, Ahmadnagar District.

280 This is similar to *Sūtrapāṭh*, "Ācār Mālikā" 180.

281 This is *Sūtrapāṭh*, "Ācār" 221.

282 Sonai (*sonai, sonaī*) is a village in present-day Nevase Taluka, Ahmadnagar District.

283 Kanadgav (*kānaḍagāva, kānaḍi gāva*) is a village in present-day Vaijapur Taluka, Aurangabad District.

284 Gangapur (*gāṅgāpura*) is a taluka headquarters in present-day Aurangabad District.

285 What had happened, that is, after Padmanabhidev's brother Jognayak took him home. See FH208.

286 Research: Baïsa said, "What kind of wish is that?" "My woman, take his blanket and baggage."

287 Phulsara (*phulasarā*), now called Phulshivara (*phulaśivarā*), is a village in present-day Gangapur Taluka, Aurangabad District.

288 Paramānubhav means "one who has the supreme experience" (*parama-anubhav*), while Paramāṇubhav means "one whose experience (*bhav*) is infinitesimally small" (*parama-aṇu-bhav*).

289 This is the beginning of *Sūtrapāṭh*, "Ācār" 239. The sutra continues, "Now I do not want to see his face."

290 Hatnaur (*hātanaura*), now called Hatnur (*hātanūra*), is a village in present-day Bhusaval Taluka, Jalgav District.

291 Kanarade (*kanaraḍe*) is a village in present-day Kannad Taluka, Aurangabad District.

292 Saegavhan (*sāegavhāṇa*) is a village in present-day Chalisgav Taluka, Jalgav District.

293 Vaguli (*vāguḷī*) is a village in present-day Chalisgav Taluka, Jalgav District.

294 Kanase (*kānase;* also spelled *kānasa*), now called Kanashi (*kanāśī*), is a village in present-day Bhadgav Taluka, Jalgav District.

295 This conversation, which illustrates Shriprabhu's typical way of speaking, is also reported in Mhaïmbhat 1984, ch. 84. Bhalugav (*bhālugāv, bhalugāv*), now called Bhalgav (*bhālagāva*), is a village in present-day Nevase Taluka, Ahmadnagar District.

296 Charthane (*cāraṭhāṇe*) is a village in present-day Jintur Taluka, Parbhani District.

297 See FH240 for the Gosavi's stay at the Brahman's home in Kanarade.

298 According to *Ajñāt Līlā* 18 (Kolte edition, Mhaïmbhat 1982), Kakos was Sadhe's paternal uncle.

299 Research: This is where he gave her the name Sadhe, saying,

"She is a simple woman from Varad." "Sadhe" means "simple one." In the version adopted for this edition, the Gosavi gives her this name, using these same words, at the end of the present chapter. Varad (*varāḍa*) is a region centering on present-day Amravati District, roughly congruent with the Vidarbha division of the modern state of Maharashtra.

300 This is the beginning of *Sūtrapāṭh*, "Ācār" 39. The sutra continues, "these three attract people to them."

301 According to the Panjabi edition (*Pūrvārdha* 275), Hard-Hearted's (Elhambhat's) mother is Samakose, his daughter is Gauraïse, and his son-in-law is Nagdevbhat (Indroba).

302 That is, they are like newborn babies.

303 Madalsa (*madaḷasā*, Sanskrit *madālasā*) is the name of a female figure in Puranic literature. In FH114, *madaḷasā* appears as the term for the carved central section of a stone pillar (B. Deshpande 2005a: 41–42).

304 Indrabhat's statement is mostly in Sanskrit.

305 Hiraïsa version: "My woman, this is the Ekadashi. Take Dados there."

306 Hiraïsa version: "Then whom should I send? You go then, Padmanabhi."

307 This is according to Rameshvarbas. According to Parasharambas, it was just a mattress.

308 Hiraïsa version: "What are you looking for, Sadhe? Sadhe, are you looking for God? Come on in. God is here."

309 This is *Sūtrapāṭh*, "Ācār" 275.

310 Hiraïsa version: After he had eaten his meal, he said, "Go to your lodgings now. It is late at night. Give Sadhe some *prasād*, my woman. Padmanabhi, go along with Sadhe."

311 The parable of the spindle is *Dṛṣṭāntapāṭh* 11: "A certain weaver went to the bazaar to get a spindle. Because the market was not open then, he went to sleep at the foot of a tree. When he looked up, he saw a straight twig on a branch. Then he said, 'What a good spindle that would make!' The spindle fell down. He took it, put it on his shoulder, and set out. Then the tree said, 'Hey, I am the wish-granting tree. I am pleased with you. Ask for something.' So he said, 'Give me another spindle in exchange for this one.'"

312 This is a day of feasting following the eleventh-day (Ekadashi) fast.

313 A thread ceremony is the ritual in which a young man is first

invested with the Brahmanical shoulder thread. The celebration would have involved a festive meal.

314 Bhadegav (*bhaḍegāva, bhaḍegāva*) is a village in present-day Pachora Taluka, Jalgav District.

315 Holi festival (*sīmugā*): a springtime festival celebrated by sprinkling people with colors and lighting a bonfire. The next day, people throw around the cooled ashes of the fire.

316 Ram's army of monkeys: the army led by Hanuman that assisted Ram, the hero of the *Ramayana,* in his quest to rescue his wife from imprisonment in Lanka. There is wordplay here, as Dados or Ramdev (here called Dev) is also called Ram.

317 *Aṅkuśmudrā* ("elephant-goad stamp") is a type of trance.

318 Hiraïsa version: "Hey! Your scripture says, 'Even if an elephant attacks, Brahmans may not enter a Jain temple.'" "Yes, Lord." "Then why did you come here?" "I came along with my Gosavi, Lord."

319 Although the Buddha appears much more frequently than the Jina as an avatar of Vishnu, there is a tradition that considers the Jain *tīrthaṅkar* Rishabha to be one (Jaini 1977).

320 Hiraïsa version: "It's a deity, isn't it?"

321 Hiraïsa version: "That's what Bhatacharya was like. He condemned the deity through his pride. Even if it is the enemy's god, should he hit it with a rock and break it? Hey, should anyone demolish a deity?" The story this refers to is found in a footnote to *Pūrvārdha* 391 in Kolte's edition (Mhaïmbhat 1982).

322 This is *Sūtrapāṭh,* "Vicār" 52.

323 Hiraïsa version: "My woman, you have come for my *darśan,* but you never come for my worship service. Why is that?"

324 They are like newborn babies. Chakradhar says the same thing about some of these same disciples in FH243.

325 Hiraïsa version: "Go with her, my woman," said the omniscient one. He sent Padmanabhidev along too. Baïse went with her and entrusted her to her companions.

326 This is *Sūtrapāṭh,* "Ācār" 66. A man's "domestic fetters," literally, his "peg and tether," are his wife and family, who chain him to worldly existence.

327 The woman Mahadaïse approaches is the one from the previous chapter.

328 See SP4 for what Mahadaïse sees when she goes there.

329 See FH329 for the sequel to this episode.

330 Dvarka: Dvaravati. Yadavas: members of Shri Krishna's tribe.

331 Hiraïsa version: "Bhat, by now your companions must have gotten far ahead."

332 A constellation necklace has twenty-seven pearls, the number of constellations in the sky.

333 Hiraïsa version: He was sitting on the right side of the veranda.

334 A shaved head is a mark of a sannyasi.

335 Sendurani (*sendurani̩*) is a village in present-day Jamner Taluka, Jalgav District.

336 Hiraïsa version: The farmer pounded the chickpeas and winnowed them, and then Padmanabhidev tied them in a bundle and brought them to the Gosavi.

337 Hiraïsa version: "Split the chickpeas yourself, grind them yourself, and make the gram pancakes yourself. You may ask people for advice, but you may not have them do it for you."

338 Erandavali (*eraṇḍavalī*), now called Erandol (*eraṇḍola*), is a taluka headquarters in present-day Jalgav District. Karanjkhed (*karañjakheḍa*) is a village in present-day Kannad Taluka, Aurangabad District. For the Southernwood festival, see FH120.

339 Hiraïsa version: He asked later, "When will you go?"

340 Hiraïsa version: He laid down some rules: "Go directly there without staying anywhere overnight. Do not put your head on Shriprabhu's holy feet for a long time. Do not sit facing him. Do not cause difficulties for Shriprabhu. Leave as soon as he sends you away. Otherwise you could cause difficulties for the god." The last sentence is the end of *Sūtrapāṭh*, "Ācār" 229.

341 Hiraïsa version: "The traveling companions are already disagreeing, before they have left!"

342 Hiraïsa version: "Someone came and made it famous. What is there in that place now? What is a ritual bath and *darśan* of Sharngadhar compared to *darśan* of Shriprabhu? What is that in comparison to this?"

343 One version: He got ten.

344 Hiraïsa version: "Go, Martanda. Cry out, 'Milk for a cowrie shell!'"

345 They could not see him in the dark.

346 Hiraïsa version: "She came for my *darśan,* but you didn't come. Why is that?" "If I come, Baïse starts insulting me right away."

347 Hiraïsa version: "Demati, you should be like a wild bull. A certain farmer is keeping watch over his haystack. There is a wild bull. When the man says, 'Shoo!' the bull takes a bite and goes away. It runs away as soon as it gets its bite."

348 Pachor (*pācora*), now called Pachora (*pācorā*), is a taluka headquarters in present-day Jalgav District.

349 Cangdev, or Cangdev Puri (*cāṅgadevapurī*) is the village around the Cangdev temple at the confluence of the Tapi and Purna Rivers, in present-day Muktainagar Taluka, Jalgav District.

350 Hiraïsa version: "My woman, he is not like other devotees. He is emotional."

351 Hiraïsa version: "My woman, that is what he saw because of his trance." According to Gopalba: The Gosavi really went into the water. Baïse saw him. He did away with that impression.

352 Savaldev (*sāvaḷadeva, sǎvaḷadeva;* "the dark-skinned god" or "the god in the shade") is a village in present-day Bhokardan Taluka, Aurangabad District.

353 Research: "People will see you. Stay here now, Mahatma."

354 The word "before" refers to the earlier incarnation, as Krishna, of the supreme God of whom Chakradhar is also an incarnation. See the next note.

355 Kubjaka was the evil king Kamsa's hunchbacked maidservant. In the fuller version of this story narrated in Kolte's edition (Mhaïmbhat 1982, *Pūrvārdha* 421), Krishna and Uddhav visit her and she puts down a seat for each of them. Krishna sits on his seat, but Uddhav sits humbly on the floor, placing his hand on the seat meant for him.

356 Valseng (*vālaseṅga*), now called Valsavangi (*vālasāvaṅgī*), is a village in present-day Bhokardan Taluka, Jalna District.

357 This Tapovan (*tapovana,* "ascetic grove,") is in present-day Bhokardan Taluka, Jalna District.

358 Masraul (*māsarauḷa*), now called Masrul (*māsrula*), is a village in present-day Buldhana Taluka, Buldhana District.

359 This Pimpalgav (*pīpaḷagāva;* "pipal-tree village") is a village in present-day Bhokardan Taluka, Jalna District.

360 Bhogvardhan (*bhogavardhana*), now called Bhokardan, is a taluka headquarters in present-day Jalna District.

361 Bameshvar (*bāmeśvara*) is a name of the god Shiva. Shela-vade (*śeḷavaḍe*), now called Sillod, is a taluka headquarters in

Aurangabad District.

362 Anave (*ānave*) is a village in present-day Bhokardan Taluka, Jalna District.

363 "If I extol…" is the beginning of *Sūtrapāṭh*, "Vicār" 163. The sutra continues, "your eyes will go to your forehead."

364 In the view of Parasharambas, this chapter should be placed along with the others that took place at the Ganapati Madh hermitage in Pratishthan, late in the *Uttarārdha* section of the text. In accordance with this view, the chapter is found as *Uttarārdha* 380 in Nagpure's edition (Mhaïmbhat 2004).

365 One-and-a-Half Man is Upadhye. See FH65.

366 See FH272.

367 This is the beginning of *Sūtrapāṭh*, "Vicār" 214. The sutra continues, "what he gives when, to which *jīva*."

368 Hiraïsa version: "Anyone who eats a mango from this tree gets a fever."

369 Research: When Lakhubaïse ate a meal, she would have Demaïse wash the bowl. One day after Lakhubaïse ate her meal, the Gosavi saw what she did. "Wash the bowl, my woman," said the omniscient one. "Your server has gone out." (This is according to Rameshvarbas. According to Parasharambas, it is an unknown *līḷā*.) For unknown (*ajñāt*) *līḷās*, see n. 20 in SP.

370 Charner (*cāranera*) is a village in present-day Sillod Taluka, Aurangabad District.

371 Unknown *līḷā:* see n. 20 in SP.

372 This is according to Parasharambas. According to Rameshvarbas, he said, "Your eighteen diseases will get tied to this pipal tree."

373 Hiraïsa version: "Martanda, this rice is all from one house."

374 This is according to Parasharambas. Research: According to Rameshvar, he said, "You've sent a heap of food, my woman. Your food arrived at a good time."

375 Hiraïsa version: "Martanda didn't tell me a thing."

376 Hiraïsa version: "My woman, why are you angry with him? His diseases cannot go away. Why would they go away? Can an oil lamp light up a kiln? The poor fellow can't tell what is good for him and what is bad."

377 Hiraïsa version: "Are you suffering from rheumatism, Nayak?" "Yes, Lord. I've been crippled by rheumatism for three years."

378 Hiraïsa version: "Nayak, take off one of your cloaks. And take off the blanket." "Lord, I can't manage without the blanket. If you still want to make me take something off, Lord Gosavi, then let me take off a cloak."

379 Hiraïsa version: "Take it off for now. Then, if you can't manage, put it back on. Why not?"

380 Hiraïsa version: He dispensed with the blanket and a cloak.

381 Hiraïsa version: He had him take off the second cloak and he had him do without the second stove. "Lord," he said, "I can do without the cloak if I must, but I can't manage without the stoves." "You can do without it for now. If you can't manage, then you can light it." He did without it.

382 Hiraïsa version: He had him get rid of the second stove and the turban. "Lord," he said, "I can do without the turban if I must, but not the stove, Lord." The omniscient one said, "You can do without it for now. If you can't manage, you can light it."

383 *Uḍīd* dal is split black lentils, and *vaḍās* are fried lentil-flour cakes.

384 Hiraïsa version: "What is this, my woman?" "Lord, I got this rice for the Nayak." "Let it be, my woman. Serve him the same things as the devotees."

385 "Food" (*anna*) is regular food, food appropriate for a proper meal, including rice and/or chapatis, as opposed to snack foods like *vaḍās*.

386 Hiraïsa version: "Did you have any trouble last night, Nayak?" "What can I tell you?" he said. He told him everything that had happened. "How are you now?" asked the omniscient one. "Now, Lord, I keep feeling, 'I must eat! I must eat!'" "So do that now," said the omniscient one.

387 This is the garment that Mahadaïse gave the Gosavi in FH259. The Hiraïsa version specifies that he wore it draped over his shoulders for six months.

388 That is, the *līḷā* took place during the Gosavi's stay in Hivarali, recounted later in *Pūrvārdha*. The Gosavi sends Bhatobas and Mahadaïse to Riddhipur in FH342.

389 Hiraïsa version: "My woman, do you know how to paint pictures?" "Lord, I don't know how to paint most kinds of pictures. I do know how to draw peacocks." "Then draw two peacocks every day."

390 Ramtirtha (*rāmatīrtha;* "Ram's *tīrtha*") is a bathing place named

for the god Ram; this one is near Karanjkhed, in Kannad Taluka, Aurangabad District.

391 Hiraïsa version: The omniscient one said, "Take a look, my woman. Is there any water-and-rice gruel?"

392 Hiraïsa version: "If he does it to you, Lord, our Gosavi, then we will do it to him."

393 This is *Sūtrapāṭh,* "Ācār" 183.

394 This is *Sūtrapāṭh,* "Vicār" 269.

395 Hiraïsa version: Baïse said, "Baba, how well Nagdev is going from one branch to another without falling!" The omniscient one said, "My woman, how much like a monkey he looks!"

396 Hiraïsa version: He had Baïse bring the blanket. He took it in his holy hand and said, "Oh, Mahatma, mend this blanket under a tree for nine hours a day for a month. Go begging for alms in the late afternoon [*Sūtrapāṭh,* "Ācār Mālikā" 53]. Eat your meal at a river and sleep in a temple. As the blanket gets repaired, your knowledge will improve."

397 Hiraïsa version: "Hey, did I tell you to mend the blanket sitting on a swing at Elhambhat's house, to eat ghee and rice on a plate with a lampstand, and to sleep on a bed with a mattress? Is that what I told you to do? What I told you was to repair the blanket at the foot of a tree for nine hours each day, to go begging for alms in the late afternoon, to eat your meal at a river, and to sleep in a temple. That is what I told you to do! Still now, if you would do this you would get a thousand years of life in the Dvapara yuga. You would have knowledge of the three times [*Sūtrapāṭh,* "Vicār Mālikā" 58]: past, future, and present. Kings would consider you divine" [*Sūtrapāṭh,* "Vicar Malika" 57]. Dev kept silent. Then the omniscient one said, "Why should that happen? The poor child has to stretch out his legs and die at home. Why should he escape that? 'Can you get a bushel's worth for a handful?' That's what they say. Can you get something eternal for a handful?"

398 Ne and T(n) precede this sentence with the following remarks: This biographical episode is from another copy. It is not from the original manuscript. It is separate here.

399 His renunciation is superficial.

400 Hiraïsa version: Indrabhat set out for the capital to get a donation. The Gosavi said to Bhat, "You go too, Monkey." "If I go there, Lord, what will I do? I am just a dolt. I don't know any scriptures." "Go

on," replied the omniscient one. "You will get the same as he does."

401 This is the festival at the full moon of the month of Shravan, in which Brahman men renew the loop of thread worn over their left shoulder and hanging down below the waist on their right side. Compare FH170.

402 She was going into labor.

403 Hiraïsa version: "Why have you come here?" He got embarrassed, and the Gosavi smiled gently.

404 The Gosavi does this, for example, in FH14, FH15, FH20, and FH21.

405 In FH91.

406 "Exclusion of Others" ("Anyavyāvṛtti"), one of the first nine chapters of the *Sūtrapāṭh,* names in turn the deities on each of the levels of the Mahanubhav system for classifying deities (the *devatācakra*), stating in each case that the deities are not the supreme God.

407 The parable of the myrobalan fruit is *Dṛṣṭāntapāṭh* 39: "There was a certain mother whose baby was not hungry. It had lost its appetite. So she rinsed its mouth with myrobalan juice. Then it got hungry. It got its appetite back. Then she nursed it."

408 Dhoreshvar (*ḍhoreśvara,* "Lord of Cattle") is a Shiva temple in Pratishthan where Chakradhar stayed in a later period of his life.

409 Hiraïsa version: "Baïse, I would have lost my status as a Mahatma." A Mahatma should be able to control such bodily functions as sneezing, yawning, farting, and sleep.

410 Dabhadi (*dābhāḍī*) is a village in present-day Badnapur Taluka, Jalna District.

411 A Rajmath (*rājamaṭha, rājamaḍha*) is a temple-hermitage dedicated to Narasimha.

412 Or, Hiraïsa version: "Those who express it don't know how to express it. When they express it, Lord, they destroy it."

413 Hiraïsa version: "What is your name, Nayak?" "They call me Vaman, Lord. Vaman." (Or, "Vaya. They call me Vaya.")

414 Vamanacharya: "Teacher Vaman," named for the dwarf incarnation of Vishnu.

415 Padali (*pāḍaḷī*) is a village in present-day Badnapur Taluka, Jalna District.

416 Research: She prepared the food the same day she arrived.

417 This is according to Parasharambas. According to Rameshvarbas,

he said, "Cook some food made with lentils here, and then you'll get it back."

418 Research: Mahadaïse removed the ones that were on her plate. He said, "Serve some to her, my woman." This happened twice.

419 Tembhurni (*ṭembhuraṇī*) is a village in present-day Japharabad Taluka, Jalna District.

420 This is according to Paraśarambas. According to Rameshvarbas, "You can do it for your people who are worn out and tired out. Ease one another's weariness." This last sentence is *Sūtrapāṭh,* "Ācār" 130.

421 This episode about Mahadaïse's brother serves as the frame story for SP13.

422 Hiraïsa version: "Give him water to drink. He crossed a river, but he did not drink any water."

423 The tenth day of the fortnight is the day before the Ekadashi, the day on which her fast was presumably to start.

424 Research: "Is it worse to have some leisure time and to be close to me?"

425 Or, Hiraïsa version: "My woman, is it worse to be in this situation than to be far, far away from me and get your eyes filled with smoke? Vriddhabaïse will prepare the food, and Lord Monkey will do the puja to me. I will accept your puja."

426 Note that, although Umaïse was menstruating and was thus assumed by everyone not to be allowed to cook, she was permitted to sit with the others to eat her meal.

427 Hiraïsa version: "You may not take pan that has been chewed."

428 Hiraïsa version: "Go to Ravasgav, my woman, and then I will give you *darśan.*"

429 According to Rameshvarbas, he had gone to the south of the hermitage. According to Parasharambas, it was to the east of the hermitage.

430 Hiraïsa version: "The original Mahatmas begged for food with these words."

431 According to a variant in Kolte's edition (Mhaïmbhat 1982, *Pūrvārdha* 470), Tikavnayak was the son-in-law of Vayanayak (and therefore Mahadaïse's brother-in-law). A variant in Nagpure's edition (Mhaïmbhat 2004, *Pūrvārdha* 433) states even more clearly: "Tikavnayak was Vayanayak's son-in-law, the husband of Mahadaïse's older sister Umaïse."

432 This idea is expressed in similar words in *Sūtrapāṭh,* "Vicār Mālikā" a61, and Mhaïmbhat 1984, ch. 280, as well as, in some versions of this text, late in "The Second Half": *Uttarārdha* 527 in Kolte's edition (Mhaïmbhat 1982); *Uttarārdha* 506 in Nagpure's (Mhaïmbhat 2004).

433 I will become an itinerant ascetic and disappear from society.

434 Hiraïsa version: "That Brahman is proud. Is it better for him to shave his head, rip up his dhoti, and take the road to the north, or for me to be Siddhanath for a little while?"

435 Mahadaïse goes to Dvaravati and comes back in FH261. This same conversation is reported in E4.

436 This is *Sūtrapāṭh,* "Ācār" 154.

CONCORDANCE

MCLI	Ne	T	K	Na	Pa	S
SP1	E1	E1	P2	P1	E1-2	E1-3
SP2	E2	E2	P3	P2	E3-4	E4
SP3	E3	E3	P3, 15	P14	E5	E5
SP4	E4	E4	P16, 463	P15	E6-7	E6-7
SP5	E5	E5	P17	P16	E7	E7
SP6	E6	E6	P18	P17	E8	E8
SP7	E7	E7	P19-20	P18	E9-10	E9-10
SP8	E8	E8	P21	P19	E11	E11
SP9	E9	E9	P22-23	P21	E12	E12
SP10	E10	E10	P25	P22	E13	E13
SP11	E11	E11	P26	P23-24	E14	E14
SP12	E12	E12	P27	P26	E15	E15
SP13	E13	E13	P28	P27	E16	E16
SP14	E14	E14	P29	P28	E17-18	E17-18
SP15	E15	E15	P30	P29	E19	E19
SP16	E16	E16	P31-32	P25	E20-22	E20-22
SP17	E17	E17	P33	P30	E23	E23
SP18	E18	E18	P34	P31	E24	E24

MCLI	Ne	T	K	Na	Pa	S
SP19	E19	E19	P35	P32	E25	E25
SP20	E20	E20	P36–37	P33	E27–28	E27–29
SP21	E21	E21	P38–40	P33–36	E29–31	E29–31
SP22	E22	E22	P41	P37	E32	E32
SP23	E23	E23	P42	P38	E33	E33
SP24	E24	E24	P43	P39	E34	E34
SP25	E25–26	E25	P44–45	P40–41	E35–37	E35–37
SP26	E27	E26	P46	P42	E38	E38
SP27	E28	E27	P47	P43	E39	E39
SP28	E29–30	E28	P48	P44–45	E40–41	E40–41
SP29	E31	E29	P49–50	P46	E26, 42–43	E26, 42–43
SP30	E32	E30	P51	P47	E44–45	E44–45
SP31	E33	E31	P52	P48	E46–47	E46–47
SP32	E34	E32	P53	P49	E48	E48
SP33	E35	E33	P54	P63	E49	E49
SP34	E36	E34	P55	P52	E50	E50
SP35	E37	E35	P56	P64	E51	E51
SP36	E38	E36	P57	P50	E52	E52
SP37	E39	E37	P59	P55	E54	E54
SP38	E40	E38	P60	P53	E55	E55
SP39	E41	E39	P61	P56	E56–57	E56–57
SP40	E42	E40	P58	P54	E53	E53
SP41	E43	E41	P62	P68	E58	E58

MCLI	Ne	T	K	Na	Pa	S
SP42	E44	E42	P63	P57	E59	E59
SP43	E45	E43	P64	P62	E60-61	E60-61
SP44	E46	E44	P65	P61	E62	E62
SP45	E47	E45	P66	P60	—	—
SP46	E48	E46	P68	P65	E63	E63
SP47	E49	E47	P69	P66	E64	E64
SP48	E50	E48	P70	P51	E65	E65
SP49	E51	E49	P71	P59	E66	E66
SP50	E52	E50	P72	P58	E67	E67
SP51	E53	E51	P73	P69	E68	E68
SP52	E54	E52	P74	P70	E69-70	E69-70
SP53	E55	E53	P75	P71-72	E71-72	E70-72
SP54	E56	E54	P76	P72	E73	E73
SP55	E57	E55	P77	P73	E74-76	E74-76
SP56	E58	E56	P78-79	P74-75	E77	E77
SP57	E59	E57	P80-81	P76	E78	E78
SP58	E60	E58	P82	P77	E79	E79
SP59	E61	E59	P83-85	P78	E80-83	E80-83
SP60	E62	E60	P86-87	P79-80	E84-85	E84-85
SP61	E63	E61	P88-90	P81-83	E86-89	E86-89
SP62	E64	E62	P91	P84	E90	E90
SP63	E65	E63	P92-93	P85, 87	E91	E91
SP64	E66	E64	P94	P86	E92	E92

MCLI	Ne	T	K	Na	Pa	S
SP65	E67	E65	P95	P88	E93	E93
SP66	E68	E66	P96	P89	E94	E94
SP67	E69	E67	P97	P90	E95	E95
SP68	E70	E68	P98	P91	E96	E96
SP69	E71	E69	P99-100	P92-93	E97-98	E97-98
SP70	E72	E70	P101	P94	E99	E99
SP71	E73	E71	P102	P94	E100	E100
SP72	E74	E72	P103	P95	E101-102	E101-102
SP73	E75	E73	P104, [128]	P96	E103	E103
SP74	E76	E74	P105-106	P97-98	E104	E104
FH1	P2	P1	P106	P98	E105-106	E105-106
FH2	P3	P2	P107	P99	P1	
FH3	P4	P3	P108	P100	P2	
FH4	P5	P4	P109	P101	P3	
FH5	P6	P5	P110	P102	P4-5	
FH6	P7	P6	P111	P103	P6	
FH7	P8	P7	P112	P104	P7	
FH8	P9	P8	P115	P107	P9-10	
FH9	P10	P9	P116	P108	P11	
FH10	P11	P10	P117	P109	P12	
FH11	P12	P11	P118	P128	P14	
FH12	P13	P12	P119	P110	P13	

MCLI	Ne	T	K	Na	Pa	S
FH13	P14	P12n	P4,[133]; A77	P3, [123]	—	
FH14	P15	P13	P132	P122	P15	
FH15	P16	P14	P132	P122a	P16	
FH16	P17	P15	P123	P113	—	
FH17	P18	P16	P125	P115	P17	
FH18	P19	P17	P113	P105	P19	
FH19	P20	P18	P127	P116	P20	
FH20	P21	P19	P120	P120	P28	
FH21	P22	P20	P121	P121	P30	
FH22	P23	P21	P122	P111	P18	
FH23	P24	P22	P126	P114	—	
FH24	P25	P23	P124	P112	—	
FH25	P26	P24	P138–139	P126–127	P31–32	
FH26	1	P25	P140	P129	P33	
FH27	2	P25	P141	P130	P34	
FH28	3	P25	P142	P131	P35	
FH29	cha	P26	P143	P132	P36	
FH30	1-2-3	P27	P144	P133	P37	
FH31	4-5-6	P28	P145	P134	P39	
FH32	7	P28	P146	P135	P40	
FH33	8	P28	P147	P136	P41	
FH34	9	P28	P148	P137	P42	

MCLI	Ne	T	K	Na	Pa	S
FH35	10	P28	P150	P138	P43	
FH36	11	P29	P154,156	P142	P44	
FH37	12	P30	P155	P143	P45-46	
FH38	13	P31	P157-158	P146-147	P47	
FH39	1	P32	P152	P140	P49	
FH40	2	P32n	P153	P141	P50	
FH41	3	P33	P151	P139	P51	
FH42	4	P33	P159	P148	P48	
FH43	5	P33	P160	P149-[150]	P52	
FH44	6	P33	P163	P152	P53	
FH45	7	P33	P164-165	P153-154	P54	
FH46	1-2	P34	P165	P155	P55	
FH47	2	P35	P166	P156	P56-57	
FH48	3	P35	—	—	P57	
FH49	4	P36	P167	P157	P58	
FH50	5	P36	P167	P157	P59	
FH51	6	P37	P168	P158	P60	
FH52	7	P37	P168	P158	P61	
FH53	1	P37	P169	P159	P62	
FH54	2	P37	P170	P160	P63	
FH55	3-4-5	P38	P172	P162	P64	
FH56	6	P39	P173	P163	P65	
FH57	1	P39	P174	P164	P66-67	

MCLI	Ne	T	K	Na	Pa	S
FH58	6	P40	P175	P165	P68	
FH59	7	P41	P176	P166	P69	
FH60	8	P41	P177	P167	P70	
FH61	9	P41	P178	P168	P71	
FH62	1	P42	P179–180	P169–170	P72–73	
FH63	2	P43	P181–183	P171–172, 194	P80–82	
FH64	3	P44	P184	P172	P83	
FH65	4	P45	P185	P174	P84	
FH66	5	P46	P186	P175	P85	
FH67	cha cha	P47	P187	P176	P86	
FH68	7	P48	P188	P177	P79	
FH69	8	P49	P189	P178	P92	
FH70	9	P50	P190	P179	P93	
FH71	10	P51	P191–193	P180–182	P102–104	
FH72	11	P52	P194	P183	P105	
FH73	12	P53	P195	P184	P107	
FH74	13	P54	P196	P185	P94	
FH75	14	P55	P197	P186	P108	
FH76	15	P56	P198	P187	P109	
FH77	16	P57	P199	P188	P110	
FH78	17	P58	P200	P189	P111	
FH79	18	P59	P201	P190	P112–113	

MCLI	Ne	T	K	Na	Pa	S
FH80	19	P60	P203	P191	P121	
FH81	20	P61	P203	P191	P122 (abridged)	
FH82	21	P62	P204	P193	P87–88	
FH83	22	P63	P208	P173	P89	
FH84	23	P64	P211	P195	P90	
FH85	24	P65	P205	P197	P74	
FH86	25	P66	P206	P198	P75	
FH87	26	P67	P207	P199	P76	
FH88	27	P68	P217–219	P206–208	P95–98	
FH89	28	P69	P222	P202	P114	
FH90	29	P70	P215	P196	P100	
FH91	30	P71	P224, U630	—	P101	
FH92	31	P72	P220	—	P99	
FH93	32	P73	P209	P205	P106	
FH94	33	P74	P221	P209	—	
FH95	34	P75	[P191]	P201	P91	
FH96	35	P76	P213	P200	P115	
FH97	36	P77	P221	[P180]	P116	
FH98	37	P78	P210	P204	P117	
FH99	38	P79	P221	[P209]	P119	
FH100	39	P80	P212	P203	P118	
FH101	40	P81	P214	P192	P120	

MCLI	Ne	T	K	Na	Pa	S
FH102	41	P82	A28	A38	—	
FH103	42	P83	P207n	—	P123	
FH104	43	P84	P225	P211	P124	
FH105	44	P85	P226–227	P212–213	P125	
FH106	1	P86	P228–229	P214	P126	
FH107	2	P86	P230	P215	P127	
FH108	3	P86	P231	P216	P127	
FH109	4	P86	P232	P217	P128	
FH110	4	P87	P233	P218	P129	
FH111	5	P88	P234	P219	P130	
FH112	6	P89	P235	P220	P131	
FH113	1	P89	P236	P221	P132	
FH114	2	P90	P237	P221	P133	
FH115	3	P91	P238	P222	P134	
FH116	4	P92	P239	P223	P135	
FH117	5	P93	P239	P223	P136	
FH118	6	P94	P239	P224	P137	
FH119	7	P95	P240	P224	P138	
FH120	8	P96	P241	P225	P139	
FH121	9	P97	P242	P226	P140	
FH122	10	P98	P243	P226	P140	
FH123	11	P99	P246	P227	P142	
FH124	12	P100	P241	P225	P141	

MCLI	Ne	T	K	Na	Pa	S
FH125	13	P101	P245	P228	P143	
FH126	1	P102	P247	P229	P144–145	
FH127	2	P102	P249	P230	P146	
FH128	1	P103	P250	P231	P147	
FH129	1–2	P104	P251	P232	P148	
FH130	6	P105	P252–255	P233–234	P149–150	
FH131	1	P105	P256	P235	P151	
FH132	2	P105	P257	P236	P152	
FH133	1	P106	P257	P236–237	P153–154	
FH134	2	P107	P257–258	P237	P155	
FH135	3	P108	P259	P238	P156	
FH136	1	P109	P260–261	P239–240	P157	
FH137	2	P109	P262	P241	P158	
FH138	3	P110	P263	P242	P158–159	
FH139	4	P110	P264	P243	P160	
FH140	1	P111	P265	P244	P161	
FH141	2,1	P111	P266	P245	P162	
FH142	2	P112	P267–270	P246–248	P163–164	
FH143	3	P112	P271	P249	P165	
FH144	4	P112	P273	P250	P166	
FH145	5	P112	P274	P251	P167	
FH146	6	P112	P275	P251	P168	
FH147	7	P112	P276	P252–253	P169	

MCLI	Ne	T	K	Na	Pa	S
FH148	8	P112	P277	P254–255	P170–171	
FH149	9	P112	P278	P256	P172	
FH150	10	P112	P280	P257	P173	
FH151	11	P112	P279	P258	P174	
FH152	1,2	P113	P281–283	P259–260	P175–176	
FH153	1	P113	P284	P261	P177	
FH154	2	P113	P285	P262	P178	
FH155	3	P113	P286	P263	P179	
FH156	4	P113	P287	P264	P180	
FH157	5	P113	P288	P265	P181	
FH158	6	P113	P289	P265	P182	
FH159	7	P113	P291	P266	P183	
FH160	1	P114	P232, 291n, 292	P217	P184–185	
FH161	2	P114	P293	P267	P186	
FH162	cha	P115	P294	P267	P187	
FH163	1	P115	P295	P267	P188	
FH164	1,2	P116	P296	P268	P189–190	
FH165	3	P117	P298	P270	P191	
FH166	4	P118	P299	P271	P192	
FH167	5	P119	P300	P272	P193	
FH168	6	P120	P301	P273	P194	
FH169	7	P121	P302	P274	P195	

MCLI	Ne	T	K	Na	Pa	S
FH170	8	P122	P303-304	P275-277	P195-197	
FH171	9	P123	P316	P278	P198	
FH172	10	P124	P305	P280	P200	
FH173	11	P125	P306	P281	P201	
FH174	12	P126	P307	P282	P202	
FH175	13	P127	P308	P283	P203	
FH176	14	P128	P309	P284	P204	
FH177	15	P129	P311	P285	P205	
FH178	16	P130	P312	P286	P206	
FH179	17	P131	P313	P287	P207	
FH180	18	P132	P317	P279	P199	
FH181	19	P133	P319	P290	P208	
FH182	20	P134	P315	P289	P209	
FH183	21	P135	P314	P288	P210	
FH184	1	P136	P318	P291	P211	
FH185	22	P137	P320	P292	P212	
FH186	1	P137	P321	P293	P213	
FH187	2	P137	P323	P294	P214	
FH188	1	P138	P324	P295	P215	
FH189	1	P139	P325	P295	P216	
FH190	1	P140	P326	P296	P217	
FH191	cha	P141	P328	P297	P219	
FH192	5	P141	P327	P298	P218	

MCLI	Ne	T	K	Na	Pa	S
FH193	14	P142	P329	P299	P220	
FH194	15	P143	P330	P300	P221	
FH195	6	P144	P331	P301	P222	
FH196	1	P145	P331	P301	P223	
FH197	‡	—	P332	P303	P224	
FH198	1	P146	P337	P308	P230	
FH199	2	P147	P338	P307	P231	
FH200	3	P148	P340	P310	P232	
FH201	4	P149	P341	P311	P233	
FH202	1	P150	P342	P312	P234	
FH203	2	P151	P343	P313	P235	
FH204	3	P152	P344	P314	P236-237	
FH205	4	P152	P345	P316	P238	
FH206	cha	P152	P346	P317	P239	
FH207	7	P153	P347	P317	P240	
FH208	2	P154	P348	P318	P241	
FH209	3	P155	P349	P319	P243	
FH210	4	P156	[U149]	[U157]	P242	
FH211	1	P156	P350	P320	P244	
FH212	2	P156	P351	[P216]	P245	
FH213	3	P156	P352	P321	P246	
FH214	1	P157	P353	P322	P247	
FH215	11	P158	P354	P324	P248	

MCLI	Ne	T	K	Na	Pa	S
FH216	2	P159	P353	P322–323	P249	
FH217	cha	P160	P355	P325	P250	
FH218	1	P160	P355	P325	P251	
FH219	2	P161	P356	P326	P252	
FH220	2	P162	P357	P327	P253	
FH221	4	P163	P358	P328	P254	
FH222	5	P164	P362	P329	P255	
FH223	6	P165	P360–361	P331	P256	
FH224	7	P166	P359	P330	P257	
FH225	6, 1	P167	P363	P332	P258	
FH226	2	P168	P364	P333	P259	
FH227	3, cha	P169	P365	P334	P260	
FH228	1	P170	P366	P334	P261	
FH229	1	P170	P367	P335	P262	
FH230	2	P171	P368	P336	P263	
FH231	1	P171	P369	P337	P264	
FH232	2	P171	—	—	—	
FH233	1	P171	P370	P338	P265	
FH234	2	P172	P371–372	P339	P266	
FH235	1	P173	P372	P340	P267	
FH236	1	P173	P373	P341	P268	
FH237	15	P173	P374	P342	P269	
FH238	1	P174	P375	P342	P270	

MCLI	Ne	T	K	Na	Pa	S
FH239	1	P174	P377	P343	P271	
FH240	2	P175	P378	P344	P272	
FH241	3	P175	P379	P345	P273	
FH242	4	P175	P380	P346	P274	
FH243	5	P176	P381-383	P347-349, 351	P275-276	
FH244	6	P177	P384	P350	P277	
FH245	7	P178	P385-386	P352-353	P278-279	
FH246	8	P179	P387	P354	P280	
FH247	9	P180	P388	P355	P281	
FH248	6	P181	P389	P356	P282	
FH249	1	P181	P393	—	P283	
FH250	2	P182	P390	P358	P284-285	
FH251	3	P183	P392	P359	P286	
FH252	4	P184	P394	P360	P287	
FH253	5	P185	P391	P358	P288	
FH254	6	P186	P395	P361	P289	
FH255	7	P187	P396	P362	P290	
FH256	4	P188	P397	P363	P291	
FH257	8	P188	P398	P364-365	P292	
FH258	9	P189	P399	P366	P293	
FH259	10	P190	P400	P367	P294	
FH260	11	P191	P401	P368	P295	
FH261	12	P192	P402	P369	P296	

MCLI	Ne	T	K	Na	Pa	S
FH262	13	P193	P403	P370	P297	
FH263	14	P194	P405	P372	P298	
FH264	15	P195	P404	P371	P299	
FH265	16	P196	P407	P374	P300	
FH266	17	P197	P408	P375	P301	
FH267	18	P198	P406	P373	P302	
FH268	12	P199	P410	P376	P303	
FH269	19	P199	P411	P376	P305	
FH270	2	P200	P412	P377	P306	
FH271	3	P201	P414	P379	P307	
FH272	4	P202	P415	P380	P308	
FH273	5	P203	P413	P378	P304	
FH274	6	P204	P416	P381	P309	
FH275	7	P204	P409	—	P310	
FH276	cha	P204–205	P417	P382	P311	
FH277	1	P205	P418	P382	P312	
FH278	2	P206	P419	P383	P313	
FH279	1	P207	P420	P384	P314	
FH280	2	P208	P421	P385	P315–316	
FH281	1	P209	P422	P386	P317	
FH282	1	P209	P423	P387	P318	
FH283	1	P210	P424	P388	P319–320	
FH284	1	P211	P424	P388	P321	

MCLI	Ne	T	K	Na	Pa	S
FH285	2	P211	P425	P389	P322	
FH286	3	P211	P426	P390	P323	
FH287	3	P211	P427	P391	P324	
FH288	1	P211	P428	P392–393	P325	
FH289	2	P212	P431	P395	P326	
FH290	3	P213	P433	P397	P327	
FH291	1	P214	P434	U380	P328	
FH292	5	P215	P430	P394	P329	
FH293	6	P216	P430	P394	P330	
FH294	7	P217	P432	P396	P331	
FH295	1,1	P218	P435	P398	—	
FH296	2	P219	P436	P399	P332	
FH297	2	P220	P437	P400	P333–334	
FH298	cha	P221	P438	P401	P335	
FH299	2	P222	P439	P402	P336	
FH300	3	P223	P440	P403	P337	
FH301	4	P224	P442	P404	P339	
FH302	5	P225	P441	P405	P338	
FH303	6	P226	P482	P445	—	
FH304	7	P227	P443	P406	P340	
FH305	8	P228	P444	P407	P341	
FH306	9	P229	P446	P409	P342	
FH307	10	P230	P448	P411	P343	

MCLI	Ne	T	K	Na	Pa	S
FH308	11	P231	P445	P408	P344	
FH309	12	P232	P447	P410	P350	
FH310	13	P233	P449	P412	P345	
FH311	14	P234	P450	P413	P351, [363]	
FH312	15	P235	P453	P415	P346	
FH313	16	P236	P455	P417	P347-348	
FH314	17	P237	P454	P416	P349	
FH315	18	P238	P451	P414	P352	
FH316	1	P238	P456	P420	P353	
FH317	2	P238	P457	P419	P354	
FH318	1	P239	P458-459	P421-422	P355-357	
FH319	2	P240	P460	P423	P358	
FH320	3	P241	P461	P424	P359	
FH321	4	P242	P462, 464	P425, 427	P360, 362	
FH322	5	P243	P467	P430	P364-365	
FH323	6	P244	P468	P431	P366	
FH324	7	P245	P465	P428	P367	
FH325	8	P246	P466	P429	P368-369	
FH326	9	P247	P469	P432	P370	
FH327	10	P248	P470	P433	P371	
FH328	11	P249	P471	P434	P372	
FH329	12	P250	P463	P426	P361	

GLOSSARY

ABAÏSE (*ābāïsē, ābaisē*) a female disciple of Chakradhar; mother of Nagdev, Umaïse, and Sarangpani; short form, Abai; also called Vriddhabaïse, "the old woman"

ADITYA (*ādītya, āditya*) a sun god

ANAKAI (*aṇakai, aṇakaiya, anakai, anakaiya, anakeya, anekai, āṇikai*) a goddess whose shrine was in one of the caves at Ellora

APDEVBHAT (*āpadevabhaṭa*) a prominent Brahman citizen of Balhegram; also called Apdev

āratī the rite of waving small oil lamps or incense in a circle in front of a deity or holy person while singing a rhythmic song

BAÏSE (*bāïsē*) Chakradhar's principal female disciple, who served as his housekeeper during the "First Half" and "Second Half" periods of his life; originally named Nagubaï or Nagubaïsē; also called *mhātārī*, "the old woman"

BATIKA (*baṭikā;* "[Brahman] student") a fond nickname for Cangdevbhat, Upadhye, Padmanabhidev, and other young men

BHAGAVAT (*bhāgavata*) (1) a devotee of Vishnu or Krishna; (2) a devotee of Chakradhar named Daï Bhagavat; (3) possibly Apdevbhat

BHAIRAV (*bhairava*) a fierce form of the god Shiva; also called Bhairavnath

BHANDAREKAR (*bhāṇḍārekāra, bhāṇḍārekara*) a Brahman man from Bhandara, originally named Nilbhat, who became an ardent devotee of Chakradhar

BHAT (*bhaṭa*) (1) a respectful term used in addressing or referring to a Brahman man; (2) a short form of Bhatobas, a nickname for Nagdev; (3) a short form of Cangdevbhat's name

BHATACHARYA (*bhaṭācārya*) the Mimamsa philosopher Kumarila Bhatta (Kumārila Bhaṭṭa)

BHUTANANDE (*bhūtānande;* "delighting in ghosts") Chakradhar's nickname for a female devotee whose original name was Maïbaï

CANGDEV (*cāṅgadeva;* "good god") the name of several holy men and yogis

CANGDEV RAÜL (*cāṅgadeva rāüḷa*) (CANGDEV RAÜL 1) a holy man based in Dvaravati who was, for Mahanubhavs, one of five incarnations of Parameshvar in human form; also called "the one from Dvaravati"; (CANGDEV RAÜL 2) Chakradhar, who is, for Mahanubhavs, a reincarnation of Cangdev Raül 1

CANGDEVBHAT (*cāṅgadevabhaṭa, cāṅgadevo bhaṭa*) Nathoba's twin brother, originally from Balhegram; a close disciple of Chakradhar; also called Bhat and Cango

CHAKRADHAR (*cakradhara;* "wheel bearer," "emperor") a reincarnation of Cangdev Raül 1 in the body of Haripal, son of a royal minister in Gujarat; often referred to as the Gosavi or "the omniscient one"; frequently addressed as Baba, meaning "father", or Lord, or with another title or nickname

DADOS (*dādosa;* "elder brother") a disciple of Chakradhar who was the previous guru of several of Chakradhar's followers, including Nagdev and Abaïse; also called Ramdev, Ram, Dev, Dado, and the Mahatma

DAÏMBA (*dāïmbā, dāyambā, dāyāmbā*) a close male disciple of Chakradhar; also called Bhoja; sometimes addressed as Daya

DAKHALE (*ḍakhale, ḍakhalā*) originally named Kheibhaṭ; a close male disciple of Chakradhar

DAKSHINESHVAR (*dakṣiṇeśvara;* "lord of the south") a name of the god Shiva

darśan the act of looking at a god or holy person; to give *darśan:* to allow someone to see a god or holy person, often oneself

DATTATREYA PRABHU, SHRI (*śrī dattātreya prabhu*) a god who is, for Mahanubhavs, one of five incarnations of the supreme God, Parameshvar, in human form

DEMAÏSE (*demāïsē*) a widow who first became a devotee of Chakradhar in Pratishthan; also called Demaï and Dematī

devatācakra a Mahanubhav theological model that categorizes and hierarchizes the many deities that are not the supreme God, Parameshvar

DVAPARA YUGA (*dvāpara yuga*) the third of the four cosmic eras, during which Shri Krishna Chakravarti lived on earth

EKADASHI (*ekādaśī*) the eleventh day of a lunar fortnight, a day of fasting for devotees of Krishna and Vishnu

ELHAMBHAT (*elhambhaṭa, yalhambhaṭa*) a Brahman man who became a follower of Chakradhar; father of Gauraïse 1, father-in-law of Indrabhat; also called Hard-Hearted Bhat

GADONAYAK (*gadonāyaka, gadonāeka*) the Yadava kings' treasurer; also called Gado the Treasurer

GAURAÏSE (*gaurāïsē;* short form, *gaurāī*) (GAURAÏSE 1) the wife of Indrabhat; (GAURAÏSE 2) the mother of Padmanabhidev

GONDO a devotee of Chakradhar from Balhegram

GOPAL (*gopāḷa*) the god Krishna as a cowherd

GORAKSHANATH (*gorakṣanātha*) a founding yogi in the Nath tradition; also called Goraksha

GOSAVI (*gosāvī;* from Skt. *go-svāmin,* "master of cows") Lord or Master; a title used in this text principally for Chakradhar, but also for Shriprabhu and Cangdev Raül; "our Gosavi": Chakradhar

HAMSARAJ (*haṃsarāja*) a female disciple of Baïse; also called Hamsubaï and Hamsubaïse

HARIDEV PANDIT (*harideva paṇḍita*) a learned man who lived in Pratishthan and belonged to the Kayastha ("Kasta") caste; also called Kasta Haridev Pandit

HIRAÏSA (*hīrāïsā, hirāïsā, hīrāïsā*) a third-generation disciple of Nagdev, famous for her quick memory, who is understood to have accurately memorized the entire *Līḷācaritra*

INDRABHAT (*indrabhaṭa*) a disciple of Dados who became a disciple of Chakradhar; husband of Gauraïse 1; originally named Nagdevbhat; also called Indroba

jīva a living being, generally human and definitely not divine

JOGNAYAK (*joganāyaka*) (JOGNAYAK 1) a tax collector; (JOGNAYAK 2) Padmanabhidev's brother

KAKOS (*kākosa;* "paternal uncle") a Brahman man

from Charthane, originally named Rupdevbhat; also called Kako

KALI YUGA the present, degenerate cosmic era

KANHARDEV (*kānharadeva*) the Yadava king Krishnadev, who reigned from 1246 to 1260; older brother of King Mahadev

KRISHNA (*kṛṣṇa*) one of five incarnations of the supreme God, Parameshvar, in human form; not, for Mahanubhavs, an incarnation of Vishnu; also called Shri Krishna Chakravarti, Hari, and Kanha

LAKHUBAÏSE (*lakhubāïsē, lakhūbāïsē, lakhumabāïsē*) a female disciple of Chakradhar from Pratishthan and a frequent companion of Demaïse; also called Lakhubaï

LAKSHMINDRABHAT (*lakṣmīn-drabhaṭa, lakṣmīdharabhaṭa*) a Brahman man from Balhegram who became a devotee of Chakradhar; also called Rake Lakshmindrabhat

līḷā ("divine play") an episode in the life of a divine incarnation; also, a chapter in this biography

MAHADAÏSE (*mahadāïsē, māhādāïsē, mahādāïsē*) a favorite female disciple of Chakradhar; the first known woman poet in Marathi; short form, Mahadaï; also called Rupai or Rupaïse, "beautiful woman"

MAHADEV (*māhādeva, māhādevo,*

māhādeo, mahadeva; "Great God," a name of Shiva) (1) King Mahadev, a king of the Yadava dynasty, who reigned from 1260 to 1270; (2) Mahadev Pathak, a Brahman man who lived at Ravasgav; (3) Mahadev Muni, an ascetic whom Mahadaïse met at Dvaravati

MAHALAKSHMI (*mahālakṣmī, māhālakṣmī, māhālakṣamī;* "Great Lakshmi") a goddess of wealth, fertility, and prosperity, either as an independent goddess or as Vishnu's wife

MAHATMA (*māhātmā, mahātmā;* "great-souled one") (1) a holy man or yogi, usually an ascetic renouncer; (2) Dados (*the* Mahatma); (3) any male follower of Chakradhar; (4) a respectful form of address sometimes used by Chakradhar for other beings

MAÏBAÏSE (*māïbāïsē*) (MAÏBAÏSE 1) original name of Shantibaïse; (MAÏBAÏSE 2) original name of Sobhage

MANIKESHVAR (*māṇikeśvara;* "lord of gems") (1) a name of the god Shiva; (2) a cave-temple at Ellora now called Kailas

MARTANDA (*mārtaṇḍa;* "the sun") a male disciple of Chakradhar who was a nephew of Baïse; also called Bhaskar

NAGDEV (*nāgadeva*) (1) Chakradhar's principal male disciple, also called Bhat, Bhatobas, Monkey, and Lord

Monkey; (2) Nagdev Upadhye, Jano Upadhye's brother, also called Nagdevbhat

NAGDEVBHAT (*nāgadevabhaṭa*) (1) the original name of Indrabhat; (2) Nagdev Upadhye, Jano Upadhye's brother; (3) Nagdevbhat the Reciter, a Brahman man from Balhegram

NARASIMHA (*narasiṃha*) the man-lion incarnation of Vishnu

NARAYAN (*nārāyaṇa*) a name of the god Vishnu

NATHOBA (*nāthobā*) a close disciple of Chakradhar, originally from Balhegram; twin brother of Cangdevbhat; nicknamed Mandalik

PADMANABHIDEV (*padmanābhideva*) a former disciple of Sarasvatbhat who became a follower of Chakradhar; son of Gauraïse 2, brother of Remnayak; also called Padmanabhi

PANDE (*pāṇḍe, pāṇḍā*) (1) a male disciple of Baïse; (2) a nickname for Sarangpandit

PANDIT (*paṇḍita*) (1) a title for a learned teacher; (2) a nickname for Sarangpandit

PANUNAYAK (*pānunāyaka, pānanāyaka*) Chakradhar's hypochondriacal landlord in Karanjkhed; nicknamed Sitalananda, "he for whom cold is bliss"

PARAMESHVAR (*parameśvara*) the singular supreme being,

incarnated in Chakradhar,
Shriprabhu, Cangdev Raül,
Dattatreya Prabhu, and Shri
Krishna

PARASHARAMBAS (*paraśarā-
mabāsa*) the editor of one
of several early versions of *God
at Play*

PARASNAYAK (*parasanāeka,
prasanāeka, prasanāyaka,
prasanāyeka, praseyā*) an
ascetic who lived in Bid and
became a follower of Chakradhar

prasād food or drink that has been
tasted by a divine being
and is reverently ingested; to
make *prasād* (said of a divine
being): to taste food, leaving
the remains to be ingested by
devotees

puja (*pūjā, pujā*) ritual worship
involving offerings of food,
flowers, and/or colored powder,
and bathing or smearing the body
with milk, water, sandalwood
paste, and/or other substances

RAM (*rāma*) (1) a nickname for
Dados, whose original name
was Ramdev; (2) the divine
hero who is the protagonist of
the Ramayana; (3) Ramtek, a
pilgrimage place of the god Ram,
northeast of Nagpur

RAMDEV (*rāmadeva;* "God
Ram") (1) original name of
Dados; (2) Kavadimba Ramdev,
"the child poet Ramdev," also
called Chinchkhedkar Ramdev,
"Ramdev from Chinchkhed";

(3) the Yadava king Ramchandra,
who reigned from 1271 to 1311,
son of Kanhardev

RAMESHVARBAS (*rāmeśvara-
bāsa*) the editor of one of
several early versions of *God at
Play*

REMNAYAK (*remanāyaka*)
Padmanabhidev's brother

SADHE (*sādhē;* "plain,
simple") Chakradhar's
nickname for Elhaïse, often
shortened to Elho, one of his
most important female disciples

SAMAKOSE (*sāmakosē*) a female
follower of Chakradhar; mother
of Elhambhat and grandmother
of Gauraïse 1; nicknamed
Madalsa

sandhyā a ritual, performed
by initiated high-caste men at
dawn, noon, and sunset, the
"junctures" (*sandhyā*) of the day,
that involves standing in a river
or a pool of water and reciting
the Gayatri mantra

SARANGPANDIT (*sāraṅgapaṇḍita*)
a learned Brahman from
Pratishthan; also called Pande
and Pandit

SARANGPANI (*sāraṅgapāṇi,
sāraṅgapāṇibhaṭa*) (1) Abaïse's
eldest son, Nagdev's brother,
who died young; (2) Grahe
Sarangpani or Sarangpanibhat,
a relative of Dados

SARASVATBHAT (*sārasvatabhaṭa*)
the former guru of Padmanabhidev; also called Sarasvatdev

SHANTIBAÏSE (*śāntibāïsē;* "peace woman") nickname of Maïbaïse 1; mother of Ekaïse and Jasamaïse and aunt of Sarangpandit

sikṣā (Skt. *śikṣā*) a rite of fellowship among Nath yogis

SHRIPRABHU (*śrīprabhu*) a divine incarnation who lived in Riddhipur and became Chakradhar's guru; also called Gundam Raül and Gosavi

SIDDHA (*sidhu, sīdha, sīdhu*) a perfected yogi; a tantric yogi

SIDDHANATH (*sidhanātha, sīdhanātha, sīdhanāthu, sīdhanāthū;* "lord of Siddhas") the god Shiva as a perfected yogi

SOBHAGE (*sobhāge, saubhāge, sobhāga;* "marital bliss") Chakradhar's nickname for Maïbaïse 2, a female disciple of Dados who became a disciple of Chakradhar; also called Sobhagbaïse

THAKUR (*ṭhākūra, ṭhākura*) a member, especially a prominent member, of a certain tribe

TIKAVNAYAK (*tikavanāyaka*) a leading Brahman citizen of Hivarali; also called Tikavdev

TIKOPADHYE (*tikopādhye*) a learned Brahman in Riddhipur

tīrtha a holy place, especially one for bathing

tulsi (*tuḷsī*) the holy basil plant

UMAÏSE (*umāïsē*) (UMAÏSE 1) Nagdev's sister, Abaïse's daughter, also called Umaï, Umai, and "woman who fasts for a month"; (UMAÏSE 2) Sarangpaṇḍit's second wife, the mother of Dhanaïse

UPADHYE (*upādhye*) one of Chakradhar's earliest and closest male disciples; also called Jano and Janopadhye or Jano Upadhye; nicknamed One-and-a-Half Man

UPASANIYE (*upāsanīye*) a male disciple who behaved outrageously while in a trance state; also called Upasani

VAMDEV (*vāmadeva*) Baïse's original guru, based in Pratishthan; a proponent of the milk-drinkers' way, a diet consisting only of dairy products; short form, Vam

VANDEV (*vanadeva;* "god of the grove") a god who resides in a grove in which the trees and other vegetation are preserved inviolate in the god's honor

VISHNUBHAT (*viṣṇubhaṭ*) a prominent citizen of Balhegram; a companion of Upadhye

vṛndāvan (Skt. *vṛndāvana*) a stand for a holy basil (tulsi) plant

YADAVA (*yādava;* "descendant of Yadu") (1) the name of a dynasty of kings, with a capital at Devgiri, who ruled the Marathi-language region of India from the late twelfth century through the early fourteenth; (2) a member of Shri Krishna's lineage

BIBLIOGRAPHY

Editions and Translations

Mhaïmbhat. 1936–1937. *Mahārāṣṭrīya ādya caritrakār Mahindrabhaṭṭa saṅkalit līḷācaritra.* Edited by Hari Narayan Nene. Vols. 1–4, Singapore: Babu Govinda Sahay.

———. 1950. *Līḷācaritra: Uttarārdha.* Edited by Hari Narayan Nene. Vol. 5. Amravati: Sarasvati Press.

———. 1964–1967. *Līḷācaritra.* Edited by S. G. Tulpule. 5 vols. Pune: Suvichar Prakashan Mandal.

———. [1980s]. *Mhāiṃma bhaṭ saṅkalīt caturtha śodhanīcā pīḍhīpāṭh: Sarvajñāce liḷā carītra.* Edited by Madhavraj Panjabi. Amravati: Madhavraj Panjabi.

———. 1982. *Mhāïmbhaṭ saṅkalit Śrīcakradhar līḷā caritra.* Edited by V. B. Kolte. 2nd ed. Mumbai: Maharashtra Rajya Sahitya-Samskriti Mandal. Original edition, 1978. Reprint, *Paṇḍit Mhaïṃbhaṭ saṅkalit Śrīcakradhar līḷācaritra,* edited by V. B. Kolte, Aurangabad: Vishvashanti Prakashan, 1977.

———. 2004. *Pāṭh Hirāïsācā: Hirāïse Upādhye śiṣye Kamaḷāüsācī Māhimbhaṭṭakṛt līḷā caritra.* Edited by Purushottam C. Nagpure. 2nd ed. Amravati: Omkar Prakashan.

———. 2007. *Ādya caritrakār ācārya Śrīmhāïmbhaṭ saṅkalit līḷācaritra: Ekāṅka.* Edited by Sushila S. Aurangabad: Kailash Publications.

Mhaïmbhat. 1977. *Leela Charitra: Ekank.* Translated [into English] by Aruna Mahajan. Hyderabad: M. Krishnadas Mahanubhav, Shri Gita Ashram.

———. 2009. *Collection of Memories by Mhaimbhat of Sarvadnya Shree Chakradhar Prabhu: "Leelacharitra."* Translated by Bhaurao Gopal Jadhav. Domegram: Raul Publication.

Sontheimer, Günther-Dietz. 1982. "God, Dharma and Society in the Yādava Kingdom of Devagirī According to the *Līḷācaritra* of Chakradhar." In *Indology and Law: Studies in Honour of Professor J. Duncan M. Derrett,* ed. G.-D. Sontheimer and Parameswara K. Aithal. Wiesbaden: F. Steiner Verlag, pp. 329–358.

Other Sources

Altekar, A. S. 1982 [1960]. "The Yādavas of Seuṇadeśa." In *The Early History of the Deccan,* ed. G. Yazdani, 2 vols. Reprint, Delhi: Oriental Books Reprint Corporation, 2:513–574.

Ashvaghosha. 2008. *Life of the Buddha.* Translated by Patrick Olivelle. New York: New York University Press.

Archarya Mahant Salkar Baba Others v. Dattatraya Others. Bombay High Court.February 27, 2015. https://www.casemine.com/judgement/in/56ea7915607dba369a6f0217.

Belvalkar, Suman. 2009. *Līḷācaritrātīl samājdarśan.* Mumbai: Popular Prakashan.

Bhavadevasuri. 1919. *Pārśvanātha caritra.* Translated by Maurice Bloomfield as *The Life and Stories of the Jaina Savior Pārśvanātha.* Baltimore: Johns Hopkins University Press.

Bhave, Vinayak Lakshman. 1924 [*Śaka* 1846]. *Mahārāṣṭra-Sārasvat.* Pt. 1. 3rd ed. Thane: Vinayak Lakshman Bhave.

———. 1928. *Mahārāṣṭra-Sārasvat.* Pt. 2. 3rd ed. Thane: Vinayak Lakshman Bhave.

Bhishmacharya. 1961. *Paṃ. Bhīṣmācārya saṃkalita niruktaśeṣa.* Edited by Yashvant Khushal Deshpande. Nagpur: Vidarbha Samshodhan Mandal.

Bidkar, Vishvanathbas. 1982. *Śrīvardhanstha śrī Viśvanāthbās Bīḍkar yāṃcā ācārband.* Edited by V. B. Kolte. Malkapur: Arun Prakashan.

Collins, Steven, ed. 2016. *Readings of the* Vessantara Jātaka. New York: Columbia University Press.

Cowell, E. B., et al., trans. 1895–1913. *The Jātaka: Or, Stories of the Buddha's Former Births.* Cambridge: Cambridge University Press.

Deshpande, Brahmananda. 2005a. "Madaḷasā." In *Mahānubhāvīy śodhnibandh,* vol. 1. Aurangabad: Raül Prakashan, pp. 37–42.

———. 2005b. "Śrīcakradharāñce Paiṭhaṇ." In *Mahānubhāvīy śodhnibandh,* vol. 1. Aurangabad: Raül Prakashan, pp. 73–94.

———. 2010. "Yādavakālīn nānevyavahār." In *Śodhamudrā,* vol. 5. Aurangabad: Kailas Publications, pp. 49–64.

Deshpande, Y. K. 1932. "Mahānubhāvāñce caritra-grantha." *Bhārat Itihās Saṃśodhak Maṇḍaḷ Traimāsik* 13: 45–57.

———, ed. 1953 [1935]. *Mahadambā: Ādya Marāṭhī Kavayitrī.* Pune: Continental Prakashan.

Dhere, Ramchandra Chintaman. 1971. "Rājmaṭhāce rahasya." In *Loksaṃskṛtīcī kṣitije.* Pune: Vishvakarma Sahityalay, pp. 47–68.

———. 1977. *Cakrapāṇi (Ādya Marāṭhī vāṅmayācī saṃskṛtik pārśva-bhūmī)*. Pune: Vishvakarma Sahityalay.

———. 1992. "Mahānubhāvīya vāṅmayātīl Baḷīpa-kathā." *Santkṛpā* 17, 3 (May): 12–23.

Digby, Simon. 1986. "The Sufi Shaikh as a Source of Authority in Medi-aeval India." *Puruṣārtha* 9: 57–77.

———. 1990. "The Sufi Shaykh and the Sultan: A Conflict of Claims to Authority in Medieval India." *Iran: Journal of the British Institute of Persian Studies* 28: 71–81.

———. 1994. "Anecdotes of a Provincial Sufi of the Dehlī Sultanate, Khwāja Gurg of Kara." *Iran: Journal of the British Institute of Persian Studies* 32: 99–109.

Eaton, Richard M. 2019. *India in the Persianate Age: 1000–1765*. Oakland: University of California Press.

Enthoven, R. E. 1920–1922 [1975]. *The Tribes and Castes of Bombay*. 3 vols. Reprint, Delhi: Cosmo Publications.

Feldhaus, Anne. 1978. "The Mahanubhavas and Scripture." *Journal of Dharma* (Bangalore) 3, 3: 295–308.

———. 1980. "The *devatācakra* of the Mahānubhāvas." *Bulletin of the School of Oriental and African Studies, University of London* 43: 101–109.

———, ed. 1983. "Introduction." In *The Religious System of the Mahānu-bhāva Sect: The Mahānubhāva Sūtrapāṭha* by Kesobas. New Delhi: Manohar.

———. 2003. *Connected Places: Region, Pilgrimage, and Geographical Imagination in India*. New York: Palgrave Macmillan.

———. 2019. "Biography as Geography." *Journal of Asian Studies* 78: 745–766.

———. Forthcoming. "The Divine Self in the *Līḷācaritra*." In *Bhakti and the Self*, ed. Martin Fuchs.

Gupta, Mahendranath. 1942. *The Gospel of Sri Ramakrishna*. Translated with an introduction by Swami Nikhilananda. New York: Rama-krishna-Vivekananda Center.

Habib, Mohammed. 1950. "Chishti Mystics [*sic*] Records of the Sultan-ate Period." *Medieval India Quarterly* 1, 3: 1–42.

Jain, Hiralal, and A. N. Upadhye. 1974. *Mahāvīra: His Times and His Philosophy of Life*. Varanasi: Bharatiya Jnanpith.

Jaini, Padmanabh S. 1977. "Jina Ṛṣabha as an *Avatāra* of Viṣṇu." *Bulletin of the School of Oriental and African Studies* 40: 321–337.

Joshi, Pralhad Narasimha. 1973. "Caritra vāṅmay." In *Marāṭhī vāṅmayācā itihās*, vol. 3, ed. Ramchandra Shripad Jog. Pune: Maharashtra Sahitya Parishad, pp. 360–404.

Kalelkar, N. G. 1950. "La Secte Manbhav." Ph.D. dissertation, University of Paris.

Kesobas. 1937. *Śrīsarvajña Cakradharnirūpit dṛṣṭānta-pāṭh.* Edited by Nilkanth Balvant Bhavalkar and Hari Narayan Nene. Nagpur: Hari Narayan Nene.

————. 1962. *Muni Keśirāj viracit mūrtiprakāś.* Edited by Vishnu Bhikaji Kolte. Nagpur: Vidarbha Samshodhan Mandal.

————. 1983. *The Religious System of the Mahānubhāva Sect: The Mahānubhāva Sūtrapāṭha.* Edited and translated with an introduction by Anne Feldhaus. New Delhi: Manohar.

————. 1986. *Śrīkeśirājvyāskṛt ratnamāḷā-stotra: Pūrvārdha.* Edited by Brahmananda Deshpande. Aurangabad: Raül Prakashan.

Kolte, Vishnu Bhikaji. 1962a. "Mahānubhāvāñce don āmnāy." In *Mahānubhāv Saṃśodhan,* vol. 1. Malkapur: Arun Prakashan, pp. 123–136.

————, ed. 1962b. "Prastāvanā." In *Muni Keśirāj viracit mūrtiprakāś* by Kesobas. Nagpur: Vidarbha Samshodhan Mandal.

————. 1975. *Mahānubhāv tattvajñān.* 4th ed. Malkapur: Arun Prakashan. Original edition, 1945.

————, ed. 1976. "Sthānsūcī." In *Sthānpothī.* Malkapur: Arun Prakashan.

————. 1977. *Śrīcakradhar caritra.* 2nd ed. Malkapur: Arun Prakashan. Original edition, 1952.

————, ed. 1982. "Prastāvanā," "Vyaktisūcī," and "Sthānsūcī." In *Mhāïmbhaṭ saṅkalit Śrīcakradhar līḷā caritra* by Mhaïmbhat. 2nd ed. Mumbai: Maharashtra Rajya Sahitya-Samskriti Mandal.

Marathe, Dattaraj. 1985. *Śrī Dattarāj Marāṭhe yāñcā lakṣan band.* Edited by V. B. Kolte. Aurangabad: Raül Prakashan.

McLeod, W. H., ed. 1980. *The B40 Janam-Sākhī.* Amritsar: Guru Nanak Dev University.

Mhaïmbhat. 1972. *Mhāïmbhaṭ-saṅkalit śrī Govindaprabhu caritra.* Edited by Vishnu Bhikaji Kolte. Malkapur: Arun Prakashan. Original edition, 1944.

————. 1984. *The Deeds of God in Ṛddhipur.* Translated and annotated by Anne Feldhaus, with introductory essays by Anne Feldhaus and Eleanor Zelliot. New York: Oxford University Press.

Molesworth, James Thomas, comp., with George and Thomas Candy.

1857. *A Dictionary, Marathi and English*. 2nd ed. Bombay: Bombay Education Society's Press. Reprint, Pune: Shubhada-Saraswat Prakashan, 2010.

Nagpure, Purushottam C., ed. 2004. "Dvitīya āvṛttī manogat," "Nivedan," "Avataraṇikā," "Vyaktisūcī," "Sthānsūcī," "Śabdakoś," and "Devatāsūcī." In *Pāṭh Hirāïsācā: Hirāïse Upādhye śiṣye Kamaḷāüsācī Māhimbhaṭṭakṛt līḷā caritra* by Mhaïmbhat. 2nd ed. Amravati: Omkar Prakashan.

Nene, Hari Narayan. 1937 [*Śaka* 1859]. *Ācārsthaḷ: Tyāgprakaraṇ, sūtreṃ 1 te 26*. Singapore: Babu Govinda Sahay.

———. 1939. "Kṛṣṇamunīceṃ anvayasthaḷa." *Bhārat Itihās Saṃśodhak Maṇḍaḷ Traimāsik* 20: 57-71.

———, ed. 1950 [*Śaka* 1872]. "Prastāvanā" (composed in 1937). In *Mahārāṣṭrīya ādya caritrakār Mahindrabhaṭ saṅkalit līḷācaritra, Bhāg 4 thā: Pūrvārdha-khaṇḍa 3 reṃ* by Mhaïmbhat. Singapore: Babu Govinda Sahay, pp. 1–10.

———, ed. 1954 [*Śaka* 1875]. "Pahilyā āvṛttīcī prastāvanā" and "Upodghāt." In *Mahārāṣṭrīya ādya caritrakār Mahindrabhaṭ saṅkalit līḷācaritra: Bhāg 1 lā: Ekāṅka* by Mhaïmbhat. 3rd ed. Singapore: Babu Govinda Sahay, pp. 9–14 and 15–52. Original edition, 1936.

Nizamuddin Auliya. 1992. *Nizam ad-din Awliya: Morals for the Heart, Conversations of Shaykh Nizam ad-din Awliya Recorded by Amir Hasan Sijzi*. Translated by Bruce B. Lawrence. New York: Paulist Press.

Novetzke, Christian Lee. 2016. *The Quotidian Revolution: Vernacularization, Religion, and the Premodern Public Sphere in India*. New York: Columbia University Press.

———. 2018. "Religion and the Public Sphere in Premodern India." *Asiatische Studien: Zeitschrift der schweizerischen Asiengesellschaft/ Études asiatiques: Revue de la Société Suisse-Asie* 72: 147–176.

Panjabi, Madhavraj, ed. n.d.(a). "Prakāśakīya don śabda," "Liḷācarītrāt yeṇāryā vyaktīce nāte sambandha," and "Śabdakoś." In *Mhāïṃma Bhaṭ saṅkalīt caturtha śodhanīcā pīḍhīpāṭh: Sarvajñāce liḷā carītra* by Mhaïmbhat. Amravati: Madhavraj Panjabi.

———, ed. n.d.(b). *Sātai rup carītra: Bhāg pahilā*. Amravati: Madhavraj Panjabi.

Pathan, Y. M. 1977. "Mahānubhāvāñcyā sāṅketik lipyā: Nirmitimī-māmāṃsā." *Marāṭhī Saṃśodhan Patrikā* 25, 1: 27-43.

———. 1982. "Caritra-abāb." In *Śrīcakradhar darśan*, ed. V. B. Kolte,

Nagarajbaba Mahanubhav, Y. M. Pathan, and P. C. Nagpure. Mumbai: Shikshan va Sevayojan Vibhag, Maharashtra Shasan, pp. 346-363.

Prakaraṇvaś. n.d. [1968]. *Prakarṇavas, arthāt prācīn Marāṭhi gadyagranth.* Edited by Madhavraj Panjabi. Amrāvatī: Mādhavrāj Pañjābī Mahānubhāv.

Priyolkar, A. K. 1965. *Mahānubhāv: Itihās prakarṇa (Marāṭhī saṃśodhanpatrikeṃtūn vegaḷīṃ kāḍhlelīṃ pṛṣṭeṃ).* Mumbai: Marathi Samshodhanmandal.

Raeside, I. M. P. 1960. "A Bibliographical Index of Mahānubhāva Works in Marathi." *Bulletin of the School of Oriental and African Studies* 23: 464-507.

———. 1970. "The Mahānubhāva *sakaḷa lipī.*" *Bulletin of the School of Oriental and African Studies* 33: 328-334.

———. 1976. "The Mahānubhāvas." *Bulletin of the School of Oriental and African Studies* 39, 3: 585-600.

———, trans. 1989. *Gadyarāja: A Fourteenth-Century Marathi Version of the Kṛṣṇa Legend.* Bombay: Popular Prakashan; London: School of Oriental and African Studies, University of London.

Ranade, Pandharinath Vishnupant. 1988. "Echoes of Ellora in Early Marathi Literature." In *Ellora Caves, Sculptures, and Architecture: Collected Papers of the University Grants Commission's National Seminar.* New Delhi: Books and Books, pp. 108-118.

Ravalobas. 1964. *Ravaḷobās-kṛt Sahyādri-varṇan.* Edited by V. B. Kolte. Pune: Pune Vidyapith.

Shahane, Ashok. 2017. "Key Document: Extracts from 'Ajakalachya Marathi vangmayavar "ksha" kiran' [An X-ray of today's Marathi literature] by Ashok Shahane." Excerpted and translated by Anjali Nerlekar. *Journal of Postcolonial Writing* 53, 1-2: 134-137. Originally published, 1963.

Smṛtisthaḷ. 1960. *Smṛtisthaḷ.* Edited by Vaman Narayan Deshpande. 2nd ed. Pune: Venus Prakashan. Original edition, 1939.

———. 1992. *In the Absence of God: The Early Years of an Indian Sect.* Translated and with an introduction by Anne Feldhaus and Shankar Gopal Tulpule. Honolulu: University of Hawai'i Press.

Solapure, Sushila, ed. 2007. "Prastāvanā," "Spaṣṭīkaraṇātmak ṭīpā," "Śabda koś," "Vyakti sūcī," and "Sthān sūcī." In *Ādya caritrakār ācārya śrīmhāïmbhaṭ saṅkalit līḷācaritra: Ekāṅka* by Mhaïmbhat. Aurangabad: Kailash Publications.

Sthānpothī. 1976. *Sthān pothī*. Edited by Vishnu Bhikaji Kolte. Malkapur: Arun Prakashan.

Thakare, Smita. n.d. [2002]. *Līḷācaritra: Saṃśodhan samīkṣā*. Amravati: Omkar Prakashan.

Tīrthamālikā. 1981. *Tīrthamālikā*. Edited by Bhaskardada Shevalikar. Phaltan: Shri Mahanubhav Bhakta Sanghatana.

Tulpule, Shankar Gopal, ed. 1966a. "Nivedan," "Prastāvanā," "Abhyāsācī Sādhane," "Ṭīpā," "Vyaktināmāñcī sūcī," "Sthalanāmāñcī sūcī," and "Devatānāmāñcī sūcī." In *Līḷācaritra: Pūrvārdha, Bhāg 1* by Mhaïmbhat. Nagpur/Pune: Suvichar Prakashan Mandal.

———, ed. 1966b. "Nivedan," "Prastāvanā," "Abhyāsācī Sādhane," "Ṭīpā," "Vyaktināmāñcī sūcī," "Sthalanāmāñcī sūcī," and "Devatānāmāñcī sūcī." In *Līḷācaritra: Pūrvārdha, Bhāg 2* by Mhaïmbhat. Nagpur/Pune: Suvichar Prakashan Mandal.

———, ed. 1972. "Nivedan," "Prastāvanā," "Abhyāsācī Sādhane," "Ṭīpā," "'Ekāṅkā'tīl vyaktināmāñcī sūcī," "'Ekāṅkā'tīl sthalanāmāñcī sūcī," and "Śabdakoś." In *Līḷācaritra: Ekāṅka* by Mhaïmbhat. 3rd ed. Pune: Suvichar Prakashan Mandal. Original edition, 1964.

———. 1973. "'Ekāṅka' Navhe, 'Ekāka'c." *Marāṭhī Saṃśodhan Patrikā* 22, 1: 97–98.

Vaïndeshkar, Avadhut Muni. 1989. *Śrī Avadhūt Munī Vaïndeśkar yāñcā brahmavidyāsāraratnākar*. Edited by V. B. Kolte. Aurangabad: Raül Prakashan.

Yativrishabha. 2012. *Ācārya Yativṛṣabha's Tiloya Pannatti*. Translated by Dasharath Jain. Delhi: Jain Granthalay.

INDEX

Karhade, 3, 413, 651n1; kitchen of, 541; land grants for, 167; law books of, 25; Madhyandin, 413; Mhaimbhat as, ix; shoulder thread of, 237, 295, 662n85, 672n229, 678n313, 684n401; in trance, 195, 227; villages of, 397; woman with cramps, 491
Brahmapuri, 155
Brahmasan, 271, 273, 665n118
Buddha, xxii, 678n319
Buddhists, 662n77
Buldhana District, 654n43, 655n60, 656nn73–74, 656n76, 659n33, 661n72, 680n358

Cangdev (person), xxxiv
Cangdev (temple), 175, 179, 181, 187, 189, 415, 529, 587, 680n349
Cangdev (village), 519, 529, 533n, 533, 680n349
Cangdev Raül, xviii, 3, 7, 651nn4–5; Chakradhar as, 7, 55, 153, 155, 191, 225, 311, 369, 389, 455, 459, 597, 607, 617, 619; Chakradhar denies being, 321; criticizes song, 177; disciples of, 15, 17, 271, 393, 607, 619; as divine incarnation, xviii, xvin1, xxvin1, 153, 155, 651n3; Dundi Raül and, 662n74; in Haripal's body, xviii, 7–9; hermit's cell of, 5, 501, 617; Karhade Brahman, 3; king's guru, 17n; leaves world, 5–7, 619; oaths on name of, 391; Shri Dattatreya Prabhu and, 3, 651n3; winnowing fan and, 3–5, 662n74 See also Chakrapani; Dvaravati: Cangdev Raül of or from;

Dvaravati: "the one from" Cangdevbhat (Batika; Bhat; Cango), 159, 169, 171, 209, 233, 241, 377, 660n45, 666n138, 666n143, 668n188, 675n277; asks to go to Parameshvarpur, 193, 659n27; banished, 343; begging bag of, 203, 205; blanket of, 205, 207, 415; brother of, 347, 670n188, 670n191 (see also Nathoba); cave ordeal and, 231, 233, 245; mother of, 297, 659n28; pawns betel-nut cutter, 221, 223; plays, 203–207, 225, 227, 660n44; poisoned, 269, 271; sand temple of, 225; sent for darśan of Shri Dattatreya Prabhu, 275, 277; told to think of Gosavi, 297; in trance, 203; victory cry by, 207, 660n50; washes dhotis, 389
Caurangi science, 345, 347, 670n195
Cauranginath, 670n195
Chakradhar (Gosavi), viii, xiv–xvi, xix, xxvin3, 5n, 7n, 13n, 55n, 229n, 651n8, 652n16; animals and, xxi, 31, 35–39, 51, 79, 81, 83, 103, 105, 107, 113, 131, 233, 259, 261, 307, 373, 407, 439, 451, 465, 481, 533, 535, 527, 581, 675n273, 679n347; aphorisms of, xxiv (see also Sūtrapāṭh); as an ascetic, x; as audience for dance or music, 179, 181, 187, 189, 477, 531; avoids the king, xxii, 315, 319, 321; bathed, 329, 469, 471, 473, 537; begs, 15, 41, 43, 73, 85, 87, 101, 355; betel nut or pan and, 21, 23, 93, 129, 167, 171, 173, 187, 189, 221, 223, 239, 251, 271, 273, 317,

145, 193–219; plays cowries, 181;
plays in water, 331, 355, 357;
plays with fan, 5; poisoned, 271–
275, 665n121; pothole observed
by, 479; praised, 59, 369; *prasād*
of, 23, 43, 45, 59, 119, 149, 167,
287, 301, 307, 327, 387, 463, 581;
prostitutes meet, 129; puja of, 61,
81, 83, 125, 127, 157, 165, 167, 183,
195, 199, 227, 271, 273, 375, 443,
457, 465, 499, 567, 609; purifies
begging bag, 203, 205, 297, 299,
553; purity and pollution rules
ignored by, 25, 115, 117, 613,
615, 655n69; robbers thwarted
by, 123, 125, 131, 133, 423; runs,
571, 573; sandals of, 135, 145,
209; sannyasis or yogis and, 97,
99, 267–271, 459; on shadow or
lotus-cloak man, 243, 247; as
Siddhanath, 615, 617; sneezes,
589, 684n409; solitary period
of, xiii, xviii–xix, xxviiin25;
son given by, 83, 85; swears by
mother, 383; on tantric rites, 243,
245; trances from, 53, 55, 87, 89,
151, 163, 289, 327, 367; *vṛndāvan*
built by, 603, 605; wanders, ix,
xviii, xix, xxv, 23, 125, 131, 147,
197, 207, 241, 243, 259, 287, 291,
331, 335, 349, 367, 371, 399, 437,
445, 479, 489, 511, 533, 541, 581,
609, 611; at waterfall, 81, 131, 417,
443; in wedding party, 91–95;
wrestler worships, 31–33; yogi's
garb or scarf of, 33, 611, 613
Chakrapani, xxvin1. *See also*
Cangdev Raül
Chalisgav Taluka, 676nn292–293

Chandori, 343, 670n190
Chandrapur District, 655n64
Chandurbazar Taluka, 660nn47–
49, 661n67
Charan Well, 259, 265, 664n109
Charner, 551, 553, 681n370
Charthane, 457, 676n296
Chaturvidh hermitage, 233, 275,
453, 662n79
Chhinnapap (Chhinnasthali), 303,
667n150
Chinchkhedkar Ramdev, 529,
658n21. *See also* Kavadimba
Ramdev

Dabhadi, 589, 684n410
Dabhvihir, 47, 653n39
Dados (Dev; Ram; Ramdev), 15,
113, 115, 241, 329, 397, 457–469,
473, 567, 663n93, 668n169,
677n305, 678n316; Abaïse
and, 321–325, 591; antics of,
672n231; Baïse and, 235, 237,
379, 479; blanket mended by,
579–581, 683n397; in Devgiri,
233, 235; disciples of, 239, 329,
457–465; dust on, 583; garment
for, 377; Gosavi fed by, 115, 117,
119; Gosavi meets, 662n86;
laughs, 591, 593; Mahadaïse
and, 457–461, 467, 493–499, 501;
Nagdev and, 321–327, 375–379,
495, 583, 674n228; pothole filled
by, 479; puja by, 197, 199, 375;
questioned, 15; relatives of, 159,
656n75; shoulder threads offered
by, 379; in trance, 115; Upadhye
and, 235–237
Daï Bhagavat, 365

ABOUT THE BOOK

Murty Classical Library of India volumes are designed by Rathna Ramanathan and Guglielmo Rossi. Informed by the history of the Indic book and drawing inspiration from polyphonic classical music, the series design is based on the idea of "unity in diversity," celebrating the individuality of each language while bringing them together within a cohesive visual identity.

The Marathi text of this book is set in the Murty Marathi typeface, commissioned by Harvard University Press and designed by John Hudson and Fiona Ross. The proportions and styling of the characters are in keeping with the typographic tradition established by the renowned Nirnaya Sagar Press, with a deliberate reduction of the typically high degree of stroke modulation: the result is a robust, modern design. The Murty Marathi typeface design therefore adopts the same core approach as that of the Murty Hindi except for some key Marathi forms; and the font adheres to the preference still found in Marathi literary publishing for a preponderance of vertical conjunct forms.

The English text is set in Antwerp, designed by Henrik Kubel from A2-TYPE and chosen for its versatility and balance with the Indic typography. The design is a free-spirited amalgamation and interpretation of the archives of type at the Museum Plantin-Moretus in Antwerp.

All the fonts commissioned for the Murty Classical Library of India will be made available, free of charge, for non-commercial use. For more information about the typography and design of the series, please visit *http://www.hup.harvard.edu/mcli*.

Printed on acid-free paper by Maple Press, York, Pennsylvania.